A Chief Justice's
Progress

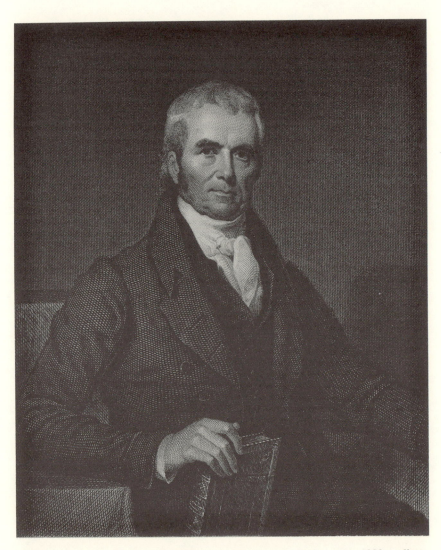

Chief Justice John Marshall in 1831. This engraving, by Asher B. Durand in 1833, replicates a portrait of Marshall by Henry Inman, said at the time to be "the best that was ever taken of him in his later life." The portrait "gives us the mature man, with all the qualities that his contemporaries ascribe to him." (National Archives)

A Chief Justice's Progress

John Marshall from Revolutionary Virginia to the Supreme Court

David Robarge

Contributions in American History, Number 185
Jon L. Wakelyn, *Series Editor*

GREENWOOD PRESS
Westport, Connecticut • London

Library of Congress Cataloging-in-Publication Data

Robarge, David Scott.
    A chief justice's progress : John Marshall from Revolutionary
Virginia to the Supreme Court / David Robarge.
        p.   cm.—(Contributions in American history, ISSN 0084–9219
; no. 185)
    Includes bibliographical references and index.
    ISBN 0–313–30858–6 (alk. paper)
    1. Marshall, John, 1755–1835.   2. Judges—United States Biography.
3. United States.   Supreme Court—History.   4. United States—
History—Revolution, 1775–1783.   I. Title.   II. Series.
KF8745.M3R63   2000
347.73′2634—dc21   99–33829
    [B]

British Library Cataloguing in Publication Data is available.

Library of Congress Catalog Card Number: 99–33829
ISBN: 0–313–30858–6
ISSN: 0084–9219

First published in 2000

Greenwood Press, 88 Post Road West, Westport, CT 06881
An imprint of Greenwood Publishing Group, Inc.
www.greenwood.com

Printed in the United States of America

The paper used in this book complies with the
Permanent Paper Standard issued by the National
Information Standards Organization (Z39.48–1984).

10 9 8 7 6 5 4 3 2

*To my wife and children, my father,
and the memory of my mother*

Contents

Photo essay begins after page 182.

Acknowledgments

Since beginning this study of John Marshall nearly 15 years ago, I have benefited in many large and small ways from the help of many people. Professor Eric McKitrick, my doctoral adviser at Columbia University, encouraged me to undertake a biographic study of Marshall and was a patient and thorough critic while the project was in the dissertation phase. Professor Robert T. Hawkes Jr., of George Mason University, was always generous with his time and friendship and offered insightful advice on several occasions. George Arnold provided his technical expertise at an important stage in the preparation of the book. Gerald K. Haines has been an understanding and accommodating supervisor. The staffs of Fairfax County Public Libraries and the George Mason University libraries were indispensable in acquiring loan materials and providing other assistance.

My family can scarcely remember a time when John Marshall did not seem like an all-too-close relation, and I will always appreciate their support, forbearance, and sacrifices. My mother and father first piqued my interest in history and unfailingly endorsed my academic pursuits. My children—Matthew, Andrew, Sarah, and Stephen—graciously went along on field trips to Marshall-related sites in Virginia and elsewhere, and often gave me late-night companionship in a lonely office. Special thanks to Matthew for helpfully taking on some unglamorous editorial chores. Lastly, my wife Cheryl has lived this book almost as deeply as I. Without her emotional support and spiritual strength, I could not have persevered.

Lorton, Virginia
October 1999

Abbreviations and Short Titles
Used in Notes

AHR   *American Historical Review*

AJLH   *American Journal of Legal History*

Call   Daniel Call, *Reports of Cases Argued and Adjudged in the Court of Appeals of Virginia*, 6 vols., 2nd ed. (Richmond: Smith, 1833)

Cranch   William Cranch, *Reports of Cases Argued and Adjudged in the Supreme Court of the United States, 1801–1815*, 9 vols. (Philadelphia: Carey and Lea, 1830–54)

JAH   *Journal of American History*

JER   *Journal of the Early Republic*

JSH   *Journal of Southern History*

Peters   Richard Peters Jr., *Reports of Cases Argued and Adjudged in the Supreme Court of the United States, from 1828 to 1843, Inclusive*, 17 vols. (Philadelphia: Nicklin, 1828–43)

PJM

The Papers of John Marshall, edited by Herbert A. Johnson et al., 9 vols. to date (Chapel Hill: University of North Carolina Press, 1974–)

VMHB

Virginia Magazine of History and Biography

Wheaton

Henry Wheaton, *Reports of Cases Argued and Adjudged in the Supreme Court of the United States, 1816–27*, 12 vols. (Philadelphia: Carey and Lea, 1816–27)

WMQ

William and Mary Quarterly

Prologue

Appointment

John Adams surely could have done without another political problem in the final winter of his beleaguered presidency. Controversy and turmoil had swirled continuously throughout his term, and an atmosphere of gloom and petulance hung over his administration during its waning months. The unifying majesty of George Washington had evaporated, and Adams—immensely learned, strongly principled, but poorly equipped to deal with the political demands of his office—struggled to keep control of events at home and abroad. Ideological strife, partisan intrigues, and policy blunders had left the once proud and ambitious Federalist Party an ineffectual, unrepresentative anachronism. The Jeffersonians, after nearly a decade of steady growth in power and sophistication, had triumphed in the 1800 national elections and soon would take over the government. The undeclared naval war with France had only just ended, the Treaty of Mortefontaine still lay unratified before the Senate, and the transatlantic peace was held hostage to developments in Europe that were beyond America's influence. Then, in mid-December 1800, Chief Justice Oliver Ellsworth's letter of resignation arrived in Washington after a two-month voyage from France.[1]

Adams had appointed Ellsworth as a member of the controversial second peace mission to France in 1799 to negotiate an end to the so-called Quasi-War. The Chief Justice—one of the Connecticut brokers of the Great Compromise at the Constitutional Convention of 1787, founding father of the federal judiciary, and devoted nationalist—helped achieve that goal. But now he was weary and sick, "[c]onstantly afflicted with the gravel and the gout in my kidneys," and eager to flee the rigors of public service and seek renewal at the spas of England and the sunny climes of Mediterranean France.[2]

Adams now faced the daunting task of selecting a replacement—a reliable Federalist who would neither enrage his political enemies nor offend the other Supreme Court justices. From both partisan and ideological perspectives, Adams and Federalists of all persuasions—High or moderate, Yankee or Southern—considered it vital that they keep watch on the Republican regime through the judiciary, the only branch of the national government they would still control after Jefferson's inauguration. Even before they lost the election, the Federalists had planned to use the courts to incorporate abstract principles of law and justice and to protect their partisan and economic interests. Speaker of the House Theodore Sedgwick bluntly stated the Federalist perspective on the tactical utility of the national courts: "[M]uch may and ought to be done to give efficiency to the government, and to repress the efforts of the Jacobins against it. We ought to spread out the judicial so as to render the justice of the nation acceptable to the people, to aid the national economy, to overawe the licentious, and to punish the guilty." In his annual address to Congress in December 1799, Adams urged the lawmakers to reorganize the federal courts to make them more powerful and efficient. After debating several measures in 1800, the Federalist-run Congress finally pushed through the Judiciary Act of 1801 in February of that year.[3]

When Adams received Ellsworth's resignation on 15 December 1800, the Judiciary Act was scheduled for debate and likely passage in just a few weeks. This timing became a crucial consideration in Adams's choice of a new chief justice.[4] The act—an awkward mixture of needed reform and blatant partisanship—contained several important provisions affecting the size, jurisdiction, and responsibilities of the federal courts. The section that most concerned Adams reduced the number of Supreme Court justices from six to five with the next vacancy. Ostensibly intended to prevent tie votes, this diminution would also prevent Jefferson from choosing a new justice for several years. The proposed reduction did, however, put pressure on Adams to nominate someone whom the Senate would confirm quickly. If he delayed his selection until the Judiciary Act came up for debate, the Republicans would likely join the Federalists in voting for it to deny Adams the chance to fill one vacancy. Also important for Adams was that he would not be able to pick an outsider for chief justice but would have to promote one of the associate justices. He was less than elated at the prospect of the aged and ill senior associate, William Cushing, or the Hamiltonian who stood next in line, William Paterson, occupying the highest judicial office in the land.

On 18 December 1800, the President nominated John Jay, governor of New York. In doing so, Adams followed the pattern, markedly unlike Washington's, of his prior two appointments. He made up his mind rapidly without consulting anyone in his cabinet or his party, and he did not even find out if Jay would accept by asking either the nominee or his associates. On the face of it, Jay seemed an excellent choice. He had served creditably as the first chief justice from 1789 to 1795 and so had the prestige necessary to satisfy the other justices. He had not betrayed Adams by aligning himself with the Hamiltonians.

Socially and ideologically, Jay was a near perfect fit: a patrician with commercial interests, a skeptic of democracy, and a nationalist in outlook. In addition, Adams and Jay had been friends since they served on the peace mission to Paris in 1782–83. The irritable and suspicious President uncharacteristically found cause for optimism in the unforeseen turn of events that Ellsworth's resignation had occasioned. Informing Jay of his nomination, Adams wrote with evident satisfaction that

it appeared to me that Providence had thrown in my way an opportunity, not only of marking to the public where, in my opinion, the greatest mass of worth remained collected in one individual, but of furnishing my country with the best security its inhabitants afforded against the increasing dissolution of morals. . . . The firmest security we can have against the effects of visionary schemes or fluctuating theories, will be in a solid judiciary.[5]

Had the President troubled to survey prominent Federalists, he would not have been surprised at their tepid response to Jay's selection. Although the Senate confirmed Jay that day after it received his nomination, Oliver Wolcott, Timothy Pickering, and other key Federalists doubted that Jay would accept. Jay, finishing his second term as governor, had announced to the state legislature that he intended to retire from public life—a widely known piece of news by mid-December. Treasury Secretary Wolcott wrote that "[t]he nomination is here considered as having been made in one of those 'sportive' humors of which our Chief is distinguished." Adams spent part of the tense days of late December devising an alternative plan if Jay refused. He informed Abigail and his son Thomas, and apparently no one else, that he would follow the line of seniority and promote William Cushing, despite the distinct possibility that the senior associate's age and infirmity might give Jefferson the chance to pick his successor. Cushing had been a cautious, workmanlike, conscientious nationalist during his nearly 11 years on the Supreme Court. Although he was increasingly feeble and often absent from the bench, Adams still preferred him to the next in line, William Paterson, whose close ties to Alexander Hamilton rendered his loyalty questionable in the President's mind. Paterson's political links did not, however, disqualify him from the succession. He definitely was Adams's second choice, as the President insisted in following the seniority principle. To the vacant seat that would follow either Cushing's or Paterson's advancement, Adams intended to nominate Jared Ingersoll, the U.S. Attorney for the Pennsylvania District and a lawyer of high stature with extensive experience arguing before the Supreme Court.[6]

Jay's reply, written on 2 January 1801, went its way south from Albany to an anxious Adams around the 13th or 14th. Jay clearly had not raised his low opinion of the federal courts since resigning the chief justiceship in 1795. He told the President that he "had left the Bench perfectly convinced that under a System so defective, it would not obtain the Energy[,] weight and Dignity which are essential to its affording due support to the national Governmt [sic]; nor acquire the public Confidence and Respect, which, as the last Resort of the Justice of the nation, it should possess." Nor did Congress show any strong inclination to improve the situation. When Jay wrote this letter, the judiciary bill was still stuck in committee. As a closing point, Jay insisted that his health could not endure the stresses of circuit riding.[7]

Jay's regrets plunged Adams into a quandary. Federalists in Congress, although not consulted up to then, were nevertheless as committed as he was to maintaining their party's lock on a six-justice Supreme Court. They sent the Secretary of the Navy, Benjamin Stoddert, to inform the President on 19 January that the House would vote on the judiciary bill the next day. Adams's plan could not work under such tight time constraints; he had to act before the bill passed or he would lose his chance to make any appointment. But William Cushing might refuse elevation to the chief justiceship, just as he had in 1796 when President Washington nominated him after Jay stepped down; and Jared Ingersoll had indicated that unless the arduous requirement of circuit riding was eliminated, he was not interested in serving on the Court. Besides the somewhat untrustworthy Justice Paterson, what other Federalist was available and confirmable on such short notice?[8]

Seemingly guided by political intuition, Adams turned to his Secretary of State, John Marshall. Marshall's quarter-century-old recollection can help us reconstruct his meeting with Adams on 19 January when the President decided to nominate him. The tall and lanky Virginian, dressed as ever in some rumpled or mismatched outfit, ambles into the President's office carrying Jay's letter. The pressures of the Administration's last weeks have tempered Marshall's usual affability with fatigue and concern, and Jay's declination, just received, adds a most nettlesome difficulty. Adams, a half-foot shorter and nearly a hundred pounds heavier, nattily attired and with hair neatly coiffured, rises expectantly from his paper-strewn desk and reads the missive with obvious chagrin. "Thoughtfully," he asks Marshall, "'Who shall I nominate now?'" "I replied that I could not tell," Marshall later writes, "as I supposed that his objection to Judge Patteson [*sic*] remained." Silently, Adams ponders the implications, and then, with a determined, almost defiant expression on his face and a "decided tone" in his voice, declares, "'I shall not nominate him.' After a moment['] hesitation," the President looks up into Marshall's dark eyes and says, "'I believe I must nominate you.'" The Secretary of State is briefly taken aback, and recalls later that he "had never before heard myself named for the office and had not even thought of it." But, "pleased as well as surprized," the loyal Federalist composes himself and dutifully "bowed in silence" at his president's summons to service.[9]

What sort of man had Adams chosen in John Marshall, and what experiences and circumstances had brought Marshall to this moment, which, in retrospect, had such a profound and enduring effect on American history? Legal scholars, historians, political scientists, judges, and attorneys regularly have ranked Marshall as our greatest chief justice.[10] His decisions on judicial review, federal-state relations, contracts, corporations, and commercial regulation—handed down during a 34-year tenure that encompassed five presidencies, a second war with Great Britain, the demise of the first American party system and the advent of the second, and the early stages of the rise of market capitalism—have had as much, if not more, influence on this country's constitutional, political, and economic development as the actions of any other single American. One of the undoubted legacies of a person of Marshall's stature is his immortalization in marble, bronze, paint, and paper. A telling symbol of Marshall's influence can be seen in the two marble bas-relief friezes along the north and south walls of the Supreme Court chamber. The tableau of 18 great lawgivers of world history includes monarchs, emperors, philosophers, scholars, and religious prophets. Only one figure is there because of his contributions as a judge: John Marshall.[11]

More pertinent for the historian is the massive body of writing about Marshall. An army of scholars, jurists, biographers, and popularizers has produced a small library about Marshall—734 titles as of 1955, according to a compilation made for the bicentennial of his birth.[12] No tally has been made recently, but the total now surely exceeds a thousand. This bibliography varies enormously in quality and utility. Much of it represents the outpouring from hagiographers or debunkers set on sanctifying or demonizing Marshall, the Supreme Court, the Constitution, or the principles on which they purportedly rest. Many of these works say far more about their authors' intellectual milieu than about Marshall's life and beliefs.[13] Probably the largest category of literature on Marshall comprises case analyses, juristic speculations, and other narrowly focused, often highly technical, studies by legal scholars. The number of comprehensive biographies of Marshall is surprisingly small. Most of them are written from strong nationalist perspectives and portray Marshall sympathetically. Noteworthy early examples are the works composed in the nineteenth century by George van Santvoord, Allan B. Magruder, and James Bradley Thayer.[14]

All were superseded by Albert J. Beveridge's four-volume *Life of John Marshall*, a masterpiece of conservative nationalist historiography written at the height of the Progressive Era by a distinguished advocate of such policies. It epitomizes the "Great Man" genre of biography with its vivid portrayal of heroes and villains against a sweeping backdrop of political events and social developments. Beveridge's treatment of Marshall is almost historicist in its appropriation of the Federalist ascendancy as a justification for the Progressives' centralizing regulatory program.[15] On its main subject, the *Life of John Marshall* is relentlessly approbatory and teleological. According to Beveridge, Marshall never errs in fulfilling his destiny of shaping the American nation and repelling the threat of Jeffersonian provincialism. Beveridge employed prodigious research and colorful "life and times" narrative to compensate for gaps in available scholarship and in Marshall's own writings.[16]

Despite its biases, Beveridge's *Life of John Marshall* has retained its durability and remains the starting point for investigations of Marshall, possibly because the most thoughtful and incisive Marshall scholars have devoted such extensive attention to the Chief Justice's jurisprudence and generally have left his biography to less able popularizers. Subsequent cradle-to-grave treatments of Marshall's life do not approach Beveridge's style and power, nor do they introduce the analytical rigor that his work lacks. Edward Corwin's *John Marshall and the Constitution*[17] is a short, judicious portrait by twentieth-century America's foremost constitutional historian. Corwin follows Beveridge's interpretations but emphasizes Supreme Court decisions at the expense of biographical narrative. David Loth's *Chief Justice*[18] offers just the opposite: a lively, anecdotal account of the man and a spotty overview of his judicial contributions. Leonard Baker's *John Marshall: A Life in Law*[19] gives a wealth of information, but the author's adulation for his subject, and his inability to discern the essential detail, render his lengthy work more a compendium of Marshalliana than a meaningful interpretation of the Chief Justice's life. Far better is Francis Stites's succinct *John Marshall: Defender of the Constitution*,[20] the most accessible study of Marshall's life and judicial career, with a balanced mix of narrative, personalities, and cases. However, publication constraints—it appeared in a biography series designed for college classroom use—prevent Stites from airing many issues thoroughly.

The most recent full-scale biography, Jean Smith's *John Marshall: Definer of a Nation*,[21] is an engagingly written life-and-times narrative in the "great man" genre with Beveridge and Baker. As one reviewer noted, however, Smith "is so enamored of the greatness of his biographical subject that little is permitted to interfere with the chief justice's seemingly inevitable march to glory . . . John Marshall the person comes alive. But John Marshall the legal thinker and craftsman is more elusive."[22] For that sort of exposition, readers should consult two recent exemplary studies: *The Great Chief Justice: John Marshall and the Rule of Law* by Charles Hobson, and *The Chief Justiceship of John Marshall, 1801–1835* by Herbert A. Johnson.[23] Hobson gives insightful attention to the best-known constitutional cases, but his special contribution is his analysis of Marshall's nonconstitutional decisions, and he is particularly effective at showing how Virginia's legal culture influenced Marshall's law practice and handling of civil cases while on the Court. Johnson offers the best one-volume assessment of Marshall's leadership of the Court, his relations with his colleagues, and the influence they had in Washington and on circuit in projecting federal power and promoting an American "common market" of economic activity.[24]

What is still lacking in the Marshall historiography is an interpretive "half-life": a biography that emphasizes the formative influences on John Marshall during the years *before* he became chief justice. After all, Marshall did not ascend to the Supreme Court until he had reached middle age. By that time, his character and attitudes were, for all practical purposes, fully formed and matured. The products of rich and varied experiences as a child of the Virginia gentry, a militiaman and Continental Army officer during the Revolution, a prominent lawyer and lawmaker in the Old Dominion, and a leading Federalist and diplomat, these traits, beliefs, and sentiments deeply affected his life and work as chief justice. Marshall's previous biographers have dealt with these early years, but often in a superficial or prefatory manner, as if the period 1755–1801 was merely a prelude to the much more important story of the chief justiceship, and from which Marshall drew but one or two large and simple lessons. Joseph J. Ellis makes the point well: "The great temptation presented by a life like Marshall's is to regard the pre-court years as a mere prologue. Then, in the triumphant phase, those magisterial Marshall opinions come marching forward in stately procession . . . The life, in effect, is subordinated to the law."[25] Marshall's pre-court years deserve detailed examination in their own right, however, for their intrinsic interest as well as for their relationship to his era and his later historical significance. In this study, I frequently pause from the march of events to reflect on crucial aspects of this part of Marshall's life, to plumb his motives and analyze the historical process in which he was involved up until 1801, and to employ and comment on other writers' contributions. Several excellent examples of this method as applied to John Randolph, "Light-Horse Harry" Lee, Abraham Lincoln, Theodore Roosevelt, and Franklin Roosevelt convinced me that a similar treatment of Marshall was feasible and warranted. The late Don E. Fehrenbacher's *Prelude to Greatness: Lincoln in the 1850s* (1962) initially enticed me to attempt such a study of Marshall.[26]

In this biography, I have concentrated the events and situations that shaped Marshall's personality and attitudes, the experiences he had, the people and environments he encountered, and the actions he took, during his first 46 years. The organization generally is chronological so as to best portray Marshall's childhood, military service, law practice, and political and diplomatic activities as a cumulative, character-forming experience. Occasionally I have departed from strict time sequence to carry a specific point to its logical end—particularly if that end falls after 1801. In addition, I have also tried to add new perspectives to the essential facts of Marshall's pre-court life by adding historical context and interpretation and, where appropriate, historiographical commentary. In doing so, I have generously used the plethora of scholarship during the past three-and-one-half decades on such key topics as Virginia's political culture and socioeconomic development, the ideology of the Revolution and the Constitution, the emerging legal and judicial profession, the dynamics of Federalism and the early American party system, and the diplomacy of an emerging nation. The study concludes with a reflective epilogue that projects beyond 1801 and draws out the implications of Marshall's early life for understanding his chief justiceship.

A word on primary sources: As a lawyer, legislator, diplomat, jurist, and historian, John Marshall could reasonably have been expected to maintain careful record and to have amassed a sizable personal archive. Quite to the contrary, however, Marshall was a haphazard record keeper who did not believe the paper paraphernalia of his life was worth preserving. He broke with the custom of his day by not retaining drafts or letterbook copies of his correspondence; he kept financial records for only a dozen years; and large portions of his personal and professional papers have been lost or destroyed.

Nonetheless, much primary source material by and about Marshall still exists, albeit scattered in many collections and repositories.[27] The Institute of Early American History and Culture at Williamsburg has collected essentially all that remains and, currently under the guidance of Charles Hobson, has produced nine superbly edited and annotated volumes of *The Papers of John Marshall* since 1974. This compilation, which so far covers Marshall's life through 1823, provides the basic information for my treatment of Marshall. In addition, Marshall wrote an autobiographical sketch of his life prior to his appointment to the Supreme Court and a five-volume biography of George Washington in which he gave his interpretation of American history through 1799.

Other records of Marshall's public life are available in several places: assorted collections of Revolutionary War records for his service in the Virginia militia and Continental Line; the journals of the Virginia House of Delegates and Council of State and editions of the ratification debates for his political career in the Old Dominion; compilations of state and federal court decisions for cases he argued as a lawyer; the diary and dispatches he composed during the XYZ Affair; the *Annals of Congress* for his brief stint in the House of Representatives; and State Department records for his tenure as Secretary of State. Also, the published papers of Marshall's contemporaries provide a wealth of opinions, descriptions, and anecdotes. The most important of these compilations include those of George Washington, Alexander Hamilton, Thomas Jefferson, John Adams, Patrick Henry, James Monroe, James Madison, George Mason, Fisher Ames, Rufus King, James Iredell, and Oliver Wolcott.

The most dangerous conceptual pitfall of the half-life is the fallacy of retrospection: using the subject's later historical reputation as a lens for viewing his early years as an unfolding chronicle that inexorably leads to whatever historical circumstance made him important. I have tried to avoid this trap by treating Marshall's life before 1801 on its own terms as he lived it, while at the same time looking at it in new ways. In doing so, however, I have not tried to force Marshall into preconceived interpretive schemes or use him as a passive medium for examining broad forces and trends. Such a study would quickly become afflicted with a debilitating historicity. Marshall would lack any iota of humanity and represent only the embodiment of static and arid ideas, themselves detached from any political or intellectual context.[28] Even if these shortcomings are avoided, judicial biography can remain, as a journalistic observer of the Supreme Court and a jurist recently noted, "a problematic enterprise . . . 'The judicial life is not enlivened by military battles, campaign rallies, cabinet meetings or diplomatic crises . . . Almost everything reduced itself to a vote on a case and a written opinion setting forth some legal position.'"[29] Marshall's public and private life before he became chief justice, in contrast, is just so enlivened in those and other ways. This study explores the social and political education of America's true founders, and the environment which influenced Marshall, and which he, in turn, helped shape.

NOTES

1. The best analyses of the circumstances of John Marshall's appointment as chief justice are Kathryn Turner, "The Appointment of Chief Justice John Marshall," *WMQ*, 3rd ser., 17 (1960), 143–63; and James R. Perry, "Supreme Court Appointments, 1789–1801: Criteria, Presidential Style, and the Press of Events," *JER*, 6 (1986), 371–410. A useful summary is Donald O. Dewey, *Marshall versus Jefferson: The Political Background of Marbury v. Madison* (New York: Alfred A. Knopf, 1970), chap. 1. Charles Warren, *The Supreme Court in United States History*, 3 vols. (Boston: Little, Brown, 1922), 1:171–84; and Albert J. Beveridge, *The Life of John Marshall*, 4 vols. (Boston: Houghton Mifflin, 1916–19), 2:547–62 are good for contemporary opinion. Henry J. Abraham, *Justices and Presidents: A Political History of Appointments to the Supreme Court* (New York: Oxford University Press, 1974), and Laurence H. Tribe, *God Save This Honorable Court: How the Choice of Supreme Court Justices Shapes Our History* (New York: Random House, 1985) exaggerate Marshall's commitment to Federalist orthodoxy ("blue-ribbon Federalism in every respect" [Abraham, 56]; "a design cut from the purest Federalist cloth Adams could have asked for" [Tribe, 56]) as a factor in his selection. Tribe also incorrectly says Marshall was Adams's second choice after John Jay.

2. Ellsworth to Adams, 16 October 1800, in Maeva Marcus and James R. Perry, eds., *Documentary History of the Supreme Court of the United States, 1789–1800*, 2 vols. (New York: Oxford University Press, 1985), 1 (pt. 1):123.

3. Sedgwick to Rufus King, 15 November 1799, in Charles R. King, ed., *The Life and Correspondence of Rufus King*, 6 vols. (New York: G. P. Putnam's Sons, 1894–1900), 3:146–47.

4. This is the main point of Turner, "Appointment of Marshall."

5. Perry, "Supreme Court Appointments," 400, 409–10; Adams to Jay, 19 December 1800, *Doc. Hist. of Sup. Ct.*, 1 (pt. 1):146. For Washington's criteria for nominating justices, see William R. Casto, *The Supreme Court in the Early Republic: The Chief Justiceships of John Jay and Oliver Ellsworth* (Columbia: University of South Carolina Press, 1995), 65–70.

6. Jay Monaghan, *John Jay: Defender of Liberty* (New York: Bobbs-Merrill, 1935), 424; Wolcott to Pickering, 28 December 1800, John Adams to Thomas B. Adams, 23 December 1800, Abigail Adams to Thomas B. Adams, 25 December 1800, *Doc. Hist. of Sup. Ct.*, 1 (pt. 2):906–07, 911; John E. O'Connor, *William Paterson: Lawyer and Statesman, 1745–1806* (New Brunswick, N.J.: Rutgers University Press, 1979), 260–61. It is not at all clear whom Jefferson would have nominated had Adams failed to fill Ellsworth's vacancy, but many scholars have assumed that Jefferson would have chosen Spencer Roane, the ardently Republican chief judge of Virginia's highest court, as chief justice, with profound consequences ensuing for the nation. There is no evidence, however, to support this speculation. See David Robarge, "Judge Spencer Roane and Jeffersonian Jurisprudence" (M.A. thesis, George Mason University, 1981), 11 n. 26; and F. Thornton Miller, "John Marshall versus Spencer Roane: A Reevaluation of *Martin v. Hunter's Lessee*," *VMHB*, 96 (1988), 313. That Jefferson might have any opportunity to appoint a chief justice explains why Marshall—writing 27 years later—claimed he expressed "fear" that Adams would nominate Cushing and advised the President to choose the younger, healthier Paterson instead. According to Marshall, Adams demurred, believing that he would hurt the senior associate's feelings in bypassing him. John Stokes Adams, ed., *An Autobiographical Sketch by John Marshall . . .* (Ann Arbor:

University of Michigan Press, 1937), 29–30 (hereafter cited as JM, *Autobiographical Sketch*).

Felix Frankfurter underscored the role of contingency in Marshall's eventual nomination:

Surely the course of American history would have been markedly different if the Senate had not rejected the nomination of John Rutledge to succeed Jay as Chief Justice, if the benign Cushing, a Federalist of different composition from Marshall's, had not withdrawn after a week and had continued as Chief Justice till his death in 1810; if Ellsworth's resignation had come later; if John Adams had persuaded Jay to return as chief justice; or if some readily imaginable circumstance had delayed Ellsworth's replacement till John Adams was out of the White House so that the new Chief Justice would have been a Jeffersonian . . . John Marshall is a conspicuous instance of Cleopatra's nose.

"John Marshall and the Judicial Function," in *Felix Frankfurter on the Supreme Court: Extrajudicial Essays on the Court and the Constitution*, ed. Philip Kurland, (Cambridge: Harvard University Press, 1970), 143–44.

7. Jay to Adams, 2 January 1801, *Doc. Hist. of Sup. Ct.*, 1 (pt. 1):146–47; Irving Dilliard, "John Jay," in *The Justices of the United States Supreme Court, 1789–1969: Their Lives and Major Opinions*, ed. Leon Friedman and Fred L. Israel, 4 vols. (New York: R. R. Bowker Co., 1969), 1:18–19; Turner, "Appointment of Marshall," 153 n. 42. Ironically, while in the House of Representatives in 1799–1800, Marshall helped draft legislation that, if passed, would have made Jay *more* willing to accept reappointment as Chief Justice. Marshall served on a committee with four other Federalists who worked on President Adams's December 1799 request for judicial reform. One provision would have eliminated the Justices' circuit-riding duties. Marshall argued at length in the committee and on the House floor in favor of "A Bill to Provide for the Better Establishment and Regulation of the Courts of the United States," but opponents of the measure succeeded in vitiating it. See the relevant editorial note and documents in Herbert Alan Johnson et al., eds., *The Papers of John Marshall*, 9 vols. to date (Chapel Hill: University of North Carolina Press, 1974–), 4:34, 111–12, 117–18; and Kathryn Turner, "Federalist Policy and the Judiciary Act of 1801," *WMQ*, 3rd ser., 22 (1965), 10–14.

8. Turner, "Appointment of Marshall," 148–49, 153–54; Perry, "Supreme Court Appointments," 405.

9. JM, *Autobiographical Sketch*, 29–30.

10. In 1972, Marshall was the only Supreme Court justice unanimously ranked as "great" by a panel of 65 law school deans, law professors, historians, and political scientists. (Louis Brandeis and Oliver Wendell Holmes Jr., came closest, with 62 and 61 votes, respectively.) Albert P. Blaustein and Roy M. Mersky, "Rating Supreme Court Justices," *Journal of the American Bar Association*, 58 (1972), 1183–89; reprinted in idem, *The First One Hundred Justices: Statistical Studies on the Supreme Court of the United States* (Hampden, Conn.: Archon Books, 1978), chap. 2. Twenty years later, over 200 scholars, judges, attorneys, and law students placed him at the top of their respective lists. The criteria on which Marshall was rated included judicial temperament, professional expertise and integrity, leadership, and writing ability. William D. Pederson and Norman W. Provizer, eds., *Great Justices of the U.S. Supreme Court: Ratings and Case Studies* (New York: Peter Lang, 1994), xviii, 14–28.

11. Besides Marshall, the other legal notables portrayed are Menes, the founder of Egypt's first dynasty; Hammurabi, ruler of Babylon; Moses; Solomon; Lycurgus, a Spartan statesman; Solon and Draco, Athenian legislators; Confucius; Octavian, the first emperor of Rome; Justinian, the Byzantine emperor; Muhammad; Charlemagne; King

John, signer of the Magna Carta; Louis IX, modernizer of France's legal system; Hugo Grotius, a Dutch lawyer who established the basis of international law; William Blackstone, the English jurist; and Napoleon Bonaparte, who influenced European civil law. See Joan Biskupic, "Lawgivers," *Washington Post*, 11 March 1998, H1.

12. James Servies, *A Bibliography of John Marshall* (Washington, D.C.: Government Printing Office, 1956). The array of official activities surrounding Marshall's 200th birthday is described in *John Marshall Bicentennial Celebration 1955. Final Report of the United States Commission for the Celebration of the Two Hundredth Anniversary of the Birth of John Marshall* (Washington, D.C.: N.p., 1955).

13. Among the more sophisticated older critiques of Marshall's political views and the effects of his jurisprudence are those by two writers in the Progressive tradition: Vernon Louis Parrington, "John Marshall: Last of the Virginia Federalists," in *Main Currents in American Thought*, 2 vols. (New York: Harcourt, Brace, 1927), 2:19–26; Max Lerner, "John Marshall and the Campaign of History," *Columbia Law Review*, 20 (1939), 396–431, and "John Marshall's Long Shadow," in *Ideas Are Weapons* (New York: Viking Press, 1943). George Dangerfield's chapter on Marshall in *The Era of Good Feelings* (New York: Harcourt, Brace and World, 1963), 157–74, picked up some of the same ideas. Wallace Mendelson offered rejoinders in "Was Chief Justice Marshall an Activist?" and "B. F. Wright on the Contract Clause: A Progressive Misunderstanding of the Marshall-Taney Era," in *Supreme Court Statecraft: The Rule of Law and Men* (Ames, Ia.: Iowa State University Press, 1985), and "Chief Justice Marshall and the Mercantile Tradition," *Southwestern Social Science Quarterly*, 29 (1948), 27–37. Probably the most thoughtful analysis of Marshall's jurisprudence from a Jeffersonian perspective is Charles G. Haines, *The Role of the Supreme Court in American Government and Politics, 1789–1835* (Berkeley: University of California Press, 1944).

14. George van Santvoord, *Sketches of the Lives, Times, and Judicial Services of the Chief Justices of the Supreme Court of the United States* (New York: Scribner, 1854); Allan B. Magruder, *John Marshall* (Boston: Houghton Mifflin, 1885); James Bradley Thayer, *John Marshall* (Boston: Houghton Mifflin, 1901).

15. *The Life of John Marshall*, 4 vols. (Boston: Houghton Mifflin, 1916–19). An illuminating discussion of Marshall's apotheosis during the Progressive period is in Michael Kammen, *A Machine That Would Go of Itself: The Constitution in American Culture* (New York: Alfred A. Knopf, 1986), 209–13. Beveridge's biographer has underscored his subject's political predilections in writing about Marshall: "[H]e swore allegiance to the gospel of nineteenth-century scientific history . . . but few historians have shown more strikingly in their work the influence of their own values, predispositions, and attitudes." John Braeman, *Albert J. Beveridge: American Nationalist* (Chicago: University of Chicago Press, 1971), 2. Similar analyses are in Claude G. Bowers, *Beveridge and the Progressive Era* (New York: Literary Guild, 1932), 554–58; Tracy E. Strevey, "Albert J. Beveridge," in *The Marcus W. Jernegan Essays in American Historiography*, ed. William T. Hutchinson (New York: Russell and Russell, 1937), 384, 388–91; and Herbert A. Johnson, "Albert J. Beveridge," in *Dictionary of Literary Biography*, Volume 17, *Twentieth-Century American Historians*, ed. Clyde N. Wilson (Detroit: Gale Research Co., 1983), 70–74. Johnson observes that Beveridge's nationalism led him to overlook Marshall's sentimental attachment to Virginia and the middling gentry culture in which he grew up. As chief justice, Marshall exhibited this attitude in his jurisprudence by moderating his nationalism with recognition of the reserved powers of the states. A century later, after large bureaucratic institutions had developed in both the public and private sectors, Beveridge regarded the states' capacity for coordinating economic activity as minimal. In his own time,

however, Marshall thought that the states' role was still important. For interesting discussions of Beveridge's research, contacts with scholars, methods of writing, comparative perspective on Marshall and Thomas Jefferson, and the publication of and reaction to the *Life of John Marshall*, see Braeman, *Beveridge*, 227–31, 244–49, 254–58, 263–69, 325–26; Bowers, *Beveridge*, 549–54, 558–60; Strevey, "Beveridge," 385–88; and Gregory M. Pfitzer, *Samuel Eliot Morison's Historical World: In Quest of a New Parkman* (Boston: Northeastern University Press, 1991), 57–64.

16. Strevey estimated that only 14 percent of Beveridge's four volumes dealt with Marshall himself, 34 percent concerned constitutional history, 32 percent political events, and 20 percent other topics. "Beveridge," 383.

17. Edward S. Corwin, *John Marshall and the Constitution* (New Haven: Yale University Press, 1919). Corwin conceded that "[my] interest in Constitutional Theory gave me the impulse [to write Marshall's biography], but I soon fell quite in love with Marshall himself." Kammen, *A Machine That Would Go of Itself*, 212–13. Herbert A. Johnson, however, has called Corwin's book a "disembodied intellectual sketch." "Beveridge," *Dictionary of Literary Biography*, 17:73.

18. David G. Loth, *Chief Justice: John Marshall and the Growth of the Republic* (New York: Greenwood Press, 1949). Similar approaches are taken in Alfred Steinberg, *John Marshall* (New York: G. P. Putnam's Sons, 1962); and John R. Cuneo, *John Marshall: Judicial Statesman* (New York: McGraw-Hill, 1975).

19. Leonard Baker, *John Marshall: A Life in Law* (New York: Macmillan, 1974).

20. Francis N. Stites, *John Marshall: Defender of the Constitution* (Boston: Little, Brown, 1981). Other helpful appraisals of Marshall's life and jurisprudence are: Herbert A. Johnson, "John Marshall," in *Justices of the Supreme Court*, 1:285–303; G. Edward White, *The American Judicial Tradition: Profiles of Leading American Judges* (New York: Oxford University Press, 1976), chap. 1; [Edward S. Corwin,] "Marshall, John," *Dictionary of American Biography*, 12:315–25; Robert K. Faulkner, "Marshall, John," *Encyclopedia of the American Constitution*, ed. Leonard W. Levy et al., 4 vols. (New York: Macmillan, 1986), 3:1205–08; and R. Kent Newmyer, "Marshall, John," in *The Oxford Companion to the Supreme Court of the United States*, ed. Kermit Hall et al. (New York: Oxford University Press, 1992), 523–26.

21. Jean Edward Smith, *John Marshall: Definer of a Nation* (New York: Henry Holt and Co., 1996). In a similar vein is Robert Wernick, "Chief Justice Marshall Takes the Law in Hand," *Smithsonian* (November 1998), 156–73.

22. Maeva Marcus in *American Historical Review*, 103 (1998), 584–85. See also Herbert Sloan's review in *Political Science Quarterly*, 112 (1997), 526.

23. Charles F. Hobson, *The Great Chief Justice: John Marshall and the Rule of Law* (Lawrence: University Press of Kansas, 1996); Herbert A. Johnson, *The Chief Justiceship of John Marshall, 1801–1835* (Columbia: University of South Carolina Press, 1997).

24. For comprehensive analyses of the Supreme Court under Marshall, see George L. Haskins and Herbert A. Johnson, *Foundations of Power: John Marshall, 1801–15* (New York: Macmillan, 1981); and G. Edward White, *The Marshall Court and Cultural Change, 1815–35* (2 vols., New York: Macmillan, 1988; abridged ed., New York: Oxford University Press, 1991).

25. Joseph J. Ellis, "Maximum Justice," *New York Times Book Review*, 1 December 1996, 14.

26. Robert Dawidoff, *The Education of John Randolph* (New York: W. W. Norton, 1979); Charles Royster, *Light-Horse Harry Lee and the Legacy of the American Revolution* (New York: Alfred A. Knopf, 1981); Don E. Fehrenbacher, *Prelude to*

Greatness: Lincoln in the 1850s (Stanford, Ca.: Stanford University Press, 1962); Douglas L. Wilson, *Honor's Voice: The Transformation of Abraham Lincoln* (New York: Alfred A. Knopf, 1998); David McCulloch, *Mornings on Horseback* (New York: Simon and Schuster, 1981); Geoffrey Ward, *Before the Trumpet: Young Franklin Roosevelt, 1882–1905* (New York: Harper and Row, 1985) and *A First-Class Temperament: The Emergence of Franklin Roosevelt* (New York: Harper and Row, 1988).

27. See Peter A. Wonders, comp., *Directory of Manuscript Collections Related to Federal Judges* (Washington, D.C.: Federal Judicial Center, 1998), 127–29.

28. Besides the many "law office histories" on Marshall—of recent note, those that inject him into the "original intent" and "interpretivist/non-interpretivist" debates—the best example of that flawed approach from the perspective of political philosophy is Robert Faulkner's *The Jurisprudence of John Marshall* (Princeton: Princeton University Press, 1968). Other works that stress Marshall's philosophy and intellectual influences are William Crosskey, "John Marshall," in *Mr. Justice*, ed. Alison Dunham and Philip Kurland (Chicago: University of Chicago Press, 1956); and Julian P. Boyd, "The Chasm That Separated Thomas Jefferson and John Marshall," in *Essays on the American Constitution*, ed. Gottfried Dietze (Englewood Cliffs, N.J.: Prentice-Hall, 1964), which perversely argue that Marshall was a strict constructionist struggling to preserve the Framers' unitary state; Saul K. Padover, "The Political Ideas of John Marshall," *Social Science*, 26 (1959), 47–70; Morton J. Frisch, "John Marshall's Philosophy of Constitutional Republicanism," *Review of Politics*, 20 (1958), 34–45; William E. Nelson, "The Eighteenth-Century Background of John Marshall's Constitutional Jurisprudence," *Michigan Law Review*, 76 (1978), 893–960; Richard A. Brisbin Jr., "John Marshall and the Nature of Law in the Early Republic," *VMHB*, 98 (1990), 57–80; several of the essays in Thomas C. Shevory, ed., *John Marshall's Achievement: Law, Politics, and Constitutional Interpretation* (Westport, Conn.: Greenwood Press, 1989); and Thomas Shevory, *John Marshall's Law: Interpretation, Ideology, and Interest* (Westport, Conn.: Greenwood Press, 1994). Most of the essays in a still useful older collection, *Chief Justice John Marshall: A Reappraisal*, ed. W. Melville Jones (Ithaca: Cornell University Press, 1955), avoid forcing Marshall into paradigms. For a critical examination of such efforts, see G. Edward White, "The Art of Revising History: Revisiting the Marshall Court," *Suffolk University Law Review*, 16 (1982), 671–85. See also the several essays in "Chief Justice John Marshall: A Symposium," *University of Pennsylvania Law Review*, 104 (1955–56), 1–68.

29. Linda Greenhouse, "Lives of the Judges," *New York Times Book Review*, 27 September 1998, 35. On the difficulties of writing judicial biographies—among them the dullness of most jurists' lives and the highly technical nature of many court decisions—see Robert M. Spector, "Judicial Biography and the U.S. Supreme Court—A Bibliographical Appraisal," *AJLH*, 11 (1967), 1–24.

Chapter 1

Childhood in the Frontier Gentry, 1755–1774

John Marshall's rise from the rude log cabin where he was born in what is now Fauquier County, Virginia, in 1755 to the Supreme Court's chambers in Washington, D.C., in 1801 culminated a story of four generations of upward mobility in space and status by the Marshall family in the fluid frontier milieu of colonial Tidewater and Piedmont Virginia. That story began with Marshall's great-grandfather Thomas, who emigrated from Wales as a carpenter in the late seventeenth century, settled in Westmoreland County in the Northern Neck region, and died a small tobacco planter in 1704. Thomas's eldest son William inherited his estate—of unknown size, but presumably a couple hundred acres—and later added to his other holdings in the region by acquiring part of a 1,200-acre tract, patented but undeveloped by other landowners and "lost for want of seating," also in Westmoreland County. In 1727, William deeded 200 acres of the property along Mattox Creek to his brother John, the Chief Justice's grandfather, for five shillings. This parcel—about the minimum size to support a family using agricultural practices of the day—seems to have been of poor quality: low, marshy, and well removed from access to the river, hence the contemporary references to John "of the Forest." This elder John nevertheless carved out a small farm and worked it successfully, growing tobacco and food crops and raising some livestock, until his death in 1752. By that time he had nearly achieved a measure of gentility, possessing a respectable estate that included 17 slaves, two stills, and other property worth £730, though no additional land. In 1753, his widow deeded 100 acres to the first of their six children, 23-year-old Thomas—the Chief Justice's father.[1]

Thomas Marshall, born in 1730, spent most of his first quarter-century on his father's farm and his own inherited estate. His early years are notable chiefly in two ways.   First, George Washington, a neighbor and possible childhood companion, apparently hired Thomas in late 1749 to assist with surveys of the vast landholdings of Lord Fairfax in what was later Frederick County in northwestern Virginia.   Thomas and George became good friends and maintained social and business contacts for years after. Second, in 1754 at age 24, Thomas married Mary Randolph Keith, the 17-year-old daughter of James Keith, an elderly Scottish parson, and Mary Isham Randolph of the prominent James River clan. Thomas's union with a Randolph tied the Marshalls to some of the first families of Virginia and made it easier for them to make their economic and political mark in the rough environs of the Piedmont and Blue Ridge frontiers.[2]

Soon after his marriage, Thomas decided to forsake his legacy—no record of sale exists, and he may have abandoned the land—and seek his fortune in the central Piedmont.[3] He likely had several motives, including the push of soil exhaustion and restive ambition, the pull of cheap land and forgotten quitrents, and a desire to avoid becoming shackled to the factorage system established by Scottish merchants who were taking over the local tobacco market. He also may have received encouragement from George Washington and Lord Fairfax. The Marshalls thus joined a large midcentury westward migration to central Virginia that comprised not former indentured servants seeking frontier homes, but prosperous—or, as with Thomas, aspiring—planters and farmers who needed new fertile land for raising tobacco, providing homesteads for their sons, and speculation.

In 1755, probably in the early spring to give time to settle in and plant a crop, Thomas set out from Westmoreland County with his young bride, two inherited slaves, and wagons of belongings, and headed for a small settlement called Germantown about 50 miles away in what was then Prince William County. The Marshall party journeyed up the Northern Neck peninsula, then turned north along the rutted tobacco trails known as the Falls Road and the German Rolling Road, a route now marked by Highways 3, 17, 634, and 610. When they arrived after a week or so, they found a region thinly settled with English gentry and yeomen and their slaves, and German and Scots-Irish small farmers. Germantown itself, believed to be the oldest settlement in what is now Fauquier County, was established in 1721 by German mining families brought over by Governor Alexander Spotswood and Baron Christopher de Graffenried to dig iron ore along the Rapidan River, who had grown dissatisfied with the arrangement and moved away. According to a county history, the area the Marshalls moved to "had natural advantages and evidently had been selected [by the original settlers] with care and foresight. There is a considerable portion of bottomland along the stream; the higher fields are well drained, but not much hilly. Licking Run is a good-sized stream, and provided a good site for a grist mill, sawmill, and other operations to be run by water power." Most of the inhabitants of Germantown had moved west by the time the Marshalls arrived. Thomas moved his wife and slaves into the abandoned homestead of the Fishbeck family (one of the first settlers of the town) a pair of small but sturdy log cabins on a slightly sloping, forested stand of unknown size a few hundred feet from Licking Run. On 24 September 1755, soon after harvest time, John, the first of their 15 children, was born.

Ten years later, Thomas moved the family about 30 miles northwest to a scenic valley in the Blue Ridge Mountains known as the Hollow, just north of the present-day hamlet of Markham. Thomas had leased 330 densely forested acres from Thomas Ludwell Lee and Richard Henry Lee, possibly using the connections his marriage afforded. The Marshalls spent probably three or four days trekking north from Germantown along the upper branch of the Dumfries Road (now U.S. 17)—an important commercial route running from the Shenandoah Valley to the Rappahannock River—to its junction with the Cool Spring Road (now State 55) where the village of Delaplane would later rise. The tired party might have rested there for the night at Thomas Watts's rough-hewn ordinary that gave the crossroads its name. Heading west into the Blue Ridge along Goose Creek was more arduous than the first leg. The road was little more than a bridle path, alternately stumpy, rocky, and muddy, meandering through thick woods. After about 10 slow, jolting miles, the Marshalls turned north into a hilly pocket surrounded by the tree-covered slopes of mountains now called Red Oak, Hard Scrabble, Blue, and Naked. In a clearing they erected a dwelling that, though characteristic of the common Virginia planter's house elsewhere, was impressively spacious and well designed for a time when almost all backwoods settlers lived in log cabins: a one-and-a-half story, four-room frame house made of whip-sawed boards and uprights nailed together, with a large stone chimney. Adjoining the structure were a small stone meat house, a one-room log cabin for the slaves, and a log stable.[4]

John would spend his next eight years in these picturesque but isolated and demanding environs. He left no detailed recollections of his childhood in Germantown and the Hollow, but he would have passed much of his time sharing in the farm labor and household chores, hunting, fishing, exploring, riding, learning crafts, and helping watch over younger siblings (eight sisters and six brothers all survived childhood) and cousins who were raised there. John also spent some of his free hours in rough-and-tumble with boys from nearby farms. "The young men within my reach were entirely uncultivated," he wrote years later, "and the time I passed with them was devoted to hardy athletic exercises."[5]

In January 1773, Thomas's rapidly growing wealth enabled him to buy his first tract of land in northern Virginia: 1,700 more conveniently located acres in the foothills of Little Cobbler Mountain, about 10 miles east of the Hollow and a few miles northwest of the present-day town of Marshall. The land there is broad and rolling, and on a rise overlooking a valley and stream, the Marshalls built a two-story, seven-room frame house with gabled roof and dormer windows. Named Oak Hill, it was the last of John's childhood homes. It also is the house commonly associated with his youth, but during this part of his life he spent less time there than in any of the family dwellings—only two years before leaving for military duty in the Revolutionary War. Oak Hill is the most attractive of the Marshall homes in Fauquier County and provides the clearest architectural measure of how far the family had advanced in place and status during the 18 years since departing the marshy lowlands along Mattox Creek.[6]

Thomas Marshall was, by all accounts, vigorous, intelligent, and ambitious. John described him as "a man to whom nature had been bountiful, and who had assiduously improved her gifts." Thomas's portrait shows him as tall, broad shouldered, and powerful, with dark eyes and a purposeful expression. He was a thoughtful man of action with a restless spirit, a public-spirited striver who parlayed hard work, family ties, local economic and political connections, successful land speculation, and favorable economic conditions into a quickly rising standard of living that by the mid-1770s put the Marshalls far ahead of most Virginians of that time who had started out in log cabins. Virginia's economy grew significantly during the mid-eighteenth century—as indicated by increases in tobacco prices, the size of export crops, the value of imports, the amount of available credit, and per capita income—and Thomas took regular advantage of these opportune circumstances to increase his wealth and landholdings. Starting as a small planter with 100 acres of mostly tobacco in Westmoreland County, he became a middling planter at Germantown, still mainly in tobacco, but also adding grain, fruit, and livestock. Speculation and settlement of the region also gave Thomas a steady source of income as a surveyor and land agent. A decade later at the Hollow, Thomas had a few hundred acres, enough to cultivate some, rent others, and let the rest lie fallow. In that location he also was better positioned to fulfill his duties as Lord Fairfax's agent. At Oak Hill, where he owned nearly 2,000 acres, he delved into land speculation. In roughly 20 years, Thomas had become a diversified and accomplished planter-speculator, able to avoid most of the pitfalls of the tobacco culture—especially debt—and to insulate his material achievements from the decline that beset Virginia's economy after 1760. He reversed the common pattern of the eighteenth-century planter family: large estates divided and bequeathed to sons who struggled under the encumbrance of debts owed to English and Scottish creditors. The typical planter obliged a part of his crop to pay for clothes, supplies, tools, and imported goods that local gentry or Scottish factors advanced to him. This need to establish credit and pay off debt drove Virginia planters and farmers to expand their landholdings. In striking contrast, Thomas Marshall built on his inheritance and augmented his holdings apparently without going into debt. His restless acquisitiveness did not derive from any need to pay off creditors, but from an impulse to improve his family's social and economic lot.[7]

Thomas Marshall assumed his first public office in 1759, and until he left Virginia 26 years later for Kentucky to accomplish much the same there, he continuously held a variety of official positions that were important in the political, legal, and economic life of Fauquier County. He was the first Marshall family member to serve in a public role. That he could politically enter the ranks of the local gentry only four years after moving to the county, and while still living in the log cabin in Germantown, indicates the respect with which prominent residents viewed his character. It also is a reflection of the unsettled nature of the Piedmont frontier, which, rather than destabilizing the gentry, actually helped it remain vital by allowing the infusion of new blood.

In 1759, the year Fauquier was split from Prince William, Thomas was appointed to two posts: county surveyor and justice of the peace. His first official duty as surveyor involved dividing the new county into districts for tax collection. Later he assumed the other functions of the frontier surveyors. As government officials, they made sure that tracts were laid out in ways that did not violate land laws. As private agents of planters or speculators, they divided patented acreage to maximize the owners' return from agriculture, rental, or sale; or they explored unpatented land to identify and map parcels that would prove most lucrative once forests were felled and roads were laid. Thomas's surveying in Fauquier, and later in Frederick County as well, provided his family with important income—John remembered that his father was often away earning fees for surveying trips, with John helping him on some as a chain carrier—and aided his later land speculation by giving him geographic insights and economic contacts.[8]

As a justice of the peace, a position he held for most of the remaining years before the Revolution, Thomas officially joined the secular institutional arm of the local oligarchy's power, the county court. Service as a justice of the peace usually was the first step in a political career in eighteenth-century Virginia and provided a vital apprenticeship in the exercise of political and social control, for it was social respect, not legal expertise, that gave the justices their broad authority. Individually, justices of the peace settled small disputes and issued court orders, but it was in their collective capacity as the county court that the "gentleman justices" influenced local affairs and received practical training in wielding authority. County courts not only ruled in certain civil and criminal matters; they also performed important economic, social, political, and administrative functions that were often more important than their judicial duties. They issued decisions, ordinances, and bylaws on matters as diverse as land titles, indentured servants and slaves, roads and public works, licenses, taxes, elections, public health and morals, professional and business practices, and charity for orphans and paupers. In short, the county courts carried out the key civic functions that affected daily life and were ideally situated to observe the activities of county residents and the effects on them of general policies adopted by the colonial government in Williamsburg.[9]

After holding its first sessions in private homes, the Fauquier County Court began meeting at Fauquier Court House, located at the intersection of Dumfries Road and the Fauquier and Alexandria pike. It was a convenient stop for wagon and coach teams, travelers, and the many people who flocked to the county seat each month to conduct official business; to work the crowds selling land, livestock, wares, and services; to pay off or collect debts; and to gossip or renew acquaintances. These monthly assemblages, full of excitement, color, and display, often resembled a carnival or country fair. They relieved the monotony and isolation of rural life and became an essential social institution of the eighteenth-century Virginia countryside. Thomas almost certainly brought John along to some of the court sessions. The young boy could hardly help but be impressed by the solemn ritual, forensic contention, and lively atmosphere. Although John never sat on a county court—a rarity for a Virginian who achieved high office—his father's service as a justice of the peace helped instill in him a lifelong loyalty to the county courts. The experience also helped instruct him in the courts' important function of mediating social conflict and encouraging orderly change. This role was vital at a time when Virginia's social cohesion was weakening under the strains of economic decline and growing criticism of the dominance of "worthy gentlemen" from evangelicals and ordinary people, whom the squirearchy in turn disparaged as "men who aim at power without merit." As late as 1830, at the Virginia constitutional convention, the Chief Justice ardently defended the county court system, claiming that "[n]o state in the union has hitherto enjoyed more complete internal quiet . . . [nor] less of ill-feeling between man and man" than Virginia because the county judges "consist in general of the best men in their respective counties. They act in the spirit of peace-makers, and allay, rather than excite, the small disputes . . . which will sometimes arise among neighbours."[10]

In 1761, two years after joining the county court, Thomas Marshall was elected to the House of Burgesses and, except for two brief interruptions, served there continuously until 1775, when he went off to war. Election as a burgess was the next step on the pathway to power in eighteenth-century Virginia, and service on the county court provided an apprenticeship for it by enabling men to practice administering the laws and observing their effects before assuming the responsibility of making them. Thomas became a burgess by winning a county election, which required "swilling the planters with bumbo," avoiding any direct solicitation of votes that would violate the genteel code that guided what passed then for campaigning, and "carrying the election"—a contemporary phase connoting that the victor earned his reward by virtue of his character, knowledge, and reputation. In addition, the genial Thomas kept on good terms with most freeholders, who found him approachable and devoted to representative government.[11]

While in the House of Burgesses, Thomas had to confront issues of greater magnitude than those he dealt with on the county court: war with the French and Indians, Britain's trade and territorial policies, currency and taxation, religion, transportation, agriculture, and land tenure, among others. He worked with some of the established or rising members of Virginia's political elite, including Peyton Randolph, Robert Carter Nicholas, George Wythe, Edmund Pendleton, Benjamin Harrison, Richard Henry Lee, Patrick Henry, Thomas Jefferson, and George Washington. Thomas was appointed to the standing committees on trade, religion, and propositions and grievances, and to several special committees and commissions. The standing committees prepared and managed most of the important business of the House. Inferential evidence indicates that Thomas sympathized with Henry's effort to shift some power away from the Tidewater squirearchy that dominated the Burgesses to the upcountry representatives. Thomas also sided early on with the Burgesses who were most critical of England's actions toward the colonies and the Assembly. When Thomas returned to the Hollow or Oak Hill, John undoubtedly heard his father's stories of the personalities and debates he had witnessed and participated in at a time when Virginians' animosity to England was building and complaints against gentry corruption were intensifying.[12]

Thomas also held other public offices in Fauquier County, and John would have acquired at least a passing familiarity with their responsibilities by listening to his father or accompanying him to governmental functions. In 1767, Thomas was appointed sheriff of the county for a two-year term. The office of sheriff, with its fee-collecting duties, control over elections, and assorted perquisites, was perhaps the most powerful local position in Virginia. For that reason, the incumbent customarily had to be the ranking justice of the peace in the county who had not previously held the post, and tenure was restricted to one or two years. In addition, Thomas was appointed in 1769–70 to the County Court in Chancery, a judicial body that heard cases without juries to resolve civil disputes for which no remedy could be found in the common law. Judges in chancery courts reached decisions by evaluating the merits of an issue and applying general principles of fairness rather than by relying on statutes and legal precedents to guide them. Thomas also served as court clerk for Dunmore (now Shenandoah) County in 1773. That he had both a utilitarian and an intellectual interest in the law may be inferred from his subscription to the first American edition of Sir William Blackstone's *Commentaries on the Laws of England*, the definitive treatise on the history, theory, and practice of English jurisprudence.[13]

Rounding out Thomas's public activities in the local gentry was his position as a vestryman for Leeds Parish of the Anglican Church, established in 1769 to encompass Fauquier County. His involvement provides some insights into how John's spiritual character was formed. Throughout Virginia, a large proportion of the justices of the peace and prominent local officials served on parish vestries. This overlap reflected the fact that the parish was a civil, as well as an ecclesiastical, jurisdiction with governmental responsibilities that went well beyond the spiritual. The essence of Anglicanism in Virginia—at least until the emergence of a strong evangelical New Light counterculture in the older parts of the colony after 1760—was, in Daniel Boorstin's apt phrase, "practical godliness," characterized by catholicity, moderation, compromise, toleration, a lack of dogma, and an emphasis on institutions rather than doctrines. Churchgoing was as much, if not more, a social custom expressing the dominance of the gentry as a spiritual discipline inculcating piety. Consequently, Thomas's substantial involvement in vestry affairs did not necessarily provide a measure of his faith. Albert Beveridge supported his assertion that Thomas was "by nature religiously inclined" by noting that he "was always a stanch churchman." There is no evidence, however, that Thomas was anything but a conventional gentry Anglican who accepted a denatured theology and practiced a civil religion. The family library contained no religious works besides the ubiquitous Bible. Thomas's most noteworthy religious act was his gift of an acre of land for a small church at the north end of Little Cobbler Mountain near the Oak Hill estate. He intended the church, then known as Cool Spring Meeting House, for use by all denominations. In contrast to Thomas, his wife Mary was a deeply reverent Anglican, and his brother William was a Baptist preacher inspired by the Great Awakening. On only one occasion did the intensifying conflict between the Anglican establishment and the Baptists in the pre-Revolutionary years directly affect him. He convinced local authorities to release William, who had been arrested after his fervent sermons rankled anti-Baptist elements in the community.[14]

John Marshall's family thus presented him with a clear choice of spiritual role models.[15] As in many other areas, Thomas's attitude predominated, at least for most of John's life. He referred to Mary Marshall—well educated, devout, and resolute—directly only in his account book and one letter. Unless a body of correspondence between them, unmentioned elsewhere, has not survived, they did not exchange letters, either. Perhaps John found his emerging personality more compatible with his affable and outgoing father than his more reserved and contemplative mother. Information on John's religious beliefs is sketchy and tainted by filiopiety and concern with demonstrating his spiritual bona fides, but it leads to the conclusion that for many years he was a deist or Unitarian who believed in an impersonal Creator as the source of ethical natural law and believed all humans were created essentially good and rational. He applauded the civic utility of religion, but otherwise he appears to have been largely indifferent to the political status of organized religion. He seems to have approved of Patrick Henry's general religious assessment bill in 1784, and although he never became a communicant in the Anglican or Episcopal Churches, he supported the Episcopal Church with money—including a pew purchase—and some lay activity while in Richmond in the early 1800s. He was skeptical of but not hostile to the New Light movement. In middle age, he dutifully attended church services at the Cool Spring Meeting House and the Monumental Church in Richmond, mainly to set an example as chief justice. The only reference to any daily devotional practice by him came decades after his death from a descendant who claimed he prayed every night before going to bed—supposedly a habit his mother taught him. By his own testimony, however, praying was "no very common practice with me."

In an interesting generational parallel, John's wife, Mary "Polly" Ambler, was intensely religious like his mother, and his deep love for "my dearest Polly" evoked in him the same respect and understanding for her spirituality as had Thomas's affection for Mary Randolph Keith. This attitude may have inclined John toward a deeper faith later in life and particularly after Polly died in 1831. He closed several letters to his wife during 1826–31 with prayers such as "that Heaven may bless you"—an invocation he had not used before. One of the better known Marshall stories from around then describes the "old gentleman's" "eloquent and unanswerable" defense of Christianity against the arguments of several doubters at a Winchester tavern. In a private letter written in 1832, Marshall observed that the human race would be benefited by greater adherence to the Bible, which he said inculcates peace. "Religion is the surest and safest foundation" of a "quiet conscience," he wrote his grandson in 1834. "The individual who turns his thoughts frequently to an omnipotent, omniscient and all perfect being, who feels his dependence on, and his infinite obligations to that being, will avoid that course of life which must harrow up the conscience." At the same time, he remained dubious about theological debates that "perplex and cannot enlighten," and he rejected the "gloomy and austere dogmas which some of [Christianity's] professors have sought to engraft on it." Memories of his mother's loving faith may have encouraged Marshall toward a spiritual change late in life. When he was nearly 70 he wrote that "precepts from the lips of a beloved mother . . . sink deep in the heart, and make an impression which is seldom entirely effaced." According to family tradition, late in life he affirmed the divinity of Christ after reading a theological work, and he planned to be confirmed as an Episcopalian but died before he could do so.

John Marshall received little formal education during his youth, but his father's native intelligence, intellectual interests, and drive for self-improvement made the Marshall household one of the "little oases of dignity and culture," in Carl Bridenbaugh's words, that dotted the Virginia frontier in the mid-eighteenth century. Virginians, a professor at the College of William and Mary College wrote in the early 1700s, "are more inclinable to read men by business and conversation, than to dive into books, and are for the most part only desirous of learning what is absolutely necessary, in the shortest and best method." Thomas Marshall, however, appears to have been determined to break with this pattern and provided John with a rudimentary classical education through home schooling and instruction by trained teachers. In addition, Thomas's prominence in the county government, which took responsibility for seeing that parents educated their children, might have induced him to set an example in his own home. The family library was substantial and sophisticated for its time and place, containing, besides the Bible, works by Livy, Horace, William Shakespeare, John Milton, John Dryden, and Alexander Pope. (The books may have come from the sizable collection of the Oxford-educated Lord Fairfax, who owned dozens of volumes of classical and contemporary literature and treatises.) John recalled that his father "gave me an early taste for history and for poetry," and that by age 12 he had transcribed (and, according to his Supreme Court colleague, Joseph Story, memorized many passages from) some of Pope's essays. In addition, as a surveyor, Thomas presumably taught John some basic mathematics and astronomy.[16]

Thomas's gentry status also afforded John the opportunity to receive some of his education away from home. There were no schools in Fauquier County until 1777, so the 14-year-old John attended an academy run by the Reverend Archibald Campbell about one hundred miles from the Hollow in Westmoreland County. The school, called Campbelltown Academy, reputedly was the best such institution in Virginia. The academy was one of three general types of schools in colonial America, the others being the English (or common) school, which stressed reading with a bit of writing and arithmetic thrown in, and the Latin (or grammar) school, which added classical languages and literature. The curriculum of an academy such as Campbelltown was less defined. "Perhaps the most that can be said of any given academy," according to Lawrence Cremin, "is that it offered what its master was prepared to teach, or what its students were prepared to learn, or what its sponsors were prepared to support, or some combination or compromise among the three." While at Campbelltown, John became a good friend of classmate James Monroe, one of whose descendants described the Reverend Campbell as "a disciplinarian of the sternest type . . . he made the school days all work and little play . . . His pupils were regarded as especially well grounded in mathematics and Latin." John more politely remembered Campbell—a classical scholar educated at the highly reputed universities in Scotland—as "a clergyman of great respectability."[17]

After a year at Campbelltown Academy, John returned home to Rosebank. His father soon retained a private tutor for John and his siblings: James Thomson, a 30-year-old Episcopalian minister from Scotland, college-educated and well versed in Greek and Latin. The vestry of Leeds Parish, which Thomas headed, chose Thomson as its minister, and he lived with the Marshalls for a year after arriving from Scotland, returning their hospitality by, and receiving a small salary for, teaching the Marshall children. Many tutors in gentry homes at this time were Anglican ministers, and Scots were especially favored for their learning, sound Protestantism, and strict code of behavior. After two years under Campbell's and Thomson's instruction, John could read Horace and Livy, the Roman poet and historian respectively, and possibly also Cicero, in Latin. Thomson may also have expressed to John his own highly critical views of British policies toward America—views such as those he conveyed in a sermon delivered five years later, in which he excoriated Parliament for denying the colonists "their just and legal rights" and loading upon them "great hardships" that "reduced the poor to great want," and exhorted his congregation "as men and Christians" to help "supply the country with arms and ammunition."[18]

The literary works that John studied at home and in school deserve comment for the way their themes fit into an intellectual trend in mid-eighteenth century America that strongly influenced the revolutionary generation of which John Marshall was a part. The authors whom he found worth mentioning in his autobiography or in remarks to associates and family—especially Horace, Livy, Cicero, Dryden, and Pope—were major figures in the Augustan Age of Latin literature in Rome in the first century B.C. or the neoclassical literary revival in seventeenth- and eighteenth-century England. In America, they were elements of one key historical source of the ideology of republicanism: the appeal to antiquity. "Such classicism was not only a scholarly ornamentation of educated Americans," writes Gordon Wood; "it helped to shape their values and their ideals of behavior." The principal ideas drawn from Americans' selective reading of antiquity were the portrayal of human existence as a struggle between virtue and vice, reason and passion; the celebration of rural life for its purity, simplicity, and frugality; the role of morality in successful statecraft; and praise for such traits as moderation, courage, dignity, and independence. These themes resonate through the works Marshall studied: Horace's *Odes*, *Epistles*, and *Satires*; Livy's *History of Rome*; and Cicero's essays and orations. Slightly modified to meet the needs of the seventeenth and eighteenth centuries, they also can be found in Dryden's heroic poetry, which extolled strong, energetic moral leadership, and Pope's essays, which equated happiness with virtue, criticized luxury, stressed the interdependence of man and society, and gave primacy to reason. Pope's works, in particular, made a lasting impression on Marshall. The *Essay on Man* was widely used in eighteenth-century America as an ethical textbook for young people as well as an aid in teaching grammar and rhetoric. In one work, it combined instruction in morals with guidance on precise expression in prose and speech. Pope's verse was frequently quoted in the newspapers, journals, and speeches that Marshall read and heard when he was older. The deistic views expressed in the *Essay on Man* may also have contributed to the lack of spirituality that characterized most of Marshall's life.[19]

John's early education also instilled in him an appreciation for belles lettres that he cultivated for his own enjoyment. He was fond of poetry—even occasionally composing his own verse—and popular novelists. He found Jane Austen's works "pleasing, interesting, equable, and yet amusing." One of his sisters-in-law recalled years after his courtship of Polly Ambler that, on visits to his future wife's home, he would "read to us from the best authors, particularly the Poets, with so much taste and feeling, and pathos, too, as to give me an idea for their sublimity which I should never have had an idea of." Among the numerous book purchases listed in his accounts are titles such as John Mason, *Spiritual Songs: or Songs of Praise*; Hugh Blair, *Lectures on Rhetoric and Belles Lettres*; Robert Burns, *Poems*; *Encyclopaedia, or a Dictionary of Arts, Sciences, and Miscellaneous Literature*; and *American Museum*, a literary magazine. Among the approximately 1,000 books currently at Marshall's house in Richmond are some 250 that he signed. They include major works of Western philosophy and political theory, legal treatises, and Roman and Latin classics.[20]

Looking back on the history of the Marshall family during the seventeenth and eighteenth centuries, one can see several themes predominating: a drive for material and social self-improvement; an ability to recognize and seize opportunity; a practical intelligence and a perceptiveness that permitted easy adaptation to changing circumstances; and an appreciation for the public responsibilities of the accomplished and successful. These qualities became distilled and concentrated in the mature character of John Marshall, in large measure through the caring yet demanding tutelage of Thomas Marshall, by far the strongest single influence on young John. In the course of moving his family to the Piedmont and Blue Ridge frontier, assuming several important government offices, and steadily advancing in affluence, status, and range of economic and social contacts, Thomas provided John with a rich upbringing, while his own intellectual instincts assured that his son would receive more sophisticated schooling than most frontier gentry children. Father and son enjoyed a close relationship—John wrote that Thomas "was my only intelligent companion; and was both a watchful parent and an affectionate, instructive friend"[21]—and John received from Thomas a practical and cultured education from which he gained exposure to political issues, legal controversies, and economic developments during a key period in Virginia's transformation from colony to state. In so educating John, Thomas was satisfying one of the essential expectations of gentry fathers. As Jack P. Greene has written,

Among the gentry, fathers sought to instill this strong sense of social duty—this powerful commitment to public service—in their sons from a very young age. They took deliberate care to transmit the political values, ideals, and attitudes of the group and to nurture that devotion to the public good that was the mark of all gentlemen of distinction. One of the most important elements in the education of young gentlemen was the constant exposure to the inner workings of governmental institutions and their early involvement in discussions of political and judicial affairs. . . . By the time they had reached manhood, sons of the gentry had an intimate knowledge of the Virginia political process and thorough preparation for the tasks for government and community leadership.[22]

For all this, John felt a deep measure of gratitude to his father. He wrote in his autobiography that "to [my father's] care I am indebted for anything valuable which I may have acquired in my youth." The Chief Justice's friend and colleague Joseph Story quoted him as saying, "My father was a far abler man than any of his sons. To him I owe the solid foundation of all my own success in life." Story remembered that "in his private and familiar conversations with me . . . he never named his father . . . without dwelling on his character with a fond and winning enthusiasm . . . he broke out with a spontaneous eloquence . . . upon his virtues and talents."[23]

John also absorbed a balanced social perception from his father. Thomas, despite his political and economic success, never became a haughty frontier parvenu, nor did he ape the cosmopolitan culture of the first families. He did not try to flaunt a false modesty more in keeping with his humble roots, and he neither scorned the less successful nor envied the better-off. This attitude, along with unpolished mannerisms acquired from frontier living, can be seen in John Marshall's "democratic demeanor" (or what Jefferson would derogate as "lax and lounging manners") that coexisted easily with his keen mind and high prestige. Examples of his common touch abound: the shabbily-dressed Chief Justice—his clothes appearing to come "from the wardrobe of some antiquated slopshop of second-hand raiment," Story wrote—ambling down a Richmond street munching on cherries out of his hat; offering to carry home an unwitting shopper's turkey; being mistaken for a butcher or errand-runner; playing marbles on hands and knees in his yard with a delivery boy; returning from market with arms laden with fresh-killed poultry and pockets stuffed with steak and chitterlings; gathering his own firewood while lodging at a tavern in North Carolina during circuit duty. One reverential writer even insisted that Marshall "ever recurred with fondness to that primitive mode of life [during his childhood], when he partook with a keen relish balm tea and mush, and when the females used thorns for pins." [24]

To stress these supposed rhapsodies over his modest origins, however, strikes the wrong emphasis and oversimplifies the character that life in the frontier gentry helped shape. Herbert Alan Johnson, an editor of the Marshall Papers, rightly observes that "Although a 'log cabin boy' by birth, [Marshall] was not the frontiersman Beveridge depicts, and he would have been puzzled by his biographer's describing him as the prototype of that paragon of all backwoodsmen, Abraham Lincoln. Marshall was a man of well-developed tastes who enjoyed the salon and carefully attended to his supply of wines." Raised in ever-more prosperous surroundings by a well-situated family with an ingrained drive for advancement, and prodded if not inspired by a dynamic and well-connected father, John was imbued with an ethos of improvement, and he welcomed the material benefits of his father's and his own accomplishments. He did not consciously fashion his rough edges later on to posture as a common man while hobnobbing with illustrious Virginians. As Gordon Wood has noted, "Marshall never acquired the cultivated elegance of his [maternal] Randolph forbears. He never shed the rough but genial manners of his frontier father." He seems instead to have sincerely and instinctively enjoyed simple hospitality and unostentatious living. After visiting Marshall when he was chief justice, Jared Sparks observed a "consistency in all things about him—his house, grounds, office, himself, bear marks of a primitive simplicity and plainness rarely to be seen combined." At the same time, though, in keeping with his unphilosophic and practical nature, Marshall did not divine deep significance in his pastoral upbringing or offer any paeans for sturdy soil-tillers as God's chosen people. Instead, the main lesson he seems to have drawn from his family's success on the Piedmont frontier is that the astute and determined pursuit of opportunity in an open and advantageous environment would and should be rewarded.[25]

Although John was well schooled by even the low contemporary standards of the gentry, the precise influence of this education on his intellectual processes and attitudes is hard to determine. In later years, he clearly showed that he accepted the major tenets of the ideology of republicanism, and that he possessed a rigorous, well-ordered mind with a capacity for incisive analysis and lucid expression. The latter may have been inherited faculties that he sharpened as a lawyer, politician, diplomat, and jurist. His classical education— which he advised his grandson "may be of great real advantage in our progress through human life"—did not inspire him toward the pure pursuit of knowledge. He was not a scholar who enjoyed learning for its own sake, nor a bookish technician who considered research an end in itself. He was a builder, not a theorizer. He had the architect's or engineer's skill at applying basic principles rather than the artist's or philosopher's talent for discovering or interpreting them. "The theories of the closet," he wrote in 1804, "must have the stamp of practice before they can be received with implicit confidence." He was well read without being erudite, thoughtful without being sophistic. His private and public writings are literate but not literary, impressive for their clarity and reasoning, devoid of pedantry and esoterica.[26]

"About the time I entered my eighteenth year [1773]," Marshall wrote in his autobiography, "the controversy between Great Britain and her colonies had assumed so serious an aspect as almost to monopolize the attention of the old and the young." During the preceding decade, which spanned most of the formative years of Marshall's youth, Great Britain's attempt to impose order on its relationship with its American colonies had revived long-standing resentments and created new sources of anger and bitterness. A myriad of political, social, economic, and ideological factors was converging to force a resolution to the growing conflict. With his childhood over, his education nearly complete, and his loyalty to Virginia's society and institutions secured, Marshall joined the revolutionary struggle and "engaged in it with all the zeal and enthusiasm which belonged to my age."[27]

NOTES

1. Albert J. Beveridge, *The Life of John Marshall*, 4 vols. (Boston: Houghton Mifflin, 1916–19), 1:12–14, 483–88, which includes texts of the wills of Thomas and John "of the Forest" and the deed of land from William to John. See also William M. Paxton, *The Marshall Family* . . . (Cincinnati: Robert Clarke and Co., 1885), passim. Although the elder John's farm was slightly smaller than the 250-acre average for older Tidewater counties outside the Northern Neck, his accumulated property was significantly more valuable than that of the typical small farmer of the region, who, according to one survey, left on average only about £16 of personal property to his heirs. Douglas Southall Freeman, *George Washington: A Biography*, 7 vols. (New York: Charles Scribner's Sons, 1949–57), 1:81, 83.

2. Beveridge, *Marshall*, 1:9–11, 17–20; William Draper Lewis, "John Marshall, 1755–1835," in *Great American Lawyers* . . . (Philadelphia: John C. Winston Co., 1907; rept., South Hackensack, N.J.: Rothman Reprints, 1971), 320; Sallie E. Marshall Hardy, "John Marshall as Son, Brother, Husband and Friend," *Green Bag*, 8 (December 1896), 479; Jean Edward Smith, *John Marshall: Definer of a Nation* (New York: Henry Holt, 1996), 23–26. There is no documentary evidence that Washington hired Thomas—no references in Washington's writings or diaries, for example—only second hand accounts passed on years later. Q.v. Beveridge, *Marshall*, 1:45–46; Freeman, *Washington*, 1:237–38; Stuart E. Brown, Jr., *Virginia Baron: The Story of Thomas 6th Lord Fairfax* (Berryville, Va.: Chesapeake Book Co., 1965), 118; T. Triplett Russell and John K. Gott, *Fauquier County in the Revolution* (Warrenton, Va.: Fauquier County American Bicentennial Commission, 1976), 35. During most of his life, John Marshall wore an amethyst ring engraved with the Keith family motto, "Veritas Vincit" (Truth Conquers). Beveridge, *Marshall*, 1:17.

3. Sources for this and the next paragraph are Beveridge, *Marshall*, 1:33–34, 485; Allan Kulikoff, *Tobacco and Slaves: The Development of Southern Cultures in the Chesapeake, 1680–1800* (Chapel Hill, N.C.: University of North Carolina Press, 1986), 141–48; T.H. Breen, *Tobacco Culture: The Mentality of the Great Tidewater Planters*

on the Eve of the Revolution (Princeton: Princeton University Press, 1985), 38, 118–19; Bruce A. Ragsdale, *A Planters' Republic: The Search for Economic Independence in Revolutionary Virginia* (Madison, Wis.: Madison House, 1996), 13–17, 36–41; Thomas P. Abernethy, *Three Virginia Frontiers* (Baton Rouge: Louisiana State University Press, 1940; rept., Gloucester, Mass.: Peter Smith, 1962), 42; Fauquier County Bicentennial Committee, *Fauquier County, Virginia, 1759–1959* (Warrenton: Virginia Publishing Co., 1959), 16–18, 33; Fairfax Harrison, *Landmarks of Old Prince William: A Study of Origins in Northern Virginia*, 2 vols. (Richmond, 1924; 2nd rept., Baltimore: Gateway Press, 1987), 1:207–21; H. C. Groome, *Fauquier during the Proprietorship: A Chronicle of the Colonization and Organization of a Northern Neck County* (Richmond, 1927; rept., Baltimore: Regional Publishing Co., 1969), 113–30, 168, 181; Charles E. Kemper, "The History of Germantown," *Bulletin of the Fauquier Historical Society,* 2 (July 1922), 125–33; idem, "The Early Westward Movement in Virginia," *VMHB,* 13 (1906), 362–70; "Germantown, Fauquier's First Settlement," *News and Notes of the Fauquier Historical Society,* 3 (summer 1981), 1–2.

Although no record of any transaction of Thomas's exists, he probably did not squat on the land but leased it instead. The territory of Prince William County had been almost fully partitioned by 1750, and much of the Germantown area was owned either by Hamilton Parish as a glebe or by some prominent local families. *Fauquier County,* 33; Harrison, *Landmarks of Old Prince William,* 1:215, 307 n. 51. Thomas's father-in-law, the Reverend James Keith, moved to Prince William County in 1733 and became the first rector of Hamilton Parish. *Fauquier County,* 194. In 1902, the Marshall Chapter of the Phi Delta Phi legal fraternity placed a memorial stone and tablet on the site of the Marshall cabins, which might have been destroyed during the Civil War. The John Marshall Birthplace Park was dedicated in 1981 by Fauquier County. Maria Newton Marshall, "The Marshall Memorial Tablet," *Green Bag,* 14 (August 1902), 372–73; *News and Notes of the Fauquier Historical Society,* 3:1 (winter 1981), 3.

4. Beveridge, *Marshall,* 1:35–39; "The Thomas Marshall Cabin," *Fauquier County, Va., Court Records,* 3 vols., comp. A. M. Seymour and W. T. Jewell, typescript at Daughters of the American Revolution library, Washington, D.C., 3:29–30; Harrison, *Landmarks of Old Prince William,* 1:247–48; *Fauquier County,* 41, 45; Rhys Isaac, *The Transformation of Virginia, 1740–1790* (Chapel Hill: University of North Carolina Press, 1982), 34; *Old Homes and Families of Fauquier County, Virginia (The W.P.A. Records)* (Berryville: Virginia Book Co., 1978), 148; author's inspections, January and May 1992, September 1994, and October 1997. A small local preservation society, Friends of the Hollow, was formed in 1981 to maintain the house. "The Hollow Needs Help," *News and Notes of the Fauquier Historical Society,* 6:4 (fall 1984), 3.

5. John Stokes Adams, ed., *An Autobiographical Sketch by John Marshall* . . . (Ann Arbor: University of Michigan Press, 1937), 4. (Hereafter cited as JM, *Autobiographical Sketch.*)

6. Beveridge, *Marshall,* 1:55–56; *Fauquier County Court Records,* 1:57–58; *Old Homes and Families of Fauquier County,* 148; Mayme Ober Peak, "Oak Hill: The Fauquier Home of Chief Justice Marshall," *House Beautiful,* 49 (April 1921), 288; Thomas's deed to John, 16 March 1785, *PJM* 1:136–37; author's inspections, January, May, and September 1992.

Thomas bought the Oak Hill property for just over £900 from Thomas Turner. Just before venturing off to Kentucky in 1785, Thomas transferred his remaining 824 acres to John (he already had sold 1,000 acres to others in 1780). In 1818, next to the original house, the Chief Justice built the much larger Federal-style mansion visible today from Interstate 66, which follows the route of the old Cold Spring Road that the Marshalls took to and from the Hollow. Marshall used the home as his principal summer retreat. He willed it to his son Thomas, but his descendants sold it in 1869. In 1965, Morris Marks, a Washington businessman, bought the property as an investment. When he died in 1993, his heirs formed the Foundation for John Marshall's Oak Hill to help find a buyer "who is sensitive to its history," but an auction in 1994 failed to bring forward such a person. A real estate broker then bought the deteriorating house and the remaining 366 acres and sold the property in several parcels. Allen Freeman, "Buyer Sought for John Marshall Estate," *Historic Preservation News*, October–November 1994, 20–21; "Justice's Home Up for Auction," *Washington Times*, 12 October 1994, Nexis 94–00758889; Jennifer Ordonez, "A Supreme Effort at Preservation In Justice's Name; Marshall Admirer Takes a Last Stand," *Washington Post*, 26 July 1998, Loudoun Co. ed., p. V7.

7. JM, *Autobiographical Sketch*, 4; Story's address in John F. Dillon, comp. and ed., *John Marshall: Life, Character and Judicial Services*, 3 vols. (Chicago: Callaghan and Co., 1903), 3:330 (hereafter cited as Dillon, *Marshall*); Francis N. Stites, *John Marshall: Defender of the Constitution* (Boston: Little, Brown, 1981), 2; Breen, *Tobacco Culture*, 125–29, 141.

8. "Minutes of the First Court," annot. H. C. Groome, *Bulletin of the Fauquier Historical Society*, no. 4 (July 1924), 387–88, 401; Groome, *Fauquier during the Proprietorship*, 178–79; James Thomas Flexner, *George Washington in the American Revolution (1775–1783)* (Boston: Little, Brown, 1967), 44; JM to Joseph Delaplaine, 22 March 1818, in Dillon, *Marshall*, 1:55; Irwin S. Rhodes, *The Papers of John Marshall: A Descriptive Calendar*, 2 vols. (Norman, Okla.: University of Oklahoma Press, 1956), 1:3–4 (hereafter cited as Rhodes, *Calendar of Marshall Papers*). Thomas received his surveyor's commission from the Trustees of William and Mary College, who appointed county surveyors until the Revolution under the terms of the school's 1692 charter. Harrison, *Landmarks of Old Prince William*, 2:65 n. 87. Virginia appointed Thomas surveyor of the western lands (Kentucky) in 1781, and George Washington chose him as collector of revenue for Kentucky in 1789. He resigned in 1797, he said, because of the "particular malevolence" of political opponents there. "Thomas Marshall," *Bulletin of the Fauquier Historical Society*, 1 (July 1922), 140–41.

9. Charles S. Sydnor, *American Revolutionaries in the Making: Political Practices in Washington's Virginia* (New York: Free Press, 1965), 76–82, 101; A. G. Roeber, *Faithful Magistrates and Republican Lawyers: Creators of Virginia Legal Culture, 1680–1810* (Chapel Hill: University of North Carolina Press, 1981), xv, 42–43; George Dargo, *Roots of the Republic: A New Perspective on Early American Constitutionalism* (New York: Praeger, 1974), 44–45.

10. Harrison, *Landmarks of Old Prince William*, 1:331–32; *Fauquier County*, 62, 78; Groome, *Fauquier during the Proprietorship*, 165–66; Roeber, *Faithful Magistrates*, 73–75, 93–95; Gordon Wood, *The Radicalism of the American Revolution* (New York: Alfred A. Knopf, 1992), 143; Beveridge, *Marshall*, 4:491.

11. Sydnor, *American Revolutionaries in the Making*, 102–4. During the 1769 election, Thomas earned a reprimand from the House of Burgesses for a self-aggrandizing lapse of character: wielding his powers as sheriff to affect the timing of a ballot to guarantee his victory. In 1769 he scheduled the election in Fauquier County on the same day as that in nearby Stafford County, hoping to discourage voting by freeholders whose support he questioned. He won by so large a margin, however, that the House seated him anyway. John G. Kolp, *Gentlemen and Freeholders: Electoral Politics in Colonial Virginia* (Baltimore: Johns Hopkins University Press, 1998), 33–34.

12. Sydnor, *American Revolutionaries in the Making*, 88–95; Beveridge, *Marshall*, 1:58, 60–65.

13. Sydnor, *American Revolutionaries in the Making*, 69–70; Rhodes, *Calendar of Marshall Papers*, 1:4; James Bradley Thayer, *John Marshall* (Boston: Houghton Mifflin, 1901), 6–7; Beveridge, *Marshall*, 1:58.

14. Bishop [William] Meade, *Old Churches, Ministers, and Families of Virginia*, 2 vols. (Philadelphia: J. P. Lippincott, 1910), 2:218; Harrison, *Landmarks of Old Prince William*, 1:282, 297–99; Sydnor, *American Revolutionaries in the Making*, 83–84; Daniel Boorstin, *The Americans: The Colonial Experience*, Vintage ed. (New York: Random House, 1958), 123–39; Isaacs, *Transformation of Virginia*, 120; Russell and Gott, *Fauquier County in the Revolution*, 19–20; *Fauquier County*, 86–87. The meeting house is now the Cool Spring Methodist Church. "Cool Spring Church," *News and Notes of the Fauquier Historical Society*, 4 (fall 1982), 1–2. The incident with William Marshall is mentioned in Louis Payton Little, *Imprisoned Preachers and Religious Liberty in Virginia*... (Lynchburg, Va.: J. P. Bell Co., 1938), 197–98.

15. Sources for this and the next paragraph are Beveridge, *Marshall*, 4:69–71; Leonard Baker, *John Marshall: A Life in Law* (New York: Macmillan, 1974), 10, 95, 751–52; Henry Howe, *Historical Collections of Virginia* . . . (Charleston, S.C., 1845; rept., Baltimore: Regional Publishing Co., 1969), 275–76; JM to Samuel F. Jarvis, 26 March 1820, *PJM*, 9:29; JM to [?], 12 September 1832, *The Calumet*, Vol. T (November–December 1832), 290–91; JM to James M. Garnett, 17 December 1830, and the Rev. Jasper Adams, 9 May 1833, in Rhodes, *Calendar of Marshall Papers*, 2:348, 417; JM to John Marshall Jr., 7 December 1834, in John Edward Oster, *The Political and Economic Doctrines of John Marshall* (orig. publ. 1914; rept., New York: Burt Franklin, 1967), 57; Hardy, "Marshall as Son, Brother, Husband and Friend," 56–57, 203–05, 480, 487; Frances Norton Mason, *My Dearest Polly: Letters of Chief Justice John Marshall to His Wife* . . . (Richmond: Garrett and Massie, 1961), 212–13, 322; "Letters from John Marshall to His Wife," *WMQ*, 2nd ser., 3 (1923), 87–89; Robert K. Faulkner, *The Jurisprudence of John Marshall* (Princeton: Princeton University Press, 1968), 35, 137, 139–40; Meade, *Old Churches, Ministers, and Families of Virginia*, 2:223; Arthur N. Holcombe, "John Marshall as Politician and Political Theorist," in *Chief Justice John Marshall: A Reappraisal*, ed. W. Melville Jones, (Ithaca: Cornell University Press, 1956), 26; JM to Thomas White, 29 November 1824, in James M. Garnett, *Lectures on Female Education*, 4th ed. (Richmond: Thomas W. White, 1825), 8.

16. Carl Bridenbaugh, *Myths and Realities: Societies of the Colonial South* (New York: Atheneum, 1965), 189; Lawrence A. Cremin, *American Education: The Colonial Experience, 1607–1783* (New York: Harper and Row, 1970), 527, 531; JM, *Autobiographical Sketch*, 4; Baker, *Marshall*, 13; Story in Dillon, *Marshall*, 3:331. Lord Fairfax's library inventory is in Brown, *Virginia Baron*, 192–93. Thomas Marshall demonstrated his technical ingenuity by inventing a surveying instrument that would convert magnetic north to true north, as the Virginia General Assembly required for all surveys made after 1772. Silvio A. Bendini, "Marshall's Meridian Instrument," *Professional Surveyor*, 7 (July/August 1987), 26ff., (September/October 1987), 60.

17. Groome, *Fauquier during the Proprietorship*, 213; Harrison, *Landmarks of Old Prince William*, 2:332; JM, *Autobiographical Sketch*, 4; Cremin, *American Education*, 500, 505; Beveridge, *Marshall*, 1:57; Baker, *Marshall*, 13; Smith, *Marshall*, 35; Harry Ammon, *James Monroe: The Quest for National Identity* (New York: McGraw-Hill, 1971), 3; W. P. Cresson, *James Monroe* (Chapel Hill: University of North Carolina Press, 1946), 8.

18. Meade, *Old Churches, Ministers, and Families of Virginia*, 2:159, 219; Beveridge, *Marshall*, 1:52–53; Louis B. Wright, *The Cultural Life of the American Colonies, 1607–1763* (New York: Harper and Row, 1957), 112; George Brydon, *Virginia's Mother Church and the Political Conditions Under Which It Grew*, 2 vols. (Philadelphia: Church Historical Society, 1948–52), 1:391; JM to John Marshall Jr., 7 November 1834 and 11 March 1835, in Oster, *Political and Economic Doctrines of Marshall*, 55, 61–62.

19. Gordon S. Wood, *The Creation of the American Republic, 1776–1787* (Chapel Hill: University of North Carolina Press, 1969; rept., New York: W. W. Norton, 1972), 48–53; Ralph Ketcham, *Presidents Above Party: The First American Presidency, 1789–1829* (Chapel Hill: University of North Carolina Press, 1984), 20–22; Agnes Marie Sibley, *Alexander Pope's Prestige in America, 1725–1835* (New York: King's Crown Press, 1949), 25–73; Maynard Mack, *Alexander Pope: A Life* (New York: W. W. Norton, 1985), 523–25.

20. Mason, *My Dearest Polly*, 277, 300–01, 332–33; JM to Story, 26 November 1826, in Oster, *Political and Economic Doctrines of Marshall*, 103; Story in Dillon, *Marshall*, 3:331–32; JM, Account Book, *PJM*, 1:329, 334, 352, 2:347, 349, 415, 427, 453, 464, 475, 479, 485. Marshall's books were dispersed to his heirs when he died. The staff of the John Marshall House Museum has tried to assemble a representative selection of the titles he is known or likely to have owned or read, but the volumes on display and in storage at the Museum do not constitute a true "library." Author's conversation with Melissa Haynes of the Museum staff, 23 November 1994.

21. JM, *Autobiographical Sketch*, 4.

22. Jack P. Greene, "Society, Ideology, and Politics: An Analysis of the Political Culture of Mid-Eighteenth-Century Virginia," in *Society, Freedom, and Conscience: The American Revolution in Virginia, Massachusetts, and New York*, ed. Richard M. Jellison (New York: W. W. Norton, 1976), 31–32.

23. JM, *Autobiographical Sketch*, 4; Story's address in Dillon, *Marshall*, 3:330.

24. Beveridge, *Marshall*, 4:61–65; Baker, *Marshall*, 755–58; Henry Howe, *Historical Collections of Virginia . . .* (Charleston, S.C., 1845; rept., Baltimore: Regional Publishing Co., 1969) 263.

25. Herbert Alan Johnson, "John Marshall," in *The Justices of the Supreme Court, 1789–1969: Their Lives and Opinions*, 4 vols., ed. Leon Friedman and Fred L. Israel (New York: R. R. Bowker Co., 1969), 1:302; Gordon Wood, "The Father of the Court," *New Republic*, 17 February 1997, 39; Herbert Baxter Adams, *The Life and Writings of Jared Sparks*, 2 vols. (Boston: Houghton Mifflin, 1893), 1:421.

26. JM to John Marshall Jr., 7 November 1834, in Oster, *Political and Economic Doctrines of Marshall*, 55; JM, *A History of the Colonies . . .* (Philadelphia: Abraham Small, 1824; rept., Fredericksburg, Va.: Citizens' Guild of Washington's Boyhood Home, 1926), 53–54. This work originally was published in 1804 as volume 1 of Marshall's biography of George Washington.

Charles F. Hobson, editor of the Marshall Papers, has given an excellent summary of the Chief Justice's intellectual qualities:

Marshall was a man of affairs—soldier, legislator, diplomat, statesman, lawyer, and judge—not a contemplative theorist. He never composed a treatise on government or jurisprudence, though he certainly possessed the intellectual ability and literary talent to produce such a work had he been so inclined. He was capable of deep thought and reflection, but his interest in law and the principles of government was not of a bookish or an academic sort. He was not a scholar-statesman like James Madison, John Adams, or John C. Calhoun; nor was he a legal commentator and publicist like Joseph Story or James Kent. . . . He pursued knowledge to derive assistance or illumination in carrying out particular public and professional tasks. His writings . . . originated in the concrete circumstances of the moment, not out of a conscious design to make an enduring statement of principles. . . . He was a creative adapter of ideas, not an original thinker who formulated new insights into the nature of government and law.

Charles F. Hobson, *The Great Chief Justice: John Marshall and the Rule of Law* (Lawrence: University Press of Kansas, 1996), x–xi.
27. JM, *Autobiographical Sketch*, 5.

Chapter 2

The Revolutionary War Experience, 1775–1781

John Marshall grew up in a political and social environment that fostered hostility to changes in Great Britain's colonial policies during the 1760s and 1770s.[1] Virginia stood at the forefront of American protests against the end of salutary neglect and of the development of a vigorous defense of the rights of Englishmen and the colonies. The gentry's strong anti-imperial attitudes were motivated mainly by political and constitutional concerns—specifically, British restrictions on the prerogatives of the House of Burgesses—rather than planter debt, western land hunger, or internal political and social disputes. Each of Parliament's major colonial enactments—particularly the Stamp Act, the Townshend Acts, and the Coercive Acts—prompted boycotts, extralegal assembly meetings, intimidation of officials, and public agitation in many areas of Virginia.

In general, frontier regions that enjoyed significant political autonomy, or derived much of their political culture, from the coastal squirearchy—such as the Virginia Piedmont where Fauquier County lay—strongly supported the movement toward independence. By 1775, protest and resistance had spread to the northern Piedmont and backcountry. County committees, originally modeled on the colonial Committees of Correspondence, had spread throughout the colony by mid-1775. Controlled by the same predominantly Anglican gentrymen who ran other local institutions, the committees created and enforced propatriot unity within the population at large. They moved forcefully against violators of nonimportation agreements and suspected loyalists and helped encourage extensive mobilization of the frontier militia. The latter function was particularly successful in the response to Governor Dunmore's seizure of powder from the colony's magazine in Williamsburg in April 1775. Hundreds of Piedmont and backwoods militiamen headed to Fredericksburg in anticipation of marching on the capital. "All the frontier counties were in motion," according to a contemporary newspaper. "Fredericksburg never was so honour'd with so many brave hearty men . . . every man Rich and poor with their hunting shirts[,] Belts and Tomahawks fixed . . . in the best manner."

In Fauquier County, anti-imperial sentiment developed early and soon pervaded the area. The Stamp Act caused the farmers and planters there to become "impatient to know their destiny—whether they are to sink under a load they say it is impossible to support, or once more be a happy people," in the words of a prominent local resident at the time. In 1774, county freeholders and gentrymen joined several other Virginia localities in castigating the Coercive Acts directed against Massachusetts. The Fauquier County Resolutions declared, among other things, that Parliament could not constitutionally tax the colonies because America's interests could not be truly represented under the current system. The Resolutions also branded anyone buying, selling, or using British tea as "an enemy to American liberty and the common rights of mankind," and called for a total commercial embargo against England. The county committee carried out the letter and spirit of the Resolutions.[2]

John Marshall's attitudes toward the conflict with Britain were formed in this increasingly contentious environment. Here, as in other areas, Thomas Marshall greatly influenced his son's thoughts and actions. Thomas was involved in a variety of political events in reaction to the renewal of imperial regulation during 1765–1775, and undoubtedly he conveyed to John his pessimistic views of what they portended for Virginia and the other colonies. Thomas made no explicit statements on the subject, but his activities made his position clear. In the Assembly, he sided early on with the Burgesses who most resisted Britain's encroachments on their power. He apparently supported Patrick Henry's remonstrations against the Stamp Act in 1765. During the next decade, Thomas attended extralegal sessions of the Assembly, voted in favor of establishing an intercolonial association to boycott British imports, approved the raising of Continental Army units from Virginia, and helped choose representatives to the second Continental Congress in 1775. John recalled when Thomas returned to Oak Hill from Richmond in the spring of 1775 after hearing Patrick Henry's "liberty or death" speech and called the oration "one of the most bold, vehement, and animated pieces of eloquence that had ever been delivered." By then, Thomas probably would have endorsed the idea of a dominion conception of the Empire, and certainly was contemplating, albeit with some trepidation, the prospects for independence from Britain.[3]

By the mid-1770s, John Marshall also would have been well aware of the philosophical and intellectual background of the Revolution. He had studied some of the important classical and neoclassical literature that contributed to the ideology of republicanism, and he recalled that he channeled some of his "zeal and enthusiasm" during 1773–75 into reading "the political essays of the day."[4] He probably was referring to, at a minimum, pieces printed in the *Virginia*

Gazette, and he may also have consulted those works on individual rights, civic humanism, constitutionalism, and imperial relations that helped develop the distinctive American theory of politics by 1776.

John Marshall joined the military struggle for independence by serving in Virginia volunteer or militia units from 1774 to 1776, when he received a commission in the Virginia Continental Line. The Virginia militia into which Marshall followed his father—Thomas presumably joined Fauquier County's first frontier defense unit soon after its formation in 1761—had reached the nadir of several decades of decline. Although Virginia had a deep-rooted militia tradition, and its seventeenth-century citizen soldiery had acquitted itself creditably in combat, by the mid-eighteenth century the colony's militia had deteriorated seriously. Dispersed settlement hindered unity and control; the reduced threat from France, Spain, and the Indians in the backcountry, combined with anxiety over slave insurrection in the Tidewater, caused the governing gentry to divert of attention and resources eastward; and militia laws were laxly enforced. Militia units throughout the colony were inexperienced, poorly equipped, badly trained, and unmotivated. For the yeoman privates, service was an inconvenience that fostered resentment toward the gentry even as it testified to their full citizenship in the community. For the gentry officers, it symbolized and solidified their prestige and leadership. The 1757 militia law idealized Virginia's social order, particularly its aspects of localism, personalized authority, and social stratification by honor, dignity, and duty. Exclusionary provisions kept the poorer sorts out of this fraternity of arms; they would instead become field substitutes for the freeholders and gentry when real war commenced. Militia musters, Edmund S. Morgan has written, were a "strange combination of camaraderie and condescension, of deference and conviviality that bound high and low together politically. It was a time for showing both the structure and the tone of society." Rather than encouraging preparedness, musters formalized the social order through ritualized martial displays and revelry. These qualities were earlier captured by the English poet John Dryden in his "Cymon and Iphigenia" (1700):

The country rings around with loud alarms,
And raw in files the rude militia swarms;
Mouths without hands, maintained at vast expense,
In peace a charge, in war a weak defence. . . .
This was the morn when, issuing on the guard,
Drawn up in rank and file, they stood prepared.
Of seeming arms to make a short assay,
Then hasten to be drunk, the business of the day.[5]

Largely in reaction to this sorry reputation, small numbers of enthusiastic, well-to-do young men in at least 27 Virginia counties and cities formed extralegal independent (also called volunteer, or gentlemen) companies between September 1774 and May–June 1775. John Marshall recalled that he started learning "the first rudiments of military exercise in an Independent company of the gentlemen of the county" of Fauquier. He and other members of these irregular auxiliary units provided their own equipment and uniforms, elected their own officers, and trained locally in small groups as it suited them instead of in the larger musters at intervals that colonial law mandated. The companies were regulated by the directives of the county Committee of Safety, for which they functioned as enforcement agents for the Continental Association's boycott of English imports. The companies proved more successful at turning out men to protest the governor's actions than at demonstrating their effectiveness as a military force. Washington later wrote that men "of the *Volunteer kind* are uneasy, impatient of Command, ungovernable; and, claiming to themselves a sort of superior merit, generally assume not only the Priviledge of thinking, but to do as they please." The egalitarianism and voluntarism on which the independent units were founded did not adapt well to stressful military situations and occasionally lapsed into disorder. This fundamental inadequacy became dangerously apparent in June 1775, when several hundred unruly volunteers from over a dozen units, joined by many vigilantes, gathered in Williamsburg and, defying their officers' orders, committed numerous acts of violence and intimidation, including raiding the Governor's Palace and detaining any royal official they thought might have some of the crown's money. "We appear rather invited to feast than fight," according to one volunteer.[6]

In August 1775, the third Virginia Convention—the extralegal assembly that met after Governor Dunmore dissolved the House of Burgesses—realized that the companies were not under adequate civil control and that the colony needed a more effective defensive force. The Convention ordered the independent units to disband and passed "[a]n ordinance for raising and embodying a sufficient force for the defence and protection of this colony." That law authorized the raising of two regiments of regular troops and 16 battalions of minutemen and placed them under strict rules and regulations to suppress the "enthusiasm" that had discredited the independent companies. The largest, best known, and perhaps most colorful minute battalion was assembled in the Culpeper District, which encompassed the counties of Culpeper, Orange, and Fauquier. By September, about 350 men had been recruited—among them Major Thomas Marshall, the third-ranking officer, and Lieutenant John Marshall.[7]

On a late summer morning in 1775, 19-year-old John, dressed in a purple or pale blue hunting shirt, trousers fringed in white, and a round black hat adorned with a bucktail, and carrying a flintlock musket, left Oak Hill and walked for a few hours to a field some 20 miles from Fauquier Court House. A company of militiamen from the Culpeper Minute Battalion had assembled there for a muster under the call of the unit captain, William Pickett, who did not attend. As his lieutenant, Marshall took command of the exercise. Several dozen men clustered about him—straight and slender at six feet tall, with a dark complexion, strong, penetrating dark brown eyes, and thick, raven-black hair. He told them that because of the fighting at Lexington and Concord in April, they would likely be called on soon to defend their country and their rights and liberties, and that it was now time to learn how to use their firearms for that purpose. Marshall ordered the sergeants to put the men in line and patiently led them through the manual of arms by word and example. After a few drills, he had the company fall out and invited it to gather around him while he discussed his understanding of what the conflict with Britain was about. His patriotic speech lasted an hour, following which the Minutemen held footraces and other athletic competitions, and then disbanded. Marshall walked the 10 miles back to Oak Hill, arriving just after sunset. Judging by this contemporary anecdote— the first detailed rendering of Marshall's involvement in the war for independence—he already bore responsibility easily, considered complex topics thoughtfully, conveyed his ideas lucidly, and exhibited leadership qualities that earned him the respect of his neighbors and peers.[8]

The uniforms and training of the men Marshall helped command embodied peculiar American ideas about warfare. The uniforms of the Culpeper Minutemen conveyed not just rustic necessity but also were a tactic of psychological warfare designed to intimidate the British. They reinforced what Daniel Boorstin has called "the myth of the omnipresent American marksman." George Washington tried to exploit this idea by issuing an order that "earnestly" encouraged "the use of Hunting Shirts, with long Breeches made of the same Cloth . . . it is a dress justly supposed to carry no small terror to the enemy, who think every such person a complete Marksman." A Culpeper Minuteman's description of his unit indicates that it took such thinking seriously:

the whole regiment appeared according to orders in hunting shirts made of strong, brown linen, dyed the color of the leaves of the trees, and on the breast of each hunting shirt was worked in large white letters the words "LIBERTY OR DEATH" and all that could procure for love or money [a] buck's tail, wore them in their hats. Each man had a leather belt around his shoulders, with a tomahawk and scalping-knife. The [yellow] flag had in the center a rattlesnake coiled in the act to strike. Below it were the words "Don't tread on me!" At the sides, "Liberty or Death!" and at the top, "The Culpeper Minute Men."

The unit's rough and menacing appearance had the more immediate effect of striking fear into the genteel locals. One of Marshall's comrades in arms wrote that "the people, hearing that we came from the backwoods, and seeing our savage-looking equipment, seemed as much afraid of us as if we had been Indians." But as the Minutemen "took pride in demeaning ourselves as patriots and gentlemen . . . the people soon treated us with respect and kindness."[9]

The Culpeper Minutemen, like other militia units throughout the colonies, modified the royal drill manual to stress simplicity over show in the exercise of arms by using the fewest possible movements to load, fire, and maneuver. The intent was to prove that determination could surmount display, or, as Timothy Pickering wrote in his simplified manual of 1775, "Away then with the trappings (as well as tricks) of the parade: Americans need them not: their eyes are not to be dazzled, nor their hearts awed into servility, by the splendour of equipage and dress: their minds are too much enlightened to be duped by a glittering outside."[10]

The Culpeper battalion apparently avoided the social divisions and political friction between gentry and nongentry which, if the Upper Valley and Southside were characteristic, impaired the effectiveness of other Piedmont and frontier militia units in Virginia. Fauquier County—as evidenced by its political practices and landholding patterns—remained strongly influenced by the Tidewater region. Although they lived in a transitional zone between east and west, Fauquier and Culpeper Minutemen did not shift their attention from the conflict with Britain over home rule to clash over who would rule at home. Small farmers' complaints about inequities in the burden of service, appointment rather than election of officers, and disparities in pay did not rise to disruptive levels in Marshall's unit as they did elsewhere.[11]

By the time Marshall joined the Culpeper Minute Battalion, the prestige of the militia had risen dramatically since the year before. A *rage militaire* had seized Virginia and the other colonies—a "passion for arms," a widespread patriotic fervor to resist royal tyranny that manifested itself not only in rhetorical excess but more tangibly in the reenergizing of militia companies. The patriots' heroic, if disorganized, performances at Concord and Bunker Hill heightened the people's confidence in the need for, and ability of, citizen soldiers to realize the purposes of republicanism. As Thomas Jefferson boasted, a "want of discipline" could be overcome by "native courage and . . . animation in the cause." Marshall later wrote that this "spirit of enthusiastic patriotism, which, for a time, elevates the mind above all considerations of individual acquisition, became the ruling passion in the American bosom." He undoubtedly found himself caught up in this emotional mix of exuberance, anxiety, chauvinism, and hostility as the Culpeper minutemen—"all fine fellows, and well armed," according to the *Virginia Gazette*—marched south to Williamsburg in October 1775 to answer an emergency call from the commander of Virginia's provisional army, Colonel Patrick Henry. Henry had summoned troops to defend the region against what Marshall termed "a small regular and predatory force" commanded by Governor Dunmore. The arduous, 150-mile march took several weeks and tested the dedication and stamina of the green militiamen. In October, the governor began raiding the coast with his Norfolk-based fleet, and in November he routed a local militia unit, declared martial law, and reaffirmed his decision to free any slaves and indentured servants who would fight for England. Dunmore, drawing support from a community of loyalist Scottish merchants, and a large portion of the residents of Norfolk who had just sworn a new oath of allegiance to the King, "made some impression around Norfolk" and "collected such a force of the disaffected and negroes, as gave him an entire ascendancy in that part of the colony," Marshall wrote.[12]

During this campaign, Marshall first faced enemy fire at the battle of Great Bridge, 12 miles south of Norfolk, on 9 December. The details of that encounter—the first clash between British soldiers and patriots since Bunker Hill, and the first Revolutionary War battle in Virginia—have been detailed elsewhere and need no reiteration here. However, a few salient facts about tactics, logistics, and military conduct warrant attention for their effect on Marshall. A combined force of over 700 Virginia regulars and militia routed some 250 British troops—over half of them regarded as unreliable "Ethiopians" and loyalists—after the King's force lost nearly half its men in a desperate but foolhardy assault by grenadiers across a narrow, 160-yard causeway against entrenched positions. The Culpeper Minutemen laid down a withering enfilade fire, and the British charge was repelled after barely 20 minutes.[13]

The Virginians' commander touted the victory as a second Bunker Hill, and patriot propaganda echoed the refrain: Once again, colonial troops, and especially the militia, had proven their competence and bravery in pitched battle against trained imperial regulars. The inference can be drawn from Marshall's own colorless accounts of his "first blood," however, that he believed the battle deserved understatement rather than acclaim. The analogy to Bunker Hill was only partially correct: Once again, British tactical miscalculation—in this case brought on by positional stalemate, harsh conditions, overconfidence, and fear that colonial reinforcements would arrive anytime—caused massive casualties and here enabled the inexperienced patriots to prevail. In addition, Marshall got a foretaste of the hardships the Continentals would suffer because of the states' inadequacies at logistics. Despite materiel requirements specified in the military law passed months before, the Virginia troops at Great Bridge were poorly equipped for battle or winter campaigning. Marshall and the other soldiers had to endure weeks of cold without enough blankets or tents, and they never had sufficient muskets or ammunition.[14]

The violent events that immediately followed the rout at Great Bridge probably had the greatest impact on Marshall. Before the battle, a loyalist merchant in Norfolk presciently observed that "[i]f the Colony Troops get possession of Norfolk, the Rifle Men will endeavour to annoy the [British] Ships [in the harbor] by taking their stand behind Houses, and firing at the officers or men who appear on the Decks, which may bring on the destruction of the Place, tho' not at this time intended by either Party." That fairly describes what happened next. Virginia troops occupying Norfolk, Marshall wrote, "frequently amused themselves by firing into the vessels in the harbour from the buildings near the water." An enraged Lord Dunmore, who had taken refuge aboard one of those ships, put up with the sniping for two weeks before ordering a landing party ashore to torch the waterfront. For no military purpose, but only to exact vengeance against Norfolk's loyalists, the Virginians let the flames spread, and then large numbers of mostly militiamen went on a three-day spree of drinking, looting, and burning that left 900 houses—two thirds of the city—in ashes before commanders on the scene restrained them. "All night the fire was so great," an American soldier wrote, "the clouds above the town appeared as red and bright as they do in an evening at sun setting." The Virginia Convention soon ordered the leveling of the remaining structures to keep the British and Tories from using them, and the last American forces evacuated the charred and desolate city in February. A state investigative commission reported that the soldiers "wantonly set fire to the greater part of the houses within the town, where the enemy never attempted to approach, and where it would have been impossible for them to have penetrated." Whatever part Marshall may have had in the near riot cannot be ascertained from his own bland rendering or other evidence, but his discomfiture with the unprofessional behavior of the militia and state regulars is clear in his comment that "[Norfolk's] destruction was one of those ill-judged measures of which the consequences are felt long after the motives are forgotten."[15]

The rampage in Norfolk graphically demonstrated to Marshall that disorder was inherent in the militia, especially when it was avenging localized wrongs. The militia's independent spirit, which ideologues and apologists touted as the reason why it was superior to a standing army, had impaired its effectiveness and inevitably would cause unruliness and unreliability. Marshall later wrote that militia "victories" such as Bunker Hill—and, it is fair to say, Great Bridge—perpetuated a dangerous self-deception:

The Americans were much elated by the intrepidity the raw troops had displayed, and the execution they had done, in this engagement. They fondly cherished the belief that courage, and dexterity in the use of firearms, would bestow advantages amply compensating the want of discipline. Unfortunately for the colonies, this course of thinking was not confined to the mass of the people. It seems to have extended to those who guided the public councils, and to have contributed to the adoption of a system, which, more than once, brought their cause to the brink of ruin. They did not distinguish sufficiently between the momentary efforts of a few brave men, brought together by a high sense of the injuries which threatened their country, and carried into action under the influence of keen resentments; and those steady persevering exertions under continued suffering, which must be necessary to bring an important war to a happy termination . . . it is not by the few that great victories are to be gained, or a country to be saved.

To Marshall, instead of proving the superiority of citizen soldiers over regulars, Bunker Hill and Great Bridge demonstrated that the patriot forces sorely needed organization and obedience—two of the hallmarks of military professionalism. The people's passion for arms would have to be controlled by a trained and disciplined professional army if the colonies were to gain their independence.[16]

In 1776, Marshall left the militia and entered the Continental Army, an experience that profoundly shaped his attitudes toward nationalism, political institutions, and the role of the military.[17] In March, on orders from the Committee of Safety, the Culpeper Minutemen and the other militia units on duty in and around Norfolk were discharged because more companies of regulars raised in the previous months had arrived in the area. Marshall's unit turned its equipment over to its replacements, went to Suffolk for dismissal from active duty, and returned home sometime in April. Marshall probably spent the next few months planting new crops and recruiting and training local men for service in the Continental Army. Meanwhile, the Virginia Convention responded to George Washington's pleas for reinforcements by providing six additional regiments for the Continental Army. On 30 July, Marshall received a commission as a lieutenant in the Third Regiment of the Virginia Continental Line. Most Fauquier men, including many former Culpeper Minutemen, joined the Third, and his father had been a major in it since March.

Soon after, Marshall joined a company that Captain William Blackwell was recruiting in Fauquier County. When the Eleventh Virginia Regiment was created in September and Daniel Morgan—the most illustrious military figure in Virginia after George Washington—was appointed its colonel in November, Blackwell volunteered his company to serve in it. Under the command of the recently promoted Morgan, who had recruited the Continental Army's first company of Virginia riflemen in 1775, the Eleventh had the potential to become an elite unit. It received special attention from Virginia authorities and the Continental command; for example, the Virginia Convention gave it higher pay than other Virginia Line units. The Eleventh, which Washington planned to use for scouting and skirmishing, was formally assigned to his army on 27 December. Blackwell's company was a 50-strong motley of frontiersmen in deerskin and frocks, Seven Years War veterans in the Virginia militia's buff and blue, and others in assorted civilian dress. In its first maneuver, the company marched over 100 miles to Philadelphia in January 1777 for smallpox inoculations. Washington had ordered all units entering the Continental Army to be vaccinated because the disease, Marshall wrote, "had proved more fatal . . . than the sword of the enemy" during the retreat across New Jersey in 1776, and recruitment was seriously hindered. Vaccinations were illegal in Virginia, however, until October 1777. After recovering from the effects of the immunization, Marshall and the rest of Blackwell's company caught up with the American forces at Princeton in April 1777 and joined the main army in early May.

Colonel Daniel Morgan was the first truly professional soldier John Marshall served under, and the "Revolutionary rifleman" undoubtedly made a powerful impression on the young captain-lieutenant (Marshall received a promotion in December). Morgan's biographer describes him as "vigorous, zestful . . . pugnacious . . . tall and muscular . . . an excellent tactician, a superb leader of men," as well as a superlative horseman and marksman. Marshall thought Morgan possessed "those peculiar qualities which fit a man for the command of a partisan corps." During the first half of 1777, Morgan concentrated on giving the Eleventh the appearance of a crack unit, despite shortages of soap, shoes, and uniforms. He also insisted that the drummers and fifers practice daily to encourage the other troops to march and maneuver in order. Morgan intended to make the Eleventh the finest regiment in the army even though it was chronically undermanned. As Marshall saw it, Morgan and other regimental commanders faced a formidable task. Besides the usual discipline problems, "more than half the troops were unacquainted with the first rudiments of military duty, and had never looked an enemy in the face." Marshall's participation in a unit trying to build a strong spirit of professionalism at a time when the *rage militaire* was dissipating reinforced his perception that the Revolution would collapse without aggressive action by a disciplined and persevering army.[18]

Marshall served in his first Continental Army staff position as Morgan's regimental adjutant during these months. Congress had stressed the importance of the adjutant function in its military organization laws, and Marshall's maturity, intelligence, and attention to detail must have been impressive enough to Morgan to earn the 21-year-old Marshall an appointment to such a key regimental post. Marshall was responsible for all the unit's administrative paperwork, compiling rolls and rosters, processing Morgan's orders and issuing directives for implementing them, and supervising daily details such as guard duties and work parties. (The writing in the regimental orderly book for April and May 1777 is entirely Marshall's.) Additionally, as a staff officer, Marshall gained insights into military decision making, the personalities and attitudes of the officer corps, the formidable administrative requirements of managing a body of diverse men to prosecute a war most effectively, and the pressures unit commanders labored under from their superiors, Congress, and civilians.[19]

By the time the 1777 campaign season began, the Continental Army's situation had partly recovered from its precarious state at the first of the year. Its fortunes had risen and fallen drastically during 1776, with the British withdrawal from Boston and the American victory at Charleston followed by humiliating defeats around New York and a perilous retreat into New Jersey. Jubilation returned after victories at Trenton and Princeton, which also largely neutralized the strong Tory presence in New Jersey. Tactically, however, Washington's daring generalship mainly enabled his exhausted army to gain time to rest and regroup at Morristown. The Revolution persisted—"The British never again came so close to snuffing out the rebellion as they did in 1776; never again the Americans so close to losing," James Kirby Martin and Mark Lender have observed—but Americans' capacity to sustain a prolonged continental struggle had been called into serious question. The campaign of 1776 had shown the limitations of a patriot army founded on a citizen soldiery energized mainly with defiance. From Marshall's point of view, the campaign had been mostly a dismal tale of militia incompetence and misplaced democracy. He blamed the loss of New York on "unsoldierly conduct" and New England troops' devotion to egalitarian practices that sought to abolish the distinctions between officers and soldiers "which are indispensable to the formation of an army suited to all the purposes of war." "It is not cause of wonder," he asserted, "that among such officers, the most disgraceful and unmilitary practices should frequently prevail and that the privates should not respect them sufficiently to acquire habits of obedience and subordination."[20]

As Marshall settled into his adjutant's duties at the Morristown encampment, an air of tentative optimism returned to the Continental Army. By the summer of 1777, its ranks, which had dwindled to below 3,000 during the winter, had swelled with new militiamen and regulars—such as Marshall's Eleventh Regiment and nine others from Virginia—and now numbered around 10,000.

Over three fourths of the army was fit for duty. Washington was uncertain where his antagonist, General William Howe, would strike next, so he deployed troops to protect the Continental Congress sitting at Philadelphia and reinforced patriot garrisons on the lower Hudson River to fend off a southerly advance by General John Burgoyne from upstate New York. Marshall and Blackwell's company participated in the latter maneuver, spending the summer on a long trek with General John Sullivan's division from Morristown to the west bank of the Hudson River near Nyack, then up to Stony Point, west to Chester, and then, once Howe's target became clear, returning through New Jersey to the Delaware River to help defend Philadelphia. Washington had his force of 17,000 march through the city, a Loyalist stronghold, to embolden the patriots there. That autumn, at Brandywine and Germantown, Pennsylvania, Marshall faced the British in his first battles as a Continental officer under Washington.[21]

At Cooch's Bridge near Brandywine on 3 September, Marshall fought with a light infantry unit that harassed some British and German battalions in the vanguard of Howe's force. At Brandywine on 11 September, Marshall and the same unit clashed several times with British troops advancing up an important road near Chadd's Ford. The concept of the light infantry had arisen recently from Britain's midcentury experience with warfare in America, particularly its strange terrain and the presence of Indians employing unconventional tactics. Light infantry units were elite, mobile forces made up of men handpicked for their bravery, stamina, agility, and marksmanship. Carrying light packs, they deployed ahead and on the flanks of the main force to serve as scouts and skirmishers. They were especially useful in woods or rough country that massed infantry could not traverse easily and for which the light infantryman's weapon, the rifle, was best suited. Very accurate but slow to load and with no bayonet, the rifle was ideal for picking off targets from a distance but of little use if a regular infantry line, carrying bayonet-tipped muskets, closed for hand-to-hand fighting. Light infantrymen thus used irregular terrain to gain an offensive and defensive advantage over their enemy. Their appearance in the Continental ranks indicated that American military leaders were adopting English models for their own purposes—in this case, as a specially trained substitute for the buckskinned Minuteman.[22]

Marshall's experience at Germantown on 4 October was less salutary. He was shot in the hand during the siege of a concentration of British soldiers holed up in a stone mansion—one of the Americans' main tactical errors. The encounter diverted both Washington's attention and badly needed American troops from more pressing action, and by wasting irreplaceable time, contributed to the disruption of Washington's intricately synchronized plan. After the battle, Marshall assumed command of his company for nearly four months when its commander fell ill and resigned his commission.[23]

At the time, the two engagements were considered serious setbacks for the Americans. The British victory at Brandywine resulted in over 1,200 American casualties (compared to 500 British) and the loss of Philadelphia. The costly repulse of the intrepid but complicated Continental attack at Germantown forced

Washington's bedraggled army to retreat to Valley Forge after suffering nearly 1,100 casualties. An outpouring of criticism fell on Washington and his generals, even though entire American units had turned and run at crucial times in both battles. Marshall later defended Washington against the charge that Howe had out-generaled him at Brandywine. Inaccurate intelligence, bad equipment, and untested, undisciplined troops—"an army decidedly inferior, not only in numbers, but in every military requisite except courage"—preordained that "the action could not have terminated in favour of the Americans." Modern commentators are not so generous. Marshall also absolved Washington of blame for the defeat at Germantown, instead implicating the faulty execution of his involved plan by inexperienced troops groping amidst "the darkness of the morning produced by a fog of uncommon density." Marshall's discussion reads more like an apologetic than an analysis, but most current assessments agree with him, acknowledging that Washington came very close to winning at Germantown despite his complex orders until, as General Anthony Wayne bitterly commented, "We ran from Victory."[24]

The defeats at Brandywine and Germantown dashed the Continental Army's heady expectations of victory in 1777 and provided a disheartening prelude to the travail of Valley Forge. Instead, after several weeks of holding actions, in mid-December he pulled his tired army back into winter quarters 18 miles northwest of Philadelphia on some hills near an iron forge where Valley Creek met the Schuykill River. Washington chose the site because it was defensible and remote from settled areas yet close enough to the British to keep watch on them. A light snow covered the ground and cold winds blew as Marshall and the other 11,000 Continentals arrived. The Virginia brigades deployed along both watercourses, with Marshall's next to Valley Creek. According to Marshall, Washington "expressed, in strong terms, his approbation of their conduct, presented them with an encouraging state of the future prospects of their country, exhorted them to bear with continuing fortitude the hardships inseparable from the position they were about to take, and endeavoured to convince their judgments that those hardships were not imposed on them by unfeeling caprice, but were necessary for the good of their country."[25]

Marshall's most detailed account of the Valley Forge encampment, found in his biography of Washington, seems rather matter-of-fact and lacks the drama one might expect from a survivor of the ordeal.[26] There are no bloody footprints in the snow, no gaunt, half-naked patriots shivering in squalid wooden huts, and few details of his own involvement. Nonetheless, Marshall's activities and the conditions he endured can be described from what is known about the experiences of the Continental officer corps and the Virginia Line.

Valley Forge became a breeding ground for grievances among the officers, whose brooding over civilian apathy and state and congressional inattention and irresponsibility flourished in the cramped huts and frigid air. Both armies had stripped the surrounding area, and supplies soon ran short. The officers' conditions—especially those of company grade like Marshall—were scarcely better at first than the private soldiers'. The officers' personal baggage, sent to

Bethlehem, Pennsylvania, before the battle of Brandywine in September, arrived at the encampment in bad condition due to pilfering and mishandling, and depreciated salaries left many of them unable to buy replacement clothes and articles. Marshall drew $27 monthly, or about £100 per year, in early 1778. This was enough income to provide some comfort before the war, but even when combined with the military pay of Marshall's father and one of his brothers and the earnings from their farm, it was insufficient under rampant wartime inflation to support their family. Besides, the money usually came late; pay was in arrears by several months throughout the period of the encampment. Marshall later described the effect these financial problems had on the officers:

[T]he depreciation of paper money . . . had become so considerable that the pay of an officer would not procure even those absolute necessaries which might protect his person from the extremes of heat and cold. The few who possessed small patrimonial estates found them melting away; and others were unable to appear as gentlemen. Such circumstances could not fail to excite disgust with the service, and a disposition to leave it . . . An officer whose pride was in any degree wounded, whose caprice was not indulged, who apprehended censure for a fault which his carelessness about remaining in the army had probably seduced him to commit, was ready to throw up a commission which, instead of being valuable, was a burden almost too heavy to be borne.[27]

Besides enduring physical hardship, Marshall also saw discipline in the ranks decline sharply. He dealt with these infractions firsthand as deputy judge advocate general (DJAG), Washington's chief legal officer at Valley Forge. In 1776, Congress, following British practice, established the position of judge advocate general to prosecute violations of military law. Subordinate DJAGs were appointed for the three territorial departments and also at the field command levels as needed. Marshall received his appointment in late November 1777—presumably, as in his previous selection as adjutant general, because superiors recognized his intelligence, maturity, and reputation—but no documentary evidence of his service exists until Valley Forge.[28]

Aside from notarial duties, Marshall must have spent most of his time as DJAG preparing for, sitting on, and writing about the almost-daily courts martial: at least 161 hearings at the brigade level and above, and an undetermined but at least equal number at the regimental level. Marshall quickly became familiar with the procedures, violations, and punishments spelled out in the 1775 military code and the harsher 1776 articles of war. He dealt with offenders charged with a range of misconduct, including theft or vandalism of military and civilian property, fraud, forgery, embezzlement, insubordination, neglect of duty, violations of sanitary rules, unauthorized firing of weapons, perjury, bounty jumping, fighting, drunkenness, gambling, fraternization, "behavior unbecoming an officer and a gentleman," sodomy, desertion, and joining the ranks of the enemy. Around 60 percent of the accused were found guilty. The tribunals Marshall worked with meted out various punishments, including reprimands, restitution, public announcement of offenses, arduous or repellent duty such as removing tree stumps or burying dead horses and offal, whipping, running the gantlet, imprisonment, cashiering, and hanging. Officers almost always were punished with disgrace, and lower-ranking soldiers with pain. In determining sentences, Marshall and the courts martial had to balance the need for order and deterrence with the fact that the army was essentially founded on voluntarism, which militated against harsh, British-style penalties such as hundreds of lashes with a cat-o'-nine tails. Washington had enjoined that "an Army without Order, Regularity, and Discipline is no better than a Commissioned Mob," but punishment could not be the sole form of discipline. If it were, not enough men would stay in the army. Instead, punishment had to secure the loyalty, respect, and obedience that characterized a professional army, while at the same time helping cultivate an internal discipline which, combined with pride, skill, and dignity, would foster "unit cohesion" and keep freedom-loving patriots in the ranks as long as the Revolution required.[29]

Virginia's dereliction in providing soldiers for the Continental Army at this crucial time magnified Marshall's disillusionment with the states' contribution to the war effort. Virginia's regulars had comprised the largest contingent from any state in Washington's army during 1776 and 1777, providing one third of his force during the second New Jersey campaign. The terms of service for the first nine Virginia regiments, however, were due to expire between January and April 1778—right in the middle of the Valley Force encampment. By early January, only 40 Virginians had reenlisted, and, despite increased bounties, just 124 had by late February. Half were discharged during the winter of 1777–78 and were not fully replaced. More officers from Virginia left the army than from any other state. When the army reached Valley Forge in December, the Virginia Line's paper strength was 4,305; when it again took the field in June, it was fallen by one fourth to 3,241. Other problems with Virginia's Line vexed Washington, including officers' requests for furloughs; by March, all the state's brigadier generals had gone home. In addition, the nasty dispute between Washington and Virginia's brigadiers over the rank of the commander of Marshall's brigade provided an unseemly display of vanity and self-interest at the highest levels of leadership at Valley Forge.[30]

While at Valley Forge, Marshall's personal contact with Washington fostered his profound admiration and respect for the commander-in-chief. Available evidence does not indicate if Marshall met Washington before joining the Continental Line. It is certain that Thomas Marshall maintained contact with Washington while living in Fauquier County, and, given what is known about John's relationship with his father, he almost certainly was made familiar with Washington's activities and temperament. John's first impressions of his future commander's military prowess and personality probably came largely from Thomas's descriptions of Washington's exploits in the Seven Years War, with heavy emphasis on the transmontane marches, the courageous defense of Fort Necessity, the massacre of General Braddock's column, the revitalization of the Virginia militia, and the capture of Fort Duquesne. Moreover, John probably gained a sense of Washington's political beliefs and character through Thomas's recounting of sessions of the House of Burgesses and various extralegal meetings in which Washington participated.[31]

Whatever doubts Marshall's first service under Washington at Brandywine and Germantown might have raised in his mind about the commander-in-chief's competence and character were erased during his intimate exposure to Washington's personal force and stoic leadership during the Valley Forge winter. As Washington's chief legal officer, Marshall would have consulted with him regularly about disciplinary problems, trials, and sentences. Washington was a shrewd judge of men, and he chose Marshall and his other young staff officers, such as Alexander Hamilton and James Monroe, with an eye toward cultivating their best qualities. In turn, their experience on his staff contributed importantly to their character and political perceptions. As Don Higginbotham has written,

Just as [Washington] surrounded himself with obviously able men, so too he brought out the best in others who served under him, individuals who moved from obscurity to play prominent parts in the war. They made every effort to measure up to his expectations. Staff officers felt a keen personal obligation to the commander in chief . . . young officers chosen to be a part of his "military family" . . . not only were intelligent but also grew in maturity and understanding of the complex problems involved in completing a revolution and creating a nation.[32]

While on Washington's staff, Marshall would have shared in the camaraderie at headquarters that took some of the harshness off the winter, and he undoubtedly felt the almost palpable lightening of spirits after Martha Washington arrived in February and cheered the bleak atmosphere, especially during the long, cold evenings. Marshall almost certainly was present at the performance of Joseph Addison's *Cato* in May. The popular play's republican themes of virtue, austerity, corruption, liberty, and tyranny must have resonated powerfully inside the audience of patriots, a sizable number of whom, like Marshall, were familiar with such classical ideas. Marshall's affable personality and hardy constitution also boosted morale. He was a natural leader who bore his responsibilities easily. According to his messmate, Captain Philip Slaughter, "If any of the officers murmured at their deprivations, he would shame them by good-natured raillery, or encourage them by his own exuberance of spirits . . . He was an excellent companion, and idolized by the soldiers and his brother officers, whose gloomy hours were enlivened by his inexhaustible fund of anecdote." When the weather warmed, the troops flocked outside, playing games such as cricket, rounders, and bowling with cannon balls. Marshall joined in these diversions and helped organize and participate in athletic events such as footraces, jumping contests, and quoits matches. Despite his lanky frame and loose-limbed carriage, he usually won. He could high jump well over five feet and was a fleet sprinter. Running in stockings partly knitted with white yarn, he earned the nickname "Silverheels."[33]

With the third year of the war drawing to a close as the chill lifted from Valley Forge, the Continental Army—and most importantly from Marshall's perspective, its officers—had come to believe steadfastly that it embodied the true principles of the Revolution, and that independence could not be achieved without it. Marshall and the Continentals had actually lived the ideals of sacrifice and duty that political leaders merely mouthed. This attitude of virtuousness and indispensability began developing while the people's passion for arms subsided throughout 1776; it gained credence with the victories at Trenton and Princeton, which enabled the Revolution to survive; and it received powerful negative reinforcement by the populace's abdication of support for the patriot cause during the adversity at Valley Forge. By mid-1778, Continental Army officers believed they were the victims of an ungrateful people. They resented Congress's treating them like mercenaries when they raised what they considered legitimate concerns about rank, salary, and pensions. They grew embittered as the states protected their own parochial interests and left the Confederation government nearly powerless to deal with the wartime financial crisis. Valley Forge had convinced the Continental Army that republican society would give them what they deserved only if they demanded it.[34]

Except for a few isolated cases, however, Marshall and the Continental officers did not let their resentment undermine their dedication to republican principles and civilian supremacy over the military. Although they had come to enjoy aspects of the warrior's life and took great pride in their survival as an army, they did not adopt militaristic or praetorian attitudes. Some of the better heeled junior officers became haughty, self-righteous, and anxious about their fame and honor. These attitudes occasionally incited them to dueling, which Marshall had to deal with in the ensuing courts martial. Marshall himself avoided these psychological traps because of his amiable character, greater sense of humility, and willingness to lead by example, not fear. His common touch enabled him to be popular with subordinates without losing their respect and obedience. Marshall could have been a model for Baron von Steuben's guidelines for company grade officers, composed at Valley Forge and later set forth in his *Regulations for the Order and Discipline of the Troops of the United States* (1779), which stressed self-control, concern for soldiers' welfare, and moderation in imposing discipline.[35]

Washington's army left Valley Forge six months to the day after it had arrived, transformed in appearance, attitude, and conduct. The company-level officers like Marshall, largely due to Von Steuben's tutelage, had expanded their conception of duty from merely leading men in combat to supervising training and maintenance of weapons and facilities, and administering headquarters directives—all previously considered sergeants' work. In addition, the baron—drawing on his familiarity with elite light troops known as *Chasseurs* in France and *Jäger* in Germany—formed and supervised the training of a light infantry brigade in which Marshall would serve. Washington's officers generally had acquired the three essential qualities of military professionalism: the expertise, responsibility, and corporate identity of officership. Marshall and his comrades-in-arms headed toward what would be the last major military encounter in the northern theater, at Monmouth Court House in New Jersey on 28 June. On that torrid day, when the heat and humidity felled as many men as hostile fire, Marshall was attached to Colonel Morgan's light infantry unit, deployed three miles away from the main contest and not directly engaged. Monmouth was a tactical draw, but it demonstrated that the Continental Army had recovered from its parlous condition of the past winter and could now hold its own in a large, open-field, pitched battle against some of Europe's finest soldiers.[36]

Monmouth was the last major revolutionary battle at which Marshall was present.[37] In early September 1778, he was promoted to captain, and in mid-September, during a realignment of Virginia regiments prompted by manpower shortages, he was put in command of the 52 men of the Eighth Company of the new Seventh (formerly the Eleventh) Regiment under Colonel Morgan. The reorganization, in response to recommendations from a congressional committee, left some officers without commands—"deranged," in contemporary parlance—and resulted in some promotions out of order of seniority. Congress's stock consequently fell even further in the eyes of Virginia Continental officers. During November, most of the Continental Army went into winter quarters near Middlebrook, New Jersey. From December 1778 to early May 1779, Marshall was on furlough in Virginia visiting his family—the first leave he had taken during two years in uniform. The personal economic cost of fighting in the Revolution came home powerfully to Marshall then. For the Marshalls and many other Continental Army families, the war took the primary income earners away from their landholdings, workshops, and businesses and caused serious financial hardship. "[H]e was greatly distressed at the straits to which 'the fortunes of war' had reduced us," his sister recalled. "When supper time arrived, mother had the meal prepared . . . and had made into bread a little flour, the last she had, which had been saved for such an occasion. The little ones cried for some. . . . [John] would eat no more of the bread which could not be shared with us."

Marshall returned to Morgan's light infantry unit in early May 1779. He served with reserve troops during "Mad Anthony" Wayne's assault on Stony Point, New York, a key British fortification on the south bank of the Hudson River, in July 1779. The next month he joined a 200-man detachment that covered "Light-Horse Harry" Lee's surprise attack on Paulus Hook, the last British garrison in New Jersey. This ended Marshall's active involvement in the fighting except for his small role in resisting Benedict Arnold's invasion of Virginia a year and one half later. By the fall of 1779, the expiration of enlistments in the Virginia Line had created a surplus of officers, so Marshall and others were sent home from the winter encampment at Morristown in December to await the call-up of new units, which never occurred. In Yorktown in early 1780, Marshall visited his father, who then commanded the newly created Virginia State Artillery. He also attended lectures on law and natural philosophy at the College of William and Mary during May–July 1780. During the year, Marshall undoubtedly worried over the military difficulties of 1780: the brutal winter and grave logistical problems that enervated Washington's army; the states' inability or reluctance to raise troops and supplies; the surrender of Charleston and the rout at Camden, South Carolina; Arnold's treason and defection; and several attempted mutinies. He also would have been distressed at Virginia's diminishing support for the war, which was evident by widespread disdain for Continental service, draft avoidance, undermanned units, and the need for frequent militia call-ups. On 12 February 1781, Marshall resigned his commission in the Continental Army.

John Marshall believed the American Revolution was "the most interesting event in the history of the human race."[38] The Revolution was the first test of his character, reputation, and beliefs and profoundly shaped his later personal and political life. The military struggle for independence also greatly influenced Marshall's thinking about nationalism and union, the roles of the state and central governments, and the compatibility of a professional military establishment with a republican order. On a personal level, his family's privation during the Revolution energized his acquisitive instincts and gave him a lifelong preoccupation with financial stability. Lastly, Marshall's mature reflections on the causes and nature of the Revolution provide insights into his political and historiographical ideas.

Marshall's socialization in the Virginia frontier gentry was broadened through service in the Continental Line, where he was exposed to the cultures and attitudes of soldiers from other states, and through contact with national authorities and institutions. He developed a more cosmopolitan, continental perspective on public affairs. Marshall later interpreted the years leading up to the Revolution as the turning point in the emergence of a national consciousness in America, and the Revolution as the completion of the process of creating *e pluribus unum*. As he wrote in his autobiography,

I had grown up at a time when a love of union and resistance to the claims of Great Britain were the inseparable inmates of the same bosom . . . when patriotism and a strong fellow feeling with our suffering fellow citizens of Boston were identical . . . when the maxim "united we stand, divided we fall" was the maxim of every orthodox American; and I had imbibed these sentiments so thoroughly that they constituted a part of my being.[39]

That perspective was powerfully informed by Marshall's painful education in the shortcomings of the state and Confederation governments during the crisis of wartime. His battlefield experience contributed to his antipathy to parochialism and made him appreciate the need for a sense of national unity, enforced by a strong central government, to preserve the achievements of independence. "I found myself associating with brave men from different states who were risking life and everything valuable in a common cause believed by all to be most precious. I was confirmed in the habit of considering America as my country, and [C]ongress as my government." He could have been describing himself when he later referred to "[m]en of enlarged and liberal minds who, in the imbecility of a general government, by which alone the capacities of the nation could be efficaciously exerted, could discern the imbecility of the nation itself . . . who felt a full value of national honour, and the full obligation of national faith; and who were persuaded of the insecurity of both, if resting for their preservation on the concurrence of thirteen distinct sovereigns." The unwillingness of parochially minded states and civilians to adequately support the Continental Army, and the incapacity of the Confederation to secure enough money and supplies, convinced Marshall that a central government endowed with substantial fiscal and economic power was necessary to secure independence and preserve the republic.[40]

Marshall's wartime experience also influenced his attitudes toward the role of a professional military in a republican society. Although Virginia's militia ranked among the colonies' most competent, an idealization of the militia and fear of standing armies were major elements of the dominant republican ideology. The Virginia Declaration of Rights, for example, referred to the militia as "the proper, natural and safe defence of a free state," whereas "standing armies in time of peace should be avoided as dangerous to liberty." Furthermore, the militia's long experience in fighting Indians and the French in the wilderness reputedly had produced a tactical expertise which the British, supposedly trained only for European-style warfare, neither possessed nor comprehended.

Marshall's encounter with the citizen soldierly, however, did not steep him in the republican militia ethos.[41] Instead, his knowledge of unprofessional behavior by Virginia's yeomen warriors, his dealings with other state militias, and his exposure to the antimilitia attitudes of Washington and the Continental Army officers, engendered in him a hostility to the concept of a citizen soldiery after he moved from the Virginia militia to the Continental Line. As a historian, he spurned the idealization of "embattled farmers" or "ragged Continentals" typical of postwar commentaries. Much to the contrary, he believed that in the first years of the Revolution, Americans were fighting two military battles: one against the British, the other against the ideological prejudice for the militia. The latter had to be won first, and America's difficulty in doing so nearly cost it victory in the former. "[I]n demonstrating its fallacy," Marshall wrote, "the independence of America had nearly perished in its cradle."

By viewing the militia's role almost exclusively in military terms, however, Marshall overlooked its crucial political contribution to the war effort. Although the militia failed to do what it was not intended to do—carry the brunt of battle—it instead became, in Don Higginbotham's phrase, a "traditional institution with revolutionary responsibilities." The militia served as an energizing and coercive mechanism for revolutionary loyalty, defining political categories, mobilizing individuals and communities to support the patriot cause, and staving off any Tory counterstrike through violence and intimidation. Marshall's exposure to the jaunty esprit de corps of the Fauquier independent company and the Culpeper Minutemen, and the vindictive elimination of loyalists in Norfolk, must have made him aware of those roles. His failure to appreciate them in his history of the Revolution partly reflects the work's military emphasis, but it also shows how his partiality toward a professional army and his nationalist beliefs limited his scholarly and political perception.[42]

During the Revolution, Marshall developed the deep admiration and respect for George Washington that formed the basis for his interpretation of Washington and the Continental Army as the only focus of allegiance for the whole country during the war. To Marshall, Washington was the incarnation of revolutionary virtue, and his signal accomplishments as military leader were epitomized at Valley Forge: "To preserve an army when conquest was impossible, to avoid defeat and ruin when victory was unattainable, to keep his forces embodied and suppress the discontents of his soldiers, exasperated by a long course of the most cruel privations, [and] to seize with unerring discrimination the critical moment when vigorous offensive operations might be advantageously carried on." Marshall's veneration of Washington also affected his historical scholarship, leading him to conceptualize the political history of America during its first decade under the Constitution as essentially the biography of one man.[43]

In the 1780s and 1790s, Marshall asserted that a permanent, professional military was necessary for, and compatible with, the survival of liberty and self-government in America. The United States, he insisted, needed a standing army and military professionalism to maintain peace, security, liberty, and stability against foreign enemies and domestic discord. His wartime experiences prepared him ideologically to support the Federalists' military policy during the 1790s, and he championed veterans' causes as a legislator and lawyer. "I partook largely of the sufferings and feelings of the army, and brought with me into civil life an ardent devotion to its interests." Yet Marshall always believed in civilian control of the military and disavowed militarism. Unlike some belligerent High Federalists, he did not see force as a positive tool of domestic governance, or consider warmongering an acceptable political or diplomatic tactic, or cling to the army as one of the last vestiges of tradition and hierarchy in a world of pell-mell democracy.[44]

The rapid impoverishment of Marshall's family during the war, to which his own distress at Valley Forge made him so sensitive, aroused in him an acquisitive urge and a captivation with financial security that would sway important decisions in his private and public life. His family's struggle may have encouraged him to decide quickly on a career in law; he began legal studies during a break in military service in the spring of 1780. In the 1780s and 1790s, he rejected several offers of public office to remain in his more lucrative legal practice. Until 1797, he restricted his political service to terms in the Virginia Assembly around which he could manage his caseload. His extensive land speculation in Virginia and Kentucky, his service on the diplomatic mission to France, and his authorship of the Washington biography were all motivated to varying degrees by monetary concerns.

Marshall made his most detailed and thoughtful judgments about the causes and nature of the Revolution in the first volume of the *Life of George Washington*, published in 1804. In this historical introduction (published in

1824 as *A History of the Colonies*), he chronicled the period 1607–1775 to "make the reader acquainted with the genius, character, and resources of the people about to engage in that memorable contest." For the years from the end of the Seven Years War to Lexington and Concord, Marshall provided a straightforward narrative of Britain's new trade and revenue measures and the colonists' reactions to them. His underlying theme was that the American Revolution was essentially a constitutional struggle over home rule within the empire. He stressed that the immediate cause of the war was the colonists' assertion of their rights of Englishmen against tighter imperial regulations. The new enactments—especially the taxes—threatened the colonial heritage of ordered liberty and the system of self-government by virtuous men based on the English Constitution that had developed over the decades. The ties between the colonies and the empire were never stronger than in 1763, but Britain's attempt to assert supremacy over what it considered dependent colonies "tore asunder all the bonds of relationship and affection that had subsisted for ages, and planted almost inextinguishable hatred in bosoms where the warmest friendship had long been cultivated." Conciliatory sentiment evaporated after blood was shed in Massachusetts, and a break with England became inevitable. "To profess allegiance and respect for a monarch with whom they were at open war was an absurdity too great to be long continued."[45]

In contrast to this emphasis on constitutional and ideological issues, Marshall gave no special attention to economics, aside from attributing Britain's new policy to its need to raise money to defer the costs of defending the frontier. "The contest with America was plainly a contest of principle," he declared, "and had been conducted entirely on principle, by both sides." Nor did Marshall draw any connections between internal colonial tensions and attitudes toward England. He offered no observations even on Virginia's sociopolitical development after 1750—a subject he knew very well—as a factor in the growth of anti-imperial, propatriot opinion. In fact, the *History of the Colonies* has scarcely any references to Virginia as an important contributor to America's colonial heritage of representative institutions and self-government. One scholar has suggested that Marshall, alienated by the Jeffersonian dominance in Virginia, instead retrospectively viewed Federalist New England as the torchbearer of liberty during the pre-Revolutionary years.[46]

Marshall's interpretation of the origins of the Revolution, which anticipates aspects of the later imperial and idealist schools of historiography, is more sophisticated than the post-Revolution nationalist histories with which his *Life of Washington* is usually compared. David Ramsay and Mercy Otis Warren, for example, saw the Revolution as the unfolding of a providential plan and described colonial-imperial relations as a simplistic, liberty-versus-tyranny dichotomy. In contrast, Marshall composed a secular exegesis grounded in individual and collective action, not impersonal forces or preordained schemes—an approach consistent with his empirical mind and suspicion of abstract theorizing and a priori reasoning. In later letters, Marshall wrote that he believed the Revolution was a war of principle and political liberty, not a

struggle against actual oppression, and that the colonies' separation from
England should have been gradual, achieved through mutual consent and
nonviolence.[47]

John Marshall returned to civilian life in February 1781 with no evident regret
at what he would miss in the Continental Army or anxiety about what awaited
him at home. Although he seemed to enjoy the fellowship, prestige, and sense
of mission of the officer corps, he did not need military rank to affirm his status
as a gentleman. Despite his family's economic woes, his social station was
secure because of his father's accomplishments in Fauquier County and his
mother's lineage. With the war stalemated—a situation that would benefit the
patriots—he believed he could take advantage of an opportunity for a discharge,
confident that he had fulfilled his obligations to the struggle. Monetary motives
entered into his decision as well. He had been admitted to the Fauquier County
bar in August 1780 and was undoubtedly eager to begin a full-time practice. He
was also eager to pursue the affections of an attractive young woman named
Mary Ambler, whom he had met in Yorktown "on a night of gentle gaiety" in
the late winter or early spring of 1779–1780.[48]

NOTES

1. Sources for this paragraph and the next are John E. Selby, *The Revolution in
Virginia, 1775–1783* (Williamsburg: The Colonial Williamsburg Foundation, 1988), 1–
4; Jack M. Sosin, *The Revolutionary Frontier, 1763–1783* (New York: Holt, Rinehart
and Winston, 1967), 94; Hamilton J. Eckenrode, *The Revolution in Virginia* (Boston:
Houghton Mifflin, 1916), chaps. 1–2; Thad W. Tate, "The Coming of the Revolution in
Virginia: Britain's Challenge to Virginia's Ruling Class, 1763–1776," *WMQ*, 3rd ser.,
19 (1962), 323–43; Jack P. Greene, *The Quest for Power: The Lower Houses of
Assembly in the Southern Royal Colonies, 1689–1776* (Chapel Hill: University of North
Carolina Press, 1963), part VI passim; Richard R. Beeman, "The Political Response to
Social Conflict in the Southern Backcountry: A Comparative View of Virginia and the
Carolinas during the Revolution," in *An Uncivil War: The Southern Backcountry during
the American Revolution*, ed. Ronald Hoffman et al. (Charlottesville: University Press of
Virginia, 1985), 234–35; Don Higginbotham, *The War of American Independence:
Military Attitudes, Policies, and Practices, 1763–1789* (Boston: Northeastern University
Press, 1983), 9.
2. T. Triplett Russell and John K. Gott, *Fauquier County in the Revolution* (Warrenton,
Va.: Fauquier County American Bicentennial Commission, 1976), 63; "Fauquier County
Resolutions," 4 August 1774, in William J. Van Schreeven, comp., and Robert L.
Scribner and Brent Tarter, eds., *Revolutionary Virginia: The Road to Independence*, 7
vols. (Charlottesville: University Press of Virginia, 1973–83), 1:134–35.
3. Albert J. Beveridge, *The Life of John Marshall*, 4 vols. (Boston: Houghton Mifflin,
1916–19), 1:64 and n. 4.; Selby, *Revolution in Virginia*, 1, 8, 49–53; Leonard Baker,
John Marshall: A Life in Law (New York: Macmillan, 1974), 24; Eckenrode,
Revolution in Virginia, 45–48; David J. Mays, *Edmund Pendleton*, 2 vols. (Cambridge:
Harvard University Press, 1952), 2:3–12; Russell and Gott, *Fauquier County*, 53–59;
Henry's Stamp Act resolutions, 29–30 May 1765, in *Revolutionary Virginia*, 1:17–18;

William Wirt, *Sketches of the Life and Character of Patrick Henry* (Ithaca: Mack, Andrus, 1848), 95.

4. John Stokes Adams, ed., *An Autobiographical Sketch by John Marshall* (Ann Arbor: University of Michigan Press, 1937), 5. (Hereafter cited as JM, *Autobiographical Sketch.*)

5. Russell and Gott, *Fauquier County*, 38; Don Higginbotham, "Military Institutions in Colonial America," in idem, *War and Society in Revolutionary America: The Wider Dimensions of Conflict* (Columbia: University of South Carolina Press, 1988), 30; John K. Mahon, *History of the Militia and the National Guard* (New York: Macmillan, 1983), 31; Allan R. Millett and Peter Maslowski, *For the Common Defense: A Military History of the United States of America* (New York: Free Press, 1984), 5–6; John Shy, "A New Look at the Colonial Militia," in *A People Numerous and Armed: Reflections on the Military Struggle for American Independence* (New York: Oxford University Press, 1976), 26–29; Frederick S. Aldridge, "Organization and Administration of the Militia System of Colonial Virginia" (Ph.D. diss., American University, 1964), 130–32, 230–38; Edmund S. Morgan, *Inventing the People: The Rise of Popular Sovereignty in England and America* (New York: W. W. Norton, 1988), 170–71; Rhys Isaac, *The Transformation of Virginia, 1740–1790* (Chapel Hill: University of North Carolina Press, 1982), 104–07; Michael A. McDonnell, "Popular Mobilization and Political Culture in Revolutionary Virginia: The Failure of the Minutemen and the Revolution from Below," *JAH*, 85 (1998–99), 947–48; Marcus Cunliffe, *Soldiers and Civilians: The Martial Spirit in America, 1775–1865* (Boston: Little, Brown, 1968), 187; James Titus, *The Old Dominion at War: Society, Politics, and Warfare in Late Colonial Virginia* (Columbia: University of South Carolina Press, 1991), 1–5, 32–41.

6. JM, *Autobiographical Sketch*, 5; William E. White, "The Independent Companies of Virginia, 1774–1775," *VMHB*, 86 (1978), 149–62; E. M. Sanchez-Saavedra, *A Guide to Virginia Military Organizations in the American Revolution, 1774 to 1787* (Richmond: Virginia State Library, 1978), 7; Russell and Gott, *Fauquier County*, 61; Aldridge, "Militia System of Colonial Virginia," 186–87; Millett and Maslowski, *For the Common Defense*, 5–6; Charles Royster, *A Revolutionary People at War: The Continental Army and American Character, 1775–1783* (New York: W. W. Norton, 1981), 50–51; John E. Selby, *Dunmore* (Williamsburg: Virginia Independence Bicentennial Commission, 1977), 26; McDonnell, "Popular Mobilization and Political Culture in Revolutionary Virginia," 954–62.

7. White, "Independent Companies," 161; Sanchez-Saavedra, *Guide to Virginia Military Organizations*, 7–8, 16; idem, "'All Fine Fellows and Well-Armed': The Culpeper Minute Battalion, 1775–1776," *Virginia Cavalcade*, 24 (summer 1974), 5; McDonnell, "Popular Mobilization and Political Culture in Revolutionary Virginia," 962–63; Virginia's militia law, passed 21 August 1775, in *Revolutionary Virginia*, 3:471.

8. Eulogy by Horace Binney in John F. Dillon, comp. and ed., *John Marshall: Life, Character, and Judicial Services*, 3 vols. (Chicago: Callaghan and Co., 1903), 3:286–88 (hereafter cited as Dillon, *Marshall*); Russell and Gott, *Fauquier County*, 65–66; Philip Slaughter, *A History of St. Mark's Parish, Culpeper County, Virginia* (Baltimore: Innes and Co., 1877), 107. Although the source on which the Binney account is based places this episode in May, it must have occurred after the Virginia Convention created the minute battalions in mid-August, and, given delays in communication and recruitment, probably took place in September. Marshall wrote many years later that the first muster was on 1 September. JM letter to [John S. Barbour], 6 February 1832, cited in Irwin S. Rhodes, *The Papers of John Marshall: A Descriptive Calendar*, 2 vols. (Norman:

University of Oklahoma Press, 1956), 2:388 (hereafter cited as Rhodes, *Calendar of Marshall Papers*).

9. John R. Elting, ed., *Military Uniforms in America: The Era of the American Revolution, 1755–1795* (San Rafael, Ca.: Presidio Press, 1974), 110; Daniel Boorstin, *The Americans: The Colonial Experience*, Vintage ed. (New York: Random House, 1958), 351; Edward W. Richardson, *Standards and Colors of the American Revolution* (Philadelphia: University of Pennsylvania Press, 1982), 136–37; Slaughter, *History of St. Mark's Parish*, 107.

10. Royster, *Revolutionary People at War*, 25–26; Higginbotham, *War of American Independence*, 47.

11. Albert H. Tillson Jr., "The Militia and Popular Political Culture in the Upper Valley of Virginia, 1740–1775," *VMHB*, 94 (1986), 286–306; idem, *Gentry and Common Folk: Political Culture on a Virginia Frontier, 1740–1789* (Lexington: University Press of Kentucky, 1991), chap. 3; Richard R. Beeman, *The Evolution of the Southern Backcountry: A Case Study of Lunenberg County, Virginia, 1746–1832* (Philadelphia: University of Pennsylvania Press, 1984), 134–35; McDonnell, "Popular Mobilization and Political Culture in Revolutionary Virginia," 964–74.

12. Royster, *Revolutionary People at War*, 25, 31; James Kirby Martin and Mark Edward Lender, *A Respectable Army: The Military Origins of the Republic, 1763–1789* (Arlington Heights, Ill.: Harlan Davidson, 1982), 31–32; Millett and Maslowski, *For the Common Defense*, 53; Don Higginbotham, *George Washington and the American Military Tradition* (Athens: University of Georgia Press, 1985), 49; Sanchez-Saavedra, "Culpeper Minute Battalion," 6; JM, *Autobiographical Sketch*, 5; Russell and Gott, *Fauquier County*, 73–75; pension application of William Burton, 1833, reprinted in *WMQ*, 1st ser., 11 (1902–3), 213–14; Eckenrode, *Revolution in Virginia*, 70–71; Selby, *Revolution in Virginia*, 68–69; JM, *Life of George Washington*, 5 vols. (Philadelphia: C. P. Wayne, 1804–7; rept., New York: Chelsea House, 1983), 1:80.

13. Elizabeth B. Wingo, *The Battle of Great Bridge* (Chesapeake, Va.: Norfolk County Historical Society, 1964), passim; Eckenrode, *Revolution in Virginia*, 80–84; Mark Mayo Boatner III, *The Encyclopedia of the American Revolution* (New York: David McKay Co., 1966), 447–48; Ivor Noël Hume, *1775: Another Part of the Field* (New York: Alfred A. Knopf, 1966), 403–40; Sanchez-Saavedra, "Culpeper Minute Battalion," 8–11; Selby, *Revolution in Virginia*, 69–74; Mays, *Pendleton*, 2:68–74; *Revolutionary Virginia*, 5:48–103; Brent Tarter, ed., "Orderly Book of the Second Virginia Regiment, September 27, 1775–April 15, 1776," *VMHB*, 85 (1977), 303–05; John R. Sellers, "The Virginia Continental Line, 1775–1780" (Ph.D. diss., Tulane University, 1968), 85–108; Russell and Gott, *Fauquier County*, 80–88; JM, *Life of Washington*, 1:81. The so-called "great bridge" was a long wooden trestle in the middle of the causeway.

14. Sellers, "Virginia Continental Line," 86; Mays, *Pendleton*, 2:71; JM, *Life of Washington*, 1:81–82; idem, *Autobiographical Sketch*, 5.

15. Sellers, "Virginia Continental Line," 108; JM, *Life of Washington*, 1:81–82; Selby, *Revolution in Virginia*, 82–84; Eckenrode, *Revolution in Virginia*, 86–88; Hume, *1775*, 447, 450, 459; Russell and Gott, *Fauquier County*, 98; Mays, *Pendleton*, 2:82.

16. Morgan, *Inventing the People*, 163; McDonnell, "Popular Mobilization and Political Culture in Revolutionary Virginia," 975; JM, *A History of the Colonies . . .* (Philadelphia: C. P. Wayne, 1804; rept., Fredericksburg, Va.: Citizens' Guild of Washington's Boyhood Home, 1926), 474–75.

17. Sources for this paragraph and the next are Sanchez-Saavedra, "Culpeper Minute Battalion," 11; *PJM*, 1:3–4, n. 1, n. 6; Sanchez-Saavedra, *Guide to Virginia Military*

Units, 38; Fred Anderson Berg, *Encyclopedia of Continental Army Units: Battalions, Regiments, and Independent Corps* (Harrisburg, Pa.: Stackpole Books, 1972), 130; JM, *Autobiographical Sketch*, 5; JM affidavits supporting pension applications by David Jamison, William Payne, and Robert Pollard, 6 February, 26 April, and 20 June 1832, JM pension application, 26 January 1833, and JM to Col. William Stark, 12 June 1832, in Rhodes, *Calendar of Marshall Papers*, 2:388, 392–94, 414; Russell and Gott, *Fauquier County*, 95, 168–70, 177; Don Higginbotham, *Daniel Morgan, Revolutionary Rifleman* (Chapel Hill: University of North Carolina Press, 1961), 56–57; Robert K. Wright, *The Continental Army* (Washington, D.C.: U.S. Army Center for Military History, 1983), 289; Sellers, "Virginia Continental Line," 69–70, 224; JM, *Life of Washington*, 1:161–62; William P. Coues, "Washington's Campaign against Smallpox in the Continental Army," *New England Journal of Medicine*, 202 (1930), 254–59.

A detailed social profile of the Continental units Marshall fought with does not exist, but the Virginia Line in general was *young*, with over 90 percent of its recruits under 25 years of age, and with a median enlistment age of 20; *not well off*, consisting mostly of farmers or the sons of tenant farmers; *parochial*, with 82 percent born in Virginia and 41 percent still living in the county of their birth; and *non-Eastern*, most soldiers coming from the Piedmont or Valley regions. Charles P. Neimeyer, *America Goes to War: A Social History of the Continental Army* (New York: New York University Press, 1996), 24.

18. Higginbotham, *Morgan*, vii–viii, 57; JM, *Life of Washington*, 1:171–73; Blackwell's company muster rolls for August–November 1777, *PJM*, 1:5–7, 9–11.

19. Wright, *Continental Army*, 30, 32, 435; John W. Wright, "Some Notes on the Continental Army," *WMQ*, 2nd ser., 11 (1931), 97–99; *PJM*, 1:4 n. 6.

20. Martin and Lender, *A Respectable Army*, 62–63; JM, *Life of Washington*, 1:119–20.

21. Martin and Lender, *A Respectable Army*, 79; Wright, *Continental Army*, 108; Wright, "Some Notes on the Continental Army," 85; Higginbotham, *War of American Independence*, 182; *PJM*, 1:4, n. 6; JM, *Life of Washington*, 1:176–77.

22. Walter Millis, *Arms and Men: A Study in American Military History* (New York: Capricorn Books, 1956), 22; Berg, *Encyclopedia of Continental Army Units*, 62; JM, *Autobiographical Sketch*, 6; idem, *Life of Washington*, 2:5–8; Beveridge, *Marshall*, 1:93–96; Sellers, "Virginia Continental Line," 253, 257, 260; Christopher Ward, *The War of the Revolution*, 2 vols. (New York: Macmillan, 1952), 1:338–45; John W. Wright, "The Rifle in the American Revolution," *AHR*, 29 (1923–24), 294–95; John F. Reed, *Campaign to Valley Forge: July 1, 1777–December 19, 1777* (Philadelphia: University of Pennsylvania Press, 1965), 88–89, 100–103; Lyon G. Tyler, "The Old Virginia Line in the Middle States during the American Revolution," *Tyler's Quarterly Historical and Genealogical Magazine*, 12 (1930–31), 24–27.

A Virginia officer recorded a humorous incident involving Marshall at Brandywine: "At ten in the night we were aroused from sleep. Lt. Marshall had raked up some leaves to sleep on, he had pulled off one of his stockings in the night (the only pair of silk stockings in the regiment), and not being able to find it in the dark, he set fire to the leaves, and before we saw it a large hole had been burnt in it. He pulled it on so, and away we went." Slaughter, *History of St. Mark's Parish*, 108.

23. *PJM*, 1:9 n. 4, 11–13; JM, *Life of Washington*, 2:22; Sellers, "Virginia Continental Line," 270–72; James Thomas Flexner, *George Washington in the Revolution (1775–1783)* (Boston: Little, Brown, 1967), 233–34; Willard M. Wallace, *Appeal to Arms: A Military History of the American Revolution* (Chicago: Quadrangle Books, 1951), 141; Ward, *War of the Revolution*, 1:362–71; Tyler, "Old Virginia Line," 28–32.

24. Royster, *Revolutionary People at War*, 146–48; JM, *Life of Washington*, 2:10–18, 22–25; Higginbotham, *War of American Independence*, 186–87; Robert Middlekauff, *The Glorious Cause: The American Revolution, 1763–1789* (New York: Oxford University Press, 1982), 393–95; Wallace, *Appeal to Arms*, 139–43; Flexner, *Washington in the Revolution*, 225–26; W. J. Wood, *Battles of the Revolutionary War, 1775–1781* (Chapel Hill: Algonquin Books, 1990), 112–14; Tyler, "Old Virginia Line," 28, 31–32; Francis Vinton Greene, *General Greene* (New York: D. Appleton, 1913; rept., Port Washington, N.Y.: Kennikat Press, 1970), chap. 6.

Virginia's troops, notably the 3rd Regiment commanded by Thomas Marshall, acquitted themselves well at Brandywine, according to contemporary accounts. "Though attacked by much superior numbers, [the 3rd Regiment] maintained its position without losing an inch of ground, until both its flanks were turned, its ammunition nearly expended, more than half of its officers, and one third of the soldiers killed or wounded," John Marshall later wrote. His father had two horses shot from under him. JM, *Life of Washington*, 2:10 n. 2.

25. Sellers, "Virginia Continental Line," 285; JM, *Life of Washington*, 2:42.

26. JM, *Life of Washington*, 2:89.

27. Alfred Hoyt Bill, *Valley Forge: The Making of an Army* (New York: Harper and Brothers, 1952), 101; John B. B. Trussell Jr., *Birthplace of an Army: A Study of the Valley Forge Encampment* (Harrisburg: Pennsylvania Historical and Museum Commission, 1976), 80, 85–87; payrolls for JM's company in *PJM*, 1:13, 15, 17–19; JM, *Life of Washington*, 2:84–85. Many accounts of Valley Forge have been written, but those by Bill and Trussell are best for the military topics discussed herein. Logistical problems that contributed to the Continental Army's suffering are described in James A. Huston, *Logistics of Liberty: American Services of Supply in the Revolutionary War and After* (Newark: University of Delaware Press, 1991). Albert Beveridge first propagated the idea that Marshall's animus toward Jefferson arose from his resentment that his cousin was not bearing the same burdens as the patriots at Valley Forge, but Jean Smith has effectively dispensed with that notion. Beveridge, *Marshall*, 1:126–30; Jean Smith, *John Marshall: Definer of a Nation* (New York: Henry Holt, 1996), 63–64 and 549 n. 197.

28. *PJM*, 1:15 n. 2; [U.S. Army, Judge Advocate General's Corps], *The Army Lawyer: A History of the Judge Advocate General's Corps, 1775–1975* (Washington, D.C.: Government Printing Office, [1975]), 7–13, 18–19; William F. Fratcher, "History of the Judge Advocate General's Corps, United States Army," *Military Law Review*, 4 (1959), 89–92, 116–17.

29. *PJM*, 1:17–22; *Army Lawyer*, 7–13; Trussell, *Birthplace of an Army*, iii, 62–75; James C. Neagles, *Summer Soldiers: A Survey and Index of Revolutionary War Courts-Martial* (Salt Lake City: Ancestry Inc., 1991), 68–280 passim; Bill, *Valley Forge*, 108–10; Noel F. Busch, *Winter Quarters: George Washington and the Continental Army at Valley Forge* (New York: Liveright, 1974), 65–66; Middlekauff, *Glorious Cause*, 415; Martin and Lender, *A Respectable Army*, 128–31; Royster, *Revolutionary People at War*, 216–29; Higginbotham, *War of American Independence*, 413–14; Stuart L. Bernath, "George Washington and the Genesis of American Military Discipline," *Mid-America*, 49 (1967), 83–100; Maurer Maurer, "Military Justice under General Washington," *Military Affairs*, 28 (1964), 8–16; Robert H. Berlin, "The Administration of Military Justice in the Continental Army during the American Revolution, 1775–1783" (Ph.D. diss., University of California at Santa Barbara, 1976), 46, 111, 121–29, 169, 184–87, 302, 305–07; Caroline H. Cox, "'A Proper Sense of Honor': The Status of Soldiers and Officers of the Continental Army, 1775–1783" (Ph.D. diss., University of California at

Berkeley, 1997), chap. 2; Paul G. Atkinson Jr., "The System of Military Discipline and Justice in the Continental Army: August 1777–June 1778," *Picket Post* (winter 1972–73), 12–23, 40–43; [General] George Weedon, *Valley Forge Orderly Book* . . . (New York: Dodd, Mead, 1902; rept., New York: Arno Press, 1971), passim. The courts martial were held in the bake house, which was available because the lack of flour meant little baking was done, and when bread was being made, the bake house was the warmest place in the encampment. Berlin, "Administration of Military Justice," 123.

30. Russell and Gott, *Fauquier County*, 243–44; Sellers, "Virginia Continental Line," 285–303; Trussell, *Birthplace of an Army*, 88–93.

31. *Diaries of George Washington, 1748–1799*, ed. John C. Fitzpatrick, 4 vols. (Boston: Houghton Mifflin, 1925), 1:316; *Diaries of George Washington*, ed. Donald Jackson, 6 vols. (Charlottesville: University Press of Virginia, 1976–79), 3:309; Russell and Gott, *Fauquier County*, 46.

32. JM, *Life of Washington*, "Preface," *PJM*, 6:233; Higginbotham, *Washington and the American Military Tradition*, 77.

33. Bill, *Valley Forge*, 144–46; Trussell, *Birthplace of an Army*, 83; Henry Howe, *Historical Collection of Virginia* . . . (Charleston, S.C., 1845; rept., Baltimore: Regional Publishing Co., 1969), 266; Albert Furtwangler, *American Silhouettes: Rhetorical Identities of the Founders* (New Haven: Yale University Press, 1988), 64–84; Beveridge, *Marshall*, 1:118–19, 132; Slaughter, *History of St. Mark's Parish*, 108.

34. Royster, *Revolutionary People at War*, 114; Richard H. Kohn, "American Generals of the Revolution: Subordination and Restraint," in *Reconsiderations of the Revolutionary War: Selected Essays*, ed. Don Higginbotham (Westport, Conn.: Greenwood Press, 1978), 107; Martin and Lender, *A Respectable Army*, 103–07, 126, 150, 152; Lawrence D. Cress, *Citizens in Arms: The Army and Militia in American Society to the War of 1812* (Chapel Hill: University of North Carolina Press, 1982), 67–73; E. Wayne Carp, *To Starve the Army at Pleasure: Continental Army Administration and American Political Culture, 1775–1783* (Chapel Hill: University of North Carolina Press, 1984), 156.

35. Don Higginbotham, "Military Leadership in the American Revolution," in *War and Society in Revolutionary America*, 96–97; Royster, *Revolutionary People at War*, 87, 193, 204ff., 212–13, 216, 220, 231–32. Marshall learned much from Von Steuben, whom he called "a real service to the American troops . . . by his skill and persevering industry, [he] effected important improvements through all ranks of the army." *Life of Washington*, 2:93. Von Steuben's contribution to the Continental Army is well described in John McAuley Palmer, *General Von Steuben* (New Haven: Yale University Press, 1937; rept., Port Washington, N.Y.: Kennikat Press, 1966), 136–61.

36. Samuel P. Huntington, *The Soldier and the State: The Theory and Practice of Civil-Military Relations*, Vintage ed. (New York: Alfred A. Knopf, 1957), chap. 1; Trussell, *Birthplace of an Army*, 57; Palmer, *General Von Steuben*, 141–42, 209–10; Martin and Lender, *A Respectable Army*, 122–24; Ward, *War of the Revolution*, 2:576–85.

37. Sources for the next three paragraphs are Sanchez-Saavedra, *Guide to Virginia Military Organizations*, 52–53; Berg, *Encyclopedia of Continental Army Units*, 136; Sellers, "Virginia Continental Line," 321–22, 325; *PJM*, 1:22 n. 8, 23–26, 27 n. 1, 33 n. 2, 35–37; JM, *Life of Washington*, 2:188 n. 1, 194 n. 1, 3:107–8; Beveridge, *Marshall*, 1:96 n. 2, 117 n. 3, 142–43; JM to Joseph Delaplaine, 22 March 1818, in Dillon, *Marshall*, 1:55; Sallie E. Marshall Hardy, "John Marshall as Son, Brother, Husband, and Friend," *Green Bag*, 8 (1896), 480; "Editorial Note," *PJM*, 1:41 and n. 9; Rhodes, *Calendar of Marshall Papers*, 1:17; Royster, *Revolutionary People at War*, 268–70, 280–82, 284, 323–24; Tyler, "Old Virginia Line," 35–37.

Thomas Marshall tried to sell George Washington some land to raise cash, but the commander-in-chief said he did not have enough money at the time. Beveridge, *Marshall*, 1:167–68. Thomas later wrote Washington that he wanted to leave the Continental infantry and command the new artillery regiment Virginia was raising. Washington, noting that Thomas's "Mathematical Abilities are sufficiently known" and that he possessed "indubitable bravery, of which he has given proofs upon every occasion," endorsed his request for change of duty. Washington to [Governor] Patrick Henry, 3 October 1777, in *The Writings of George Washington*, ed. John C. Fitzpatrick, 39 vols. (Washington, D.C.: Government Printing Office, 1931–44), 9:301–2.

38. JM to William Theodore Dwight, 7 August 1827, quoted in Rhodes, *Calendar of Marshall Papers*, 2:282; JM, *Autobiographical Sketch*, 5.

39. Daniel R. Gilbert, "John Marshall and the Development of a National History," in *Early Nationalist Historians*, vol. 4 of *The Colonial Legacy*, ed. Lawrence H. Leder (New York: Harper and Row, 1973), 4:190–92; JM, *Autobiographical Sketch*, 9.

40. JM, *Autobiographical Sketch*, 9–10; idem, *Life of Washington*, 4:89.

41. Sources for this paragraph and the next are E. Wayne Carp, "Early American Military History: A Review of Recent Work," *VMHB*, 94 (1986), 277; "Virginia Declaration of Rights," enacted 12 June 1776, in *Revolutionary America*, 7:449–50; Martin and Lender, *A Respectable Army*, 65–66; JM, *Life of Washington*, 1:157; Sylvia Neely, "Mason Locke Weems's *Life of George Washington* and the Myth of Braddock's Defeat," *VMHB*, 107 (1999), 56–58.

42. Don Higginbotham, "The American Militia: A Traditional Institution with Revolutionary Responsibilities," in *Reconsiderations on the Revolutionary War*, 90–96; Shy, "New Look at Colonial Militia," 216–20.

43. JM, "Preface" to *Life of Washington*, in *PJM*, 6:233; Frank Shuffelton, "Endangered History: Character and Narrative in Early American Historical Writing," *The Eighteenth Century*, 34 (1993), 237–42.

44. JM, *Autobiographical Sketch*, 5, 10; Richard H. Kohn, *Eagle and Sword: The Federalists and the Creation of the Military Establishment in America, 1783–1802* (New York: Free Press, 1975), 252, 284–85; Stephen G. Kurtz, *The Presidency of John Adams: The Collapse of Federalism, 1795–1800* (rept., New York: A. S. Barnes and Co., 1961), chap. 14 passim; Higginbotham, *Washington and the American Military Tradition*, 2.

45. JM, *History of the Colonies*, 366; idem, "Preface" to *Life of Washington*, in *PJM*, 6:234; idem, *Life of Washington*, 1:90.

46. Arthur H. Shaffer, *The Politics of History: Writing the History of the American Revolution, 1783–1815* (Chicago: Precedent Publishing, 1975), 99; JM, *History of the Colonies*, 401.

47. JM to John Elliot, 23 April 1810, *Massachusetts Historical Society Proceedings*, 2nd ser., 14 (1900), 355; JM to Edward Everett, 2 August 1826, Rhodes, *Calendar of Marshall Papers*, 2:268; Shuffelton, "Endangered History," 231–37. For analyses of JM's treatment of the prelude to the Revolution, see Gilbert, "John Marshall and the Development of a National History"; William Raymond Smith, *History as Argument: Three Patriot Historians of the American Revolution* (The Hague: Mouton and Co., 1966), 118–29; Shaffer, *Politics of History*, passim; and Michael Kraus and Davis D. Joyce, *The Writing of American History*, rev. ed. (Norman: University of Oklahoma Press, 1985), 72–73. Other examinations of the *Life of Washington* are George H. Callcott, *History in the United States, 1800–1860: Its Practice and Purpose* (Baltimore: Johns Hopkins University Press, 1970); Harvey Wish, *The American Historian: A Social-Intellectual History of the Writing of the American Past* (New York: Oxford

University Press, 1960); Bert Loewenberg, *American History in American Thought* (New York: Simon and Schuster, 1972); William Alfred Bryan, *George Washington in American Literature, 1775–1865* (New York: Columbia University Press, 1952); and Marcus Cunliffe, "Introduction" to Chelsea House edition of *The Life of Washington*. Neither these nor Marshall's principal biographers discuss the *History of the Colonies* in any detail.

48. Beveridge, *Marshall*, 1:148.

Chapter 3

Lawyer and Lawmaker in the Old Dominion, 1781–1787

For John Marshall, the several years after he left the Continental Army were a time of professional, political, and personal maturation. He established a thriving legal practice and within a short time became one of the most eminent lawyers in Virginia, whose bar was among the most renowned in the nation. His service in the House of Delegates and the Council of State earned him high prestige, enabled him to meet influential friends and make essential political and professional connections, and contributed to the shaping of his views on the public issues of the day. Also during this period, Marshall became a fixture in Richmond's civic and cultural life, speculated heavily in western lands and dabbled in frontier politics, and married his eventual lifetime companion. His experiences in these years would have provided early evidence for Henry Adams's observation that "[l]aw and politics were the only objects of Virginian thought; but within these bounds the Virginians achieved triumphs."[1]

Writing to a prospective biographer in 1818 at age 62, Marshall recalled that "[f]rom my infancy I was destined to the bar."[2] From that vantage point, such may well have seemed the case, for by then he had been a lawyer and jurist for almost four decades and had spent nearly two of them in the paramount position of the American legal profession. As one reconstructs the biographical background of his legal and judicial achievements, however, a complex picture emerges, one that comprises paternal encouragement, self-initiative, specific circumstances and events, and broad political trends and changes in attitudes toward lawyers and the law. Moreover, Marshall and his parents do not appear to have considered that he take up other occupations available to the son of a prominent member of the gentry. He briefly tried but did not care for the planter's life, and no one ever seems to have thought him better suited to be a merchant, clergyman, or physician.

In his youth, Marshall accumulated knowledge and experience, much of it made available by his father Thomas, that prepared him well for his chosen vocation. Since around 1750, the practice of law had been considered a proper pursuit for members of the Virginia gentry. Thomas, who had no legal training, decided to provide John with greater opportunities for developing what interest in law his son already had shown. For example, Thomas encouraged John to accompany him to sessions of the Fauquier County Court. There, amidst the occasionally raucous activities of court day, John received his first exposure to lawyers and judges, legal institutions, procedures, and customs, and the personal drama of legal conflict, and he probably came away having learned at least a superficial practical lesson in the role of law in helping maintain social order. As a teenager, John spent many hours in the Hollow, by fireside or candlelight after the farm chores were done for the day, reading the four volumes of Blackstone's *Commentaries* that his father had bought. No evidence, however, substantiates the family tradition that John walked 36 miles a day to read law with, and clerk for, an attorney in Warrenton.[3]

Marshall first became directly involved in legal affairs during his military service in the Revolution. As a lieutenant in the Culpeper Minute Battalion, he participated in his first legal proceeding: a court-martial, held in December 1775 at Great Bridge, Virginia, of some militiamen charged with desertion or sleeping on duty. In the winter and spring of 1778–1779 at Valley Forge, Marshall served as one of 15 deputy judge advocates general (DJAGs) in the Continental Army and worked as George Washington's chief legal officer during the encampment. Besides performing the duties of a clerk and notary, he prosecuted infractions of military law ranging from tardiness to treason. "Prosecute" should not, however, be taken in its modern adversarial sense, for Revolutionary courts-martial were not so much adjudicative proceedings as evidentiary hearings. They had no judge or jury, and the accused had no right to counsel, although he could cross-examine witnesses. Revolutionary War DJAGs normally did not argue cases and often said little during the proceedings, which consisted mostly of principals giving statements rather than responding to questions. Marshall's main functions were to compile evidence, assure the attendance of witnesses, swear in the officers on the court-martial, and instruct them on the applicable law, derived from the 1776 Articles of War, army regulations, and military customs. The frequency with which courts-martial were held at Valley Forge—more than one a day—put a premium on speed and simplicity, not protracted discourse, intensive interrogation, and legal arcana. Most trials of junior and noncommissioned officers took less than a day. Courts-martial of higher ranking officers presented more of a challenge to the DJAG because the accused's interest in preserving his honor frequently produced a more elaborate defense that tested the prosecutor's "courtroom" abilities.[4]

Considering the physical and psychological stresses Marshall already labored under at Valley Forge, the heavy caseload, lack of assistance, scant rewards, and confrontations with disgruntled soldiers and officers must have taxed his faculties and character. At least from the account of one contemporary, though, he bore the strain well and kept his equable and discerning temperament both inside and outside the hearing room:

[A]ll those who intimately knew him affirmed that his capacity was held in such estimation by many of his brother officers, that in many disputes . . . he was constantly chosen arbiter; and that officers, irritated by differences or animated by debate, often submitted the contested points to his judgment, which being given in writing, and accompanied, as it commonly was, by sound reasons in support of his decision, obtained general acquiescence.

Marshall's service as DJAG further familiarized him with legal concepts and procedures and gave him firsthand experience in quasi-judicial settings. In his civilian practice, however, he would not have found knowledge of military law very useful because of its specialized nature. As Sir Matthew Hale, the influential English jurist, wrote in his *History of the Common Law of England* (1713), military law was "something indulged, rather than allowed as law." "The necessity of Government, Order, and Discipline in an Army, is that only which can give those laws a Countenance." Marshall remained a DJAG on paper until he resigned from the army in February 1781, but he did not serve in that capacity after Valley Forge.[5]

While visiting his father in Yorktown in the spring of 1780, Marshall decided to take advantage of a slow period in the war to acquire his only formal legal education: three months of lectures at the College of William and Mary by George Wythe, the newly appointed Professor of Law and Police. At the time, Virginia was the only one of the original 13 states without a prescribed training period for aspiring lawyers. Practical experience was preferred over preparatory studies. Marshall's previous reading and tutoring in classical literature and languages and prominent English literary works enabled him to meet the informal or customary requirements for academic study of the law in Virginia. Besides attending college, he could have chosen from among several other avenues for legal training, such as apprenticing under an attorney in London, an American city, or somewhere in Virginia; clerking in a county court; or entering one of the English Inns of Court. It is not known how much influence Thomas Marshall had on John's decision, but the family's financial straits and the war eliminated expensive study in England as an option, and John would not have found the other choices very appealing. Reading law in an attorney's office or clerking in a court had well-deserved reputations for drudgery, as frequently the apprentice or clerk was relegated to copying documents and performing fact-grubbing research and had little time left for organized study. Much of that time was spent reading cases and memorizing decisions. In addition, the master lawyer often was too busy or, in some instances, too haughty to spend much time with his menial apprentices.[6]

Marshall, having decided to learn law at the academy, could have picked one of the several American colleges established outside Virginia during the colonial period that remained open during the war: Harvard, Yale, the College of New Jersey (now Princeton), the College of Rhode Island (now Brown), the College of Philadelphia (now Pennsylvania), Queen's College (now Rutgers), or Dartmouth. None of these institutions had specialized law courses, but their curricula prepared young men for more comprehensive legal study, and college training increasingly was becoming expected of, and necessary for, a successful lawyer in America. Instead, Marshall opted for Wythe's short course at William and Mary, probably for a number of reasons. The religious affiliation of some of the schools may have precluded them. The College of Rhode Island was Baptist; Harvard and Yale were Congregationalist; and Queen's College was Calvinist; whereas Kings College and William and Mary had the preferred Episcopal connection. The College of Philadelphia and the College of New Jersey were suitable, the latter having attracted several prominent young Virginians (notably James Madison), but other circumstances inclined Marshall toward attending the local school. It was not feasible for him to make a lengthy commitment outside Virginia just then. His military obligation had not ended yet, and, depending on what course the war took, he could have been returned to active duty at any time. He probably also did not want to leave his family until the fighting was over, or be too far away from Mary Ambler, the object of his romantic intentions, who was living in Yorktown then. Lastly, attendance at William and Mary was emerging as a credential for legal prominence in Virginia. For example, during the years just before the Revolution, a growing percentage of lawyers admitted to practice before the General Court—the colony's highest-ranking judicial body—were educated at William and Mary.[7]

Some of William and Mary's increased appeal to prospective lawyers such as Marshall resulted from the efforts of Governor Thomas Jefferson, who served as an ex officio member of the College's Board of Visitors. As part of his program to reform public education in Virginia, Jefferson in 1779 persuaded the visitors to change the curriculum and faculty by abolishing the chairs of divinity and Oriental languages and establishing new professorships in modern languages, medicine, and law. The professorship of law was the first such faculty position at an American college. After 1750, some law began to appear in college curricula in America, but only as an aspect of other subjects such as politics, theology, or philosophy. Not until George Wythe became a professor at William and Mary were law and jurisprudence presented as a separate discipline.[8]

Marshall arrived at the College in time for the spring term, which began on 1 May 1780. At age 25, he probably was among the older of the approximately 80 students there. The campus was nondescript and somewhat run-down, described by Jefferson a year later as an assemblage of "rude, mis-shapen piles, which, but that they have roofs, would be taken for brick-kilns," and providing only "an indifferent accomodation" [sic] for about a hundred students. Wartime inflation had driven nominal tuition up drastically; one of Marshall's classmates despaired that his father could not pay the 4,000 pounds of tobacco needed for board and fees. Wythe's one term of lectures would have cost the Marshalls slightly under 1,000 pounds of tobacco, the tuition charge for a full year's study under two professors. Because students had to pay for room and board and all other expenses, the Marshalls' cash-strapped condition probably forced John to lodge with a local acquaintance of his father's or possibly of Jaquelin Ambler's, his future father-in-law.[9]

George Wythe was the most esteemed member of the William and Mary faculty. A prominent gentryman, he had served as Virginia's colonial attorney general and also had held seats in the House of Burgesses, the Continental Congress (where he had signed the Declaration of Independence), and the House of Delegates. In 1780, he was appointed a justice of the High Court of Chancery and the Court of Appeals, the latter the state's supreme court. He served, along with Jefferson and Edmund Pendleton, on a commission to revise the laws of the Commonwealth to make them consistent with the ideals of the Revolution. Wythe was one of the preeminent members of the Virginia bar and a well-known legal educator, widely sought as a tutor for ambitious planters' sons. One of his students, William Munford, recalled the appeal Wythe had for the prospective Virginia lawyer: "Nothing would advance me faster in the world than the reputation of having been educated by Mr. Wythe, for such a man as he casts a light upon all around him." When Marshall first met him, Wythe was 54 years old, of medium height but stooped and frail looking, with a bulbous balding head and a hatchet face. He had a courtly and reserved manner, a speculative but not quick intellect, an acute concern for honor and integrity, and cosmopolitan tastes balanced by occasional dogmatism on matters of principle.[10]

Wythe also was an innovative and demanding teacher who conceived his purpose as producing not just competent lawyers but also leaders in public life—or, as he put it in a letter to John Adams, "to form such characters as may be fit to succede [sic] those which have been ornamental and useful in the national councils of America."[11] By the spring 1780 term, Wythe had developed a rigorous course combining theory and practice and consisting of readings and lectures supplemented with moot courts and mock legislative sessions. At the twice-weekly lectures, Marshall heard Wythe expound upon the theory and philosophy of law, drawing heavily on Blackstone's *Commentaries* (1765–69); Matthew Bacon's *New Abridgement of the Law* (1766–69), a standard treatise on English law; *The Acts of Assembly . . . in the Colony of Virginia* (1769), the major compilation of local legislation; and works of political thought by Montesquieu, Hume, and other Enlightenment figures.

Wythe's study of English legal history may have inspired him to revive and adapt the practice of "mooting," or staging court sessions and parliamentary debates. Marshall and his classmates met in Williamsburg's old Capitol, recently abandoned when the government moved to Richmond, once or twice a month for moot court and every Saturday for moot legislature. Each was held before an audience of local residents. Wythe and the other professors presided over the "court," and Wythe, sitting in a raised, high-backed chair, maintained order as Speaker of the House when the "legislature" was in session. Marshall and the other students had to prepare and argue cases that Wythe assigned, and draft and debate bills, some of which drew on Wythe's recent work on revising Virginia's pre-Revolution laws. In addition, Wythe expected Marshall and his classmates to read and take notes on various treatises on English law and legal history and procedure, and to delve into some of the numerous compilations of English cases.

At the time, Marshall ventured no opinions about Wythe's demanding curriculum, nor did he later reflect on how it influenced him. In just three months, he could have received only an introduction to the theory and substance of the law. As one of his classmates wrote at the time, "those who finish this study in a few months either have strong natural parts or else they know little about it." For the most part, Marshall learned his law while he practiced it. The most immediate use that Wythe's classes had for Marshall would have come from the mock trials and assembly sessions. They would have given Marshall a feel for speaking and debating in public, preparing cases and bills, and working with courtroom and parliamentary procedures. In addition, Marshall may have come away from Wythe's classes and mootings with a few basic ideas that contributed to the more complex conceptions of jurisprudence and constitutionalism he developed later and applied in some of his most famous decisions. Among these ideas of Wythe's were construing statutes as narrowly as required to reach the appropriate resolution of the case at hand; avoiding extravagant, imaginative interpretations; using a clear sense of the statute's meaning and intent as the basis for a decision; and always recurring to the truism that law's predictability rests on statutes interpreted in accordance with accepted judicial doctrines. In addition, Marshall's necessarily cursory examination of Montesquieu's and Hume's political ideas probably underscored for him the importance, respectively, of the role of an independent judiciary in maintaining balance among the branches of government, and the need to dispense with a priori notions when addressing real-life legal disputes.[12]

Marshall also partook of other attractions William and Mary had to offer. College rules entitled students to attend the lectures of two professors, so Marshall chose those given by the president of the College, the Reverend James Madison, in natural philosophy—a contemporary term for an interdisciplinary study of physics and chemistry. Marshall also joined Phi Beta Kappa, "being recommended as a gentleman who would make a worthy member," according to the chapter's minutes. Founded at William and Mary in 1776, Phi Beta Kappa principally was a social, literary, and debating society. During Marshall's attendance, it entertained such questions as "Whether the Execution of Charles the First was justifyable"; "Whether the rape of the Sabine women was just"; and "Whether in Civil War any person is justifyable in remaining Neuter." Marshall joined in a debate on "Whether any form of Government is more favorable to public virtue than a Commonwealth"; he seems to have argued against the proposition. Among the members of the fraternity were Marshall's future Supreme Court colleague and biographical collaborator, Bushrod Washington, and his future Jeffersonian antagonist, Spencer Roane. Between classes and debates, Marshall took his meals with the other students at a "college table"—beer, toddy, and spirits were available, and in warm weather the students were not required to wear coats or even shoes—and he left a lasting testament to his presence at the college by carving his initials in the plaster of a wall in the Wren building.[13]

One other aspect of Marshall's legal education warrants attention: his law notes—a calf-bound notebook containing over 200 manuscript pages of references, abstracts, and notations on 70 subjects, mostly civil, arranged alphabetically from "Abatement" to "Limitation of Actions." The law notes indicate the authorities most often relied on and the sorts of legal controversies that arose most often in Virginia law at that time. The purpose of the notes was to give Marshall a convenient summary of the common law as then practiced in Virginia. Marshall did not take the notes as Wythe lectured, but instead compiled them outside class. Law students and newly minted lawyers often copied legal material from sources into their own notebooks, a process generally known as "commonplacing," as a method of self-education. Marshall commonplaced mainly from two printed sources: Bacon's *New Abridgement of the Law*, and *The Acts of Assembly . . . in the Colony of Virginia*. Marshall's citations from Bacon are weighted heavily toward King's Bench and High Court of Chancery reports, perhaps indicating a contemporary preference for the case law that those tribunals handed down. Marshall also cited several other English treatises, including those by Hale, William Hawkins, and Sir Edward Coke. It is not known whether Marshall consulted these works directly or relied on Bacon's and Blackstone's citations of them, but at a minimum the references indicate that such studies were considered important sources for a Virginia lawyer of that era. Marshall substituted Virginia statutory material for some Parliamentary citations to make the notes more useful in his future practice.[14]

The influence of Blackstone on Marshall's legal thought, which almost all his biographers have emphasized without analysis, is difficult to determine, and a case could be made that it may have been less significant than usually supposed. For example, Marshall included relatively few passages from the *Commentaries* in his law notes, cited them infrequently in his arguments, and did not mention Blackstone in any correspondence. Nevertheless, Marshall probably drew some general and specific lessons from the English jurist that are worth noting.

The publication of numerous editions of the *Commentaries* after 1770 helped create a "vogue of Blackstone" that had an indirect and diffuse impact on American politics, constitutional thought, and legal education and procedure. The *Commentaries* imparted a rudimentary knowledge of the law to previously untutored Americans, and—ironically, considering that Blackstone was a Tory who believed in a constitutional monarchy—helped instill in influential Americans a devotion to the English common law as the basis for the rights of Englishmen which they believed Parliament was violating. In addition,

Marshall gleaned from Blackstone less a particular exposition of English law than a sense of law as a science comprehensible through a methodology of legal reasoning. Writing in an accessible style, Blackstone infused the study of law with the rationalism of the Enlightenment, considering legal principles as universal as those of physics. As James Wilson, probably Blackstone's most influential American disciple, would later write, "Law should be studied and taught as a historical science." A lawyer or judge could use this rational, deductive approach to apply statutes and constitutional provisions in individual cases by analyzing, in succession, their language, context, intent, and spirit—a more expansive approach than the crabbed traditional view advocated by Blackstone's juristic predecessor, Sir Edward Coke. For Marshall, whose unspeculative mind possessed formidable powers of logic and argumentation, Blackstone's science of law held a strong appeal that is evident in some of his major Supreme Court opinions. The most notable examples, perhaps, are *Marbury v. Madison* (1803), which asserted the Supreme Court's authority to review congressional acts, and *McCulloch v. Maryland* (1819), which upheld the constitutionality of the national bank using a broad construction of the "necessary and proper" clause in Article I, section 8 of the Constitution.[15]

Even by contemporary standards, Marshall's formal legal training was slight, but it suited his temperament and intellect. Research and scholarship never were Marshall's forte, as suggested by his (probably apocryphal) remark to Joseph Story after announcing a decision: "Now, Story, that is the law; *you* find the precedents for it." Wythe's class gave Marshall an adequate grounding in the law while sparing him months of isolation reading arcane legal tomes that had little immediate value in the courtroom. His quick study at William and Mary and his later on-the-job education enabled him to approach and analyze legal problems more intuitively and less rigidly. Besides, technical learning often did not help American lawyers practice before judges whose legal education frequently was as limited as their own, if not more so. Such lay jurists were unimpressed by torrents of citations and Latinisms—they tended to dismiss them as pedantry and obfuscation—and had more interest in adapting general legal principles to novel circumstances, a pursuit at which Marshall excelled.[16]

Marshall finished his studies at William and Mary at the end of the term in late July 1780, but before he could start his practice, he had to pass an examination and receive a license. The exact procedure he followed is unclear because the pre-Revolutionary process no longer was followed and the legislature had not yet enacted new guidelines for licensing attorneys. Marshall presumably did the same as other lawyers around this time. He obtained a recommendation from a city or county court—probably Richmond, Williamsburg, or Fauquier—and petitioned Governor Jefferson for a license. The governor then appointed at least two experienced lawyers, including possibly the attorney general, to examine Marshall to whatever degree they deemed necessary to satisfy themselves of his competency. They reported to

Jefferson that Marshall had passed the examination, and sometime between 31 July and 14 August the governor issued his license.[17]

Marshall then had to present his license to the city or county court where he intended to practice and take an oath before he could take cases to the bar. Marshall chose Fauquier County, not Williamsburg or Richmond, probably for several reasons. Richmond, the new capital, was the center of Virginia's legal profession, and many talented and prestigious lawyers had established practices there. A neophyte attorney like Marshall would have had difficulty building a clientele and was customarily expected to "apprentice" in a county court. In addition, he probably wanted to be near his family—his mother and several siblings were living at Oak Hill—after their lengthy wartime separation. Lastly, 14-year-old Mary Ambler, residing with her father in Yorktown, was too young to marry yet. Marshall apparently figured he could spend a couple of dutiful years at the Fauquier County bar, gaining legal experience and adding to his estate, before moving to Richmond, where he could satisfy his professional ambition and also be nearer to the comely young woman who had captivated him while in Williamsburg. On 28 August 1780, according to Fauquier County Court records, "John Marshall, Gent., produced a license from his Excellency the Governor to practice law and took the oaths prescribed by act of Assembly."[18]

Most of the next two years passed uneventfully and, it seems safe to say, somewhat tediously, for Marshall. He had little legal work to do, even after the Virginia courts reopened following George Washington's defeat of Lord Cornwallis in October 1781. (They had closed in January 1781 when Benedict Arnold led a small British invasion force up the James River and attacked Richmond.) County records indicate that Marshall was involved in only one minor civil suit during 1781–82, and no available evidence suggests he conducted an office practice of drafting wills, deeds, and other legal papers. He probably spent most of his time tending to the family plantation at Oak Hill, which had deteriorated during the war. In September 1780, the restless Marshall decided to rejoin the Continental Army in Philadelphia after Virginia refused to raise the troops Washington needed. Marshall walked the nearly 170 miles, his long legs striding up to 35 miles a day. When he arrived after two weeks on the road, his hair, beard, and clothing looked so shabby that the first tavern he went to for lodging turned him away. While he was with the army, he received another smallpox vaccination. The one he received while in the Continental Army apparently had not taken, Virginia law made inoculation extremely difficult, and Marshall may have wanted to be protected against the disease before asking Mary Ambler to be his wife.[19]

In November, Marshall returned to Virginia as part of a contingent led by General Nathaniel Greene and Baron von Steuben, whom Washington had charged with raising and commanding a new army to confront Cornwallis. Greene took over the Continental forces in the Carolinas, and Von Steuben undertook the task of rebuilding Virginia's militia and finding reinforcements for the army. Marshall participated in the baron's recruitment drive, which produced about 1,500 men by year's end. In January 1781, Marshall joined in Virginia's feeble military response to Arnold's attack on the Richmond area that sent the government and many notables fleeing into the countryside. A small mixed force of Continentals and militia, Marshall among them, ambushed Arnold's troops while they were heading back toward the Chesapeake Bay. According to Marshall's later account, the Americans "gave [the British] one fire with some effect; but, on its being partially returned . . . broke and fled in the utmost confusion."[20]

After these few months of excitement, Marshall resigned his commission in the Continental Army and returned to the slow-paced life of a country lawyer and planter. He was anxious to establish his practice at the center of the Commonwealth's legal and political life, and he wanted to be near Mary, so he decided to run for a seat in the House of Delegates from Fauquier County in April 1782. Service in the assembly was not lucrative by itself—delegates received only a small per diem allowance—but it was an essential step in the advancement of a young man's financial and political fortune. In Richmond, Marshall could meet influential lawyers, politicians, and officials who could refer clients to him and admit him to their fraternity of power. In addition, Marshall could more conveniently pursue his courtship of Mary, now at the marrying age of 16 and living in the capital with her father, who had become a member of the governor's cabinet after moving from Yorktown. No details of Marshall's election are available. Presumably it resembled those genteel and ritualized contests described earlier, although in some ways politics in Fauquier County had the competitive characteristics of the nearby Northern Neck. Marshall certainly benefited from his father's stature in the county. Unconfirmed family tradition holds that Marshall received all votes but one, and that Thomas "[took] the delinquent [freeholder] to task [and] inflicted upon him a good whipping."[21]

Marshall arrived in Richmond in May 1782 to take his oath of office and attend his first session of the House of Delegates. He encountered a frontier community less than a mile square with a boomtown atmosphere and few amenities.   Nearly half of Richmond's approximately 1,000 residents had arrived in the past three years and came from all strata of society: political leaders and lawyers; merchants and peddlers; craftsmen, laborers, tars, and chattels; and idlers and drifters. About 55 percent of the population was white; most of the rest were slaves. Nearly all of the 300 or so houses were made of wood, one or two stories high and scattered on two heights divided by a brook called Shockoe Creek. The legislature met in two small frame buildings on an abandoned commercial lot near the James River. The delegates' home was an empty warehouse also used for large public social functions such as dances and banquets. Richmond also had a wharf area, some storehouses, a marketplace, several inns and taverns, one church (an underused Anglican facility), and one newspaper (the *Virginia Gazette*). The unpaved streets, plied by creaking wagons and painted carriages, lacked sidewalks and were covered with mud or dust except for the occasional piles of ashes and cinders that served as footpaths at intersections. Richmond had grown too fast for comfort since the late 1770s, and the city trustees had to enact several ordinances concerning fire safety, sanitation, animal control, transportation, and street maintenance in 1782–83. Crime remained chronic, and thievery—especially horse stealing—and "disorderly houses" thrived in the unsettled environment.[22]

By becoming a delegate, Marshall had joined the most influential branch of Virginia's government. The framers of the state constitution of 1776 had sought to strip power from the executive and upper house and restore the assembly to the preeminence it enjoyed in the colonial era. The House, which met biannually in the spring and fall, had exclusive power to originate legislation; the Senate could only approve, reject, or amend bills (except for proposed revenue laws, which it could not alter); and the governor had no veto. The House also joined the Senate in selecting the governor, treasurer, Council of State (which helped administer the laws), attorney general, and judges above the county level.[23]

Marshall's first term in the House covered the periods 25 May–2 July and 9–29 November 1782.[24] During the session, he experienced a style of politics familiar to him from Fauquier County: oligarchic, personalized, and nonideological. The assembly had undergone a slight "democratization" during the Revolution. Delegates, chosen by freeholders who met a low property qualification, did not have to satisfy any special property requirement themselves and could be reelected. More frontiersmen's buckskins and farmers' homespun could be seen on the assembly floor than before the war; and the proceedings tended to be less decorous. According to a European traveler at the time, "It is said of the Assembly: It sits; but this is not a true expression, for these members show themselves in every possible position rather than that of sitting still, with dignity and attention." Still, the overwhelming number of delegates came from established, and often interrelated, families, owned large farms or plantations or practiced professions, and had served in public office before.

A small group of leaders—principally Patrick Henry, Richard Henry Lee, Henry Tazewell, and Speaker John Tyler—organized the delegates into loose, shifting alliances that resembled coteries more than factions. These coalitions of mostly gentlemen, possessing "much good intention, but little knowledge of the science" to which they were called, wrote Jefferson, engaged in congenial contests mainly over questions arising from the economic disruption of the Revolution and the postwar depression: taxation, debtor relief, paper money, and British debts. Henry led a debtor-oriented alliance. What little opposition he faced gravitated toward Tazewell. Votes on specific issues defined the coalitions, not sets of principles or consistent attitudes toward groups of issues—insofar as any alignments are discernible, because turnover and absenteeism were high. Personalities usually decided elections, and alliances lacked durable constituencies. Consistent voting patterns based on region, economic interest, or ideology, and contentious factionalism had not yet emerged in the polite politics of the Commonwealth.

When the Virginia legislature was in session, most lawmakers boarded at Richmond's several taverns (also known as inns and ordinaries), which included Formicola's, The Bird in the Hand, Hogg's, Galt's, Cowley's, Bowler's, and The Swan. Marshall roomed at the most popular of these, Formicola's, located on Main Street between 15th and 17th Streets and named for and operated by a Neapolitan who had been *maitre d'hotel* to Virginia's last colonial governor. Marshall slept upstairs in one of two large rooms crowded with beds and ate, drank, politicked, gossiped, and played cards, billiards, and backgammon downstairs with "generals, colonels, captains, senators, assemblymen, judges, doctors, clerks and crowds of gentlemen of every weight and calibre [*sic*] . . . [who] sat all together about the fire, drinking, smoking, singing and talking ribaldry," according to a foreign traveler. It is not known whether Marshall and delegates from different coalitions or sections gravitated toward specific taverns, as early nineteenth century senators and representatives did with boardinghouses in Washington. Were that so, Richmond's taverns might have played a similar key role in the political sociology of the House of Delegates, facilitating the formation of factional and sectional allegiances by serving as a combination of fraternity house and political club for legislators with shared interests and loyalties. At least in the early 1780s, however, the taverns probably had the opposite effect on Marshall and his fellow legislators. They reinforced the consensual, oligarchic, personalized qualities of Virginia politics by homogenizing delegates of disparate views and backgrounds in communal living situations.[25]

During his first term, Marshall was chosen to serve on two of the House's standing committees—Courts of Justice, and Privileges and Elections—and several select committees appointed to draft bills and reports. The legislation he worked on included measures to reorganize the militia, "to form a plan of national defense against invasion," and to facilitate surveying of "vacant & unappropriated Lands . . . on the Eastern Waters." The House soon passed the latter two. Not enough roll calls were recorded in this session to provide evidence of a pattern or predisposition in Marshall's votes, and there are no records of his votes on some important measures such as the repeal of a 1781 law granting Congress the authority to levy a duty on imports; the repeal of a law reopening Virginia's courts to cases involving debts owed to British creditors; and measures raising and apportioning equally the tax on land. He opposed a bill to supply troops for the Continental Army, possibly because his experience as a company officer made him question the state's resolve to support the recruits adequately. "Capt. Marshall," Edmund Randolph advised James Madison, "a young man of rising character, will make a furious onset for the abolition of the draft." (The bill passed on the last day of the session.) One historian has placed Marshall in the anti-Henry bloc led by Henry Tazewell, many members of which became procreditor nationalists and Federalists later in the decade. Whatever effect—if any—Marshall's first stint in the legislature had on his emerging political perspective, he did come away more skeptical of his colleagues' ability to surmount narrow concerns and pursue the common good. In February 1783, he wrote to a friend that "[t]he grand object of the people is still, as it has ever been, to oppose successfully our British enemies and to establish on the firm base of certainty the independence of America. But in the attainment of this object an attention to a variety of little interests & passions produces such a distracted contrariety of measures that tis sometimes difficult to determine whether some other end is not nearer the hearts of those who guide our Counsels."[26]

In the fall 1782 session, the House of Delegates and the Senate elected Marshall to fill an unexpected vacancy on the Council of State, or Privy Council. The Council served as the state government's executive branch and the governor's cabinet. Under the 1776 Constitution, it lacked the power and prestige it had before the Revolution, although the governor still had to seek its advice and consent. Older, more experienced political leaders had less interest in serving on it, so the legislature turned to younger men such as Marshall, James Monroe, James Madison, William Short, and Beverly Randolph. Some luminaries in the government resented Marshall's presence on the Council; Judge Edmund Pendleton wrote that "Mr. Marshall . . . is clever, but I think too young for that department, which he should rather have earned as a retirement and reward, by ten or twelve years hard service in the Assembly."[27]

Beginning on 30 November, Marshall served on the Council for 18 months and gained experience in a wide range of governmental matters from the perspective of the executive branch. (The state constitution prohibited simultaneous service in the legislature and on the Council, so Marshall did not return to the House until after he resigned from the Council in April 1784.) He signed the proceedings of 200 meetings and missed few sessions. He and his fellow councilors met, usually every day, in a brick house on the hill across 12th Street from the governor's residence. They dealt with, among many routine concerns, appointments of minor officials such as tobacco inspectors and surveyors, requests from neighboring states for extradition of fugitives, and delegations of authority to militia officers fighting Indians on the frontier. The Council also appointed Marshall and his friend James Monroe to report on the state solicitor general's efforts to settle Virginia's wartime accounts with the national government. "[W]e have reason to suspect," they wrote, "great abuses have taken place and very dishonourable misapplications of the public money [have been made.]"[28]

Marshall addressed one important constitutional issue while on the Council. Acting under a 1778 law, Governor Benjamin Harrison tried to get the councilors to join him in removing from office a county magistrate accused of "diverse gross misdemeanors," including theft from an estate and dereliction of duty. In February 1783, Marshall signed a Council opinion declaring that "the Law authorizing the Executive to enquire into the Conduct of a Magistrate . . . is repugnant to the Act of Government[,] contrary to the fundamental principles of our constitution[,] and directly opposite to the general tenor of our Laws." This opinion, when considered with a decision by Chancellor George Wythe in *Commonwealth v. Caton* the previous year, indicated that many prominent

Virginians believed that the state's governmental system contained a serious constitutional flaw: It failed to distinguish between constitution and statute, between fundamental law and legislation, and was susceptible to abuse of power by the legislature, which conceivably could change the constitution at will. Fear of this possibility inspired an unsuccessful campaign, led by James Madison, to revise the constitution in 1783. Marshall did not comment directly on this effort, but by their actions, he and the other members of the Council and the judiciary made an early attempt to establish that the state constitution was fundamental law that superseded, and must be the reference point for, all governmental actions. Marshall and the other councilors, through an opportune denial of power to themselves, were able to create a check on possible "democratic despotism." Governor Benjamin Harrison did not agree, however, and when the legislature reconvened in May 1783, he reported the issue to the Assembly. Marshall and the councilors submitted their own report to the delegates by way of rebuttal. The House evidently resolved the dispute in the Council's favor; the justice of peace in question was tried in court instead.[29]

On 3 January 1783, Marshall married Mary "Polly" Ambler after a three-year courtship.[30] Regrettably for the historian, the details of their romance and marriage are clouded in family sentimentality and quaint reminiscence. The most reliable evidence, however—the letters from "J. Marshall" to "My Dearest Polly"—substantiates the unanimous description of their relationship by relatives, friends, and associates as loving and devoted. For almost 50 years they were faithful and affectionate companions, even though Polly's chronic debility after the mid-1780s severely restricted their activities and tried John's patience and energy. When Marshall wrote in an 1823 decision of "the sacredness of the connection between husband and wife," and that "the sweetness of social intercourse, the harmony of society, the happiness of families, depend on that mutual partiality which they feel, or that delicate forbearance which they manifest towards each other," his heart, as well as his intellect, was speaking.

Polly was the second of four daughters of Jaquelin Ambler and Rebecca Burwell, who had spurned Jefferson in favor of him. Jaquelin Ambler came from one of Virginia's first families and was an educated, courtly, and successful businessman and collector of customs in Yorktown. By 1779, the disruptions of the Revolutionary War, especially the cutoff of shipping into the port, had reduced the Ambler family to "poverty and perplexity of every kind," Polly's sister Eliza recalled, and Jaquelin had to move his family from a mansion to a row house. Their new dwelling, however, happened to be next door to the quarters of Colonel Thomas Marshall, commander of the Virginia State Regiment of Artillery and head of the Yorktown garrison. Colonel Marshall often visited the Ambler home and watched over the daughters when their father made frequent trips to Williamsburg as a member of the Council of State. According to Eliza Ambler, Thomas read the girls letters that John had sent him and told them about his son's battlefield experiences. "Perhaps no other officer that had been introduced to us excited so much interest, Eliza remembered. "We had been accustomed to hear him spoken of by all as a very *paragon* . . . Our expectations were raised to the highest pitch" when Colonel Marshall told them that "the gay-hearted young captain . . . called Silverheels" was coming to visit soon after Christmas 1779. "[T]he little circle of York was on tip-toe awaiting his arrival."

The ardor of all but one of the Ambler daughters was dampened when Marshall arrived at the formal ball organized in his honor in March 1780. After beholding his "awkward figure, unpolished manners, and total negligence of person," according to Eliza, they "lost all desire of becoming agreeable in his eyes." Fourteen-year-old Polly, however, "diffident beyond all others" but possessing a "superior discernment and solidity of character," already had "resolved to set her cap at him," and nothing in that first encounter dissuaded her. "She with a glance divined his character and understood how to appreciate it . . . Under [Marshall's] slouched hat there beamed an eye that penetrated at one glance the inmost recesses of the human character; and beneath the slovenly garb there dwelt a heart replete with every virtue." The striking contrast between the tall, rough-edged, good-natured John and the petite, refined, shy Polly added to the intensity of that love-at-first-sight introduction.

Marshall soon undertook what he later described as an "ardent & assiduous" courtship that he recalled fondly to Polly many years later:

I begin with the ball at York, and with the dinner on the fish at your house the next day: I then retrace my visit to York, our splendid assembly at the Palace in Williamsburg, my visit to Richmond where I acted Pa for a fortnight, my return the ensuing fall and the very welcome reception you gave me on your arrival from Dover, our little tiffs & makings up, my feelings while Major Dick was courting you, my trip to the cottage, the lock of hair, my visit again to Richmond the ensuing fall, and all the thousand indescribable but deeply affecting instances of your affection or coldness which constituted for a time the happiness or misery of my life.

When Marshall became bored or distracted while copying dull legal references in his notebook, he instead made affectionate jottings in the margins—versions of Polly's name, sometimes with his own linked to it, as in "John, Maria" and "John Marshall, Miss Polly Am." He could conduct this long-distance romance much more easily when the Amblers moved from Yorktown to Richmond in June 1780 after it became the new capital and when he began attending sessions of the House of Delegates in 1782. In June 1780, Marshall and his friends organized a ball at the vacant Governor's Palace in honor of "the Misses Ambler" when the family was passing through Williamsburg on the way to Richmond. "The entertainment in itself," Eliza Ambler wrote soon after, "was like most of the entertainments of the present time, simple and frugal as to its viands, but of the brilliancy of the company too much cannot be said." She further noted that Marshall "was devoted to my sister."

After Polly reached the marriageable age of 16 in 1782, Marshall—then 27—decided to propose. According to somewhat overdramatized family tradition, she said no, he rode off in a huff, and she cried inconsolably. Her cousin, a silent witness to the scene, secretly snipped a lock of her hair, caught up with the rejected suitor, and gave it to him. Marshall, believing Polly had sent it, renewed his suit, and they were married soon after. They exchanged vows in an evening ceremony at "The Cottage," her cousin's plantation in nearby Hanover County. The contents and value of Polly's dowry are unknown, but, given the Amblers' financial predicament, it probably was neither extensive nor valuable. As wedding presents, John's father gave him three horses and a slave. John and Polly moved into a tiny rented wood house with one story and two rooms in Richmond, where he had resided since his election to the Council of State in November 1782.[31]

Marshall's political accomplishments so far had been respectable but undistinguished, and it was his achievements as a lawyer that secured his reputation by the late 1780s as one of Virginia's leading public figures. As noteworthy as Marshall's stature is the speed with which he attained it. He did not begin practicing law full time until mid–1784 after resigning from the Council of State. (For the first year of their marriage, he and Polly lived off his income from civil list fees, transactions involving land warrants and military pay certificates, agricultural sales at Oak Hill, and a few small legal fees.) Yet during the next two years, Marshall's practice grew rapidly in both caseload and earnings, and he gained a place of distinction in Virginia's legal fraternity, reputedly among the nation's finest. His quick rise to professional prominence and prosperity resulted from the coincidence of several personal, political, and institutional factors. He successfully applied his impressive intellectual and forensic skills as a courtroom advocate almost always on behalf of economically and politically influential clients, at a time of heavy litigation, expanding opportunities for lawyers, and increasing prestige for the legal profession.[32]

William Wirt, one of the foremost lawyers of the early national period, wrote in 1803 that "[m]en of talents in this country . . . have been generally bred to the profession of law. . . . The bar in America is the road to honour." Marshall and other lawyers in Virginia did not, however, always enjoy that lofty reputation. A distinct class of professional, trained lawyers did not develop there until well into the eighteenth century. For much of the Commonwealth's colonial period, lawyers faced pronounced hostility from merchants and planters, who controlled the county courts, handled their own legal affairs, and wanted to keep outsiders with dubious credentials and questionable ties to the Crown or royal government from gaining social and political influence at their expense. This aversion was manifested in efforts initially to ban lawyers and, when those failed, to intensively regulate their qualifications, licensing, income, and conduct.[33]

The prestige of lawyers in Virginia began rising toward the mid-eighteenth century as economic and social changes increased demand for their services, not the least on the part of merchants and planters. Economic change, population growth, frontier expansion, widespread land speculation and indebtedness, evermore complex commercial relationships, and an increasingly intricate body of common and equity law produced a massive rise in litigation that far surpassed the ability of laymen to handle. In turn, merchants and planters, recognizing the need for a trained bar to interpret English legal materials and apply them in Virginia's courts to new situations, developed a keen interest in legal education and encouraged their sons to pursue law as a career. Practicing law in the county courts also helped introduce young gentry to politically influential members of the squirearchy and enabled lawyers to move into positions of political power, especially in the House of Burgesses. By the time Marshall's father began introducing him to the idea of a legal career, law had become a vocation of advancement, enabling men to satisfy their economic and social ambitions while affording them opportunities to prepare for political leadership. On the eve of the Revolution, lawyers had secured a place at the top of the Virginia gentry.[34]

The Revolution helped Virginia's lawyers dispel some of their mercenary reputation. By encouraging defiance to British rule in various ways—as when 16 eminent attorneys signed the Nonimportation Agreement in 1770—they demonstrated their republican virtue and public spirit. Governor Dunmore's closure of the Commonwealth's courts in 1774 because of a dispute over legal fees further energized perhaps the most politically astute and articulate group in the colony to organize anti-imperial sentiment. "In no country perhaps in the world is the law so general a study," Edmund Burke observed in a speech to Parliament in 1775, and it "renders [Americans] acute, inquisitive, dexterous, prompt in attack, ready in defense, [and] full of resources." Virginia's lawyers also benefited from the widely held contemporary perception that, as Thomas Paine proclaimed in 1776, "In America the law is king"—i.e., that law played a central role in the birth of the republic. Patriot lawyers, tutored in the British constitution and common law, framed their arguments largely in legal and constitutional terms that drew heavily on the vocabulary of the English Whigs and, writes Kermit Hall, were "natural leaders of a highly legal revolution." "Lawyers did not cause the American Revolution, but they did define its intellectual boundaries . . . they were essentially attempting to define the nature of the rule of law as it applied under colonial circumstances." Their influence in shaping the events leading to independence was far out of proportion to their numbers in the population. Historically, members of the legal profession have assumed key positions in the governing elites of new nations, and revolutionary Americans were especially open to a system of authority based on principles of law and contract. "A society under law tended to translate into a social order in which lawyers ruled," R. Kent Newmyer has aptly noted.[35]

The Revolutionary experience of Virginia's lawyers was not entirely favorable, however, and several persistent areas of vulnerability had appeared by the time John Marshall began his legal studies in 1780 and would confront him to varying degrees through most of his legal career. Defendants from all social classes accused lawyers of profiting from the economic hardship of the war by enriching themselves off increased suits involving debt, insolvency, foreclosure, and recovery of property. Lawyers became the convenient targets of an animus to the English common law and legal precedents, which were at times irrationally viewed as relics of tyranny. They also faced criticism from humbler Virginians, used to the participatory rituals of court days, who now contended that lawyers engaged in an "undemocratic" profession that used an abstruse, inaccessible language and seemed mainly to benefit the better-off. Some of this antipathy was shown in new regulations on attorneys' licensing, fees, and conduct.[36]

Marshall found other conditions in the 1780s generally favorable for the novice lawyer, as the war had created several opportunities for advancement. The recently reopened courts had a large backlog of business, much of it consisting of civil suits arising from wartime dislocations, population movements, and the postwar economic downturn. The shortage of money was a boon to lawyers. It caused many controversies over debts, taxes, and contracts, partly because planters delayed payments until good harvests came in or tried to shirk their obligations entirely. Senior members of the bar vacated their practices to assume judicial positions in the postrevolutionary state courts, eliminating a source of competition for ambitious young lawyers such as Marshall. Lastly, Marshall had a waiting clientele. "My extensive acquaintance in the army was of great service to me," he wrote in his autobiography. "My numerous military friends . . . took great interest in my favour, and I was more successful than I had reason to expect." He took over the clients of other lawyers, most notably Edmund Randolph's in 1786, when they entered public office or left the state, and he handled the Ambler family's extensive litigation as well. Marshall's account book shows the overall growth in his practice. In 1784, he was involved in about 100 legal matters from which he earned just under £500; in 1785, around 150 with income of nearly £850; in 1786, about 120 earning him approximately £1,075; and in 1787, over 330 with an income around £1,100. By 1787, what Marshall called his "immense load of professional business" began forcing him to decline appointments to public office.[37]

The low income figures for Marshall's practice in the early 1780s are attributable not only to his small clientele but also to the lack of circulating currency in Richmond then. High inflation rates and Virginia's aggressive payment of its wartime debt had removed large amounts of money from circulation. Consequently, many of Marshall's clients may have paid their fees in kind, especially with tobacco but also with books, home furnishings, and services, and Marshall did not record those transactions in his account book. Marshall supplemented his cash flow with money from purchasers of Kentucky land who gave him their payments for his father's surveys. Marshall temporarily added the funds to his own income to make up shortfalls and then passed on the fees to the appropriate state agency, thereby giving himself a short-term, interest-free loan. This commingling of funds was not considered improper at the time.[38]

Lawyers traditionally have had three functions: as advisors, they counsel clients on how to conduct legal or other business; as agents, they undertake legal transactions; and as advocates, they represent parties in litigation. Marshall occasionally performed the first two functions, but from the start, he built his reputation on the third. He seemed temperamentally unsuited to an office practice—what John Adams disparaged as "fumbling and raking amidst the rubbish of Writs, indightments, Pleas, ejectments, enfiefed, illatebration and a 1000 other lignum Vitae words that have neither harmony nor meaning"—and sometimes his carelessness with detail resulted in the dismissal of his suits.[39]

Marshall excelled, however, in trial work, particularly at the appellate level. Most of his extensive practice comprised civil cases arising from efforts to secure the payment of a debt, recover property, or resolve a disputed commercial transaction, land claim, or will. Over 80 percent of his cases for which documentation exists were suits for the recovery of a debt—not surprising in an agricultural economy based on credit rather than circulating currency—and he almost always represented the creditor plaintiff. Marshall's most frequent clients were merchants, planters, and large farmers. His highest fees came from the first two, who often became embroiled in complicated chancery suits and contested land speculations and commonly used the courts as a collection agency when they had exhausted other means. A much smaller part of Marshall's practice involved defending criminals. His legal work before the superior courts was much more sophisticated and demanding than what he had performed in the county courts. He and the other select group of lawyers appearing at the state bar received more time to argue their cases and were expected to investigate extensively only one or two issues, highlighting the applicable rules of law derived from English common law and equity precedents. This was but one of several features of the Virginia legal system that enabled Marshall to best apply his intellectual assets.[40]

During most of the 1780s, Marshall argued nearly all his cases in Virginia's superior courts. As in the colonial period, most of the state's better lawyers—whether well trained and experienced, or, like Marshall, skilled and ambitious—gravitated from the county courts toward the more remunerative commercial clientele of the capital. The superior courts Marshall practiced in were the General Court, the High Court of Chancery, and the Court of Appeals, which (along with the Court of Admiralty, where Marshall never appeared) were established under the 1776 constitution and a series of enactments during the next three years. The General Court, consisting of five judges who met four times a year, assumed the common law jurisdiction over civil and criminal matters that its pre-Revolutionary namesake had, and it also possessed appellate jurisdiction over the county and corporation courts. The Court of Chancery heard original cases in equity and appeals of chancery suits from the county courts. During this period of Marshall's practice, it had three judges, two of whom were among the Commonwealth's most esteemed legal figures—Edmund Pendleton and George Wythe. The Court of Appeals at this time was not a separate court but was composed of all 11 superior court judges, who met for six days twice a year to review appeals from the decrees, judgments, and sentences of the above-mentioned tribunals when the controversy was valued at £50 or more or involved a freehold or franchise. Marshall was admitted to the bar of the Court of Appeals in April 1785. He was only the sixth lawyer accorded that privilege.[41]

Much of Marshall's success as a lawyer is attributable to how he fashioned his lawyerly style to suit his intellect and personality. He quickly established the pattern of argument he would use in hundreds of cases and decisions as a lawyer and jurist over the next half century. Never fond of courtroom theatrics and rhetorical flourishes, Marshall relied instead on his abilities to learn quickly, reason logically, discern basic principles, and analyze an opponent's argument on the spot. He could easily penetrate the fog of intricacies in civil suits, which made up nearly all of his caseload. He recognized that he was poorly trained, even by the low standards of the time, and so he did not try to contest more learned counsel by prooftexting treatises or piling on precedents. Instead, he apprised himself of his opponents' positions by listening to their presentations. He then offered declarative, concise, unpedantic arguments based on seeming truisms—"By this rule let the question be tried," he asserted typically in a 1786 case—and, after recasting the issues in his own terms, in a syllogistic pattern reached the conclusion appropriate to the case at hand. He used simple, direct words and phrases, frequently stopped to summarize the points he had made, and smoothly shifted to new topics. Depending on the case, he would argue that precedents contradicted the authority of a case on which opposing counsel was relying, or that the case was not applicable to the current controversy, or that precedents were not binding because they did not address all issues now under dispute, or simply that no previous cases applied. Marshall especially preferred to close arguments. Presenting his clear, to-the-point statement of the case as the last word was an effective tactic for persuading judge and jury.[42]

The best contemporary description of Marshall's forensic technique comes from Francis Gilmer, who, on the advice of his father-in-law, the renowned lawyer William Wirt, studied Marshall in court. Gilmer recounted that

So perfect is his analysis, that he extracts the whole matter, the kernel of the inquiry, unbroken, undivided, clean and entire. In this process, such is the instinctive neatness and precision of his mind that no superfluous thought or even word, ever presents itself and still he says everything that seems appropriate to the subject.

This perfect exemption from any unnecessary encumbrance of matter or ornament is in some degree the effect of an aversion for the labour of thinking. So great a mind, perhaps, like large bodies in the physical world, is with difficulty set in motion. That this is the case with Mr. Marshall's is manifest, from his mode of entering on an argument both in conversation and in a publick debate.

It is difficult to rouse his faculties; he begins with reluctance, hesitation, and vacancy of eye; presently his articulation becomes less broken, his eye more fixed, until finally, his voice is full, clear, and rapid, his manner bold, and his whole face lighted up, with the mingled fires of genius and passion; and he pours forth the unbroken stream of eloquence, in a current deep, majestic, smooth, and strong.

He reminds one of some great bird, which flounders and flounces on the earth for a while before it acquires the impetus to sustain its soaring flight.

The characteristic of his eloquence is an irresistible cogency, and a luminous simplicity in the order of his reasoning. His arguments are remarkable for their separate and independent strength, and for the solid, compact, impenetrable order in which they are arrayed.

He certainly possesses in an eminent degree the power . . . of mastering the most complicated subjects with facility, and when moving with his full momentum, even without the appearance of resistance.[43]

This method and style showed not only Marshall's honest appreciation of his abilities and limitations, but also proved to be valuable in the legal culture of eighteenth-century Virginia, which had no tradition of extensive schooling in theory or procedure, and where decisions were often reached after citationless argument.[44] In this common law environment, to quote the English jurist Lord Mansfield, "Precedents serve to illustrate principles and give them a fixed certainty." The law comprises not "particular cases, but . . . general principles, which run through the cases and govern the decision of them." Marshall was, a nineteenth-century commentator wrote,

a *common law lawyer*, in the best and noblest acceptation of the term. He was educated for the bar at a period, when Digests, abridgments and all the numerous facilities, which now smooth the path of the law student were unknown. . . . It was thus no easy task to become an able lawyer, and it required no common share of industry and perseverance to amass sufficient knowledge of the law, to make even a decent appearance in the forum. Mr. Marshall succeeded, in a comparatively short time, to muster the elements of the common law, and to place himself at the head of the profession in Virginia.

Marshall's courtroom audience of yeomen jurors and gentlemen judges—the latter drawn from the ranks of lawyers trained, like himself, by colonial era practices—were more impressed with arguments relying on clearly stated premises and common sense than ones laden with English case references and Latin legal jargon. Not surprisingly, at this early stage in his legal career, Marshall seems not to have begun developing a personal philosophy of law or to have operated under a set of axioms—for example, that law is a body of principles that transcends individual cases—so one cannot yet conclude that his rhetorical technique had deeper origins.

On the contrary, common law practices of the day were intellectually confining. They forced Marshall to think about law narrowly as a series of procedures ("forms of action") used to enforce specific legal demands, rather than as a system of abstract rules and precepts. Common law pleadings, for example, were largely routine operations, samples of which Marshall could have found in numerous books of precedents. This element of his practice, which took a sizable proportion of his time and effort, tested his ingenuity only when he had to choose the most advantageous form of action when more than one was applicable to a case. Special pleading, which provided a much better gauge of a lawyer's abilities, was not extensively practiced in Virginia's courts. Although Marshall learned much substantive law during these first years at the bar, he had to apply that knowledge within the procedural boundaries in which it had developed. He could not yet systematically study broad legal topics, such as torts or contracts—treatises on them were not yet available—although he did at least buy works on evidence and equity when they became accessible.

In their effort to humanize Marshall, historians probably have made too much of his rusticity in describing his legal style. Nearly every biographer, for example, has mentioned the story of the wealthy merchant who spurns recommendations that he retain Marshall because he cannot believe such a supposedly fine lawyer would dress so slovenly. The merchant uses all but five dollars of his money to hire a distinguished-looking attorney donning a powdered wig and black coat. This well-appointed lawyer then argues against the scruffily clad Marshall in another suit and loses, after which the merchant contritely asks if Marshall will take his case for the remaining five dollars. Marshall agrees, joking about the power of a wig and coat. A. G. Roeber rightly cautions that such anecdotes appearing after 1800 deserve to be treated skeptically. Lawyers in the early nineteenth century, acting out of self-interest, sought to portray their profession as compatible with republican society.[45]

Marshall learned equally important lessons about the role of law and the judiciary in a republican system from the other side of the bar—the judges who heard the cases he participated in, especially Edmund Pendleton, presiding judge of the Court of Appeals, and George Wythe, chancellor of the High Court of Chancery. "These eminent jurists," writes Charles Hobson, "personified qualities of judicial dignity and integrity that Marshall sought to emulate." Pendleton displayed "a style of leadership in which the court most often spoke through the presiding judge and a practical approach to the art of judging that emphasized substance over technicalities," whereas Wythe "epitomized the independent-minded jurist." From both, Marshall gained an appreciation for the broad discretion judges had in determining what case law was relevant, to follow or reject precedents depending on whether they conformed to basic legal principles. Through the proper exercise of this discretion, judges could make new situations fit the law, as Virginia's common law culture required. Distinguishing between the legislative will and just law grew even more difficult in the post-Revolutionary years, when judges had to construe all the new statutes of the Commonwealth as well as English and colonial precedents. Doing so demanded intellectual creativity of a practical sort, which Marshall possessed in abundance. It is no wonder that he admired the most creative of pre-Revolutionary English judges, Lord Mansfield, whom he later called "one of the greatest Judges who ever sat on any bench, & who has done more than any other to remove those technical impediments which grew out of a different state of society, & too long continued to obstruct the course of substantial justice." Marshall came away from the first years of his legal practice believing that the judge's duty was to discover and apply legal principles to real-life controversies without assuming the role of lawgiver.[46]

The Fairfax lands, with which Marshall would have a lifelong connection as attorney, speculator, and jurist, figured prominently in his early practice. A large body of litigation arose from a disputed claim of title to a portion of

Thomas, Lord Fairfax's huge landholdings in the Northern Neck. The original suit, filed in 1749, was decided against him in 1771. Both sides appealed, but the Revolution disrupted the proceedings. Lord Fairfax died in 1781, and his executors were substituted as defendants the following year. In 1786, the Virginia Court of Appeals heard arguments in *Hite v. Fairfax*, Marshall's most important early case and his first appearance before that tribunal. He knew the Fairfax holdings well, having grown up on, and helped his father survey, lands derived from the Fairfax title. These personal ties notwithstanding, Marshall's involvement in such a prominent suit at age 30 with barely two years of full-time practice shows the high professional stature he had achieved. He was the lead attorney for Fairfax's executors, and two of the state's most notable lawyers, Attorney General Edmund Randolph and John Taylor of Caroline, argued for the plaintiff. Contrary to contemporary and subsequent misimpressions, the *Hite* case did not directly concern the legitimacy of the Fairfax title to the Northern Neck proprietary. Nonetheless, this phase of the litigation took on a legally unwarranted political importance because it coincided with the Virginia legislature's attempts to sequester alien lands on the common law principle that aliens could not hold lands in the state.[47]

At the appellate hearing, which required six days of oral arguments, Marshall avoided the pathos of the controversy that Hite's counsel stressed—"poor deluded frontier settlers . . . versus a powerful, uncompromising feudal landlord," as one historian has termed it. Instead, Marshall—arguing last, as he preferred—contended, in his usual direct, logical way, that the wisdom of granting Fairfax's title was not open to judicial scrutiny, and that the title itself was valid: "[I]f he have not title, he could not convey one." Underlying Marshall's presentation was his first expression of the sanctity of contracts, a view that ran against the tendency of some state legislatures in the 1780s to annul contracts in pursuit of vaguely egalitarian goals—a feature of what was known as "democratic despotism." His arguments must have had some effect on the judges. In what appears to have been a compromise ruling, the court decided for Hite in the case at hand but upheld the validity of the rest of Fairfax's title. The decision did not settle the matter, however, for it allowed other parties who obtained land from Hite to pursue claims against Fairfax in the Court of Chancery under the terms of the 1771 ruling. Marshall represented many of the claimants in these derivative suits. He would remain personally and professionally involved with the Fairfax lands for many years after, and he was directly affected by a milestone Supreme Court ruling—*Martin v. Hunter's Lessee* (1816)—dealing with the Fairfax lands and decided while he served as chief justice.[48]

Revolutionary War veterans provided Marshall with another sizeable part of his legal business. He represented them in disputes over land warrants, back pay, and pensions they had received from Virginia and the Confederation Congress. Establishing clear title to the land grants was a complicated legal procedure, and primitive surveying techniques and Virginia's practice of granting more land than was available assured an abundance of disputes.

Marshall's father, a public surveyor and land speculator in Kentucky by the mid-1780s, referred many aggrieved veterans to his son. "They knew," Marshall wrote later, "that I felt their wrongs, and sympathized in their suffering, and had partaken of their labors, and that I vindicated their claims upon their country with a warm and constant earnestness." Self-interest combined with Marshall's benevolence. He had his own, and some of his relatives', substantial wartime land grants to protect as well, and any legal victory on behalf of a veteran client would bolster the Marshall clan's claims.[49]

On 1 April 1784, Marshall resigned from the Council of State after the General Court, apparently concerned with the intermingling of executive and judicial functions, ruled that members of the Council could not also be practicing lawyers who argued cases in the state courts. Marshall could not afford to give up his legal practice, yet he did not want to lose his official entree into Virginia's governing elite, so "[I] made a small excursion into Fauquier [County] to enquire into the probability of my being chosen by the people, should I offer as a candidate [for delegate] at the next election." His interest in remaining in state politics surpassed his distaste for certain characteristics of the legislature. For example, he found it "surprising that Gentlemen of character cannot dismiss their private animosities, but will bring them in the Assembly," and he complained that, aside from one tax measure, "this long session [1783] has not produced a single bill of Public importance." Even though he lived in Henrico County, under state law Marshall could run for office anywhere he owned land. Marshall calculated that the odds were in his favor—despite the absence of his father, who had moved to Kentucky the previous year—and on 26 April, the freeholders of Fauquier sent him to the House for a second time.[50]

Virginia's politics at mid-decade had changed dramatically from what Marshall had experienced during his first term. The personalized politics of harmony and cohesion of the early 1780s, with its piecemeal approach to matters of policy, had ended, a casualty of the worsening postwar depression that intensified social and economic divisions and caused bitter political disputes. Increasingly, organized factions in the legislature contended over interrelated issues—such as tax and debtor relief, payment of British debts, court reform, and church establishment—in debates that often contained a marked ideological content. Marshall's second term in the House coincided with this transformation, and by the time the session ended in January 1785, he had clearly sided with the creditor-nationalist faction led by James Madison, who had returned to state politics after serving in the Confederation Congress for several years. Marshall's legislative experience at this time also provided him with a disillusioning education in the perils of popular politics. He left the House even more skeptical of the virtues of republicanism and increasingly pessimistic about the ability of the state and Confederation governments to deal with the problems besetting the country.[51]

"Mr. Henry arrived yesterday," Marshall wrote Monroe in May 1784 as the legislative session opened, "& appears as usual to be chargd [sic] high with postponement of the collection of the taxes. If you wish to see a part of the first speech he will make on this subject versified[,] turn to Churchill's prophecy of famine & read his description of the highlands of Scotland." Marshall's uncharacteristically cynical comment about the assembly's champion of debtors and small farmers shows how, at least in his own mind, the tenor of political discourse was changing, as well as where his own sympathies were beginning to lie. He was well aware of Madison's efforts in the Confederation Congress to expand its powers and implement a nationalist program, especially in granting the Congress greater taxation authority, and of Madison's intention of making Virginia a "bold Example" that "would have Influence on the other States." Marshall endorsed this goal and worked to implement it in several areas of policy, notably British debts and court reorganization. At the same time, his positions on those and other issues occasionally reflected his personal or professional allegiances to institutions or economic and social groups.[52]

Of all the subjects the House debated this session, the repayment of prewar debts owed to British merchants caused the deepest divisions in Virginia politics and had the greatest implications for the United States.[53] The issue involved the sanctity of private contracts, national treaty obligations, and large amounts of money—at least £2 million—owed by some of the most prominent political figures in the state. From their perspective, the situation was bad enough for Jefferson to assert that "the planters were a species of property annexed to certain mercantile houses in London." Under the terms of the 1783 peace treaty, states could not legally impair the collection of debts, but the Virginia legislature that year barred the payment of British debts until Britain offered compensation for slaves that its armies had seized during the war. An additional justification for the state's policy had arisen by early 1784: Britain was violating the treaty by keeping garrisons in the northwest on territory Virginia had not formally ceded to the national government. Opponents of British debt payment also cited general economic hardship in the state and the lack of hard currency need to pay the debts.

The Commonwealth's position troubled Marshall, who voted for an unsuccessful attempt to repeal the ban on debt payment. He objected to any hindrance to debt collection on contractual grounds, preferring, like Richard Henry Lee, that Americans remain "the honest slaves of Great Britain, than . . . become dishonest freemen." Marshall also believed that the ban gave Britain a pretext for retaining its forts in the northwest—which might someday adversely affect his western landholdings—and undercut the power and prestige of the national government. "I ever considered [the repayment law] as a measure tending to weaken the federal bands which in my conception are too weak already," he wrote Monroe. No record exists, however, of his vote on Madison's compromise plan for installment payments that the legislature favorably considered but never formally enacted in the fall 1784 session.

Marshall helped draft two other laws that would strengthen the national government. He worked on a bill to change the method of apportioning the debts the states owed the Confederation, from land values to population. The former method had never worked well, and Congress had unsuccessfully proposed an amendment to the Articles of Confederation, making the latter the rule. The legislature, with Patrick Henry and George Mason representing the popular opinion against paying the debts, voted down the proposal. Marshall also helped develop a bill authorizing Congress to pass retaliatory trade laws, in response to its request that the states grant it greater authority to regulate trade. This measure passed, in keeping with Virginia's pattern of supporting such grants.[54]

Marshall supported, at least in principle, one of Madison's pet projects: the restriction of Virginia's foreign trade to two ports, Alexandria and Norfolk. The idea behind this mercantilist scheme, which Madison launched from his position as chairman of the Committee on Commerce, was to centralize the state's trade and develop a powerful class of merchants and financiers who could compete with rivals in Baltimore and Philadelphia and keep out the Scottish factors on whom Virginia planters had grown so dependent during the colonial years. The Port Bill also was part of the state government's effort to develop a coherent commercial plan in the absence of British regulation, and would have improved the collection of duties, helped control smuggling, and given preference to American-built and -owned shipping. The measure ran into strong opposition, however, from economic interests in the locales that were not favored, and from merchants and others "devoted from either interest or prejudice to the British trade," Madison contended. To build support, three other towns were quickly logrolled into the measure. Marshall subscribed to the general intention of the bill and believed its initial version would "produce many happy effects," even though Richmond was not included. He voted against the final measure, however, in part reflecting the view of the merchants and planters in the Richmond area with whom he had close political ties and whom he represented in his legal practice. He also probably took note of the critical petitions from Fauquier County, whose residents complained that they would have to pay more to transport their goods to the five designated ports.[55]

As a lawyer, Marshall gave special attention to the hotly debated issue of court reorganization, which also had important political and economic ramifications. The surge in litigation in the early 1780s had generated strong pressure from creditors to expedite lengthy and costly suits and create new courts more supportive of their interests. Borrowing from an older effort at legal reform led by Jefferson, Pendleton, and Wythe, Madison proposed setting up new assize (or circuit) courts run from Richmond. Marshall, already serving on the Standing Committee on Courts of Justice, was appointed to a committee that prepared a circuit court bill that Madison sponsored. Though enacted in December 1784, the new system was never put into effect, largely owing to opposition from justices of the peace and county court lawyers. Marshall had presciently suggested six months earlier that this might happen:

Those Magistrates who are tenacious in authority will not assent to any thing which may diminish their ideal dignity & put into the hands of others a power which they will not exercise themselves. Such of the County Court lawyers too as are suspicious that they do not possess abilities or knowledge sufficient to enable them to stand before judges of law are opposd [*sic*] from motives of interest to any plan which may put the distribution of justice into the hands of judges.

Marshall was also concerned about the legal and economic impact this opposition would have on creditors. He criticized those delegates "who really appear to be determind [*sic*] against every Measure which may expedite and facilitate the business of recovering debts & compelling a strict compliance with contracts. These are sufficient to throw impediments in the way of any improvements in our judiciary system tho they are not so powerful as to shut up our courts altogether." Marshall would revisit this issue during the next few years when, as a private citizen, he tried to encourage court reform but encountered the same localist "opposition from selfish individuals."[56]

Another controversial matter Marshall and the delegates debated this term was Patrick Henry's proposal for a general tax assessment in support of the Christian religion. Marshall, along with most other Episcopalians and some Presbyterians, approved of the measure, and he also voted for a companion bill to incorporate the Episcopal Church. He may have been motivated by a concern with combating the decline in public virtue or, less likely, from a thoughtful sense of promoting civil religion. Probably, though, he wanted to help preserve the religious institution in which he had grown up and which had played such a vital public role in Virginia's colonial period. The assessment and incorporation bills would help accomplish this by creating a source of public funding for the church, establishing its legal independence, and confirming title to its glebe lands. Although Marshall's vote on a resolution favoring a general assessment was not recorded, he opposed a parliamentary move by Madison to delay a vote for a year so that antiassessment forces—mostly rural Baptists and other dissenting denominations—could organize, and he was "apprehensive" that Henry's "favorite measure must miscarry." It did so the following year, but Marshall was not in the House then to try to prevent that from occurring.[57]

Also during the session, Marshall attempted, in a small yet symbolic way, to affirm his revolutionary sentiments by supporting a relief bill for Thomas Paine. The author of *Common Sense* had contributed the profits from that and other writings to the war effort, had no regular income, was living largely off friends' charity, and spent much of his time trying to win remuneration from Congress and the states for his services on behalf of the Revolution. Acting on the suggestion of Washington—who queried Madison, "Must the merits of *Common Sense* continue to glide down the stream of time unrewarded by this country?"—Marshall and a House committee brought in a bill to grant Paine a modest parcel of public land. The other delegates rejected the proposal, however, possibly because Paine argued against Virginia's western land claims in his 1780 pamphlet *Public Good*.[58]

By the end of the 1784 term, Marshall had grown frustrated at the legislature's failure to address meaningfully such pressing problems as the money shortage, war debt, taxation, British creditors, and court reorganization.

"Not a bill of public importance, in which an individual was not particularly interested[,] has passed," he complained, with some exaggeration, to Monroe, and decided not to seek reelection. During his first two terms in the House, Marshall had not independently articulated a political program nor built a reputation as a coalition leader, influential orator, perceptive vote counter, or clever parliamentarian. He nonetheless, largely through strength of character, confirmed his place as a rising figure in Virginia's public life. His colleagues respected his intelligence and industry, and his amiable nature helped him work effectively behind the scenes, as in committees where delegates fashioned compromises on the language of draft bills. He appears to have gone out of his way to avoid confrontations with legislative opponents. When Marshall left the House in January 1785, he was recognized as a loyal yet conciliatory supporter of Madison's nationalist agenda, with a consistent yet not strongly ideological approach to economic and political issues, principled yet far more amenable to appeals to reason than to passion.[59]

Although Marshall remained out of the legislature until 1787, he gained further political and governmental experience through several other public activities at the state and local levels. He was a founding member of the Virginia Constitutional Society, a small group of politically involved men from Richmond and Williamsburg "associated for the purpose of preserving and handing down to posterity those pure and sacred principles of liberty which have been derived to us from the happy event of the late glorious revolution," and whose main activity appears to have been discussing issues scheduled to come before the Assembly. Marshall ran for attorney general in 1786 when the incumbent, Edmund Randolph, became governor after Patrick Henry stepped down. This was the first and only time Marshall sought an elective position outside the legislature, and the only time he lost a political contest. On this occasion, he overestimated his standing within the House and Senate—which selected the attorney general by joint ballot—and lost to James Innes, a friend from the Continental Army and a prominent lawyer and popular public figure, although Madison wrote that Marshall still got a "handsome" vote. Marshall also served the Commonwealth in some quasi-public capacities around this time. In October 1786, the General Assembly chose him as one of six commissioners charged with arbitrating claims for tobacco destroyed in a warehouse fire in Richmond. He and the commissioners were authorized to hold hearings and swear in witnesses to determine how much tobacco was lost. Two months later, Marshall was again chosen to arbitrate a claim by a Philadelphia merchant that Virginia owed him payment in specie for military supplies he had provided during the war; the state wanted to pay him in nearly worthless paper currency. Some observers might have expected that Marshall, the son-in-law of Virginia's treasurer, might side with the state, but he and the other arbitrator decided in the merchant's favor on the simple grounds that once two parties make a contract, one of them cannot arbitrarily change its terms.[60]

Marshall also kept busy in the municipal affairs of Richmond during the mid-1780s. In July 1785, he was elected to the city's governing body, the

Common Hall, receiving the second highest number of votes among 75 candidates for 16 positions. In recognition of his professional reputation, as well as of the votes he had received, the aldermen of Richmond selected Marshall to be city recorder, responsible for prosecuting actions for the city, signing legal and administrative orders, and maintaining municipal records. He regularly attended the monthly sessions of the Common Hall, which addressed the problems of the state capital undergoing rapid economic and population growth.[61]

Another of Marshall's duties as recorder involved meeting with the mayor and aldermen together as the Richmond City Hustings Court. This panel had original jurisdiction over criminal and civil cases arising within the capital. It served the same function for Richmond as the county courts did in the countryside, and its members had the same powers as justices of the peace. Among the court's activities in which Marshall participated—both as a lone magistrate and as a member of the full body—were criminal arraignments, misdemeanor and felony prosecutions (including slaves), civil suits (mostly debt and tax collections and minor torts), probate proceedings, and hearings for assorted legal matters such as powers of attorney, indebtedness, and business partnerships. The court also performed other municipal duties such as appointing and supervising city officials, setting prices for public accommodations, and granting business licenses. Marshall presided over several sessions of the full court when the mayor was absent. After holding these various offices for nearly three years, Marshall resigned from the Common Hall in March 1788, presumably because of the demands of his legal practice and his political activities on behalf of the proposed federal Constitution.[62]

Marshall kept his private life filled during these years as well, as befitted a gregarious member of the local elite. As his account book indicates, he eagerly took part in Richmond's social activities, attending seasonal dances (then called "assemblies") and horse races and joining a club at Formicola's tavern. He also was a member of the Sons of St. Tammany, which performed charitable works and in 1784 provided "a sumptuous entertainment" for state officials, and he was an active Mason. He joined the Order while in the Continental Army and in 1786 became deputy grand master of a lodge in Richmond. Besides participating in the Masons' annual Festival of St. John the Evangelist and other fraternal functions, as city recorder he helped organize a lottery to pay for construction of the first lodge hall in the city (and reputedly the first solely Masonic building in the United States). In addition, Marshall spent part of his leisure time gambling at whist and backgammon, started a lifelong habit of frequenting the theater, attended the Episcopal Church, supported the Richmond Subscription Library, was a member of the fire company, and contributed to a relief fund for victims of a fire in 1787 that destroyed much of the core of the city.[63]

Marshall's family life during the 1780s was a mixture of joy, sorrow, and devotion. His and Polly's first child, Thomas, was born in July 1784. Their second, Rebecca, followed in June 1786 but lived only five days. Several months later, Polly, only 20 years old, suffered a miscarriage. The successive tragedies caused her to have a mental breakdown—"Mrs. Marshall . . . is Insane," Jefferson's daughter wrote; "the loss of two Children is thought to have Occationed [sic] it"—and apparently brought on the chronic nervous exhaustion, compounded by congenital anemia and possibly a gynecological disorder, that would enfeeble her for the rest of her life. Marshall, judging by entries in his account book, hired a local woman to help care for his wife and took over the management of his household, assuming duties, such as going to the market and purchasing items for the home, that Polly would have performed had she been well. Around this time, he also began his efforts—often commented upon by friends, descendants, and biographers—to keep noises from disturbing Polly by, among other things, shushing dogs and horses in the middle of the night and asking Richmond officials not to peal bells. Polly's weakened condition meant she had to endure long recoveries after childbirth, such as followed the arrival of another son, named Jaquelin after her father, in December 1787. Her frequent pregnancies—she eventually bore 10 children, the last in 1805 when she was nearly 40—very likely kept her from ever regaining full health. Her mind remained sharp and her personality pleasant for the most part despite her semi-invalid state. Marshall wrote years later that

Her judgment was so sound and so safe that I have often relied upon it in situations of some perplexity. . . . Though serious as well as gentle in her deportment, she possessed a good deal of chaste, delicate, and playful wit, and if she permitted herself to indulge this talent, told her little story with grace, and could mimic very successfully the peculiarities of the person who was its subject. She had a fine taste for belle-lettre reading. . . . This quality, by improving her talents for conversation, contributed not inconsiderably to make her a most desirable and agreeable companion.[64]

Marshall remained close to his brothers and sisters as well. Three of his sisters decided not to accompany their father to Kentucky and lived with him and Polly at various times in Richmond, first at their small rented house on Shockoe Hill and then in another house he apparently bought in 1785. Entries in Marshall's account book show that he gave his siblings money—especially his younger brother James—bought them clothes, and even paid for dancing lessons. Besides his family, according to 1785 tax lists, Marshall had to provide for two slaves, two horses, and 12 head of cattle—an indication of how far he had come financially from the single guinea that family tradition says he had on his wedding day.[65]

Along with his experience in the Revolutionary War and his association with Madison's political agenda, Marshall's involvement in western affairs significantly shaped his emerging nationalist perspective. His extensive speculation in frontier land and his attention to politics in Kentucky, where most of his and his family's landholdings outside Virginia were located, expanded his political vision beyond his home state and encouraged him to think about how the abstract foreign policy goals of European powers directly affected the welfare of the new nation. As part of this more cosmopolitan perspective, Marshall advocated a greater role for the state government in binding east and west commercially and politically, and, as the decade passed, he became more concerned that the national government was not strong enough to protect its frontiers from hostile foreign designs.[66]

Throughout the early and mid-1780s, Marshall aggressively speculated in western land, especially in Kentucky, where several Marshalls—including his father, his brother James, and his cousin Humphrey—developed extensive economic and political interests. Marshall's motives for this speculation, of course, were mainly financial: to acquire assets that would grow in value at a time when hard money was in short supply and paper currency was grossly depreciated. For the Virginia gentry, there was hardly any other way to get rich. Also, until about 1785, he considered following his father to Kentucky—"a country to which my nearest connexions will certainly move & which in all probability will be ultimately my place of residence"—and so needed land for a homestead. To keep resources available for that purpose, Marshall did not buy property in Richmond until 1785. After mid-decade, however, he was professionally and politically tied to Richmond and apparently thought no more about going west. He wrote that "[m]y present plan is to pass my summers at Oak Hill and my winters here in Richmond." In March 1785 he bought a half-acre lot in the center of the capital.[67]

Virginia, acting upon the terms of its 1609 charter, first asserted a direct claim over the Kentucky region in 1777 when it established Kentucky County. Two years later, the state passed a law providing for three types of claims to land in the region (by settlement, purchase, or military bounty), opened a land office in Richmond to handle sales, and set aside a large district in Kentucky for veteran grantees. Enlisted men were allotted 200 acres, officers substantially more. After validating all claims for which surveys had been completed, Virginia offered the remaining lands for sale at £40 per 100 acres with no limit on how much an individual could buy.[68]

Marshall's first interest in Kentucky land derived from his wartime service allotment of 4,000 acres, which he divided equally between Virginia and Kentucky. He also acquired many warrants (paper titles to land) from the state land office or by assignment from original purchasers. Living in Richmond gave him easy access to both sources.[69] In addition, Marshall formed a partnership with his father, who first went to Kentucky in 1780 under special permit from Virginia's governor to locate land warrants, was appointed surveyor of Fayette County in 1781, and moved there permanently in 1782. Under their arrangement, not unusual for the time, John obtained the warrants, sometimes with the advice of Thomas, who knew the best parcels; Thomas conducted a survey; and John filed papers with the land office. Father and son also were well positioned to serve as agents for other claimants—among them George Washington and James Monroe—by acquiring warrants and filing caveats (disputes of other claims to the same land) on their behalf, and to speculate in depreciated warrants. "I have been maneuvering amazingly to turn your warrants into cash," John advised Monroe in April 1784. "If I succeed I shall think myself a first rate speculator." Virginians' craving for Kentucky land peaked around then, by which time Kentucky's population had risen from an insignificant level before the Revolution to nearly 20,000, and large speculators had acquired most of the remaining tracts. During the 1780s and 1790s, Marshall or his assignees—principally his father and brothers—received grants to over 150,000 acres.[70]

Marshall was not in the House of Delegates in 1781 and 1783 when it considered the cession of Virginia's western lands to the Confederation—the major territorial issue affecting the state during the 1780s—nor did he comment on the matter later. His views on Western affairs can be ascertained, though, by looking at his voting record on frontier-related legislation, his support for building economic and transportation links between eastern and western regions, and his endorsement of Kentucky statehood. Marshall voted for three frontier-related laws that the House of Delegates considered in the 1784 session. He probably believed they would remove sources of instability and tension in the west and help protect his and his family's landholdings there. He supported a highly controversial extradition bill requiring that Virginia deliver up for trial to a requesting foreign power any fugitive from that country who had fled to Virginia. Madison, the law's sponsor, intended it to discourage filibustering in Spanish and Indian territory and to eliminate a dangerous flash point in the Commonwealth's relations with foreign nations and native tribes. The House passed the law in November. In addition, Marshall considered "advantageous to this country" an unsuccessful proposal of Henry's to provide financial incentives for white men to marry Indian women. Marshall and the measure's other supporters hoped it would improve relations with the Indians and help pacify the frontier, but he lamented to Monroe that "Our prejudices . . . oppose themselves to our interests & operate too powerfully for them." Lastly, Marshall voted for a bill allowing Virginia's cash-poor western counties to pay back taxes in hemp instead of specie. Normally he would not have approved of such so-called "commutable" measures, largely because the state lost money when the goods were auctioned, but in this case he apparently calculated that reducing frontier animosity was preferable to adhering to a fiscally orthodox view.[71]

Marshall's speculation in Kentucky land was always informed by a keen attention to political developments in the region—"I interest myself much in the happiness of the western country," he wrote—and he was intrigued at the prospect of Kentucky serving as an experiment in post-Revolution constitution making. He believed that "no people on earth possess a fairer prospect of political happiness than do the inhabitants of Kentucky." Perhaps largely because most came from Virginia, he thought Kentuckians could write a constitution "formed with more experience & less prejudice" than the original 13 states, which were led by "persons whose political ideas grew entirely under a Monarchy" and who "introduced principles unnecessary & perhaps improper, in a Republic by guarding against the influence of the crown where no crown exists."[72]

Marshall had a strong interest in creating commercial connections between Virginia's eastward-flowing rivers and the Mississippi and Ohio River's westward-coursing tributaries. He believed such links had several benefits. They would enhance the value of Virginians' western landholdings, enrich Tidewater merchants and planters, develop the state's ports, foster political unity between the older states and the frontier, reduce the West's reliance on the Mississippi and Ohio for transport, and curtail the threat foreign powers posed to America's commerce. Spain had closed the Mississippi to American commerce in 1784, and Marshall thought surrendering American navigation rights on the river was "dishonourable and injurious" and "[could not] conjecture how this opinion is to be supported." The notion of linking the Virginia and Mississippi river systems was conceived in the mid-eighteenth century but received a great boost from George Washington and Thomas Jefferson in the 1770s and 1780s. As a result of their initiative—best conceptualized in Washington's lengthy letter to Governor Benjamin Harrison in 1784—the state legislature in the fall 1784 term approved several resolutions providing for funding, surveys, ancillary internal improvements, and incorporation of the Potomac Company and the James River Company to improve navigation on those rivers with the goal of connecting them to the Mississippi and Ohio tributaries.[73]

Marshall considered these laws as being "of the utmost consequence" to Virginia and Kentucky and bought stock in both the Potomac and James River Companies. He was especially engaged with the latter, which intended to connect the James with the Great Kanawah River in what is now West Virginia and then with the Ohio. Richmond merchants aggressively peddled subscriptions to this plan, and soon residents of the capital had bought nearly all the shares needed to pay for cutting canals and building locks and other works. Marshall also voted to grant a 10-year monopoly to inventor James Rumsey to develop his novel design for a steamboat. Rumsey's odd contraption consisted of two boats joined between by a paddle wheel that moved poles hung over the sides of the boats. When the wheel turned, the poles walked along the stream bed and pushed the boat against the current. Marshall thought Rumsey's invention would provide a crucial technological link in the scheme to connect east and west and eliminate the foreign threat to American trade. The monopoly grant to Rumsey, he wrote, was "of as much perhaps more consequence than any other bill we have passed" that term, and, once the steamboat began plying the watercourses made navigable by the river company's improvements, "communication between us will be easy, and we shall have but little occasion to contest the navigation of the Mississippi." Rumsey's design failed, but the James River Company's limited improvements around Richmond aided transportation and raised land values in the Piedmont. Marshall remained privately and officially involved in the company's activities and the issue of western waterways for many years—perhaps most prominently when he led a state-commissioned survey of several rivers in southwestern Virginia in 1812.[74]

Developments in Kentucky politics forced Marshall to temper his optimism that constitutionally the West would mature faster than the older regions or that economically it could be connected to the East. Separatist enthusiasm in Kentucky, initially concentrated among small farmers who had not secured their land claims, waxed and waned throughout the early 1780s but rose again toward mid-decade when prominent speculators and merchants and nearly every key figure in Virginia politics embraced the idea of Kentucky's separating from the Old Dominion. These latter-day advocates of statehood complained about Richmond's inability to administer properly or protect a distant region where they held valuable property, and about land and revenue laws they perceived as unjust, such as the 1784 tax on land grants over 1,400 acres. Spain's closure of the Mississippi to Virginia trade in 1784, and the prospect that treaty negotiations with Madrid might produce a 25-year extension of that ban, won other supporters for separation, who viewed it as a step toward independence and special commercial arrangements with Spain. Statehood champions differed, however, over how to disengage from Virginia. One of two main factions called for immediate independence and sought to wrest power from the other faction, which wanted to effect a legal separation under which Virginians' land titles were guaranteed. This latter group included Thomas Marshall in its ranks.[75]

John Marshall agreed with their position. "It is impossible," he wrote to a former legal colleague who had moved to Kentucky, "that we can, at this distance, legislate wisely for you, and it is proper that you should legislate for yourselves." Putting aside previous musings about Kentucky serving as a laboratory of republicanism, he now merely hoped that "the business [could] be done with wisdom and temperance." He did not comment on the concurrent deliberations by the House of Delegates and several statehood conventions in Kentucky during 1785–87, which finally arrived at a consensus—mainly incorporating Richmond's terms—that a new state of Kentucky must join the Confederation, validate all Virginia land grants, and tax nonresident landowners at the same rates as residents. The movement to overhaul the Articles of Confederation and the debate over ratification of the proposed constitution overtook events in Kentucky, however; the statehood issue became the concern of the new national government and remained unresolved until 1792.[76]

In the meantime, Marshall grew increasingly troubled that more frequent intrigues and military actions on the frontier by Spain, Britain, and American soldiers and freebooters would cause a flare-up of hostilities that the national government was too weak to control. "I very much fear that the conduct of some unthinking men in the western country will embroil us with Spain unless there be some more vigorous interposition of government than we seem disposed to make," he wrote to a Confederation official in March 1787. Marshall believed that on the whole matter of protecting America's commercial interests in the west against foreign threats, there had been much talk but little action—"as we have been *fortiter in modo*, I dare say we shall be *suaviter in re*"—and he gave no indication that he thought the situation would improve short of a substantial overhaul of the Confederation system.[77]

Marshall's involvement with frontier issues and Kentucky lands provided an immediate context in which he could place the growing discontent with the national government apparent in Virginia and throughout the country. His western dealings also reinforced his allegiance to Madison's nationalist program and helped frame his perspective on the coming debate over the proposed constitution. Having gained extensive experience in public office during the past several years, and enjoying a sterling reputation as a lawyer and lawmaker, Marshall was well positioned to emerge on the national political scene by serving as an effective advocate for ratification of the new charter of government.

NOTES

1. Henry Adams, *History of the United States of America*, 9 vols. (New York: Charles Scribner's Sons, 1889–91), 1:134.

2. JM to Joseph Delaplaine, 22 March 1818, in John F. Dillon, comp. and ed., *John Marshall: Life, Character and Judicial Services,* 3 vols. (Chicago: Callaghan and Co., 1903), 1:55. (Hereafter cited as Dillon, *Marshall*.)

3. A. G. Roeber, *Faithful Magistrates and Republican Lawyers: Creators of Virginia Legal Culture, 1680–1810* (Chapel Hill: University of North Carolina Press, 1981), 73–75, 93–95; Frances Norton Mason, *My Dearest Polly: Letters of Chief Justice John Marshall to His Wife* . . . (Richmond: Garrett and Massie, 1961), 7; Herbert Alan Johnson, "John Marshall," in *The Justices of the Supreme Court, 1789–1969: Their Lives and Opinions*, ed. Leon Friedman and Fred L. Israel, 4 vols. (New York: R. R. Bowker Co., 1969), 1:288–89; "Subscribers in Virginia to Blackstone's *Commentaries*," *WMQ*, 2nd ser., 1 (1921), 183.

4. Brent Tarter, ed., "Orderly Book of the Second Virginia Regiment," entry for 7 December 1775, in *VMHB*, 85 (1977), 302; [U.S. Army, Judge Advocate General's Corps,] *The Army Lawyer: A History of the Judge Advocate General's Corps, 1775–1975* (Washington, D.C.: Government Printing Office, [1975]), 7–13, 18–19, 23; William Fratcher, "History of the Judge Advocate General's Corps, United States Army," *Military Law Review*, 4 (1959), 89–90, 116–17; *PJM*, 1:15 n. 2; Robert Berlin, "The Administration of Military Justice in the Continental Army during the American Revolution, 1775–1783" (Ph.D. diss., University of California at Santa Barbara, 1976), 82–83, 102, 121–29, 184–87; Maurer Maurer, "Military Justice under General Washington," *Military Affairs*, 28 (1964), 9–10, 13–14.

5. *Army Lawyer*, 24; Maurer, "Military Justice under Washington," 9; Berlin, "Administration of Military Justice in the Continental Army," 89–90, 302.

6. John Stokes Adams, ed., *An Autobiographical Sketch by John Marshall* (Ann Arbor: University of Michigan Press, 1937), 6 (hereafter cited as JM, *Autobiographical Sketch*); *PJM*, 1:37, 41; Alfred Z. Reed, *Training for the Public Profession of the Law* . . . (New York: Carnegie Foundation, 1921), 82–83; Alan M. Smith, "Virginia Lawyers, 1680–1776: The Birth of an American Profession" (Ph.D. diss., Johns Hopkins University,

1967), chap. 5 passim; Anton-Hermann Chroust, *The Rise of the Legal Profession in America*, 2 vols. (Norman: University of Oklahoma Press, 1965), 1:30–37; Charles Warren, *A History of the American Bar* (Boston: Little, Brown, 1911), 164–77; E. Lee Shepard, "Lawyers Look at Themselves: Professional Consciousness and the Virginia Bar, 1770–1850," *AJLH*, 25 (1981), 9; W. Hamilton Bryson, "The History of Legal Education in Virginia," *University of Richmond Law Review*, 14 (1979–80), 155–63; Jay Alexander, "Legal Careers in Eighteenth Century America," *Duquesne Law Review*, 23 (1984–85), 632–39. Only about 100 American lawyers-to-be, nearly all from affluent families, studied at the Inns of Court between 1750 and 1776. Beverly Zweiben, *How Blackstone Lost the Colonies: English Law, Colonial Lawyers, and the American Revolution* (New York: Garland Publishing, 1990), 26–27.

7. Smith, "Virginia Lawyers," 89–90, 115–16, 120; Chroust, *Rise of the Legal Profession in America*, 1:37.

8. Dumas Malone, *Jefferson the Virginian* (Boston: Little, Brown, 1948), 284–85; Reed, *Training for the Profession of Law*, 114, 116; Daniel Boorstin, *The Americans: The Colonial Experience*, Vintage ed. (New York: Random House, 1958), 204; Alonzo Thomas Dill, *George Wythe, Teacher of Liberty* (Williamsburg: Virginia Independence Bicentennial Commission, 1979), 41–42; Robert B. Kirtland, "George Wythe: Lawyer, Revolutionary, Judge" (Ph.D. diss., University of Michigan, 1986), 114–15; Richard Beale Davis, *Intellectual Life in Jefferson's Virginia, 1790–1830* (Chapel Hill: University of North Carolina Press, 1964), 51–52; Charles T. Cullen, "New Light on John Marshall's Legal Education and Admission to the Bar," *AJLH*, 16 (1972), 345; Bryson, "History of Legal Education in Virginia," 171–73.

9. Thomas Jefferson, *Notes on the State of Virginia*, ed. William Peden (New York: W. W. Norton, 1982), 150, 152; John Brown to Col. William Preston, 6 July 1780, in "Glimpses of Old College Life," *WMQ*, 1st ser., 9 (1900), 22; William Clarkin, *Serene Patriot: A Life of George Wythe* (Albany, N.Y.: Alan Publications, 1970), 143; Fred B. Devitt Jr., "William and Mary: America's First Law School," *William and Mary Law Review*, 2 (1960), 434; Lyon G. Tyler, *The College of William and Mary . . .* ([Williamsburg: College of William and Mary, 1917]), passim.

10. Kirtland, "Wythe," 48ff; Dill, *Wythe*, 42–43; Imogene Brown, *American Aristides: A Biography of George Wythe* (East Brunswick, N.J.: Associated University Presses, 1981), 174–98.

11. Sources for this paragraph and the next are Dill, *Wythe*, 44; Cullen, "New Light on Marshall's Legal Education," 346; Joyce Blackburn, *George Wythe of Williamsburg* (New York: Harper and Row, 1975), 102–03; Brown, *American Aristides*, 203; John Brown to William Preston, 6 July 1789, in Robert Hughes, "William and Mary, the First American Law School," *WMQ*, 2nd ser., 2 (1922), 41–42. A. G. Roeber adds that "Wythe believed that to secure a republican legal culture, the commonwealth would have to rely on an elite cadre of professionally trained lawyers and judges, who were not only technically skilled but also broadly educated in republican letters." *Faithful Magistrates and Republican Lawyers*, 167.

12. John Brown to William Preston, 15 February 1780, in Hughes, "William and Mary," 41; Brown, *American Aristides*, 203; Kirtland, "Wythe," chaps. 8 and 10 passim. Montesquieu's *Spirit of the Laws* (1750) and Hume's *Treatise of Human Nature* (1739) figured prominently in Wythe's course. See also William E. Nelson, "The Eighteenth-Century Background of John Marshall's Constitutional Jurisprudence," *Michigan Law Review*, 76 (1978), 893–960.

13. JM, *Autobiographical Sketch*, 6; Lyon G. Tyler, "Original Records of the Phi Beta Kappa Society," *WMQ*, 1st ser., 4 (1896), 215; Oscar M. Voorhees, *The History of Phi Beta Kappa* (New York: Crown Publishers, 1945), 11–13; Leonard Baker, *John Marshall: A Life in Law* (New York: Macmillan, 1974), 64; "Historical and Genealogical Notes," *WMQ*, 1st ser., 9 (1901), 142; E. G. Swem, "Some Notes on the Four Forms of the Oldest Building of William and Mary College," *WMQ*, 2nd ser., 9 (1928), 288.

14. William F. Swindler, "John Marshall's Preparation for the Bar—Some Observations on His Law Notes," *AJLH*, 11 (1967), 207–13; "Law Notes: Editorial Note" and notes, *PJM*, 1:38–87; Cullen, "New Light on Marshall's Legal Education," 347–48. The original notebook is in the library of the College of William and Mary.

15. David A. Lockmiller, *Sir William Blackstone* (Chapel Hill: University of North Carolina Press, 1938), 172–83; Dennis R. Nolan, "Sir William Blackstone and the New American Republic: A Study of Intellectual Impact," *New York University Law Review*, 51 (1976), 731–68; Daniel Boorstin, *The Mysterious Science of the Law: An Essay on Blackstone's "Commentaries,"* (Boston: Beacon Press, 1958), 20–25, 35–36; idem, *Americans: Colonial Experience*, 202; George M. Curtis, "The Virginia Courts during the Revolution" (Ph.D. diss., University of Wisconsin, 1970), 23–25; Zweiben, *How Blackstone Lost the Colonies*, chap. 5; James Wilson, "Study of the Law," in *The Works of James Wilson*, ed. Robert G. McCloskey, 2 vols. (Cambridge: Harvard University Press, 1967), 1:70; Christopher Wolfe, *The Rise of Modern Judicial Review: From Constitutional Interpretation to Judge-Made Law* (New York: Basic Books, 1986), 18–19; R. Kent Newmyer, *Supreme Court Justice Joseph Story: Statesman of the Old Republic* (Chapel Hill: University of North Carolina Press, 1985), 41.

16. Albert J. Beveridge, *The Life of John Marshall*, 4 vols. (Boston: Houghton Mifflin, 1916–19), 4:119; Edward S. Corwin, *John Marshall and the Constitution* (New Haven: Yale University Press, 1919), 116; Boorstin, *Americans: Colonial Experience*, 200.

17. Cullen, "New Light on Marshall's Legal Education," 348–51; "Law Notes: Editorial Note," *PJM*, 1:40 and n. 9; Smith, "Virginia Lawyers," 290–98; Reed, *Training for the Law*, 67; Raymond B. Blackard, "Requirements for Admission to the Bar in Revolutionary America," *Tennessee Law Review*, 15 (1938), 116–27.

18. Cullen, "New Light on Marshall's Legal Education," 351; "Law Notes: Editorial Note," *PJM*, 1:41 and n. 9; Beveridge, *Marshall*, 1:161.

19. JM, *Autobiographical Sketch*, 7; Beveridge, *Marshall*, 1:162–63, citing JM's statement quoted in *Southern Literary Messenger*, 2 (February 1836), 183. Virginia's 1777 inoculation law required that all justices in the subject's county give written permission, and that all neighbors within two miles must consent. Any physician who violated these restrictions faced a fine of $10,000. W. W. Hening, ed., *The Statutes at Large . . .*, 13 vols. (Richmond: Bartow, 1819–23), 9:371.

20. John E. Selby, *The Revolution in Virginia, 1775–1783* (Williamsburg: The Colonial Williamsburg Foundation, 1988), 221–25; John McAuley Palmer, *General Von Steuben* (New Haven: Yale University Press, 1937; rept., Port Washington, N.Y.: Kennikat Press, 1966), 237–50; Francis Rives Lassiter, "Arnold's Invasion of Virginia," *Sewanee Review*, 9 (1901), 78–93, 185–203; Malone, *Jefferson the Virginian*, 336–40; JM, *The Life of George Washington*, 5 vols. (Philadelphia: C. P. Wayne, 1804–7; rept., New York: Chelsea House, 1983), 3:107–08.

21. Beveridge, *Marshall*, 1:202; Baker, *Marshall*, 90; John Gilman Kolp, *Gentlemen and Freeholders: Electoral Politics in Colonial Virginia* (Baltimore: Johns Hopkins University Press, 1998), 80. Jean Smith suggests that Marshall may have resigned from

88   A CHIEF JUSTICE'S PROGRESS

the army not to "pay attention to my future prospects in life," as he wrote in his autobiography, but because of animus toward Baron von Steuben. JM, *Autobiographical Sketch*, 6; Smith, *John Marshall: Definer of a Nation* (New York: Henry Holt, 1996), 84–85 n. A letter Marshall wrote to General Greene in April 1781 that might have explained his decision to resign is missing. *PJM*, 1:87.

22. JM's oath of office, 25 May 1782, *PJM*, 1:87–88; Harry M. Ward and Harold E. Greer, Jr., *Richmond during the Revolution, 1775–1783* (Charlottesville: University Press of Virginia, 1977), x, 8–9, 16, 66–70, 109–11; Beveridge, *Marshall*, 1:165–66, 171–72; Virginius Dabney, *Richmond: The Story of a City* (Garden City, N.Y.: Doubleday and Co., 1976), chap. 4 passim; W. Asbury Christian, *Richmond: Her Past and Present* (Richmond: L. H. Jenkins, 1912), 23; Johann Schoepf, *Travels in the Confederation* (1783), excerpted in *A Richmond Reader, 1733–1983*, ed. Maurice Duke and Daniel P. Jordan (Chapel Hill: University of North Carolina Press, 1983), 12–17; Samuel Mordecai, *Richmond in By-Gone Days* . . . (Richmond: West and Johnson, 1856), 54, 59; Marianne P. B. Sheldon, "Richmond, Virginia: The Town and Henrico County to 1820" (Ph.D. diss., University of Michigan, 1975), chaps. 2–6 passim.

23. Virginia Constitution of 1776, in Francis Newton Thorpe, ed., *The Federal and State Constitutions, Colonial Charters, and Other Organic Laws of the States, Territories, and Colonies* . . ., 7 vols. (Washington, D.C.: Government Printing Office, 1909), 7:3815–16; Jackson Turner Main, *The Sovereign States, 1775–1783* (New York: Franklin Watts, 1973), 156–59; Hamilton J. Eckenrode, *The Revolution in Virginia* (Boston: Houghton Mifflin, 1916), 164–65; Allan Nevins, *The American States during and after the Revolution, 1775–1789* (New York: Macmillan, 1924), 148; Selby, *Revolution in Virginia*, 116–17; George B. Oliver, "A Constitutional History of Virginia, 1776–1860" (Ph.D. diss., Duke University, 1959), 229–33, 243.

24. Sources for this paragraph and the next are Norman K. Risjord and Gordon DenBoer, "The Evolution of Political Parties in Virginia, 1782–1800," *JAH*, 60 (1973–74), 963–66; Norman K. Risjord, *Chesapeake Politics, 1781–1800* (New York: Columbia University Press, 1978), 71–73, 81–84; Gordon DenBoer, "The House of Delegates and the Evolution of Political Parties in Virginia, 1782–1789" (Ph.D. diss., University of Wisconsin, 1972), chap. 2 passim; Ward and Greer, *Richmond during the Revolution*, 45; Thomas Jefferson to Edmund Randolph, 15 February 1783, in *The Papers of Thomas Jefferson*, ed. Julian P. Boyd et al., 27 vols. to date (Princeton: Princeton University Press, 1950–), 6:246–49; Joseph Jones to James Madison, 14 June 1783, in *The Papers of James Madison*, ed. William T. Hutchinson et al., 17 vols. (Chicago and Charlottesville: University of Chicago Press, 1962–91), 7:143–45; Randolph to Jefferson, 15 May 1784, quoted in Richard R. Beeman, *Patrick Henry: A Biography* (New York: McGraw-Hill, 1974), 130; Harry Ammon, *James Monroe: The Quest for National Identity* (New York: McGraw-Hill, 1971), 35–36; Jackson Turner Main, "The American Revolution and the Democratization of the Legislatures," *WMQ*, 3rd ser., 22 (1966), 396, 402–03; idem, *Political Parties before the Constitution* (Chapel Hill: University of North Carolina Press, 1973), 244–45, 249. Main adds that even his own protean categories of "cosmopolitan" and "localist" do not describe Virginia's political alignments during the 1780s.

25. Ward and Greer, *Richmond during the Revolution*, 49–50; Dabney, *Richmond*, 36; Schoepf, *Travels in the Confederation*, in *Richmond Reader*, 15; James Sterling Young, *The Washington Community, 1800–1828* (New York: Columbia University Press, 1966), 98–107.

26. *Journals of the House of Delegates of the Commonwealth of Virginia* (Richmond: Thomas W. White, 1828), October 1782 sess., 10–45 passim; "Legislative Bill," 30 November 1782, *PJM*, 1:89–91; Edmund Randolph to James Madison, 20 June 1782, *Papers of Madison*, 4:358; Risjord, *Chesapeake Politics*, 84; DenBoer, "Evolution of Political Parties in Virginia," 40–43; Emory G. Evans, "Private Indebtedness and the Revolution in Virginia, 1776–1796," *WMQ*, 3rd ser., 28 (1971), 358; John J. Reardon, *Edmund Randolph: A Biography* (New York: Macmillan, 1974), 57–58; JM to William Pierce, 12 February 1783, *PJM*, 1:95.

27. JM, *Autobiographical Sketch*, 7; *PJM*, 1:92 n. 9; *Journals of the Council of the State of Virginia*, 5 vols. (Richmond: Division of Purchase and Printing, 1971–82), 3:184; W. P. Palmer et al., eds., *Calendar of Virginia State Papers . . .*, 11 vols. (Richmond: N.p., 1875–93), 3:386; Beveridge, *Marshall*, 1:209–10; Charles Sydnor, *American Revolutionaries in the Making: Political Practices in Washington's Virginia* (rept., New York: Free Press, 1965), 63; Thorpe, ed., *Federal and State Constitutions*, 7:3817–18.

28. *Journal of the Council of State*, 3:184–344 passim; Ward and Greer, *Richmond during the Revolution*, 49; Beveridge, *Marshall*, 1:210; Ammon, *Monroe*, 37–38; Baker, *Marshall*, 90; JM et al., "Report to the Council of State," 25 March 1783, *PJM*, 1:99–100; Thorpe, ed., *Federal and State Constitutions*, 7:3815, 3817.

29. "Council of State Opinion," 20 February 1783, *PJM*, 1:96–97; *Papers of Madison*, 6:347 n. 5; Thad W. Tate, "The Social Contract in America, 1774–1787: Revolutionary Theory as a Conservative Instrument," *WMQ*, 3rd ser., 22 (1965), 384; Gordon Wood, *The Creation of the American Republic, 1776–1787* (Chapel Hill: University of North Carolina Press, 1969; rept., New York: W. W. Norton, 1972), 274–75; Nevins, *American States during and after the Revolution*, 193–95; *Journal of the House of Delegates*, May 1783 sess., 14, 22; Smith, *Marshall*, 96, 562 n. 58. The magistrate was John Price Posey of New Kent County. In 1788, he was hanged after a conviction for arson. *PJM*, 1:96 n. 2.

30. Sources for this discussion of the Marshall-Ambler romance and marriage are "Marriage Bond," 1 January 1783, *PJM*, 1:92–93 and n. 4; JM, *Autobiographical Sketch*, 6–7; Mason, *My Dearest Polly*, chaps. 1–2; Elizabeth D. Coleman, "Till Death Did Them Part," *Virginia Cavalcade*, 5 (autumn 1955), 14–19; Elizabeth Ambler Carrington's letters in "An Old Virginia Correspondence," *Atlantic Monthly*, 84 (1899), 536–37, 546–48; "Letters from John Marshall to His Wife," *WMQ*, 2nd ser., 3 (1923), 86; *Green Bag*, 9 (1896), 481; *Sexton v. Wheaton*, 8 Wheaton 229 at 239 (1823); JM to Polly, 23 February 1824, quoted in Mason, *My Dearest Polly*, 262–63; Beveridge, *Marshall*, 1:148–54, 159–60, 163–67, 170–71; Francis N. Stites, *John Marshall: Defender of the Constitution* (Boston: Little, Brown, 1981), 15–18; Baker, *Marshall*, 57–61, 71–73; Smith, *Marshall*, 70–73, 85; Lyon G. Tyler, ed., *Encyclopedia of Virginia Biography* (New York: Lewis Historical Publishing Co., 1915), s.v. "Ambler, Jaquelin," 2:335; Bishop [William] Meade, *Old Churches, Ministers, and Families of Virginia*, 2 vols. (Philadelphia: J. P. Lippincott, 1910), 1:103–08; William M. Paxton, *The Marshall Family . . .* (Cincinnati: Robert Clarke and Co., 1885), 42–45; "Account Book," *PJM*, 1:296 n. 26. The "Major Dick" mentioned as Marshall's romantic rival in his 1824 letter to Polly was Alexander Dick, an officer in the Virginia Line. *PJM*, 5:207 n. 4.

31. The cousin's surreptitious snipping probably did not occur; more likely, Polly did the cutting herself and sent him off with the lock of hair. Jean Smith probably gives the lovestruck couple too much intellectual credit when he proposes that a work of Alexander Pope's that they both supposedly read, *The Rape of the Lock*, guided their thoughts during the incident. In this case, a simple romantic explanation seems best. In

any event, Polly placed the snippet of her hair inside a locket and wore it around her neck constantly thereafter. When she died, Marshall wore it for the rest of his life. The locket is on display at the John Marshall House Museum in Richmond. Smith, *Marshall*, 85–86.

32. JM, *Autobiographical Sketch*, 7; "Account Book," *PJM*, 1:291, 295, 297–98, 300–301.

33. William Wirt, *Letters of the British Spy* (orig. publ. 1832; rept., Chapel Hill: University of North Carolina Press, 1970), 206; Charles Warren, *A History of the American Bar* (Boston: Little, Brown, 1911), 8, 39–44; Chroust, *Rise of the Legal Profession in America*, 1:27–28, 266–77; Francis R. Aumann, *The Changing American Legal System: Some Selected Phases* (Columbus: Ohio State University Press, 1940; rept., New York: DaCapo Press, 1969), 20–21, 24–26; Roeber, *Faithful Magistrates and Republican Lawyers*, 32, 47, 53, 71; Smith, "Virginia Lawyers," 280–99; Richard Beale Davis, *Intellectual Life in the Colonial South, 1585–1763*, 3 vols. (Knoxville: University of Tennessee Press, 1978), 3:1601–2; Philip Alexander Bruce, *Institutional History of Virginia in the Seventeenth Century*, 2 vols. (New York: G. P. Putnam's Sons, 1910), 1:561–69; E. Lee Shepard, "'This Ancient and Honorable Class of Men': Practicing the Law in Old Virginia," *Virginia Cavalcade*, 36 (spring 1987), 149.

34. Smith, "Virginia Lawyers," 13–23, 72–75; Chroust, *Rise of the Legal Profession*, 1:52, 285–92; Sydnor, *American Revolutionaries in the Making*, 17; Warren, *History of the American Bar*, 46–49; Roeber, *Faithful Magistrates and Republican Lawyers*, 145; Shepard, "'This Ancient and Honorable Class of Men,'" 149.

35. Gordon S. Wood, *The Radicalism of the American Revolution* (New York: Alfred A. Knopf, 1992), 107, 210; Roeber, *Faithful Magistrates and Republican Lawyers*, 156 n. 79, 161; Smith, "Virginia Lawyers," 339–43; Shepard, "'This Ancient and Honorable Class of Men,'" 149–50; Edmund Burke, "Speech on Moving Resolutions for Conciliation with the American Colonies," 22 March 1776, in *Burke's Speech on Conciliation with America*, ed. Charles R. Morris (New York: Harper and Brothers, 1945), 31–32; Wood, *Creation of the American Republic*, chap. 7 passim; Robert A. Ferguson, *Law and Letters in American Culture* (Cambridge: Harvard University Press, 1984), 11–12; Thomas Paine, *Common Sense*, ed. Isaac Kramnick (New York: Penguin Books, 1982), 98; Jack P. Greene, "From the Perspective of Law: Context and Legitimacy in the Origins of the American Revolution," *South Atlantic Quarterly*, 85 (1986), 56–77; Erwin R. Surrency, "The Lawyer and the American Revolution," *AJLH*, 8 (1964), 125–35; Kermit L. Hall, *The Magic Mirror: Law in American History* (New York: Oxford University Press, 1989), 50, 53; Seymour Martin Lipset, *The First New Nation: The United States in Historical and Comparative Perspective* (New York: W. W. Norton, 1979), 67; Newmyer, *Story*, xvi; Jack M. Sosin, *The Aristocracy of the Long Robe: The Origins of Judicial Review in America* (Westport, Conn.: Greenwood Press, 1989), chap. 12.

36. Chroust, *Rise of the Legal Profession*, 1:14–17, 54–57, 261–63; Warren, *History of the American Bar*, 214–15, 224–25; Roeber, *Faithful Magistrates and Republican Lawyers*, 113.

37. Chroust, *Rise of the Legal Profession*, 2:34; Shepard, "Lawyers Look at Themselves," 3–4; Roeber, *Faithful Magistrates and Republican Lawyers*, 172; JM, *Autobiographical Sketch*, 7; W. A. Low, "Merchant and Planter Relations in Post-Revolutionary Virginia, 1783–1789," *VMHB*, 61 (1953), 314–16; JM to John Ambler, 7 May 1784, *PJM*, 1:122; Smith, *Marshall*, 101; JM to Beverley Randolph, 6 August 1787, *PJM*, 1:234; "A General View of Marshall's Practice," *PJM*, 5:liii–liv; JM,

"Account Book," *PJM*, 1:295–400 passim; Irwin S. Rhodes, *The Papers of John Marshall: A Descriptive Calendar*, 2 vols. (Norman: University of Oklahoma Press, 1956), 1:32–33, 38–39, 43, 61–62 (hereafter cited as Rhodes, *Calendar of Marshall Papers*); Reardon, *Randolph*, 88, citing *Virginia Independent Chronicle*, 22 November 1786.

38. Ward and Green, *Richmond after the Revolution*, 141; Risjord, *Chesapeake Politics*, 98–99; Smith, *Marshall*, 99–100, 564 n. 92.

39. Chroust, *Rise of the Legal Profession*, 1:xiv–xvii; Adams to Charles Cushing, 1 April 1756, in L. Kilvin Wroth and Hiller B. Zobel, eds., *Legal Papers of John Adams*, 3 vols. (Cambridge: Harvard University Press, 1965), 1:lii; "General View of Marshall's Practice," *PJM*, 5:lv–lvi; JM to John Breckinridge, ca. 20 May, 10 June 1791, ibid., 2:91–92, 94–95.

40. "General View of Marshall's Practice," *PJM*, 5:liv–lv, lviii; "Editorial Note," *PJM*, 5:3, 5, 7–8; JM, "Account Book," numerous entries for legal fees, *PJM*, 1:295–413 passim; numerous cases in *PJM*, 1:126–252 passim; Charles F. Hobson, *The Great Chief Justice: John Marshall and the Rule of Law* (Lawrence: University Press of Kansas, 1996), 30–31; Rhodes, *Calendar of Marshall Papers*, 1:48–56, 61–64; Charles T. Cullen, "St. George Tucker and Law in Virginia" (Ph.D. diss., University of Virginia, 1971), 87.

41. Roeber, *Faithful Magistrates and Republican Lawyers*, 121; Shepard, "'This Ancient and Honorable Class of Men,'" 154; "The Court System of Post-Revolutionary Virginia," *PJM*, 5:xxviii–xxx; "Editorial Notes," *PJM*, 5:53, 451; Thorpe, *Federal and State Constitutions*, 7:3817–18; Cullen, "St. George Tucker," 38–43.

42. *Hite v. Fairfax* (4 Call 69–81 [1786]), *PJM*, 1:157; Gale Lee Richards, "A Criticism of the Public Speaking of John Marshall prior to 1801" (Ph.D. diss., University of Iowa, 1950), 379–405, 412–31; Hobson, *Great Chief Justice*, 32–33. A good example of Marshall's method of argument in his earlier cases is *Ashton v. West* (1786), *PJM*, 1:178.

43. Francis Walker Gilmer, *Sketches, Essays, and Translations* (Baltimore: F. Lucas, 1818), 23–24.

44. Sources for this paragraph and the next are "General View of Marshall's Practice," *PJM*, 5:lix; Hobson, *Great Chief Justice*, 26–28; Julius Goebel, "The Common Law and the Constitution," in W. Melville Jones, ed., *Chief Justice John Marshall: A Reappraisal* (Ithaca: Cornell University Press, 1956), 108–11; Chroust, *Rise of the Legal Profession*, 1:21–22; "Common Law Procedure in Virginia," *PJM*, 5:xxv, xxxiii, lx, lxii; Gustavus Schmidt, "Reminiscences of the Late Chief Justice Marshall," *Louisiana Law Journal*, 1 (1841), 81–83 (emphasis in original); JM, "Account Book," *PJM*, 1:334, 341.

45. Henry Howe, *Historical Collections of Virginia* . . . (Charleston: N.p., 1845; rept., Baltimore: Regional Publishing Co., 1969), 266; Roeber, *Faithful Magistrates and Republican Lawyers*, chap. 7 passim, esp. 241ff.

46. Hobson, *Great Chief Justice*, 33–43; *Livingston v. Jefferson* (1 Brockenbrough 209 [1811]), *PJM*, 7:284.

47. "*Hite v. Fairfax*: Editorial Note," *PJM*, 1:150–52; Stanley P. Smith, "The Northern Neck's Role in American Legal History," *VMHB*, 77 (1969), 281–83; Josiah L. Dickinson, *The Fairfax Proprietary* (Front Royal, Va.: Warren Press, 1959), 9–11 and Appendix, I–LVII; Stuart E. Brown, Jr., *Virginia Baron: The Story of Thomas 6th Lord Fairfax* (Berryville, Va.: Chesapeake Book Co., 1965), 74–117 passim; H. C. Groome, *Fauquier during the Proprietorship* . . . (Richmond: N.p., 1927; rept., Baltimore: Richmond Publishing Co., 1969), 30–81; John A. Treon, "*Martin v. Hunter's Lessee*: A Case History" (Ph.D. diss., University of Virginia, 1970), chap. 1; "Marshall and the

Fairfax Litigation from the Compromise of 1796 to *Martin v. Hunter's Lessee*: Editorial Note," *PJM*, 8:109.

48. Reardon, *Randolph*, 72; Smith, "Northern Neck in American Legal History," 281; JM, "*Hite v. Fairfax*: Argument in the Court of Appeals," *PJM*, 1:153–64; derivative cases listed in *PJM*, 1:188–92, and Rhodes, *Calendar of Marshall Papers*, 1:48–56; *Leith v. Hite* et al., (1790), *PJM*, 5:62–71; JM, "List of Fees," *PJM*, 2:104–07. In *Martin v. Hunter's Lessee*, the Supreme Court asserted its right to review decisions of state courts. It overruled the Virginia Court of Appeals, which had declared unconstitutional section 25 of the Judiciary Act of 1789 that provided for certain appeals of state court rulings to the national judiciary. Marshall recused himself from the Court's deliberations because of his family's interest in the case; his brother James owned the tract of land at issue.

49. Henry Flanders, *The Lives and Times of the Chief Justices of the Supreme Court of the United States*, 2 vols. (Philadelphia: T. and J. W. Johnson and Co., 1881), 2:303; Baker, *Marshall*, 78–79, 86; Stites, *Marshall*, 23; Irwin S. Rhodes, "John Marshall and the Western Country: The Early Days," *Historical and Philosophical Society of Ohio Bulletin*, 18 (1960), 123ff. Thomas Marshall's attachment to western lands began with his appointment by Governor Jefferson in early 1780 to conduct a preliminary survey of the Kentucky territory.

50. JM to [Governor] Benjamin Harrison, 1 April 1784, *PJM*, 1:118 and n. 8; JM to James Monroe, 17 April 1784, *PJM*, 1:120–21 and n. 7; JM to Leven Powell, 9 December 1783, *PJM*, 1:109; JM, *Autobiographical Sketch*, 7.

51. Risjord, *Chesapeake Politics*, 122, 132–35, 161–66; Risjord and DenBoer, "Evolution of Political Parties in Virginia," 966; DenBoer, "House of Delegates and Political Parties in Virginia," 33–46; Herbert Sloan and Peter S. Onuf, "Politics, Culture, and the Revolution in Virginia: A Review of Recent Work," *VMHB*, 91 (1983), 279–80; Gordon S. Wood, "Interests and Disinterestedness in the Making of the Constitution," in *Beyond Confederation: Origins of the Constitution and American National Identity*, Richard Beeman et al., eds. (Chapel Hill: University of North Carolina Press, 1987), 74–75.

52. JM to Monroe, 15 May 1784, *PJM*, 1:123; Ralph Ketcham, *James Madison: A Biography* (New York: Macmillan, 1971), 159; Irving Brant, *James Madison: The Nationalist* (Indianapolis: Bobbs-Merrill, 1941), 316. Marshall's literary allusion was to Charles Churchill, *The Prophecy of Famine* (1763), part of which reads:

No living thing, whate'er its food, feasts there,
But the Cameleon, who can feast on air.
No birds, except as birds of passage, flew,
No bee was known to hum, no dove to coo.
No streams as amber smooth, as amber clear,
Were seen to glide, or heard to warble there.
Rebellion's spring, which thro' the country ran,
Furnished, with bitter draughts, the steady clan.

53. Sources for this paragraph and the next are Risjord, *Chesapeake Politics*, 110–16; Risjord and DenBoer, "Evolution of Virginia Political Parties," 964–65; DenBoer, "House of Delegates and Political Parties in Virginia," 33–35; Evans, "Private Indebtedness and the Revolution in Virginia," 349, 359–63; Nevins, *American States during and after the Revolution*, 337; *Journal of the House of Delegates*, May 1784 sess., 41; JM to Monroe, 2 December 1784, *PJM*, 1:130; Francis H. Rudko, *John*

Marshall and International Law: Statesman and Chief Justice (Westport, Conn.: Greenwood Press, 1991), 17–21, 24–31.

54. *Journal of the House of Delegates,* May 1784 sess., 11–12; E. James Ferguson, *The Power of the Purse: A History of American Public Finance, 1776–1790* (Chapel Hill: University of North Carolina Press, 1961), 209; Richard B. Morris, *The Forging of the Union, 1781–1789* (New York: Harper and Row, 1987), 151; Merrill Jensen, *The New Nation: A History of the United States during the Confederation, 1781–1789,* Vintage ed. (New York: Alfred A. Knopf, 1965), 402.

55. *Journal of the House of Delegates,* May 1784 sess., 61; Risjord, *Chesapeake Politics,* 135–37; Brant, *Madison,* 315; Drew R. McCoy, *The Elusive Republic: Political Economy in Jeffersonian America* (Chapel Hill: University of North Carolina Press, 1980; rept., New York: W. W. Norton, 1982), 15–16; idem, "The Virginia Port Bill of 1784," *VMHB,* 83 (1975), 288–93; JM to Charles Simms, 16 June 1784, *PJM,* 1:124; DenBoer, "House of Delegates and Political Parties in Virginia," 66–68; Myra L. Rich, "The Experimental Years: Virginia, 1781–1789" (Ph.D. diss., Yale University, 1966), 150–65.

56. Roeber, *Faithful Magistrates and Republican Lawyers,* 189–93; Risjord, *Chesapeake Politics,* 181–82; Brant, *Madison,* 356–57; JM to Charles Simms, 16 June 1784, *PJM,* 1:124. Roeber notes that "supporters of [court] reform were linked to more cosmopolitan views and demands of merchants, lawyers, and diversified planters than were opponents." *Faithful Magistrates and Republican Lawyers,* 199 n. 85.

57. *Journal of the House of Delegates,* May 1784 sess., 19, 27, 79, 82; JM to Monroe, 2 December 1784, *PJM,* 1:131; Risjord, *Chesapeake Politics,* 205–10; DenBoer, "House of Delegates and Political Parties in Virginia," 36–39; Brant, *Madison,* 343–49; Thomas F. Buckley, *Church and State in Revolutionary Virginia, 1776–1787* (Charlottesville: University Press of Virginia, 1977), 71–112, 194. Buckley erroneously suggests that Marshall's support for the assessment bill contributed to his election defeat the following year. As noted below, Marshall chose not to run, and for other reasons.

58. *Journal of the House of Delegates,* May 1784 sess., 86; Beveridge, *Marshall,* 1:213–14; Brant, *Madison,* 319–20; Eric Foner, *Tom Paine and Revolutionary America* (New York: Oxford University Press, 1976), 189, 192; Peter S. Onuf, *The Origins of the Federal Republic: Jurisdictional Controversies in the United States, 1775–1787* (Philadelphia: University of Pennsylvania Press, 1983), 90–91.

59. JM to Monroe, 2 December 1784, *PJM,* 1:130.

60. "Virginia Constitutional Society Subscription Paper," 13 April 1785, *PJM,* 1:140–42; J. G. Roulhac Hamilton, "A Society for the Preservation of Liberty," *AHR,* 32 (1927), 550–52, 702–93; Bess Furman, "Signed, Sealed—and Forgotten! The Story of a Premier Promoter of the Constitution," *Daughters of the American Revolution Magazine,* 71 (1937), 1004–09; Baker, *Marshall,* 96–100; Beveridge, *Marshall,* 173, 473; *Dictionary of American Biography,* 5:486–87, s.v. "Innes, James"; Madison to George Washington, 1 November and 4 December 1786, in *The Writings of James Madison,* ed. Gaillard Hunt, 9 vols. (New York: G. P. Putnam's Sons, 1900–1910), 2:282, 294; Hening, ed., *Statutes,* 12:280; "Arbitrator's Award," 28 December 1786, *PJM,* 1:198; *Papers of Madison,* 3:21 n. 1; *Papers of Jefferson,* 6:321–24.   The Virginia Constitutional Society included many prominent Virginians among its members, such as James Madison (the president of William and Mary), James Madison, Jr. (the future president of the United States), Edmund Randolph, Richard Henry Lee, John Blair, and Phillip Mazzei. The organization met at least three times but then became inactive. *PJM,* 1:140 n. 7, 141–42. The Philadelphia merchant was Simon Nathan. The Assembly

accepted the arbitrators' decision and authorized the executive to issue land warrants to pay his claim. *PJM*, 1:198 n. 3.

61. Rhodes, *Calendar of Marshall Papers*, "Recorder for Town of Richmond," 1:34–36; "Hustings Court Session: Editorial Note," *PJM*, 1:169–70.

62. "Hustings Court Session," *PJM*, 1:170–71; JM to [Mayor] John Beckley, March 1788, ibid., 249; Virginia Common Hall Records, 1782–1792, and Richmond City Hustings Court Order Books 1 and 2, cited in Rhodes, *Calendar of Marshall Papers*, 1:34–36.

63. "Subscription," 9 January 1788, *PJM*, 1:248–49 and ns. 9 and 1–2; "Account Book," *PJM*, 1:299 and ns. 34 and 37, 303 and n. 58, 306 and n. 71, 313, 315 and n. 20, 317 and n. 26, 319 and n. 40, 320 and n. 46, 321 and n. 48, 329, 336, 342 and n. 40, 368, 399 and n. 73; David K. Walthall, *History of Richmond Lodge, No. 10* (Richmond: Ware and Duke, 1909), 22, 34–35; JM to Edward Everett, 22 July 1833, in John E. Oster, *The Political and Economic Doctrines of John Marshall* (orig. publ. 1914; rept., New York: Burt Franklin, 1967), 98; Christian, *Richmond*, 28; Ward and Greer, *Richmond after the Revolution*, 49. Marshall was such a devotee of the stage that a new civic theater that opened in Richmond in 1838 was named in his honor. The repertoire of traveling and resident companies that Marshall saw in Richmond is discussed in Martin S. Shockley, "The Richmond Theatre, 1780–1790," *VMHB*, 60 (1952), 421–36.

64. Notations in Marshall Family Bible, 24 July 1784, 15 and 20 June 1786, 3 December 1787, and entries in Marshall's Account Book, in *PJM*, 1:125, 168 and n. 7, 243, 308 and n. 80, 356 and n. 96, 399 and n. 68; Mason, *My Dearest Polly*, 343–44; C. M. S., "The Home Life of Chief Justice Marshall," *WMQ*, 2nd ser., 12 (1932), 67–69. After graduating from Princeton in 1803, Thomas Marshall practiced law in Richmond and served in the state legislature until health problems forced him to retire to Oak Hill. In 1835, while passing through Baltimore to see his dying father in Philadelphia, Thomas was struck on the head by a falling brick and killed. John Marshall, in the last stages of a fatal liver ailment, was never told of his son's death before succumbing to his illness a week later. Jaquelin Marshall studied medicine but did not establish a practice, choosing instead to lead a quiet and unindustrious life with his wife at an estate not too far from Oak Hill. He died there in 1852. *PJM*, 1:125 n. 3, 243 n. 3; Paxton, *Marshall Family*, 90–92, 99.

65. JM, "Account Book," *PJM*, 1:296 and n. 26, 297 n. 27; 319 n. 39, 320 n. 45, 332–33 n. 97; Henrico County Titheable Book, cited in *Calendar of Marshall Papers*, 1:38.

66. Some instructive parallels between Marshall's and George Washington's mix of personal and political motives for speculating in western lands, and how they fit into the developing Federalist persuasion, can be found in Rick W. Sturdevant, "Quest for Eden: George Washington's Frontier Land Interests" (Ph.D. diss., University of California at Santa Barbara, 1982); John Lauritz Larson, "'Wisdom Enough to Improve Them': Government, Liberty, and Inland Waterways in the Rising American Empire," in *Launching the "Extended Republic": The Federalist Era*, ed. Ronald Hoffman and Peter J. Albert (Charlottesville: University Press of Virginia, 1996), 223–48; and Andrew R. L. Clayton, "Radicals in the 'Western World': The Federalist Conquest of Trans-Appalachian North America," in *Federalists Reconsidered*, ed. Doron Ben-Atar and Barbara B. Oberg (Charlottesville: University Press of Virginia, 1998), 77–96.

67. JM to Arthur Lee, 17 April 1784, *PJM*, 1:119–20; JM to Charles Simms, 16 June 1784, *PJM*, 1:125; Rhodes, "Marshall and the Western Country," 120ff. The lot Marshall bought is located at 400 N. 8th Street and is now occupied by the Federal Building. Smith, *Marshall*, 104, 566 n. 123.

Humphrey Marshall had a multifaceted life that deserves its own full treatment. The son of Thomas Marshall's brother John, he was born in 1760 in Fauquier County and fought during the Revolution, reaching the rank of captain-lieutenant in the Virginia artillery. In 1782, he settled in Kentucky and became deputy surveyor for Fayette County, working in his uncle's office. He received a warrant for 4,000 acres of land that year, and by the time he died in 1841 had become one of the largest landholders (with over 400,000 acres) and wealthiest citizens in Kentucky. He also was a prominent attorney, voted for ratification of the proposed U.S. Constitution at the Virginia convention in 1788, and became a Federalist partisan in an overwhelmingly Jeffersonian state. As a U.S. Senator in the mid-1790s, he voted for the Jay Treaty. His harsh tongue and rapierlike pen gained him many political enemies, among them Henry Clay, against whom he fought a duel in 1809 (both men were slightly wounded, Clay more seriously). In 1806, Humphrey and Joseph H. Daveiss, the district attorney for Kentucky and John Marshall's brother-in-law, wrote articles in a local paper publicizing rumors that Aaron Burr and James Wilkinson were involved in a Spanish-backed conspiracy to separate the western region from the rest of the United States. In 1810, Marshall established the only Federalist newspaper in Kentucky and two years later wrote the first formal history of the state.   Although that chronicle's political interpretations are self-serving and untrustworthy, its facts are considered reliable for the most part. *Dictionary of American Biography*, 12:309–10, s.v. "Marshall, Humphrey"; Humphrey Marshall, *The History of Kentucky . . .* (Frankfort, Ky.: George S. Robinson, 1824); Robert V. Remini, *Henry Clay: Statesman for the Union* (New York: W. W. Norton, 1991), 53–56; Milton Lomask, *Aaron Burr: The Conspiracy and the Years of Exile, 1805–1836* (New York: Farrar, Straus, Giroux, 1982), 138. See also the many references to Marshall in Patricia Watlington, *The Partisan Spirit: Kentucky Politics, 1779–1792* (New York: Atheneum, 1972).

68. Risjord, *Chesapeake Politics*, 220; Thomas P. Abernethy, *Western Lands and the American Revolution* (Charlottesville: University of Virginia Institute for Research in the Social Sciences, 1937; rept., New York: Russell and Russell, 1959), 224–25; Watlington, *Partisan Spirit*, 11–14.

69. "Marshall's Kentucky Lands: Editorial Note," *PJM*, 1:100–101; Watlington, *Partisan Spirit*, 39–43, 111–14, 156–57, 204; Rhodes, "Marshall and the Western Country," 124–25; *Dictionary of American Biography*, 12:309–10, 313–14, s.v. "Marshall, Humphrey" and "Marshall, James Markham"; Randolph W. Church, "James Markham Marshall," *Virginia Cavalcade*, 13 (spring 1964), 22–29; "Land Bounty Certificate," and "Military Land Warrant," both dated 30 November 1782, *PJM*, 1:91–92; "Land–Office Warrant No. 4583," 7 April 1780, *PJM*, 1:104; Lloyd D. Bockstruck, *Revolutionary War Bounty Land Grants Awarded by State Governments* (Baltimore: Genealogical Publishing Co., 1996), 334; Gaius M. Brumbaugh, *Revolutionary War Records. Volume I, Virginia . . .* (Lancaster, Pa.: Lancaster Press, 1936), 104; Willard Rouse Jillson, *Old Kentucky Entries and Deeds* (Louisville, Ky.: Standard Publishing Co., 1926), 124–25, 245, 348, 432. Marshall's father received two warrants for over 8,000 acres in Kentucky; his brother James received two for nearly 4,700 acres; and his cousin Humphrey received one for 4,000. Jillson, *Old Kentucky Entries and Deeds*, 124, 348, 384, 432; John H. Gwathmey, *Historical Register of Virginians in the Revolution: Soldiers, Sailors, Marines, 1775–1783* (Richmond: Dietz Press, 1938), 502; Bockstruck, *Revolutionary War Bounty Land Grants*, 333–34; Brumbaugh, *Revolutionary War Records*, 104, 106.

70. Watlington, *Partisan Spirit*, 20–21, 40–41; *Dictionary of American Biography*, 12:329, s.v. "Marshall, Thomas"; "Marshall's Kentucky Lands," *PJM*, 1:101–102; Stites, *Marshall*, 22–23; various land-related documents in *PJM*, 1:104–05, 164–68, 248, 250; JM letters to James Monroe, 3 January, 19 February, 17 April, 2 December 1784, *PJM*, 1:113, 115, 121, 132; numerous entries for JM warrants, grants, surveys, and caveats in Rhodes, *Calendar of Marshall Papers*, 1:20–24, 26, 33, 38, 40, 43–44, 69.

Thomas Marshall and his other sons would own the better part of 400,000 acres of Kentucky lands. Thomas, following the architectural pattern he set earlier in Virginia, lived in a two-story log house he built that was markedly more elaborate than the primitive log cabins then found in Kentucky. Called Buck Pond, it was located in what is now Woodford County. Thomas owned over 100,000 acres when he died in 1802. Besides land in Kentucky, John Marshall also acquired other parcels in Fauquier County, such as the 268 acres he bought in October 1787. Watlington, *Partisan Spirit*, 70 n. 130; "Deed," 18 October 1787, *PJM*, 1:240; Rhodes, "Marshall and the Western Country," 123.

71. *Journal of the House of Delegates*, October 1784 sess., 41, 95; Beveridge, *Marshall*, 1:235–40; Brant, *Madison*, 359–60; JM to Monroe, 2 December 1784, *PJM*, 1:131; Robert D. Meade, *Patrick Henry, Practical Revolutionary* (Philadelphia: J. P. Lippincott, 1969), 264–65.

72. JM to Arthur Lee, 17 April 1784, *PJM*, 1:120.

73. Kent Druyvesteyn, "With Great Vision: The James River and Kanawha Canal: A Pictorial Essay," *Virginia Cavalcade*, 22 (winter 1972), 22–26; Wayland F. Dunaway, *History of the James River and Kanawha Company* (Columbia University Studies in History, Economics, and Public Law, vol. 104, no. 2, 1922; rept., New York: AMS Press, 1969), 9–28; James Thomas Flexner, *George Washington and the New Nation (1783–1793)* (Boston: Little, Brown, 1970), 73–78; Malone, *Jefferson the Virginian*, 378; Risjord, *Chesapeake Politics*, 240–42; JM to George Muter, 11 February 1787, *PJM*, 1:204; JM to Thomas Marshall, 17 January 1787, *PJM*, 1:202; JM, *Life of Washington*, 4:77–80; John L. Larson, "'Bind the Republic Together': The National Union and the Struggle for a System of Internal Improvements," *JAH*, 74 (1987–88), 363–87; Philip M. Rice, "Internal Improvements in Virginia, 1775–1860" (Ph.D. diss., University of North Carolina, 1948), chap. 3.

74. JM's subscriptions in *PJM*, 1:306, 344, 356; JM to Monroe, 2 December 1784, *PJM*, 1:130–31; JM to Muter, 7 January 1785, *PJM*, 1:134–35; Flexner, *Washington and the New Nation*, 79; Dunaway, *History of the James River and Kanawha Company*, 28–38, 50–55, 75, 100–104; Risjord, *Chesapeake Politics*, 245.

75. Watlington, *Partisan Spirit*, chaps. 2–3 passim; Risjord, *Chesapeake Politics*, 234–38; Abernethy, *Western Lands*, 249–55, 262–67, 296–309, 319–28; Jensen, *New Nation*, 334–35; Morris, *Forging of the Union*, 223, 225.

76. JM to George Muter, 7 January 1785, *PJM*, 1:133–34; Risjord, *Chesapeake Politics*, 237–40; Abernethy, *Western Lands*, 346–53.

77. JM to George Muter, 7 January 1785 and 11 February 1787, JM to Arthur Lee, 5 March 1787, *PJM*, 1:133–34, 204–6. The Latin phrases mean "strong in manner" and "gentle in deed."

Chapter 4

Virginia Nationalist, 1787–1791

John Marshall spent much of his public time and energy in the late 1780s and early 1790s trying to preserve the accomplishments and ideals of the Revolution in which he had fought. He believed, with good reason, that the increasingly unsettled political conditions of the mid–1780s threatened republican values and institutions, and he joined the nationalists' campaign to reform the Confederation. Serving as an important champion of the Framers' Constitution in a state that was essential to its adoption and success, at the Virginia ratifying convention Marshall advocated a stronger central government, with expanded fiscal, military, and judicial authority, as the best means of enabling the new nation to secure its independence and define itself politically and economically. He later played a prominent part in the ensuing ideological and proto-partisan conflicts over Alexander Hamilton's financial program, which was highly unpopular in Virginia. Marshall spurned national office for personal reasons, but he became a leader of the state's dwindling cadre of Washington administration supporters at a time when the former Antifederalists' growing domination of Virginia politics was forcing Federalists in the Commonwealth to break with the new government or pay a high political price.

By early 1787, the men whom Marshall later called the "enlightened friends of republican government" and "the wise and thinking part of the community," and whom historians commonly refer to as "nationalists," perceived that the republic was in peril because of the Confederation's inadequate powers and the state legislatures' abuses of authority. From these nationalists' vantage point—the contrary views of some modern historians, notably Merrill Jensen and his students, aside—the nation was in sorry shape. The postwar depression dragged on in many places, and Virginia's economy, which had recovered temporarily by mid-decade, was sliding into another downturn, largely because of falling tobacco prices. "Chesapeake planters," according to Richard B. Morris, "returned once more to their chronic condition of depression, characterized by lack of specie and an increasing indebtedness to British merchants above and beyond prewar debts which in many cases remained to be settled." Widespread economic distress, exacerbated by a money shortage, left many states unable to pay debts owed to the Confederation for prosecuting the war, and to indemnify British subjects for wartime losses, without raising taxes. The lingering depression and higher tax burden raised political and social tensions—most seriously in Massachusetts, but also in Virginia—and some state legislatures tried to stanch potential instability with prodebtor policies such as annulling contracts, delaying creditors' lawsuits, suspending tax collections, and printing paper money. The feckless Confederation lacked the constitutional authority, political will, and financial means to raise adequate revenue, regulate commerce, persuade the states to grant it more power, or defend the national interest against Great Britain and Spain, which continued to cause trouble on the western frontier.[1]

Of the many domestic and foreign problems enfeebling the Confederation, three stand out as key influences on Marshall's decision to join the campaign to expand the powers of the national government and restrict those of the states: separatism and intrigue on the frontier, state legislatures' abuses of power, and political and social unrest. Marshall's interest in the first subject was discussed in the previous chapter and need only be mentioned here. He was quite critical of the second development, which Jefferson referred to as "elective despotism"—state assemblies passing paper money and debtor relief laws and other measures that harmed creditors and violated individual property rights—even though Virginia's legislature was not notorious for enacting such laws. Nonetheless, in early 1787 Marshall feared the influence of debtor interests in the Virginia assembly, and he later wrote that

the general tendency of state politics convinced me that no safe and permanent remedy could be found but in a more efficient and better organized general government. The questions . . . which were perpetually recurring in the state legislatures and which brought annually into doubt principles which I thought most sound, which proved that everything was afloat, and that we had no safe anchorage ground, gave a high value in my estimation to that article in the constitution which imposes restrictions on the states.[2]

Domestic instability seems to have bothered Marshall more than any other development during the 1780s. He commented extensively on the uprising in Massachusetts in mid-1786 to early 1787 known as Shays's Rebellion. Extralegal committees and "out-of-doors" had run Massachusetts' western region conventions since around 1774. From this environment of confrontation arose protests by "Regulators," to the accompaniment of Revolutionary rhetoric and egalitarian sentiments, that led to the closing of courts, the intimidation of officials, and, eventually, violence. Faced in the mid-1780s with declining prices, bad harvests, mortgage foreclosures, high taxes, and imprisonment for debt, some 2,000 distressed farmers and laborers led by a former militia captain, Daniel Shays, took up arms. The rebels forcibly shut down several courts responsible for debt collection and effectively took control of a few counties. Their apparent objective, underscored by Shays's attack on a federal arsenal, was to overthrow the state government.[3]

This populist insurgency shocked and angered Marshall. It struck hard at his Virginia gentryman's sense of orderly representative government and aroused in him a fear that the Revolution had set in motion leveling forces that American political institutions might not be able to control. Contributing to Marshall's dismay was his belief—widely shared at the time—that Massachusetts had the soundest constitution of any state and should have been the last place where such an upheaval might occur. In January 1787, an alarmed Marshall—possibly influenced by Henry Knox's widely circulated letter to George Washington in September 1786 that described "12 or 15,000 desperate and unprincipled men" on the march seeking "a common division of property, [and] annihilation of all debts"—declared that "[a]ll is gloom in the eastern states."

Massachusetts is rent into two equal factions and an appeal I fear has by this time been made to the God of battles. . . . Whatever may be the cause of these dissentions or however they may terminate . . . they deeply affect the happiness and reputation of the United States. . . . These violent, I fear bloody, dissentions in a state I had thought inferior in wisdom and virtue to no one in the union, added to the strong tendency which the politics of many eminent characters among ourselves have to promote private and public dishonesty[,] cast a deep shade over that bright prospect which the revolution in America and the establishment of our free governments had opened to the votaries of liberty throughout the globe. I fear, and there is no opinion more degrading to the dignity of man, that these have truth on their side who say that man is incapable of governing himself. I fear we may live to see another revolution.[4]

Writing later as a partisan historian, Marshall ascribed the "formidable and wicked rebellion" in Massachusetts to wartime indebtedness, high taxes, "lax notions concerning public and private faith," and "erroneous opinions which confound liberty with an exemption from legal control." These factors combined to foster a "disorderly spirit . . . cherished by unlicensed conventions, which, after voting their own constitutionality, and assuming the name of the people, arrayed themselves against the legislature," vented their hostility against Revolutionary veterans' pensions and taxes, and demanded circulation of paper money. "Against lawyers and courts," however, "the strongest resentments were manifested; . . . in many instances, tumultuous assemblages of people arrested the course of law, and restrained the judges from proceeding in the execution of their duty." Marshall thought Shays's uprising delivered a mortal blow to the Confederation and "demonstrated . . . the indispensable necessity of clothing government with powers sufficiently ample for the protection of the rights of the peaceable and quiet, from the invasions of the licentious and turbulent part of the community."[5]

Massachusetts officials' concessions to the insurgents and the Confederation's reluctance to send federal troops against them only intensified the spirit of sedition, according to Marshall; "the forbearance of the government was attributed to timidity rather than to moderation" and "the ordinary recourse to the power of the country was found an insufficient protection." A small, privately recruited force, however, routed the poorly organized, poorly led rebels by February 1787. Marshall lauded the suppression and encouraged harsh punishment of the perpetrators to set an example for future dissidents. A month after Shays's defeat, he wrote that "their [Massachusetts'] government will now stand more firmly than before the insurrection provided some examples are made in order to impress on the minds of the people a conviction that punishment will surely follow an attempt to subvert the laws & government of the Commonwealth."[6]

The rebellion in Massachusetts also evoked in Marshall and other nationalists a sense of urgency because the contagion of backcountry resistance soon spread from Massachusetts into New England and as far south as South Carolina. Virginia experienced its own minor episodes of protest and violence against debt and tax collection. These incidents undoubtedly worried Marshall, although he did not mention them specifically. In April 1787, residents of Caroline County formed an association to boycott the sale of property for debt. In May, the courthouses in King William and New Kent Counties were burned down, and all records were destroyed. In August, "disorderly people of desperate circumstances" in Amelia County obstructed the session of the debtor court, according to Beverly Randolph, and in Greenbrier County "the course of Justice has been mutinously stopped, and associations entered into against the payment of taxes," James Madison reported. Throughout Virginia in 1787, he informed Jefferson, "the prisons and Court Houses and clerks' offices [have been] willfully burnt."[7]

The spread of domestic unrest in the wake of the Confederation's timid response to Shays's uprising was especially galling for Marshall as a Continental Army veteran with strong sympathies for the many former military colleagues he had as friends, associates, and clients in Virginia. These veterans resented the Confederation for failing to pay their military pensions—Marshall, for example, wrote understandingly of the Newburgh conspirators that they "had wasted their fortunes and their prime of life in unrewarded service, fearing, with reason, that Congress possessed neither the power nor the inclination to comply with its engagements to the army"—and for disbanding the army, leaving only a tiny force incapable of dealing with frontier disorders, separatist threats, Indian raids, Spanish intrigues, and British troops still on American territory. Many of these disgruntled ex-officers consequently banded together with some nationalist-minded politicians and financiers to form what Richard B. Morris has aptly termed the "military-fiscal complex" that worked on the state and national levels to strengthen the military and fiscal powers of the Confederation. Marshall falls in this grouping because his political views and legislative record favored a stronger central government; as a lawyer, he advocated the interests of veterans, creditors, and merchants; and he had extensive connections to land speculators and financiers outside Virginia. The "complex" began as a circle of energetic and opportunely placed men, centered in the middle states but supported by public creditors and sympathizers elsewhere, linked with a shared cosmopolitan perspective on political and economic matters and with ties to the group's dominant figure, Robert Morris. They were, according to Marshall, "sincerely disposed to do ample justice to the public creditors . . . and to that class of them particularly whose claims were founded in military service." The nationalists' efforts to enhance the Confederation's powers had stalled by 1786, but the agrarian unrest of 1786–87 revitalized them by raising the specter of insurrection at a time when the Confederation lacked the means and will to suppress it.[8]

Thus, Marshall and other "men of enlarged and liberal minds," as he later called them, "could discern the imbecility of the nation" and "perceive the dangers to which these young republics [the states] were exposed, if not held together by a cement capable of preserving beneficial connexion; . . . felt the full value of national honour, and the full obligation of national faith; and . . . were persuaded of the insecurity of both, if resting for their preservation on the concurrent of thirteen distinct sovereigns." Marshall and these nationalists "struggled with unabated zeal for the exact observance of public and private engagements" because "the faith of a nation, or of a private man[,] was deemed a sacred pledge, the violation of which was equally forbidden by the principles of moral justice, and of sound policy" which dictated that "the distresses of individuals . . . were to be alleviated only by industry and frugality, not by a relaxation of the laws, or by a sacrifice of the rights of others." More specifically, these men espoused "a regular administration of justice, and . . . a vigorous course of taxation," and "[b]y a natural association of ideas, they were also in favour of enlarging the powers of the federal government, and of enabling it to protect the dignity and character of the nation abroad, and its interests at home."[9]

With those purposes in mind, Marshall, "though devoted to my profession, entered with a good deal of spirit" into Virginia politics again. He was elected for the third time to the House of Delegates on 2 April 1787, representing Henrico County, and attended the fall session beginning in mid-October.[10]

The Constitutional Convention in Philadelphia adjourned just a month before the House of Delegates session opened, and practically everything that occurred during the fall term fell in the shadow of the Framers' work. The proposed Constitution dominated the delegates' discussions and directed their deliberations. Marshall and his fellow members drafted, argued, and enacted laws and resolutions, and talked and dined in taverns and private homes, with a brooding awareness that their actions would directly influence the outcome of the ratification struggle in Virginia and possibly the country. Even issues of no constitutional import were seen as measures of prevailing moods. The constitutional debate had captured the public's attention like nothing since the

Revolution, and for the first time in years, there was a quorum on the first day of the House session. The delegates received the proposed Constitution from Governor Edmund Randolph on 15 October when the term opened, and 10 days later they unanimously authorized a ratification convention. After that, Marshall and his colleagues took up several familiar but crucial issues—British debts, paper money and debtor relief, navigation of the Mississippi, reform of the state court system—with a keen eye toward winning support for their views on ratification.[11]

The House of Delegates had become more polarized regionally and ideologically during the mid-1780s and was roughly divided into two loose coalitions when Marshall rejoined it.[12] The voting blocs can be discerned from analyses of the roll calls on mostly economic legislation during the 1785–87 sessions. One bloc comprised mainly delegates from the Piedmont and Southside who displayed a basically localist perspective and usually sympathized with the interests of debtors, small farmers, the less well off, and social newcomers. This set of delegates opposed paying debts to the British and taking power away from the county courts, and supported laws that deferred payment of private debts, lowered taxes, and established a paper currency. The other, larger bloc consisted mostly of delegates from the lower James River Valley—Marshall was one—the Northern Neck, and the West who, for the most part, had a nationalist or cosmopolitan outlook and normally backed the interests of creditors, merchants, large planters, professionals, the well-to-do, and established families. These delegates supported enforcement of treaty obligations and expanding the state court system, and opposed laws that altered contracts and inflated the currency.

Terms such as "faction" and "party" are inappropriate for these alignments, however, and the regional and economic distinctions described above must not be thought of as a simplistic, hard-and-fast, Beardian-type dichotomy. The blocs had not coalesced fully and had no organizations or defined constituencies, and personalities still greatly affected the outcomes of many elections. Marshall's election in April 1787 exemplifies the last point. His decision to run seems to have occasioned little if any opposition or comment, and his mere announcement was tantamount to success even though he had not held state office since 1784.

By the time the fall session ended in January 1788, Marshall had been involved with several measures or activities that promoted the interests of the nationalist-creditor bloc and helped improve the prospects for ratification of the proposed Constitution. The legislation Marshall worked on and supported that was most directly linked in debate to the draft Constitution was the repeal of laws impeding the collection of British debts. This proposal drew fire from opponents who feared that the Constitution's grant to federal courts of jurisdiction over "Controversies . . . Between a State, or the Citizens thereof, and foreign states, Citizens, or Subjects," and the national supremacy clause in Article V, would intrude the national government into economic matters properly left to individuals and the states. Marshall helped draft the repeal law passed on 12 December with an amendment suspending it until Britain complied with all terms of the peace treaty; he voted against including the amendment. Marshall also served on a special House commission which concluded that the Confederation had inadequately reimbursed Virginia for Revolutionary War expenses when the state ceded its western lands in 1784. The commission's finding on this sensitive subject probably encouraged proratification sentiment by adding to the evidence of the Confederation's unreliability. In addition, Marshall helped write a bill for establishing district courts, which creditors had long sought to speed up debt suits that tended to languish in the county courts. Marshall voted against the final bill, but for reasons unrelated to debtor-creditor matters. During this session, the House also established a sinking fund to pay off Virginia's war debt, enacted some minor debtor relief legislation, and passed resolutions condemning paper money and asserting that Virginians had a God-given right to navigate the Mississippi River. Marshall's positions on these matters are not recorded, but, judging from his other votes and views, it is likely that he would have supported all of them.[13]

The motion on 25 October to summon a convention to consider the proposed Constitution created "a great ferment," according to Edmund Randolph. Marshall recalled that "Mr. P. Henry, Mr. G. Mason, and several other gentlemen of great influence were much opposed to it, and permitted no opportunity to escape of inveighing against it and of communicating their prejudices to others." Although most Virginians believed the legislature should submit the Constitution to a state convention, the important question was, on what terms? During debate, Henry and Mason claimed that the key resolution, "That a Convention should be called, according to the recommendation of Congress," implied that the convention could not propose amendments—which they hoped to use to eviscerate the draft Constitution. Marshall thought the Constitution should be considered as it stood, but, realizing that the adopt-or-reject attitude would make the proratification side appear authoritarian and intransigent, he immediately offered compromise language that the proceedings of the Philadelphia Convention "be submitted to a convention of the people, for their full and free investigation and discussion." He chose this wording carefully. Without mentioning possible amendments, it neither precluded them nor suggested that Virginia would oppose the Constitution without them. Marshall's "happy and politick resolution," as Randolph described it, prevented the antiratification forces from setting the convention's ground rules. With no other state conventions having yet met, Marshall did not want Virginia—already perceived as one of the crucial states in the contest—to send the signal that the Constitution could be ratified only with significant changes. The House approved his change unanimously.[14]

The delegates also agreed, while appropriating funds to pay the expenses for the convention, to set aside other monies in case it adopted amendments that required a second national convention to consider them. Marshall and the other supporters of ratification opposed a second convention because they believed it would give antiratification forces another opportunity to weaken the

Constitution. Marshall and his allies failed to block the funding resolutions in the committee of the whole, but they were able to work out compromise language so that the final measures contained no references to a second convention. Next, supporters and opponents of ratification—by this time widely referred to as "Federalists" and "Antifederalists"—agreed to set the date for the convention as late as possible, in June 1788, but did so for different tactical reasons. Federalists wanted to capitalize on any momentum that prior ratifications had built up, while Antifederalists sought time to organize alliances with kindred spirits in other states, and to convert a general uneasiness toward the Framers' constitution into a broad, concerted opposition.[15]

As 1787 ended, proponents of ratification grew gloomier about their prospects for success. Marshall recalled that "[i]n the course of the [House of Delegates] session, the unceasing efforts of the enemies of the constitution made a deep impression; and before its close, a great majority showed a decided hostility to it." Before the session began, Madison had declared to Jefferson that "a very decided majority of the Assembly is said to be zealously in favor of the New Constitution." As the session wound down, he informed Washington that "the present Assembly may perhaps be regarded as pleading most powerfully the cause of the new Government, for it is impossible for stronger proofs to be found than in their conduct, of the necessity of some such anchor against the fluctuations which threaten shipwreck to our liberty." Madison perceived that opinion on the Constitution in Virginia had formed into three blocs: "The first for adopting without attempting Amendments . . . the 2d. party which urges amendments . . . [and] a third class, at the head of which is Mr. Henry." Marshall—along with, most prominently, George Washington, Henry ("Light-Horse Harry") Lee, and Madison—fell into the first category, probably the smallest of the three. Those who supported ratification with "a few additional Guards in favor of the Rights of the States and of the people" included George Mason, Edmund Randolph, Edmund Pendleton, Richard Henry Lee, and George Wythe. Joining Henry in the "third class"—which "concurs at present with the patrons of amendments, but will probably contend for such as strike at the essence of the System"—were, among others, William Grayson, Benjamin Harrison, John Tyler, and Spencer Roane. (The second group, which wanted amendments, actually was split into two subgroups that differed over whether to add them either before or after ratification.)[16]

These alignments took shape amid an unprecedentedly extensive and thorough public debate in Virginia that began soon after the Framers left Philadelphia and ended nine months later with the Antifederalists having won the support of most eligible voters—60 percent, according to the best recent estimate. Federalists and their opponents fully aired their views through dozens of newspaper articles, publications, speeches, and meetings throughout the state. As a start, the text of the Constitution was quickly made available to the public. It first appeared in a Virginia newspaper only a few days after the Philadelphia Convention adjourned; within weeks, it was printed in several more papers and as broadsides and pamphlets; and the state assembly ordered 5,000 more copies for public distribution. In addition, Marshall and other Virginians had access to a voluminous array of local and out-of-state commentaries, pamphlets, anthologies, and reports of proceedings and debates in other states' conventions, which covered, in polemical or analytical fashion, all aspects of the Constitution's history, theory and mechanics. The first numbers of *The Federalist* appeared in Virginia newspapers in December 1787, and the first volume of the book version was available the following April, at which time Marshall bought his own copy. Marshall may also have attended two proratification functions held in the Richmond area in late 1787. The first, a rally in Henrico County in October, was one of at least eight such meetings that Federalists used as forums to extol the Constitution and instruct state legislators to support the calling of a state convention. The second was a series of debates by the Union (or Political) Society of Richmond during November and December, which led to a lopsided vote in favor of ratification. The result was noted in the letters of several prominent Virginians and in some out-of-state newspapers.[17]

Virginia's decision to approve or reject the proposed Constitution, however, would rest not on majority sentiment forged through the free and open exchange of ideas, but with 173 men chosen by freeholders in elections held throughout the state on the first scheduled court day in March. Marshall did not say when or how he decided to stand for election as a delegate to the ratifying convention. George Washington or James Madison may have prevailed upon him to run, but the circumstances of his return to state politics in early 1788 suggest that he needed no prodding. The election in Henrico County where Marshall ran was held on 3 March. The other candidates were Edmund Randolph, perceived as a mild Antifederalist although he kept his exact views to himself, and William Foushee, the decidedly Antifederalist county sheriff and former mayor of Richmond. Sentiment in Henrico leaned heavily against the Constitution, although Richmond—not yet entitled to its own convention delegate—was strongly Federalist. No accounts of the campaign in Henrico exist, but Marshall and his opponents probably resorted to the traditional Virginia methods of "treating" the freeholders and making speeches at the polling place on election day. On 29 February, Randolph wrote that "Marshall is in danger, but F. [Foushee] is not popular enough on other scores to be elected, altho he is perfectly a Henryite." When the last vote was cast four days later, Marshall had edged past Foushee, 198 to 187, while Randolph finished well ahead with 373 votes; the two highest votegetters went to the convention. Marshall later attributed his victory to "private affections," and he no doubt drew nearly all his support from clients, veterans, Masons, political associates, and friends and relatives in and around Richmond.[18]

In Henrico County and throughout Virginia, all the constitutional discourse, newspapers "teem[ing] with the productions of temperate reason, or genius, and of passion," as Marshall described them, public meetings, and hotly contested elections in many counties did not seem to excite the voters. Turnout for Virginia's first single-issue election was very low, suggesting that the animated debate took place mainly among members of the politically active urban and planter elite, and that most Virginians outside cities with newspapers or areas with ready access to them either knew little about the issues surrounding the proposed Constitution, were confused by the relative merits of preratification or postratification amendments, or registered their vague wariness about the whole process by staying away from the polls.[19]

The statewide results diminished some of Marshall's and the other Virginia Federalists' earlier pessimism, as most reliable accounts soon after the election gave them a slight majority in the upcoming convention. Proratification delegates had won the Tidewater, Northern Neck, and Valley regions, while antiratification sentiment dominated the Southside and the Piedmont. Quite a few delegates, however, went on record as undecided. The western districts held the balance, and signs that Kentucky would go Antifederalist worried Marshall and his compatriots. They knew that Kentucky had several good reasons to oppose the Constitution, especially the near surrender of navigation rights on the Mississippi under the unratified Jay-Gardoqui Treaty; Congress's reluctance to admit the District of Kentucky, separated from Virginia in September 1787, into the Union; the provision in Article I, section 8 granting qualified federal authority over the militia; and the remoteness of the federal court system, which would have jurisdiction over many economic suits involving Kentuckians. The bad news came in April: Kentucky had elected a predominantly Antifederalist delegation. As June drew near, Marshall and his Federalist allies lived with the anticipation that at the convention they would face a powerful and sophisticated opposition with political, oratorical, and intellectual abilities at least equal to their own. Unlike in the northern states, where notable proponents of the Constitution had eclipsed their relatively unknown and inexperienced rivals, Marshall and the Virginia Federalists had to contend with a group of Antifederalists every bit as prominent and capable as themselves.[20]

The convention opened on Monday, 2 June—a hot, dry day, the latest in a drought that had parched the countryside around Richmond for weeks. The dusty streets of the city had bustled the night before with horses, carriages, and coaches carrying delegates, visitors, and their attendants, shouting instructions to liverymen and calling for directions from passersby. (The stagecoach company had moved up its schedule a day and added vehicles to ensure that the delegates arrived on time.) The taverns and rooming houses—such as the Swan, where George Mason, Patrick Henry, James Madison, and Edmund Pendleton stayed, and Formicola's, which was Marshall's favorite—had been completely booked weeks earlier, and that Sunday evening, a merchant recalled, they were filled until late with the din of "debate & altercation in all companies." Although his mind was occupied with thoughts about the next day's events, Marshall no doubt found time to fret about how all the noise and commotion outside his home would upset Polly's delicate constitution. In anticipation of frequent entertaining while the convention was in session, he had spruced up his wardrobe and stocked up on wine and food.[21]

The next morning, Marshall walked the several blocks to the convention's first session at the Old Capitol, a three-story clapboard building about 50 feet square at Cary and Fourteenth Streets. The structure, which still served as Virginia's temporary statehouse, was too small and warm to hold the delegates and crowds of spectators comfortably, so after selecting a president and dispensing with a few parliamentary matters, the convention decided to meet the next morning at the nearby New Academy, an elegant, French-style school with a commodious assembly hall used for balls, concerts, and plays. For the next three and one-half weeks, Marshall and the other delegates met there daily, except Sunday, from 9:00 or 10:00 A.M. until around 4:00 P.M. They assembled on the main floor, while hundreds of onlookers packed the boxes and galleries above them. "We have every day a gay circle of ladies to hear the debates," wrote one delegate, "and have the pleasure of believing them all Federalists."[22]

Never before had Marshall been in such distinguished company. The Virginia convention surpassed all other state assemblages—and probably was second only to Philadelphia's—in the intellect, rhetorical ability, political skill and experience, and social stature of its delegates, and nowhere outside the Framers' meeting were the Constitution and its implications examined with such thoroughness, intensity, and insight. The delegates included scions of the gentry, large planters, leading legislators, lawyers, and jurists, as well as merchants, professionals, and small farmers. Three fourths had served in the legislature, and 20 were among the state's wealthiest men. Although three of the Commonwealth's notables were absent—George Washington, Thomas Jefferson, and Richard Henry Lee—most of Virginia's ablest public figures attended, including Madison, Mason, Henry, Pendleton, Edmund Randolph, George Wythe, Paul Carrington, John Tyler, William Grayson, George Nicholas, John Blair, Wilson Cary Nicholas, James Innes, Henry Lee, Benjamin Harrison, Archibald Stuart, William Fleming, and Nathaniel Burwell.[23]

Although many of these eminencies made important informal and private contributions to the convention, just 23 of the delegates spoke during the session, and only seven shaped the debate. The principal Federalist participants were Madison, Pendleton, Randolph (who declared his support for ratification just as the convention opened), George Nicholas, and Marshall; the key Antifederalists were Henry (he spoke on 18 of the 23 days) and Mason. When the debates formally began on 4 June, eight states had already ratified. The outcome in Virginia would influence, if not determine, the result in the upcoming New York convention, and Marshall and his fellow delegates knew that without those states' ratifications, the "more perfect union" probably would be only a hollow alliance.

The Federalist leaders considered Marshall a potential parliamentary asset and brought him into their planning conclaves, but his overall role in the debates was less significant than the labors of Madison, Pendleton, Randolph, and Nicholas, and his early activities at the convention were unnoteworthy. His first important work was on a committee that determined the validity of delegates' elections. After gathering evidence in several disputes, however, the committee replaced only one. Marshall did not speak in debate during the first week and instead listened and learned, as he did in court, while the two sides carried out their respective strategies. The Antifederalists—especially the theatrical Henry, whom Marshall derogated as a rabble-rouser—launched a wide-ranging but disorganized attack on a few of the Constitution's vulnerable points, particularly its alleged illegitimacy and the dangers it purportedly posed to American liberty. The Federalists, in contrast, presented a somewhat more methodical and cohesive defense of the Framers' work, using an assortment of theoretical, political, and historical arguments to justify specific clauses and provisions. Over the next two weeks, Marshall would become fully engaged in the activities on the convention floor, speaking in debate three times and providing key rebuttals of powerful Antifederalist arguments. His speeches offer important insights into his and the Federalists' perspectives on the fiscal, military, and judicial powers of the proposed national government. He also joined in the evening politicking at Richmond's taverns and public houses, where his congeniality combined with the plentiful food and drink to make him a persuasive advocate for ratification.[24]

Before examining Marshall's addresses, note should be taken of some of the biases and shortcomings of the three principal sources for his speeches and for the Virginia convention generally—David Robertson's *Debates and Other Proceedings of the Convention of Virginia* (1788), Jonathan Elliot's *Debates in the Several State Conventions* (1836), and Hugh Grigsby's *History of the Virginia Federal Convention of 1788* (1890–91)—and the ways in which those problems might affect an understanding of Marshall's ideas. Some Antifederalists, notably Mason, questioned whether Robertson, chosen by the Federalist majority, would fairly serve as the convention's stenographer, and at times he could not hear the speeches or, according to some delegates, he recounted them inaccurately. Marshall, for example, many years later reportedly claimed that "if my name had not have been prefixed to the speaches [*sic*] I never should have recognized them as productions of mine," although he did not say where or how Robertson's rendering was faulty. Regarding Elliot's compilation, contemporaries knew that it was highly inaccurate, and a recent analysis suggests that Elliot altered his edition to advance the political ideas of John C. Calhoun. Obvious doctoring is not readily discernible in Marshall's remarks, but a few open-ended statements, contradictions, and imprecisions could be attributed to Elliot's supposed predilections. In any event, the differences between the work of the Federalist Robertson and the Jacksonian Democrat Elliot are insignificant, at least where Marshall is concerned. Finally, Grigsby's detailed secondary account is mildly sympathetic to the Antifederalists, and although he favorably portrays Marshall, he does not convey the sharpness of Marshall's arguments that is evident in the primary sources.[25]

Marshall first rose before the convention on 10 June, "a tall young man, slovenly dressed in loose summer apparel, with piercing black eyes," according to eyewitnesses. His friend James Monroe, an Antifederalist, had just finished a scholarly exegesis of classical and contemporary political systems, but Marshall did not intend to answer him or to complement the speeches of Lee and Randolph from the day before. Instead, Marshall had prepared his address the previous weekend as the premier public expression of his approval of the Constitution, and as his rebuttal of Henry's harsh attacks of 7 and 9 June on the proposed revenue power of the new government. He probably appeared on this occasion, his first major public address, in the same stiff manner he would display in a courtroom a few years later: "His voice is dry and hard; his attitude, in his most effective orations, was often extremely awkward; as it was not unusual for him to stand with his left foot in advance, while all his gestures proceeded from his right arm, and consisted merely in a vehement, perpendicular swing of it, from about the elevation of his head, to the bar." In a long, loosely structured discourse, Marshall parried most of Henry's thrusts and asserted most of the Federalists' tenets: a pessimistic view of human nature; the need for a "well-regulated democracy" protected by a strong central government with adequate powers over "the sword and the purse"; the inability of the Confederation to protect private property, to reform itself, or to defend the nation from hostile foreign powers; and the use of history and experience as guides for the people's representatives. As ever, Marshall spoke as a lawyer, not a politician, relying on the strength of his arguments and his incisive criticism of his opponents' positions and reasoning, not on the power and style of his rhetoric.[26]

Marshall's speech pleased the Federalist leaders—Madison, for example, said he had "entered into the subject with a great deal of ability"—and they decided to let him refute charges by Mason, Henry, and William Grayson that the Constitution would deprive the states of authority over their militias and introduce one of the gravest threats to republicanism, a standing army. In a short and pointed address on 16 June, Marshall endorsed the Constitution's provisions for a small national military establishment and a federalized militia, with some Whiggish safeguards included. Diversified state control of the militia would be ineffective in a national crisis, he argued; "It is . . . necessary to give the Government that power in time of peace, which the necessities of war will render indispensable, or else we shall be attacked unprepared." Marshall used the Federalists' rhetorical appropriation of popular sovereignty to contend that bestowing this power on the central government would not endanger liberty: "[A]s the Government was drawn from the people, the feelings and interests of the people would be attended to . . . When the Government is drawn from the people . . . oppressive measures will not be attempted." He further noted that the Constitution did not divest the states of their traditional authority to arm and train citizen-soldiers. Marshall's views on military preparedness and centralized control, drawn in large part from his Revolutionary War experience, conformed to the essential principles of Federalist military theory, which was well developed by 1788. His address prompted immediate impassioned replies from Henry and Grayson.[27]

For the next three days, Marshall sat quietly while the delegates debated slavery, a bill of rights, the treaty-making power, and presidential election procedures. Then the discussion turned once again to the contentious issue of the federal judiciary. From the opening of the convention, Henry had attacked the Constitution's provisions for a national court system, playing upon fears of federal judges serving as collection agents for British creditors or seizing frontiersmen's land on behalf of eastern speculators. On 19 June, Mason presented a lengthy criticism of the new system as auguring the destruction of the state courts and the erosion of individual liberties, and Henry added more extravagant oratory about justice's imminent demise. Edmund Pendleton, the Commonwealth's most venerated jurist and the Virginia Federalists' elder statesman, had not yet recovered from an illness and gave a halting, barely audible reply while tottering on crutches. The Federalist leaders knew that unless they responded more effectively to Mason and Henry on this highly charged issue, they could lose several crucial votes. They turned to Marshall to give a point-by-point rebuttal.[28]

Marshall proceeded to make his ablest speech of the convention. Relying either on his own careful notes or a transcript from the convention's stenographer, he prepared a detailed rejoinder to Mason's speech that drew on his knowledge of legal procedures, court jurisdictions, and the development of legal systems. He did not present a positive theoretical or practical case for the proposed national courts. Instead, he employed his characteristic unremitting logic to turn the Antifederalists' points against them with carefully framed arguments that demonstrated the factual misstatements, analytical inconsistencies, and unsupportable presumptions that underlay their criticisms that the Constitution would override state and local courts and laws and did not guarantee a federal right of trial by jury. Marshall also asserted that the national courts could protect liberty by exercising judicial review over congressional acts. Finally, he noted that federal and state courts shared jurisdiction over many kinds of cases. (It seems safe to say—although Marshall dared not do so then—that he preferred more national uniformity of law, and probably believed that, as the only practical way to uphold the supremacy clause in Article V, the federal courts had authority to review state laws as well.)[29]

After Marshall's speech, the debate subsided. The crucial arguments had been made, and the heat, anxiety, and pressure for decision had taken their toll of the delegates. No one was sure which side would win when George Wythe on 24 June moved that the convention "should ratify the Constitution, and that whatsoever amendments might be deemed necessary, should be recommended to the consideration of Congress which should first assemble under the Constitution." After final pleas from Henry and Randolph—the former's forebodings were drowned out by a violent thunderstorm——the roll was called the next day on an Antifederalist resolution to ratify with amendments. The vote, conducted alphabetically by county, was so close that a Federalist victory was not assured until the roll call reached 82–80 against the resolution; the final tally was 88–80. The delegates then voted 89–79 to ratify without prior amendments, and Virginia became the tenth and most important state so far to approve the Constitution. Marshall's last activities at the convention involved serving on two committees that prepared a form of ratification—the official document that would be sent to Congress—and drafted 40 amendments to recommend to Congress, a 20-article declaration of rights and 20 structural changes intended to preserve the power of the states. No details of Marshall's work on these committees exist, but presumably he tried to restrain efforts to reduce the national government's authority. After approving the committees' work, the convention then adjourned with "due decorum and solemnity," according to Madison.[30]

For the next several days, Richmond remained quiet. "There is no rejoicing on account of the vote," lawyer Spencer Roane observed. "It would not be prudent to do so, and the federalists . . . do not exult in their success." The victors were "either wise enough, or polite enough, to make no procession or parade," according to a local newspaper. Marshall probably attended some of the celebrations that were finally held on the Fourth of July, when the city's greens, taverns, and dining rooms reverberated with cannon salutes, cheers, and toasts to "American union and public liberty" and to "the great epoch of American honor, happiness, and glory." For his contribution to bringing about the *novus ordo seclorum*, Marshall earned £13.[31]

Historians and political scientists have studied Virginia's ratifying convention more than any other because its approval of the Constitution was indispensable to the charter's success. Edmund Randolph did not exaggerate when he told the delegates on the final day of debate that their choice was between "union or no union." Many scholars have attempted to explain the crucial outcome in Virginia by identifying the key economic, political, social, and ideological dynamics that they believe motivated or determined the delegates' votes. Most of these studies have stressed one or more starkly contrasting qualities as representing the vital distinctions between the Federalists and Antifederalists. These polarities have included personalty and realty, cosmopolitanism and localism, commercialism and agrarianism, elitism and democracy, youth and age, energy and inertia, prestige and inferiority, court and country, and even good and evil. Other examinations have taken issue with some of these dichotomies but have still been confined by them. A recent cliometric analysis tested the Virginia delegates' votes against many socioeconomic variables and concluded that the Federalists tended to be relatively wealthy, better educated, and younger, and had out-of-state experiences, contacts, or loyalties derived from Continental Army service or economic interests.[32]

John Marshall fell into nearly every socioeconomic category of Virginia's delegates that voted marginally to overwhelmingly Federalist. He was a moderately wealthy professional living in a commercial city, and a Continental Army veteran with economic connections outside the Old Dominion. In his own analysis of Virginia's ratification, however, and in his recollection of his own motivations, Marshall ascribed support for the Constitution "at least as much to casual circumstances as to judgement" and to the influences of powerful individuals in close contests. "So balanced were parties in some of them," Marshall wrote in his biography of Washington, "and so small, in many instances, was the majority in its favour, as to afford strong ground for the opinion that, had the influence of character been removed, the intrinsic merits of the instrument would not have secured its adoption."[33]

In explaining his vote for ratification, Marshall stressed his sentiment of nationalism formed from his allegiance with the Patriot side during the Revolution, his service in the Continental Army, and his exposure to the weaknesses of the state governments during and after the war.

I had grown up at a time when a love of union and resistance to the claims of Great Britain were the inseparable inmates of the same bosom;—when patriotism and a strong fellow feeling with our suffering fellow citizens of Boston were identical;—when the maxim "united we stand, divided we fall" was the maxim of every orthodox American; and I had imbibed these sentiments so thoughroughly [sic] that they constituted a part of my being. I carried them with me into the army where I found myself associated with brave men from different states who were risking life and everything valuable in a common cause believed by all to be most precious; and where I was confirmed in the habit of considering America as my country, and congress as my government. I partook largely of the sufferings and feelings of the army, and brought with me into civil life an ardent devotion to its interests. My immediate entrance into the state legislature opened to my view the causes which had been chiefly instrumental in augmenting those sufferings, and I was consequently a determined advocate for its adoption.[34]

The ratification debate taught Marshall several valuable political lessons and probably changed the way he conceived that politics should be conducted. It underscored for him the changes that had occurred in Virginia politics during the 1780s and showed him the usefulness of tactics and techniques that he and the Federalists would employ in later battles with the Republicans. Marshall recognized that issues—increasingly, ideological ones—rather than personalities were becoming the primary factors in political contests because they polarized opinion and enhanced the role of the electorate. The struggle over ratification also showed Marshall the importance of a well-organized, more sophisticated effort to publicize views, identify interests, predict votes, and obtain commitments of support. Moreover, the debate required Marshall and the other Virginia Federalists to refocus their attention from local to national issues, and they began building a political network outside the state that would give them timely information and assessments from well-placed allies in Philadelphia, New York, and elsewhere.[35]

This nationalization of Virginia's politics would profoundly affect Marshall, forcing him out of the private sphere into which he wanted to withdraw. "I willingly relinquished public life to devote myself to my profession . . . My practice had become very considerable, and I could not spare from its claims on me so much time as would be necessary to maintain such a standing in the legislature as I was desirous of preserving," he wrote years later. But as much as he preferred to concentrate on his law practice and his family, with at most occasional excursions into local and state politics, his prominence at the convention and his contacts with key figures in the new federal government drew him out of his provincial domain into the realm of national affairs. Recognizing the fragility of the Federalists' victory, he decided, after a brief respite, to resume active engagement in securing that victory by promoting and defending the Washington administration's policies in the Virginia House of Delegates.[36]

In the nine months after the ratifying convention, Marshall witnessed the Federalists in Virginia suffer several serious political setbacks. During the fall 1788 assembly session, the Antifederalists tried to regain what they had lost in the convention and assert control of Commonwealth politics. Outnumbering the Federalists nearly two to one, Antifederalists in the House of Delegates unseated a prominent Federalist representative, passed a resolution calling for a second convention, helped choose two Antifederalist U.S. senators, and sent an address to Congress affirming their opposition to the Constitution in its present form. Led by Patrick Henry, the Antifederalists were better organized than the Federalists, whose leaders, James Madison and Henry Lee, were in New York at the final meetings of the Continental Congress. St. John de Crèvecoeur wrote to Jefferson about "how rankly antifederal" the Assembly had become, and Richard Bland Lee lamented that "the friends of the new government, being all young and inexperienced, form but a feeble band against them." Virginia Federalists recovered some ground in the elections for U.S. representatives and presidential electors held in early 1789—Federalist candidates won seven of 10 congressional seats and nine of 12 contests for elector—but these victories were less clear-cut than they seemed. Several of the Federalist representatives wanted substantial changes in the Constitution, and the public's expectation that George Washington would be chosen president exaggerated the support for Federalist electors. Most Virginia Federalists were despondent by the time the new government began functioning in the spring of 1789.[37]

Marshall, believing that the Antifederalists' resurgence threatened "those great principles of public policy which I considered as essential to the general happiness," decided to return to state politics in 1789. In December 1788, the legislature passed an act giving Richmond its own delegate, and friends and colleagues pressed Marshall to represent the strongly Federalist capital in the fall 1789 assembly session. Marshall wrote that he "yielded to the general wish . . . partly because I found the hostility to the [national] government so strong in the legislature as to require from its friends all the support they could give it." He ruled out holding national office, however, as a way to help the Federalist administration. He declined President Washington's nomination as U.S. district attorney for Virginia—even at the risk of embarrassing the chief executive, as the Senate had already confirmed him—and fended off pleas that he run for the House of Representatives seat from the mid-Tidewater district. Marshall was not then willing to inconvenience his personal and professional life or to possibly reduce his influence in Virginia by moving to New York or becoming closely identified with the national government. He decided, though, that serving for a few months in the state assembly near his home was a less disruptive yet politically useful way for him to answer the call of duty he was hearing. In late April 1789, he was elected to the House of Delegates for the fourth time.[38]

Marshall and the other Federalist delegates began their work in mid-October a bit inauspiciously.[39] The roof of the unfinished state Capitol building leaked, and a flu outbreak felled many legislators. They also were thrown off balance because the Washington administration and the Federalist Congress had engaged in controversies or enacted policies that had weakened them politically in Virginia and strained their relations with political allies in the northern states. First came the matter of executive titles and ceremony. The Federalists had sought to bestow legitimacy on the new government by imparting to it a Roman standard of duty, dignity, and simplicity.   Intentions aside, however, the seriocomic bickering in Congress over how to address the president and whether Washington's somewhat aloof and formal conduct of presidential business smacked of monarchism had raised sincere questions about the Federalists' devotion to republican values among Virginians, who prided themselves on their adherence to such ideals. The debate—which Marshall blandly recounted in his biography of Washington—not only made him and the Federalist minority in Virginia targets of political attack by erstwhile Antifederalists there; it also opened a rift between them and northern Federalists, who were the strongest advocates of a more "aristocratic" presidential etiquette.

Second, two of the Federalists' revenue measures, the protective tariff and the duty on shipping tonnage, tested Marshall's and the Virginia Federalists' loyalty to the administration and their willingness to maintain a national perspective on economic issues.   The tariff measure clearly protected only northern manufactures; coverage for some southern staples, including tobacco, meant little because they were not imported, and Virginians would have to pay more for items that were. Virginia Federalists could do little, however, but suppress their sectional concerns and support the tariff as essential for helping establish the financial soundness of the new government. Madison's proposed tonnage regulations would have required that American-built and -owned ships bringing goods into American ports pay lower duties than foreign vessels; that ships from countries with which the United States had commercial treaties pay a higher duty; and that ships from all "other powers" pay the highest duties. Madison's intention was twofold: to encourage a domestic merchant fleet and to discriminate commercially in favor of France, with which the United States had a trade treaty, and against Great Britain, with which it did not.

Marshall—judging from his approval of an earlier navigation proposal of Madison's, the Port Bill of 1784—and most Virginia Federalists would have endorsed the first motive, but the second posed a dilemma. As Marshall later wrote, "a great deal of sensibility was discovered." Although discrimination against Britain would have benefited southern trade by helping pry open the

West Indies market, discrimination of any sort between American and foreign shipping meant higher freight rates on southern produce carried in foreign vessels and might, at least in theory, enable New England shippers to monopolize the coastal trade by taxing foreign ships out of competition. Beyond the concerns of sectional economic interests, the debate over tonnage discrimination brought to the surface latent ideological differences between northern Anglophiles—such as Hamilton and Adams—who wanted to persuade Britain to relax its trade regulations while remaining commercially attached to it, and southern Anglophobes—particularly Madison and Jefferson—who sought to liberate America from economic dependence on Britain. Marshall and the Virginia Federalists were squeezed between forces of partisanship, loyalty to Washington, sectional interest, and political weakness. Even when writing about the controversy 15 years later, Marshall still had not sorted out all the countervailing demands. In the end, Congress dropped the provision discriminating against British shipping and imposed higher duties on all foreign vessels. An indication of the contradictory influences besetting Virginia Federalists can be seen in the votes of Chesapeake-region Federalists in the House of Representatives: They divided evenly, including those with important seaports in their districts.[40]

Marshall and the Virginia House of Delegates spent much of the contentious fall 1789 term arguing over the 12 constitutional amendments that Congress, fulfilling a condition that a number of states had set for ratifying the Constitution, passed and sent to the states on 25 September.[41] During the summer, Edmund Randolph gave Madison a preview of the debate that followed:

The amendments, proposed by you, are much approved by the strong federalists here . . . being considered as an anodyne to the discontented. Some others, equally affectionate to the union, but less sanguine, expect to hear at the next session of assembly, that a real melioration of the constitution was not so much intended, as a soporific draught to the restless. I believe . . . that nothing, nay not even the abolishment of direct taxation would satisfy those who are most clamorous . . . [Patrick Henry] still asks for the great desideratum, the destruction of direct taxation.

Notwithstanding his reservations about some of the amendments, Randolph led the ratification effort.

Marshall supported him but did not have a key role. He voted against a resolution that the state legislature urge Congress to reconsider the amendments the Virginia ratifying convention had recommended but that Congress did not adopt. The resolution fell only one vote short, and a milder version passed overwhelmingly. Nevertheless, Marshall and the Federalists could still draw some encouragement from the outcome, which was the first indication since the convention that a significant number of elected representatives in Virginia had some confidence in the national government. The House then approved all 12 amendments. Marshall's votes are not recorded. Although he did not believe the Constitution needed amending, he almost certainly supported doing so now to broaden approval of the new government. When the state senate, controlled by former Antifederalists, balked and rejected four of the amendments, Marshall joined a conference committee that unsuccessfully tried to resolve the two chambers' differences. The dispute delayed Virginia's ratification of the Bill of Rights for two years.

Marshall devoted most of the balance of his time during the term to committee work. He served on the two principal standing committees, Privileges and Elections and Courts of Justice, and on several special committees that drafted bills on court and penal reform, revision of the state legal code, cession of land for the national capital, and Kentucky statehood. Marshall also cast two illustrative votes on religious and fiscal matters. Consistent with his establishmentarian views, he sided with the legislative majority against the Baptists' perennial petition to revoke the privileges of the Episcopal Church. In a departure from his previous record, however, he voted against a "commutable" bill that would have allowed payment of taxes in agricultural produce instead of specie. Marshall had approved of such a deviation from orthodox, procreditor fiscal practices during the economic distress of the immediate postwar years, but he now apparently believed that the economic upturn of 1789 warranted a return to traditional revenue-raising methods. In furtherance of that approach, Marshall helped write a bill for the collection of back taxes in Botetourt County, a measure that was part of the delegates' effort to broaden the collection of debts owed to the Commonwealth. On balance, Marshall was pleased with the delegates' accomplishments during the session. Just after adjournment, he wrote to a lawyer acquaintance that "the last assembly preservd [sic] the little reputation which is still left to the old dominion."[42]

Marshall ran again for election to the House of Delegates in the spring of 1790 to assist the Washington administration during the bitter debate over Treasury Secretary Alexander Hamilton's financial program. Marshall was one of only a few Federalists in Virginia who stood against the prevailing sentiment and supported all the essential features of Hamilton's plan. He did so principally because he believed the program was vital to the nation's economic welfare and the new government's political success. Marshall probably had at least a passing familiarity with some of the theories of political economy on which Hamilton based his ideas—principally David Hume's essays on commerce, industry, money, and credit—but his own views on the value of a commercial society assisted by an active central government were based on less abstruse, more practical concerns about how best to establish national credit, foster unity, and encourage economic growth. Not beholden to self-limiting ideologies such as agrarianism or mercantilism, Marshall was willing to grant the new administration political and constitutional flexibility to experiment with novel ways of making the economy sound and prosperous, to protect property rights, and to promote commerce and release entrepreneurial energy.[43]

Marshall did so, however, at great political risk. In supporting what Forrest McDonald has called "a government-channeled, government-encouraged, and sometimes government-subsidized system of private enterprise for personal profit," Marshall faced powerful opposition in Virginia from localistic, agrarian former Antifederalists and, increasingly, anti-Hamilton Federalists who trimmed their nationalism to fit the fashions of state politics. Unlike those more accommodating Federalists, Marshall was willing to compromise Virginia's parochial interests to promote harmony within the national Federalist organization and, most importantly, to prevent sectional discord. Marshall feared that southern opposition to Hamilton's program could be, as Hamilton warned, "the first symptom of a spirit which must either be killed or will kill the constitution of the United States."[44]

The controversy over financial policy began right after Hamilton issued his first Report on Public Credit in January 1790 and quickly took on an ideological and sectional cast. Hamilton had proposed that the federal government resolve the serious problem of Revolutionary War debt—over $56 million owed by the national authority to foreign and domestic creditors, and another $25 million by the states to foreign creditors, Continental Army veterans, and merchants who held public securities promising future payment. Hamilton recommended that the federal government fund the foreign and domestic debt at par—by enabling creditors to exchange depreciated securities for new interest-bearing bonds at face value—and assume over 80 percent of the state debts. Financial troubles had largely caused the Confederation's failure, and most Americans agreed that the new government had to resolve the nation's confused debt situation and restore its credit standing at home and abroad. Paying off the foreign debt in full and devising a method for funding the national debt were givens. The outcry arose over the way Hamilton had suggested doing the latter, and over the whole notion of assumption. Nowhere was the hostility to his plan more intense than in Virginia.[45]

Most Virginians opposed Hamilton's proposed funding methods, not because they wanted to avoid paying the national debt, but for reasons of fairness, sectional interest, and ideology.[46] Virginians considered their state a model of fiscal probity. Between 1784 and 1790, Virginia obligated 80 percent of its revenue to retiring Revolutionary War debts owed to Congress and reduced its balance due from over £4 million to less than £1 million. Accordingly, most Virginians were loath to be taxed to pay off the large national debt that would accrue when the federal government issued bonds to fund the foreign and domestic debt at par. Besides this matter of equity, ideological overtones of republicanism, Anglophobia, and agrarianism pervaded the arguments of Virginians who opposed Hamilton's plan. They believed that northern commercial and financial interests, economically and ideologically allied to Britain and with growing influence in the new government, would reap a windfall. Although current owners of public securities included ex-Continental officers, storekeepers, professionals, and large landowners from all over the country, distrustful Virginians claimed that northern merchants, speculators, and brokers with questionable scruples had increased their share during the frenzy of exchanges after the national government was formed, and that New York City dominated the country's financial markets because speculators there received "insider" information from federal legislators and officials.

Most Virginians, in short, feared that Hamilton's funding plan would help create a corrupt, English-style "court," controlled by northern monied interests who would subordinate agriculture to commerce and force America away from the republican principles on which it was founded. Opposition even came from members of Richmond's financial community, who might have been expected to ally themselves with their northern counterparts in taking advantage of the funding plan. Instead, they directed their resentment toward the speculators who descended on the state from the north to buy up securities from war veterans and widows. In the House of Representatives, moreover, Virginia's delegation provided nine of the 13 votes cast for Madison's modification of Hamilton's plan that allowed the government to discriminate between current and original holders of securities and thereby reduce the profits from come-lately speculation.

Marshall, like most of his educated contemporaries, was aware of how a funded debt had been used to try to stabilize the English economy after the Glorious Revolution of 1689. He also had some firsthand familiarity with the policy through his dealings in the House of Delegates with Virginia's sinking fund, which was set up in 1787 to allow the state to buy public securities and redeem some of the principal on the state debt, and which had worked fairly well. In addition, Marshall had a small personal stake in funding's success; he owned some military and state certificates whose value would increase under the plan. (In 1791, they were worth almost £2,000.) Beyond these matters, however, Marshall had more substantial reasons for endorsing Hamilton's funding scheme. He shared the treasury secretary's belief that it would serve two purposes: Economically, it would establish the national government's creditworthiness; politically, it would secure the loyalty of commercial and financial elites from all sections to the new government. The attainment of both goals would prevent a repetition of two of the circumstances that helped doom the Confederation, financial collapse and disunity. Marshall probably also agreed with those Virginia Federalists who opposed Madison's discrimination idea as a dangerous innovation and a violation of private contracts.[47]

Hamilton's assumption plan ran into even stiffer opposition in Virginia than his funding scheme, and all Marshall and other Federalists could do was deflect some of the attacks and try to moderate the harsh tone of the debate. Assumption's critics offered several practical, political, and ideological reasons for their view. The state had paid off most of its debt, and they did not want to shoulder the burdens of northern states that had not. Virginia's outstanding claims against the national government had not been completely reconciled, and an immediate assumption of the debt might shortchange the state. The opponents of assumption also contended that it was unconstitutional. Nowhere, they asserted, did the Constitution give the national government authority to intrude into state financial affairs. As a corollary, they feared that the northern merchants and speculators whom they saw as gaining control of the federal government would take over direction of Virginia's finances as part of a massive centralization of power.[48]

By the time Marshall and the other delegates met for the fall 1790 session, Congress had approved Hamilton's financial program in a sectional compromise that broke a lengthy stalemate. Hamilton agreed to secure enough northern votes to place the national capital along the Potomac River, instead of in Philadelphia, in exchange for Madison's pledge to obtain southern support for assumption. In late July and early August, the assumption and funding measures became law. On 3 November, an outraged Patrick Henry came out of retirement to introduce resolutions in the House of Delegates decrying assumption as "repugnant to the Constitution" and "dangerous to the rights and subversive of the interests of the people." Marshall opposed the resolution, and he and his Federalist colleagues, trying to preserve something from a losing situation, drafted a less vitriolic measure that condemned assumption on every ground that Henry used except its unconstitutionality. Marshall was willing to compromise on policy, politics, and ideology, but would not—could not—concede the constitutional question. He knew that without a broad interpretation of the Constitution, Hamilton's nationalist financial program was a dead letter. Marshall and his allies lost by nearly a two-to-one margin, however; Henry's version passed easily; and three weeks later the Virginia legislature sent to Congress a memorial that denounced Hamilton's plan in the language of liberty, Anglophobia, agrarianism, and strict construction.[49]

Marshall and the Virginia Federalists scarcely had time to recover from their defeat on assumption before they had to contend with another controversial aspect of Hamilton's financial program, the national bank. In December 1790, Hamilton issued his second Report on Public Credit in which he proposed that the federal government charter a national bank to hold government funds, issue banknotes, help the Treasury conduct fiscal policy, and provide credit for business investment. As with funding and assumption, most Virginians opposed the idea for political and ideological reasons. They perceived the national bank as further evidence of sinister collaboration between the Washington administration and northern mercantile and financial interests. Virginia Federalists in the House of Representatives continued their pattern of siding with former Antifederalists when sentiment back home required by voting against the bill incorporating the Bank of the United States that passed in February 1791.[50]

Marshall strongly endorsed the bank plan as a critical component of Hamilton's financial structure, and, no doubt to his great relief, he had less difficulty defending it in Virginia than he had with the other features of the treasury secretary's program. The bank proposal did not provoke the same hostility in the Old Dominion that funding and assumption had, even though constitutionally it was more questionable than either. The state legislature, for example, did not issue a formal protest as it had against assumption. Three

factors probably were responsible for this widespread quiescence: Most of
Hamilton's program had been enacted, so opposing the bank seemed fairly
pointless; politicians and their constituents were tired of wrangling over
financial issues; and the bank bill promised to aid Virginia's commercial
interests without threatening harm to others who would not directly benefit from
it. Under these conditions, the bank's alleged unconstitutionality—asserted by,
among others, Madison, Jefferson, and Randolph inside the administration, and
jurist St. George Tucker and political theorist and lawyer John Taylor of
Caroline inside Virginia—was largely irrelevant. Marshall believed, of course,
that the Constitution gave the federal government authority to charter a bank.
The arguments Hamilton made in his "Opinion on the Constitutionality of the
Bank," which relied heavily on a broad construction of the "necessary and
proper" clause in Article I, section 8, so resonated with Marshall that he used
many of them practically verbatim almost 30 years later in his own landmark
Supreme Court opinion affirming the bank's constitutionality, *McCulloch v.
Maryland* (1819).[51]

Marshall was out of the legislature when Hamilton proposed the other aspects
of his program, the national mint and the whiskey tax, and when he issued his
Report on Manufactures. Marshall did not comment on them at the time, but it
is safe to say, judging from his attitudes and actions concerning the rest of
Hamilton's plan, that he approved of them as well—once again going against
the dominant view in Virginia, where opponents of the proposals employed
now-familiar political, ideological, and sectional arguments against them.[52]

The intense debate over Hamilton's program deepened Marshall's
understanding of economic theory and practice and clarified and broadened his
conception of the proper role of government in commercial and financial
activity.[53] Most historians, especially those in the Progressive tradition, have
concentrated on Marshall's Supreme Court decisions affirming the sanctity of
contracts and defending property rights to interpret him as an advocate of laissez
faire capitalism. That perspective, however, only partially conveys the premises
of his economic jurisprudence, and it is decidedly inaccurate when his views on
political economy in the 1780s and 1790s are considered—if for no other reason
than that "capitalism" would not be established in America until the market
revolution of the Jacksonian era. Nor was Marshall a mercantilist in the sense
of subordinating the economy to purposes of the state.

Instead, Marshall championed a mixed economy as the best way to "promote
the general welfare." Ever since he entered Virginia's political and legal circles
in the early 1780s, he had worked with, represented, befriended, and voted on
behalf of, members of the state's economic elite—merchants, bankers, land
speculators, insurance brokers, financiers, turnpike and canal builders,
entrepreneurs—who wanted to use government to spur development and
investment. Marshall did not believe that merely leaving energetic interests to
combine resources on their own would accomplish much. Instead, he had a
more dynamic conception of economic endeavor that entailed a supportive role
for government, guiding private enterprise into its most productive channels and

imparting predictability to commercial transactions. In Virginia, this support so far had been limited to chartering business corporations, granting them special tax exemptions and other privileges, and affording legal protection to their property, and did not encompass developing native industry (except during the Revolution) or levying taxes specifically for internal improvements.

During the battle over Hamilton's plan, however, Marshall moved intellectually beyond his experience with Virginia's limited system of mixed enterprise. Besides expanding his knowledge of political economy to include complicated matters of credit, debt, banking, taxes, and currency, he also came to appreciate the potential benefits of greater government involvement in the economy—especially the importance of a strong federal government that could limit state regulation of property and trade that would inhibit commerce. He drew a distinction between the state governments' promotion of enterprise that would have national benefits and state-based mercantilism that would impair the growth of the national economy. Marshall had already couched his support for the Constitution partly in economic terms—"[the Confederation] takes away the incitements to industry, by rendering property insecure and unprotected. It is [the Constitution] that will promote and encourage industry"—that were consistent with the "common market" philosophy of the economically minded Framers. During 1790–91 he worked as hard as he did for Hamilton's program because he believed it would best accomplish the Constitution's objectives in political economy.

Finally, during the controversy over Hamilton's financial plan, Marshall witnessed, and to some degree helped bring about, an important phase in Virginia's political development. The legislative coteries that gathered around personalities when Marshall first joined the legislature in the early 1780s, and then aligned themselves over mostly economic issues in the mid- and late 1780s, had, by 1792, developed into two recognizable factions with fairly coherent ideologies and agendas. Recent studies of political factionalism in Virginia during the years 1788–91 indicate that although Federalists during ratification split into Federalists and Republicans in the early republic's party system, most Antifederalists gravitated toward the emerging Republican organization. For example, of the 61 delegates at the 1788 convention who favored ratification and whose later careers can be traced, 38 became Federalists and 23 joined the Republicans. In contrast, of the 40 delegates who opposed ratification and can be subsequently identified, all but two became Republicans. As new domestic and foreign issues arose after 1791, the new national party structure was superimposed over the established factional alignments in Virginia. From Marshall's perspective, this meant that by the early 1790s he was, at least in Virginia, politically isolated—a member of a tiny pro-Hamilton splinter group in a band of outnumbered and disorganized Federalists, many of whom disapproved of the Washington administration's policies and voted with its opponents, in a state where former Antifederalists dominated a highly polarized political environment. This situation must have made Marshall—who had sought public office only as a necessary step toward private prominence and

from a sense of civic duty, and not from a fondness for the political life itself—
doubly glad to leave further conflicts over the new government to those who
truly enjoyed them, especially now that the federal financial policies he had
labored for had become the law of the land.[54]

After the 1791 session of the House of Delegates, Marshall "again withdrew
from the assembly, determined to bid a final adieu to political life," he wrote
later. With the foundations of Hamilton's program in place, and with Virginia
and the nation benefiting from them and from improved economic conditions,
Marshall saw no need to divert more energy and attention from his family and
law practice by staying in the legislature. Assumption had resulted in a net
federal contribution to the state's treasury and enabled it to cut taxes in 1792;
prices for wheat, one of Virginia's key commodities, had risen steadily since
late 1790; and the nation's foreign and domestic credit was sound. After two
arduous sessions in the legislature working to bring those conditions about,
Marshall was eager to forswear politics and devote himself to his wife, children,
and profession, and to enjoy his new house that was completed in late 1790.
The handsome, spacious, and unpretentious two-and-one-half story dwelling of
Federal design, which eventually had outbuildings for a kitchen, stable, laundry,
slave quarters, and a law office, still stands at what is now Ninth and Marshall
Streets in downtown Richmond. His private intentions aside, during the next
few years, intensifying partisan conflict between Federalists and Republicans,
especially over foreign policy, would pull Marshall back into the public sphere
and make him, after Washington, the Federalists' most important spokesman in
the South.[55]

NOTES

1. JM, *Life of George Washington*, 5 vols. (Philadelphia: C. P. Wayne, 1804–7; rept.,
New York: Chelsea House, 1983), 4:123; Alan Schaffer, "Virginia's 'Critical Period,'"
in *The Old Dominion: Essays for Thomas Perkins Abernethy*, ed. Darrett Rutman,
(Charlottesville: University Press of Virginia, 1964), 152–70; Richard B. Morris, *The
Forging of the Union, 1781–1789* (New York: Harper and Row, 1987), chap. 6, esp.
144–48; Norman K. Risjord, *Chesapeake Politics, 1781–1800* (New York: Columbia
University Press, 1978), 161–65; Myra L. Rich, "The Experimental Years: Virginia,
1781–1789" (Ph.D. diss., Yale University, 1966), 207–8.

2. Gordon S. Wood, *The Creation of the American Republic, 1776–1787* (Chapel Hill:
University of North Carolina Press, 1969; rept., New York: W. W. Norton, 1972), 403–
13; Thomas Jefferson, *Notes on the State of Virginia*, ed. William Peden (New York: W.
W. Norton, 1982), 120; JM to Arthur Lee, 5 May 1787, *PJM*, 1:206; John Stokes
Adams, ed., *An Autobiographical Sketch by John Marshall* (Ann Arbor: University of
Michigan Press, 1937), 10 (hereafter cited as JM, *Autobiographical Sketch*).

An example of Virginia's reluctance to adopt anticreditor laws occurred in 1786; the
House of Delegates rejected paper money proposals, calling them "unjust, impolitic,
[and] destructive of public and private confidence." Risjord, *Chesapeake Politics*, 174–
79; Ralph Ketcham, *James Madison: A Biography* (New York: Macmillan, 1971), 172.

3. David P. Szatmary, *Shays's Rebellion: The Making of an Agrarian Insurrection* (Amherst: University of Massachusetts Press, 1980), chaps. 2–6; Morris, *Forging of the Union*, 258–66; Richard D. Brown, "Shays's Rebellion and the Ratification of the Federal Constitution in Massachusetts," in *Beyond Confederation: Origins of the Constitution and American National Identity*, ed. Richard Beeman et al., (Chapel Hill: University of North Carolina Press, 1987), 115–16; Forrest McDonald and Ellen Shapiro McDonald, "On the Late Disturbances in Massachusetts," in *Requiem: Variations on Eighteenth-Century Themes* (Lawrence: University Press of Kansas, 1988), 59–83; Harold E. Cox, "Federalism and Anti-Federalism in Virginia, 1787: A Study of Political and Economic Motivations" (Ph.D. diss., University of Virginia, 1958), 166–68.

4. JM to James Wilkinson, 5 January 1787, *PJM*, 1:200–201.

5. JM, *Life of Washington*, 4:137–38, 144.

6. JM to Arthur Lee, 5 March 1787, *PJM*, 1:206; JM, *Life of Washington*, 4:138.

7. Morris, *Forging of the Union*, 265; Gordon DenBoer, "The House of Delegates and the Evolution of Political Parties in Virginia, 1782–1792" (Ph.D. diss., University of Wisconsin, 1972), 80–82; Beverly Randolph to Edmund Randolph, 8 September 1787, in *The Papers of James Madison*, ed. William T. Hutchinson et al., 17 vols. (Chicago: University of Chicago Press, 1962–91), 10:161 n.; James Madison to Thomas Jefferson, 6 September 1787, in *The Papers of Thomas Jefferson*, ed. Julian P. Boyd et al., 27 vols. to date (Princeton: Princeton University Press, 1950–), 12:103–4.

8. JM, *Life of Washington*, 4:47–48; Morris, *Forging of the Union*, chap. 2; E. James Ferguson, *The Power of the Purse: A History of American Public Finance, 1776–1790* (Chapel Hill: University of North Carolina Press, 1961), 109–76, 242–43, 249–50.

9. JM, *Life of Washington*, 4:89–90, 120–21.

10. JM, *Autobiographical Sketch*, 10; "Record of Attendance," 15 October 1787, *PJM*, 1:240 and n. 1.

11. DenBoer, "House of Delegates and Political Parties in Virginia," 112; Merrill Jensen et al., eds., *The Documentary History of the Ratification of the Constitution*, 10 vols. to date (Madison: State Historical Society of Wisconsin, 1976–), 8:57–58, 110–16 (hereafter cited as *DHRC*).

12. Sources for this paragraph and the next are Norman K. Risjord and Gordon DenBoer, "The Evolution of Political Parties in Virginia, 1782–1800," *JAH*, 60 (1973–74), 967–70; Jackson Turner Main, *Political Parties before the Constitution* (Chapel Hill: University of North Carolina Press, 1973), chap. 9; DenBoer, "House of Delegates and Political Parties in Virginia," 94, 112.

13. U.S. Constitution, Article 3, section 2; *Journals of the House of Delegates of the Commonwealth of Virginia* (Richmond: Thomas W. White, 1828), October 1787 sess., 79–95 passim; *DHRC*, 8:xxvii, xxxi; "Report of the Commissioners on Illinois Accounts," 2 January 1788, *PJM*, 1:243–46; Ferguson, *Power of the Purse*, 216–17; *The Papers of George Mason*, ed. Robert Rutland, 3 vols. (Chapel Hill: University of North Carolina Press, 1970), 3:1027–37; DenBoer, "House of Delegates and Political Parties in Virginia," 82–87.

14. John J. Reardon, *Edmund Randolph: A Biography* (New York: Macmillan, 1974), 127; JM, *Autobiographical Sketch*, 8; *DHRC*, 8:110–16; Albert J. Beveridge, *The Life of John Marshall*, 4 vols. (Boston: Houghton Mifflin, 1916–19), 1:246–47.

15. Reardon, *Randolph*, 128; *DHRC*, 8:183–93; *Journal of the House of Delegates*, October 1787 sess., 77, 95; Risjord, *Chesapeake Politics*, 300.

16. JM, *Autobiographical Sketch*, 8–9; Madison to Jefferson, 24 October 1787, *Papers of Jefferson*, 12:283–84; Madison to Jefferson, 9 December 1787, and to George Washington, 14 December 1787, *Papers of Madison*, 10:312, 327; Jon Kukla, "'A

Spectrum of Sentiments': Virginia's Federalists, Antifederalists, and 'Federalists Who Are For Amendments,' 1787–1788," *VMHB*, 96 (1988), 277–96; F. Claiborne Johnston Jr., ed., "Federalist, Doubtful, and Antifederalist: A Note on the Virginia Convention of 1788," *VMHB*, 96 (1988), 333–44; Risjord, *Chesapeake Politics*, 295–300.

17. Jackson Turner Main, *The Antifederalists: Critics of the Constitution, 1781–1788* (New York: W. W. Norton, 1974), 285–86; *DHRC*, 8:3, 4, 17–19, 57–58, 170–72, 180–83, 9:633, 652–54; "Account Book," *PJM*, 1:409; DenBoer, "House of Delegates and Political Parties in Virginia," 119–20.

18. Edmund Randolph to James Madison, 29 February 1788, and *Virginia Independent Chronicle*, 5 March 1788, both in *DHRC*, 9:592; DenBoer, "House of Delegates and Political Parties in Virginia," 150–51; Steven R. Boyd, *The Politics of Opposition: Antifederalists and the Acceptance of the Constitution* (Millwood, N.Y.: KTO Press, 1979), 105–6; JM, *Autobiographical Sketch*, 10.
Marshall had several encounters with Foushee after the election. He represented Foushee in a two-year-long suit that they finally won in 1791. Foushee, a physician, delivered Marshall's son John James in February 1792, and opposed Marshall at a public meeting about the Jay Treaty in Richmond in April 1796. Foushee was president of the James River Company during 1789–1818 and in 1793 helped run a stock subscription drive to open a branch of the Bank of the United States; Marshall invested in both undertakings. Foushee succeeded him in the House of Delegates after the 1797 term. Lastly, Marshall, as chief justice on circuit duty in Richmond in 1807, ran the grand jury on which Foushee served that indicted Aaron Burr. *PJM*, 2:370–71 n. 63, 434; Beveridge, *Marshall*, 2:139–40 n. 2, 152, 3:413; *A Register of the General Assembly of Virginia, 1776–1918*, ed. E. G. Swem and John W. Williams (Richmond: Bottom, 1918), 49.

19. JM, *Life of Washington*, 4:149; Richard R. Beeman, *The Old Dominion and the New Nation, 1788–1801* (Lexington: University Press of Kentucky, 1972), 3; *DHRC*, 9:561–63; DenBoer, "House of Delegates and Political Parties in Virginia," 139–42.

20. *DHRC*, 9:626–31; DenBoer, "House of Delegates and Political Parties in Virginia," 162–67; Patricia Watlington, *The Partisan Spirit: Kentucky Politics, 1779–1792* (New York: Atheneum, 1972), 148–51, 155–56; Robert A. Rutland, *The Ordeal of the Constitution: The Antifederalists and the Ratification Struggle of 1787–1788* (Norman: University of Oklahoma Press, 1966), 189, 197–98; Forrest McDonald, *We the People: The Economic Origins of the Constitution* (Chicago: University of Chicago Press, 1958), 256–58; Johnston, ed., "Federalist, Doubtful, and Antifederalist," 334–36.

21. Hugh B. Grigsby, *The History of the Virginia Federal Convention of 1788 . . .*, 2 vols. (Richmond: Virginia Historical Society, 1890; rept., New York: DaCapo Press, 1969), 1:25; David J. Mays, *Edmund Pendleton*, 2 vols. (Cambridge: Harvard University Press, 1952), 2:227; *DHRC*, 9:897; Henry Mayer, *A Son of Thunder: Patrick Henry and the American Republic* (New York: Franklin Watts, 1986), 396; Beveridge, *Marshall*, 1:319; Helen Hill Miller, *George Mason: Gentleman Revolutionary* (Chapel Hill: University of North Carolina Press, 1975), 285; Robert D. Meade, *Patrick Henry: Practical Revolutionary* (Philadelphia and New York: J. P. Lippincott, 1969), 342; "Account Book," *PJM*, 1:403–13 passim.

22. Grigsby, *History of the Virginia Convention*, 1:67; Ketcham, *Madison*, 254; Mayer, *Son of Thunder*, 399; *DHRC*, 9:897; Reardon, *Randolph*, 138; Samuel Mordecai, *Richmond in By-Gone Days . . .* (Richmond: West and Johnson, 1856), 210.

23. DenBoer, "House of Delegates and Political Parties in Virginia," 191–92; McDonald, *We the People*, 269–81.

24. "The Virginia Ratifying Convention: Editorial Note," *PJM*, 1:255; Meade, *Henry*, 344.

25. [David Robertson,] *Debates and Other Proceedings of the Convention of Virginia, Convened at Richmond, on Monday the 2d of June, 1788* . . . (Petersburg, Va.: David Robertson, 1788; 2nd ed., 1805); Jonathan Elliot, ed., *The Debates in the Several State Conventions on the Adoption of the Federal Constitution* . . . (Philadelphia: Lippincott, 1836); *DHRC*, 9:904–06; Richard R. Beeman, *Patrick Henry: A Biography* (New York: McGraw-Hill, 1974), 149; Miller, *Mason*, 285; Meade, *Henry*, 343–44; Thomas H. Bayly's memorandum of conversation with JM, [1832], quoted in *PJM*, 1:256 n. 7; James H. Hutson, "Riddles of the Federal Constitutional Convention," *WMQ*, 3rd ser., 44 (1987), 411–13.

26. Grigsby, *Virginia Federal Convention*, 1:176; [William Wirt,] *The Letters of the British Spy* (orig. pub. 1803; rept., Chapel Hill: University of North Carolina Press, 1970), 179; JM, "Speech," *PJM*, 1:256–70 (also in *DHRC*, 10:1115–27; Robertson, *Debates*, 2:28–40; and Elliot, *Debates*, 3:223–36); Gale Lee Richards, "A Criticism of the Public Speaking of John Marshall Prior to 1801" (Ph.D. diss., University of Iowa, 1950), 212–20.

27. Elliot, *Debates*, 2:254; JM, "Speech," *PJM*, 1:273–74 (also in *DHRC*, 10:1306–8; Robertson, *Debates*, 3:11–13; and Elliot, *Debates*, 3:419–20); Richard H. Kohn, *Eagle and Sword: The Federalists and the Creation of the Military Establishment in America, 1783–1802* (New York: Free Press, 1975), 86.

28. Mays, *Pendleton*, 2:262–63.

29. "The Virginia Ratifying Convention: Editorial Note," *PJM*, 1:254 and n. 4; JM, "Speech," *PJM*, 1:275–85 (also in *DHRC*, 10:1430–39; Robertson, *Debates*, 3:124–33; and Elliot, *Debates*, 3:551–62).

30. Mays, *Pendleton*, 2:267–68; Lisle A. Rose, *Prologue to Democracy: The Federalists in the South, 1789–1800* (Lexington: University of Kentucky Press, 1968), 7 and n. 13; *DHRC*, 9:899–900; Beeman, *Old Dominion and New Nation*, 11–12; Leonard Baker, *John Marshall: A Life in Law* (New York: Macmillan, 1974), 137. With a few exceptions, the final vote replicated a forecast that some Virginia Federalists made soon after the delegates were elected during the spring. Johnston, ed., "Federalist, Doubtful, and Antifederalist," passim. The delegation from Kentucky territory voted 10–3 against ratification. Marshall's cousin Humphrey voted to ratify, mainly because he was concerned about Indian and European threats to the frontier. Watlington, *Partisan Spirit*, 155–56.

31. Spencer Roane to Philip Aylett, 28 June 1788, *New York Journal*, 8 July 1788, and *Virginia Independent Chronicle*, 9 July 1788, quoted in Mayer, *Son of Thunder*, 438, 441; *DHRC*, 10:1566.

32. The most noteworthy of these interpretations—some of which deal with ratification generally and do not focus on Virginia—are Charles A. Beard, *An Economic Interpretation of the Constitution of the United States* (New York: Macmillan, 1913); McDonald, *We the People*; Robert E. Thomas, "The Virginia Convention of 1788: A Criticism of Beard's *An Economic Interpretation of the Constitution*," *JSH*, 19 (1953), 63–72; Merrill Jensen, *The New Nation: A History of the United States during the Confederation, 1781–1789*, Vintage ed. (New York: Alfred A. Knopf, 1965); Main, *Political Parties before the Constitution* and *Antifederalists*; Cecilia M. Kenyon, "Men of Little Faith: The Anti-Federalists on the Nature of Representative Government," *WMQ*, 3rd ser., 12 (1955), 3–43; Stanley Elkins and Eric McKitrick, "The Founding Fathers: Young Men of the Revolution," *Political Science Quarterly*, 76 (1961), 181–216; Rutland, *Ordeal of the Constitution*; James H. Hutson, "Court, Country, and the

Constitution: Antifederalism and the Historian," *WMQ*, 3rd ser., 38 (1981), 337–68; J. Thomas Wren, "The Ideology of Court and Country in the Virginia Ratifying Convention of 1788," *VMHB*, 93 (1985), 389–408; George Bancroft, *The History of the United States of America*, 6 vols. (Boston: Little, Brown, 1885), 4:6–7, 207, 367; and Forrest McDonald, *E Pluribus Unum: The Formation of the American Republic* (Boston: Houghton Mifflin, 1965), 1. Norman K. Risjord gives the cliometric analysis in *Chesapeake Politics*, 316–17, and, in more detail, in "Virginians and the Constitution: A Multivariant Analysis," *WMQ*, 3rd ser., 31 (1974), 613–32. Probably the most satisfactory synthesis of the economic, political, social, and ideological dynamics of ratification is Wood, *Creation of the American Republic*, part 5.

33. JM, *Life of Washington*, 4:150.

34. JM, *Autobiographical Sketch*, 9–10.

35. Risjord and DenBoer, "Evolution of Political Parties in Virginia," 971–72; Risjord, *Chesapeake Politics*, 277.

36. JM, *Autobiographical Sketch*, 11.

37. Beeman, *Old Dominion and New Nation*, 14–21, 56; Risjord, *Chesapeake Politics*, 322–30; St. John de Crèvecoeur to Jefferson, 20 November 1788, *Papers of Jefferson*, 14:274. In contrast, the U.S. Congress was lopsidedly Federalist; no more than 11 of 59 representatives, and only two out of 20 senators, were Antifederalists. Stanley Elkins and Eric McKitrick, *The Age of Federalism* (New York: Oxford University Press, 1993), 33.

38. JM, *Autobiographical Sketch*, 12–13; George Washington to JM, 30 September 1789, JM to Washington, 14 October 1789, and Washington to JM, 23 November 1789, *PJM*, 2:41–44; DenBoer, "House of Delegates and Political Parties in Virginia," 259–60. No details of Marshall's election are available.

39. Sources for this paragraph and the next are Susan L. Foard, "Virginia Enters the Union: A Legislative Study of the Commonwealth, 1789–1792" (M.A. thesis, College of William and Mary, 1966), 17; Elkins and McKitrick, *Age of Federalism*, 46–50; John C. Miller, *The Federalist Era, 1789–1801* (New York: Harper and Row, 1960), 6–10; Forrest McDonald, *The Presidency of George Washington* (New York: W. W. Norton, 1975), 25–26, 29–30; Risjord, *Chesapeake Politics*, 342–43; JM, *Life of Washington*, 4:169–72.

40. JM, *Life of Washington*, 4:186–89; Elkins and McKitrick, *Age of Federalism*, 65–74; Risjord, *Chesapeake Politics*, 344–46; Miller, *Federalist Era*, 14–19; McDonald, *Presidency of Washington*, 32–34; Drew R. McCoy, *The Elusive Republic: Political Economy in Jeffersonian America* (Chapel Hill: University of North Carolina Press, 1980; rept., New York: W. W. Norton, 1982), 137–45.

41. Sources for this paragraph and the next are Randolph to Madison, 30 July 1789, quoted in Foard, "Virginia Enters the Union," 33, also 34–39; Risjord, *Chesapeake Politics*, 355–57; Reardon, *Randolph*, 181–82; Beveridge, *Marshall*, 2:57–58; Beeman, *Old Dominion and New Nation*, 61–66; *Journal of the House of Delegates*, October 1789 sess., 101–2.

42. *Journal of the House of Delegates*, October 1789 sess., 4, 8, 10–11, 87–88, 113, 117; Foard, "Virginia Enters the Union," 44–45, 194; JM to Archibald Stuart, [?] December 1789, *PJM*, 2:47.

43. For the theoretical bases of Hamilton's financial ideas, see Elkins and McKitrick, *Age of Federalism*, 107–13, 258–61; Forrest McDonald, *Alexander Hamilton: A Biography* (New York: W. W. Norton, 1982), 35–37, 84–85, 160–61; and John R. Nelson, Jr., *Liberty and Property: Political Economy and Policymaking in the New Nation, 1789–1812* (Baltimore: Johns Hopkins University Press, 1987), chaps. 2–4.

44. Forrest McDonald, "Capitalism and the Constitution," in *How Capitalistic Is the Constitution?*, ed. Robert A. Goldwin and William A. Schambra (Washington, D.C.: American Enterprise Institute, 1982), 71; Hamilton to John Jay, 13 November 1989, *The Papers of Alexander Hamilton*, ed. Harold Syrett et al., 27 vols. (New York: Columbia University Press, 1961–81), 7:149–50.

45. Ferguson, *Power of the Purse*, 289–325; McDonald, *Hamilton*, 117–88; idem, *Presidency of Washington*, 47–75; Elkins and McKitrick, *Age of Federalism*, 92–131; Miller, *Federalist Era*, 36–53. Marshall gives a thorough and nonpartisan account of Hamilton's plan and the reaction to it in *Life of Washington*, 4:210–27.

46. Sources for this paragraph and the next are Ferguson, *Power of the Purse*, 255, 258, 265, 301; Beeman, *Old Dominion and New Nation*, 68–70; Rose, *Prologue to Democracy*, 10–11; DenBoer, "House of Delegates and Political Parties in Virginia," 281; and Risjord, *Chesapeake Politics*, 365. Some data support the Virginians' suspicions of Hamilton's plan: 30 percent of the state's securities were held by nonresidents and 22 percent by fewer than two dozen large speculators; and 95 percent were held by secondary purchasers. Whitney K. Bates, "Northern Speculators and Southern State Debts: 1790," *WMQ*, 3rd ser., 19 (1962), 32–33, 42–43.

47. Foard, "Virginia Enters the Union," 42; Ferguson, *Power of the Purse*, 233; "Receipt," 10 February 1792, *PJM*, 2:109; Risjord, *Chesapeake Politics*, 366.

48. Ferguson, *Power of the Purse*, 304–10; Beeman, *Old Dominion and New Nation*, 72–73; Risjord, *Chesapeake Politics*, 366–67.

49. *Journal of the House of Delegates*, October 1790 sess., 35–36; Risjord, *Chesapeake Politics*, 366–67; Miller, *Federalist Era*, 52; Beeman, *Old Dominion and New Nation*, 78–81; DenBoer, "House of Delegates and Political Parties in Virginia," 283; Foard, "Virginia Enters the Union," 69–78.

50. McDonald, *Hamilton*, 192–94; Miller, *Federalist Era*, 55–56; Elkins and McKitrick, *Age of Federalism*, 226–27; Risjord, *Chesapeake Politics*, 404–05.

51. Elkins and McKitrick, *Age of Federalism*, 229–33; Miller, *Federalist Era*, 58–59; Dumas Malone, *Jefferson and the Rights of Man* (Boston: Little, Brown, 1951), 341–44; Reardon, *Randolph*, 197–99; Robert A. Rutland, *James Madison: The Founding Father* (New York: Macmillan, 1987), 96–97; McDonald, *Hamilton*, 200–202, 205–9; Beeman, *Old Dominion and New Nation*, 116–17. Marshall gives an even-handed account of the bank debate in *Life of Washington*, 4:240–44.

52. Miller, *Federalist Era*, 63–66; McDonald, *Hamilton*, 195–97, 232–36; Elkins and McKitrick, *Age of Federalism*, 258–61; Rose, *Prologue to Democracy*, 37; JM, *Life of Washington*, 4:236–40.

53. Sources for this discussion of Marshall's views on political economy are Joseph Dorfman, "John Marshall: Political Economist," in *Chief Justice John Marshall: A Reappraisal*, ed. W. Melville Jones (Ithaca: Cornell University Press, 1956), 124–44; Wallace Mendelson, "Chief Justice Marshall and the Mercantile Tradition," *Southwestern Social Science Quarterly*, 29 (1948), 27–37; Bruce A. Campbell, "John Marshall, the Virginia Political Economy, and the *Dartmouth College* Decision," *AJLH*, 19 (1975), 40–65; idem, "Law and Experience in the Early Republic: The Evolution of the Dartmouth College Doctrine, 1780–1819" (Ph.D. diss., Michigan State University, 1973), 246–47, 313; Rich, "Experimental Years," 224–26; R. Kent Newmyer, *Supreme Court Justice Joseph Story: Statesman of the Old Republic* (Chapel Hill: University of North Carolina Press, 1985), 60–61, 115–16, 125–26; idem, *The Supreme Court under Marshall and Taney* (New York: Thomas Y. Crowell Co., 1968), 81; Robert K. Faulkner, *The Jurisprudence of John Marshall* (Princeton: Princeton University Press, 1968), 19, 130–31, 134–35; Robert Johnson, "Government Regulation of Business

Enterprise in Virginia, 1750–1820" (Ph.D. diss., University of Minnesota, 1958), chaps. 7–8; Janet Riesman, "Money, Credit, and Federalist Political Economy," in *Beyond Confederation*, 128–61; James W. Ely Jr., *The Guardian of Every Other Right: A Constitutional History of Property Rights* (New York: Oxford University Press, 1992), 48–53; David Schultz, "Political Theory and Legal History: Conflicting Depictions of Property in the American Political Founding," *AJLH*, 37 (1993), 464–95; Stuart Bruchey, "The Impact of Concern for the Security of Property Rights on the Legal System of the Early Republic," *Wisconsin Law Review* (1980), 1135–58; JM, "Speech," 10 July 1788, *PJM*, 1:266; idem, *A History of the Colonies* . . . (Philadelphia: C. P. Wayne, 1804), 42ff; Herbert Alan Johnson, "John Marshall," in *The Supreme Court Justices: Illustrated Biographies, 1789–1995*, ed. Clare Cushman, 2 vols. (Washington, D.C.: Congressional Quarterly, 1993), 1:65.

54. DenBoer, "House of Delegates and Political Parties in Virginia," 285–87, 294–97; Risjord and DenBoer, "Evolution of Political Parties in Virginia," 975–77; Norman K. Risjord, "The Virginia Federalists," *JSH*, 33 (1967), 487–88; Beeman, *Old Dominion and New Nation*, 82–87.

55. Elkins and McKitrick, *Age of Federalism*, 265; JM, "Construction Account," *PJM*, 2:8–12; Leonard Baker, "John Marshall's Federalist House," *Washington Post*, 28 March 1971, G1; The John Marshall Foundation, untitled guidebook to the John Marshall House in Richmond (N.p., n.d.), passim; Mary Wingfield Scott, *Houses of Old Richmond* (New York: Bonanza Books, 1941), 21–23.

Chapter 5

Southern Federalist (I), 1791–1797

For the first few years of the 1790s, John Marshall focused his attention on adapting his law practice to a new legal environment and participating in important cases concerning Virginians' debts to British creditors, the legal rights of corporations, and a scandal among the gentry. He continued his high level of involvement in Richmond's civic and social affairs, as well as attending to a family life beset with more childhood tragedy. Despite his earlier intentions, the pull of politics proved too strong to resist, especially after diplomatic disputes intensified partisan conflict and raised the prospect of war with Great Britain. By mid-1793, Marshall led the influential Federalist faction in Richmond and had become one of the party's key operatives in Virginia. He returned to the House of Delegates in 1795–96 to defend the Washington administration against Republican attacks on its foreign policy. By 1797, Marshall had settled his personal finances sufficiently, through the long-sought purchase of some Fairfax lands, to consider assuming a significantly more substantial public role on behalf of the new president, John Adams.

Marshall conducted his law practice during these years in a legal system that had undergone two major changes since the pre-Constitution period.[1] In December 1788, the General Assembly completely altered the structure of the judiciary, and in late 1792 it thoroughly revised the state laws. The first change came about because the legislature had failed—with the district court act of January 1788, superseding an unimplemented 1784 law—to find a way to administer justice more efficiently at the local level. The assembly seemed unable to avoid antagonizing county court judges, who would lose power, and appellate judges, who would have to ride circuit. They refused to abide by the 1788 act and petitioned the assembly for redress, claiming that the law assigned them new duties without compensation and undermined the independence of the judiciary by leaving them vulnerable to intimidation. The judges' actions caused such an uproar that Governor Edmund Randolph had to call the legislature into special session while the constitutional ratifying convention was still underway.

The assembly broke the impasse during its fall 1792 session by overhauling the judiciary. Under the new arrangement, the tradition-bound and slow-moving General Court—the superior court just above the county level—was decentralized into 18 districts and its cadre of judges was expanded. These district courts had almost the entire jurisdiction of the old General Court and quickly took over its backlog of cases. A new five-judge Court of Appeals was created as the state's highest judicial tribunal. The judges Marshall argued before most often were Edmund Pendleton, Paul Carrington, Peter Lyons, William Fleming—all respected, moderate jurists—and Spencer Roane, a young Jeffersonian ideologue. In addition, the High Court of Chancery was reduced to one judge—Marshall's law school teacher, George Wythe. Chancery proceedings were also reformed to reduce the notorious delays and tortuous procedures that hampered creditors from recovering debts. Marshall practiced in this court system, with a few minor modifications, for the rest of his career as a lawyer.

Marshall found the new system inconvenient at first, but it soon proved to be quite lucrative. In the initial years after the reorganization, he had to spend a fair amount of time—at least several weeks each year—in the districts where his pending General Court cases had been redocketed. This requirement posed no great difficulty when the courts were in Petersburg and Fredericksburg—indeed, Marshall and many other prominent lawyers avidly sought admission to practice in the latter—but he also had to face the hardships of frequent travel to outlying districts in the Shenandoah Valley, Southside, and Eastern Shore. Because of his professional and personal ties to Richmond, Marshall had no interest in becoming a circuit-riding attorney, and the new judiciary law enabled him to avoid that situation. It created a demand for lawyers to practice in the new district courts, giving Marshall and other established, Richmond-based attorneys the opportunity to turn over distant cases to eager novice lawyers trying to build clienteles outside the capital. Marshall gave his suits joined in the Charlottesville and Prince William districts to John Breckinridge, in the Staunton court to Archibald Stuart, and in Petersburg to William Branch Giles. Marshall profited from these informal business relationships; in exchange for the divested cases, he received referrals of suits that those lawyers wanted filed in the new Court of Appeals or the High Court of Chancery. Between 1789 and 1791, Marshall concentrated his district court practice in Richmond, Petersburg, and Fredericksburg, but afterward he tried to clear his workload of suits from outside the capital and focus on practicing before the Commonwealth's highest courts and the United States Circuit Court of Virginia. He stopped taking new cases in Fredericksburg in 1791 and passed on his unfinished cases there to Charles Lee, a future U.S. attorney general, in 1793. By mid-decade, Marshall had confined his legal activities to the most prestigious and remunerative forums, the state appellate and federal courts.[2]

The other major change in Virginia's legal environment that Marshall had to contend with during these years was the legislature's revision of state laws to resolve confusion about which English statutes remained in force after the Revolution and how recent enactments had affected them. The state's political leadership knew that some laws had to be adapted to new circumstances and that others needed to be abolished. Several attempts during the 1770s and 1780s to revise the laws and adopt a code—led by Thomas Jefferson, Edmund Pendleton, George Wythe, and James Madison—had made only piecemeal progress, largely because the assembly was preoccupied with prosecuting the war and dealing with postwar economic issues. Moreover, among legal matters, the legislature considered court reform more pressing than revisal because judges' power was directly at stake in the former. Between 1787 and 1792, however, growing concern about the muddled condition of the Commonwealth's laws prompted the legislature to appoint three successive commissions that worked on the problem of legal revision. While in the House of Delegates in 1789–90, Marshall served on the second commission and a subgroup that determined that well under half of the English and Virginia laws still in effect were relevant and enforced; recommended that a 1776 ordinance adopting pre-1607 English laws be repealed; and urged the appointment of a revisal commission with broad authority to devise a legal code. This third body finished the task of revisal. It consolidated older statutes into several dozen concise bills and combined them with the Declaration of Rights, the Virginia Constitution, and other laws passed since 1776 to form a simplified legal code known as the Revisal of 1792.[3]

The revised legal code, along with the annual accretion of new statutes and cases, formed a larger proportion of the citations and precedents on which Marshall relied in his arguments. In post-Revolutionary Virginia's courts, he found a tactical advantage in referring to laws and decisions that had been "strip[ped] of all vestiges of [their] earlier monarchical aspects and [brought] into conformity with republican principles," as Julian Boyd has described them. In the short term, however, Marshall still had to rely mostly on English law, whose rules and principles remained the dominant authority in Virginia until well into the nineteenth century. His arguments in the Court of Appeals, for example, cite over two dozen collections of cases in various English courts dating from the reign of Elizabeth I. Marshall owned or borrowed the reports, all of which were available in recent editions, but he probably first consulted treatises, digests, or abridgements in preparing his briefs. By using such shortcuts, Marshall was not avoiding research; like nearly all his contemporaries, he took advantage of common-sense timesavers. Despite his reputation as a slack scholar while chief justice, Marshall as a lawyer was a thorough researcher. His civil briefs are filled with citations of cases, statutes, and sources, some of them obscure or archaic. At the same time, he knew that one sure way to lose a case was to bore a judge or jury with an argument larded with references to King's Bench, Yelverton, or Lord Raymond, so he saved those for his written filings. He adjusted his approach in chancery proceedings, where displays of erudition did not have the same soporific effect.[4]

Marshall continued to take on almost exclusively civil cases during this period; his account book records fees from only a few felony clients.[5] As in previous years, he represented mostly plaintiff creditors of various occupations—merchants, planters, and farmers in particular—who sought payment for goods, enforcement of contracts, or recovery of debts. Although he earned a comfortable income averaging over £1,000 a year, he depended on small, statutorily set fees statutorily set fees from many clients involved in litigation rather than retainers from a wealthy few. (That situation may explain why he hurriedly finished a letter to a friend in 1789 with, "A client is just come in—pray heaven he may have money.") He received the highest fees from work in the Virginia Court of Appeals, where he won 67 of 125 cases. The largest category of cases that Marshall participated in before that tribunal involved disputes over the inheritance of land and slaves. These often exceedingly complex cases tested Marshall's facility with arcane principles of property law, his knowledge of the technical rules for construing wills, and his ability to ferret out English citations, on which lawyers in legacy suits relied because American precedents were lacking. Other cases in which he participated in state court concerned suits by titleholders to recover real estate from squatters and assorted breaches of contract. In the federal circuit court, to which he was admitted in 1790, Marshall represented mainly merchants from New York, Philadelphia, and Baltimore, some commercial firms from London, and many Virginia debtors under suit from British creditors.

Marshall also handled many creditors' appeals from chancery decisions that had overturned lower court verdicts in their favor. These cases raised the perennial question of the relationship between law and equity. Marshall usually argued that the debtor had received a full and fair hearing before a jury—in other words, that common law procedures and principles had been properly applied—and that allegations of error should be pleaded in an appellate tribunal, not in an equity (chancery) court that did not stress the common law. Some of Marshall's chancery cases had little intrinsic import but involved legal principles of potentially broad impact. For example, a 1794 case about the comparative effects of repealing versus suspending a statute, which may seem like arid legal casuistry, required Marshall to undertake an intricate analysis of rules of statutory construction and legislative intent—major themes of many of his Supreme Court decisions. The court accepted much of his reasoning as the basis for its ruling for his client; it also found that the legislature had not inadvertently created a void in inheritance law into which the common law must intrude, but instead had preserved the statutory law. This distinction significantly affected how the chancery courts would deal with certain legacy suits.

The most numerous class of cases Marshall took on during his legal career—over 100 during the 1790s—concerned suits initiated in the 1790s by British subjects to recover debts Virginians had contracted before the Revolution.[6] (In

1791, the British government estimated the value of the debt exceeded £2,300,000.) These actions stemmed from pervasive anti-British sentiment in Virginia during the 1780s. Although the fourth article of the 1783 peace treaty with Great Britain stated that "creditors on either side shall meet with no lawful impediment to the recovery of the full value in sterling money, of all bona fide debts heretofore contracted," the Virginia Assembly in 1783 directed that state courts remain closed to British creditors. Virginians feared an onslaught of suits that would undermine the state's already shaky finances. The federal courts, established under the Judiciary Act of 1789, seemed to offer a better opportunity for British creditors; the Federalist judges who held an overwhelming majority of the seats on the federal bench were more sympathetic to British interests than were the mostly Antifederalist judges on the Virginia courts. During the next several years, the U.S. Circuit Court in Virginia heard hundreds of such cases, or approximately three fourths of its docket. Many of the plaintiffs were English consignment merchants and Scottish representatives of Glasgow trading houses; the latter had taken over Virginia's tobacco market before the Revolution. Their suits covered several types of obligations, including, in descending order of frequency, defaulted bonds, unliquidated debts for goods sold and delivered ("book debts"), and unpaid bills of exchange.

Marshall almost always represented the defendants in these cases for reasons of personal friendship, professional acquaintance, financial reward, political advantage, state loyalty, and national honor. Sometimes his clients were Commonwealth bluebloods, such as the Byrds, Randolphs, and Harrisons, but more often they were middling and humbler planters and merchants. On rare occasion, a British merchant retained Marshall. By indirectly defending Virginia's challenge to the federal government's treaty-making authority, however, Marshall seemingly contradicted his support as a legislator for repealing Virginia's impediments to British debtors, as well as his overall nationalist perspective. A lawyer, of course, has to represent his clients as best he can, sometimes at the cost of his personal views. Marshall did not, however, deny that federal treaties took precedence over state laws. What he tried to show in these cases was that at least some of Virginia's actions were not "lawful impediments" under the peace treaty. His argument was based on vested rights, not states rights.

The British plaintiffs met serious obstacles in the federal courts. Most debts that smaller Scottish factors sought to recover fell below the $500 minimum for federal jurisdiction; these merchants ran the retail trade throughout the Piedmont, and the disqualification of their suits eliminated a large percentage of potential litigation. More important for Marshall, Virginia debtors entered, in addition to the regular common law pleas, a set of special pleas that raised questions of law that the courts would have to decide before juries could address any issues of fact. These pleas, eventually numbering four, declared that the debtors' payments made to the state loan office under a 1777 sequestration law legally discharged the debt; that two other wartime acts, which vested all British subjects' property in the state government and prohibited recovery of British debts not assigned before May 1777, were still in effect; that British violations of the seventh article of the peace treaty, pertaining to the confiscation of slaves and the continued occupation of forts in the Northwest, abrogated the peace treaty; and that the dissolution of the colonial relationship on 2 July 1776 annulled the British plaintiffs' rights of recovery.

Marshall apparently was heavily involved in formulating these pleas. They were so lengthy and so frequently employed that he found it convenient to have them printed, using two sets of forms for different types of legal actions. Regardless of whether Marshall and other attorneys for the Virginia debtors thought they could win on the merits of the special pleas, filing them served useful purposes: prolonging the cases until the plaintiffs might consider settling or withdrawing; giving clients time to recover financially so they could afford an adverse judgment; and delaying until a diplomatic resolution to the British debt problem was reached—preferably an accord that would shift responsibility for the debtors' obligation to the state treasury. The judges were in no hurry, either, to decide the weighty constitutional issues embodied in the pleas, such as whether a federal treaty superseded state law, whether British violations had voided the peace treaty, and whether the judiciary had the authority to declare it so. The judges' reluctance to take on these issues is evident in the fact that they heard no arguments until 18 months after the first suits were filed. Moreover, Marshall and the debtors' other lawyers knew that even if the judges ruled against the special pleas, their clients' cases would go before juries whose members mirrored the strong anti-British feeling among Virginians and who could be expected to help the defendants in most cases.[7]

No courts heard any arguments on the British debt cases until November 1791, when Marshall represented Thomas Walker, a physician, soldier, explorer, land speculator, and legislator from Albemarle County, in a suit filed in federal circuit court by William Jones, a partner in the Bristol trading firm of Farell and Jones. Walker was a frequent client of Marshall's, and Jones was plaintiff in over 20 recovery suits. *Jones v. Walker* became the test case for determining the validity of the special pleas and attracted an array of Virginia's ablest lawyers. During a weeklong hearing in a packed Richmond courtroom, two associate justices of the U.S. Supreme Court and a U.S. District Court judge heard a formidable battery of lawyers—Marshall, Patrick Henry, Alexander Campbell, the U.S. district attorney for Virginia, and James Innes, the Commonwealth's attorney general—argue for defendant Walker against John Wickham, Jerman Baker, Andrew Ronald, and Burwell Starke on behalf of plaintiff Jones. A stenographic report of the proceedings was lost, and the only surviving record of the arguments is a speech of Henry's published over 25 years later but based on the original transcript. Marshall presumably gave his usual dispassionate analysis of the essential issues in the special pleas—which were framed to emphasize the ongoing dispute with Great Britain over peace treaty violations—and Henry's high-sounding forensics took up three days. Both efforts went for naught; one member of the court had to leave suddenly for personal reasons, and the other two declined to issue a ruling by themselves. Twice in 1792, two-judge panels reheard the case but refused to decide it.[8]

A full circuit court, consisting of Chief Justice John Jay, Associate Justice James Iredell, and District Judge Cyrus Griffin, finally convened in May 1793. By then, the plaintiff Jones had died, and all of his many suits had to be revived by special writs in the name of his estate's administrator, John Tyndale Ware. To prevent another postponement, the court ordered that one of those suits, against prominent Richmond merchant Daniel Hylton, be revived in Ware's name. *Ware v. Hylton* thus became the new test case for the special pleas. Hylton retained the same four lawyers—Marshall, Henry, Campbell, and Innes—whom Thomas Walker had used. The court heard the case from 24 May to 7 June; Marshall argued his points on the 29th and 30th. His own notes have been lost, but Justice Iredell scrawled several pages of disjointed words and phrases which, when used with materials on the 1796 appeal of the case, make Marshall's main contentions evident. Besides extrapolating from the special pleas, he also discussed some of the constitutional issues, such as the authority of states relative to the federal treaty-making power, that judges previously had avoided. His essential point was that the peace treaty repealed conflicting state laws prospectively but could not undo actions taken while the sequestration act was in effect. The arguments of Marshall and the other lawyers impressed Justice Iredell—he praised their "ingenuity . . . depth of investigation, and . . . power of reasoning" as "fully equal to any thing I have ever witnessed"—and one observer reported that "Marshall, it was acknowledged by all hands, excelled himself in sound sense and argument—which is saying an immensity."[9]

Despite their compelling rhetoric, Marshall and his colleagues lost the case. The court unanimously rejected three of the special pleas—those pertaining to peace treaty violations, the dissolution of the colonial relationship, and the state law limiting recovery to prewar debts—but by a 2–1 vote affirmed the fourth plea, that payments into the state loan office under Virginia's 1777 sequestration law legally discharged debts owed to British creditors. After the decision, British creditors routinely won their suits. Marshall lost every British debt case in which he represented the defendant; the only suits he won were the few in which his client was the British creditor. Even though Ware carried most of his points, he decided to appeal the circuit court's finding on loan office payments to the U.S. Supreme Court, a determination reinforced by a jury verdict that denied him interest on the amount that Hylton had not yet paid. Marshall traveled to Philadelphia in January–February 1795—his first trip outside Virginia since marching with Continental troops to New York and New Jersey in 1779—to be admitted to practice before the Supreme Court and to participate in the justices' first hearing of *Ware v. Hylton*. The Court granted continuances then and at a second hearing in August. Final arguments began on 6 February 1796 and lasted for five days. Marshall, in his only appearance before the Supreme Court arguing a case, and Campbell represented Hylton; opposing them were a noted Philadelphia lawyer, Edward Tilghman, joined by William Lewis and Alexander Wilcocks.[10]

Marshall reiterated the main points he had used in the earlier hearings to support the one special plea before the Court. His presentation was characteristically straightforward, cogent, logical, and precise. William Wirt, one of Virginia's most prominent attorneys and later attorney general under James Monroe and John Quincy Adams, heard Marshall's argument and recalled that in contrast to Campbell's "Apollonian airs," Marshall "spoke, as he always does, to the judgment merely and for the simple purpose of convincing." His main assertion was that Hylton's voluntary payments to the state treasury under the terms of the 1777 debt law, which was confiscatory in nature, fully discharged his client's obligation to Ware. He also stressed that under the unique circumstances of the Revolution, Virginia was a sovereign state when it passed its debt sequestration laws; that those laws were valid because "property is the creature of civil society, and subject, in all respects, to the disposition and controul [sic] of civil institutions"; and consequently that a treaty ratified later by a new national government could not repeal valid state statutes merely by inference. Marshall avoided directly disputing the plaintiff's constitutional point that treaties were supreme over state laws because he probably anticipated that the Court would disagree with Virginia's contrary view. Instead, he sought to persuade the Justices that a "fair and rational construction" of the peace treaty would lead them to conclude that Virginia was correct in this instance, that loan office payments were not lawful impediments.[11]

The justices were not convinced. In a 4–1 decision issued on 7 March, they rejected Marshall's "ingenious, metaphysical reasoning and refinement upon the words, debt, discharge, [and] extinguishment" as contradicting accepted principles for interpreting treaties, and held that article 4 of the peace treaty annulled Virginia's 1777 debt law and allowed British debtors to pursue recovery. The outcome was not surprising. Besides having several circuit court precedents to rely on, the justices, all Federalists, were certain to have rebuffed Marshall's challenge to the primacy of the federal government. Marshall left no personal thoughts about the decision. One can safely surmise, though, that he felt a variety of emotions: frustration that all the time and effort he had expended arguing the special pleas in dozens of cases since 1793 had gone for nothing; relief that he had fulfilled his professional responsibility to his Virginia clients; and satisfaction at the experience of arguing before the Supreme Court. The only known remuneration Marshall received for all his work on Daniel Hylton's behalf was £7 in 1793, and Hylton soon was in no position to pay any more. In 1797, a jury assessed him over $6,000 in damages, principal and interest, which he paid with 36 slaves, five horses, two mules, 30 head of cattle, 24 head of sheep, and 300 barrels of corn. Hylton went bankrupt satisfying this and other judgments, and creditors drove him into debtor's prison for several years.[12]

Marshall built his law practice while the American economy was undergoing rapid commercial growth that prompted, and was in turn reinforced by, changes in the roles of law, lawyers, and judges in promoting economic development. During the 1780s and 1790s, he experienced the first phase of the abandonment of customs and technicalities of the English common law, many of which inhibited enterprise with traditional regulations, in favor of an "instrumental" conception of law that emphasized the "release of energy." Under this new paradigm, law, as interpreted by lawyers and judges, was to be adapted to rapidly changing commercial circumstances, encourage productive use of resources and capital, impart legal predictability, and protect property, new mediums of exchange, contracts, and corporate charters from "democratic" or "moral economy" regulation. Marshall and nearly all of his political, economic, and legal associates, allies, and friends in Virginia shared this new attitude toward the role of law in fostering development and investment. Not surprisingly, the jurist Marshall most admired was Lord Mansfield, who refashioned key elements of English commercial and contract law, as Marshall wrote in an 1811 Supreme Court decision, "[to] remove those technical impediments which grew out of a different state of society."[13]

In this changing legal environment, Marshall refined his views affirming the sanctity of contracts—which he had expressed earlier in *Hite v. Fairfax* (1786)—in a significant case involving the school where he received his legal education.[14] *Bracken v. College of William and Mary* (1790) arose because the Board of Visitors in 1779 tried to revise extensively the school's curriculum, and to eliminate some professorships and create others. As part of the overhaul, they dismissed the Reverend John Bracken, a professor of classics. Bracken contended that the visitors had exceeded their authority under the college's 1693 charter and sought a writ of mandamus directing the visitors to reinstate him. In December 1790, the Virginia Court of Appeals heard arguments from Marshall, who had represented the board since the suit began in 1787, and John Taylor of Caroline for Bracken. In essence, Marshall asserted that the actions of a private corporation were immune from government regulation as long as they could reasonably be construed as not violating the terms of its charter. The court unanimously denied Bracken's request for a mandamus. Although ignoring Marshall's point that the court lacked jurisdiction over "private eleemosynary institutions," the judges agreed with him that the college's charter should be interpreted broadly to give the Board of Visitors "power to make such laws for the government of the college, from time to time, *according to their various occasion and circumstance*, as to them should seem most fit and expedient" (Marshall's emphasis).

The *Bracken* case involved education and eleemosynary institutions, but Marshall could easily apply his logic against regulation of business corporations—such as the transportation, banking, and entrepreneurial endeavors in which he was personally or professionally involved—as violating contract rights spelled out in their charters. In *Bracken*, Marshall laid the foundation on which he built his historic Supreme Court decision in *Dartmouth College v. Woodward* (1819). In that case, he explicitly ruled that a corporate charter was a contract protected from state government alteration under Article I, section 10 of the U.S. Constitution. As one legal scholar has noted, "The Chief Justice's reasoning in 1819 was in certain respects grounded upon premises only one step removed from the reasoning of Marshall, the lawyer, in 1790." Another historian of Marshall observes that "[the idea] that a corporate charter was a kind of contract, perhaps one that was constitutionally protected, was perfectly consistent with Marshall's Virginia experience." Marshall had been professionally tied to Richmond's urban, commercial interests since he began his practice. He regularly invested in enterprises dealing with river and road transportation and bought stock in banks and insurance companies. By the time of the *Bracken* case, the Commonwealth had chartered corporations involved with internal improvements. Marshall, who had invested with two of them—the Potomac River Company and James River Company—recognized the special role the corporate form of organization had in raising capital and encouraging enterprise. He believed charters, as contracts between investors and state governments, must have constitutional protection to provide some legal stability during a time of rapid commercialization, and to prevent interference from authorities responding to socioeconomic pressure groups— mainly debtors and farmers—who opposed the economic activities of people such as Marshall's clients, business associates, and legal colleagues.

While he was an advocate of and investor in corporations, Marshall realized that their right of contract would occasionally collide with the equally valid right of the individual to hold property. This conflict was highlighted when entrepreneurs and investors undertaking government-sponsored internal improvements sought to have the state exercise its eminent domain power to take property owners' land. Virginia, like most states, had no general law or constitutional provision requiring that it pay "just compensation" to owners of lands it appropriated for public works, although such stipulations usually were written into legally binding agreements between landholders and road builders or canal cutters. Marshall participated in one such case in 1792, when the Potomac River Company, a state-chartered corporation, proposed to dig a channel through some land which Governor Henry Lee owned but which the legislature had condemned. Either the company or the governor asked Marshall for his opinion on whether Lee should be compensated for some of the land before or after the canal was dug. Marshall had his own conflicting interests in this instance—he was a stockholder in the company and a friend of Lee—but on the general principle, he came down on the side of the property owner: "I conceive that any law which is to wrest from an individual his property without his consent must be construed strictly, and rather narrowed than enlarged." Marshall tried to be judicious, asking only that corporations respect others' property rights while exercising their own. Doing so, he believed, would not impede commercial activity. On the contrary, the status of corporations would improve if property rights received widespread respect because corporate charters were contracts, and contract rights were a type of property right.[15]

The most sensational case Marshall participated in during his legal career was also Virginia's most famous criminal proceeding of the eighteenth century: *Commonwealth v. Randolph* (1793).[16] The case concerned lurid allegations of incestuous adultery and infanticide made against 23-year-old Richard Randolph and his 17-year-old sister-in-law Ann Cary "Nancy" Randolph in late 1792 and early 1793. This Gothic *cause célèbre* brought together political rivals—John Marshall, the Federalist, joined with his longtime opponent, Patrick Henry, to defend a member of one of the state's most influential families, the Randolphs—in a striking display of elite cohesion in the face of scandal. Moreover, Marshall, whose mother was a Randolph, had a family reputation to protect.

Richard Randolph was the son of John Randolph of "Matoax," a brother of John Randolph of Roanoke and a stepson of St. George Tucker, the esteemed judge and lawyer. On 30 September or 1 October 1792, he, his dour wife Judith, and the charming and attractive Nancy took a short carriage ride to visit "Glenlyvar," the home of their cousin Randolph Harrison. Soon after arriving, Nancy, who suffered from chronic "colic," complained that she did not feel well and went to bed early. During the night, screams of pain, loud voices, heavy footsteps, and other commotion came from the guests' bedrooms and roused the household. Nancy asked for and was given a dose of the opiate laudanum. When examined the next day, she was quiet but extremely pale. She had lost a fair amount of blood; much of her bedding had been stripped, and stains were evident on the stairs and elsewhere. After a few days of bed rest, Nancy recovered and left Glenlyvar with Richard and Judith, and the party believed the unpleasant episode would be kept quiet.

Soon, however, rumors emanated from the slave quarters that Nancy had given birth to Richard's child, and that he had strangled it. One slave even claimed to know where Richard had tried to hide the dead baby in a pile of old shingles. The story spread throughout much of southern Virginia, and the Randolphs had to find a way to stop it from sullying their reputation. Probably at St. George Tucker's suggestion, Richard in early 1793 tried to arrange an action of slander to vindicate his honor, but Nancy's father declined his request to join in a contrived suit. Resolved to fight, Richard had little choice but to flush his accusers into the open. In late March, he announced in several newspapers that he intended to appear before the Cumberland County Court at its next session "to answer in the due course of law, any charge or crime which any person or persons whatsoever shall then and there think proper to alledge [*sic*] against me." Also around this time, Richard retained the legal services of John Marshall and—after his initial hesitation supposedly was overcome by a proffered fee of £250—Patrick Henry. On 21 or 22 April, Richard appeared before at least one of the justices of the peace, who decided that the matter warranted a hearing by the whole county court. He spent several days in jail, as required under law, until the examination of evidence on 29 April.[17]

The judges listened to Richard, various Randolph relations, and other witnesses delicately describe Richard and Nancy's supposed "imprudent familiarities" with each other; her insistence on undressing only around her servant; her request for the drug gum guaiacum—a common remedy for colic that also relieved morning sickness and sometimes induced premature labor—

and "appearances which would justify the suspicion of a Birth or abortion" in her bedroom. Under Virginia law, the slaves' allegations were inadmissible through direct testimony, although one cousin did refer to them secondhand. No written ruling exists, but the judges apparently concluded that Nancy had either miscarried or delivered a stillborn child, and that while she and Richard may have been guilty of adultery—or "criminal conversation," in contemporary legal parlance—no evidence conclusively pointed to a murder. Without retiring to deliberate, the magistrates dismissed the case. *Commonwealth v. Randolph* resulted in Richard's exoneration, at least legally and officially.

Several questions about Marshall's exact part in all of this remain unresolved. What kind of legal service or advice did he provide for Richard Randolph before the hearing? Did he attend the hearing, and if so, what did he do there? Did he, for example, make any statements or question any witnesses? And what exactly are Marshall's "notes of evidence," the principal source of information about the case? Did he take them during the proceedings or compose them afterward, and if the latter, why?

There is no record of what advice Marshall gave Richard before the hearing, or that the two met or even corresponded, although some communication must have occurred. Along with St. George Tucker, Marshall might have suggested that Richard pursue some avenue of legal redress. Circumstantial evidence strongly indicates that Marshall was at Cumberland County Court in late April in some lawyerly capacity, but not necessarily as one of Richard's courtroom advocates; that responsibility apparently fell to Henry. Nor do Marshall's "notes of evidence," dated around 29 April, help sort things out. If anything, they suggest at least three possibilities for Marshall's involvement in the case.

The first theory, upon which all secondary accounts of the affair are based, contends that Marshall took the notes during the hearing. By this theory, the notes are, in effect, an informal transcript of the "trial," and, conveniently for the biographer, provide a neat courtroom climax: Marshall, following Henry's incisive cross-examination of snooping Randolph relatives, seals the case with a telling analysis of the most damning evidence—Richard and Nancy's purported "fondness" toward one another, her apparent pregnancy and request for gum guaiacum, the bloodstains in the bedroom, and the alleged concealment of the dead child—and turned the contentions of Richard's accusers back on themselves.[18]

The "trial" was actually more like an informal coroner's inquest—Richard had not yet been charged with any crime—but the same procedures of questioning witnesses, presenting arguments, and rendering a verdict would have been followed. In retrospect, it might seem risky for Marshall to have waited to listen to all witnesses before preparing his crucial closing statement, but he could quickly grasp the essential points of a case and knew how to think on his feet, and this matter was transparent compared to the intricate civil suits with which he had so much experience. A telling point against this theory, however, is the quality of the notes: They seem too thorough and well crafted for Marshall to have composed them amid the tension and distractions of the hearing. On other occasions when he took notes during proceedings, he only jotted down sentence fragments, words, and abbreviations. Moreover, although evidence of Henry's courtroom theatrics—notably his mock outrage at one tryingly meddlesome cousin—exists elsewhere, nowhere except in the notes is there any documentation of Marshall's so-called "summation." Thus, the most-used explanation for the notes seems the least likely.

Two other, more plausible interpretations of the notes start with the premise that Marshall compiled them after Richard's hearing for use either in defending Nancy at a separate inquest or as a reference for the Randolph family to employ in responding to persistent rumors. Evidence exists to support either theory, and both explain the notes' clarity and comprehensiveness, but neither is conclusive. Regarding the first, Nancy was never officially accused of any crime, but both she and her cousin John Randolph recalled that she had been questioned, and Marshall's notes imply as much. There are no indications, such as records of fees or references to travel to Cumberland County, that Marshall represented Nancy in any legal manner after Richard's hearing, but he could have used his or someone else's rough notes—since lost—of that proceeding to prepare the extant document for Nancy's lawyer. The last paragraph of the notes, however, may be read as supporting the idea that the Randolphs intended to use them to rebut continued allegations of Nancy's wrongdoing. The words sound as though Marshall wrote them not to convince a group of judges but to persuade a much larger audience that in Nancy's case, "[c]andor will not condemn or exclude from society, a person who may be only unfortunate."[19]

Without further evidence—such as Marshall's own copy of the notes; John Randolph and an unknown person transcribed the only existing versions of the original—Marshall's precise legal role in the scandal cannot be better clarified. The episode continued to embarrass the Randolphs for years, and Marshall reentered it sixteen years later. Richard Randolph died in 1795, and Nancy, lacking an estate of her own, had to live with his family under most unpleasant, and possibly abusive, conditions. In 1809, she met Gouverneur Morris, a well-known Federalist politician from New York, who hired her as his housekeeper and soon planned to marry her. Morris, a longtime acquaintance of Marshall's, wrote "to ask you frankly the Reputation Miss Randolph left in Virginia, and the Standing she held in Society." Morris claimed that he did not believe the calumnies he had heard against her but wanted to avoid giving the Federalists' political opponents a weapon to use against him and his party. Marshall responded with a discreet overview of the affair, noted that opinion on Richard and Nancy's guilt was divided at the time, that those who thought Nancy was "the victim of a concurrent of unfortunate circumstances" included "those ladies with whom I am connected," and that the episode did not consign her to outcast status. He was not asked for his own judgment and did not give it. The recitation of facts reassured Morris, and he wed Nancy soon after.[20]

A concluding postscript: The probable truth of what happened in September–October 1792 may have come out several years after Gouverneur Morris and Nancy married. In 1814, John Randolph of Roanoke, seemingly overcome with jealousy and hatred that could be attributed to his earlier unrequited love for Nancy and his growing mental instability, wrote a letter to Morris rehashing the details of the scandal. He also circulated the letter in Virginia. Nancy responded in a January 1815 letter that she also sent to several notable Virginians. She admitted that she had borne a child—dead—but that Richard was not the father; Theodorick Randolph, Richard and John's brother, was. She and Theodorick had been engaged, but her father opposed their marriage because Theodorick's inheritance was encumbered by a British debt. He died in February 1792, just after what Nancy recalled as "the scene which began the history of my sorrows." Richard "knew every circumstance" about the two lovers, but, "a man of honor" in Nancy's eyes, said nothing and became her close but platonic companion. After Nancy sent her letter, the controversy faded away. If Marshall ever knew about Theodorick, he never let on. He did not consider it legally or politically beneficial to either his clients or Virginia's squirearchy to admit that anything untoward had happened that autumn night at Glenlyvar.[21]

Marshall's other noteworthy legal activities from the late 1780s to 1797 further demonstrate the scope of his professional connections and interests, his stature in the state bar, and the demand for his legal expertise. He served as acting attorney general of Virginia from October 1794 to March 1795. The incumbent, James Innes, received the approval of the governor and the Council of State to ask Marshall to assume those duties while Innes went to Kentucky on a political and diplomatic mission for President Washington. During those six months, Marshall rendered eight opinions, most on civil matters ranging from the law of salvage and a sheriff's fraudulent sale of land to pay tax arrearages, to a registrar's lack of authority to issue land patents and the date to be used by an appointee for posting bond and security of office. Marshall's two most important opinions dealt with the constitutional issue of concurrent state and federal authority over the militia. The controversy arose after Congress in May 1794 authorized the president to requisition militias because of the threat of war with Great Britain or France, and after Washington in August had called up several state militias, including Virginia's, to help suppress the Whiskey Rebellion in western Pennsylvania. In one opinion, Marshall argued that when delinquent militiamen were subject to both federal and state fines, the former should take precedence. In the other opinion, he contended that after their call-up, militia officers served under the authority of the federal government, even though the governor had formally requisitioned them, and must obey presidential orders and abide by federal law. Marshall, from the Virginia ratifying convention in 1788 to a U.S. circuit court opinion in 1815, consistently held that state authority over the militia was concurrent in areas where federal law did not apply but otherwise was subordinate to national authority.[22]

In addition to filling in as attorney general, Marshall also provided advice to the Richmond and Alexandria city governments, answered George Washington's questions about debt recovery and disputed land claims, filed legislative petitions for individuals claiming that Virginia owed them for wartime supplies, served on a panel that decided whether to commit mentally unstable persons, and, at the request of the legislature, worked ex officio on a committee to collect all the state's property laws. Marshall's 1793 opinion for the Richmond Common Hall, the city's governing council, on a jurisdictional dispute over a tract of land is notable for his assertion that "I am myself inclined to construe Acts literally"—a position that his later critics would claim was scarcely accurate but that, as Charles Hobson has amply demonstrated, properly characterized his interpretive inclinations then and later. Marshall's work on the compilation of property laws, intended to help resolve rapidly multiplying disputes over land holdings, became one of the early steps leading to the publication of Hening's *Statutes*, an indispensable reference for Virginia legal history.[23]

In the 1790s, Marshall also participated in two prominent social activities—in one as host, in the other as member—that reflected and helped secure his prominence in the Virginia bar. In the early part of the decade, he began his tradition, lasting until the 1830s, of inviting some 30 legal colleagues to a banquet at his new home one Sunday each month. These "lawyers' dinners," as they came to be called, usually lasted from midafternoon until late evening and, by all accounts, included many courses of food and wine served in the large dining room, along with lively conversation encouraged by the convivial host. Marshall's dinners became one of the premier events on Richmond's social calendar and were a private source of professional identity and unity for the capital's legal elite. They provided a relaxed setting in which courtroom and political rivals could smooth over differences and exchange ideas and information about cases, clients, and public affairs. Marshall probably came up with the idea for the lawyers' dinners to break the social isolation that Polly's debility often forced him into, but, as in his political activities, the needs of his congenial and gregarious personality advanced his professional reputation and reinforced his social prestige as well.[24]

Marshall was a founding member of another social institution of Richmond's legal and professional illuminati, the Quoit Club, later known as the Barbecue Club. Founded in 1788 by a group of local lawyers and businessmen, the club met every Saturday between May and October about a mile west of Marshall's house at a small resort called Buchanan's Spring, named for the Episcopalian minister on whose farm it was located. Except for limiting its membership to thirty, the Quoit Club had only one other rule: Discussions of politics, business, or religion were prohibited, with transgressors fined a case of champagne (which members would drink at the next meeting). Instead, Marshall and his fellow members—most of them attorneys, merchants, and planters he knew well from his law practice and political activities—directed their energies to disposing of a huge repast of barbecued suckling and tubs of liquor punch and playing backgammon or quoits, a game much like horseshoes but using large metal rings. These weekend gatherings, which Marshall faithfully attended until the 1830s, produced many anecdotes about him, including reminiscences about his dead-eye accuracy at "ringing the meg" with the heavy, rough-hewn iron quoits he favored (most players used lighter brass rings); his childlike exuberance during close matches; and his feigned gravity in arguing before a "tribunal" that adjudicated a dispute over whether his throw had won (it did, the "court" decided). Some of the recollections are probably apocryphal, but the fact that numerous stories exist at all is an indication of the cheerful regard in which his contemporaries held him. Moreover, from the standpoint of his profession, the club had similar effects as his lawyers' dinners, even though substantive discussions supposedly did not occur.[25]

Marshall remained heavily engaged in Richmond's civic and social life during the early and mid-1790s. If anything, his activities had increased when compared with the previous several years. Most significant from the standpoint of the capital's welfare was his participation, as an officer in the city militia, in two efforts to maintain order during periods of widespread public anxiety: the months following the slave revolt in the French colony of St. Domingue in 1791, and the yellow fever epidemic that ravaged Philadelphia in the summer and fall of 1793. Richmond had a large enough population by 1790 to warrant its own militia regiment, and in August 1791, Marshall was sworn in as the unit's colonel. Also that year, slaves in the Caribbean colony of St. Domingue (Haiti) launched a bloody uprising against their French masters. This revolutionary act sent a wave of fear throughout slaveholding regions of the South and elicited groundless rumors of conspiracies and weapons caches and hushed talk about the "French island." At least two violent incidents did occur in Virginia in 1792: a gang of slaves raided a plantation in Charles City County and killed an overseer, and elsewhere another group of slaves attacked a member of a slave patrol. The arrival of several hundred desperate French refugees in Norfolk in July 1793, who fled the island after slaves stormed the port city of Cap François, heightened white Virginians' apprehension and produced more false intelligence about "Intended Risings." In August and September 1793, state officials heard allegations that slave insurrections probably would occur any moment in Richmond, Petersburg, Yorktown, Norfolk, Portsmouth, and several counties in the lower Chesapeake region. Marshall passed on one such report to Governor Henry Lee: a letter describing a purported plot in Powhatan County by 300 slaves and the escape of several "negro foremen," including one "with a Sworde."[26]

As commander of the capital's militia detachment, Marshall administered the orders of the governor and lieutenant governor to organize security detachments, guard the armory, and "perform such duty as you may think conducive to the public safety of the City." Marshall attended to logistical and administrative matters and did not have to deploy the militia, as the rumors of imminent violence proved unfounded. Besides his militia duties, he also contributed to a private relief fund for the French refugees. (In 1794, the General Assembly approved a public fund for the refugees. Marshall was not a delegate then but presumably would have voted for the relief.)[27]

Marshall never expressed any strong proslavery views, advanced only legalistic and unemotional positions in the slavery-related cases he was involved in, was bothered by the crueler aspects of the institution, and was a benign master to his own slaves. Yet the St. Domingue insurrection outraged him because of the threat it posed to the plantation-based gentry society to which he was politically and professionally devoted. In his biography of Washington, it was one of the few subjects—most of which also concern instability of one sort or another—about which Marshall made no pretext of objectivity. He described the rebellion as the "early and bitter fruits" of the French revolutionists' "mad and wicked project" of spreading their "malignant philosophy" of egalitarianism to the West Indies, where the slaves engaged in a "fury" of massacre, rape, and pillage against the whites. Instead of "slow and cautious steps which gradually introduce reform without ruin," "oceans of blood" were spilled for the "attainment of some fancied untried good." Such overwrought prose is uncharacteristic of Marshall's otherwise bland narrative style—even granting the ideological point he was trying to score against French radicalism and its domestic ally, the Republicans—and, when read along with his attacks on Shays's Rebellion and the Whiskey Rebellion, underscores the importance he placed on order, stability, and security. The Caribbean uprising may also have started Marshall thinking about the possibility of colonizing free blacks in Africa as a way to prevent racial strife. Some years later, he became head of the Richmond chapter of the American Colonization Society.[28]

In October 1793, Marshall helped enforce Richmond's quarantine against what one historian has called "the most appalling collective disaster that had ever overtaken an American city": the yellow fever epidemic that had killed nearly 5,000 Philadelphians (almost 10 percent of the population) and paralyzed the national government since it broke out in August. News of "the plague or some other infectious disease" reached Richmond in mid-September, and the Council of State immediately subjected all ships from Philadelphia and the West Indies, where the disease had also struck, to a 20-day quarantine off an island near Norfolk. In mid-October, Governor Henry Lee learned that a woman had died of yellow fever after arriving in Richmond a few days earlier from Philadelphia. Lee ordered Marshall, in his capacity as militia commander, to visit the ship on which the woman had traveled. Marshall boarded the *Phoenix*, anchored across the James River off Manchester, and closely questioned the vessel's captain, a passenger, a cabin boy, and a sailor about its activities in Philadelphia. He concluded that the ship might have been infected and, after reporting to the Council of State, supervised the movement of the *Phoenix* to the quarantine site. Although Marshall did not know it, he was not in danger of contracting the disease through his contact with the passengers. Yellow fever is not contagious, and unless isolating the ship kept some stowaway mosquitoes from flying ashore, the state's policy cannot be credited with the fact that no cases of the disease were reported in Virginia that summer and fall.[29]

Marshall returned to political office in Richmond in June 1794. Six years after resigning from the Common Council, the city's governing board, he was elected for a second time. Soon after, the other members of the Council offered him the mayoralty, but he refused, presumably because he believed that the duties of that office would take too much time away from his legal practice. He remained on the Council until at least May 1795, when the existing records end. He and his fellow aldermen worked on problems of congestion, sanitation, and safety stemming from Richmond's rapid growth; by 1795 the capital had nearly 5,000 inhabitants, a 25 percent increase in just five years. They also oversaw the capital's continued recovery from the devastating fire of 1787, which had destroyed most buildings in the city. Businessmen built more corn and wheat mills, tobacco warehouses, and small factories along the waterfront, and residents continued spreading farther up the hills to the north, east, and west. The new houses, like Marshall's, usually were made of brick, and by mid-decade a foreign visitor noted that few wooden ones remained. In addition to responding to these major changes in Richmond's character, Marshall and the other councilors also dealt with everyday municipal matters such as licensing taverns, arranging for street repairs, and collecting taxes.[30]

As an active Mason, Marshall participated in the order's social and charitable functions such as the annual ball and the celebration of St. John's feast day. In 1793–95 he was elected grand master of the order in Virginia. Marshall also contributed money to and was an officer of the Amicable Society, formed in 1788 to assist travelers and strangers to the capital. In 1794, Marshall helped found the Mutual Assurance Society, one of America's oldest fire insurance companies, and received a policy for his house two years later. When members later questioned the legality of the society, Marshall, as an assembly delegate, introduced a bill affirming its establishment. He also helped manage a bridge lottery and a lead mine sale, subscribed to the public library, served as executor for the estate of the popular tavern keeper Serafino Formicola, and was a member of one of the Jockey Clubs, which set rules and raised purses for biannual horse races attended by Richmond's elite. Lastly, Marshall's account book is filled with evidence of his full social life, with numerous references to plays, balls, Fourth of July and Washington's birthday celebrations, St. Tammany festivals, and even the circus.[31]

Despite his heavy schedule of professional, civic, and social activities, Marshall stayed close to his family. In addition to caring for Polly and his children, Marshall regularly gave money to his brothers Louis and Alexander— they replaced James, who had left Richmond, as the main beneficiaries of his largesse—and to his sister Lucy, who lived with him and Polly until her marriage to John Ambler (Polly's cousin) in May 1791. Marshall also provided two tutors at different times for his eldest son, Thomas. One was the Reverend John DuBois, a Roman Catholic priest who had fled revolutionary France in 1791, settled in Richmond, and taught classical languages, arithmetic, and bookkeeping. The other was Eldridge Harris, a Richmond schoolmaster who reopened the Richmond Academy in 1794 and taught a similar curriculum.[32]

Marshall's family life mostly was marred with tragedy during this period. Only one of the three children Polly bore between 1789 and 1795 survived childhood. In 1792, four-month-old John James and three-year-old Mary Ann died within two months of each other. Marshall recounted the wrenching circumstances of his infant son's death in a letter he wrote many years later to his friend Joseph Story, who had just lost a child:

You ask me if Mrs. Marshall and myself have ever lost a child. We have lost four—three of them bidding fairer for health and life than any that have survived them. One, a daughter about six or seven[,] was brought fresh to our minds by what you say of yours. She was one of the most fascinating children I ever saw. She was followed within a fortnight by a brother whose death was attended by a circumstance we can never forget. When the child was supposed to be dying[,] I tore the distracted mother from the bedside. We soon afterwards heard a voice in the room which we considered as indicating the death of the infant. . . . [I went] into the room and found him still breathing. I returned [and] as the pang of his death had been felt by his mother and [I] was confident he must die, I concealed his being alive and prevailed on her to take refuge with her mother. . . . The child lived two days, during which I was agonized with its condition and with the occasional hope, though the case was desperate, that I might enrapture his mother with the intelligence of his restoration to us. After the event had taken place[,] his mother could not bear to return to the house she had left and remained with her mother a fortnight. I then addressed her a letter in verse in which our mutual loss was deplored, our lost children spoken of with the parental feeling which belonged to the occasion, her affection for those who survived was appealed to, and her religious confidence in the wisdom and goodness of Providence excited. The letter closed with a pressing invitation to return to me and her children.

Nor could Marshall and his wife long enjoy the arrival of another daughter, also named Mary, in September 1795, as his sister Lucy died soon after. The deaths of John James and Mary Ann no doubt drew Marshall closer to his other children and probably caused Polly to withdraw further from her expected child-rearing role. Marshall, whose letters indicate he was an affectionate and attentive father, would have assumed even more responsibility for his children's upbringing, just as he had gradually taken over the management of his household's domestic affairs in the absence of his wife.[33]

Marshall supported his family well with the income he drew from his law practice, which averaged almost £1120 annually between 1789 and 1795, when his account book ends. His earnings fluctuated instead of growing steadily, with a high of £1,427 in 1790 and a low of £973 in 1792, but in most years his income was twice as large as his expenditures and easily gave him enough to improve his family's living standard steadily. According to personal property lists and tax records from the mid-1790s, Marshall owned nine slaves, four horses, and one coach or carriage. He also possessed 520 acres of land in Fauquier County, an unknown acreage of farmland in or near Richmond, and a house and two lots in the city. His house at the corner of Ninth and I Streets, which he built for just over £1,200 between 1788 and 1790, and several outbuildings were located in the fashionable "Court End" of the capital and had appreciated in value to nearly £2,000 by 1796. The house itself was unostentatiously decorated, reflecting the simple, comfortable life its practical and unpretentious owner enjoyed. Marshall could easily walk to the capitol building, and his neighbors included a number of relatives and professional associates—among them Jaquelin Ambler, Edward Carrington, Daniel Call, William Wirt, Thomas Ritchie, John Wickham, Philip Nicholas, and Spencer Roane.[34]

Marshall loyally supported Federalist domestic and foreign policies while in the state legislature in the early 1790s. He had espoused Alexander Hamilton's Bank of the United States (BUS) during the October 1790 session, and he now endorsed the opening of a branch in Virginia to link the state's economy and political system to the national government. Marshall and other BUS stockholders, however, could not overcome opposition from Republicans who were averse to allowing any extension of Hamilton's financial apparatus into Virginia. In an effort to persuade reluctant BUS officials to act, Marshall and 125 other persons and businesses in July 1792 petitioned the BUS. They noted Richmond's "centrical situation" in Virginia trade and finance and suggested that "a Scheme . . . now in agitation for the establishment of a State Bank in the said City" would preclude the BUS from participating in Virginia's economic development. In addition, the petitioners did not want to surrender resulting political benefits to the Republicans, who wanted to create a state-based banking system as a foil to the Federalists' national network. The assembly granted a charter for the Bank of Richmond in December 1792, and Marshall, sensing that prospects for a BUS branch in the capital had dwindled, agreed to serve as one of 10 superintendents of a stock subscription for the state-chartered bank. The drive to sell $400,000 in stock began in May 1793 but soon faltered.[35]

Marshall believed the failure to establish a BUS branch in Virginia impaired economic growth and investment, and caused financial disruptions which lowered some of the state's agricultural prices so much that farmers stopped growing some crops and lost market share to mid-Atlantic competitors. He sarcastically observed, however, that "good democrats & real friends of this country" blamed "Hamilton, Jay & the Devil" for the lower prices. Marshall kept with the issue and raised the BUS branch idea again in 1795 while in the assembly. He was chairman of a special House of Delegates committee that brought in a bill authorizing at least one BUS branch in Virginia. The delegates overwhelmingly passed the measure, which Marshall and its advocates intended as a display of pro-BUS sentiment. At the next session, the House rejected a bill to charter a state bank in Norfolk. Marshall voted for that measure, probably because he had resigned himself to the fact that a BUS branch would not be established but believed another state-chartered bank was needed (the first had opened in Alexandria in 1792) to promote financial stability and economic growth. A BUS branch was finally set up in Norfolk in 1800, apparently with little opposition. By then, even many Republicans recognized the utility of Hamilton's Bank. Once the national bank's branch was established in Virginia, Marshall switched his position on a state-chartered bank. After the Bank of Virginia was created in 1803–4, he declared that he "would not trust a single dollar to it," noting that "[t]he monied here have many objections to it[,] the most essential of which is that it is entirely under the control of the state & will of course as they think be rather a political than a money institution."[36]

By the early 1790s, Marshall had not yet developed strong views about foreign affairs because they had little influence in his life except for the rare instances when, as with the British debt cases, they brought him legal business. Like most Americans, Marshall understood international developments in the context of their impact on domestic politics rather than for their implications for American foreign policy. More than anything else, this connection between foreign affairs and partisan politics explains why the 1790s was, in Marshall Smelser's phrase, an Age of Passion, not an Age of Reason. Politics during much of the decade, according to John Howe, "was gross and distorted, characterized by heated exaggeration and haunted by conspiratorial fantasy. Events were viewed in apocalyptic terms with the very survival of republican liberty riding in the balance." The Federalists were often caught in a "Jacobin Phrenzy" resulting from the international ramifications of the seminal event of the era, the French Revolution. As Jefferson observed at the time, "The sensations [the French Revolution] has produced here . . . have shown that the form our own government was to take depended much more on the events of France than anybody had before imagined." Marshall recalled that during the Revolution's early reformist stage he was "strongly attached to France" and "sincerely believed human liberty to depend in a great measure on the success of the French revolution." For him initially, the Revolution helped legitimize the American republic and his own role in bringing it into being. He grew increasingly troubled, however, as the Revolution lapsed into radicalism, riots, and terror during 1792, and he soon considered "the idea that a republic was to be introduced and supported by force" to be "a paradox in politics." By early 1793, when news of King Louis XVI's execution and France's declaration of war against Great Britain reached America, Marshall was ready to join Federalists outside Virginia in openly rejecting the Revolution and France, linking the Republicans to "massacres . . . turbulence and violence," and defending England against its Gallic and Francophile enemies.[37]

Marshall displayed much political courage in taking such positions in Virginia then. Animus toward Britain remained strong in the state because of English contempt for American maritime rights, the British debt litigation, and the association of Hamilton's financial program with English "court" corruption. Meanwhile, optimism about the French Revolution in the Old Dominion persisted even among some Federalists. After a disastrous 1792 congressional election in which all antiadministration candidates won, the lone consistent administration supporter lost, and Federalists were left with only four of 19 seats, Marshall's state party allies tried to recover by acting and voting like Republicans even more than they already had.[38]

The outrageously provocative behavior of France's mercurial new minister to the United States, Citizen Edmond Charles Genet, in the several months after he arrived in April 1793 temporarily ended this Francophile phase in Virginia politics and directly involved Marshall in national politics for the first time since

the ratification convention.   The young and impetuous Genet landed in
Charleston, South Carolina, with grandiose objectives: arousing separatism in
the West, persuading the United States to accept France's interpretation of
current treaties while negotiating a new one, and liquidating America's large
wartime debt to France.   After arranging to have some privateers outfitted in
Charleston, he journeyed up the coast to Philadelphia to present his credentials,
receiving tumultuous acclaim almost all along the way.   He passed quickly and
quietly through Federalist Richmond just as President Washington issued the
neutrality proclamation declaring that the United States would "adopt and
pursue a conduct friendly and impartial toward the belligerent powers."   After
several weeks of indiscreet and increasingly tense dealings with an unreceptive
administration, Genet announced that he would take his case directly to the
American people, who he believed would reject neutrality and embrace the
Revolution.   Genet's further miscalculations and misconduct and what Marshall
termed his "lofty offensive style" alienated his Republican supporters and in
August prompted the administration to request his recall.[39]

Genet's blunders politically rejuvenated Marshall and the Virginia Federalists,
who now found advantage in criticizing France.   Marshall's later description of
his own attitude mirrored those of his party colleagues at the time: "My
partiality to France . . . did not so entirely pervert my understanding as to render
me insensible to the danger of permitting a foreign minister to mingle himself in
the management of our affairs, and to intrude himself between our government
and people."   Virginia Federalists organized a series of public protest
meetings—a participatory tactic they had effectively employed during
ratification, and similar to one Hamilton, Rufus King, John Jay, and other
Federalists had recently used in several northern states.   Marshall skillfully
planned the first and largest rally in Virginia, on 17 August in Richmond. He
got Chancellor George Wythe to preside—a clever touch, as the presence of a
close associate of Jefferson's gave the impression that the Republicans approved
of the meeting. Those attending adopted resolutions and a memorial, drafted by
a committee that Marshall headed, endorsing American neutrality ("no madness
or folly could ever be so supreme as to involve us again in European contests"),
praising President Washington ("your conduct has been uniformly calculated to
promote [the American people's] happiness and welfare"), and castigating
Genet ("foreign influence, which history informs us has been the bane of more
than one republic"). Federalist rallies in other counties during the next several
weeks—at least one of which Marshall helped instigate—passed similar
resolutions, and the Republicans, caught off guard, scrambled to stage
counterprotests.[40]

Marshall and James Monroe, with the latter directing the Republican
rejoinder, then carried the debate over the French Revolution into the Richmond
press.   In an exchange of nine articles lasting from early September to early
December, under the pseudonyms "Agricola" for Monroe and "Aristides" and
"Gracchus" for Marshall, they restated now-familiar doctrines and charged each
other's parties with dangerous loyalties to foreign powers that threatened

America's independence and republican form of government. Their prose and argumentation never reached the quality of Hamilton and Madison's earlier "Pacificus"-"Helvidius" letters on neutrality and often lapsed into clumsy *ad horrendums* and puerile *ad hominems*. Marshall's articles were especially inconsistent, leading to later speculation that he might not have written all of them. With one exception—the first Gracchus letter, which stands out for its powerful logic and direct language—Marshall's pieces never established a clear position against Genet's interloping and spent too much time discursively rebutting Agricola's accusations that the Federalists were crypto-monarchists. Marshall failed to use the literary equivalent of his courtroom technique; he did not counterattack by turning his opponent's arguments against them. Perhaps Marshall, more accustomed to drafting dry legal briefs, did not feel comfortable with polemics; he might have been distracted by other personal and professional matters; or possibly he was perfunctorily expounding his side of a public disputation he had arranged with his old friend Monroe. A leading scholar of the Genet affair notes, though, that Marshall's letters were "far livelier than Monroe's . . . Marshall had a lighter and more ironical touch than his opponent."[41]

By the time Marshall and Monroe waged their *guerre de plume*, the Genet affair had died down, and a Jacobin regime had taken over in France. Genet, a Girondist, was ordered to return to France. Rightly fearing for his life, he sought and was granted asylum in America. His cometlike presence in 1793— bright and fleeting—left a permanent mark on Marshall, the Federalists, and American politics. Party solidarity, ideological cohesion, and popular political participation in the Old Dominion reached new heights. More than ever before, Marshall and the Virginia Federalists had to take sides, define their principles, and seek public support. They became more willing—out of necessity, as the minority party—to use "democratic" techniques such as mass appeals, petition campaigns, and propaganda, as long as steady Federalist hands were guiding the "people out of doors." Marshall may have had misgivings about this trend toward, in Rufus King's words, "the Government be[ing] carried on by town meetings, and those irregular measures which disorganize the Society, destroy the salutary influence of regular Government and render the Magistracy a meer Pageant," but he and the Virginia Federalists had little alternative if they were to have any influence in a Republican-controlled state. In addition, because of the Genet episode, Marshall also came to believe steadfastly that American neutrality toward European affairs was essential to the national interest, and he moved closer to accepting Hamilton's total commitment to peaceful relations with Great Britain, and to equating the Federalists' good with the public good. He reflected on the personal and political effects of this polarization in his autobiography:

The resentments of the great political party which led Virginia had been directed toward me for some time, but [his activities against Genet] brought it into active operation. I was attacked with great virulence in the papers . . . With equal vivacity I defended myself and the measures of the government. My constant effort was to show that the conduct of our government respecting its foreign relations were such as a just self-respect and a regard for our rights as a sovereign nation rendered indispensable, and that our independence was brought into real danger by the overgrown and inordinate influence of France.[42]

Although the urgency of the Genet affair soon passed, Marshall remained involved in the controversy over America's policy toward the Anglo-French war. In June 1794, Congress passed the Neutrality Act, which prohibited U.S. citizens from enlisting in the service of a foreign power, and foreign armed vessels from fitting out in American ports. In August, Governor Henry Lee ordered Marshall and a militia regiment to Smithfield, in Isle of Wight County near Norfolk, to enforce the act's ban on privateering by preventing some French sympathizers from outfitting a ship. The locals had threatened a federal marshal who had seized the suspect vessel, and the militia from the area had done little to help the official. General Marshall—he had been elected brigadier in December—must have looked awkwardly resplendent in the new uniform of "dark blue coat, shirts lined with buff, capes, lapells and cuffs buff, buttons yellow, epaulets gold, one on each shoulder, block cocked hatt with black cockade, black stock & boots" as he and his detachment of several hundred men, including cavalry, peacefully resolved the "arduous and unpleasant" situation and secured the ship. In a report to the governor, Marshall remarked that the local militia commanders "seem not to have been sufficiently impressed with the importance of maintaining the sovereignty of the laws" but that after he arrived, "the [militia] of the county are as prompt as could be wished in rendering any service required from them," and "a more proper mode of thinking is beginning to prevail."[43]

The intensifying partisan strife soon produced two manifestations of widespread pro-Republican opinion—one peaceful, one violent—that greatly troubled Marshall because he, like nearly all Federalists, attributed them to radical democratic ideas introduced from France and encouraged by the Revolution's Republican apologists. The spontaneous formation of some three dozen Democratic Societies during 1793–94 and the outbreak of the Whiskey Rebellion in Pennsylvania and elsewhere in mid-1794 forced Marshall to confront fundamental issues such as the role of popular movements in a representative political system, the extent of the federal government's coercive power over the states, and the place of a professional standing army in a republic still imbued with the militia ethos.

Scattered along the East Coast but concentrated in the mid-Atlantic states, the ardently Republican and Francophile Democratic Societies—a combination of voluntary association, political club, and pressure group—tried to direct an inchoate populist impulse in favor of France against the Washington administration's policy of neutrality in the Anglo-French conflict. Unlike the extremely energetic societies in Pennsylvania, however, the chapters in Virginia were not very effective. Several societies formed—most in the Norfolk-

Portsmouth area, along with one each in Prince William and Wythe counties—but had little influence and engaged mostly in uncontroversial, low-level political activity. Some levied propagandistic charges against the Washington administration; the Norfolk and Portsmouth society disavowed the neutrality proclamation in a lofty sounding "Declaration of Sentiments and Principles"; the Prince William society, in its "Dumfries Resolutions," disapproved of sending John Jay on a diplomatic mission to England; and the Wytheville society distributed copies of Tom Paine's *Rights of Man*. None of the societies in Virginia lasted longer than a year, and some embarrassed the Republicans they purported to help.[44]

The inhabitants of backcountry Pennsylvania produced a massive volume of whiskey (as many as one quarter of the nation's stills was located there) and even used it as a substitute currency. They had refused to pay the federal excise tax on spirits levied in 1791—one of Hamilton's revenue measures—and in mid-1794 their low-key but slowly growing defiance erupted into violent mass resistance, fomented in part by two local Democratic Societies. Mobs attacked excise collectors, destroyed the property of distillers who paid the tax, robbed the mails, disrupted court proceedings, and threatened to march on Pittsburgh. Antiexcise violence spread into at least four counties in Virginia and several jurisdictions in Kentucky. In one episode that Marshall surely heard about, protesters burned an effigy of his father, the superintendent of revenue for the Ohio district, and threatened his father's deputies. President Washington resolved to suppress this first armed challenge to the new government and called on the governors of Pennsylvania, Virginia, Maryland, and New Jersey to mobilize nearly 13,000 militia. Virginia's quota of 3,300 came mostly from Federalist strongholds in the west. By the time the troops reached the Pittsburgh area in October, however, the rebels had dispersed. No hostile fire occurred, and only 20 persons were arrested; two were convicted of treason, and Washington pardoned both.[45]

In the context of the French Terror and the Whiskey Rebellion, the Democratic Societies heightened Marshall's abiding aversion to political instability and his suspicion of mass movements operating outside of representative institutions or without elite guidance. Recalling that a "democratic" uprising in Massachusetts had helped bring down the Confederation only seven years before, Marshall appears to have repudiated the wisdom of the "people out of doors." Hewing to the questionable Federalist position that the chapters in Pennsylvania had sparked the rebellion there, Marshall linked the societies with the Jacobin clubs in France and observed that the demise of both organizations after Robespierre's execution was no coincidence: "As if their destinies depended on the same threat, the political death of the [Jacobin clubs] was the unerring signal for that of the [Democratic Societies]."[46]

Marshall did not accompany Virginia's militia contingent to fight the rebels in Pennsylvania, probably because his sick wife and young children, his busy law practice, his service as acting attorney general, and his efforts to buy some of the Fairfax lands required that he remain at home. But he heartily supported President Washington's "prudent vigour" in calling out the militia to suppress the "treasonable practices" and "multiple outrages" that "threatened to shake the government of the United States to its foundations." Like most Federalists, Marshall exaggerated the threat the ragtag insurrectionists posed. For example, he later described them as "organized assemblages of factious individuals . . . under the imposing garb of watchfulness over liberty, concealed designs subversive of all those principles which preserve the order, the peace, and the happiness of society." Marshall knew, however, that as a matter of principle, the national government sometimes had to use force to preserve the rule of law, and that as a political imperative, the Washington administration had to prove it could maintain civil order and enforce national law against recalcitrant citizens. Thomas Jefferson acidly remarked that "an insurrection was announced and proclaimed and armed against, but could never be found," and although a good deal of Federalist hyperbole and opportunism surrounded the rebellion, it nevertheless was a genuine expression of widespread hostility to Federalist policies, a popular movement tinctured with violence that demanded a decisive response from a national government still only five years old.[47]

The rebellion also drove home to Marshall some lessons he had learned during the Revolution about the dangers of the national government relying on an untrained, locally administered militia as its first line of defense against domestic and foreign threats. In the early 1790s, Virginia's frugal Republican-controlled government left the militia underfunded, understaffed, and underequipped, exacerbating quarrels among officers and between units (such as the dispute between infantry and grenadiers that Marshall brought to the governor's attention in July 1794). During the uprising in Pennsylvania, militia officials in Virginia reported that shortcomings in the state militia law and popular support for the rebels hampered mobilization. Many militiamen evaded the draft by paying fines or running away, and draft riots broke out in at least two counties. For a nationalist such as Marshall, the rebellion provided further proof, if any were needed, that the national government must have a professional standing army responsive to its will if it was going to meet its obligations to protect the country's security. Marshall, who accepted the tenets of Federalist military policy—preparedness, centralization, and professionalization—now realized that even the military system he had argued for in the Virginia ratifying convention—concurrent national and state authority over the locally run militia, and national authority over a military establishment that now existed mostly on paper—was inadequate.[48]

Lastly, the rebellion further weakened the political position of Marshall and the Federalists in Virginia. The Republican-dominated General Assembly capitalized on antiexcise opinion to attack President Washington and Governor Lee and to extend its control over the executive branch. The legislature passed a resolution criticizing the administration's use of federal troops in Pennsylvania and, when Lee was there leading Virginia's militia units, it invoked a 1788 law that prohibited state officials from accepting federal appointments, declared the governorship vacant, and elected a Republican to replace him. The Federalist minority, most of whom had regularly voted with the Republicans in a desperate effort to maintain influence, was too feeble to resist. The Republicans' action marked the first time that a major Virginia official had been chosen because of his stand on national issues and demonstrated the widening interrelationship between local and national affairs. As Marshall and the Virginia Federalists sought to keep their position from slipping further, they would find themselves drawn more and more into national politics. Not that Marshall found that prospect encouraging or inspiring; he complained to a friend that "the[re ap]pears to me every day to be more folly, envy, malice & damnd rascality in the world than there was the day before & I do verily think that plain downright honesty & unintriguing integrity will be kickd out of doors."[49]

"The public and frequent altercations in which I was unavoidably engaged weakened my decision never again to go into the [state] legislature," Marshall recalled, as probably did the Federalists' loss of the congressional district of Richmond in the spring 1795 elections. Marshall was chosen for a fifth term in the House of Delegates largely because his high reputation and strong personal appeal transcended factionalism. As he later described the process, when he showed up at the courthouse to vote, a freeholder demanded that a poll be taken for him. Marshall demurred, suggesting he might run next time. He then cast his ballot and left. The freeholder persisted that Marshall stand for election and voted for him. The balloting was suspended while the principal freeholders hurriedly discussed this unexpected development. That evening, Marshall learned of his victory. His reluctant return to the assembly followed the pattern of his legislative service since his first term 13 years before. Each time, he did not seek office to advance himself along the path to higher office, but usually to help political allies or defend policies in which he strongly believed.[50]

An outbreak of hostility to the Jay Treaty in early and mid-1795 soon tested Marshall's resolve and political skill, made him the de facto leader of Virginia's Federalists, and earned him high praise from watchful Federalist leaders in Philadelphia, New York, and elsewhere. The immediate purpose of the Jay Treaty was to prevent a war with Great Britain provoked by British interference with American neutral shipping—specifically, their seizure of some 300 vessels and impressment and imprisonment of crews—and from their restrictions on American trade with the British West Indies. "We fear & not without reason a war," Marshall wrote in early 1794. "[T]he outrages committed upon us are beyond human bearing. . . . pray Heaven we may weather the storm." The Washington administration could not afford hostilities with Britain, largely because Hamilton's financial system depended on tariff revenue from British exports to the United States. The American special envoy, Chief Justice John Jay, was also instructed to resolve grievances stemming from the 1783 peace treaty: on Britain's side, its refusal to evacuate its forts in the Northwest or to compensate slaveowners for chattels confiscated during the war; and for the United States' part, state laws impeding British citizens' collection of debts owned by Americans. Most Republicans believed Jay's appointment showed that Anglophiles controlled the administration and would sell out to the British. Virginians remembered that in 1784 Jay had tried to negotiate away their right to navigate the Mississippi River.[51]

The Jay Treaty was signed in November 1794, but the administration intended to kept its contents secret until after the Senate's special session in June. After two weeks of closed-door deliberations, the Senate ratified the treaty without the highly controversial article 12 restricting American trade with the West Indies. After the treaty's provisions were publicized through a press leak in late June, an unprecedentedly impassioned national debate ensued. Marshall recalled that "the whole country was agitated. . . . The commotion . . . seemed to rush through the Union with a rapidity and violence which set human reason and common sense at defiance." Public meetings convened in many cities, and President Washington was inundated with remonstrances and petitions of all sorts. Mobs burned John Jay's effigy and copies of the treaty and attacked the houses of British officials. The intensity of the denunciations is mainly attributable to many Americans' perception that the treaty forced them to choose between pride and prosperity: avoiding a costly war with Britain and losing indispensable British trade meant returning to a semicolonial relationship.[52]

Most important from Marshall's perspective, Virginians overwhelmingly opposed the treaty. From commercial towns to countryside, and at public meetings throughout the state, they expressed outrage that the treaty had failed to win compensation for Southern slaveowners, recognized British land titles in America, established procedures for restoring confiscated Loyalist property and securing payment of debts owed to British creditors, retained restrictions on neutral shipping and the West Indies trade, surrendered for 10 years the right to impose discriminatory duties on British ships and goods, and probably would harm relations with France while putting America back into a state of dependence on Britain. Critics of the treaty believed it was, as Marshall later wrote, "a degrading insult to the American people; a pusillanimous surrender of their honour; and an insidious injury to France." The only support for the treaty in Virginia came from the western counties because of the provisions requiring Britain to evacuate its posts in the Northwest. Criticism of the treaty was so widespread that, unlike during the Genet affair, the Federalists, with one exception, did not counterattack with their own rallies. In contrast, treaty opponents even held a meeting in Richmond chaired by George Wythe—a double slap at the Federalists, because the capital was a Federalist stronghold and Wythe had presided at the 1793 rally that Marshall organized against Genet.[53]

Marshall completely opposed this trend and became the Jay Treaty's most adamant defender in Virginia. He did so out of loyalty to the president, the administration, and the Federalist party; because he believed an Anglo-American war at a minimum would be militarily and financially disastrous for the United States; because he did not want his president and his party to suffer a humiliating political defeat over a foreign policy issue; and, from a personal standpoint, because recognition of British land titles would help him acquire some of the Fairfax lands. As with the French Revolution and the question of neutrality, Marshall viewed the Jay Treaty mainly as a problem of domestic politics, not foreign policy. He recognized that the United States had little ability to influence British diplomacy and that it would remain dependent on British trade for the foreseeable future. He knew from Virginia's unsuccessful efforts in the 1780s, for example, that developing a preferential trading relationship with France while limiting British commercial inroads was practically impossible. Moreover, Marshall keenly perceived the Jay Treaty's impact on American political parties, processes, and ideologies, and he later wrote, "I determined to make myself master of it."[54]

Marshall returned to the House of Delegates in November 1795 and immediately took up the cause of defending the treaty. By then the controversy had waned—the president's signature on the treaty had moderated the public discussion—and critics of the treaty in the assembly tried instead to persuade their congressional representatives to deny appropriations for it on the constitutional ground that Congress's authority to regulate foreign trade had been infringed. Almost as soon as the term opened, the delegates skirmished over a resolution lauding the efforts of Republican U.S. Senators Henry Tazewell and Stevens T. Mason against the treaty. Marshall spoke for three hours in favor of Charles Lee's amendment that declared the state legislatures had no authority to interfere in foreign affairs or to judge the actions of national legislators, but the resolution passed as written, 100 to 50.[55]

Taking a cue from Senator Tazewell, assembly Republicans submitted a resolution urging that the Constitution be amended to give the House of Representatives a role in ratifying treaties, to prohibit federal judges (such as Federalist Chief Justice Jay) from holding other offices, and to limit (mostly Federalist) senators to three-year terms and strip them of their impeachment authority. Although Marshall must have known that Congress would not pass these proposals, he did not even want the delegates to consider them. He probably realized that the Republicans were using the resolution to try to persuade Congress to reconsider the Jay Treaty in 1796 while providing themselves with a popular issue for the next year's presidential election. Accordingly, Marshall contended on the floor that the proper constitutional course for treaty opponents to take was to stop having the assembly undermine the treaty and instead have the House of Representatives render it inoperative by refusing to appropriate funds for its implementation. He also rebutted the critics' argument that the president could not negotiate treaties that limited the congressional commerce power and must have the House of Representatives' assent to pacts that required funding. He later wrote that "there was perhaps never a political question . . . which was susceptible of more complete demonstration . . . I had reason to know that a politician even in times of violent party strife maintains his respectability by showing his strength; and is most safe when he encounters prejudice most fearlessly. There was scarcely an intelligent man in the house who did not yield his opinion on the constitutional question."

Supreme Court Justice James Iredell heard Marshall's speech and reported that "there were few members who were not convinced by Mr. Marshall's arguments as to its being constitutional, which few members thought it was before the debate began, and some of the speakers had the candor to acknowledge their conviction, though not in the House." Marshall was trying to buy time to allow Federalists in Congress to mobilize against their opponents. He and his allies failed, however, as the resolution proposing the amendments passed 88–32. The assembly then forwarded the proposals to the other state legislatures.[56]

Although the Jay Treaty dominated the assembly session, Marshall also worked on a few matters of state concern. As in previous terms, he was appointed to the Privileges and Elections, Propositions and Grievances, and Courts of Justice standing committees. He also served on committees that revised the penal code and drafted bills to allow branches of the BUS in Virginia; to permit the state government to supply county prisons, change equity procedures in debt cases, and raise the salaries of judges on the High Court of Chancery; and to authorize state subscriptions of stock to the James River and Potomac canal companies. There is no record of Marshall's vote on the Potomac River Company's successful attempt to secure public funds for completing its canal around the Great Falls, but his record indicates he would have backed the measure. Largely because of the contentious debate over the Jay Treaty amendments, Marshall could hardly wait for the term to end. "The legislature is considerd as growing worse & worse," he wrote Charles Lee. "It is to be hopd their session will soon determine [*sic*]."[57]

Marshall's advocacy of the Jay Treaty won him accolades from national Federalist leaders and expanded his role as an informal advisor to the administration, which already had solicited his views on legal aspects of Anglo-American relations and Supreme Court appointments, and had asked him to represent it in cases arising from the new carriage tax. When Marshall went to Philadelphia in February 1796 to argue one of the British debt cases, he met, among others, George Cabot, Fisher Ames, Theodore Sedgwick, and Rufus King. Because, in Marshall's words, "a Virginian who supported with any sort of reputation the measures of the government was such a *rara avis*," he was "received by them all with a degree of kindness which I had not anticipated." In recognition of his contribution, President Washington in March considered appointing him as one of the two Americans on the five-member joint commission that would arbitrate debt disputes under the Jay Treaty. Marshall had already turned down two presidential appointment offers, as U.S. attorney for Virginia in 1789 and as attorney general in 1795. Washington, who thought so highly of Marshall that he had wanted him to succeed the disgraced Edmund Randolph as secretary of state in 1795, was understandably wary of offering another federal position without some assurance of success. The president inquired of Marshall's friend Charles Lee, who replied with the usual litany of personal and professional reasons that Marshall himself had given before. Still determined to get Marshall in his service, Washington tried again in July with the ministry to France that James Monroe soon would vacate. Marshall declined yet again.[58]

By the time Marshall reentered the debate over the Jay Treaty in the spring of 1796, public sentiment had swung broadly in its favor. When the House of Representatives took up the treaty in March, the Federalists were riding a surge of popularity produced by military victory over the Indians in the Northwest, a treaty with Spain that won everything Americans had wanted in the Mississippi region, and an economic windfall from wartorn Europe's demand for American goods. Newspaper articles, petitions, and public meetings clearly showed widespread unease that the House's efforts to kill the Jay Treaty would cause an international crisis. Marshall helped organize and spoke at one of the key rallies, in Richmond on 25 April. He wrote at the time that it "was more numerous than I have ever seen at this place & after a very ardent & zealous discussion which consumd the day a decided majority declared in favor of a resolution that the welfare & honor of the nation requird us to give full effect to the treaty." "The ruling party in Virginia are extremely irritated at the vote today." Elsewhere, the state legislatures went along with the popular current and refused to endorse the Virginia amendments, apparently out of reluctance to challenge President Washington. The antitreaty majority in the House steadily diminished, and on 30 April the Federalists won the necessary funds by a 51–48 vote.[59]

During the Jay Treaty controversy, Marshall, as he had done during the Genet episode, helped advance a trend toward popular politics that, although useful for the Federalists in the short term, hurt them in the long run. The previously mentioned rally in Richmond, for example, was significant because for the first time the organizers of such a meeting in Virginia did not control the proceedings or present a stacked audience with a set of prewritten resolutions to approve. Instead, 300 to 400 freeholders and nonfreeholders—the latter included at the Federalists' insistence—listened to arguments from both sides and voted on resolutions prepared afterward. Although the treaty debate in general left Marshall more disappointed with popular politics, especially when foreign policy was involved, he knew that in Virginia the minority Federalists had no choice but to broaden their appeal with "democratic" tactics. Marshall did not seem to realize, however—and he was hardly alone in this failing—that the Federalists did not have the resources of organization, leadership, or ideology to compete against the Republicans in the more populist political environment that they themselves were helping to bring into being.[60]

All of which left the Virginia Federalists suffering from a debilitating identity crisis as they entered the election of 1796. In many ways they could call themselves Federalists in name only. Their need to survive politically in an increasingly Republican state forced them to compromise beliefs and muddle over differences with the dominant party. Although this tactic enabled them to participate on the state level—Federalists held important positions in Virginia's government—it severely weakened their stature in the national party. No Virginia Federalists except Marshall had truly national perspectives, and, aside from the policy of neutrality, they had opposed all major administration initiatives. Their political trimming was too crass and too superficial; it left them with a constituency too thinly spread to be effective. Consequently, they had abdicated a potentially vital role in keeping the national party competitive. Under Marshall's leadership, the Virginia Federalists might have served as a model for bridging the exclusivist attitude of the Northern-controlled Federalist leadership and the populist emphasis of the Republicans. They had their own internal social division between planters and lower gentry to provide a pattern. But neither Marshall, nor anyone else of note for that matter, seemed to recognize that opportunity; and as the 1796 election would show, the Federalists could no longer rely on the Augustan majesty of George Washington to keep them in power in a more pluralistic system dominated by new elites claiming, with good reason, to be the exemplars of Revolutionary republicanism.[61]

Marshall enjoyed good relations with most of his Republican opponents in Virginia even while he emerged as the state's leading Federalist when partisan animosity often strained or sundered friendships. Marshall had been an "intimate friend" of George Mason's, socialized and shared cases with William Branch Giles, and wrote an introduction for him when he went off to Congress. Marshall's dealings with Judge Spencer Roane of the Court of Appeals were still respectfully professional. Republicans' occasional personal attacks rankled Marshall—for example, accusations that he had improperly used money from the BUS to buy the Fairfax lands—and family members reported that he was the subject of malicious gossip about his lack of formal education, his casual manners and dress, and his fondness for wine. Late in life, Marshall claimed the Republicans "attacked with great virulence in the papers" because of his opposition to Citizen Genet. Although he exaggerated the extent of their resentment, his views on the French Revolution may have made Jefferson and Madison withdraw him from consideration for a diplomatic mission to New Orleans to negotiate with Spain. For the most part, however, Marshall's easygoing nature and the ties he had developed with Republican lawyers and politicians through social clubs and his own private dinners kept him on at least cordial terms with most partisan rivals among Virginia Republicans. One exception that must have bothered him greatly was James Monroe. Friends since boyhood, they fell out because of ideological differences over France and broke off contact until the early 1800s.[62]

Another exception, and the most glaring, was Thomas Jefferson. Marshall and his distant cousin—both of their mothers were Randolphs—never seemed to like each other, and the partisan and ideological acrimony of the 1790s turned them into irreconcilable enemies. Family heritage may have had a part, as the Randolphs had disowned Marshall's grandmother while Jefferson's forebears enjoyed good standing in the clan. The specific cause of the men's difficulties possibly occurred in 1781, when Marshall began courting Mary Ambler, the daughter of Rebecca Burwell and Jacquelin Ambler. Some 20 years before, Rebecca had spurned Jefferson's somewhat inept attempt to woo her and instead chose Jacquelin. As one scholar of the Marshall-Jefferson relationship has noted, "Marshall may have married into his antagonism for Jefferson"; Jefferson may have displaced onto Marshall any deep-seated jealously or resentment he bore toward the Amblers. Also in 1781, then-Governor Jefferson and other state government leaders on two occasions fled from British strike forces under Benedict Arnold and Banastre Tarleton. The former sacked parts of the capital, and the latter nearly captured Jefferson at Monticello. Marshall had fought with the militia against Arnold's troops, and he and some of the Amblers, perhaps in public, contrasted his actions with those of Jefferson, who, wrote one of the Ambler daughters, went "scampering" over the countryside with the rest of the government and "took neither rest nor food until he was safely out of Tarleton's reach." During the Revolution, Marshall developed a powerful disdain for state political leaders, and he may have seen Jefferson's feckless wartime administration, epitomized in the flight from Tarleton's dragoons, as symbols of the failure of the states to support the Continental Army.[63]

During the 1780s, Marshall and Jefferson generally shared the same nationalist outlook—although Marshall was somewhat more critical of the Confederation and the state legislatures—and both supported ratification of the Constitution. Their differences widened over Hamilton's financial plan—especially the BUS, which Marshall believed was constitutional and Jefferson did not—and they began to question each other's devotion to republican principles. By 1792, Marshall's growing prominence in Virginia politics and his loyalty to the Federalists had become a threat to Jefferson and the Republicans. When Jefferson found out that Hamilton wanted Marshall to run for the House of Representatives, he suggested to the Republican leader in Virginia, James Madison, that Marshall instead be shunted off to the state court and kept out of Congress; "I think nothing better could be done than to make him a judge." It is not clear what led Jefferson to believe Hamilton had "plyed [Marshall] well with flattery and solicitation" so convincing that Marshall "expressed half a mind to come." There is no evidence that Hamilton communicated any such interest directly to Marshall—Washington possibly conveyed the idea secondhand—or that Marshall would have responded favorably. He still considered himself obliged to stay out of national politics for personal and professional reasons.[64]

As a result of the conflicts and intrigues over the Washington administration's foreign policy, Marshall and Jefferson came to view one another as blind ideologues whose slavishness toward Great Britain and France, respectively, imperiled America's independence and security. Marshall's active support of the Jay Treaty, for example, prompted Jefferson to unleash the most splenetic comment by either man against the other so far:

Though Marshall will be able to embarras [sic] the republican party in the assembly a good deal, yet upon the whole his having gone into it will be of service. He has been, hitherto, able to do more mischief acting under the mask of Republicanism than he will be able to do after throwing it plainly off. His lax lounging manners have made him popular with the bulk of the people of Richmond; & a profound hypocrisy, with many thinking men of our country. But having come forth in the plenitude of his English principles the latter will see that it is high time to make him known.

For his part, Marshall by now may have realized that the squire of Monticello was at heart an aristocrat and disdained Jefferson as a democratic *poseur*. The cousins' strikingly contrasting personalities—Marshall was convivial and relaxed, Jefferson tended to be touchy and prim—as well as their different forensic abilities—Marshall was adept at quick summation and improvisation before a jury and could deliver a speech effectively, whereas Jefferson was lost in the courtroom without careful notes and had no gift for debate—accentuated their political differences. Marshall held his fire for the time being, but his political and diplomatic experiences in the 1790s convinced him that the Federalists' relinquishing power to Jefferson and his Francophile allies would be "the fruitful source of woe to our country."[65]

Marshall's work as a lawyer for and against Jefferson during the 1790s in several cases involving the estate of Jefferson's father-in-law, John Wayles, almost certainly contributed to their growing hostility toward each other. As one of the executors of the estate of Wayles, who died in 1773, Jefferson inherited over £4,000 in debt owed to the Bristol merchant house of Farell and Jones and became a party to several lawsuits concerning the debt's liquidation. The executors of the estate of another Marshall cousin, Richard Randolph, also were litigants in some of those cases. Marshall advised and represented both the Wayles and the Randolph executors, who at various times were adversaries or partners in the suits. An increasingly vexed Jefferson had not prevailed so far in achieving a legal resolution to his indebtedness, and he perhaps came to question the quality of Marshall's legal work on his behalf. In 1795, the whole matter assuredly took on a strong personal cast when Randolph's executors retained Marshall to defend them in a debt suit filed by Jefferson and Wayles's other executors. They sought to void some of the Randolph estate's land sale deeds to gain access to real assets to pay off their own debt to the Farell and Jones house. After four and one half years of intricate and abstruse proceedings, Marshall and the Randolph executors won a favorable decree from the Virginia Court of Appeals. Marshall must have relished besting Jefferson's side in court, but he left no comments on the outcome. According to Dumas Malone, "the whole of [Jefferson's] later life was colored by the fateful Wayles inheritance, which first enriched and then impoverished him," and he surely blamed Marshall for a good portion of his predicament. Marshall was as unforgiving, writing in 1830 that "I have never believed firmly in [Jefferson's] infallibility. I have never thought him a particularly wise, sound and practical statesman [and] I have not changed this mode of thinking."[66]

The retirement of George Washington confronted Marshall and the Federalists with their gravest challenge yet.[67] The leadership of the "Patriot King" had become so personalized that despite all the Federalists' accomplishments— establishing a sound national economy, pacifying the frontier, maintaining peace with European powers, securing internal order, gaining access to the Mississippi

River—the people gave Washington nearly all the credit, and the party's reputation benefited little. Moreover, the Federalists had grown so accustomed to Washington's presence in office, and so reliant on reverence for the Constitution and on political patronage to keep themselves in power, that they were ill-prepared to deal with the political requirements of succession: finding a worthy successor to Washington who enjoyed broad popular support, and mobilizing their followers for victory in the election.

The "official" candidate, John Adams, compounded the Federalists' other political liabilities, especially in Marshall's home state. Virginians, like nearly all Southerners, disliked Adams intensely because of his Yankee manners, speech, and ideas, and because they considered him an apologist for monarchism and privilege. Federalist leaders knew that to win any southern electors, they either had to find an attractive Southerner to run with Adams or replace him with another candidate. Alexander Hamilton, who despised Adams as much as anyone, tried to enlist Marshall to help explore the second alternative. Hamilton had his colleague Rufus King write Marshall in early 1796 about enticing Patrick Henry to run for president. They believed that only Henry had the stature and popularity to defeat Jefferson in Virginia, and they trusted Marshall with this sensitive political mission. Marshall declined, claiming he had too little contact with Henry to approach him on so delicate a matter. Implicit in Marshall's reply, however, was a hint of disapproval at this sort of conspiracy, as well as his expressed concern that publicity about the proposition might "become an unpleasant circumstance" for the Federalists and split the party. Instead, Marshall had Henry Lee do the errand. The solicitation was futile, and the Federalists were stuck with Adams.[68]

By the end of Washington's second term, a functioning two-party system had developed in Virginia, and most of the leaders' remaining work consisted of developing techniques of mobilization and control, such as maintaining discipline in the legislature and improving mechanisms for popular participation. Federalist support in Virginia was far-flung and hard to muster, especially when the party's candidate was so unpopular. The Federalists were strongest in Richmond and adjacent counties, Williamsburg, and parts of the Tidewater, the Northern Neck, the upper Shenandoah Valley, and the far southwestern portion of the state. The Federalists running for presidential elector—Virginia was one of six states that picked electors by popular vote—adopted vague, nonpartisan stances toward the candidates and tried unsuccessfully to concentrate on foreign and domestic policies as a way to keep attention off Adams. Foreign influence in American politics again became an issue because of the meddling of French minister Pierre Adet, and Federalist hopes briefly revived. In November, Adet publicly announced a break in diplomatic relations with the United States and blamed the Federalists, who seized on the opportunity to decry the "Jacobins'" egregious effort attempt to promote Jefferson's election. This diversion did not prevent the disastrous outcome; only one Federalist was chosen among the 21 Virginia electors.

Nationally, Adams won by three electoral votes over Jefferson, followed by Thomas Pinckney of South Carolina and Aaron Burr of New York.[69]

The Federalists did better in the Virginia congressional elections, capturing or holding three seats, and nationally they won more congressional seats than ever before. Despite the gains, Marshall seemed morose and bitter at the Republicans' victory, which he believed they had achieved through deceit.

The insidious attempt which is made to ascribe the aggressions made on us by France to the British treaty & the partiality of our government for Britain, tho it has been provd a thousand times to be the most shameless insult on truth & common sense, still succeeds. That party has laid such fast hold on the public mind in this party of Virginia that an attempt to oppose sinks at once the person who makes it. The elections for the State legislature go entirely against the foederalists [sic] who are madly & foolishly as well as wickedly styled a british party.[70]

Marshall, of course, favored Adams over Jefferson, but he expressed no opinions on his party's candidate, did little to aid Adams during the election, and declined to take part in a scurrilous attack on Jefferson's reputation. Some Federalists in the Northern Neck tried to impeach Jefferson's revolutionary credentials by claiming he had supported independence because he was heavily in debt to British merchants when the Revolution broke out, and that just after the war these creditors retained Marshall to sue him. Marshall denied that he had ever filed a legal action against Jefferson or that he knew anything of Jefferson's finances or the sources of the rumor. Otherwise, Marshall was uninvolved in the election. Like his Virginia Federalist colleagues, Marshall acted as if he knew what he was against far better than what he was for. Still, his antipathy to the Republicans seems, in retrospect, less moralistic and ideological than that of the northern Federalists—probably because his temperament was more equable and accommodating, he lacked religious passion to inform his political beliefs, and he had experience in being in the political minority. His attitude toward parties fell toward the orthodox end of the contemporary spectrum of views. He seems to have instinctively preferred the nonpartisanship of Washington, but political realities in Virginia kept him from disavowing parties as pernicious factions or decrying organized dissent as seditious. Although he did not approve of the idea of legitimate opposition, he had to accept the emergence of a more pluralistic system and saw some value in the establishment of a permanent opposition simply as a way for the Federalists to survive in Virginia.[71]

Partisanship had become so pervasive that the retiring president's fellow Virginians even clashed over how to express publicly their gratitude for his leadership. In April 1796, Marshall had been elected to his sixth and last term in the House of Delegates, and at the November–December session he served on a Republican-controlled committee charged by the full House with preparing an address to Washington to mark the president's departure from public life. The committee produced some stiffly worded sentences that, unlike the motion authorizing the address, did not mention that the President had governed "wisely." This petty insult aroused Marshall's ire. He and other Washington loyalists introduced an adulatory substitute declaring that Washington's administration had been "marked by wisdom in the Cabinet, valor in the field, and by the purest patriotism in both" and "had essentially contributed to establish and maintain the happiness and prosperity of the nation." Marshall worked harder than anyone to get this language passed, but he lost by three votes, and the Republicans then made the address even more frigid. "To what has America fallen!" Marshall privately lamented.[72]

Marshall otherwise found the House term uneventful. He again served on the major standing committees as well as a few special drafting committees that dealt with the state's boundaries with Kentucky and Maryland and several minor legal, administrative, and financial matters. No noteworthy votes by him are recorded.[73]

Marshall devoted a substantial portion of his time, energy, and resources in the early and mid-1790s to land speculation and western development. His compelling interest as an investor and a nationalist is particularly evident in his acquisition of more western land and his further support for companies seeking to build commercial and, he hoped, political ties between east and west. In 1789, Marshall bought a number of Revolutionary land warrants; in 1791, he received a grant for 1,000 acres in Kentucky; and in 1794 and 1796, he received 2,000 acres of land in the Ohio Territory for his wartime service. He would eventually hold over 41,000 acres in his own name. As a lawyer, Marshall defended the claims of a group of veterans—and, indirectly, his own holdings— against challenges involving colonial-era Cherokee titles granted but later voided by Virginia. Moreover, Marshall continued buying shares in the Potomac River Company and the James River Company, which planned to connect those rivers to the tributaries of the Mississippi and Ohio Rivers.[74]

By far the largest and most complicated land transaction Marshall participated in was his purchase of a portion of the 5.2 million-acre Fairfax proprietary in the Northern Neck, one of the largest and potentially most profitable landholdings in the United States.[75] He probably first thought about owning some of the Fairfax lands in the early 1780s and had several motives for pursuing the idea. He had grown up in and was fond of the region; he held title to the home his father had built at Oak Hill in Fauquier County; he had decided to remain in Virginia instead of moving to Kentucky; and he was keenly interested in establishing his family's financial security, which at this time in Virginia usually meant owning land. Marshall's subsequent involvement with the proprietary during the late 1780s and 1790s comprises an intricate story that advances simultaneously on several overlapping legal, legislative, political, and financial tracks: the efforts of Lord Fairfax's heir to secure title to the lands; Virginia's actions to appropriate parts of them; and Marshall's moves on behalf of the heir to resolve the dispute with Virginia, finance his own purchase of choice proprietary holdings, and gain legal protection from either the Commonwealth or the federal government for his prospective title. After setting his mind on acquiring part of the Fairfax lands, Marshall cleverly and tenaciously pursued his goal through practically all feasible legal, political, and financial avenues. In addition, his preoccupation with the Fairfax lands had a crucial effect on his political career. It forced him to confine his political activity to Virginia for most of the 1790s until he had secured his title to the lands and was guaranteed financing for buying them outright. Only then did Marshall consider himself free to consider political activity outside Virginia; only then would his transformation from a provincial to a national political figure be complete.

The immense Fairfax tract, stretching over 100 miles from the Potomac River in southeastern Fairfax County westward into present-day West Virginia, consisted of three categories of land: unappropriated wilderness (or "waste") lands, which accounted for nearly half the total; a similar amount of appropriated lands granted to individuals who paid quitrents; and just over 200,000 acres of valuable "manor" lands reserved for the personal use of the Fairfax family. The manor lands were divided into four tracts: Leeds, approximately 150,000 acres in Loudoun, Fauquier, Frederick, and Shenandoah Counties; South Branch, nearly 55,000 acres in Hampshire and Hardy Counties; Gooney Run, just under 14,000 acres in Warren County; and Greenway Court, where the manor house was located. Marshall wanted to buy these manor lands, and they became available to him as a result of the tortuous conflict, in which he emerged as the driving force, between the Commonwealth and Lord Fairfax's heir.

Just after the Revolution ended, the General Assembly, motivated by strong anti-British sentiment and looking for ways to relieve Virginia's financial distress, began removing the Fairfax proprietary's escheat and taxation protections, sequestering tenants' quitrents, and selling title to portions of the waste lands.[76] Even though Lord Fairfax was a citizen of the Commonwealth when he died in 1781, the state contended that under the common law his nephew and heir, Denny Martin Fairfax—a British subject—could not inherit property in Virginia. Denny Fairfax claimed that his title to his uncle's proprietary lands was valid under the 1783 Treaty of Peace, and he instituted various legal actions to stop the state from selling or granting patents to them. In turn, the Commonwealth and American land speculators filed suits against him. Between 1786 and 1796, Marshall represented Fairfax in several of these litigations: a pre-Revolutionary claim by a land speculator to part of the waste lands (*Hite v. Fairfax*, discussed in chapter 3); hearings on caveats (protests) that Fairfax took out against speculators seeking patents to the waste lands; a state ejectment action brought against Fairfax by one of those patent-seekers; escheat proceedings brought by Virginia against the manor lands; and a federal ejectment action filed by Fairfax against a land speculator, David Hunter, who had received title from Virginia to some of the unappropriated lands. Marshall was the "hidden litigant" in these suits. He wanted to protect his potential title to the lands he would buy from Fairfax by securing Fairfax's own title to them first.

By 1792, no definitive judgment on any legal point in the controversy had been reached.   Marshall's prospects of acquiring a Fairfax tract rose dramatically that year when Denny Fairfax, 68 years old and discouraged by doubts that the title he had held for over a decade would ever be affirmed, decided not to settle in Virginia but instead to return to England, sell the Leeds and South Branch manor lands, and continue collecting rents from his other holdings.   As Fairfax's attorney, Marshall probably had an inside line on the manor sales.   He did not have enough personal wealth to buy them alone, however, so he organized a syndicate with one of his brothers, James, and a brother-in-law, Rawleigh Colston, to pool resources and secure financing.   In December 1792 or January 1793, James traveled to London, where in February he signed a contract with Fairfax on behalf of the syndicate to buy the manor lands for £20,000.   A year later, the syndicate members still had not raised the full sum and renegotiated with Fairfax to split the purchase.   They would first buy South Branch Manor for £6,000, and then Leeds Manor for the balance. The syndicate apparently intended to use John Marshall's profits from the sale of stock in the BUS, as well as other unknown monies, to buy South Branch. Two implicit conditions covered the entire deal, which was to be closed on 1 February 1794: Fairfax would not transfer title until the syndicate paid in full, and the syndicate would not pay until Fairfax's legal dispute with Virginia seemed resolved.[77]

Meanwhile, more inconclusive legal developments compounded the financial uncertainty Marshall and his partners faced.   In the state ejectment suit mentioned above, *Hunter v. Fairfax* (1794), Marshall won only a conditional victory for his client.   Appearing before Judges St. George Tucker and Thomas Nelson in Winchester in November 1793, he unequivocally asserted that the Treaty of Peace granted Denny Fairfax clear title to the proprietary lands and protected them from future confiscation—in short, that the treaty overrode Virginia's common law prohibiting alien inheritance.   The judges, however, accepted only part of Marshall's argument.   They affirmed Fairfax's title for the time being but were not willing to limit absolutely the state's power to appropriate British subjects' land.   They ruled that the 1785 confiscation act conflicted with the peace treaty but permitted the Commonwealth to take land through a formal inquest of office as set forth in a 1779 law.   Fairfax's title to the 788 acres at issue in the case—and by extension to any tract contested in the future, such as the manor lands the Marshall syndicate wanted—remained vulnerable to political maneuverings within the state's legal system.   Fairfax could foresee losing his more than 2,000,000 acres of waste lands piece by piece through countless inquests, a legal erosion that would have undermined the Marshall syndicate's title as well.

Concurrently, the Commonwealth adopted a new tactic of moving against the manor lands, which previously it had left alone.   In December 1793, the General Assembly, probably incensed at federal court judgments in favor of British creditors, passed resolutions calling for suspension of the peace treaty and more vigorous use of escheat proceedings.   The latter resolution, despite its general language, was obviously intended to inspire challenges to the Fairfax title. The *Hunter v. Fairfax* ruling forestalled immediate moves to take the waste lands, but the state tried to confiscate the manor lands through escheat proceedings. Escheators in three counties containing manor lands held inquests of office during February–August 1794—Marshall may have represented Fairfax in all of them[78]—and juries decided for the state each time. In October, a district court rejected Fairfax's challenge to one of those decisions, whereupon Fairfax appealed to the Court of Appeals. At the time, Marshall was acting attorney general and would have been expected to represent the Commonwealth against Fairfax, but in these unusual circumstances, Virginia used a special counsel.

Marshall thought the state government would delay Fairfax's appeal until the ratification of the Eleventh Amendment to the U.S. Constitution, which would deny the federal courts jurisdiction over any case brought against a state by a citizen of another state. The proposed amendment—Virginia ratified it in November 1794—would prevent Fairfax from appealing an expected unfavorable decision by the Virginia Court of Appeals to the Federalist-dominated Supreme Court, which was more likely to uphold his rights under the peace treaty. To counter the advantage the state would gain from the amendment, Marshall undertook several maneuvers that highlight his legal ingenuity and his pertinacity. First, in December he advised that Fairfax suggest to the American treaty negotiators in England that they request explicit recognition of the Fairfax title in the new treaty. (Marshall did not then know that what would be called Jay's Treaty had already been signed.) Second, in February 1795, Marshall decided to assert his and his syndicate partners' claim of title to the manor lands under equity law. (By then, another brother-in-law, John Ambler, and Henry Lee had contracted with the syndicate to buy Leeds Manor.) Marshall prepared a bill against the state for consideration by the High Court of Chancery and hoped the chancellor, George Wythe, would issue a decree before the Court of Appeals heard Fairfax's appeal in May. To expedite the lengthy chancery process, Marshall asked Governor Robert Brooke and the Council of State, both defendants in his action, to forego standard preliminary procedures. Not surprisingly, they refused. The evidence is unclear whether Marshall pursued this equity case further.[79]

Marshall next capitalized on an opportunity to bring the Fairfax title question before the federal courts. His goal all along had been to move the dispute out of Virginia's courts by turning it into a federal question to be decided by more sympathetic federal courts on the basis of the national government's treaty-making power and the supremacy clause of Article V of the U.S. Constitution. News of the signing of Jay's Treaty, article nine of which guaranteed British subjects' land titles in the United States, reached Richmond in March 1795. Marshall quickly filed an ejectment action in the U.S. Circuit Court for Virginia on Fairfax's behalf against the speculator Hunter, who had declared his intention of appealing the 1794 ejectment decision against him. Marshall wanted to preempt a Virginia court decision that probably would be based on the common law or state law and not on either the peace treaty or Jay's Treaty.

By initiating Fairfax's suit in the U.S. Circuit Court, Marshall assured that any appellate ruling had to address all aspects of the title dispute. Moreover, beyond the issues of the case, the nationalist Marshall may have had a larger constitutional purpose: establishing the federal courts' authority to review state laws.

In June 1795 in Richmond, Marshall faced two associates from the Richmond legal fraternity whom Virginia had retained for Hunter, Alexander Campbell and John Wickham, in arguments before Supreme Court Justice James Wilson and U.S. District Judge Cyrus Griffin. No report of the case, *Fairfax's Lessee v. Hunter*, exists, but the arguments that Marshall and his opponents presented can be inferred from the long statement of facts stipulated to by the parties that was submitted to the court before the hearing. Justice Wilson and Judge Griffin ruled in favor of Fairfax. Hunter—at first with the state's support, and later on his own—appealed to the U.S. Supreme Court, which docketed the case for argument in February 1796.[80]

A frustrated Marshall—still without a conclusive federal court ruling for Fairfax, and with the state appellate court still delaying a decision on Fairfax's escheat appeal—attended the fall 1795 session of the House of Delegates. The legislators debated a resolution denying that the federal courts had authority to decide cases affecting titles to lands that the Commonwealth had granted to its citizens, but then decided to table the motion. Marshall pressed his own claims to the manor lands in the state courts. In a carefully calibrated move, he had his attorney, Charles Lee, go to the district court in Dumfries in December 1795 on behalf of the syndicate and file a challenge to the Fauquier County inquest's decision against Fairfax's title to the manor lands. He further instructed Lee to arrange his pleas so as to bring about an adverse ruling, which he would then appeal to the Court of Appeals and, expecting no satisfaction there, to the Supreme Court. He and his partners, unlike the British subject Fairfax, could take an unfavorable state court decision into federal court because the Eleventh Amendment, ratified in February 1795, did not apply to them.[81]

Marshall traveled to Philadelphia in February 1796 to argue the British debt case *Ware v. Hylton* before the Supreme Court. He had also prepared for the scheduled hearing of *Hunter v. Fairfax's Lessee*. In January, however, Hunter petitioned the Court for a postponement, contending that Virginia's withdrawal of legal support left him unprepared to pursue his appeal. Marshall expected the Court to grant Hunter's wish and was very annoyed at the prospect; he wrote to Polly that "[m]y own cause I greatly fear will not be taken up & I shall be under the very disagreeable necessity of returning without any decision." The delay at least kept him from being put in the strange situation of arguing contradictory positions in two major cases at the same time before the same court. In *Ware v. Hylton*, Marshall contended that Virginia's laws regarding British creditors superseded the peace treaty, but he insisted that the opposite applied to the Fairfax title dispute. Given his deep personal interest in the latter controversy, one could safely conclude that he believed the case for the supremacy of treaties over state laws was far stronger. Then, in July, Hunter's lawyer, Alexander

Campbell, committed suicide. Anxious that Campbell's death would "be usd as the instrument for delay of our cause," Marshall asked John Wickham to replace Campbell but was refused. Although Marshall was not sure the Supreme Court would hear the case, he began another trip to Philadelphia in July but stopped at Mt. Vernon when he heard that Hunter was going to seek another postponement. Further delay would be a "serious calamity," he complained, but the Supreme Court granted a continuance in August.[82]

Marshall received more bad news during these months about the failure of Jaquelin Ambler, Robert Morris, and James Marshall to procure funding for the syndicate's purchase of the manor lands. John Marshall's ties to Morris, a freewheeling financier and merchant and compulsive land speculator with some interests in Virginia, dated to the late 1780s when he represented Morris in complicated commercial litigation in the chancery court. In the early 1790s, John and James Marshall borrowed from Morris to buy stock in the BUS. After James became engaged to Morris's daughter in 1794 or 1795 and was appointed secretary of the financier's North American Land Company, Morris offered to underwrite the manor lands purchase with European loans. In December 1795, Morris sent James to meet with bankers in the Netherlands and France while he himself negotiated with associates in England. (The Fairfax lands were but a small part of the holdings for which the North American Land Company sought financing.) None of the solicitations succeeded, however, for several reasons. Money and credit were tight throughout Europe because of the Continental wars; several English banks failed in early 1796; and European financiers considered Morris a bad risk because he had seriously overextended himself in other ventures. Lacking alternatives, Morris turned to American sources. At John Marshall's request, he tried but failed to buy a block of BUS stock. Marshall apparently never considered selling, or even offering as collateral, any of his western lands, even though that would have taken care of the syndicate's shortfall. He was fixated on possessing land and for the time being was willing to live without assured financing for the manor lands as long as he did not have to part with any real estate he already owned.[83]

The Fairfax title controversy was moving toward some sort of resolution by the time the General Assembly met in November 1796.[84] By then, the principal parties to the dispute—the Commonwealth, the Marshall syndicate, and, by now almost incidentally, Denny Fairfax—appeared willing to compromise. The state government had come under increasing pressure to settle the affair from holders of titles it had issued in the unappropriated tracts. For example, soon after the legislature convened, it received a petition from 219 residents of several counties in the waste lands region imploring the Assembly to enact "some safe and speedy Remedy" for protecting their titles. Moreover, Virginia also probably realized that Marshall's neat legal maneuvers and the Jay Treaty's guarantee of alien landholding rights made certain an eventual Supreme Court ruling in Fairfax's favor. Under these circumstances, the governor and the Council of State decided to concede the manor lands to the Marshall syndicate and Denny Fairfax in the hope of gaining what they really wanted—title to the unappropriated lands. For his part, John Marshall came to the Assembly session intending to press his advantage and reach a settlement affirming the syndicate's claim to the manor lands; he was ready, if necessary, to surrender Denny Fairfax's claim to the unappropriated lands.

The above-mentioned petition went to the Committee for Courts of Justice on which Marshall sat, and during the next week the committee framed a compromise proposed by Marshall that was quite similar to what he and the state government both had in mind. The terms were simple: Fairfax would transfer title to the "waste and unappropriated" lands to Virginia, and the state would recognize Fairfax's title to the "specifically appropriated" (manor) lands. Marshall, after insisting that language be added that the syndicate could use later to increase the acreage of the manor lands, accepted the arrangement on behalf of his partners and Denny Fairfax on 24 November. The Assembly wrote the settlement into law on 10 December.

The legislature also gave Marshall another victory by effectively ending David Hunter's appeal of the U.S. Circuit Court's ruling for Fairfax. In November 1796, Hunter had petitioned the Assembly to help pay for his legal actions against Fairfax—the real reason for his requests to the Supreme Court for postponements, he revealed in a letter to Alexander Hamilton—but the assembly turned him down. Because he did not go forward with his appeal, the Supreme Court at its February 1797 term issued a *non prosequitur* judgment against Hunter. With the compromise legislation passed, Marshall did not need a final Supreme Court ruling as badly as before, but he probably would have felt more secure if his title were supported by a federal court decision than a repealable state law.

Marshall and the syndicate still faced the problem of financing the manor lands purchase: no loan, no land. The most they could secure, through James Marshall's negotiations with Dutch and English bankers and Robert Morris's efforts with the latter and in the United States, was about one third of the £22,000, including interest, due for all the manor lands. Sometime in January 1797, James Marshall apparently overcame initial difficulties in Holland and obtained a sizable loan; his account book contains a 25 January entry for "£7700 paid the Revd. Denny Fairfax." John Marshall—still loath to part with any of his western lands, even when the deal was falling into place—and his partners pressed Morris to raise more money. In April, Morris reluctantly mortgaged some lots he held as speculations in the future District of Columbia. In August, Marshall and the syndicate paid an additional £2,625 to Fairfax, making final the transfer of the South Branch, Greenway Court, and Gooney Run manors, a total of 58,959 acres. On 30 August, Denny Fairfax conveyed the South Branch lands to James but retained the more attractive Leeds tract until the syndicate paid the balance. After Morris's credit in Europe collapsed in 1797 and he went bankrupt the next year, Marshall and his partners had to try to secure the remaining £15,000 for Leeds Manor by themselves. They had scant cause for optimism. The market for land in the United States had weakened significantly because European investors—on whom American land speculators such as

Marshall had counted to make quick, large purchases—found the returns higher in making loans to European governments fighting the French. Marshall and the syndicate found themselves in a tightening financial bind. They owned a great deal of land but had too few buyers to earn a large enough profit quickly enough to meet their other obligations and avoid losing their entire investment.[85]

By gaining legal protection for the syndicate's title through adroit legal and political maneuvers, Marshall had surmounted the main obstacle blocking his entrance into national affairs. He could not have left Virginia or accepted appointments to federal office until then without seriously harming his litigation strategy. After the legislative compromise, he found himself free to travel outside the state and raise his standing with Federalist leaders, and to accept appointments to positions in the national government. At the same time, he bore most of the remaining financial burden of the Fairfax lands purchase. Soon, however, Marshall would reap unexpected political and monetary benefits from deteriorating relations between the United States and France.

NOTES

1. Sources for this paragraph and the next are David J. Mays, *Edmund Pendleton*, 2 vols. (Cambridge: Harvard University Press, 1952), 2:273–74, 297–30; Charles T. Cullen, "St. George Tucker and Law in Virginia" (Ph.D. diss., University of Virginia, 1971), chap. 5 passim, esp. 100–120; *PJM*, editorial notes at 1:291 and 5:xxxi–xxxii, 60–61, 451, 453; A. G. Roeber, *Faithful Magistrates and Republican Lawyers: Creators of Virginia Legal Culture, 1680–1810* (Chapel Hill: University of North Carolina Press, 1981), 205–07; John Reardon, *Edmund Randolph: A Biography* (New York: Macmillan, 1974), 161–62; profiles of judges in 4 Call i–vi. For the political preliminaries on the January 1788 law, see Norman K. Risjord, *Chesapeake Politics, 1781–1800* (New York: Columbia University Press, 1978), 183–84. Marshall favorably described the new system in a letter to Albert Gallatin, 3 January 1790, *PJM*, 2:48–50. Marshall, as a member of the House of Delegates' Committee on Courts of Justice, helped draft the repeal of the 1784 assize court law and the new district court law, but then—perhaps anticipating the judges' complaints—voted against it. "Legislative Bill," 3 January 1788, *PJM*, 1:248; *Journal of the House of Delegates of the Commonwealth of Virginia* (Richmond: Thomas W. White, 1828), October 1787 sess., 85, 105–6, 132.

2. Cullen, "St. George Tucker," 117–18; Roeber, *Faithful Magistrates and Republican Lawyers*, 210–11; *PJM*, editorial notes at 1:292 and 5:lvi, 4; JM to John Breckinridge, 22 June 1789, 28 March 1790, to Archibald Stuart, ca. March 1790, to William Branch Giles, 25 March 1790, to Charles Lee, 15 April 1793, *PJM*, 2:25–26, 51, 52, 54, 160.

3. Charles T. Cullen, "Completing the Revisal of the Laws in Post-Revolutionary Virginia," *VMHB*, 82 (1974), 84–99; idem, "St. George Tucker," chap. 6; Susan Foard, "Virginia Enters the Union: A Legislative Study of the Commonwealth, 1789–1792" (M.A. thesis, College of William and Mary, 1966), 164–70; Dumas Malone, *Jefferson the Virginian* (Boston: Little, Brown, 1948), 261–63; Alonzo T. Dill, *George Wythe, Teacher of Liberty* (Williamsburg: Virginia Independence Bicentennial Commission, 1979), 37–39, 57–58; *Journal of the House of Delegates*, October 1789 sess., 4, October 1790 sess., 41, 121–22, 161.

4. See, e.g., the cases in *PJM*, 2:26–27, 72–81, 5:424–25, 458–61, and passim; Mays, *Pendleton*, 2:300–301; Charles F. Hobson, *The Great Chief Justice: John Marshall and the Rule of Law* (Lawrence: University Press of Kansas, 1996), 31.

5. Sources for this paragraph and the next are *PJM*, editorial notes at 5:163–65, 455, and 465; legal fees recorded in "Account Book" for 1787–95, *PJM*, 1:368–413 and 2:335–498 passim; cases at *PJM*, 2:282–89 and 5:166–200, 215–27; JM to Archibald Stuart, [December 1789], *PJM*, 5:47–48; and numerous cases cited in 3 and 4 Call, 1 Washington, Wythe's chancery reports, and the district court record books for Accomack and Northhampton, Augusta, Frederick, Northumberland, Prince Edward, Prince William, and Franklin counties and for Fredericksburg, most accessibly cited in Irwin S. Rhodes, *The Papers of John Marshall: A Descriptive Calendar*, 2 vols. (Norman: University of Oklahoma Press, 1956), 1:62–63, 73–75, 82–91, 97–118, 122–47, 149–58, 174–201, 209–30, 238–57, 269–83 (hereafter cited as Rhodes, *Calendar of Marshall Papers*).

6. Sources for this paragraph and the next three are Charles F. Hobson, "The Recovery of British Debts in the Federal Circuit Court of Virginia, 1790 to 1797," *VMHB*, 92 (1984), 176–87, 193; Samuel Flagg Bemis, *Jay's Treaty: A Study in Commerce and Diplomacy* (New York: Macmillan, 1923), 103 n. 19; editorial notes and cases in *PJM*, 5:259–406; and numerous cases from the U.S. Circuit Court of Virginia order books and record books for 1791–96, most accessibly cited in Rhodes, *Calendar of Marshall Papers*, 1:122, 150, 174–83, 210–15, 217, 239–45, 269–76; Risjord, *Chesapeake Politics*, 452; Charles Warren, *The Supreme Court in United States History*, 3 vols. (Boston: Little, Brown, 1922), 1:99; John A. Treon, "*Martin v. Hunter's Lessee*: A Case History" (Ph.D. diss., University of Virginia, 1970), 98.

7. Marshall and the debtors' attorneys seemed to have worked together to develop a common legal strategy. In late October 1790, an advertisement appeared in Richmond newspapers for a meeting on 1 January 1791 at Eagle Tavern for "persons who are, or may hereafter be engaged or interested in any suits instituted by British Creditors or their agents. . . . the sole object of this proposition is to provide for a fair and legal investigation of the several claims that may be exhibited, in order to [reach] an equitable issue." *PJM*, 2:333.

8. Editorial notes and documents on *Jones v. Walker* in *PJM*, 5:264–94; William Wirt Henry, *Patrick Henry: Life, Correspondence, and Speeches*, 3 vols. (New York: Charles Scribner's Sons, 1891), 3:601–48; Hobson, "Recovery of British Debts," 187–89; Frederick T. Miller, "Juries and Judges versus the Law: Virginia from the Revolution to the Confrontation between John Marshall and Spencer Roane" (Ph.D. diss., University of Alabama, 1986), 31–33.

9. "*Ware, Administrator of Jones, v. Hylton, 1790–1796*: Editorial Note," *PJM*, 5:295–96; "Argument in the Circuit Court, 29–30 May 1793," *PJM*, 5:300–313; Miller, "Juries and Judges versus the Law," 163–64 n. 10; Leonard Baker, *John Marshall: A Life in Law* (New York: Macmillan, 1974), 159–60; Frances H. Rudko, *John Marshall and International Law: Statesman and Chief Justice* (New York: Greenwood Press, 1991), 17–21, 24–31.

10. Hobson, "Recovery of British Debts," 189–92; editorial notes in *PJM*, 3:5 and 5:296; *PJM*, 2:309 n. 2; cases in U.S. Circuit Court of Virginia cited in n. 6 above; Julius Goebel Jr., *Antecedents and Beginnings to 1801*, Volume 1 of the Oliver Wendell Holmes Jr. Devise History of the Supreme Court (New York: Macmillan, 1971), 750; Miller, "Juries and Judges versus the Law," 34–36, 164 n. 13.

Marshall had one other direct involvement with the Supreme Court around this time. In February 1797 the state of Virginia retained him as counsel in *Hollingsworth v. Virginia*, a suit filed by the Indiana Company five years before to force the state to recognize the validity of the company's deed to nearly 200,000 acres of land in what is now West Virginia. Marshall advised Governor James Wood not to enter a plea because the Eleventh Amendment, which would eliminate the federal courts' jurisdiction over suits against a state by citizens of another state, would soon be ratified and render the case moot. Marshall was right. In February 1798, after President John Adams declared that the amendment had been ratified, the Supreme Court ruled that it lacked jurisdiction in *Hollingsworth v. Virginia* and dismissed the Indiana Company's suit. James C. Brandow, "John Marshall's Supreme Court Practice: A Letter Comes to Light," *Journal of Supreme Court History*, 1 (1995), 73–76.

11. Albert J. Beveridge, *The Life of John Marshall*, 4 vols. (Boston: Houghton Mifflin, 1916–19), 2:192, citing John P. Kennedy, *Memoirs of the Life of William Wirt*, 2 vols. (Philadelphia, 1849), 2:76; Marshall's arguments in *PJM*, 3:7–14 and 5:317–25.

12. Goebel, *Antecedents and Beginnings*, 751–54; Warren, *Supreme Court in U.S. History*, 1:66; Miller, "Juries and Judges versus the Law," 36–38; JM, "Account Book," *PJM*, 2:309; "Judgment," *PJM*, 5:328–30 n. 2. Marshall's advocacy of Virginia's side in the case notwithstanding, his true sympathies may be divined from the fact that as chief justice he wrote four opinions upholding *Ware v. Hylton*. Herbert A. Johnson, *The Chief Justiceship of John Marshall, 1801–1835* (Columbia: University of South Carolina Press, 1997), 230–31.

13. Morton J. Horwitz, *The Transformation of American Law, 1780–1860* (Cambridge: Harvard University Press, 1977), chaps. 1–6 passim; James Willard Hurst, *Law and the Conditions of Freedom in the Nineteenth-Century United States* (Madison: University of Wisconsin Press, 1956), chap. 1; Joseph Dorfman, "John Marshall: Political Economist," in *Chief Justice John Marshall: A Reappraisal*, ed. W. Melville Jones (Ithaca: Cornell University Press, 1956), 136; Forrest McDonald, *Novus Ordo Seclorum: The Intellectual Origins of the Constitution* (Lawrence: University Press of Kansas, 1985), 114; *Livingston v. Jefferson*, (1811), *PJM*, 7:284.

14. Sources for this paragraph and the next are the editorial note and Marshall's argument in *Bracken v. College of William and Mary* (1790), *PJM*, 2:67–81; Florian Bartosic, "With John Marshall from William and Mary to Dartmouth College," *William and Mary Law Review*, 7 (1966), 259–66; Bruce A. Campbell, "John Marshall, the Virginia Political Economy, and the *Dartmouth College* Decision," *AJLH*, 19 (1975), 40–65.

15. Horwitz, *Transformation of American Law*, 63–64; JM, "Opinion," *PJM*, 2:108; Michael W. McConnell, "Contract Rights and Property Rights: A Case Study in the Relationship between Individual Liberties and Constitutional Structure," in *Liberty, Property, and the Foundations of the American Constitution*, ed. Ellen Frankel Paul and Howard Dickman (Albany: State University of New York Press, 1989), 141–68.

16. Sources for this discussion are William Cabell Bruce, *John Randolph of Roanoke, 1773–1833*, 2 vols. (New York: G. P. Putnam's Sons, 1922), 1:107–21; Henry, *Life of Henry*, 2:490–93; H. J. Eckenrode, *The Randolphs: The Story of a Virginia Family* (Indianapolis: Bobbs-Merrill, 1946), 171–87; Jonathan Daniels, *The Randolphs of Virginia* (Garden City, N.Y.: Doubleday and Co., 1972), 135–49; Baker, *Marshall*, 139–53; Francis Biddle, "Scandal at Bizarre," *American Heritage*, 12 (August 1961), 10–13, 79–82; Robert D. Meade, *Patrick Henry: Practical Revolutionary* (Philadelphia: J. P. Lippincott, 1969), 417–20; "*Commonwealth v. Randolph*: Editorial Note" and "Notes of Evidence," *PJM*, 2:161–78. A fairly effective novelistic treatment of the scandal is in Robert S. Bloom, *A Generation of Leaves* (New York: Ballantine Books, 1991), 347–420.

17. Jean Smith, Marshall's most recent biographer, states that Marshall "devised the strategy [used by Richard Randolph and described below] that ultimately brought the matter to a head." Most evidence suggests, however, that St. George Tucker recommended Randolph's first steps and that Marshall became involved later as the episode entered its procedural phase. Smith correctly notes that no documentation proves that Henry received the enormous sum of £500 for his services, as stated in some accounts. According to local court records, Richard Randolph paid him £140—still a huge amount at the time. Marshall either received no fee, which seems unlikely, or neglected to record one in his account book, which would be more in character for him. Smith, *John Marshall: Definer of a Nation* (New York: Henry Holt, 1996), 150, 574 n. 31.

18. *PJM*, 2:175–78.

19. Ibid., 178.

20. Morris to JM, 2 and 28 December 1809, and JM to Morris, 12 December 1809, *PJM*, 7:219–24; Max M. Mintz, *Gouverneur Morris and the American Revolution* (Norman: University of Oklahoma Press, 1970), 234–35; Anne Cary Morris, ed., *The Diary and Letters of Gouverneur Morris . . .*, 2 vols. (New York: Charles Scribner's Sons, 1888), 2:515–16.

21. John Randolph to Ann Randolph Morris, 31 October 1814, and Ann Randolph Morris to John Randolph, 16 January 1815, quoted in Bruce, *Randolph*, 2:274–75.

22. Opinions in *PJM*, 2:290–314 passim.

23. "Account Book," *PJM*, 2:335–37; JM, "Opinion," ca. 15 June 1793, *PJM*, 2:188–92; George Washington to JM, 15 August 1788, JM to Washington, 5 September 1788, Washington to JM, 17 March, 5 and 11 April 1789, *PJM*, 2:5–7, 17–20; JM's petitions for John A. Chevallie and James Markham, 5 and 15 October 1792, *PJM*, 2:125, 127; JM to Beverley Randolph, 29 January 1789, Beverley Randolph to JM, 4 February 1789, *PJM*, 2:14–15; Baker, *Marshall*, 172; Hobson, *Great Chief Justice*, 191–208.

24. Frances Norton Mason, *My Dearest Polly: Letters of Chief Justice John Marshall to His Wife . . .* (Richmond: Garrett and Massie, 1961), 57–59; Baker, *Marshall*, 184; Beveridge, *Marshall*, 3:394; Francis Stites, *John Marshall: Defender of the Constitution* (Boston: Little, Brown, 1981), 43; C. M. S., "The Home Life of Chief Justice Marshall," *WMQ*, 2nd ser., 12 (1932), 67–69.

25. William H. Gaines Jr., "Bench, Bar, and Barbecue Club," *Virginia Cavalcade*, 5 (autumn 1955), 8–13; Edmund Berkeley Jr., "Quoits, the Sport of Gentlemen," *Virginia Cavalcade*, 15 (summer 1965), 11–21; Edward S. Corwin, *John Marshall and the Constitution* (New Haven: Yale University Press, 1919), 202–05; Samuel Mordecai, *Richmond in By-Gone Days . . .* (Richmond: West and Johnson, 1856), 261–63; George Wythe Munford, *The Two Parsons; Cupid's Sports; The Dream; and The Jewel of Virginia* (Richmond: J. D. K. Sleight, 1884), 326–41; Beveridge, *Marshall*, 2:182–85; Baker, *Marshall*, 102–6; Stites, *Marshall*, 43; Smith, *Marshall*, 160–61; Henry Flanders, *The Lives and Times of the Chief Justices of the Supreme Court of the United States*, 2 vols. (orig. publ. 1855–58; rept., Philadelphia: T. and J. W. Johnson, 1881), 2:517–20; *PJM*, 2:461–62 n. 65.

26. "Militia Duty: Editorial Note," *PJM*, 2:180; Herbert Aptheker, *American Negro Slave Revolts* (New York: Columbia University Press, 1943), 210–15; Robert McColley, *Slavery and Jeffersonian Virginia*, 2nd ed. (Urbana: University of Illinois Press, 1973), 107; Winthrop D. Jordan, *White over Black: American Attitudes toward the Negro, 1550–1812*, Penguin ed. (Chapel Hill: University of North Carolina Press, 1968), 391–92; Virginius Dabney, *Richmond: The Story of a City* (Garden City, N.Y.: Doubleday and Co., 1976), 51–52; Thomas O. Ott, *The Haitian Revolution, 1787–1804* (Knoxville:

University of Tennessee Press, 1973), chaps. 3–4; Donald R. Hickey, "America's Response to the Slave Revolt in Haiti, 1791–1806," *JER*, 2 (1982), 361–80; Paul Finkelman, "The Problem of Slavery in the Age of Federalism," in *Federalists Reconsidered*, ed. Doron Ben-Atar and Barbara B. Oberg (Charlottesville: University Press of Virginia, 1998), 149–52; Robert Mitchell to JM, 23 September 1793, JM to Henry Lee, 26 September 1793, *PJM*, 2:210–11. As many as 10,000 French fled Haiti on over 100 ships, which sailed into Norfolk during 7–11 July 1793. Those refugees who did not stay in Virginia went on to other Eastern Seaboard cities. Alexander DeConde, *Entangling Alliance: Politics and Diplomacy under George Washington* (Durham, N.C.: Duke University Press, 1958), 273, 275 n. 1.

27. James Wood to JM, 23 August 1793, JM to Henry Lee, 23 September 1793, Henry Lee to JM, 26 September 1793, *PJM*, 2:200–201, 209, 211; "Account Book," *PJM*, 2:463 and n. 71.

28. JM, *Life of George Washington*, 5 vols. (Philadelphia: C. P. Wayne, 1804–7; rept., New York: Chelsea House, 1983), 5:36–37.

29. J. H. Powell, *Bring Out Your Dead: The Great Plague of Yellow Fever in Philadelphia in 1793* (Philadelphia: University of Pennsylvania Press, 1949), v, 239; JM, affidavits and letters in *PJM*, 2:217–21.

30. W. Asbury Christian, *Richmond: Her Past and Present* (Richmond, L. H. Jenkins, 1912), 30; Beveridge, *Marshall*, 2:172; Marianne P. B. Sheldon, "Richmond, Virginia: The Town and Henrico County to 1820" (Ph.D. diss., University of Michigan, 1975), chaps. 2–6 passim; Francois Alexandre de la Rochefoucauld-Liancourt, *Travels through the United States of North America* (London, 1800), excerpted in Maurice Duke and Daniel P. Jordan, eds., *A Richmond Reader, 1733–1983* (Chapel Hill: University of North Carolina Press, 1983), 24; Mary Wingfield Scott, *Houses of Old Richmond* (New York: Bonanza Books, 1941), 6, 27–32; Charles H. Ambler, *Thomas Ritchie: A Study in Virginia Politics* (Richmond: Bell Book and Stationery Co., 1913), 13–16.

31. Berkeley, "Quoits," 11–12; Mordecai, *Richmond in By-Gone Days*, 188, 255–56; Christian, *Richmond*, 35, 46–47; "Account Book," *PJM*, 2:355–498 passim; "Notice of Public Auction," 21 December 1791, *PJM*, 2:101–2; "Memorial," 15 November 1794, and "Fire Insurance Application, ca. 24 February 1796, *PJM*, 2:296–97, 3:16. When anti-Masonic sentiment grew strong in the 1830s, Marshall minimized his earlier involvement with the order. *PJM*, 2:418–19, 421.

32. "Account Book," *PJM*, 2:355–498 passim, under entries for JM's siblings and children.

33. JM to Joseph Story, 26 June 1831, in John Oster, *The Political and Economic Doctrines of John Marshall* (orig. publ. 1914; rept., New York: Burt Franklin, 1967), 135–36; Mason, *My Dearest Polly*, 60–62; *PJM*, 2:321 and n. 5, 323. Marshall's letter to Polly has been lost.

34. "Account Book," *PJM*, 2:353, 380, 408, 431, 444–45 n. 94, 449, 471, 474 n. 18, 485; JM to James Breckinridge, 12 October 1793, *PJM*, 2:217 and n. 9; deeds dated 7 July 1789 and 4 January 1791, *PJM*, 2:28–29, 85; "Construction Account," October 1788–November 1790, *PJM*, 2:8–12; "Fire Insurance Application," ca. 24 February 1793, *PJM*, 3:16; JM's personal property lists in Rhodes, *Calendar of Marshall Papers*, 1:65; Leonard Baker, "John Marshall's Federalist House," *Washington Post*, 28 March 1971, G1; The John Marshall Foundation, untitled guidebook for the John Marshall House (Richmond: N.p., n.d.); Scott, *Houses of Old Richmond*, 21–23; author's visits, July 1991 and July 1994. The half-acre lot on which Marshall built his house cost £150. In 1791, he bought an adjacent half-acre lot for £50. I Street was renamed Marshall Street in 1845 to honor the late chief justice. Marshall's house remained with his

descendants until the early 1900s, when the City of Richmond acquired it. It was then entrusted to the Association for the Preservation of Virginia Antiquities, which still maintains it.

35. "Petition," ca. 1 July 1792, *PJM*, 2:118–20.

36. Beveridge, *Marshall*, 2:141; Bruce A. Campbell, "Law and Experience in the Early Republic: The Evolution of the Dartmouth College Doctrine, 1780–1819" (Ph.D. diss., Michigan State University, 1973), 243; George T. Starnes, *Sixty Years of Branch Banking in Virginia* (New York: Macmillan, 1931), 19, 24–25; William W. Hening, ed., *The Statutes at Large . . .*, 13 vols. (Richmond: Bartow, 1819–23), 13:599; James O. Wettereau, "The Branches of the First Bank of the United States," *Journal of Economic History*, supplement to 2 (1942), 76–77; Risjord, *Chesapeake Politics*, 473–75, 669 n. 19; "The Bank of the United States. Petitions of Virginia Cities and Towns for the Establishment of Branches, 1791," *VMHB*, 8 (1901), 287–95; Bray Hammond, *Banks and Politics in America from the Revolution to the Civil War* (Princeton: Princeton University Press, 1957), 145–46, 172; JM to Henry Tazewell, 11 January 1795, and to James M. Marshall, 2 February and 1 April 1804, *PJM*, 2:308, 6:256, 278; Kathryn R. Malone, "The Fate of Revolutionary Republicanism in Early National Virginia," *JER*, 7 (1987), 34–43.

37. Marshall Smelser, "The Federalist Period as an Age of Passion," *American Quarterly*, 10 (1958), 391–419; idem, "The Jacobin Phrenzy: Federalism and the Menace of Liberty, Equality, and Fraternity," *Review of Politics*, 13 (1951), 457–82; idem, "The Jacobin Phrenzy: The Menace of Monarchy, Plutocracy, and Anglophilia, 1789–1798," *Review of Politics*, 21 (1959), 239–58; John R. Howe, "Republican Thought and the Political Violence of the 1790s," *American Quarterly*, 19 (1967), 147–65, quote at 150; Jefferson to Thomas Mann Randolph, 7 January 1793, in *The Papers of Thomas Jefferson*, ed. Julian P. Boyd et al., 27 vols. to date (Princeton: Princeton University Press, 1950–), 25:30; John Stokes Adams, ed., *An Autobiographical Sketch by John Marshall . . .* (Ann Arbor: University of Michigan Press, 1937), 13 (hereafter cited as JM, *Autobiographical Sketch*); DeConde, *Entangling Alliance*, 173–81; Stanley Elkins and Eric McKitrick, *The Age of Federalism* (New York: Oxford University Press, 1993), 308–11; JM, *Life of Washington*, 5:49–52, 54.

Mason, *My Dearest Polly*, 66, 95, mentions Marshall's "many" French friends in Richmond but refers only to the traveling noble Francois Alexandre de la Rochefoucault-Liancourt as a dinner guest in the mid-1790s. There are no other documentary references to French residents in Virginia who might have influenced Marshall's attitudes toward France and the Revolution.

Several works state that two incidents involving Marshall's relatives and France explain much of his rising antipathy toward the Revolution. In 1794, one of his brothers, James, visited France as President Washington's confidential agent to negotiate for the release of the Marquis de Lafayette, whom the Jacobins had imprisoned for his alleged monarchist sympathies. Another brother, Louis, supposedly was a medical student in Paris but was jailed and sentenced to death for his involvement in counterrevolutionary activities, and then was rescued from execution through John and James's intervention. See, e.g., Beveridge, *Marshall*, 2:33–34; Randolph W. Church, "James Markham Marshall," *Virginia Cavalcade*, 13 (spring 1964), 26; Mason, *My Dearest Polly*, 64–65. However, the Prussians and Austrians, not the Jacobins, imprisoned Lafayette; and Louis Marshall could not have been in Paris at the time family tradition claims he was. John Marshall wrote that Washington sent James to Berlin to negotiate for Lafayette's release. JM, *Life of Washington*, 5:213; Baker, *Marshall*, 292–93, citing William Buchanan,

"Louis Marshall, M.D." (M.A. thesis, Washington and Lee University, 1941); *PJM*, 7:56 n. 2.

38. Richard R. Beeman, *The Old Dominion and the New Nation, 1788–1801* (Lexington: University Press of Kentucky, 1972), 122–25; Risjord, *Chesapeake Politics*, 422–23.

39. Beeman, *Old Dominion and New Nation*, 122–33; DeConde, *Entangling Alliance*, 182–310; Albert H. Bowman, *The Struggle for Neutrality: Franco-American Diplomacy during the Federalist Era* (Knoxville: University of Tennessee Press, 1974), chap. 3; Harry Ammon, *The Genet Mission* (New York: W. W. Norton, 1973), passim; Elkins and McKitrick, *Age of Federalism*, 330–65; Forrest McDonald, *The Presidency of George Washington* (New York: W. W. Norton, 1975), 123–29; Lisle A. Rose, *Prologue to Democracy: The Federalists in the South, 1789–1800* (Lexington: University of Kentucky Press, 1968), 424–30; Washington's Proclamation of Neutrality, 22 April 1793, in John C. Fitzpatrick, ed., *The Writings of George Washington*, 39 vols. (Washington, D.C.: Government Printing Office, 1931–44), 32:430–31.

40. JM, *Autobiographical Sketch*, 13–14; "Resolutions" and "Address," 17 April 1793, *PJM*, 2:196–200; James Monroe to Jefferson, 3 September 1793, *The Writings of James Monroe*, ed. Stanislaus Murray Hamilton, 7 vols. (New York: G. P. Putnam's Sons, 1898–1903), 1:274; Ammon, *Genet Mission*, 135–40; idem, "The Genet Mission and the Development of American Political Parties," *JAH*, 52 (1965–66), 730–33; Risjord, *Chesapeake Politics*, 428–29; Robert Ernst, *Rufus King, American Federalist* (Chapel Hill: University of North Carolina Press, 1968), 189–93.

No evidence supports the assertion in John A. Carroll and Mary W. Ashworth, *George Washington: First in Peace*, 1793–1799 (New York: Charles Scribner's Sons, 1957), 129 n. 21, that Marshall forced the resolutions through the Richmond meeting over Wythe's opposition. Cf. Ammon's article, 730-31, 732 n. 26. Ammon suggests that Hamilton may have arranged the Richmond rally either through Marshall or Marshall's brother-in-law, Edward Carrington, to whom Hamilton was close; but Ammon also notes that no available documentation supports his idea.

41. Harry Ammon, "Agricola versus Aristides: James Monroe, John Marshall, and the Genet Affair in Virginia," *VMHB*, 74 (1966), 312–20; Philip Marsh, "James Monroe as 'Agricola' in the Genet Controversy," *VMHB*, 62 (1954), 472–76; JM, *Autobiographical Sketch*, 14; Baker, *Marshall*, 197, 796 n. 7; Rudko, *John Marshall and International Law*, 14–16. Smith, *Marshall*, 174 and 582 n. 32, makes some interesting suggestions about why Marshall chose his pseudonyms. As the Athenian statesman Aristides, Marshall was criticizing the pretensions of Citizen Genet. As the Roman plebian Gracchus, he was refuting Monroe's charge that the Federalists favored monarchy.

42. Ammon, *Genet Mission*, 33; idem, "Genet Mission and American Political Parties," passim; Elkins and McKitrick, *Age of Federalism*, 359–60; Rose, *Prologue to Democracy*, 50, 81; JM, *Autobiographical Sketch*, 14.

43. Henry Lee to JM, 8 July 1793, 18 April and 21 July 1794; James Wood to JM, 22 August 1793; and JM to Henry Lee, 23 and 28 July 1794, in *PJM*, 2:183–84, 200, 265, 273–78; "Editorial Note: Militia Duty," *PJM*, 2:182–83; Beveridge, *Marshall*, 2:103–6; Baker, *Marshall*, 174–75; Charles Royster, *Light-Horse Harry Lee and the Legacy of the American Revolution* (New York: Alfred A. Knopf, 1981), 141.

44. Beeman, *Old Dominion and New Nation*, 111, 121, 134; Eugene P. Link, *Democratic-Republican Societies, 1790–1800* (New York: Columbia University Press, 1942), 13–16, 164; Philip S. Foner, ed., *The Democratic-Republican Societies, 1790–1800: A Documentary Sourcebook of Constitutions, Declarations, Addresses, Resolutions, and Toasts* (Westport, Conn.: Greenwood Press, 1976), 345–55; Matthew

Schoenbachler, "Republicanism in the Age of Democratic Revolution: The Democratic-Republican Societies of the 1790s," *JER*, 18 (1998), 237–61; Risjord, *Chesapeake Politics*, 430, 441; Noble Cunningham, *The Jeffersonian Republicans: The Formation of Party Organization, 1789–1801* (Chapel Hill: University of North Carolina Press, 1957), 62–66; Elkins and McKitrick, *Age of Federalism*, 457–61. The society in Fayette County, Kentucky, where Thomas Marshall lived, emphasized how improved French-American relations would reduce tensions on the frontier with Spain. Foner, ed., *Democratic-Republican Societies*, 357–73.

45. Thomas P. Slaughter, *The Whiskey Rebellion: Frontier Epilogue to the American Revolution* (New York: Oxford University Press, 1986), 99, 117–18, 151, 169; Leland D. Baldwin, *Whiskey Rebels: The Story of a Frontier Uprising* (Pittsburgh: University of Pittsburgh Press, 1939), 105, 206–7; *PJM*, 3:46 n. 4; Risjord, *Chesapeake Politics*, 446; Elkins and McKitrick, *Age of Federalism*, 461–74; Forrest McDonald, *Alexander Hamilton: A Biography* (New York: W. W. Norton, 1982), 297–302; John C. Miller, *The Federalist Era, 1789–1801* (New York: Harper and Row, 1960), 155–59; Richard H. Kohn, *Eagle and Sword: The Federalists and the Creation of the Military Establishment in America, 1783–1802* (New York: Free Press, 1975), 157–70.

46. JM, *Life of Washington*, 5:171–73. At the same time Marshall could, without contradiction, be a member of the Masons, which were politically active for the Federalists but were not "self-created" and were founded for fraternal, not political, purposes. John L. Brooke, "Ancient Lodges and Self-Created Societies: Voluntary Association and the Public Sphere in the Early Republic," in *Launching the "Extended Republic": The Federalist Age*, ed. Ronald Hoffman and Peter J. Albert (Charlottesville: University Press of Virginia, 1996), 316–23, 340–42.

47. "Editorial Note: Militia Duty," *PJM*, 2:183; JM, *Life of Washington*, 5:157–66, 171–72; Lawrence D. Cress, *Citizens in Arms: The Army and the Militia in American Society to the War of 1812* (Chapel Hill: University of North Carolina Press, 1982), 121, 124; Baker, *Marshall*, 301; Beveridge, *Marshall*, 2:86–91.

48. Cress, *Citizens in Arms*, 81, 94, 97ff., 121, 124; Beeman, *Old Dominion and New Nation*, 102–8; Slaughter, *Whiskey Rebellion*, 213–14; Baldwin, *Whiskey Rebels*, 223; Charles Royster, *A Revolutionary People at War: The Continental Army and American Character, 1775–1783* (New York: W. W. Norton, 1981), 341; Kohn, *Eagle and Sword*, 76–80, 86, 88, 137, 281 n.; Marcus Cunliffe, *Soldiers and Civilians: The Martial Spirit in America, 1775–1865* (Boston: Little, Brown, 1968), 180–86; Arthur A. Ekirch, *The Civilian and the Military: A History of the American Antimilitarist Tradition* (Colorado Springs: Ralph Myles, 1972), 24–31; Don Higginbotham, *The War of American Independence: Military Attitudes, Policies, and Practice, 1763–1789* (Boston: Northeastern University Press, 1983), 449–62; JM, *Life of Washington*, 4:137; U.S. Constitution, Article I, section 8, Article II, section 2, Article IV, section 4; Jacob E. Cooke, ed., *The Federalist Papers* (Middletown, Conn.: Wesleyan University Press, 1961), nos. 24–29 at 152–87; JM, speeches on 10 and 16 June 1788, *PJM*, 1:261, 273–74; idem, opinions on 10 October and ca. late 1794, *PJM*, 2:291, 305–07.

49. Royster, *Light-Horse Harry Lee*, 134; Beeman, *Old Dominion and New Nation*, 134–36; Risjord, *Chesapeake Politics*, 447–48; JM to Archibald Stuart, 27 March 1794, *PJM*, 2:261–62.

50. JM, *Autobiographical Sketch*, 14–16; Risjord, *Chesapeake Politics*, 449.

51. Principal sources for this discussion of the Jay Treaty debate are Jerald A. Combs, *The Jay Treaty: Political Battleground of the Founding Fathers* (Berkeley: University of California Press, 1970), chaps. 10–11; Bradford Perkins, *The First Rapprochement: England and the United States, 1795–1805* (Berkeley: University of California Press,

1967), chap. 3; Richard Buel Jr., *Securing the Revolution: Ideology in American Politics, 1789–1815* (Ithaca: Cornell University Press, 1972), chap. 3; Elkins and McKitrick, *Age of Federalism*, chap. 9; DeConde, *Entangling Alliance*, chap. 4; McDonald, *Presidency of Washington*, chap. 8. Marshall's relatively objective account is in *Life of Washington*, 5:180–92, 201–10.

52. JM to Archibald Stuart, 27 March 1794, *PJM*, 2:262.

53. Beeman, *Old Dominion and New Nation*, 137–51; Rose, *Prologue to Democracy*, 119–29; Risjord, *Chesapeake Politics*, 450–60; Thomas J. Farnham, "The Virginia Amendments of 1795: An Episode in the Opposition to Jay's Treaty," *VMHB*, 75 (1967), 75–88; JM, *Life of Washington*, 5:184.

54. *Journal of the House of Delegates*, November 1795 sess., 26–29, 71–72; Stephen G. Kurtz, *The Presidency of John Adams: The Collapse of Federalism, 1795–1800* (rept., New York: A. S. Barnes, 1961), 21–23.

55. Myra L. Rich, "The Experimental Years: Virginia, 1781–1789" (Ph.D. diss., Yale University, 1966), chaps. 4–5; JM, *Autobiographical Sketch*, 17.

56. Farnham, "Virginia Amendments of 1795," 88; Kurtz, *Presidency of Adams*, 24–25; JM, *Autobiographical Sketch*, 17–19; Griffith J. McRee, ed., *The Life and Correspondence of James Iredell*, 2 vols. (New York: D. Appleton, 1858), 2:456; JM to Alexander Hamilton, 25 April 1796, *PJM*, 3:24; *Journal of the House of Delegates*, November 1795 sess., 91–92; Beveridge, *Marshall*, 2:133–36, 141–43. Smith, *Marshall*, 180–81 and 584 n. 69, mistakenly places Marshall's speech in the November 1796 assembly session.

57. *Journal of the House of Delegates*, November 1795 sess., 4, 5, 12, 14, 50, 53, 113, 119, 131; Risjord, *Chesapeake Politics*, 480; JM to Charles Lee, ca. December 1795, *PJM*, 2:330.

58. JM, *Autobiographical Sketch*, 19–20; Edmund Randolph to JM, 19 October 1794, JM to Randolph, 27 October 1794, *PJM*, 2:293–94; Tench Coxe to JM, 1 February 1795, *PJM*, 2:309–10 and ns. 2 and 3; Warren, *Supreme Court in U.S. History*, 1:141–42; George Washington to JM, 30 September 1789, JM to Washington, 14 October 1789, Washington to JM, 26 August 1795, JM to Washington, 31 August 1795, *PJM*, 2:319–20; Charles Lee to Washington, 20 March 1796, quoted in Beveridge, *Marshall*, 2:201–2.

59. JM to Alexander Hamilton and to Rufus King, both 25 April 1796, *PJM*, 2:22–24; sources cited in notes 52 and 53 above.

60. The Federalists' use of rallies, festivities, rituals, and other forms of "celebratory politics" to mobilize public support for their policies is discussed in David Waldstreicher, *In the Midst of Perpetual Fetes: The Making of American Nationalism, 1776–1820* (Chapel Hill: University of North Carolina Press, 1997), chaps. 2 and 3; and Simon P. Newman, *Parades and the Politics of the Street: Festive Culture in the Early Republic* (Philadelphia: University of Pennsylvania Press, 1997), chaps. 2–6.

61. Beeman, *Old Dominion and New Nation*, 156–57; Elkins and McKitrick, *Age of Federalism*, 517–18; Rose, *Prologue to Democracy*, 69–74.

62. George Mason to John Mason, 12 July 1791, *The Papers of George Mason*, ed. Robert A. Rutland, 3 vols. (Chapel Hill: University of North Carolina Press, 1970), 3:1230; JM to James Madison, 29 November 1790, *PJM*, 2:66; Beveridge, *Marshall*, 2:99–103; Madison to Jefferson, 17 July 1793, *The Papers of James Madison*, ed. William T. Hutchinson et al., 17 vols. (Chicago: University of Chicago Press, 1962–91), 15:31–32; Harry T. Ammon, *James Monroe: The Quest for National Identity* (New York: McGraw-Hill, 1971), 81–82. The Marshall-Monroe friendship might have

suffered its first strain when Marshall opposed Monroe's bid for a U.S. Senate seat in 1790. Monroe to Jefferson, 20 October 1790, *Papers of Jefferson*, 17:607.

63. Donald O. Dewey, *Marshall versus Jefferson: The Political Background of Marbury v. Madison* (New York: Alfred A. Knopf, 1970), 31–32; Beveridge, *Marshall*, 1:144 n. 2; Smith, *Marshall*, 11; Malone, *Jefferson the Virginian*, 359. In his *Life of Washington*, 3:127–28, Marshall gives a brief account of the military action but does not mention Jefferson.

64. Jefferson to Madison, 29 June 1792, *Papers of Jefferson*, 24:133.

65. Jefferson to Madison, 26 November 1795, *Papers of Madison*, 16:134–35; Dewey, *Marshall versus Jefferson*, 38; Elkins and McKitrick, *Age of Federalism*, 205; Julian P. Boyd, "The Chasm that Separated Thomas Jefferson and John Marshall," in *Essays on the American Constitution*, ed. Gottfried Dietze (Englewood Cliffs, N.J.: Prentice-Hall, 1964), 3–20.

66. *Eppes et al. v. Lomax* (1791), cited in Rhodes, *Calendar of Marshall Papers*, 1:138; *Wayles's Executors v. Randolph et al.*, *PJM*, 5:117–60; Malone, *Jefferson the Virginian*, 441–45; JM, "Opinion," 1 April 1791, *PJM*, 2:89–90; letters and documents in *Papers of Jefferson*, 15:642–77, 20:166–67; JM to Henry Lee, 25 October 1830, quoted in Smith, *Marshall*, 12. The missing Marshall-Jefferson correspondence between July 1794 and November 1795 probably dealt with the Wayles estate litigation; the letters are calendared in *PJM*, 2:273, 279, 317–18, 321–23.

67. Sources for this discussion of the 1796 election are Kurtz, *Presidency of Adams*, chaps. 4–9; Manning J. Dauer, *The Adams Federalists* (Baltimore: Johns Hopkins University Press, 1953), chap. 3; Elkins and McKitrick, *Age of Federalism*, 513–19; McDonald, *Presidency of Washington*, 177–83; Page Smith, *John Adams*, 2 vols. (Garden City, N.Y.: Doubleday and Co., 1962), 2:898–914; Risjord, *Chesapeake Politics*, 506–9, 512–15; Rose, *Prologue to Democracy*, 123–38; and Beeman, *Old Dominion and New Nation*, 159–68.

68. JM to Rufus King, 19 April and 24 May 1796, *PJM*, 3:21–22, 28. Marshall was not involved in, nor did he then or later comment on, Hamilton's subsequent attempt to deny Adams the presidency by getting Federalist electors in the South to split their votes between Adams and Thomas Pinckney, thereby giving the victory to Jefferson.

69. Norman K. Risjord and Gordon DenBoer, "The Evolution of Political Parties in Virginia, 1782–1800," *JAH*, 60 (1973–74), 977–80; Beeman, *Old Dominion and New Nation*, 151–52, 155; Risjord, *Chesapeake Politics*, 468–505 passim; Rose, *Prologue to Democracy*, 82–84; Bowman, *Struggle for Neutrality*, chap. 11; DeConde, *Entangling Alliance*, chaps. 13–14; Dauer, *Adams Federalists*, 106; JM, *Life of Washington*, 5:240–42.

70. JM to Charles Lee, 20 April 1797, *PJM*, 3:70–71.

71. Kurtz, *Presidency of Adams*, 164; Richard Hofstadter, *The Idea of a Party System: The Rise of Legitimate Opposition in the United States, 1780–1840* (Berkeley: University of California Press, 1969), 16–39, 86–102.

72. Beveridge, *Marshall*, 159–62; *Journal of the House of Delegates*, November 1796 sess., 22, 28, 63–65, 70–71; JM to James Iredell, 15 December 1796, 3:59; Beveridge, *Marshall*, 2:159–64. Marshall recounts the episode inaccurately in his *Autobiographical Sketch*, 20–21.

73. *Journal of the House of Delegates*, November 1796 sess., 3–99 passim.

74. "Account Book," *PJM*, 2:363, 367, 382, 474, 477; "Grant," 8 February 1791, "Bounty Land Surveys," 25 November 1794, "Bounty Land Grant," 20 February 1796, *PJM*, 1:106–7, 2:298, 3:15; "Marshall's Kentucky Lands: Editorial Note," *PJM*, 1:102; Irwin S. Rhodes, "John Marshall and the Western Country: The Early Days," *Historical*

and Philosophical Society of Ohio Bulletin, 18 (1960), 125; Thomas Marshall to Edmund Randolph, 15 September 1789, cited in Rhodes, *Calendar of Marshall Papers*, 1:77; *Thomas Marshall et al. v. George Rogers Clark*, 4 Call 268 (1791).

75. General sources for this section are the editorial notes in *PJM*, 2:140–49, 5:228–34, and 8:108–13; H. C. Groome, *Fauquier during the Proprietorship: A Chronicle of the Colonization and Organization of a Northern Neck County* (Richmond, 1927; rept., Baltimore: Regional Publishing Co., 1969), chap. 10; Stuart E. Brown, Jr., *Virginia Baron: The Story of Thomas 6th Lord Fairfax* (Berryville, Va.: Chesapeake Book Co., 1965), passim; Josiah L. Dickinson, *The Fairfax Proprietary* (Front Royal, Va.: Warren Press, 1959), passim; Treon, "*Martin v. Hunter's Lessee*," passim; Charles Hobson, "John Marshall and the Fairfax Litigation: The Background of *Martin v. Hunter's Lessee*," *Journal of Supreme Court History*, 2 (1996), 36–41.

76. *Escheat* refers to the government's power to seize the property of someone who dies without legal heirs. *Ejectment* is a lawsuit by a rightful titleholder to recover property occupied by another person who has no lawful title to it.

77. JM to Richard Henry Lee, 18 January 1793, "Articles of Agreement," 1 February 1793, JM to Archibald Stuart, 22 January 1794, "Deed," 1 February 1794; *PJM*, 2:138–39, 150–56, 253–58.

78. Marshall's account book contains references to his trips to the inquests; *PJM*, 2:472, 475, 482.

79. JM to Robert Brooke, ca. 2 March 1795, Brooke to JM, 2 March 1795, *PJM*, 2:312–13; Royster, *Light-Horse Harry Lee*, 172.

80. Case documents are in *PJM*, 5:236–49.

81. JM to Charles Lee, ca. December 1795, *PJM*, 2:329–30.

82. "Petition for Postponement," 22 January and 29 July 1796, *PJM*, 5:252, 254–55; JM to Polly, 3 February 1796, to Henry Lee, 18 July 1796, *PJM*, 3:3–4, 35–36.

83. Barbara Ann Chernow, "Robert Morris: Land Speculator, 1790–1801" (Ph.D. diss., Columbia University, 1974), 154–55, 176; documents for *Morris v. William Alexander and Co.* in *PJM*, 5:92–111; Beveridge, *Marshall*, 2:199–206; Ellis P. Oberholtzer, *Robert Morris, Patriot and Financier* (rept., New York: Burt Franklin, 1968), 321–22; Church, "James Markham Marshall," passim; Robert Morris to JM, 29 December 1795, 3 May, 16 June, 24 August 1796, *PJM*, 2:329, 3:25, 29, 42.

84. Sources for this and the next two paragraphs are: JM to John Wise, 24 November 1796, *PJM*, 3:54–55; *PJM*, 5:255–56, 8:109–10; Hobson, "Marshall and the Fairfax Litigation," 41–42. Hunter revived his cause in the early 1800s and obtained a reversal of the district court judgment by the state Court of Appeals in 1810. That decision led to two very significant Supreme Court decisions concerning federal-state relations: *Fairfax's Devisee v. Hunter's Lessee* (1813) and *Martin v. Hunter's Lessee* (1816). *PJM*, 5:230.

85. Beveridge, *Marshall*, 2:210; Robert Morris to JM, 23 January 1797, *PJM*, 3:63; text of deed in *Marshall v. Conrad*, 5 Call 264 at 370 (1805); Royster, *Light-Horse Harry Lee*, 173–74. Ironically, James Marshall inadvertently reopened the question of the validity of Fairfax's title in the *Marshall v. Conrad* case, which began in 1799 when he filed an ejectment action in the Winchester District Court in furtherance of his claim to certain lots in the town. He based his claim on the nonpayment of rents which he said had passed to him in Denny Fairfax's 1797 deed conveying the manor lands. Marshall lost in the district court but won on appeal in 1805. *PJM*, 6:278 n. 3; JM to James Marshall, 1 April 1804, *PJM*, 6:277; Hobson, "Marshall and the Fairfax Litigation," 43.

Marshall's father Thomas, a prominent Virginia public figure, landholder, and Continental Army officer. Intelligent and ambitious, he was probably the strongest influence in shaping young John's character. (National Archives)

Marshall's mother Mary, a reserved and devout homemaker whom Marshall respected but was not close to. She came from one of the first families of Virginia, the Randolphs. (National Archives)

Marshall's second childhood home, the Hollow, in northern Fauquier County, Virginia. Its present decrepit state makes it hard to appreciate that the house's architectural features, such as split-board sides, pane glass windows, and two full stories, were unusually "fancy" for the Blue Ridge frontier in the 1760s. (Author photo)

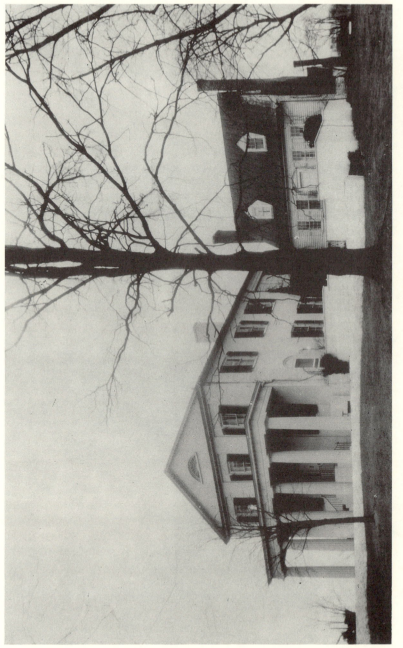

Marshall's third and best known childhood home, Oak Hill, also in northern Fauquier County, Virginia. His father built the smaller structure in the early 1770s. Like the Hollow, its design was quite sophisticated for its time and place. Marshall added the larger dwelling after inheriting the property and used it mainly as a summer home. (National Archives)

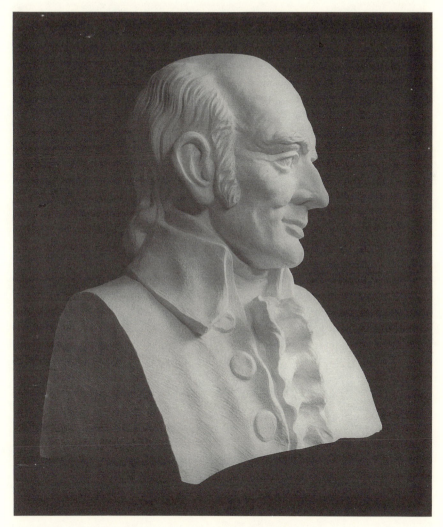

George Wythe, Marshall's law professor at the College of William and Mary. During his brief tutelage under Wythe, Marshall learned basic principles of law and courtroom forensics. (National Archives)

Marshall's beloved wife Mary, whom he usually referred to in correspondence as "my dearest Polly." This portrait, done during the 1820s when she was around 60, shows the toll that years of medical maladies and at least 10 pregnancies took on the pretty and petite 16-year-old Marshall married in 1783. (National Archives)

Marshall's Federalist-style home in Richmond, built to his specifications in 1790. The simple but elegant structure reflects Marshall's tastes, which combined the practical with the aesthetic. He hosted his famous "lawyers' dinners" amid its humble but refined furnishings. (National Archives)

This engraving, based on a physiognotrace by Charles Balthazar Julien Fevret de Saint-Mémin in 1808, captures Marshall's handsomeness, physical power, and strength of character. (National Archives)

Chapter 6

Diplomatic Interlude: The XYZ Mission, 1797–1798

John Marshall became a special envoy to France because the signing and ratification of the Jay Treaty had sent United States-French relations into a precipitous decline that threatened to turn into full-scale war. The French government interpreted the treaty as a de facto Anglo-American alliance and a unilateral renunciation by America of the 1778 accords that had made the United States and France virtual allies. During 1795–97, France launched a limited sea war against American ships transporting goods to English ports. France claimed the right to retaliate for U.S. failure to enforce against Britain the provision of the 1778 treaty that "free ships make free goods." French raiders seized over 300 American ships and confiscated or destroyed over $55 million worth of American property in the most intense period of the "Quasi-War" during 1796–97. Meanwhile, in 1796, the United States recalled its blatantly Francophile minister, James Monroe, from Paris, and French diplomats in America tried to stifle the Jay Treaty by using propaganda and intrigue to prevent its ratification and by openly intervening in the presidential election on behalf of Thomas Jefferson, who Paris hoped would render the treaty meaningless. In December 1796, the French government refused to receive the new American minister, Charles Cotesworth Pinckney, and expelled him from the country.[1]

Franco-American relations continued their downward spiral after John Adams's election. In early March 1797, just before the inauguration, the French government decreed that American vessels carrying enemy goods of any kind—not just contraband—would be subject to seizure; that American sailors serving on English ships would be treated as pirates; and that all American ships must carry a list of crew and passengers or face capture. In a speech to Congress in May, Adams declared that further French depredations "ought to be repelled with a decision which shall convince France and the world that we are not a degraded people, humiliated under a colonial spirit of fear and sense of inferiority, fitted to be the miserable instruments of foreign influence, and regardless of national honor, character, and interest." Adams did not want to go to war, however, without trying diplomacy one more time. Drawing on the experience of the crisis with Britain in 1794–95, and with bipartisan support, he decided to appoint a special envoy to France. If this last effort failed, he would ask Congress to authorize preparations for war.

John Marshall was not the president's first choice for the assignment, nor was he even considered at all until the cabinet insisted that Adams add one or two envoys besides Pinckney, then minister-in-exile in the Netherlands. After naming Francis Dana for the second position, Adams solicited the cabinet's opinions on the remaining appointment. At the bottom of a questionnaire he circulated, the president listed several names: James Madison, John Marshall, Ludwell Lee, Thomas Lee, Bushrod Washington, and William Vans Murray. Adams had not met Marshall but probably put him on the list because he had supported the Federalists during the Genet and Jay Treaty controversies, had a reputation as a moderate who was skeptical but not hostile toward France, and had been George Washington's first choice to replace Monroe as minister to Paris in 1796. The cabinet then dropped Madison for partisan reasons—he had already indicated he would refuse anyway—and Adams and his secretaries agreed on Marshall as the third envoy. The nominations went to the Senate on 31 May and were approved on 5 June with little opposition; Marshall was confirmed by a vote of 22 to 6. Dana then declined the appointment owing to ill health, and the president submitted Elbridge Gerry's name instead.[2]

Marshall later noted that this was "the first time in my life that I had ever hesitated concerning the acceptance of office," but he soon made up his mind. Secretary of State Timothy Pickering learned less than a week after Marshall's confirmation that he would accept. Why was Marshall so willing, even eager, to accede finally to a federal nomination, especially one that would take him overseas for potentially many months and disrupt his family life and law practice? He had a mixture of patriotic, partisan, and private motives. He firmly believed that the United States must avoid war with France for the same economic and military reasons that he had advocated peace with Britain a few years before, and—acting upon themes from Washington's Farewell Address that resonated so powerfully with him—to help check the ideological and partisan strife, originating in disputes over foreign policy, that he saw subverting American politics. Somewhat contradictorily, Marshall also feared for the Federalists' political future and hoped that helping end the conflict with France would enable his party to stay in power and check the Republicans' growing influence.[3]

On the personal side, Marshall, then interested in raising his reputation in Federalist circles, wanted to use the diplomatic crisis to establish fully his national stature. "I will confess," he recalled, "that the eclat which would attend a successful termination of the differences between the two countries had no small influence over a mind in which ambition, though subjected to controul, was not absolutely extinguished." The trip to Europe also gave Marshall an inexpensive opportunity to investigate sources of financing for the Fairfax lands purchase. He planned to stop in London on the way back to help his brother James negotiate loans for the balance their syndicate owed on the Fairfax manor lands. (The brothers realized by then that Robert Morris's connections would avail them little.) Later writers, beginning with Thomas Jefferson, would claim that Marshall agreed to the appointment primarily because the money would take care of his financial worries, but that conclusion is greatly exaggerated. It is true that Marshall almost doubled his income while on the mission. He collected nearly $20,000—$9,000 as salary, the rest for expenses—when he returned a year later, and some evidence suggests he might have used as much as $6,000 for an installment on the manor lands contract. The premium he earned as an envoy, however—roughly $4,500—was not enough to relieve him of the Fairfax burden, let alone markedly improve his family's standard of living. Moreover, it is not clear whether Marshall knew how much he would earn before he accepted the nomination.[4]

Even with all these considerations in favor of accepting the appointment, Marshall probably would not have agreed if he thought his law practice would be seriously damaged. "The mission was temporary, and could not be of long duration," he later wrote. "I should return after a short absence, to my profession, with no diminution of character, &, I trusted, with no diminution of practice. My clients would know immediately that I should soon return & I could make arrangements with the gentlemen of the bar which would prevent my business from suffering in the meantime."[5]

Marshall received his commission on 5 June and quickly prepared to go. About that time, he learned that Polly was pregnant again, and, knowing how hard her labors were, he surely felt deep hesitation about leaving just then. He probably figured, though, that her nearby parents and sisters could look after her, and that his principal servant, Robin Spurlock, could manage the household. Polly begged her husband not to go and reacted with hurt and some bitterness when she could not dissuade him, relatives recalled. Marshall was cheered somewhat when about 50 friends in Richmond held a farewell banquet in his honor at the Eagle Tavern. He left for Philadelphia on horseback around the 20th, stopped at Mt. Vernon for a day to see and discuss affairs with George Washington, and sailed from Alexandria to the capital, arriving on 1 July. He met John Adams for the first time at a private dinner that evening; he found the President to be "a sensible plain candid good temperd man" and was "much pleasd with him." (Adams, in turn, thought Marshall was "a plain Man, very Sensible, cautious, guarded, learned in the Law of Nations.") Marshall also dined with Robert Morris and observed the financier's distress; "a heavy gloom hangs around [the family] which only their good sense restrains them from showing." Marshall had expected to sail within a week or so and passed the time at business in meetings with the president and secretary of state, and at leisure attending dinners, going to plays, and visiting old acquaintances and meeting new ones. At a lavish Fourth of July dinner with "a very large company" of senators and representatives, he "experienced from them the most flattering attention." Despite the diversions, he became both homesick for his "much loved and absent wife" and anxious to leave, especially as the departure date kept slipping. "This dissipated life does not long suit my temper," he wrote Polly. "I am sick to death of this place."[6]

Finally, Marshall left Philadelphia on the 17th for New Castle to board the brig *Grace*, and the next day he began the seven-week transatlantic voyage. The mission would be his first and last time outside the United States.[7] Marshall found the trip enjoyable. He had comfortable accommodations, was hardly ever seasick, imbibed from his own stock of porter, wine, and brandy, read many books, and conversed with his two companions—his secretary and a friend's son who was making a tour of Europe—and two other passengers who he thought were Dutch but actually were Frenchmen traveling under false passports. The most exciting time of the crossing occurred as the *Grace* approached the Dutch coast, when sailors from British warships boarded three times. They were unfailingly cordial to Marshall, who thought they were trying to curry favor with Americans.

The ship put in at Amsterdam on 29 August. After spending a few days there, probably talking to bankers about money for the Fairfax lands purchase, Marshall set out for The Hague to meet Charles Cotesworth Pinckney. Three more weeks of waiting followed as the two envoys sought word of Gerry's arrival. Marshall did not care for The Hague, finding its society unapproachable for an American. Moreover, the manner in which the French subjugated the Netherlands and the way the Dutch in turn "relinquish[ed] national independence for individual safety" steeled his resolve to prevent the same fate from befalling the United States. He derived what limited pleasure he had mostly from a nearby theater and from time spent with Pinckney. He had never met his Federalist colleague from South Carolina but was "very much pleasd [*sic*]" to find out that they shared critical attitudes about the course of events in France and modest expectations for the success of their mission. He later described the portly, pleasant and dutiful Pinckney as "a sensible man, and one of high and even romantic honour." (Pinckney would later call Marshall "a man of extensive ability, of manly candour, and an honest heart.") Marshall and Pinckney finally left for Paris without Gerry. Word of his arrival on the 18th overtook them en route, but he still did not reach Paris until 4 October.

By the time Marshall and his associates reached the French capital, a significant change had occurred in France's political leadership that promised to make their position much more difficult. Hardliners, aided by the army, had taken over the governing Directory in a coup in early September. The new ruling group, strongly anti-American, annulled elections the previous March that had produced a legislature interested in conciliation with the United States.

They also purged opponents from the government and suppressed public and journalistic criticism. "All power," Marshall reported to Pickering, "is now in the undivided possession of those who have directed against us those hostile measures of which we so justly complain"; or, as he later wrote more bluntly, "This revolution blasted every hope of an accomodation [*sic*]." Privately, Marshall did not conceal his contempt for the violence, oppression, and betrayal into which the revolution had degenerated—"That [France] is not and never will be a republick is a truth which I scarcely dare whisper even to myself. It is in America and America only that human liberty has found an asylum," he wrote to Charles Lee—but he knew he could not let his personal feelings detract from the purpose of the mission.

I am sensible . . . that we have nothing to do with the internal revolutions of a sovereign nation which decides on its own fate. No remark on it will be made by me, nor will any sentiment be utterd which can have the appearance of intermedling, even in thought, with their proper concerns. Our business is to labor the accomodation of differences & to that sole object will all our efforts tend. France may assume what form of government she pleases & may administer it as she pleases—our object & our duty remain the same.[8]

The "object & duty" of Marshall, Pinckney, and Gerry was spelled out in the instructions Pickering had written in July. Marshall no doubt thought about them long and hard during his voyage. Cautious, nonbelligerent, and clear-cut in tone and content, they were well suited to his predisposition to avoid conflict and settle differences in a rational, straightforward way. He and his colleagues were to "'terminate our differences in such manner, as without referring to the merits of our respective complaints and pretensions, may be the best calculated to produce mutual satisfaction and good understanding.'" The envoys' main objective was to preserve American neutrality, not to "wound [France's] feelings or to excite resentment." They were instructed to try to recover damages for losses to American shipping, but they were not to insist on a set sum or immediate payment, and they had a good deal of flexibility in determining how, or even whether, to seek redress. The envoys were prepared to forego the "free ships, free goods" principle of the 1778 treaty and agree that the United States would treat France's and Great Britain's maritime trade the same. They were also expected to seek an end to the mutual defense clause of the 1778 alliance. Pinckney further instructed the envoys not to agree to any loan, or to violate any previous treaties (especially the Jay Treaty), or to permit any limits on trade to which America was entitled under international law.[9]

The French, for their part, would not be expecting much of an accommodating spirit in the envoys—particularly Marshall. Soon after his appointment was announced, France's consul in New York reported home that Marshall "is a man of a very pronounced character who hides neither his support for the English cause nor his distance from anything that favors French interests." Adams's selection of Marshall was "an expression of intent on the part of the president which is as astonishing as [the anti-French] views contained in his address to Congress."[10]

Marshall and the other Americans in the envoys' party—Pinckney, his wife and daughter, three secretaries, and Gerry—moved into three floors of a large four-story townhouse a few blocks from the Foreign Ministry. Marshall and Gerry took small ground-level apartments that opened onto a courtyard; the Pinckneys and the secretaries each got an entire floor to themselves. The frugal Marshall must have winced at the exorbitant rent—his share was 350 francs a month—especially since, according to Gerry and Pinckney's wife, the furnishings were "not very fresh," there were no towels, the mirrors were cracked, the chimneys "smoaked," and the rooms were directly above a noisy stable. The seedy habitation they shared did, however, encourage communication and cooperation among the envoys, at least initially. Later, as the mission foundered because of French procrastination and intrigue, the close quarters intensified the envoys' personal differences and afforded too many opportunities for rancorous hallway encounters, especially between Marshall and Gerry.[11]

Marshall, Pinckney, and Gerry soon had their first contact with the crafty, venal, and unscrupulous foreign minister, Charles-Maurice de Talleyrand-Périgord. (As it turned out, they would have only two more encounters, months later.) They granted Talleyrand's request for a supposedly short delay in the opening of formal negotiations, and so began a well-known sequence of events over the next four months: Talleyrand's stalls, insults, and transparent efforts to intimidate, demoralize, and divide the Americans, whom he never officially received and with whom he never openly negotiated; repeated attempts by his agents, known as W, X, Y, and Z in later American documents, to solicit some $250,000 in bribes and to pressure the Americans into contravening their instructions by agreeing to a loan of roughly $12 million; Pinckney's ringing response of "No! No! Not a sixpence!" which came to epitomize the Americans' moral rectitude in the face of European cynicism and corruption; the envoys' bickering over how seriously to take France's threats to declare war on the United States; their falling out over Gerry's independent back-channel negotiations; and Marshall's and Pinckney's abrupt departure from Paris in April 1798 while Gerry lingered on as a diplomatic salvage-seeker. "History will scarcely furnish," Marshall wrote later, "the example of a nation, not absolutely degraded, which has received from a foreign power such open contumely, and undisguised insult."[12]

This familiar chronology does not need recounting here, but several topics pertaining to Marshall's actions and attitudes deserve closer examination for the way they influenced the outcome of the mission and for indicating whether he missed opportunities to achieve other results. Among these subjects are the trustworthiness of the historical evidence, most of which came from Marshall's pen; the initial attitudes about France and the mission which he brought to Paris, and how they were reinforced while he was there; some of Marshall's purported misconceptions; the ways in which he allegedly departed from the traditional portrayal of his involvement; and the sources of information he drew upon to reach and justify his conclusions.

The principal sources for the XYZ Affair are Marshall's "hastyly sketchd journal," containing "a curious account of transactions at Paris" from early October 1797 to mid-April 1798, and eight dispatches to the secretary of state, written mainly by Marshall during the same period. It has been suggested, reasonably enough, that Marshall may have started the journal—the only continuous account of the mission—because he wanted to have a private record to refer to during potential controversies to follow. Not surprisingly, Marshall put himself and Pinckney on the right side of any dispute with Gerry and unrelentingly ascribed duplicitous motives to the French. At the same time, the journal, albeit inadvertently, occasionally shows Marshall in a negative light. His attitudes toward the French and Gerry, by his own words, became more adamant, more suspicious, and more disdainful as Talleyrand's informal approaches and Gerry's unauthorized feelers persisted. The dispatches replicate much of the journal and follow its interpretations. The politically astute Marshall must have considered the possibility that the Adams administration would exploit the messages for political gain, perhaps by publicizing their contents, and he surely grasped the domestic implications of framing the negotiations in such stark, anti-French terms. He approached the problem as if he were arguing a legal case. The longer dispatches almost read like briefs, laying out evidence and presenting tight, logical arguments for an unseen judge and jury. Yet Marshall's exegeses were not tendentious or distorted. By all indications he did not write anything in either the journal or the dispatches that was false, and both his colleagues—even Gerry, with whom he fundamentally disagreed over what was going on—signed the dispatches. This lends credibility to the journal, on which the dispatches were based.[13]

Early in the mission, perhaps even before it began, Marshall made several fundamental judgments about French intentions from which he never departed, no matter how hard Talleyrand, X, Y, Z, Gerry, and others tried to persuade him. Marshall's keen intelligence and unshakeable nerve—in this case, the latter might be characterized as constructive obstinacy—kept the mission on track despite powerful temptations and changing circumstances. His guiding conclusion, from which all others derived, was that France, though "at present it seems to me to be radically hostile to our country," did not want war with the United States and would not declare war if the mission failed. Marshall believed that France sought, more than anything else, to keep the United States out of its conflict with Great Britain until arms or diplomacy resolved it. Although "continu[ing] us in an humble state of dependent solicitation" and gaining American neutrality by default, "this haughty ambitious government is not willing to come to an absolute rupture with America during the present state of war with England but will not condescend to act with justice or to treat us as a free and independent nation."[14]

Marshall thought the French government was bluffing when it threatened to invade Britain, even after the Treaty of Campo Formio freed France of the military threat from Austria and opened the way for a cross-channel assault. If France did attack Britain, war with America was still unlikely because the Directory could not fight simultaneous land and naval campaigns against two enemies, particularly when one was located an ocean away. Toward the end of the mission, Marshall believed that France's military preparations were a ploy to conceal secret talks with Britain; this notion reinforced his conclusion that the envoys could break off talks without fearing war with France. Marshall did not "lose perspective" and start taking French saber rattling at face value, as Pinckney's biographer has suggested. If so, why would he have sought to end the negotiations when that would increase the chance of war? Instead, Marshall held exactly the opposite view: He concluded that the French threats were hollow, and so he could spurn the back-channel contacts and, in the end, move to call off the talks over matters of protocol and principle, thus preserving peace while keeping the political high ground.[15]

Marshall also discerned that Talleyrand and his agents were lackeys of the Directory, had little or no authority to negotiate meaningfully, and were trying to dupe the envoys into becoming tools for French efforts to manipulate American partisan politics. Keenly attuned to the Farewell Address's admonitions against foreign meddling in domestic affairs, Marshall believed that one of Talleyrand's main motives in avoiding formal negotiations was to bolster France's stature in America. Marshall reasoned that Talleyrand wanted to maneuver the envoys into an untenable situation and force them to break off the mission, thereby enabling the Republicans to benefit from the Federalists' diplomatic failure. "[T]here can be no doubt," Marshall wrote in his journal, "of [France's] policy in one respect—she will keep up and cherish . . . her party in the United States. Whether then she is disposed to treat rather than to part with us, or to part rather than treat with us, she will do the one or the other with a view to this her primary object." "What a lesson to those who would admit foreign influence into the United States!" he declared to Washington.[16]

Marshall remained perceptive, realistic, and strong-willed throughout the XYZ episode and turned a practically impossible situation to maximum advantage. Nevertheless, he has been charged with some misconceptions, missteps, and inconsistencies that, although not disabling to the mission, might have improved prospects for a productive outcome had he avoided them. Probably the most basic criticism was his alleged exaggeration of the United States' importance to France. In a reprise of American attitudes in the years before the Jay Treaty, Marshall supposedly seemed to think that the most important consideration for the French government should have been how its actions would affect the United States. He did not adequately appreciate how insignificant America was in the minds of French policy makers, the argument goes, especially when it was weighted against Paris's other foreign and domestic concerns. All the days of effort he expended on his long and thoughtful "Memorial" to Talleyrand, which set forth in great detail U.S. positions on points of conflict with France, were wasted because he assumed that the French government would accord some importance to those views. Marshall's mistake is evident in France's response to the "Memorial"—all it did was step up the shipping war. This line of reasoning, however, is purely speculative and lacks supporting evidence. Analyses of the XYZ affair that draw on French sources make it patently clear that the Directory had no interest in America. As just one example, its minutes for the entire period of the mission do not refer to the United States at all except when mentioning a possible "loan," which the envoys' instructions expressly forbade them from considering.[17]

Marshall's writings during and about the mission have also been read as revealing an "innocents abroad" naivete, which if true would show a trait that Marshall did not display at any other time. He insisted, according to this view, that France deal with America—"incapable of duplicity . . . [and] with the pride of conscious integrity"—as an equal and independent nation. At times he supposedly made simplistic comparisons between American honor and European corruption, and appeared sincerely offended at the impropriety of clandestine talks and bribes, which he later called "degrading intercourse." One feeler particularly outraged him. Marshall had served as the Virginia attorney for one of Talleyrand's interlocutors, Caron de Beaumarchais, who now offered to turn over £50,000 of the settlement Marshall had won for him to the French government as partial payment of the bribe. Marshall refused, partly because the judgment had been appealed, partly because he found the idea reprehensible. Beneath his visceral reaction, however, lay an insightful reading of French tactics. He knew from the Genet affair and from early contacts with Talleyrand's emissaries that the governments of Revolutionary France had dispensed with all customary protocols of international diplomacy, and he quickly grasped the fact that he was dealing with a system of organized extortion. Marshall then turned the situation in America's favor. Although steadfastly advocating his country's interests and leaving no plausible avenue of negotiation unexplored, he presented the mission's record in a way that would turn American public opinion powerfully against France and perhaps create a scandal in Europe that might force the Directory to negotiate purposefully.[18]

Marshall supposedly showed more flexibility as the mission dragged on, but there is no convincing evidence for that conclusion, largely because he saw no reason to depart from the firm course he had set. He might have been growing uneasy about keeping the envoys united and about the political implications for the Federalists if responsibility for failure could not unequivocally be laid on France, but next to nothing suggests he was more willing to bargain than he admitted in his journal, even though the Directory considered him more approachable than Pinckney. Various signs that he was—for example, at times he suggested he was amenable to going back on the envoys' pledge not to negotiate with agents, may have authorized Gerry's private call on Talleyrand, considered paying a bribe if France stopped attacking American ships, and was willing to return to the United States to discuss a loan with the government— were tactical maneuvers, nothing more. He never seriously contemplated paying the *douceur* that Talleyrand's agents demanded, or leaving France. Although it is scarcely surprising that the homesick Marshall, in his more doleful moments, might have thought of returning to America, he knew that seeking clarification of the envoys' instructions would work strongly to France's advantage. It would shift the onus of rejection to the United States—exactly what he was trying to avoid—while allowing France to continue preying on American vessels during the fracas that an envoy's return would set off in the United States.[19]

Marshall's insistence that the French did not want war put him at odds with Gerry, who believed just as firmly that they did. Gerry insisted on maintaining contact—any contact—with the French government out of fear of French military might and the harmful effect war would have on America. From Marshall's standpoint, however, Gerry's approach was appeasement without a purpose; as he wrote to Rufus King, the American minister in London, "submission has its limits." In Marshall's estimation, Gerry's increasingly anxious efforts at back door diplomacy promised only talk for talk's sake and played into French hands by making the envoys appear disunited. Marshall might have started the mission thinking favorably of Gerry. Although he had not known the independent and unpredictable Yankee before the mission, Marshall had heard from the American minister to The Hague, William Vans Murray, that Gerry possessed "a tender and friendly heart" and was "a man of cordiality . . . [who] will cooperate with you with sincerity and kindness." Murray warned Marshall, though, that Gerry "seems to believe . . . that there is a very powerful British party in America" and "mistakes . . . our commercial operations for political influence." The envoys' differences emerged almost immediately over Thomas Paine's proposal, probably formulated by Talleyrand during the summer of 1797, that the United States declare itself an unarmed neutral and essentially abrogate the Jay Treaty; they widened during the tedious dealings with X, Y, and Z; and they became unbridgeable by the time Marshall wrote the "Memorial" to the foreign minister, which Gerry almost refused to sign. Marshall had several altercations with his nervous and irascible colleague but tried not to let personal animosity prompt him to call for ending the mission until circumstances allowed him to make France appear at fault.[20]

In reaching and affirming his judgments, Marshall drew on a variety of sources for information. His brothers Louis and James had been in Paris in 1797—in medical school and on business, respectively—and conveyed their impressions to Pinckney, who undoubtedly passed them on to him. James's insights probably proved especially valuable. He knew one of Talleyrand's agents—Jean Conrad Hottinguer, a Swiss banker later referred to as X—directly from their recent negotiations over the loan that enabled the Marshall syndicate to buy some of the Fairfax lands. From the key vantagepoint of London, Rufus King encouraged Marshall and his colleagues to resist French importunings, to keep patient in the face of French delays, and to remain resolute against French demands. The opinions of King—who thought Marshall's "head is one of the best organized of anyone that I have known"—carried special authority because he was a Federalist ally of Marshall's, was familiar with British policy toward the French-American conflict, and was sensitive to how the envoys' actions would affect London's decisions. Marshall also received useful political, military, and diplomatic intelligence from Vans Murray. It has been suggested that Marshall could have used Vans Murray as his own agent for private negotiations with Talleyrand, but that notion seems fanciful given the way the French responded to any of the envoys' attempts to communicate with them except on their terms.[21]

Marshall's regular contact with the American community in Paris—a melange of diplomats, merchants, land agents, and intellectuals residing on the Left Bank near the envoys—reinforced his skepticism toward the French government. The American "colony" or "club" knew far more about the French government's practices and personalities than Marshall, Pinckney, or Gerry did, but their Francophile attitudes, born of self-interest and ideology, disqualified their advice in Marshall's mind. Most were Jeffersonians, some were radical republicans who wanted to see Great Britain subdued and Europe remade through revolution, and all hoped the United States would concede to French demands and avoid hostilities that would disrupt their comfortable situations. Marshall did not care for these people, spurned most of their advice, and ignored them when Talleyrand began using them to pressure him and the other envoys. He sensed in them a divided loyalty—he snippishly referred to one as "an American I believe by birth"—that might develop in the United States if French influence continued to infect American politics. He also disliked how, as Pinckney put it, "the American Jacobins here pay [Gerry] great court."[22]

Marshall's homesickness, frustration, and anxiety over Polly's pregnancy mounted as the mission stalled with no end in sight. "Oh God how much time & how much happiness have I thrown away!" he moaned to Polly; and to Charles Lee, he "cursed a thousand times the moment when a sense of duty inducd me to undertake this painful embassy." He found Paris's "incessant round of amusement" to be a welcome relief from the long stretches of diplomatic inaction, his loneliness, and the wrangling with Gerry, and he clearly found the salons, theaters, and sights more interesting than the limited range of activities found in rustic Richmond. "Every day," he wrote Polly, "you may see something new magnificent and beautiful, every night you may see a spectacle which astonishes and inchants the imagination . . . All that you can conceive and a great deal more . . . is to be found in this gay metropolis." He took a liking to some of the French decorative arts as well, buying several items as gifts for his wife or as home furnishings—among them a mahogany sewing box, a porcelain coffee or chocolate service, and an ebony and ormolu mantel clock—and he would eventually acquire more French furniture for the Richmond house. He also had Parisian artists produce two likenesses of himself: a miniature portrait, probably intended as a memento for Polly; and a small terra cotta bust, erroneously thought for many years to have been done by the noted sculptor Jean Antoine Houdon. The provincial yet cultured Marshall considered Paris's vibrant social life at once privately alluring and publicly repugnant. Even as he savored Parisian delectations, he derided them as empty "dissipation" and believed the capital offered "very little . . . which interests the heart." "I suspect it woud not be easy to find a friend. I woud not live in Paris to be among the wealthiest of its citizens." Marshall may also have deplored the cosmopolitan luxury of French society that violated his republican sensibilities and, in the classical paradigm prevalent then, that augured France's decline and eventual demise.[23]

While in Paris, Marshall was implicated in the only purported moral transgression of his entire life.[24] In mid-November 1797, Marshall and Gerry moved from their shabby apartments—where, Marshall wrote, he lived "in the style of a miserable old batchelor without any mixture of female society"—into sumptuous rooms in the mansion of the Marquise Reine-Philiberte Rouph de Variacourt, better known as Madame de Villette. She was the 35-year-old widow of a licentious marquis and a disciple of the French *philosophe* Voltaire. Her house was chock with Voltairiana, including his robe and some of his letters, a bust of him under which she burned incense, and, displayed in a glass jar in the drawing room, his heart. Aside from these cultish obsessions, Madame de Villette was, by Marshall's and other's accounts, intelligent, engaging, and attractive (Voltaire called her *belle et bonne*), and well connected to Parisian salon society. Marshall and Gerry spent a good deal of time with her during the next several months. They passed most afternoons in conversation and French lessons, dined together frequently, attended the theater and opera (Marshall once forgot a meeting with Pinckney because he had gone with Madame to see Voltaire's play *Mahomet*), and spent occasional weekends with her and another French woman at her country estate.

All of this merriment, Marshall told his wife with interesting understatement, "renders my situation less unpleasant." No credible evidence suggests that the relationship between Marshall and his landlady went beyond what he called "respectful friendship." As a recent treatment of the episode has concluded: "Had it been otherwise, somebody would almost certainly have told on somebody, or at least dropped innuendoes; somebody in the American colony in Paris [with which Madame de Villette had close ties] would at least have gossiped about Madame's morals. But so far as is known, nobody did." The best explanation for Marshall's behavior is the most obvious: Thousands of miles from his home and family in a strange country whose language he did not understand, bored and frustrated at the mission's seeming failure, he was desperately lonely and, when afforded the opportunity, sought the regular companionship of, in his words, "a very sensible & . . . very amiable lady whose temper, very contrary to the general character of her country women, is domestic." Madame de Villette, in turn, very likely found much appealing in Marshall—by French standards, a towering six feet tall with a lean and well muscled physique, compelling black eyes, courtly manners, and an ingratiating sense of humor. Marshall had no fear that their social encounters would scandalize the mission, given what he apparently considered the lax moral standards of French high society. Republicans later tried to put a political twist on the story in an effort to slander him and Pinckney. They claimed that

Madame de Villette was one of Talleyrand's agents (W) and had tried to use her charms to extract the bribes and loans her master wanted from the envoys. These allegations have crept into recent accounts of the XYZ "affair" but are likewise unfounded.

By March 1798, a denouement to the XYZ affair seemed near. After two months, Talleyrand finally responded to the "Memorial" that Marshall had spent several weeks writing. Marshall's document, over 20,000 words long and constructed like a compendious legal brief, justified the conduct of the United States in its conflict with France and asserted its claims against the French government. Marshall showed a solid grasp of international law, although his repeated effort to reconcile parts of the Jay Treaty with the 1778 treaty with France and to prove that America had not backed away from the "free ships, free goods" principle is occasionally strained. Talleyrand's reply rehashed French grievances but raised the idea that the Directory would deal only with "that one of the three [Gerry], whose opinions, presumed to be more impartial, promise . . . more of that reciprocal confidence which is indispensable." Talleyrand calculated that Marshall and Pinckney were ready to leave France anyway and was giving them the chance to do so without having to order them out. A few days later, the foreign minister's secretary reaffirmed the proposal, telling Marshall that unless he and Pinckney applied to leave the country, they would be expelled.[25]

Marshall saw through this tactic, which he later described as "a trial of skill between the minister and ourselves . . . he endeavouring to force us to demand our passports, we endeavouring to impose on him the necessity of sending them." Marshall dashed off a contentious response to Talleyrand that scotched the idea of any envoy's staying on alone; they were all determined to remain and negotiate, if only the French government would treat them seriously. Marshall forced the cagey foreign minister to take the step that would end the mission. After Gerry agreed to stay, Talleyrand gave Marshall and Pinckney their passports. Marshall left Paris on 16 April and reached Bordeaux six days later, where he booked passage on the *Alexander Hamilton*—"a very excellent vessel but for the sin of the name which makes my return in her almost as criminal as if I had taken England in my way." He sailed for the United States on the 23rd, "bid[ding] . . . an eternal adieu to Europe . . . & to its crimes."[26]

NOTES

1. The following sources provided background on Franco-American relations at this time: Alexander DeConde, *The Quasi-War: The Politics and Diplomacy of the Undeclared War with France, 1797–1801* (New York: Charles Scribner's Sons, 1966), chaps. 1–2; Albert H. Bowman, *The Struggle for Neutrality: Franco-American Diplomacy during the Federalist Era* (Knoxville: University of Tennessee Press, 1974), chaps. 11 and 13; Marvin R. Zahniser, *Uncertain Friendship: American-French Diplomatic Relations Through the Cold War* (New York: John Wiley and Sons, 1975), 69–73; Stanley Elkins and Eric McKitrick, *The Age of Federalism* (New York: Oxford

University Press, 1993), 498–513; Paul A. Varg, *Foreign Policies of the Founding Fathers*, Pelican ed. (Baltimore: Penguin Books, 1970), chap. 3; Reginald Horsman, *The Diplomacy of the New Republic, 1776–1815* (Arlington Heights, Ill.: Harlan Davison, 1985), 67–78; Lawrence S. Kaplan, *Colonies into Nation: American Diplomacy, 1763–1801* (New York: Macmillan, 1972), chap. 9; Gerard H. Clarfield, *Timothy Pickering and American Diplomacy, 1795–1800* (Columbia: University of Missouri Press, 1969), chaps. 3–6, 8; George A. Billias, *Elbridge Gerry: Founding Father and Republican Statesman* (New York: McGraw-Hill, 1976), 253–63; William Stinchcombe, *The XYZ Affair* (Westport, Conn.: Greenwood Press, 1980), chaps. 1–2; "Mission to France: Editorial Note," in *PJM*, 3:73–79.

2. *PJM*, 3:79; Stinchcombe, *XYZ Affair*, 21–22, 31 n. 27. The Senate approved Pinckney's nomination by a 20–4 vote, Dana's by 22–6, and Gerry's by 21–6. Marshall's cousin Humphrey, from Kentucky, voted against Gerry. Manning Dauer, *The Adams Federalists* (Baltimore: Johns Hopkins University Press, 1953), 130.

3. John Stokes Adams, ed., *An Autobiographical Sketch of John Marshall* (Ann Arbor: University of Michigan Press, 1937), 21 (hereafter cited as JM, *Autobiographical Sketch.*)

4. JM, *Autobiographical Sketch*, 22; *PJM*, 3:80 and n. 7.

5. JM, *Autobiographical Sketch*, 22.

6. Frances Norton Mason, *My Dearest Polly: Letters of Chief Justice Marshall to His Wife* . . . (Richmond: Garrett and Massie, 1961), 89–90; JM to Polly, 24 June, 3, 5, 10, 11, 12, 14 July 1797, to Caesar Rodney, 1 July 1797, *PJM*, 3:92–102; John Adams to Elbridge Gerry, 17 July 1797, *The Works of John Adams*, ed. Charles Francis Adams, 10 vols. (Boston: Little, Brown, 1850–56), 8:549.

7. Sources for this paragraph and the next are JM to Polly, 20 July, 3 and 9 August, 9 September 1797, to Edward Carrington, 2 September 1797, to Timothy Pickering, 2 September 1797, to George Washington, 15 September 1797, to Charles Lee, 22 September 1797, *PJM*, 3:120–24, 128–31, 141, 147; JM, *Autobiographical Sketch*, 24; Stinchcombe, *XYZ Affair*, 51; Charles Cotesworth Pinckney to Rufus King, 4 April 1798, quoted in Albert J. Beveridge, *The Life of John Marshall*, 4 vols. (Boston: Houghton Mifflin, 1916–19), 2:334.

8. JM to Pickering, 9 and 15 September 1797, to Washington, 15 September 1797, to Charles Lee, 22 September and 25 October 1797, *PJM*, 3:138–49, 251; JM, *Autobiographical Sketch*, 23.

9. Pickering to envoys, 15 June 1797, *PJM*, 3:102–19. Some scholars have claimed or suggested that Marshall had a large hand in drafting the instructions, but there is no convincing evidence for this conclusion. See the discussion in Elkins and McKitrick, *Age of Federalism*, 871 n. 108.

10. Alexander Hauterive's correspondence with Pierre Adet in May and June 1797, quoted in Jean Smith, *John Marshall: Definer of a Nation* (New York: Henry Holt, 1996), 187.

11. Stinchcombe, *XYZ Affair*, 54; Marvin R. Zahniser, *Charles Cotesworth Pinckney, Founding Father* (Chapel Hill: University of North Carolina Press, 1967), 165–66; *PJM*, 3:300 n. 6, quoting letters by Gerry and Mary Pinckney.

12. JM, *The Life of George Washington*, 5 vols. (Philadelphia: C. P. Wayne, 1804–7; rept., New York: Chelsea House, 1983), 5:261.

13. "Paris Journal," *PJM*, 3:158–242; JM's dispatches to Pickering, *PJM*, 3:255–67, 276–92, 305–7, 317–24, 325–26, 381–82, 402–11, and 460; JM to Pickering, 11 April 1798, *PJM*, 3:486; JM, *Autobiographical Sketch*, 23; "Paris Journal: Editorial Note," *PJM*, 3:153–58; Elkins and McKitrick, *Age of Federalism*, 550.

14. JM to Washington, 24 October 1797, to Charles Lee, 3 November 1797, to Pickering, 27 November 1797, *PJM*, 3:270, 273, 303–5; JM, "Paris Journal," 4 and 10 February 1798, *PJM*, 3:197, 199.

15. JM to Washington, 8 March 1798, *PJM*, 3:400; Zahniser, *Pinckney*, 173.

16. JM, "Paris Journal," 4 February 1798, *PJM*, 3:196; JM to Washington, 15 September 1797, *PJM*, 3:141.

17. JM, "Memorial," 17 January 1798, *PJM*, 3:331–81. Elkins and McKitrick, *Age of Federalism*, 549–79 passim, is the most effective statement of these points.

18. Elkins and McKitrick, *Age of Federalism*, 357–58; JM, "Paris Journal," *PJM*, 3:170–74, 176–77, 276–87.

19. Stinchcombe, *XYZ Affair*, 65–66, 100; Billias, *Gerry*, 270–72; JM, "Paris Journal," 20–21 October 1797, and envoys to Pickering, 22 October 1797, *PJM*, 3:166–68, 255–65.

20. Billias, *Gerry*, 253–54; JM to Rufus King, 24 December 1797, *PJM*, 3:315; Vans Murray to JM, 24 September 1797, *PJM*, 3:150; Thomas Paine to envoys, 11 October 1797, *PJM*, 3:243–45; JM, "Paris Journal," 11 October 1797, 26 February, 3 and 6 March 1798, *PJM*, 3:160–61, 202–7, 220, 223–24. It is not known if before he left for France, Marshall had heard of the prescient evaluation that Secretary of War James McHenry made of Gerry. After hearing Gerry proposed as an envoy, McHenry remarked, "If . . . it was a desirable thing to distract the mission, a fitter person could not perhaps be found. It is ten to one against his agreeing with his colleagues." Bernard C. Steiner, *The Life and Correspondence of James McHenry* (Cleveland: Burrows Brothers, 1907), 224. Gerry's friend Abigail Adams, with characteristic acerbity, observed that "Poor Gerry always had a wrong kink in his head." Smith, *Marshall*, 200.

21. Stinchcombe, *XYZ Affair*, 52; *PJM*, 3:164 n. 17; King to JM, 23 and 30 December 1797, *PJM*, 3:313–15, 325; Robert Ernst, *Rufus King: American Federalist* (Chapel Hill: University of North Carolina Press, 1968), 258–60; JM to and from Vans Murray, 24 September, 17 October, 2 and 9 November 1797, *PJM*, 3:149–50, 251–52, 272–73, 292–93; Peter P. Hill, *William Vans Murray: Federalist Diplomat* (Syracuse: Syracuse University Press, 1971), 57–58.

22. JM, "Paris Journal," 11 October, 1797, *PJM*, 3:160; Stinchcombe, *XYZ Affair*, 68–69 and chap. 5 passim, esp. 77–80 and 95–98.

23. JM to Polly, 27 November 1797, *PJM*, 3:299; Stinchcombe, *XYZ Affair*, 98–100; The John Marshall Foundation, untitled guidebook for the John Marshall House (Richmond: N.p., n.d.); Andrew Oliver, *The Portraits of John Marshall* (Charlottesville: University Press of Virginia, 1977), 6–7, 9–17.

24. Sources for this paragraph and the next are Stinchcombe, *XYZ Affair*, 66–68, 108; JM to Polly, 27 November 1797, *PJM*, 3:300–01 and n. 7; envoys to Nathaniel Cutting, 27 February 1798, *PJM*, 3:395; JM to Pinckney, 17 December 1797, *PJM*, 3:311–12; JM to Fulwar Skipwith, 21 April 1798, *PJM*, 3:464; *PJM*, 3:318 n. 7; Zahniser, *Pinckney*, 175–76; S. G. Tallentyre, *The Life of Voltaire*, 3rd ed. (New York: G. P. Putnam's Sons, n.d.), 517, 524–25, 553, 561, 564–66; Jean Orieux, *Voltaire ou La Royauté de L'Esprit* (Paris: Flammarion, 1966), 784–86; DeConde, *Quasi-War*, 51–52; Billias, *Gerry*, 268; John C. Miller, *Crisis in Freedom: The Alien and Sedition Acts* (Boston: Little, Brown, 1951), 148–49; Elkins and McKitrick, *Age of Federalism*, 867 n. 68; Beveridge, *Marshall*, 2:380 n. 1, 409–10; Baker, *Marshall*, 312–13; Mason, *My Dearest Polly*, 113; Smith, *Marshall*, 215–18. John Wood's "history" of the Adams administration, published in 1802, accused Marshall and Pinckney of indiscreet behavior while in France.

25. JM, "Memorial," 17 January 1798, *PJM*, 3:331–81; idem, "Paris Journal," 22 March 1798, *PJM*, 3:233; Frances Rudko, *John Marshall and International Law: Statesman and Chief Justice* (New York: Greenwood Press, 1991), chap. 3.

26. JM, *Autobiographical Sketch*, 24; JM to Talleyrand, 3 April 1798, JM to Pinckney, 21 April 1798, *PJM*, 3:428–59, 463.

Chapter 7

Southern Federalist (II), 1798–1801

John Marshall sailed into New York on 17 June 1798 after 53 days at sea and, skipping a reception in his honor, promptly set out for Philadelphia to report to President Adams. On the evening of the 19th, six miles outside the capital, he met a welcoming party consisting of Secretary of State Timothy Pickering, three troops of cavalry in full regalia, and dozens of local residents riding in carriages or on horses, and on foot. As the cavalcade entered the city, "the streets, the windows, and even the tops of the houses . . . were crowded with people, whose voices seemed to vie with the joyful peal from the steeple of Christ Church" and the thundering of cannon, according to a local newspaper. Marshall was escorted to his lodgings at O'Eller's Tavern, and, during the next several days, he was inundated with congratulations from throngs of public officials, prominent citizens, and other well wishers. The storm of approbation climaxed at a testimonial banquet that Federalists in Congress held at O'Eller's on the 23rd. Over 120 admirers, including members of the cabinet, Supreme Court justices, army officers, congressional leaders, and Catholic and Episcopal bishops, feted him. The evening's most memorable toast—"Millions for Defense but not a cent for Tribute!"—became a Federalist shibboleth for the whole XYZ affair. Marshall "seemed to be rather disconcerted" by all this lavish attention and behaved throughout like a "very modest man," an eyewitness recalled.[1]

Marshall's triumphal return continued after he left for Winchester, where Polly was staying with a relative, and Richmond on 25 June. Excited crowds, ceremonial militia escorts, cannon firings, and bell ringings greeted him all along the route. His reception in Richmond was as ebullient as that in Philadelphia. In addition to the usual displays and congratulations, 200 residents from the vicinity held a banquet for Marshall at Buchanan's Spring, where the Barbecue Club met. The governor, members of the Council of State, and veteran officers from the Continental Army showed up to laud Marshall. Responding to an address from citizens of the capital, Marshall called for national unity in the face of a foreign threat: "Desirable as is at all times a due confidence in our government, it is peculiarly so in a moment of peril like the present, in a moment when the want of that confidence must impair the means of self defense, must increase a danger already but too great, and furnish, or at least give the appearance of furnishing, to a foreign real enemy, those weapons which have so often been so successfully used." A local newspaper effused that "[w]hen future generations peruse the history of America, they will find the name of Marshall on its sacred page as one of the brightest ornaments of the age."[2]

Marshall had drafted the envoys' dispatches so as to place his own strong interpretation on the negotiations, and with an eye toward influencing the public debate over the mission.[3] But he could hardly have anticipated that private diplomatic communications would make him a national hero and, a year later, propel him into his first national political office; or that they would so heighten partisan antagonism that, according to Thomas Jefferson, "intimate friends cross the street to avoid meeting, and turn their heads another way, lest they should be obliged to touch their hats." Marshall's dispatches, written between late October 1797 and early January 1798, did not reach Philadelphia until 4 March. During that long interval, rumors of failure proliferated, fed by scattered, unconfirmed news of developments in Europe purveyed by travelers and correspondents. "Are our commissioners guillotined," wondered George Washington, "or what else is the occasion of their silence?" Partisan sniping intensified, and the political tension had become almost palpable when the envoys' reports arrived in the capital. On 5 March, President Adams told Congress that the mission had failed, but, after promising to release deciphered versions of the dispatches, he decided to withhold them lest the envoys' security be jeopardized. Adams also announced that a state of limited war with France existed and called on Congress to strengthen the nation's defenses. Members of both parties demanded that Adams produce the dispatches. Indignant Republicans thought he was concealing information and trying to incite a war scare, and belligerent Federalists wanted to humiliate France and its American allies.

Publication of the papers—the Federalist-controlled Congress ordered the printing of 10,000 copies of the whole correspondence—set off an explosion of outrage against France, manifested in public rallies and addresses, petitions to Congress, bellicose newspaper articles and sermons, popular new songs like "Adams and Liberty" and "Hail Columbia," the wearing of black cockades, and fervid prophecies of French invasions and slave uprisings. Between March and July, Congress passed 20 defense measures (including acts expanding the army and creating a navy department), suspended trade and abrogated all treaties with France, and enacted controversial laws against aliens and critics of the government. The day before Marshall left Philadelphia, Adams declared that "I will never send another Minister to France without assurances that he will be received, respected, and honored as the representative of a great, free, powerful, and independent nation." Adams had initially decried the envoys' "pedantic, timorous" behavior but soon realized that Marshall's dispatches had given him an ideal political opportunity.

Although Marshall recalled years later that the dispatches' "effect on public opinion had fully equalled my anticipations," he probably had some misgivings at the time that the situation had gotten a bit out of hand. He had not wanted war, yet he had contributed to the war scare then underway. He had criticized the Republicans for manipulating diplomacy for political gain, yet the ideologues of his party were wielding his dispatches as a partisan weapon. In Fredericksburg, he saw a graphic display of the fervor he had helped incite. While attending the theater, he watched a brawl erupt in the audience when the house musicians played the "President's March," a tune associated with the Federalists. Apparently trying to calm the frenzy, Marshall made no belligerent public statements and gave only bland endorsements of the Federalists' military preparedness moves. For example, in response to a New Jersey militia unit's spread-eagle resolution, he asserted that "all honorable means of avoiding war should be essayed before the sword be appealed to." In private, he counseled Pickering and Adams that France did not want to declare war against the United States and that its bullying tactics should not be misconstrued. Marshall's attempt to distance himself somewhat from what Jefferson later derided as the "X.Y.Z. dish cooked up by Marshall" led some Republicans to believe at the time, with Jefferson, that "he is not hot enough for his friends" and that he faced difficult relations with his party confederates.[4]

Marshall's friends in Virginia did not share that assessment and soon began pressuring him to run for the House of Representatives.[5] Federalists held only four of 19 congressional seats, and Marshall looked like a sure winner in the current climate. Selecting him as a candidate was part of the Federalists' "Southern strategy" of running popular Southerners, such as Marshall and Patrick Henry, in opposition strongholds in the region to dispel the idea of a Republican monolith. Typically, however, Marshall resisted. "I returned to Richmond with a full determination to devote myself entirely to my professional duties," he recalled. His financial situation was still tenuous—he had not yet been paid for his diplomatic services, and payments for the Fairfax lands were overdue—and he did not want to disrupt his family life again with the demands of public office. "My refusal was peremptory, and I did not believe it possible that my determination could be shaken. I was however mistaken."

George Washington, whom Marshall respected more than anyone save his father, employed his considerable powers of persuasion upon Marshall during a visit to Mount Vernon in early September 1798. "I can never forget the manner in which [Washington] treated this objection" that private concerns precluded Marshall from carrying out his civic duty. The former president and

Revolutionary commander, adopting his best Cincinnatus persona, insisted in "a very earnest conversation" that perilous times demanded that citizens forego personal interests and work for the national good, and presented himself as a model for Marshall to emulate. "My resolution yielded to this presentation," and Marshall agreed to run for the House seat in the Richmond district. He had come to feel "with increasd force," he wrote later in the campaign, that "the obligations of duty to make sacrafices [*sic*] & exertions for the preservation of American Union and independence" and "the reality of the danger which threatens them"—namely, a Republican takeover. Marshall's attitude toward his prior political service suggests he was not dissembling. He did not seek electoral office as a preliminary to a higher public position. He had enough disdain for politicians' compromises and deceits to spurn the legislative life for its own sake and as a vehicle for political self-promotion. Similarly, he would not accept an appointment to national office—as secretary of state—until 1800, and he did so then for much the same reason that he agreed to run for Congress in 1798: his concern for the fate of the Federalists and the effect their eclipse would have on the national welfare.

Worsening American-French relations revived the Virginia Federalists. They had been diligently rallying their forces since the poor showing in the 1796 elections, and they moved quickly to exploit Marshall's news of the envoys' maltreatment in France. Marshall's political allies in Richmond had developed close ties with national party leaders and got some help from Secretary of State Pickering, who ordered that 1,800 copies of the dispatches be distributed throughout the state. Marshall helped link the Richmond and Alexandria factions, in part by including in the Fairfax land deal a relative of the latter city's party leader. Virginia Federalists also used the now-standard participatory techniques they had employed so effectively in the Genet and Jay Treaty controversies to mobilize broad support for the Adams administration. Public meetings sent petitions to the president and Congress, party newspapers ran polemical articles, and Fourth of July celebrations turned into proadministration rallies. Federalists in the Richmond district disseminated copies of a Francophobic tract called "The Cannibal's Progress, or the Dreadful Horrors of the French Invasion," supposedly an account of France's incursion into Germany in 1796. Citizens of Norfolk even raised a private fund of more than $16,000 to help build and outfit ships to be lent to the federal government for operations against the French navy. Around the time Marshall returned to Virginia, Federalists there, and in the South generally, had fashioned an ideology of sorts—anti-Jacobin but not Anglophilic, nationalist but cautious about grand Hamiltonian schemes, ardently patriotic but not militaristic—and had reached an unprecedented level of popularity, substantially expanding an increasingly cohesive party organization beyond the Tidewater and making inroads in Republican-dominated areas.[6]

Marshall's race for the Sixth Congress in 1799 would be a key indicator of the Federalists' strength. Unlike the times he ran for the state assembly, when personalities and local political trends were most important, national issues such as the Alien and Sedition Acts and states' rights dominated his campaign for the House. The influence of Marshall's personal popularity was diluted because he had to seek support from a broader constituency than before. The Richmond district encompassed not only the Federalist-controlled capital (which Edmund Randolph disparaged as "little more than a colony of Philadelphia") and Henrico County, but also Hanover, New Kent, Charles City, and James City counties, all majority Republican. Moreover, by the time Marshall began his campaign, the Federalists' political fortunes had declined markedly because the administration's military buildup and prosecution of Republican journalists were so unpopular in Virginia. In a year of wide and rapid swings in political attitudes, Marshall stood to become a victim of controversial policies set in Philadelphia and had to struggle to maintain the stature that the outpouring of post-XYZ nationalism had given him.[7]

Marshall also faced a formidable opponent in John Clopton, a two-term incumbent from a family of local notables. Clopton had been a Continental Army officer, a member of the House of Delegates from 1789 to 1791, and a successful lawyer before representing the Richmond City district in Congress for two terms beginning in 1795. He was well connected, well organized, and politically perceptive. Just after Marshall's XYZ dispatches arrived in Philadelphia, he circulated a letter in which he disavowed his party's Francophile tendencies and uncategorically affirmed his "sentiments of love for this my native land." His views on the major issues did not differ much from Marshall's, and his personal popularity rivaled his opponent's. In addition, Virginia's voters at the time did not seem to show any particular animus toward incumbents; the rate of return for the state's congressional delegation in 1798, 57 percent, was only slightly below the national average of 62 percent and was four points above the rate in 1796.[8]

"The conflict of parties in this state is extremely ardent," Marshall wrote just after the campaign began, and he later recalled that it "was contested with unusual warmth." The Republicans could not allow such a prominent Federalist to seize one of their seats in Jefferson's and Madison's home state, and they worked hard to defeat what Jefferson would later call the "federalism & Marshalism" that corrupted Richmond. The Republicans launched bitter attacks against Marshall's character, motives, and tactics. "The jacobin presses . . . teem with publications of which the object is to poison still further the public opinion and which are level'd particularly at me," Marshall complained. He was charged with, among other things, running for Congress only to better position himself for a cabinet appointment; spending too much on barbecues and liquor; throwing Republican tracts into bonfires at a rally and dancing around them with his supporters; and appealing for votes from Scottish merchants and former Tories.[9]

Marshall seemed surprised and hurt by the intensity and scurrility of his opponents' attacks, and by the time the campaign ended, he had become more disgusted than ever with partisan politics. "Nothing I believe more debases or pollutes the human mind than faction," he wrote his brother James. He also realized, however, that disfavor toward his candidacy went far beyond the "malignant calumnies . . . profusely bestowd on me." "The exertions made against me by particular characters throughout this state & even from other States," he wrote Washington, "have an activity & a malignancy which no personal considerations woud [sic] excite." He knew that his race against Clopton was only a small episode in a remorseless struggle for national power waged between two ideologically polarized parties. This fact was made clear to him in the way two issues, the Alien and Sedition Acts and the Virginia and Kentucky Resolutions, dominated the electoral debate.[10]

The Alien and Sedition Acts, particularly the latter, significantly contributed to the Federalists' loss of public support during the latter months of 1798 and tarnished Marshall's reputation in Virginia. The acts shifted discussion away from France and the XYZ Affair—Marshall saw this happening as early as August—and forced him and other Federalist candidates onto the defensive as critics charged the Adams administration with violating cherished liberties. Marshall did not like the Sedition Act and said so, but in a way that he thought would avoid antagonizing both Republicans and High Federalists.[11]

In early October, Marshall and an anonymous "Freeholder" exchanged letters that were printed in several Virginia newspapers. Besides inquiring into Marshall's views on foreign alliances and his commitment to the Constitution, the Freeholder asked whether Marshall supported the Alien and Sedition Acts, and if not, whether he would work to repeal them if elected. In his only public statement during the campaign, Marshall wrote that he did not believe the Acts were unconstitutional, but had he been in Congress at the time, he would have opposed them "because I think them useless; and because they are calculated to create, unnecessarily, discontents and jealousies at a time when our very existence, as a nation, may depend on our union." On repeal, Marshall would vote as his constituents wanted; privately, he did not think any action was warranted because the laws were due to expire anyway, and he strongly opposed renewing them.[12]

The "Freeholder letters" permitted Marshall to rebut Republican attacks that he advocated censorship of the Federalists' adversaries. Marshall accepted the Federalists' position that the Sedition Act, by allowing truth to be used as a defense in criminal libel cases, was more libertarian than the English common law previously in effect. At the same time, he had to address the fact that most Americans were sensitive to perceived infringements on a free press; as he wrote to Washington a few months later, "an act operating on the press in any manner, affords to its opposers arguments which so captivate the public ear, which so mislead the public mind that the efforts of reason to correct false impressions will often fail of success."[13]

By adopting this "constitutional but unwise" position, Marshall could partly disassociate himself from the High Federalists without moving too far toward the Republican view. He put himself on record as the election process commenced to defuse the issue and would not be baited into further public skirmishing over the Sedition Act. He declined, for example, to respond when a

Republican polemicist named "Curtius" criticized the "Freeholder" answers in December 1798 and January 1799, and instead let several of his supporters reply. The Sedition Act had hurt the Federalists so badly in Virginia that he probably saw nothing to gain and much to lose in being associated personally with a long-running debate that kept the issue before the public.[14]

Marshall knew that enforcing the Sedition Act in Virginia would ruin his election chances, and he no doubt was appalled at Secretary of State Pickering's badly timed inquiries into charges that John Clopton had committed seditious libel. To avoid antagonizing party leaders, however, Marshall had to move cautiously to scotch efforts to prosecute Clopton. He tried to impress upon Pickering, who initiated all prosecutions under the Sedition Law, that the political situation in the Richmond area was unique and demanded delicate handling. "It requires to be in this part of Virginia to know the degree of irritation which has been excited and the probable extent of the views of those who excite it." Marshall also may have approached his brother-in-law, Edward Carrington—a prominent Richmond Federalist with good connections to the northern wing of the party—to intercede with Pickering on his behalf. Carrington, responding to Pickering's request for information about Clopton, wrote that there was no evidence against Marshall's opponent and advised the secretary to drop the subject, which he did.[15]

Marshall's attempt in his "Freeholder" letter to follow a middle way outraged more dogmatic Federalist leaders in the North and threatened to undermine his standing in the national party. "Marshall's politicks will not prove sound according to New England ideas," observed George Cabot; Timothy Pickering claimed he had "not met with one good federalist who does not regret [Marshall's] answer"; Theodore Sedgwick declared that Marshall had "degraded himself by a mean & paltry electioneering trick" that was "mysterious & unpardonable"; and Fisher Ames, who thought little of Virginians to begin with, called him a "False Federalist" and fulminated that "[n]o correct man . . . whose affections and feelings are wedded to the government, would give his name to the base opposers of the law . . . Excuses may palliate, future zeal in the cause may partially atone, but his character is done for." Marshall's Yankee critics could safely strike this pose of purity that was available only to either an ensconced majority or a carping minority. He, on the other hand, was in a position to win something of value to his party, a congressional seat in the Jeffersonian heartland; but despite his personal appeal, he knew he could lose if he hewed to party orthodoxy, particularly over the despised Sedition Act. He further demonstrated his independence by declining Pickering's request that he write a polemical essay on the whole XYZ episode. He replied that he was too busy and wanted to avoid "news paper [sic] altercations." Actually, Marshall probably did not want the High Federalists to manipulate his words for political ends as they had after he returned from France, and he did not want to stir up so much anti-French sentiment that President Adams could not pursue the diplomatic approach he endorsed.[16]

Marshall became less engaged in the other main issue in the campaign, states rights versus national supremacy. In December, the Virginia legislature passed resolutions drafted by James Madison that called on states to use their sovereign powers to obstruct enforcement of the Alien and Sedition Acts. Marshall thought the "very serious & alarming" resolutions were the handiwork of "men who will hold power by any means rather than not hold it; & who woud prefer a dissolution of the union to the continuance of an administration not of their own party." The Federalists in the assembly—led by another of Marshall's brothers-in-law, George Keith Taylor, Henry Lee, and probably with some help from Marshall himself—wrote a minority address defending the Acts as well as Federalist policies throughout the 1790s. Historians used to credit Marshall with sole authorship of the address, but recent scholarship has pointed out differences between his views and the document—the latter, for example, approved the efficacy of the Acts and called for nationalizing the common law—that suggest he was at most a collaborator. The evidence is not conclusive, however, and Marshall may have been trying to gain votes and recoup some Federalist backing he had lost with the "Freeholder" letter. Such was the perception of Theodore Sedgwick, who called the address "a masterly performance . . . General Marshall . . . has, by it, in some measure atoned for his pitiful electioneering epistle." The House of Delegates refused to publish the minority address, so the Federalists printed and circulated it as a campaign tract. A tedious and prolix apologia, it had little effect.[17]

Beyond this behind-the-scenes effort, Marshall stayed away from the Virginia Resolutions. Considering that their constitutional premises were so antithetical to his nationalism, it seems surprising that he would pass up a chance to set forth his views, however unsystematically developed, on federal-state relations and the judiciary's role in resolving disputes between the levels of government. Possibly Marshall realized that the Resolutions really were peaceful appeals to public opinion and not concealed calls to arms, as some Federalists tried to portray them. He may have confronted them more directly had they been well received in Virginia, but he did not need to because the reaction to them in the state generally was negative, and Clopton was put on the defensive. In any event, with the election in Virginia so focused on the Alien and Sedition Acts and the Virginia and Kentucky Resolutions, Marshall did not have to deal with the issues that dominated the campaigns in other states—the standing army and the taxes needed to fund the Federalists' expansion of the military.[18]

Foreign affairs—specifically, the conflict with France—intruded into the campaign in its closing months, but Marshall adeptly took advantage of the issue. On 18 February, President Adams announced that he would send a second mission to France to accomplish what the XYZ envoys had not. Adams's declaration infuriated the High Federalists and irreparably divided the party, but Marshall welcomed the move. He believed that an accord with France was not only in the national interest but would bring the Federalists political dividends in Republican-dominated regions. Once again, he could play both sides of the issue, distancing himself from party extremists while arguing that the administration's defense buildup had convinced France at last to receive another minister and accord him due respect. By then, most leading Federalists believed a commitment to expanding the army precluded negotiations with France, but Marshall had no intellectual difficulty moving along both tracks simultaneously. He did, however, have to disassociate himself from the unpopular recruitment program for the provisional army.[19]

As the April election approached, the outcome remained in doubt. Both parties intensified their activity at all levels, mobilizing popular support and trying to solicit endorsements from political luminaries. One such Republican attempt turned into a costly blunder that benefited Marshall. Some of Clopton's supporters spread a rumor that Patrick Henry opposed Marshall's election because the candidate belonged to the "aristocratic" party in Virginia. Henry weighed in on Marshall's side with his characteristic vehemence.

Independently of the high gratification I felt from his public ministry, he ever stood high in my esteem as a private citizen. His temper and disposition were always pleasant, his talents and integrity unquestioned. These things are sufficient to place that gentleman far above any competitor in the district for Congress . . . Tell Marshall I love him, because [in France] he felt and acted as a Republican, as an American . . . I really should give him my vote for Congress, preferably to any citizen in the state at this juncture, one only excepted [Washington].

This letter circulated widely and lost the Republicans some votes. Still, they remained confident. Just before the election, Jefferson concluded that "[t]he tide is evidently turning . . . from Marshall's romance." Marshall agreed; "The fate of my election is extremely uncertain," he wrote to his brother James around the same time.[20]

The balloting at the Richmond courthouse green on 24 April followed customary practices. Marshall and Clopton "treated" the freeholders with whiskey and thanked each citizen for his vote, which was given verbally before election officials and the candidates. The crowd was more raucous than usual— a spurious story that Republicans had cached arms to resist enforcement of the Alien and Sedition Laws had made many people tense—and several fights broke out. Both parties made strenuous efforts to get out the vote, and sketchy information suggests that participation was unusually high.[21]

Marshall won by between 108 and 114 votes. His victory was a bellwether of significant Federalist gains in Virginia. In the liveliest campaign since ratification, the Federalists took eight of 19 of the state's seats in the House of Representatives—a net gain of four and their highest total ever, showing newfound influence in the Southside and Northern Neck regions. In the House of Delegates, they added 15 seats, although the Republicans retained clear control. The Federalists' show of strength—which "astonished every one," according to Jefferson—was part of a broad resurgence by the party throughout the South and, somewhat less so, in New England that largely resulted from the outpouring of nationalism after the XYZ Affair and gave the Federalists a 20-seat majority (up from six) in the upcoming Sixth Congress. Their achievement in Virginia, the Carolinas, and Georgia, where they won 22 of 37 seats, seemed to suggest that the center of power in the party was shifting south. Marshall embodied the post-XYZ nationalist sentiment to most voters in the Richmond district, and, when combined with his glowing personal and professional reputation and expressions of support from Washington and Henry, enabled him to offset Clopton's imposing credentials.[22]

The elections did not produce a permanent shift in voting allegiance in Virginia, however, and Federalist gains proved to be fragile and transitory. They resulted more from the Federalists' exploitation of a singular circumstance, and from temporary developments such as the announcement of the second peace mission to France, than from a significant change in the people's political preference. The patriotic fervor of 1798 ebbed throughout the following year—Jefferson remarked that the Alien and Sedition Acts were "powerful sedatives of the [South's] XYZ inflammation"—as did the sense of national purpose on which the Federalists were basing their hopes. Marshall pessimistically seems to have feared that the outcome was only a deviation from a steady course toward nationwide defeat. In his correspondence after the elections, he emphasized what the Federalists had failed to accomplish rather than what they had achieved, deplored the "baneful influence of a legislature hostile perhaps to the Union," and entered Congress more prepared to fight a holding action than to implement a clear vision of the future.[23]

Not much is known about Marshall's activities in Virginia during the eight months between his election and the opening of the congressional session in December. What documentation that does exist indicates he continued trying to rebuild his law practice, attended court sessions outside Richmond, wrote to Secretary of State Pickering explaining why he believed the United States should not recognize any French claims against American property without reciprocity, corresponded with Washington about military appointments, sold parcels of his Fairfax holdings, and visited his sick father in Kentucky. He followed battlefield developments in Europe and presumably attended the funeral of Patrick Henry, who died in June. His feeble (and again pregnant) wife and young children no doubt took up much of his free time.[24]

In late November, Marshall left for the convening of the Sixth Congress, which met in Philadelphia between December 1799 and May 1800. He appeared with his credentials and took his seat on 2 December. He immediately found the factional intrigue and partisan discord extremely worrisome. About his own party, he wrote to his brother James that

the situation of our affairs with respect to domestic quiet is much more critical than I had conjectured. The eastern people are very much dissatisfied with the President on account of the late mission to France. They are strongly disposd to desert him & to push some other candidate. King or Ellsworth with one of the Pinckneys—most probably the general, are thought of. . . . Perhaps this ill humor may evaporate before the election comes on—but at present it wears a very serious aspect.

Marshall was equally concerned about conflict with the Republicans:

[T]here are such different views with respect to the future, such a rancarous [*sic*] malignity of temper among the democrats, such an apparent disposition . . . to propel us to a war with Br[itain] & to infold us within the embrace of France[,] such a detestation & fear of France among others [that] I look forward with more apprehension than I have ever done to the future political events of our country.[25]

Much of Marshall's activity during his five months in Congress can be seen as his effort to rescue the Federalist Party from self-destruction and oblivion by persuading it to adopt more popular policies without sacrificing its core beliefs and renouncing its warrant, as the party of enlightenment and virtue, to national leadership. Indeed, he would argue that some aspects of party "orthodoxy" actually violated the principles from which the Federalist persuasion derived. Marshall was, as one commentator has observed, "strategically a good Federalist, [but] he reserved the right to tactical independence" as he tried to build a centrist faction based first and foremost on support for President Adams—especially on seeking a rapprochement with France. A convincing retrospective case has recently been made that this strategy was destined to fail, that "Federalism possessed none of the resources—of spirit, will, imagination, or responsiveness" to become a "reconstituted and chastened" political alternative to the Republicans. Rather, "the response of Federalism was that of righteousness under siege, and amounted to little more in the end than a sterile defense of constituted order against the forces of insubordination and sedition." But in late 1799–early 1800, Marshall did not see things that way or believe that the Federalists had any choice but to try. Moreover, he seems to have thought the Virginia Federalists' experience, as a moderate opposition well versed in participatory politics and without the disabling anti-Jacobin paranoia of their Yankee counterparts, could serve as an example for the national party. It would give at least some Federalists a basis on which to accept, as a purely practical necessity, the idea of being an alternative. The composition of the Sixth Congress gave Marshall some cause for hoping that he might successfully use Virginia Federalism as a model. The Federalists had a 20-seat majority, and most of the party's newly elected members, many of them from the South, were more inclined than the extremist faction to back Adams. For example, most of Marshall's colleagues in Virginia's House delegation—with 19 seats, the largest in the 106-member chamber—were moderates who strongly endorsed Adams.[26]

Marshall's tenuous relationship with northern Federalist leaders who dominated the party's elements in the national government complicated his task of creating a Federalist alternative. They respected his intelligence and political talents—"He possesses great powers and has much dexterity in the application of them . . . we can do nothing without him," Speaker of the House Theodore Sedgwick wrote—but most had not forgiven him for failing to endorse the Alien and Sedition Acts, and his independent streak angered and troubled them. Some adopted a patronizing attitude toward Marshall, writing about him as if he were a wayward cousin needing strong correction and a proper home. Sedgwick believed Marshall "would have been a more decided man had his education been on the other side of the Delaware." George Cabot claimed he displayed "the faults of a Virginian. He thinks too much of that State, & he expects the world will be governed according to the rules of Logic. I have seen such men often become excellent legislators after experience has cured their errors. I hope it will prove so with Genl. M.[arshall], who seems calculated to act a great part." Oliver Wolcott asserted that Marshall "will read and expound the constitution as if it were a penal statute."[27]

Marshall would confront these varied challenges as he dealt with a wide range of political, economic, diplomatic, and military issues during the fast-paced first session, held amid rising popular disaffection toward the Federalists—as expressed in the petitions that flooded Congress earlier in the year—and growing anticipation that the coming presidential election would bring a new regime into power. Marshall and the other Federalists spent much of their time fending off Republican attacks on unpopular measures such as the Alien and Sedition Acts and the army while trying to avert a permanent schism in their own party. As the session proceeded, Marshall in effect became the floor leader of the proadministration voting bloc in the House, supplanting Harrison Gray Otis and Robert Goodloe Harper.[28]

Marshall's early efforts at straightening out his party met with mixed success. First, he tried to induce Federalist leaders in the House to recognize the party's bisectional makeup by selecting a Southerner as speaker—the three previous speakers had come from the middle states or New England—and he worked on behalf of John Rutledge of South Carolina, a former associate justice and, briefly, chief justice of the Supreme Court. The Yankee faction eventually prevailed, however, in choosing Theodore Sedgwick of Massachusetts, an intractable ideologue and vehement opponent of Adams's conciliatory French policy, to preside over the chamber. Next, when Sedgwick chose Marshall to be chairman of a committee to prepare the House's reply to Adams's speech opening the session, Marshall tried to unite all House factions by dodging controversy. He composed an anodyne response that probably left most members unsatisfied but was sufficiently bland to arouse no debate. The address, which wandered over issues such as Fries's Rebellion, judicial reform, the second mission to France, the Jay Treaty, and the Federalists' military buildup, mildly reflected Adams's positions on them and "passed with silent dissent," according to Oliver Wolcott.[29]

George Washington's death on 14 December, scarcely two weeks into the session, enabled Marshall to demonstrate both his enduring affection toward his former commander and his keen sense of political opportunity. On the 18th, he interrupted the House's proceedings to announce, "in a voice that bespoke the anguish of his mind, and a countenance expressive of the deepest regret," the "distressing intelligence" of the former president's passing, and he moved that the members adjourn at once. The next day, Marshall delivered a short eulogy stressing nationalistic themes and raising the specter of disunion if partisan strife persisted. He also introduced resolutions, which Henry Lee drafted, directing that memorial efforts be started. Marshall would head a committee "to consider . . . the most suitable manner of paying honour to the memory of the man, first in war, first in peace, and first in the hearts of his country." Within a week, the committee recommended that a marble monument, most likely an equestrian statue, be erected in the Capitol, and that Washington's family be asked to allow him to be buried under it. Although Marshall sincerely grieved over Washington's death, he also knew that the event gave the Federalists their last chance to wrap themselves in the ex-president's mantle (or, in this case, his burial shroud) and, as they had done so often while he was alive, invoke the personification of American nationhood—"our Washington," Marshall called him—as a justification for their continued control of the government to forestall the grim prospect of a Republican takeover.[30]

When Marshall considered substantive legislation, he tried to keep the Federalists focused on issues of national interest and away from narrow partisan concerns. He was not very successful, partly because he tried to accomplish too much. His pursuit of party harmony required that he side with the administration bloc on some issues, with the High Federalists on others, and sometimes cobble together compromises that satisfied no one. On occasion, he would try—as with the federal bankruptcy law and the Republican effort to disband the army—to temper the Federalist position with procedural or symbolic moves that would broaden legislative support. In other instances— notably with the disputed elections bill and repeal of the Sedition Act—Marshall had strong enough convictions to risk breaking with his party after failing to persuade it to renounce what he considered to be politically foolish positions. In the end, he could not build a centrist faction or bring the High Federalists toward the mainstream. The only person who seemed pleased with Marshall's congressional labors—and in the end, he would be more important than anyone—was John Adams.

Marshall's work on behalf of a national bankruptcy law gave him his last chance as a legislator to promote a Hamiltonian economic objective. Marshall served on a committee that spent a month drafting a uniform law based on British statutes. Federalist advocates of what Congressman James A. Bayard called "one great commercial Republic" wanted a national bankruptcy law to support mercantile credit, promote interstate commerce, and encourage financial ventures. They strongly opposed state insolvency laws for creating confusion and uncertainty, inhibiting national economic development, and encouraging aimless speculation, and wanted the federal government to exercise its plenary authority in this area. Congress had tried but failed by narrow margins to enact such a measure after financial panics in 1792 and 1797. An odd coalition of Republicans, who opposed expanding national power, and tight-money Federalists, who thought bankruptcy laws undermined contract rights and encouraged profligacy, defeated those efforts. The bill reported out of committee in 1800 would end the common law practice of imprisonment for debt—a feature Marshall must have found appealing because his friend Robert

Morris was jailed in Philadelphia in 1797 after declaring bankruptcy—and transfer legal actions to the federal district courts. To win votes for the controversial law, Marshall included a novel provision that required juries to determine the fact of bankruptcy and set the amount of the debt. This concession to Republican populism irritated some High Federalists but probably saved the bill, which passed when Speaker Sedgwick broke a tie vote.[31]

The bankruptcy bill was closely related to another Federalist proposal that Marshall strongly backed: restructuring the national court system. Sedgwick wrote that the bankruptcy bill would "render it absolutely necessary to spread out the national judicial by a creation of new districts and Judges," and a Republican congressman described the judiciary bill as "the eldest child of the bankrupt system." Indeed, Marshall and the same group of Federalists drafted both the judiciary statute and the bankruptcy law. With the judiciary bill, Marshall's party intended to strengthen the Federalist-dominated courts— especially by giving them authority to review state judicial decisions—and preserve the national judiciary as a source of Federalist influence in a future Republican-controlled government. The party's attitude toward the importance of the national courts had changed substantially since the Judiciary Act of 1789 was passed. At that time, the Federalists were interested generally in assuring that the authority of the United States was enforceable through the courts, but their thoughts on the subject were not as unified and focused as might have been expected, and they regarded the national judiciary as somewhat of an abstraction. The 1799 court bill, in contrast, shows the extent to which pragmatic political calculations now drove Federalist thinking about the judicial branch. The measure's most significant provisions would have reduced the number of Supreme Court justices from six to five; abolished the current district courts and organized a new system of districts and circuits; substantially extended the circuit courts' and Supreme Court's jurisdiction; and authorized the former to compel removal of suits from the state to the federal courts.[32]

Marshall spoke several times on the House floor in favor of the bill. He believed it made worthwhile changes in the power and organization of the federal courts. Its blatant partisanship probably troubled him, but he apparently shared Wolcott's view that "there is no way to combat the state opposition but by an efficient and extended organization of judges, magistrates, and other civil officers." Republican opponents struck out the bill's more egregious features, but Marshall and his fellow committeemen wrote a revised version that included most of what the Federalists wanted. Congress eventually passed it in early 1801. In addition, Marshall helped add provisions that would benefit him personally by minimizing the problem of Virginians' hostility to his Fairfax speculations. One section gave the new circuit court in Fredericksburg jurisdiction over cases involving the Fairfax lands; another raised the financial threshold for filing civil suits in federal courts well above the value involved in most Fairfax cases. Marshall thus got a double benefit: He achieved a longtime goal of getting Fairfax lands cases into the federal courts, which would be more sympathetic to him than Virginia's judges; and he was protected from much litigation that might have arisen otherwise.[33]

The question of what to do about the army put Marshall in a dilemma that tested his allegiances to the Federalists, President Adams, and his own beliefs.[34] The Hamiltonians' military establishment, which they had created piecemeal during the 1790s in response to threats of war with Britain, the Indians, and France, and which they expanded during the atmosphere of anxiety and suspicion of 1798–99, was in deep trouble. Fears of a professional standing army and opposition to the taxes needed to support it were growing everywhere south of New England, and the Republicans—some of whom were also afraid that zealous Federalists might use troops to interfere with the upcoming election—seized the moment to strike at this vulnerable point. On 1 January 1800, Representative John Nicholas of Virginia moved that the July 1798 and March 1799 acts enlarging the army be repealed. He contended that disbanding the army would not affect ongoing negotiations with France, and that borrowing money for military expenditures would show that the United States was weaker than it claimed to be. The High Federalists, implacably committed to their army and uncertain how the mission to France might turn out, refused to countenance any demobilization.

Marshall surely realized that disbanding the so-called New Army would win the Federalists some votes and also please President Adams, who never wanted it. But on military issues, Marshall thought like a Hamiltonian, and he was not ready to go that far. Never worrying that the army might become a Federalist praetorian guard, he spoke and voted against Nicholas's motion, which was defeated after several days of debate. By then, though, he apparently calculated that some compromise was in order and pushed hard for a proposal that would halt new enlistments while keeping the army until a peace agreement with France appeared likely. As the congressional session ended, support for the army had eroded so badly that even belligerent Federalists decided they must deny the Republicans a tactical victory by doing the inevitable. In early May, the House passed a demobilization measure containing Marshall's proviso that soldiers would be discharged at the president's discretion when he believed relations with France warranted it.

In his speeches and private remarks, Marshall stated his purely practical rationale for retaining the army. "The whole world is in arms & no rights are respected but those which are maintained by force." France was negotiating only because of the United States' military capability: "To supplicating America even discussion was denied. America armed and immediately a different language was used, and the rights of an independent nation were allowed her." At the same time, he recognized how great a political liability the army had become, and he privately conceded that the Republicans reflected the public will on higher military expenditures. "I am apprehensive," he wrote his brother, "that our people would receive with very ill temper a system which should keep up an army of observation at the expence of the annual addition of five million to our debt." In the current diplomatic context, however, he publicly argued that national security could not be held hostage to economics, and that a frugal nation could lose its independence if it considered debt a more fearsome adversary than foreign enemies. "Suppose this had been the language of '75—Suppose at the commencement of our revolution, a gentleman had risen on the floor of congress, to compare our revenues with our expences—what would have been the result of the calculation?"[35]

Lastly, Marshall may have concluded that taking the position he did at that time would repair some of the political damage the Federalists, the administration, and he had recently sustained. Adams had staked his reputation on a settlement with France, and Marshall believed that a firm military posture was essential to achieving one. Although the army had become, in Stephen Kurtz's words, "the *bête noire* of Federalism," a diplomatic breakthrough in Paris might help Adams and the Federalists execute another XYZ-style political coup and put the army back in good stead. For Marshall himself, association with such achievements would help restore some of his prestige with Federalist leaders. His positions on other military issues during the congressional session—opposing a Republican effort to make soldiers imprisonable for debt, voting against a portion of the Marine Corps bill that would subject that service's officers to trials in civilian courts, and supporting a bill to establish a military academy—may have been influenced by immediate political concerns as well as long-standing promilitary attitudes. Those attitudes, moreover, were shaped largely by Marshall's Revolutionary War experience, through which he understood that the Continental Army, and particularly the officer corps, was not a bulwark of aristocracy but a socially diverse cohort more American than military in its culture. As a result, he appreciated how the permanent military preserved and protected republican values instead of threatening them.[36]

Marshall did not stand down from his "constitutional but unwise" position on the Sedition Act when it came up for repeal in January 1800. In his "Freeholder" letter, he had said he would vote on repeal as his constituents wanted. Accordingly, he supported a Republican repeal proposal, which carried by only two votes. He also opposed a retrograde Federalist attempt to make the same offenses spelled out in the Sedition Act punishable under the common law of seditious libel. Previously, the Federalists had argued that the Sedition Act, by allowing truth as a defense, improved on the common law. In an effort to help salvage something of the earlier Federalist position, Marshall backed another Republican proposal to allow truth as a defense in libel proceedings; this measure passed by four votes. An indication that Marshall did not quite embrace the emerging libertarian interpretation of seditious libel arose when the Senate tried to punish Republican editor William Duane for criticizing the Disputed Elections Bill. Marshall believed the move was clumsy, but he noted that it was not unprecedented and had wide support, and so he did not oppose it.[37]

Probably the best example of how Marshall tried to save the Federalists from their own folly, even at great risk to his political fortunes, was his scuttling of the Disputed Elections Bill.[38] Also known as the Ross Bill after its senatorial sponsor, the measure was a witless and probably unconstitutional attempt by extreme Federalists to alter the presidential election returns. The Ross Bill would have given a "Grand Committee" of six senators and six representatives (picked by a Federalist-controlled Congress) and the chief justice an unappealable veto over the validity of contested votes by presidential electors. The bill was intended to resolve a deadlock in the Pennsylvania legislature over choosing presidential electors. Because that state would likely go Republican in 1800, some Federalists wanted to find a way to deny Vice President Jefferson, the probable opposition candidate, its crucial electoral votes.

Ross's proposal "excited more feeling than any other subject which has come before us," Marshall reported. He thought the bill was unconstitutional as well as politically disastrous and set aside his personal and political hostility toward Jefferson to prevent its passage. Under Article II of the Constitution, he observed, the House of Representatives was responsible for choosing a president if no candidate received a majority of electoral votes; the House and Senate could only count electoral votes as full, separate bodies, and could not delegate that responsibility to a mixed committee; and inclusion of the chief justice in the process violated the separation of powers. He did believe, though, that the national government had some authority to regulate presidential elections—for example, to investigate alleged fraud and illegalities. He spoke on the floor, met privately with other members, and led a select redrafting committee that removed the most offensive terms from the Ross Bill. Under the revised version, the Grand Committee had only a fact-finding responsibility, and the House and Senate could override its findings. These changes prevented the Ross Bill from doing what its originators had intended and effectively killed it. Speaker Sedgwick accused Marshall of "dissipating our majority." The House passed a bill containing Marshall's modifications; the Senate refused to endorse the changes, with all Federalist senators voting against them; and the bill died when Congress adjourned.

No issue that Marshall addressed during the session evoked from him such a powerful and elaborate defense of the Adams administration than the extradition case of Thomas Nash, alias Jonathan Robbins.[39] Nash had been arrested in Charleston, South Carolina, in mid-1799 on charges of participating in a murderous mutiny on a British Royal Navy frigate. The British invoked article 27 of the Jay Treaty and requested his extradition. Nash claimed he was an American citizen named Jonathan Robbins, had been impressed into service in the British navy, and served on the vessel on which the mutiny occurred but had not participated in it. Congress had not yet passed legislation to implement article 27, and no federal court had clear authority to assist in its execution. After a federal judge decided that the decision rested with the executive branch, Adams looked into the case at the request of the British minister and approved Nash's extradition. The sailor was court-martialed and hanged. Republicans were enraged at this apparent subservience to Britain and charged that the administration had interfered improperly with the courts to deny Nash a trial. The incident became the most contentious issue of the congressional session beginning in February 1800. As with the Jay Treaty and the XYZ Affair, the Republicans demanded that the president document the executive branch's conduct and, as Marshall wrote his brother, "Every stratagem seems to be usd [sic] to give to this business an undue impression." The administration provided records supposedly showing that Nash was not Robbins. Federalists and Republicans traded resolutions approving and censuring Adams, and an acrimonious debate ensued for more than two weeks until Marshall closed off all discussion with what may have been the most forceful and convincing speech of his career.[40]

Marshall, who had already spoken briefly during some of the earlier parliamentary jousts, took the floor on 7 March after extended discourses from Republicans Edward Livingston and Albert Gallatin.[41] Seemingly irked over the tedious and protracted debate, he insisted that the members evaluate the available evidence and come to closure on the matter. Despite his speech's length—it took three hours to deliver and filled 22 columns of small type in the *Annals of Congress*—it could be reduced to two essential points. First, the facts of Nash's case—especially his failure to prove his American citizenship, and Britain's jurisdiction over him when he committed his crimes—required that the United States surrender him under the terms of the Jay Treaty. Second, American courts had no jurisdiction over international disputes arising from implementation of treaties because such problems technically were not legal cases but "questions of political law." Extradition was one of those questions. Furthermore,

The case was in its nature a national demand made upon the nation. The parties were the two nations. They cannot come into court to litigate their claims, nor can a court decide on them. Of consequence the demand is not a case for judicial cognizance.

The President is the sole organ of the nation in its external relations . . . the demand of a foreign nation can only be made on him. He is charged to execute the laws. A treaty is declared to be a law. He must then execute a treaty, where he and he alone possesses the means of executing it.[42]

Marshall's rhetorical tour de force provides a case study of the exegetical methods that he had used so effectively as a lawyer and that he would employ as chief justice: reducing intricate questions to a few basic suppositions, following a clear analytic line, relying mostly on force of logic while also buttressing arguments with some references to authorities and documents, and using counterhypotheses to answer rebuttals. His view on extradition was not opportunistic but followed the one he had taken 16 years before in the House of Delegates. At that time, he approved of extraditing any Virginian wanted on criminal charges in another country. His advocacy of judicial restraint may seem to contradict perhaps his most famous Supreme Court decision, *Marbury v. Madison* (1803), where he expanded the courts' power relative to the other branches. In cases concerning international law, treaty obligations, neutral rights, and foreign affairs generally, however, he continued to insist that the judiciary should accede to the political branches' prerogatives, and he consistently believed that the courts should try to preserve their legitimacy by avoiding political questions. In his speech, Marshall had presented the first important examination of the constitutional roles of the presidency and the judiciary in interpreting and fulfilling treaty obligations. During the nineteenth century, several state courts followed his interpretation in deciding extradition cases.[43]

Marshall offered this categorical defense of Adams's position for several diplomatic and political reasons. He believed the United States must uphold its treaty obligations to gain and keep the respect of other nations, and it also must affirm the rule of international law and not act capriciously like less civilized countries. He also resented that the Republicans were again using foreign policy as a partisan issue and potentially damaging the national security by antagonizing Great Britain. Moreover, he feared that the affair would harm the Federalists politically and help the Republicans win the election. His speech was so effective, however, that the Republicans could not muster a response. After Marshall sat down, some House members urged Gallatin to reply; he reportedly said, "Gentlemen, answer it yourself; for my part I think it unanswerable." A motion to censure Adams failed the next day by a 61–35 vote, and a resolution approving the president's conduct passed on 10 March by 62–36. A few skirmishes occurred on the floor in April, but the Nash-Robbins imbroglio died away for the rest of the session. Marshall's speech received widespread publicity and eliminated the subject as a campaign issue.[44]

Marshall's other most noteworthy activities during the Sixth Congress concerned western lands. He served as chairman of a committee that drafted legislation to accept from Connecticut over 3,000,000 acres of territory west of Pennsylvania and south of Lake Erie that the state had reserved from its 1786 cession of land claimed under its colonial charter. Marshall wanted the national government to acquire this tract, known as the Western Reserve, because he supported the establishment of a federal domain in the west to encourage settlement and extend the nation's influence. In addition, even though westward expansion would undercut the value of his Virginia lands, appreciation of his holdings in Kentucky would more than offset the loss. Marshall also continued his long-standing assistance to Revolutionary War veterans by introducing a bill to give them federal land patents in the areas Virginia had ceded in the Ohio Valley. Both chambers approved the bill late in the session.[45]

By the time Congress adjourned in May, the Federalists had permanently split into extremist and administration factions despite Marshall's attempts to find common ground between them. The party never had a working majority during the session because of defections to the Republican side, yet moderate Federalists did not coalesce into a centrist bloc that could wield influence on the floor. As a result of Marshall's unsuccessful efforts toward that end, his standing in the party had changed dramatically. His reputation with President Adams had risen sharply, largely because of the Nash affair, but the High Federalists held him in even lower esteem because of what they viewed as his breach of party principles. Theodore Sedgwick offered a good synopsis of their opinion of Marshall, who as the session opened "was looked up to as the man whose great and commanding genius was to enlighten & direct the national councils" by administration supporters but was considered "temporizing" and "feeble" by other Federalists. Now, although conceding that Marshall had several admirable qualities—among them friendliness, honesty, and "almost unequalled" reasoning powers—Sedgwick contended that he was "attached to pleasures . . . indolent" and had "a strong attachment to popularity" that he was "indisposed to sacrifice to his integrity."[46]

Marshall left the session early for Richmond to attend the U.S. Circuit Court and to revive his dwindling law practice during the summer recess. Whatever inclination he had to remain in politics after his frustrating experience in Philadelphia was rendered moot by the news that Adams had nominated him to become secretary of state.[47]

Marshall became the fourth secretary of state because John Adams finally made up his mind to remove High Federalist intriguers from his cabinet and replace them with men he could trust.[48] By early May 1800, Adams decided he had put up long enough with the disloyal connivances of Secretary of State Timothy Pickering, Secretary of War James McHenry, and Secretary of the Treasury Oliver Wolcott. These Hamiltonian holdovers from Washington's second term irreconcilably opposed the president's efforts to reach a settlement with France and worked behind the scenes to sabotage them. They blamed Adams for the Federalists' political distress and decided that the party's only chance to retain the presidency was to conspire against his candidacy and back Charles Cotesworth Pinckney instead. On 3 May 1800, a caucus of congressional Federalists hatched a scheme to do this.

When Adams learned of the plot, he moved quickly to quash it. He forced McHenry to resign and fired Pickering. He tried to replace McHenry with Marshall, who first heard about his nomination when he dropped by the War Department just before leaving Philadelphia. He "was a good deal struck with a strange sort of mysterious coldness which I soon observed in the countenance of Mr. McHenry, with whom I had long been on terms of friendly intimacy." Marshall did not understand what the chief clerk meant by congratulating him "on being placed at the head of that department" and was "really surprised" to learn that Adams had selected him. He declined, at the time citing the press of private business and later adding that he did not consider himself qualified. Adams did not withdraw Marshall's nomination, however, and the Senate approved it on 9 May. Marshall legally served as secretary of war for four days, although he never performed any duties.[49]

After dismissing Pickering, who stubbornly refused to resign as requested, Adams sent Marshall's name to the Senate on 12 May, and confirmation followed almost immediately. (Samuel Dexter, from Massachusetts, succeeded Marshall at the War Department.) Presumably Adams wanted Marshall to be his secretary of state because he appreciated Marshall's proadministration labors in Congress and was impressed with his diplomatic abilities, as displayed in the

XYZ Affair, and his political discernment. Most important, Adams by this time
wanted loyal and dependable men in his cabinet.

Marshall, by then back in Richmond, pondered for a while over whether to
accept the appointment. "I never felt more doubt than on the question of
accepting or declining this office," he recalled. He realized that his legislative
service had severely hurt his law practice and that he could never reconstruct it
without leaving Congress for good. He needed a steady source of income to
meet interest payments on the Fairfax loans, and the salary of the secretary,
$5,000 a year, surpassed what he had earned as a lawyer in his best years. He
also knew that his political adversaries in Virginia were organizing to defeat
him, and that a probable Republican victory in the presidential contest made his
own reelection unlikely. By joining the administration, Marshall believed he
could best serve the country and the Federalists. He could promote policies he
believed were in the national interest while using his access to Adams to try to
keep the president from further wrecking the party. Marshall keenly respected
Adams's independence and refusal to truck with the Hamiltonians, but he knew
that the only hope for the Federalists lay in party harmony. As head of the
cabinet, Marshall would have an ideal vantage point for reining in Adams and
helping to bring the Federalists a brief but vital period of unity. In agreeing to
serve, Marshall overrode the wishes of his wife, who did not want to leave
Richmond again after six months in Philadelphia—least of all for the
undesirable environs of the new capital city of Washington.[50]

Marshall's selection elicited little comment from either Republicans or High
Federalists, probably because they figured he was the best they would get from
Adams. Even the extremists on either side sounded temperate. Benjamin
Bache's *Aurora*, one of the most acerbic Jeffersonian newspapers, suggested
that Marshall was less prejudiced against France than Pickering and might help
smooth relations with that country. Meanwhile, Timothy Pickering, Theodore
Sedgwick, and Charles Cotesworth Pinckney apparently succeeded in placating
the Hamiltonians. Pickering told them that the office "was never better filled";
Sedgwick called the appointment "a fortunate event"; and Pinckney assuringly
stated that "you may rely on [Marshall's] federalism, & be certain that he will
not unite with Jefferson & the Jacobins." Marshall recalled that he got along
well with all cabinet members except Wolcott, who thought Marshall was a
political enemy of Pickering, McHenry, and himself. Their relations soon
improved, however. After Marshall had been in office for four months, Wolcott
wrote that "I consider Gen. Marshall and Mr. Dexter as more than secretaries—
as state conservatores—the value of whose services ought to be estimated, not
only by the good they do, but by the mischief they have prevented."[51]

By early June, Marshall had taken up his post in the steamy morasses and
dense woods of Washington, shortly after the rest of the government had
arrived. Except for brief trips to Richmond to argue a legal case and visit his
family, he did not leave the capital until the following year. Marshall had had
no reason to visit Washington before then and probably thought Richmond in
the 1780s was luxurious compared with the rough, slovenly village that was the

new seat of the national government. Washington was set amid a scene of natural beauty—rolling hills, lush forests, flowering meadows, and rich farmland—but was notorious for its noxious living conditions and showed minimal progress toward, and seemed to have little chance of achieving, Pierre L'Enfant's grand design. One congressman called it "both melancholy and ludicrous . . . a city in ruins," and a senator wrote that there was "nothing to admire but the beauties of nature." Its most prominent features were a hill toward the east, on which the Capitol building was slowly rising; a lower elevation of land a mile to the west, where the president's nearly completed residence stood; and, between them, a tidal marsh through which a sluggish creek ran and a causeway of sorts (later to become Pennsylvania Avenue) had been cut. A few other unlit, stump-lined avenues entered and disappeared into the surrounding forests or trailed off into orchards, fields, or pastures. Cattle, pigs, and chickens roamed the rutted streets, which lay deep in mud or dust depending on the season. Several dozen incommodious private homes, boarding houses, and hotels, along with assorted rude shops, lay in small clusters around either hill. A couple hundred more were scattered over the several miles between the busy port of Georgetown and the Eastern Branch (now called the Anacostia River). Few residents could afford to meet the requirements of the building code (which President Jefferson waived in 1801). Marshall roomed with Secretary of War Dexter at the Washington City Hotel and Tavern, also known as Tunnicliff's, across from the Capitol. Only three religious facilities graced the capital: a small Catholic chapel, a tobacco barn that Episcopalians used, and a corridor in the Treasury Department building, where Presbyterians gathered. A racetrack, a theater, the Marine Corps band, and two newspapers offered the main diversions besides the dinners, receptions, and dances of the political crowd. This "scattered, unformed, uncouth" hamlet had slightly over 3,000 residents, barely 100 government employees, and their families, servants, and slaves. Treasury Secretary Wolcott observed that "the people are poor . . . As far as I can judge they live like fishes, by eating each other."[52]

Such were the mean conditions in which Marshall took up his duties as America's chief diplomatist. For nearly three months, his office was situated near the Treasury Building, one of a handful of two-story, red brick warehouselike structures where the executive departments conducted their business. At the end of August, the State Department moved from this location near the president's home to a row house a few blocks away on Pennsylvania Avenue. From there, Marshall supervised nine employees in Washington (a chief clerk, seven clerks, and a messenger) and nearly 70 emissaries overseas: six ministers or chargés d'affaires in Paris, London, The Hague, Berlin, Lisbon, and Madrid; a consul general in Algiers; several dozen consuls or vice consuls; and almost a dozen commercial agents. Much of Marshall's work, or that which he delegated to his clerks, was the routine fare of foreign affairs at the time: responding to dispatches from consuls and ministers, notes from foreign diplomats in the United States, letters from merchants whose ships or cargoes had been seized, reports from bankers and agents who handled official American accounts overseas, and pleas on behalf of sailors impressed into foreign navies.[53]

Besides those mundane matters, Marshall spent the rest of his official time dealing with four important foreign policy issues: resolving disputes with Great Britain over implementation of the Jay Treaty; concluding peace negotiations with France; clearing up territorial controversies with Spain; and developing a modus vivendi with the Barbary Pirates. On all of these questions, Marshall adopted the role of counselor to and administrator for President Adams but did not have a large hand in shaping diplomatic strategies. Although some Hamiltonians, among them Oliver Wolcott, believed that "the secret of Mr. A[dams]'s satisfaction [with Marshall's performance] was that he obeyed his Secretary of State without being conscious of it," in reality the president retained full control of foreign policy. Marshall advised Adams, helped devise means for carrying out his plans, and effectively implemented his decisions, but Adams set the diplomatic course Marshall followed. Marshall definitely regarded his function as that of secretary. That said, it should be noted that Adams rarely if ever countermanded anything Marshall did, and he never disapproved of any of Marshall's letters of instruction to ministers abroad. Even if Marshall disagreed with the president on an important point, he never took advantage of Adams's protracted absence in Quincy, Massachusetts, to direct diplomacy against the chief executive's wishes.[54]

As secretary of state, Marshall consistently acted according to certain themes, principles, or attitudes about diplomacy in general and American foreign policy in particular. They included preserving American independence by remaining neutral in European conflicts, encouraging commercial ties with Europe, separating the national interest from ideological and partisan controversy, and establishing a corpus of international law to provide apolitical juristic solutions to disputes among nations. Marshall probably derived most of these maxims from Washington's Farewell Address and had enunciated several of them during his 1798–99 congressional campaign. He did not use them then only as rhetorical contrivances to win votes, however; he believed in and practiced them.[55]

For Marshall, the key to a successful foreign policy was avoiding political entanglements with Europe and remaining neutral in conflicts among the European powers. "We have avoided, & we shall continue to avoid, any political connections which might engage us further than is compatible with the neutrality we profess," he wrote to Rufus King, the American minister in London, "and we have sought, by a conduct just & friendly to all, to be permitted to maintain a position which, without offence to any, we had a right to take." But Marshall ascribed to the Federalist version of neutrality, which required that Great Britain receive priority. He contended that France had tried to exploit the American-French alliance to make the United States weak and dependent. Moreover, the United States must preserve its economic stability, support Hamilton's financial program, and protect its commercial shipping. Doing so required close economic ties to Britain. This de facto alliance could be justified as purely in the national interest without reference to ideology, and accordingly would help develop a stronger sense of nationhood and detach foreign policy from domestic partisan politics.[56]

Marshall was secondarily interested in encouraging the establishment of a body of international law that could regulate conflict and promote commerce among nation states. He was particularly interested at this time in aspects of neutral rights and maritime law, which the conflicts with Britain, France, Spain, and the Barbary states all underscored. European scholarship on international law was antiquated and American legal precedents were few, but Marshall studied and tried to use them as the foundation for dealings with European governments. For example, in his instructions to King in September 1800, Marshall displayed a thorough familiarity with international maritime law, particularly on neutral rights and contraband, and made a strong case for the American viewpoint. He was not in office long enough to achieve much in this area, but some of his international law opinions as chief justice were cited in English proceedings as late as the 1920s.[57]

Marshall's most pressing diplomatic concern was breaking the deadlock with Great Britain over articles six and seven of the Jay Treaty, which addressed compensation for the debts owed by Americans to British creditors and for American property seized or destroyed during the European wars of the 1790s. The two countries had established arbitration commissions to deal with those issues. The negotiations of the debts commission, which met in Philadelphia, were particularly combative, largely because the British majority continually outvoted and browbeat the American representatives. During the summer of 1799, the Americans decided to boycott the meetings. In protest, the British government ordered its members of the war damages commission, which sat in London, to do the same. In April 1800, just before Marshall became secretary of state, Foreign Minister Lord Grenville hinted that the British wanted to avoid further disagreement and might accept a lump-sum payment for the outstanding debts. Marshall at first wondered if making such a payment might "afford just cause of discontent to France" by appearing to violate American neutrality, but President Adams insisted that the United States could negotiate whatever method of debt resolution it deemed appropriate and that "[n]o foreign country has anything to do with it." Marshall reached the same judgment and instructed King to negotiate a settlement of no more than $2,500,000. The government of William Pitt resigned before details could be worked out, but the movement on both sides eased the way for the Convention of 1802. Under that accord, the United States paid the British government £600,000, and a commission heard claims and distributed the amount between 1803 and 1811. British merchants claimed losses of £1,400,000, so as a group they lost about 60 percent of the amount the American debtors owed them. Marshall reacted with some bitterness when the Jefferson administration trumpeted the diplomatic achievement that had eluded him and Adams. In 1802 he wrote King of his "mortifying reflection" that had the Federalists remained in office, "the payment of a specific sum woud [sic] then have been pronouncd, by those who now take merit to themselves for it, a humiliating national degradation, an abandonment of national interest, a free will offering of millions to Britain for her grace & favor, by those who sought to engage in a war with France, rather than repay, in part, by a small loan to that republic, the immense debt of gratitude we owe her. Such is & such I fear will ever be human justice!"[58]

Marshall could not make any headway on the other problems in U.S. relations with Britain: the capture and condemnation of American merchant ships, impressment of American seamen, and closure of ports to American vessels. Britain, broadly defining contraband, had captured more American vessels trying to run its blockade in the Caribbean and the Gulf of Mexico, and it also kept its West Indies ports closed to American ships. British depredations against American commercial shipping were more than a problem of diplomacy because they forced up insurance rates sharply and gave the Republicans another issue with which to attack the Federalists. The Adams administration issued protests, and Marshall instructed King to issue a demarche to the British Foreign Ministry. In his lengthy letter to the minister, Marshall clearly and rigorously set forth the precepts of American neutrality while asserting U.S. resolve to defend its principles, by force if necessary.

Separated far from Europe, we mean not to mingle in their quarrels . . . we have avoided, & we shall continue to avoid, any political connections which might engage us further than is compatible with the neutrality we profess; and we have sought, by a conduct just & friendly to all, to be permitted to maintain a position which, without offence to any, we had a right to take.

The aggressions [of foreign powers] . . . have forcd us to contemplate, & to prepare for, war . . . But this is a situation of necessity, not of choice. It is one in which we are placed—not by our own acts—but by the acts of others; & which we change, so soon as the conduct of others will permit us to change it. . . . We still pursue peace. We will embrace it if it can be obtained without violating our national honor or our national faith, but we will reject, without hesitation, all propositions which may compromit [sic] the one or the other.

The United States, however, would not and probably could not take stronger action then, and the various naval controversies went unresolved until the War of 1812. Marshall's letter indicates, however, that he was trying to effect in diplomacy the same tack toward the center that he was pursuing in some areas of domestic policy. He realized that, as Fisher Ames noted, "the hardest thing for the Federalists to bear was the charge of British influence," and he tried to regain some political support for his party by carefully recrafting its image as a bastion of Anglophilia.[59]

The second mission to France, consisting of Oliver Ellsworth, William Vans Murray, and William R. Davie, had departed in November 1799 and was well underway when Marshall took office six months later.[60] Several interrelated factors had markedly improved the chances for an accord. France had a new government—led by Napoleon Bonaparte, who seized power in the coup d'etat of 18 Brumaire in November 1799—with the resolve, strategic perspective, and ability to end the Quasi-War; and the American commission had the authority to negotiate a settlement acceptable to the American public, which by then had become weary and frustrated with the Quasi-War. As the talks dragged on through the summer of 1800, Adams grew despondent over the thought of asking Congress to declare war against France. Marshall was not surprised at the lack of progress. Before taking office, he had suspected the French might stall until military events in Europe and political developments in America—specifically, a change in administrations—turned in their favor. After Napoleon's coup, though, Marshall became "greatly disposd to think that the present [French] government is much inclind to correct, at least in part, the follies of the past." He advised the president to be patient despite signs of another stalemate. Even if the envoys returned empty-handed, he told Adams, war was unnecessary because France had already taken steps toward recognizing America's neutral rights. Marshall had little role in the negotiations besides offering counsel to Adams, and no available evidence suggests he dealt directly with the envoys.[61]

An agreement followed quickly in September after the American envoys decided to disregard their specific instructions. Although the Convention of 1800[62] did not require the French to pay reparations for American shipping losses but left the matter to future negotiations, and did not specifically recognize the right of the United States to abrogate previous treaties, it renewed most-favored-nation commercial relations, more clearly defined contraband, and recognized the neutral rights principles of the 1778 model treaty. News of the accord reached Washington in early December; envoy Davie arrived in America with copies of it on the 11th; and Adams, displeased with its terms but realizing that he had no acceptable alternative, sent it to the Senate on the 15th. There it received a mixed reception. Republicans criticized some provisions but urged ratification. Prominent High Federalists—including Wolcott, Ames, Sedgwick, Otis ("another chapter in the book of humiliation"), Gouverneur Morris, and John Rutledge—damned the agreement, especially the deferral of spoliation claims. Only moderate proadministration Federalists supported ratification at first. Marshall favored ratification but was "far very far from approving" of the treaty and expressed concern about how it contradicted some articles of the Jay Treaty. He correctly predicted that the Senate would reject the treaty without changes. Although he believed rejection of the accord would "utterly ruin the Federal party and endanger our internal tranquillity," neither he nor Adams was able to sway recalcitrant party members. Having lost the election, the president was even weaker than before, and Marshall's influence diminished accordingly. To the Federalists' surprise—itself a sign of how out of touch the party had become—the treaty proved to be popular throughout the country, and, after expected British objections failed to arise, enough Federalists changed their minds to allow a conditional ratification one day before Marshall became chief justice.[63]

The Pinckney Treaty of 1795 had settled the major controversies in American-Spanish relations, but Marshall had to address Spain's violation of U.S. neutral rights and deal with an American breach of the treaty in the Florida region. Spain had allied itself with France in 1796 during the latter's war with Britain. While the Quasi-War was underway, Spain fulfilled its obligation to help France by seizing American vessels, allowing French consuls in Spanish territory to confiscate those ships unlawfully, and outfitting privateers that sailed under French commissions and harried American shipping. Marshall advised Adams that these "enormous abuses & injuries" required "a very serious remonstrance," and he firmly instructed the American minister in Madrid, David Humphreys, to affirm U.S. neutral rights and call on the Spanish king to abide by Spain's agreements with it. Marshall's demand was a pure assertion of principle; the American navy, busy countering the French in the Caribbean, was not able to take on the Spanish fleet at the same time. Ultimately, the United States would have had to fall back on the British line if wider naval hostilities broke out. Given Anglo-American tensions then, Marshall's and Adams's position was something of a gamble. The controversy faded with the Convention of 1800 and the end of the European wars.[64]

Marshall apparently calculated that trying to conciliate with Madrid on neutral rights by helping it suppress an Indian insurgency in Spanish Florida would send the wrong signal. An adventurer named William Augustus Bowles wanted to establish an independent Indian state in Florida, and after a force of Creeks under his command captured a Spanish fort in early 1800, he united several other tribes in his cause. Bowles's actions—which the Spanish believed had British backing—violated article 5 of the Pinckney Treaty, by which the United States and Spain agreed to maintain peace and harmony among the Indians in the Florida region. Adams wanted to send American troops there to help the Spanish fight the Indians, but Marshall convinced him that the presence of a U.S. force in Florida would raise Spanish suspicions. Bowles's filibustering subsided, but the matter of Florida was not resolved until Spain renounced its claims in the area in the Adams-Onís treaty of 1819.[65]

Marshall found carrying out American treaty obligations to the extortionist Barbary states of North Africa to be personally frustrating and politically demeaning, but all he could do was swallow his pride and put up with what one historian has called the "bribes, tributes, insults, [and] haggles." By 1799, the United States had ratified pacts with Algiers, Tripoli, and Tunis that cost it $1,000,000 up front and traded later payments of money, military supplies, and jewels for "protection" for American shipping. Marshall often found himself diverted from matters of greater import to implement those agreements. For example, he spent many hours trying to get a reliable accounting of what the United States owed the Barbary states, looking for a source of gems for the Bey of Tunis, and arranging for the purchase and transport of goods for the North African rulers. At no point did Marshall advise the president to send the Federalist-built navy—either alone or in concert with European countries—to protect American vessels, liberate enslaved American seamen, and put an end to the pirates' shakedown. Although he and Adams found the tributes "exorbitant and unwarrantable," they preferred to act militarily only if provoked; then they would consider aiding a European move against the Barbary states. Until that situation arose, Marshall—drawing on his experience with the Jay Treaty—suggested paying off the North Africans with one last lump sum of nearly $290,000. Congress appropriated $256,000, but Marshall's proposal went no further. The Republicans inherited the Barbary problem and eventually settled it with force.[66]

Besides conducting foreign policy, the State Department at this time had many domestic responsibilities akin to those of a British Home Office, and they took up a fair amount of Marshall's time. He had to concern himself with granting patents and copyrights, issuing passports, taking the census, supervising the Mint, recording land patents, printing and distributing copies of federal laws and government documents, drafting and delivering commissions of appointment to office, overseeing the administration of the territories, and safeguarding the Seal of the United States. The secretary of state also superintended the federal justice system, as the attorney general then had only an advisory role. Marshall instructed federal district attorneys and marshals and corresponded with judges. Moreover, now that the government had moved to Washington, Marshall had the thankless task of monitoring the construction of public buildings and roads in the new capital. Probably the most sensitive aspect of that duty for Marshall was ensuring that the White House was ready for occupancy on time. In addition, Marshall had one ex officio assignment of note while he was secretary. He served on a federal commission that met with counterparts from Georgia to settle the state's boundary dispute with the United States and to receive proposals for partial or total cession of the state's territorial claims. The matter was still unresolved when he left office in May 1801.[67]

Although the XYZ mission supposedly brought Marshall a monetary windfall, his financial situation did not improve during the last few years before he became chief justice. Lack of records, such as an account book, make generalizing about his income and worth difficult, but Marshall apparently acquired no important new assets—personal property lists for 1797–1801 show him with a few horses and coaches or chariots and about a dozen slaves—and he never rebuilt his law practice to its previous lucrative level. Marshall seems to have lived mainly off the "extra" money he received from his diplomatic service. He received several thousand pounds from selling off most of the 56,000-acre South Branch Manor of the Fairfax lands, but he had to obligate that money to fulfill his contract to buy the former proprietary's prize tract, the 106,000-acre Leeds Manor. By spring 1800, Marshall's financial prospects were sufficiently uncertain that the $5,000 annual salary for a cabinet post was a powerful inducement for him to accept President Adams's nomination as secretary of state.[68]

Marshall never resumed a full-time law practice after returning from Paris because of the distractions of politics and public service. "[O]n becoming a candidate for Congress I was given up as a lawyer, and considered generally as entirely a political man," he recalled. When he returned to Richmond after Congress adjourned in May 1800, he found potential clients reluctant to engage him because he would have to abandon their suits when he left for Washington for the winter House session. Because of this perception that he was no longer committed to the legal profession, Marshall got few new cases and spent most of his time handling continuances or appeals of old ones. Moreover, he was solicited for advice much less frequently in the late 1790s, and his correspondence for those years contains far fewer exchanges with friends and associates on legal matters.[69]

What remained of Marshall's practice had most of the same characteristics as in preceding years. It involved almost exclusively civil litigation, most originating in disputes over commercial property and contracts, land titles, wills, and debts. A few members of Virginia's first families were among his clients, and he worked with and against Thomas Jefferson in separate suits. Some of his cases involved British merchants' claims against Virginians, but as a result of article six of the Jay Treaty, most of those disputes went before the Anglo-American arbitration commission. Marshall's cases were heard in state and federal courts in Richmond; unlike in earlier times, he did not have to travel to county and state district courts outside the capital. His argumentation, particularly the simplification of complex facts into one or two basic points and the discernment of the fundamental points of law at issue, was as effective as ever.[70]

The most noteworthy case Marshall was involved with during the late 1790s concerned slavery and provides the best evidence against simplistic generalizations that he unalterably defended and legitimized the "peculiar institution."[71] *Pleasants v. Pleasants* (1799) provided a classic test between the laws of property and the right to liberty. The case originated in a will, executed in 1771, directing that the more than 400 bequeathed slaves of John Pleasants be freed at age 30 if state law so allowed. In 1782, the General Assembly passed a law authorizing private manumission, but Pleasants's legatees did not release their slaves at the time prescribed in the will. The estate's executor, Robert Pleasants, a Quaker and antislavery activist, unsuccessfully petitioned the Assembly on the slaves' behalf in 1790 and 1791 and soon after filed suit in the High Court of Chancery. In 1798, Chancellor George Wythe, who had strong antislavery views, handed down an unprecedentedly broad decision in the slaves' favor, which the Pleasants legatees quickly appealed.[72]

Marshall joined the litigation at this point as one of Robert Pleasants's two attorneys. Marshall had represented Pleasants in a British debt suit in the early 1790s. In November 1798, he and his colleague John Warden argued against Edmund Randolph and John Wickham at the Court of Appeals in Richmond. Marshall, typically, spoke last. Probably having concluded that Wythe's moralistic decree would not stand in full, he avoided idealistic rhetoric and relied on narrow legal points to support the will's terms. The key issue he had to address in this complicated case was whether the common law rule against "perpetuities"—conditions that prevented inheritance from occurring beyond a reasonable time—applied when the slaves themselves became heirs of an "estate" of freedom at age thirty. Marshall contended that slaves had a legally enforceable right of inheritance. The judges—Spencer Roane, Paul Carrington, and Edmund Pendleton—took several months to reach a decision that showed Marshall's strategy had been sound. In May 1799, they delivered three opinions that together affirmed the validity of John Pleasants's will while sharply curtailing the more far-reaching aspects of Wythe's decree. Marshall accordingly may also have taken away from the case the lesson that judicial self-restraint, especially on controversial topics, can help enhance judicial power.[73]

Marshall's arguments and the Court of Appeals ruling typify his cautious, temperate approach to the issue of slavery. The human tragedy touched him, as when he represented slaves, evidently pro bono, in three suits for freedom before the court of appeals. In another instance, he showed a reluctance to break up slave families. During an estate suit, he offered a narrow interpretation of inheritance law that would have prevented the sale of slaves to pay a testator's debts. He also wanted to limit the residual power slavery could exert over the free black. In the Assembly he worked on a bill to punish the stealing of free persons or selling them as slaves, and he opposed a measure requiring emancipated slaves to leave the state within a year and authorizing the sale of poor free blacks into slavery. At the same time, however, Marshall sometimes represented the masters' interests, as in a 1795 suit for freedom, and in Congress he voted against debating the slave trade or altering the fugitive slave law to prevent "disquiet and jealousy." Marshall, then, had the same attitude toward slavery as many of his fellow Virginians in the late eighteenth century. He harbored a long-range hope that slavery might disappear, but he never held any illusions about that coming to pass. He did not believe the legal system was the appropriate venue for decreeing emancipation, but he did agree that freedom could be dispensed one step at a time as the case warranted, adhering to principles of law and to precedent and avoiding reasoning that might, as Judge Roane wrote in his opinion in *Pleasants*, "agitate and convulse the Commonwealth to its center." The Gabriel insurrection plot that seized Richmond and vicinity in 1800 could only have reinforced Marshall's resolve to follow that carefully measured course.[74]

The usually good-humored Marshall became more dispirited throughout the year 1800 as the Federalists' prospects for retaining power dimmed.[75] The dismal Virginia House of Delegates session in the winter of 1799–1800 had driven home to him how fleeting the Federalist resurgence after the XYZ affair had been, and presaged many of the problems the party would encounter during the election year. The Federalists in the Assembly lost every major legislative battle. The determined Republican majority swept aside feeble opposition and purged Federalists from the offices of governor, speaker, and clerk; adopted Madison's defense of the Virginia Resolutions, the *Virginia Report*; passed resolutions protesting the expansion of the standing army and the taxes to pay for it, and the application of the English common law in America; and changed the state's election rules to their advantage by switching from a district to a winner-take-all system. The last measure deprived Adams of any chance to win electors from Virginia.[76]

The Virginia Federalists' weakness became even clearer after the spring 1800 state elections. According to James Monroe, at least 25 Federalists lost their seats to staunch Republicans. Most painfully for Marshall, his party could not even hold on to his congressional seat in a special election held after he became secretary of state. "Ill news from Virginia," he reported to Harrison Gray Otis. "To succeed me has been elected by an immense majority one of the most decided democrats in the union." Littleton Waller Tazewell, an arch-Jeffersonian, had trounced John Mayo by a margin three times larger than Marshall's in 1799. The Federalists' stature had fallen so far in the Old Dominion that the state organization would not even use the party's name; its slate of electors was called "The American Republican Ticket." "What survived the [state] election of 1800 was an unorganized handful of assemblymen, whose Federalist voting habits originated more from western sectionalism and ethnic interests than party ideals," according to Norman K. Risjord. These depressing developments led Marshall, the only Federalist left with a statewide reputation, to observe that "[t]here is a tide in the affairs of nations, of parties, & of individuals. I fear that of real Americanism is on the ebb."[77]

Even though Marshall was either in Washington or Richmond throughout the "campaign," he took no active part in party machinations. Apparently he was too busy with his diplomatic duties, or he had decided that a Federalist defeat was inevitable, or that taking sides in the party infighting between Hamiltonians and Adamsites would be too divisive. He evidently did not try to encourage contact between Federalist leaders in the north and in Virginia, and his only involvement in party maneuvers was involuntary. At the congressional Federalists' caucus in Philadelphia in April—where the scheme to deny the presidency to Adams was devised—Charles Cotesworth Pinckney proposed that Marshall be the party's vice presidential candidate. The South Carolinian contended that Marshall could win more votes in Virginia than any other Federalist. Party members from the mid-Atlantic region did not like the idea, however, and Marshall would not have aided a plan disloyal to Adams. Pinckney then agreed to run in the number two slot.[78]

Perhaps Marshall's chief, albeit somewhat passive, contribution to the Federalist effort was serving as a conciliator and opponent of extremism within the party, as he had tried to do in Congress. He believed the Federalists could avoid a fatal split only by supporting the policies of the Adams administration, no matter how much they despised the president himself. He told at least one correspondent that Hamilton's splenetic against Adams's conduct and character should "never [have] been seen by any person." (Hamilton intended that the pamphlet would circulate privately among Federalists, but somehow Burr got a copy and gave it to a Republican newspaper, with predictable results.) Evidence is scanty, but Marshall appears to have had some success in restraining the president from further attacking the Hamiltonians after the cabinet shake-up in May. For Adams's last State of the Union address in November, Marshall wrote a draft stressing unity and recounting the Federalists' domestic and foreign accomplishments since 1789. Lastly, in an incongruous display of party loyalty, Marshall's anyone-but-Jefferson attitude prevented him from disavowing the High Federalists' plan to supplant Adams with Pinckney. He may have decided that the Federalists' last, best chance lay in harmony, and, in the perverse politics of 1800, that meant tacitly going along with a political conspiracy which had an outside chance of denying Jefferson the presidency. He may also have thought that not enough moderate Federalists would desert Adams for Pinckney to make the plan work, so he did not have to do anything to stop it. Marshall surely knew, though, that if the plan failed, it would complete the Federalists' self-destruction and deliver the Republicans a free gift of victory.[79]

Some Hamiltonians appreciated Marshall's attempts to keep the Federalists together. Theodore Sedgwick, for example, wrote that "there is not a man in the U.S. of better intentions [than Marshall] and he has the confidence of all good men—no man regrets more than he does the disunion which has taken place and no one would do more to heal the wounds inflicted by it. . . . [But] his efforts will . . . prove ineffectual." Sedgwick's prediction came true largely because Marshall and the Federalists faced a host of other problems besides factionalism, some of them affecting Marshall and his associates in the party's southern wing. By 1800, many southern Federalists who were Adams's chief allies against the Yankee extremists had, under the influence of heightened sectional suspicion, sided with Hamilton and the vice presidential candidate from South Carolina, Charles Cotesworth Pinckney. In addition, the ideological limitations of the southern Federalists became more apparent during the campaign. Although successful up to then, their "democratic" tactics could no longer conceal their commitment to elitist government by the "worthy." Lastly, saddled with an unpopular incumbent, southern Federalists tried to evade the problem of Adams by ignoring him, crediting "[o]ur government" with achieving peace and prosperity and defending the Constitution, and trying to scare the voters with charges of Republican radicalism and irreligion.[80]

Marshall generally seemed to have been aware of the Federalists' deep-seated difficulties, but he could not resist the understandable temptation to look for superficial answers—"I believe . . . much of the strength of jacobinism is attributable to the direct tax [to support the army]—[it is] a snare which has been long set for the federalists & in which they have at length permitted themselves to be taken"—or to grasp at straw hopes, such as a procedural deadlock in Pennsylvania that might leave "our case . . . not absolutely desperate." But by late October he had given up. "I pray devoutly (which is no very common practice with me), that the future administration may do as little harm as the present & the past."[81] The Federalists got no boost from the Convention of 1800, for news of the settlement did not arrive until December— too late to affect balloting for electors. (The accord might have benefited the

Federalists when the House deliberated over the Burr-Jefferson tie, but more intraparty fighting eliminated that possibility.)

All states had completed the months-long voting process by December, and the final tabulation put Jefferson and Burr in a tie with 73 votes each; Adams finished third with 65; Pinckney came in fourth with 64; and Jay received one. The outcome was closer than the pessimistic Marshall had expected. He may have based his forecast on the trends in Virginia, which held its election in early November using the at-large system the Republicans had pushed through the previous spring. Jefferson defeated Adams by approximately 21,000 to 6,000— a margin greater than the two-to-one majority the Republicans held in the assembly—despite an active local Federalist organization, an aggressive partisan press, and invocations of the cult of Washington. The president led in scarcely half a dozen of the state's 94 counties, and even there won mainly because of the electors' own prestige, not his or the party's appeal. The Federalists narrowly lost Richmond and barely won the commercial hub of Norfolk.[82]

In January, the House of Representatives prepared to assume its constitutional duty to break the Jefferson-Burr deadlock. "I take no part & feel no interest" in the election outcome, Marshall claimed. "Having myself no voice in the election, and in fact scarcely any wish concerning it, I do not intermeddle with it." He did not mean to say that he did not care who won, but rather that he could not bring himself to choose between Burr and Jefferson. He was as ambivalent as the election returns. At first, he considered Jefferson and Burr "a choice of evils" and was "really . . . uncertain who would be the greatest," but he seemed influenced by the fact that most observers around him preferred the New Yorker. "It is not beleivd that he woud weaken the vital parts of the constitution, nor is it beleivd that he has any undue foreign attachments." When Hamilton sought Marshall's support for Jefferson, he declined. He expressed "almost insuperable objections" to his cousin the vice president.

His foreign prejudices seem to me totally to unfit him for the chief magistracy of a nation which cannot indulge those prejudices without sustaining deep & permanent injury. In addition . . . Mr. Jefferson appears to me to be a man who will embody himself with the house of representatives. By weakening the office of President he will increase his personal power. He will diminish his responsibility, [and] sap the fundamental principles of the government. . . . The Morals of the Author of the letter to Mazzei cannot be pure.

Based on what Hamilton had told him, Marshall concluded that Burr was "more to be feard & may do more immediate if not greater mischief," but he could not work for Jefferson's election. By refusing to endorse either candidate, Marshall also hoped to preserve his reputation by squelching rumors that Burr intended to keep him on as secretary of state in return for his backing.[83]

Despite Marshall's studied neutrality, other equally baseless rumors circulated in Washington that he was part of a Federalist intrigue to prevent the Republicans from winning the presidency. Some suspicious Republicans— among them Jefferson, Gallatin, and Monroe—accused him of suggesting that if the House of Representatives divided evenly between Jefferson and Burr, the full Congress could break the deadlock by appointing someone else, perhaps John Jay or even Marshall himself. Marshall did not respond to demands that he disavow the "plot," discussion of which was soon overtaken by events in the House, where the Federalists were "play[ing] their most desperate game yet" by trying to organize enough votes to elect Burr. After 36 ballots over six days of continuous voting, which ended only when one representative from Delaware withdrew his vote, Jefferson was elected president and Burr vice president.[84]

The election of 1800 left the Federalist Party broken and demoralized, at least temporarily, as the first national transfer of political power in the history of the republic removed from control of the executive and legislative branches the leaders who claimed to have created that republic and to have preserved and protected it though the trials of its turbulent infancy. The outcome also spelled the end of Federalism in Virginia as an organized political force. The party retained strength in the west, but it had lost its center of influence in Richmond and the Tidewater and had little sway in the state government in subsequent years. Many Federalists in the Old Dominion left politics, or intended to. Even before the final outcome, Marshall had planned to stay in Washington only until the change of administrations and then return to Richmond to his law practice and his family. "If my present wish can succeed," he wrote to Pinckney, "I shall never again fill any political station whatever." One day in mid-February, however, John Adams had a different idea.[85]

John Adams had offered John Marshall a seat on the Supreme Court in 1798 but evidently had not thought about appointing his secretary of state to replace Chief Justice Oliver Ellsworth until their meeting in the White House on 19 January 1801. Adams took rather a gamble in selecting Marshall again, as he could not be sure the Senate would confirm his nominee before the Judiciary Act of 1801 went into effect and prevented him from making an appointment. Still, the president was satisfied that he had chosen a reliable nationalist and "a gentleman in the full vigor of middle age in the full habits of business and whose reading in the science [of law] is fresh in his head."[86]

Marshall recalled years later feeling "unfeignedly gratified" when Adams offered him the chief justiceship. One can understand that he might have felt flattered that the president had called on him in a time of dire trouble to fill a position of potentially great influence. One can as easily appreciate his feeling perturbed at the prospect of being burdened with the leadership of an as yet constitutionally inferior branch; facing the stresses of circuit riding; spending long periods away from his home, sick wife, and children; and earning less than he could from practicing law. His reluctance might be evident in the fact that he did not officially communicate his acceptance to Adams for two weeks. During that time, Marshall probably gauged the political impact of his appointment, especially the chances that it might get caught up in Federalist feuding or become a target of Republican attacks—either of which would have caused the Supreme Court's already low prestige to suffer. On the other side, he may have considered that, except for a few months each year when the court was in session or he was riding circuit, he would be free to work on the biography of George Washington he had agreed to write.[87]

One key reason why Marshall agreed to become chief justice appears to have been his intention to use the Supreme Court as a counterweight to the Republicans, who would soon dominate the other branches of the federal government. Marshall and the Federalists had accepted defeat and peacefully transferred power to their political enemies, not because they considered the Jeffersonians a legitimate opposition, but because they believed failure to relinquish office would violate the whole American experiment in republican government. That said, the Federalists would use whatever influence they had—and they were well entrenched in the national judiciary—to rally their supporters and return their party to its rightful place. A strong Supreme Court and a determined chief justice were essential if the judiciary were to accomplish its part in that daunting task. "In 1801," Robert Wiebe has written, the Supreme Court "stood high but exposed, a vulnerable salient whose authority could have been neutralized by a little legislative pruning and a lot of Republican indifference." Now Marshall and the Federalists had the opportunity to prevent that from happening, and their key agency would be the chief justiceship—a void waiting to be filled by a man with the right combination of conviction, intellect, political astuteness, and personality. Marshall, whose friendliness and self-effacement concealed a resolute will and deep self-confidence, believed he was that man.[88]

Probably most compelling for Marshall, though, was a deeper motive: the opportunity to shape the nation's constitutional development by giving substance and force to its highest court, to look "beyond the confines of strict law to the needs of a vigorous nation entered upon the task of occupying a continent," in Bernard Schwartz's words. Marshall would be able with his own hand and mind to fill in America's constitutional outline and provide "the transfiguring thought that the judge normally is not called upon to impose on society." The appointment offered him a lofty and spacious mission that he must have seen as a near-perfect consummation of his public life up to then. A man with Marshall's formative genius could not fail to perceive the immense implications of the occasion. It presented him with the best opportunity to act on his commitment to shaping American society according to the values he had derived from the Revolution and the founding period. As with many other members of the revolutionary generation, he was extremely conscious of the difference he had made in forming the society in which he lived. His sense of "firstness" was acute, and for him politics was highly personalized. Having been through the creation of the republic in the Revolution and its renovation when the Constitution was written and ratified, he was now afforded the responsibility for preserving it—a duty he could not in good conscience forswear for any personal or transient reasons.[89]

Adams sent Marshall's nomination to the Senate on 20 January.[90] It met some disorganized resistance from Hamiltonians, who delayed confirmation for a

234 A CHIEF JUSTICE'S PROGRESS

week while they tried to persuade Adams to choose Associate Justice William Paterson instead. What Senator Jonathan Dayton described as the High Federalists' "grief, astonishment, & almost indignation" had two sources. First, they questioned Marshall's loyalty to the party and doubted how reliably he would implement Federalist orthodoxy from the bench. They complained that he was too faithful to Adams and too independent-minded to be trusted. Second, the Hamiltonians had expected Adams to appoint Paterson and interpreted his selection of Marshall as yet another aspersion cast upon their judgment.

Dayton attributed Adams's decision to "debility or derangement of intellect" and led a compromise effort to persuade him to pick Paterson for chief justice and Marshall for the vacated associate's seat. Adams refused, and the Hamiltonians had to relent. They realized that Marshall was the best they would get from Adams—or, as Dayton put it, "lest another not so well qualified and more disgusting to the Bench, should be substituted"—and wanted to approve a nomination before the judiciary bill was reported out of committee. The Republicans were oddly muted throughout the brief debate over Marshall's nomination, and even afterward only the vituperative *Aurora* and the libelous James Callender had much to say about it. On 27 January, the Senate unanimously confirmed Marshall as the fourth chief justice.

NOTES

1. JM to Timothy Pickering, 18 June 1798, *PJM*, 3:467; addresses from the Gloucester County, N.J., grand jury and militia to JM, and his replies, 22 and 25 June 1798, *PJM*, 3:468–71; Thomas Jefferson to James Madison, 21 June 1798, in *The Writings of Thomas Jefferson*, ed. Paul Leicester Ford, 10 vols. (New York: G. P. Putnam's Sons, 1892–99), 8:439–40; Albert J. Beveridge, *The Life of John Marshall*, 4 vols. (Boston: Houghton Mifflin, 1916–19), 2:344–45, 348–50; Leonard Baker, *John Marshall: A Life in Law* (New York: Macmillan, 1974), 283–84; David Loth, *Chief Justice John Marshall and the Growth of the Republic* (New York: Greenwood Press, 1949), 140–41; Frances N. Stites, *John Marshall: Defender of the Constitution* (Boston: Little, Brown, 1981), 65; Jean Smith, *John Marshall: Definer of a Nation* (New York: Henry Holt, 1996), 234–36.

2. *PJM*, 3:475–84; Beveridge, *Marshall*, 2:351–54; Nancy M. Merz, "The XYZ Affair and the Congressional Election of 1799 in Richmond, Virginia" (M.A. thesis, College of William and Mary, 1973), 13–14. A recent study of how the XYZ effusions fit into a broader political and social context that melded local and national concerns—and continued the elitist Federalists' paradoxical, but politically necessary, employment of "the people out of doors" as allies—is David Waldstreicher, *In the Midst of Perpetual Fetes: The Making of American Nationalism, 1776–1820* (Chapel Hill: University of North Carolina Press, 1997), chaps. 2–3 generally and 160 on the XYZ Affair (though Marshall's triumphal return is not mentioned). See also Rosemarie Zagarri, "Festive Nationalism and Antiparty Partyism," *Reviews in American History*, 26 (1998), 504–9.

Polly had given birth to their fourth child, John, on 13 January, three days after her father, Jaquelin Ambler, had died. Her grief slowed her recovery from the difficult labor and may have caused a nervous collapse by early spring. She went to Winchester to recuperate at the home of one of Marshall's sisters, and Marshall met her there on 28 June. The family spent the next several weeks together. Polly was still not well enough to accompany Marshall when he left for Richmond on 3 August with his new son. *PJM*, 3:468 n. 3, 486 n. 9; JM to George Washington, 22 June 1798, *PJM*, 3:468; JM to Polly, 18 August 1798, *PJM*, 3:486–87 and n. 3; Beveridge, *Marshall*, 2:371 n. 1; Frances Norton Mason, *My Dearest Polly: Letters of Chief Justice John Marshall to His Wife . . .* (Richmond: Garrett and Massie, 1961), 113–23.

3. Sources for this paragraph and the next are John W. Kuehl, "The Quest for Identity in an Age of Insecurity: The XYZ Affair and American Nationalism" (Ph.D. diss., University of Wisconsin, 1968), chaps. 3–5; Alexander DeConde, *The Quasi-War: The Politics and Diplomacy of the Undeclared War with France, 1797–1801* (New York: Charles Scribner's Sons, 1966), 59–108; Stephen G. Kurtz, *The Presidency of John Adams: The Collapse of Federalism, 1795–1800* (rept., New York: A.S. Barnes and Co., 1961), chap. 13; Ralph Adams Brown, *The Presidency of John Adams* (Lawrence: University Press of Kansas, 1975), chap. 5; Stanley Elkins and Eric McKitrick, *The Age of Federalism* (New York: Oxford University Press, 1993), 581–99; Gerard H. Clarfield, *Timothy Pickering and American Diplomacy, 1795–1800* (Columbia: University of Missouri Press, 1969), chap. 8; Richard Buel, Jr., *Securing the Revolution: Ideology in American Politics, 1789–1815* (Ithaca: Cornell University Press, 1972), 163–83; Page Smith, *John Adams*, 2 vols. (Garden City, N.Y.: Doubleday and Co., 1962), 2:952–74; Beveridge, *Marshall*, 2:339–43, 351; John Bach McMaster, *A History of the People of the United States from the Revolution to the Civil War*, 8 vols. (New York: Appleton and Co., 1921), 2:376–87; Thomas M. Ray, "'Not One Cent for Tribute': The Public Addresses and American Popular Reaction to the XYZ Affair, 1798–1799," *JER*, 3 (1983), 401–02; Washington to James McHenry, 4 March 1798, *The Writings of George Washington*, ed. John C. Fitzpatrick, 39 vols. (Washington: Government Printing Office, 1931–44), 36:179; Pickering to JM, 24 July 1798, *PJM*, 3:475; *PJM*, 3:274 n. 4.

4. John Stokes Adams, ed., *An Autobiographical Sketch by John Marshall* (Ann Arbor: University of Michigan Press, 1937), 25 (hereafter cited at JM, *Autobiographical Sketch*); *PJM*, 3:475 n. 9; address from and response to Gloucester County, N.J., militia, 25 July 1798, *PJM*, 3:470–71; Elkins and McKitrick, *Age of Federalism*, 596; William Stinchcombe, *The XYZ Affair* (Westport, Conn.: Greenwood Press, 1980), 120; Kurtz, *Presidency of Adams*, 339–40; Smith, *Adams*, 2:971; Lisle A. Rose, *Prologue to Democracy: The Federalists in the South, 1789–1800* (Lexington: University of Kentucky Press, 1968), 200–201; Jefferson to James Madison, 21 June 1798, and to Pendleton, 29 January 1799, *Writings of Jefferson*, 8:439, 9:27. Jefferson got much of his intelligence on Marshall's views from Edward Livingston, who shared the coach Marshall rode from New York to Philadelphia. Marshall must have known that Livingston, one of Jefferson's political allies, would report all he heard to the Republican leader and presumably saw this as a chance to get his message across through an interlocutor his rivals would trust. Smith, *Marshall*, 235.

5. Sources for this paragraph and the next are JM, *Autobiographical Sketch*, 25–26; JM to James K. Paulding, 4 April 1835, in John E. Oster, *The Political and Economic Doctrines of John Marshall* (orig. publ. 1914; rept., New York: Burt Franklin, 1967), 190–92; JM to Pickering, 11 April 1798, *PJM*, 3:485–86; "Congressional Election Campaign: Editorial Note," *PJM*, 3:494–95; Merz, "XYZ Affair and Congressional Election of 1799 in Richmond," 16–17; Beveridge, *Marshall*, 2:374–79; Smith, *Marshall*, 240–41; *Diaries of George Washington, 1748–1799*, ed. John C. Fitzpatrick, 4 vols. (Boston: Houghton Mifflin, 1925), 4:283–84; Washington to Bushrod

Washington, 27 August 1798, in *Writings of Washington*, 36:420; JM to Washington, 8 January 1799, *PJM*, 4:4.

6. Rose, *Prologue to Democracy*, 139, 143–48, 154–57, 161–62, 165–72, 187–88, 191–97; Richard R. Beeman, *The Old Dominion and the New Nation, 1788–1801* (Lexington: University Press of Kentucky, 1972), 176–79; Norman K. Risjord and Gordon DenBoer, "The Evolution of Political Parties in Virginia, 1782–1800," *JAH*, 60 (1973–74), 981; Norman K. Risjord, *Chesapeake Politics, 1782–1800* (New York: Columbia University Press, 1978), 535; Buel, *Securing the Revolution*, 230–31; Kurtz, *Presidency of Adams*, chap. 3; Pickering to JM, 24 July 1798, *PJM*, 4:475; Merz, "XYZ Affair and Congressional Election of 1799 in Richmond," 21; Ray, "'Not One Cent for Tribute,'" 401–2. Cf. the main themes of Southern Federalist ideology with its northern counterpart, as described in James M. Banner Jr., *To the Hartford Convention: The Federalists and the Origins of Party Politics in Massachusetts, 1789–1815* (New York: Alfred A. Knopf, 1970), chap. 1; John C. Miller, *The Federalist Era, 1789–1801* (New York: Harper and Row, 1960), 108–22; and Linda K. Kerber, *Federalists in Dissent: Imagery and Ideology in Jeffersonian America* (Ithaca: Cornell University Press, 1970), esp. chap. 6. After 1800, Southern Federalists started sounding more like their Yankee compatriots; see Kerber, *Federalists in Dissent*, and James H. Broussard, *The Southern Federalists, 1800–1816* (Baton Rouge: Louisiana State University Press, 1978), chap. 21, esp. 307–13.

7. Donald O. Dewey, *Marshall versus Jefferson: The Political Background of Marbury v. Madison* (New York: Alfred A. Knopf, 1970), 39; Edmund Randolph to James Madison, 8 January 1798, in *The Papers of James Madison*, ed. William T. Hutchinson et al., 17 vols. (Chicago: University of Chicago Press, 1962–91), 16:450; Smith, *Marshall*, 242; Elkins and McKitrick, *Age of Federalism*, 581–618; Kurtz, *Presidency of Adams*, chap. 14; Brown, *Presidency of Adams*, chap. 10; Risjord, *Chesapeake Politics*, 541; Myron F. Wehtje, "The Congressional Elections of 1799 in Virginia," *West Virginia History*, 29 (1968), 252–59.

8. Merz, "XYZ Affair and Congressional Election of 1799 in Richmond," 17–19, 22–23; *Dictionary of American Biography*, 4:230–31, s.v. "Clopton, John"; Anthony Upton, "The Road to Power in Virginia in the Early Nineteenth Century," *VMHB*, 62 (1954), 263–64; "Congressional Election Campaign: Editorial Note," *PJM*, 3:496, 499 n. 2; Rudolph M. Bell, *Party and Faction in American Politics: The House of Representatives, 1789–1801* (Westport, Conn.: Greenwood Press, 1973), 8.

9. JM to Pickering, 1 and 15 October 1798, JM to Washington, 1 May 1799, *PJM*, 3:511, 516, 4:12; JM, *Autobiographical Sketch*, 26; Jefferson to James Monroe, 26 March 1800, quoted in Noble E. Cunningham Jr., *The Jeffersonian Republicans: The Formation of Party Organization, 1789–1801* (Chapel Hill: University of North Carolina Press, 1957), 139; Beveridge, *Marshall*, 2:409; Baker, *Marshall*, 312; Smith, *Marshall*, 248; Patrick Henry to Archibald Blair, 8 January 1799, in William Wirt Henry, *Patrick Henry: Life, Correspondence, and Speeches*, 3 vols. (New York: Charles Scribner's Sons, 1891), 2:591–94.

10. JM to Washington, 8 January 1799, JM to James Markham Marshall, 3 April 1799, *PJM*, 4:4, 10; Wehtje, "Congressional Elections of 1799 in Virginia," 261.

11. JM to Pickering, 11 August 1798, *PJM*, 3:485.

12. "From a Freeholder" and "To a Freeholder," 19 and 20 September 1798, *PJM*, 3:502–6. See also JM to Pickering, 11 August 1798, *PJM*, 3:485, in which Marshall wrote that he was "extremely sorry" that "a great many well meaning men" thought the laws were unconstitutional.

13. Marshall had been involved with at least two civil libel cases—one as an attorney in 1790, the other as an advisor to a colleague in 1794—but did not participate in any criminal libel suits. *Lewis v. Dicken* (1790), *PJM*, 2:56–57; JM to Archibald Stuart, 28 May 1794, *PJM*, 2:267–68, and to Washington, 8 January 1799, *PJM*, 4:3. Two studies of the Sedition Act that represent the Federalist and Jeffersonian views, respectively, are Leonard Levy, *Emergence of a Free Press* (New York: Oxford University Press, 1985), and James Morton Smith, *Freedom's Fetters: The Alien and Sedition Laws and American Civil Liberties* (Ithaca: Cornell University Press, 1956).

14. Baker, *Marshall*, 306–7; Smith, *Marshall*, 244, 246, 600 ns. 67, 70. Marshall never seems to have thought through the problem of the Sedition Act and displayed a somewhat muddled view of it even two years later. In an exchange of letters with St. George Tucker over the prosecution of Jeffersonian "journalist" James Callender, Marshall claimed that the president had no influence over such prosecutions (even though the district attorneys who brought such cases served at his pleasure), said he privately opposed the move against Callender as politically maladroit, and hinted that he now might have some reservations about the Act's constitutionality (without explaining why he changed his mind). Letters of 6 and 8 November 1800, *PJM*, 6:4–5, 14–15. See also Richard Hofstadter, *The Idea of a Party System: The Rise of Legitimate Opposition in the United States, 1780–1840* (Berkeley: University of California Press, 1969), 106–9.

15. JM to Pickering, 22 October 1798, *PJM*, 3:520; "Congressional Campaign: Editorial Note," *PJM*, 3:497; Merz, "XYZ Affair and Congressional Election of 1799 in Richmond," 29–32; Smith, *Marshall*, 600 n. 68.

16. Beveridge, *Marshall*, 2:389–93; Smith, *Marshall*, 244–45; Fisher Ames to Christopher Gore, 18 December 1798, in *Works of Fisher Ames . . .*, ed. Seth Ames, 2 vols. (Boston: Little, Brown, 1854), 1:246; Merz, "XYZ Affair and Congressional Election of 1799 in Richmond," 33–34; Winfred E. Bernhard, *Fisher Ames: Federalist and Statesman, 1758–1808* (Chapel Hill: University of North Carolina Press, 1965), 278. Some more perceptive Federalists, such as Cabot and Pickering, recognized the realities of Virginia politics. After some reflection, the former wrote that "Some allowance . . . should be made for the influence of the Atmosphere of Virginia which doubtless makes everyone who breathes it visionary &, upon the subject of Free Govt., incredibly credulous; but it is certain that Marshall at Philadelphia would become a most powerful auxiliary to the cause of order and good government, and therefore we ought not to diminish his fame which would ultimately be a loss to ourselves." Cabot to Rufus King, 26 April 1799, in Charles R. King, *The Life and Correspondence of Rufus King*, 6 vols. (New York: G. P. Putnam's Sons, 1894–1900), 3:9. The Republicans, through imitation, conceded the effectiveness of Marshall's approach; Clopton's supporters used the same public-letter technique to spread their candidate's views. Beeman, *Old Dominion and New Nation*, 205; Merz, "XYZ Affair and Congressional Election of 1799 in Richmond," 29. Marshall's exchange of letters with Pickering, 4, 15, and 18 October 1798, is in *PJM*, 3:512, 516–18.

17. JM to Washington, 8 January 1799, *PJM*, 4:4; "Congressional Election Campaign: Editorial Note," *PJM*, 3:498–99 and n. 1; Baker, *Marshall*, 309–10; Beveridge, *Marshall*, 2:402, 405–6; Sedgwick to King, 20 March 1799, *Life and Correspondence of King*, 2:581; Beeman, *Old Dominion and New Nation*, 196–98; Rose, *Prologue to Democracy*, 190, 213–15; Risjord, *Chesapeake Politics*, 539–41; Kurtz, *Presidency of Adams*, 336–39.

18. Philip G. Davidson, "Virginia and the Alien and Sedition Acts," *AHR*, 36 (1931), 336–42; Buel, *Securing the Revolution*, 219–22; Kurtz, *Presidency of Adams*, 359–66;

Risjord, "Virginia Federalists," 504–5; Wehtje, "Congressional Elections of 1799 in Virginia," 256–57; Smith, *Marshall*, 247 and 601 n. 77.

19. Charles Lee to John Adams, 14 March 1799, in *The Works of John Adams*, ed. Charles Francis Adams, 10 vols. (Boston: Little, Brown, 1856), 8:628; Oliver Wolcott to Fisher Ames, 29 December 1799, in George Gibbs, *Memoirs of the Administrations of Washington and John Adams . . .*, 2 vols. (New York: Van Norden Co., 1846), 2:314; Kurtz, *Presidency of Adams*, 383, 389; Elkins and McKitrick, *Age of Federalism*, 606–7; Rose, *Prologue to Democracy*, 220.

20. Henry to Archibald Blair, 8 January 1799, Henry, *Henry*, 3:592–93; Rose, *Prologue to Democracy*, 216–22; Jefferson to Edmund Pendleton, 22 April 1799, *Writings of Jefferson*, 9:64–65; JM to James Markham Marshall, 3 April 1799, *PJM*, 4:10.

21. "Congressional Election Campaign: Editorial Note," *PJM*, 3:501; Merz, "XYZ Affair and Congressional Election of 1799 in Richmond," 51, 59–60; Beveridge, *Marshall*, 2:413–15; Smith, *Marshall*, 249–50; George Wythe Munford, *The Two Parsons; Cupid's Sports; The Dream; and The Jewels of Virginia* (Richmond: J. D. K. Sleight, 1884), 208–10.

22. Merz, "XYZ Affair and Congressional Election of 1799 in Richmond," 52–54; "Congressional Election Campaign: Editorial Note," *PJM*, 3:501; Norman K. Risjord, "The Virginia Federalists," *JSH*, 33 (1967), 503–4; Jefferson to Tench Coxe, 21 May 1799, *Writings of Jefferson*, 9:69–70; Cunningham, *Jeffersonian Republicans*, 134; Manning J. Dauer, *The Adams Federalists* (Baltimore: Johns Hopkins University Press, 1953), 233; Beeman, *Old Dominion and New Nation*, 209–10; Stinchcombe, *XYZ Affair*, 126–27; Wehtje, "Congressional Elections of 1799 in Virginia," 252, 257; Kuehl, "Quest for Identity," chap. 7; idem, "Southern Reaction to the XYZ Affair: An Incident in the Emergency of American Nationalism," *Kentucky Historical Society Register*, 70 (1972), 21–49; idem, "The XYZ Affair and American Nationalism: Republican Victories in the Middle Atlantic States," *Maryland Historical Magazine*, 67 (1972), 1–20.

23. Rose, *Prologue to Democracy*, 196; Elkins and McKitrick, *Age of Federalism*, 620–21; JM to Washington, 16 May 1799, *PJM*, 4:15; Jefferson to Gerry, 26 Jan 1799, quoted in Kurtz, *Presidency of Adams*, 361.

24. *PJM*, 4:13–31 passim. Thomas Marshall died in 1802. By his will, executed in 1798, John Marshall inherited the family estate in Fauquier County, Oak Hill, and three large land tracts in Kentucky. Irwin S. Rhodes, "John Marshall and the Western Country: The Early Days," *Historical and Philosophical Society of Ohio Bulletin*, 18 (1960), 123 and n. 24.

25. JM to James Markham Marshall, 16 December 1799, *PJM*, 4:45. Polly, six months pregnant, accompanied Marshall. Their eighth child, James Keith Marshall, was born in February.

26. Elkins and McKitrick, *Age of Federalism*, 24, chap. 15 passim, esp. 691–93; John C. Roche, ed., *John Marshall: Major Opinions and Other Writings* (Indianapolis: Bobbs-Merrill, 1967), xxv; Rose, *Prologue to Democracy*, 237; and, generally, Dauer, *Adams Federalists*; Kurtz, *Presidency of Adams*; Brown, *Presidency of Adams*; and Jean S. Holder, "The John Adams Presidency: War Crisis Leadership in the Early Republic" (Ph.D. diss., The American University, 1983). Oddly, in his autobiography, Marshall slights his congressional service, dispensing with it in a brief paragraph (26–27).

27. Sedgwick to Rufus King, 29 December 1799, and Cabot to King, 20 January 1800, *Life and Correspondence of King*, 3:163, 84; Wolcott to Fisher Ames, 29 December 1799, Gibbs, *Memoirs*, 2:314. See also Sedgwick to King, 26 July 1799, *Life and Correspondence of King*, 3:69: "[Marshall] may and probably will give a tone to the

federal politics South of the Susquehanna. . . . There never has been an instance where the commencement of a political career was so important as that of General Marshall."

28. Elkins and McKitrick, *Age of Federalism*, 615; Samuel Eliot Morison, *The Life and Letters of Harrison Gray Otis*, 2 vols. (Boston: Houghton Mifflin, 1913), 1:165; Brown, *Presidency of Adams*, 166–68.

29. Patrick J. Furlong, "John Rutledge Jr. and the Election of a Speaker of the House in 1799," *WMQ*, 3rd ser., 24 (1967), 432–36; Rose, *Prologue to Democracy*, 232–33; Wolcott to Ames, 29 December 1799, Gibbs, *Memoirs*, 2:314; "Congressional Career: Editorial Note," *PJM*, 4:32 and n. 8; "Address," 6 December 1799, *PJM*, 4:39–43. The New England faction had already punished Rutledge for criticizing the Jay Treaty by defeating his nomination for chief justice but four years later was just as determined to keep him out of the speaker's chair. After three fractious meetings of the party caucus, Rutledge instructed Marshall to withdraw his name in favor of Sedgwick, largely to prevent the Republicans from exploiting the Federalists' infighting to elect their own candidate as speaker.

30. *Annals of Congress*, 6th Cong., 1st sess., 203; "Motion," "Speech," and "Resolutions," 18, 19, and 23 December 1799, *PJM*, 4:46–49; JM, *The Life of George Washington*, 5 vols. (Philadelphia: C. P. Wayne, 1804–7; rept., New York: Chelsea House, 1983), 5:275–81; JM to Charles Hanson, 29 March 1832, Oster, *Political and Economic Doctrines of Marshall*, 60; Bernard Mayo, *Myths and Men* (New York: Harper and Row, 1963), 48–49. Barry Schwartz, *George Washington: The Making of an American Symbol* (New York: Free Press, 1987), chap. 3; Simon P. Newman, "Principles or Men? George Washington and the Political Culture of National Leadership," *JER*, 12 (1992), 477–507; and idem, *Parades and the Politics of the Street: Festive Culture in the Early American Republic* (Philadelphia: University of Pennsylvania Press, 1997), pp. 68–82, describe the popular veneration of Washington that the Federalists hoped to exploit through numerous commemorative rites, symbolic funerals, proclamations of mourning, and memorial orations that soon followed his death. Vice President Jefferson's absence from the official memorial services in Philadelphia surely fed Marshall's antipathy toward his cousin. Dumas Malone, *Jefferson and the Ordeal of Liberty* (Boston: Little, Brown, 1962), 442–43.

31. "Legislative Bill," 6 January 1800, *PJM*, 4:52; "Congressional Career: Editorial Note," *PJM*, 4:34; Charles Warren, *Bankruptcy in United States History* (Cambridge: Harvard University Press, 1935), 10–21; Peter J. Coleman, *Debtors and Creditors in America: Insolvency, Imprisonment for Debt, and Bankruptcy, 1607–1900* (Madison: State Historical Society of Wisconsin, 1974), 3–17; Drew R. McCoy, *The Elusive Republic: Political Economy in Jeffersonian Virginia* (Chapel Hill: University of North Carolina Press, 1980; rept., New York: W. W. Norton, 1982), 178–84; Morton Borden, *The Federalism of James A. Bayard* (Columbia University Studies in the Social Sciences, 1955; rept., New York: AMS Press, 1968), 62–70; Buel, *Securing the Revolution*, 207–8; Sedgwick to King, 11 May 1800, *Life and Correspondence of King*, 3:236; Joseph Dorfman, "John Marshall, Political Economist," in *Chief Justice John Marshall: A Reappraisal*, ed. W. Melville Jones (Ithaca: Cornell University Press, 1956), 132. The 1800 law soon was regarded as an inequitable failure; it did not help small creditors recover debts, but it relieved "plungers, speculators, promoters, and manipulators" of theirs. In 1803, the Republican-controlled Congress repealed the Bankruptcy Act, and no new federal bankruptcy legislation was enacted until 1841. Coleman, *Debtors and Creditors in America*, 20; Warren, *Bankruptcy in U.S. History*, 21.

32. Sedgwick to Henry van Schaak, 15 January 1800, and John Dawson to Madison, 30 March 1800, quoted in Kathryn Turner, "Federalist Policy and the Judiciary Act of

1801," *WMQ*, 3rd ser., 22 (1965), 10 n. 33, and 10–14; pertinent entries from *PJM*, 4:111–12 and 117–18; Elkins and McKitrick, *Age of Federalism*, 64.

33. Wolcott to Ames, 29 December 1799, in Gibbs, *Memoirs*, 2:316; Turner, "Federalist Policy and the Judiciary Act of 1801," 15–22, 27–29.

34. Sources for this paragraph and the next are Richard H. Kohn, *Eagle and Sword: The Federalists and the Creation of the Military Establishment in America, 1783–1802* (New York: Free Press, 1975), 174–75, 219–55, 260–63; Lawrence D. Cress, *Citizens in Arms: The Army and Militia in American Society to the War of 1812* (Chapel Hill: University of North Carolina Press, 1982), 137–49; Kurtz, *Presidency of Adams*, 307–33, 366; Beveridge, *Marshall*, 2:476–81; Arthur A. Ekirch, *The Civilian and the Military: A History of the American Antimilitarist Tradition* (Colorado Springs: Ralph Myles, 1972), 40–42; Elkins and McKitrick, *Age of Federalism*, 714–19, 730–31; *PJM*, 4:33 and n. 4, 53–54 n. 1.

35. Speeches on 7 and 20 January 1800, *PJM*, 4:53–58, 76–78; JM to Charles Dabney, 20 January 1800, and to James Markham Marshall, *PJM*, 4:45, 75–76; Gale Lee Richards, "A Criticism of the Public Speaking of John Marshall Prior to 1801" (Ph.D. diss., University of Iowa, 1950), 260–79. See also *Life of Washington*, 5:273: "America, supplicating for peace, had been spurned with contempt . . . America, in arms, was treated with some respect."

36. Kurtz, *Presidency of Adams*, 366; Beveridge, *Marshall*, 2:445–48; *Annals of Congress*, 6th Cong., 1st sess., 521–22, 623–24, 691–92, 713–16.

37. "Congressional Career: Editorial Note," *PJM*, 4:37; JM to James Markham Marshall, 4 April 1800, *PJM*, 4:121–22; *Annals of Congress*, 6th Cong., 1st sess., 251–55, 369, 395–96, 403–4.

38. Sources for this paragraph and the next are Beveridge, *Marshall*, 2:452–58; Elkins and McKitrick, *Age of Federalism*, 730; Dauer, *Adams Federalists*, 244; Buel, *Securing the Revolution*, 208–9; JM to James Markham Marshall, 4 April 1800, "Amendment," ca. 16 April 1800, and "Committee Report," 25 April 1800, *PJM*, 4:123–24, 128–30, 138–45; "Congressional Career: Editorial Note," *PJM*, 4:136–37; Sedgwick to King, 11 May 1800, *Life and Correspondence of King*, 3:237–38.

39. This discussion is based on Larry D. Cress, "The Jonathan Robbins Incident: Extradition and the Separation of Powers in the Adams Administration," *Essex Institute Historical Collections*, 111 (1975), 99–121; Ruth Wedgwood, "The Revolutionary Martyrdom of Jonathan Robbins," *Yale Law Journal*, 100 (1990), 229–368; Beveridge, *Marshall*, 2:458–75; "Congressional Career: Editorial Note," *PJM*, 4:35–36; Smith, *Marshall*, 258–62.

40. JM to James Markham Marshall, 28 February 1800, *PJM*, 4:81.

41. In September 1799, a long defense of Adams's actions appeared in the *Virginia Federalist*, a Richmond newspaper. Many years later, the piece was attributed to Marshall. It has some similarities in style to Marshall's writings, and it raised, in a preliminary fashion, some of the points he declaimed upon in his House speech. "Communication," ca. 7 September 1799, *PJM*, 4:23–28; Wedgewood, "Revolutionary Martyrdom of Jonathan Robbins," 338.

42. "Speech," 27 February 1800, and "Speech," 7 March 1800, *PJM*, 4:79–80, 82–109. Cress and Wedgewood provide evidence, not readily available in 1799–1800, that Nash probably was the American citizen, Jonathan Robbins, he claimed to be.

43. Richards, "Criticism of Public Speaking of Marshall," 306–50; *Journal of the House of Delegates of the Commonwealth of Virginia* (Richmond: Thomas W. White, 1828), October 1784 sess., 41–42; Francis H. Rudko, *John Marshall and International Law: Statesman and Chief Justice* (New York: Greenwood Press, 1991), 87–89; Benjamin

Ziegler, *The International Law of John Marshall: A Study of First Principles* (Chapel Hill: University of North Carolina Press, 1939), passim; Charles Warren, *The Supreme Court in United States History*, 3 vols. (Boston: Little, Brown, 1922), 1:319–20, 426, 432, 2:40–42.

44. "Amendment," 2 April 1800, "Amendments," 29 April 1800, JM to Reuben George, 16 March 1800, *PJM*, 4:114, 120, 146–47; William B. Hatcher, *Edward Livingston, Jeffersonian Republican and Jacksonian Democrat* (University: Louisiana State University Press, 1940), 52–54; Walter Pincus, "Censure: A Debate with a Past," *Washington Post*, 19 November 1998, A27.

45. Beveridge, *Marshall*, 2:446; "Committee Report" and "Legislative Bill," 21 March 1800, "Speeches," 7 and 8 April 1800, "Legislative Bill," 17 April 1800, *PJM*, 4:115–16, 126, 130; committee report text in Oster, *Political and Economic Doctrines of Marshall*, 205–21; Benjamin Hibbard, *A History of the Public Land Policies* (New York: Macmillan, 1924), 11; Frederick Merk, *History of the Westward Movement* (New York: Alfred A. Knopf, 1978), 114–15; David M. Roth, *Connecticut: A History* (New York: W. W. Norton, 1979), 120.

46. Sedgwick to King, 11 May 1800, *Life and Correspondence of King*, 3:237.

47. Charles Lee to JM, 13 May 1800, and "Commission," 13 May 1800, *PJM*, 4:149 and n. 4.

48. Sources for the background on Marshall's appointment are Brown, *Presidency of Adams*, 168–69; Clarfield, *Pickering and American Diplomacy*, 213–14; Elkins and McKitrick, *Age of Federalism*, 735–36; and Smith, *Adams*, 2:1027–29.

49. JM to Adams, 8 May 1800, *PJM*, 4:148–49; JM, *Autobiographical Sketch*, 27–28.

50. Charles Lee to JM, 12 May 1800, and "Commission," 13 May 1800, *PJM*, 4:149–50; JM, *Autobiographical Sketch*, 28–29; Mason, *My Dearest Polly*, 142–44.

51. (Philadelphia) *Aurora*, 27 May and 4 June 1800, quoted in Smith, *Marshall*, 268; Sedgwick to King, 26 September 1800, *Life and Correspondence of King*, 3:309; JM, *Autobiographical Sketch*, 29; Wolcott to Ames, 10 August 1800, Gibbs, *Memoirs*, 2:458.

52. JM to Adams, 17 September 1800, *PJM*, 4:280; "Secretary of State: Editorial Note," *PJM*, 4:158; Beveridge, *Marshall*, 3:1–10; Bob Arnebeck, *Through a Fiery Trial: Building Washington, 1790–1800* (Lanham, Md.: Madison Books, 1991), 569–70; Kenneth Bowling, *The Creation of Washington, D.C.: The Idea and Location of the American Capital* (Fairfax, Va.: George Mason University Press, 1991), 237–38; James Sterling Young, *The Washington Community, 1800–1828* (New York: Columbia University Press, 1966), chaps. 2 and 4; Constance McLaughlin Green, *Washington: Village and Capital, 1800–1878* (Princeton: Princeton University Press, 1962), chap. 1; Gaillard Hunt, ed., *The First Forty Years of Washington Society . . .* (orig. publ. 1906; rept., New York: Frederick Ungar, 1965), 9–16; John W. Reps, *Washington On View: The Nation's Capital since 1790* (Chapel Hill: University of North Carolina Press, 1991), 40, 42, 46, 48, 60, 64; Christian Hines, *Early Recollections of Washington City* (Washington, D.C.: N.p., 1866), passim; Wilhelmus B. Bryan, *A History of the National Capital . . .*, 2 vols. (New York: Macmillan, 1914), 1:357–86; Smith, *Marshall*, 277; Wolcott in Gibbs, *Memoirs*, 2:377; George L. Haskins and Herbert A. Johnson, *Foundations of Power: John Marshall, 1801–15*, Volume 2 of the Oliver Wendell Holmes Jr., Devise History of the Supreme Court (New York: Macmillan, 1981), 74–78. In 1799, Marshall, his brother James, and another man had bought seven lots in the capital near what is today Lafayette Park. *PJM*, 8:200 n. 1.

53. John C. Proctor, ed., *Washington, Past and Present*, 4 vols. (New York: Lewis Historical Publishing Co., 1930), 1:69–70; Beveridge, *Marshall*, 3:3; Leonard D. White, *The Federalists: A Study in Administrative History, 1789–1801* (New York: Free Press,

1948), 128, 134–35; "Appendix: Miscellaneous Papers," *PJM*, 4:341–49; Appendices I and II, *PJM*, 6:501–23, 530–36.

54. George Van Santvoord, *Sketches of the Lives, Times and Judicial Services of the Chief Justices . . .*, 2nd ed. (Albany: Weare C. Little, 1882), 398; "Secretary of State: Editorial Note," *PJM*, 4:160.

55. "To a Freeholder," 20 September 1798, and JM to Posey, 30 January 1799, *PJM*, 3:504–5, 4:5–6.

56. JM to King, 20 September 1800, to Thomas Posey, 30 January 1799, *PJM*, 4:5–6, 286; Albert H. Bowman, *The Struggle for Neutrality: Franco-American Diplomacy during the Federalist Era* (Knoxville: University of Tennessee Press, 1974), 427–29; Robert K. Faulkner, *The Jurisprudence of John Marshall* (Princeton: Princeton University Press, 1968), 41ff.

57. Warren, *Supreme Court in U.S. History*, 2:27–28; Van Santvoord, *Sketches of . . . the Chief Justices*, 434–35; Thomas Shaw Craigmyle, *John Marshall in Diplomacy and in Law* (New York: Charles Scribner's Sons, 1933), 81–82, 86–87. Cf. Ziegler, *International Law of Marshall*, 97: "[Marshall was] lost . . . in the vast field of international law when he did not have the guiding hands of the more learned counsel in the profession to lead him." That may have been true only earlier. In 1794, Marshall admitted to a client that he was "little versd in marine law as I never practisd in the courts of admiralty & never turnd my attention to the subject." JM to Charles Simms, 12 December 1794, *PJM*, 2:301.

58. Brown, *Presidency of Adams*, 153–55; Andrew J. Montague, "John Marshall," in *The American Secretaries of State and Their Diplomacy*, ed. Samuel Flagg Bemis, 18 vols. (rept., New York: Cooper Square Publishers, 1963), 1:259–73; Bradford Perkins, *The First Rapprochement: England and the United States, 1795–1805* (Berkeley: University of California Press, 1967), 116–20, 138–41; Rudko, *Marshall and International Law*, 22–24, 106–9; King to JM, 22 April 1800, *PJM*, 4:132–37; JM to Adams, 24 June, 21 and 26 July, 12 August 1800, *PJM*, 4:169, 184, 191, 214–15; JM to King, 23 August, 4 December 1800, *PJM*, 4:233–40, 261–62; JM to Samuel Sitgreaves, 2 December 1800, *PJM*, 6:30–33; Adams to JM, 1, 11, and 22 August 1800, *PJM*, 6:199, 212, 229; King to JM, 12 January and 5 August 1802, *PJM*, 6:102–4, 121–22; JM to King, 5 May 1802, *PJM*, 6:119.

59. JM to Edward Thornton, 3 February 1801, *PJM*, 6:67–69; to King, 20 September 1800, *PJM*, 4:283–97; "Memorandum on Foreign Affairs," 2 February 1801, *PJM*, 6:65–66; Montague, "Marshall," 265–73; Ames to Christopher Gore, 29 December 1800, *Works of Ames*, 1:287. Adams wrote Marshall that he read the letter of instruction to King "with some care and great pleasure. I think it very proper that such a letter should be sent." The President was "so fully satisfied with the Representations and Reasonings in it" that he arranged for the letter to be sent to London at the first opportunity. Adams to JM, 3 October 1800, *PJM*, 4:313.

60. Background on the second mission and the ensuing treaty comes from Elkins and McKitrick, *Age of Federalism*, 662–90; DeConde, *Quasi-War*, 223–58; Bowman, *Struggle for Neutrality*, chaps. 14–17; Brown, *Presidency of Adams*, chap. 13; Lawrence D. Kaplan, *Colonies into Nation: American Diplomacy, 1763–1801* (New York: Macmillan, 1972), chap. 10; and Rudko, *Marshall and International Law*, 100–103.

61. JM to Adams, 21 July, 25 August, 17 September 1800, JM to King, 23 August 1800, *PJM*, 4:185, 240, 279.

62. The use of the term "convention" was a literary artifice that showed how interested the two sides were in accommodating each other. They avoided the word "treaty" so that

France could argue that the older bilateral agreements had not been abrogated, and the United States could claim that those same accords had been superseded.

63. Envoys to JM, 4 October 1800, *PJM*, 4:315–19; JM to Charles Cotesworth Pinckney, 18 December 1800, JM to Alexander Hamilton, 1 January 1801, JM to King, 18 January 1801, *PJM*, 6:41, 47, 57; King to JM, 31 October 1800, *PJM*, 4:338–39; Otis to Hamilton, 17 December 1800, in *The Papers of Alexander Hamilton*, ed. Harold Syrett et al., 27 vols. (New York: Columbia University Press, 1961–81), 25:260; Robert E. Welch Jr., *Theodore Sedgwick, Federalist* (Middleton, Conn.: Wesleyan University Press, 1965), 210. The Senate rejected the convention on 23 January 1801, 16 to 14—well short of the necessary two thirds, and with Federalists casting all negative votes—but approved it on 3 February, 22 to 9.

64. JM to Adams, 6 September 1800, JM to David Humphreys, 8 and 23 September 1800, 5 January 1801, *PJM*, 4:262, 266–73, 298–302, 6:50, 515ff.; *PJM*, 4:180 n. 1; Samuel Flagg Bemis, *Pinckney's Treaty: A Study of America's Advantage from Europe's Distress, 1783–1800* (Baltimore: Johns Hopkins University Press, 1926), chaps. 12–13.

65. Adams to JM, 11 August 1800, JM to Adams, 12 August 1800, JM to Carlos Martinez de Yrujo, 15 August 1800, Robert Liston to JM, 25 August 1800, JM to Liston, 6 September 1800, *PJM*, 4:210, 213–14, 222–23, 241–42, 263–64; Montague, "John Marshall," 279–80; Rudko, *Marshall and International Law*, 109–11.

66. Numerous documents in *PJM*, vols. 4 and 6 passim, esp. Pickering to JM, 17 May 1800, and JM to Richard O'Brien, 29 July 1800, 4:151–53, 192–93; JM to Roger Griswold, 15 January 1801, *PJM*, 6:54; JM, "Memorandum on Foreign Affairs," [2 February 1801], *PJM*, 6:65–66; Glenn Tucker, *Dawn Like Thunder: The Barbary Wars and the Birth of the U.S. Navy* (Indianapolis: Bobbs-Merrill, 1963), chap. 7 and passim; Rudko, *Marshall and International Law*, 103–05; Montague, "John Marshall," 280–81; "Secretary of State: Editorial Note," *PJM*, 4:159–60; Robert J. Allison, *The Crescent Obscured: The United States and the Muslim World, 1776–1815* (New York: Oxford University Press, 1995), chap. 1.

67. White, *Federalists*, 132–33, 136–44; "Secretary of State: Editorial Note," *PJM*, 4:160; documents in *PJM*, 4:167–68, 172, 175, 181–85, 192, 206–7, 211–12, 243–44, 246, 277, 279, 330, 332, 336–37, 6:51–52.

68. See *PJM*, vols. 3–4 passim, 6:543–45, and Irwin S. Rhodes, *The Papers of John Marshall: A Descriptive Calendar*, 2 vols. (Norman: University of Oklahoma Press, 1956), 1:65–66, 314–18, 345–48, 371–74, 435–38 for numerous deeds and JM's personal property lists (hereafter cited as Rhodes, *Calendar of Marshall Papers*).

69. JM, *Autobiographical Sketch*, 28. On Marshall's declining legal caseload, see *PJM*, 5:562–63; Rhodes, *Calendar of Marshall Papers*, 1:333–45, 358–70, 429–35, 463–66; and Daniel Call, *Reports of Cases Argued and Adjudged in the Court of Appeals of Virginia*, 6 vols., 2nd ed. (Richmond: Peter Cottom, 1824), vols. 1–4 passim.

70. Legal sources cited in note 69, and also cases in *PJM*, 5:534–55. The cases involving Jefferson were *Ware v. Jefferson et al.* (1798), most conveniently summarized in Rhodes, *Calendar of Marshall Papers*, 1:335–36; and *Eppes and Jefferson v. Randolph et al.*, 2 Call 183 (1799). On the debt cases, see Charles F. Hobson, "The Recovery of British Debts in the Federal Circuit Court of Virginia, 1790 to 1797," *VMHB*, 92 (1984), 199; and Risjord, *Chesapeake Politics*, 454.

71. E.g., Fred Rodell, "The Great Chief Justice," *American Heritage*, 7 (1955–56), 110–11; Olive A. Taylor, "Blacks and the Constitution: Chief Justice John Marshall," *Washington Post*, 4 July 1987, A19; Taylor interview with Bill Moyers on "In Search of the Constitution," Public Broadcasting System, 16 April 1987; and, in a more scholarly

vein, Donald M. Roper, "In Quest of Judicial Objectivity: The Marshall Court and the Legitimation of Slavery," *Stanford Law Review*, 21 (1969), 532–39.

72. Details of the lawsuit come from *PJM*, 5:541–49; James H. Kettner, "Persons or Property? The Pleasants Slaves in the Virginia Courts, 1792–1799," in *Launching the "Extended Republic": The Federalist Era*, ed. Ronald Hoffman and Peter J. Albert (Charlottesville: University Press of Virginia, 1996), 136–55; and 2 Call 270ff. On Robert Pleasants and Quaker antislavery activities, see Robert McColley, *Slavery and Jeffersonian Virginia*, 2nd ed. (Urbana: University of Illinois Press, 1973), 156–59. Winthrop Jordan discusses subsequent efforts to restrict private manumissions in *White over Black: American Attitudes toward the Negro, 1550–1812*, Penguin ed. (Chapel Hill: University of North Carolina Press, 1968), 574–78.

73. Charles F. Hobson, *The Great Chief Justice: John Marshall and the Rule of Law* (Lawrence: University Press of Kansas, 1996), 42.

74. *Coleman v. Dick and Pat*, 1 Wash. 233 (1793); *Hannah v. Davis* (1787), *PJM*, 1:218–21; "Opinion," March 1792, *PJM*, 2:112–16; *Shelton v. Barbour*, 2 Wash. 64, (1794); *Journal of the House of Delegates*, October 1787 sess., 126, 128–29, 141; Smith, *Marshall*, 162–63; *Annals of Congress*, 6th Cong., 1st sess., 3 January 1800, 245; Douglas R. Egerton, *Gabriel's Rebellion: The Virginia Slave Conspiracies of 1800 and 1802* (Chapel Hill: University of North Carolina Press, 1993), chaps. 5–7, 9–11. Marshall's signing of a petition for mercy for a free black woman who killed a slavecatcher who had mistaken her for a runaway was less an indication of an enlightened attitude toward race relations than an effort to redress a gross injustice. "Petition," 12 September 1793, *PJM*, 2:207–9; Smith, *Marshall*, 161–62.

75. Background and details about the 1800 election come from Cunningham, *Jeffersonian Republicans*, chaps. 7–9; Dumas Malone, *Jefferson and the Ordeal of Liberty* (Boston: Little, Brown, 1962), chap. 30; Miller, *Federalist Era*, chap. 14; Brown, *Presidency of Adams*, chap. 14; Rose, *Prologue to Democracy*, chap. 7; Elkins and McKitrick, *Age of Federalism*, 726–54; and the studies of Virginia and the South by Risjord, Beeman, and Broussard cited in the next note.

76. Risjord, *Chesapeake Politics*, 550–57; Beeman, *Old Dominion and New Nation*, 211–16; Broussard, *Southern Federalists*, 23–25; Malone, *Jefferson and the Ordeal of Liberty*, 460–61; *PJM*, 7:184 n. 4. Marshall wrote in 1808 that under the general ticket system "the voice of the minority is lost." Letter to Charles Cotesworth Pinckney, 21 September 1808, *PJM*, 7:183.

77. James Monroe to Jefferson, 26 April 1800, in *The Writings of James Monroe*, ed. Stanislaus Murray Hamilton, 7 vols. (New York: G. P. Putnam's Sons, 1898–1903), 3:175–76; JM to Harrison Gray Otis, 5 August 1800, *PJM*, 4:205; Merz, "XYZ Affair and Congressional Election of 1799 in Richmond," 60; Beveridge, *Marshall*, 2:515; Broussard, *Southern Federalists*, 28, 199–214, 263–68; Risjord, *Chesapeake Politics*, 556–57; Beeman, *Old Dominion and New Nation*, 223.

78. Elkins and McKitrick, *Age of Federalism*, 734–35; Broussard, *Southern Federalists*, 18, 23. Jean Smith (*Marshall*, 270) states that Marshall, his brother-in-law Edward Carrington, and Henry Lee wrote the election statement of the Federalist state committee in Virginia that was circulated in May 1800. Aside from some rough parallels with views Marshall stated elsewhere, there is no other evidence that he participated in drafting the statement (a portion of which is in Cunningham, *Jeffersonian Republicans*, 227–28).

79. JM to St. George Tucker, 18 November 1800, *PJM*, 6:14–15; Jacob E. Cooke, *Alexander Hamilton* (New York: Charles Scribner's Sons, 1982), 220–24; Milton Lomask, *Aaron Burr: The Years from Princeton to Vice President, 1756–1805* (New

York: Farrar, Straus, and Giroux, 1979), 257–58; Smith, *Adams*, 2:1043–45; Adams's speech documents in *PJM*, 6:7–14.

80. Sedgwick to King, 26 September 1800, *Life and Correspondence of King*, 3:309; Rose, *Prologue to Democracy*, 239, 266, 283–88; Beeman, *Old Dominion and New Nation*, 223–24, 229–31; Broussard, *Southern Federalists*, 19–22; Malone, *Jefferson and the Ordeal of Liberty*, 479–82.

81. JM to Richard Peters, 3 October 1800, *PJM*, 4:336.

82. Beeman, *Old Dominion and New Nation*, 232–34; Risjord, *Chesapeake Politics*, 560–61; Broussard, *Southern Federalists*, 29–30.

83. JM to Edward Carrington, 28 December 1800, to Charles Cotesworth Pinckney, 18 December 1800, to Hamilton, 1 January 1801, *PJM*, 6:41, 45, 47. Marshall was referring to Jefferson's notorious 1796 letter to Philip Mazzei, in which, according to a thirdhand English translation, he criticized "an Anglican monarchical, & aristocratical party . . . whose avowed object is to draw over us the substance, as they have already done the forms of the British government." The Federalists were "apostates . . . Samsons in the field & Solomons in the council, but who have had their heads short by the harlot England." Marshall commented on the Mazzei letter in the appendix of volume 5 of the *Life of Washington*. See also Malone, *Jefferson and the Ordeal of Liberty*, 267–68, 302–07, and Beveridge, *Marshall*, 2:536–39.

84. Baker, *Marshall*, 347–48; Beveridge, *Marshall*, 2:539–44; Smith, *Marshall*, 14; Warren, *Supreme Court in U.S. History*, 1:182–83; Dewey, *Marshall versus Jefferson*, 43; Beeman, *Old Dominion and New Nation*, 235; Monroe to Jefferson, 6, 18, and 27 January 1801, *Writings of Monroe*, 3:253–57; Malone, *Jefferson and the Ordeal of Liberty*, 496; Elkins and McKitrick, *Age of Federalism*, 747–50.

85. JM to Pinckney, 18 December 1800, *PJM*, 6:41. See sections on Virginia in David Hackett Fischer, *The Revolution of American Conservatism: The Federalist Party in the Era of Jeffersonian Democracy* (New York: Harper and Row, 1965), and Broussard, *Southern Federalists*, chap. 14.

86. Adams to Elias Boudinot, 26 January 1801, in *Documentary History of the Supreme Court of the United States, 1789–1800*, ed. Maeva Marcus and James R. Perry, 4 vols. to date (New York: Columbia University Press, 1985–), 1, pt. 2:922. Late in Marshall's life, Adams wrote to him that "[m]y gift of John Marshall to the people of the United States was the proudest act of my life. . . . I have given to my country . . . a Hale, a Holt, or a Mansfield." Warren, *Supreme Court in U.S. History*, 1:178.

87. JM, *Autobiographical Sketch*, 30; JM to Adams, 4 February 1801, *PJM*, 6:73.

88. Hofstadter, *Idea of a Party System*, 130–31, 141; Robert H. Wiebe, *The Opening of American Society from the Adoption of the Constitution to the Eve of Disunion* (New York: Alfred A. Knopf, 1984), 223.

89. Bernard Schwartz, *A History of the Supreme Court* (New York: Oxford University Press, 1993), 36; Elkins and McKitrick, *Age of Federalism*, 78.

90. Marshall's confirmation is discussed in Kathryn Turner, "The Appointment of Chief Justice John Marshall," *WMQ*, 3rd ser., 17 (1960), 156–62; James R. Perry, "Supreme Court Appointments, 1789–1801: Criteria, Presidential Style, and the Press of Events," *JER*, 6 (1986), 407–8; John E. O'Connor, *William Paterson: Lawyer and Statesman, 1745–1806* (New Brunswick, N.J.: Rutgers University Press, 1979), 260–62; Gertrude Wood, *William Paterson of New Jersey, 1745–1806* (Fair Lawn, N.J.: Fair Lawn Press, 1933), 167–68; Beveridge, *Marshall*, 2:553–57; Dewey, *Marshall versus Jefferson*, 14–15.

Chapter 8

Chief Justice, 1801–1835

When John Marshall became America's premier judicial officer, he was 45 years old, and his public and private identities were fully formed. He possessed a vision of what America could and ought to become as a people and a nation, but he confronted dynamic, unforeseen, and at times threatening forces to which he had to respond personally, politically, and institutionally. The manner in which Marshall sought to achieve his public goals, and the degree of success he had in doing so, can be described and interpreted through the three distinctive leadership roles he took on as chief justice. These roles were usually interrelated but sometimes discrete, and Marshall either fashioned them for himself, some more quickly and resolutely than others, or assumed them because of changing historical circumstances, or immediate political disputes, or both. First, and most important for the Supreme Court's place in American history as a governmental institution, Marshall was a judicial statesman who, as the most influential member of the Court in its first half-century, guided it in creating a powerful and independent judiciary and establishing a consistent, widely accepted, practical, and durable body of constitutional law. As one of the leading Federalists directly engaged in the debate over the judiciary during the ratification period, he knew as well as anyone what the purposes of the "least dangerous branch" were to be, and, operating in an incremental, opportunistic way, he went about accomplishing them. Second, and most significant for the Court's impact on daily life and the material world, he was a constitutional and economic nationalist, developing and adjusting the federal "common market" by according constitutional protection to property rights and corporations, restricting state mercantilism, and promoting investment and expansion through the agency of the federal courts. The Marshall Court was a vital element of the transformation of American law that occurred during the metamorphosis of the United States from a republican to a liberal-capitalist society between the Revolutionary and Jacksonian periods. Lastly, having spent two decades as a lawyer and politician before his appointment as chief justice, Marshall was a profoundly political jurist whose judicial statecraft and economic objectives interwove his constitutional decisions with the era's most salient and controversial public issues. He initially tried to salvage Federalism as a party and a political order through the national judiciary and the legal profession, but by the end of his life, he saw it eclipsed by a new political system that he decried but that, ironically, was complementary to, and reinforced by, an expanding economic revolution to which his decisions contributed so prominently.

This final chapter, then, will not attempt to synopsize or analyze the Supreme Court decisions and constitutional and legal development during Marshall's 34-year tenure as chief justice, nor to synthesize hundreds of interpretations into a few dozen pages, nor to comprehensively narrate the balance of Marshall's life. Instead, it will present an impressionistic, and occasionally episodic, projection of the major themes of Marshall's early years into his service on the Court, showing how his experiences, character traits, and legal and political views up to 1801 manifested themselves in the judicial and partisan controversies in which he became involved subsequently. It will concentrate on discerning the behavioral patterns in Marshall's statements and actions, taking the events of his chief justiceship on their own terms rather than explaining them through an imposed philosophical framework. This biographical approach seems more fruitful than trying to apply ideological categories to his ideas ex post facto— Marshall did and said this, Locke or Montesquieu or whoever wrote that, therefore Marshall believed in or was a ____. Scholars' attempts at this are illuminating up to a point but suffer from a logical and empirical inability to prove the positive. All the assorted ideas claimed as predominant influences on Marshall—Locke's liberalism, classical republicanism, laissez faire economics, English juristic ideas, Hobbes's individualism, and Machiavelli's realism, among them—were part of the intellectual milieu in which he became a public man. Scant convincing evidence—for example, the educational curricula he studied under, the books he owned or mentioned in letters, frequent references in his opinions, correspondence, and public writings—exists to show that any one or two of them affected him more pronouncedly than others. Moreover, these excursions often read effects back into causes, employ classifications developed much later that the persons being examined were not aware of, or assume that people's ideological reference points do not change over time. Like most political leaders in the early republic, Marshall evinced various ideas in varying proportions at different times in different circumstances. Lacking curiosity toward philosophical subjects, he probably imbibed these conceptions more through osmosis than any other process. Marshall was a man of the world, not of the mind, and it is there that his contribution to the history of the early republic can best be understood.[1]

Marshall officially accepted Adams's nomination as chief justice and received his commission of office from the president on 4 February 1801. On a cold and rainy morning, Marshall walked through the mud on Pennsylvania Avenue to the Capitol, where the Supreme Court was holding its first session in Washington. In what a contemporary described as a "half-finished Committee room, meanly furnished, and very inconvenient," which the Senate had allowed the Court to use only two weeks before, he presented his commission and was sworn in as the fourth chief justice. As an indication of the low regard with which the Court was held then, few persons attended the event, and the press scarcely took note of it. The proceedings that Marshall oversaw during the six-day session were routine. The justices granted some motions for continuances, admitted several lawyers to practice, heard arguments in one case, and then adjourned. The only change of note was Marshall's donning of a plain black robe, in the style of the judges of Virginia's courts and in contrast to the scarlet and ermine of the King's Bench or the colored academic gowns that the justices had worn previously. Marshall's adoption of simple republican attire may have had a prosaic motive—he did not like fancy clothes—but intentionally or not, it subtly symbolized the leadership style he planned to adopt—one based on character and intellect rather than rank and custom—and of his intention to remove the Court and American constitutional law from partisan politics by dispensing with English trappings that perpetuated the association between Federalism and Anglophilia.[2]

One of the most important elements in Marshall's role as a judicial statesman was his judicial philosophy: his perspective on the appropriate function of the federal courts under the Constitution, the methodology by which he reached his decisions, and the manner in which he retained significant control over the Court for so many years. His judicial philosophy in turn largely derived from his institutional interest in establishing and consolidating the power of an independent federal judiciary, which as of 1801 was the weakest branch of government, beleaguered by instability and uncertainty. One of Marshall's most immediate objectives for achieving that goal over the long term was fixing the prerogatives of the chief justice, a feeble office in 1801 that he transformed into a major governmental force. He spoke for the Court when it handed down rulings or decided who would if he were in the majority. He presided both in open session and at conference. At the former he allowed full and open argument, sometimes lasting days in the more significant cases, thereby performing a public education and legitimization function intended to assure the people that the Supreme Court made up its mind only after fairly weighing all sides. At conferences with his colleagues, Marshall established the agenda of the discussions by setting out the issues and stating his own opinion first. Lastly, he maintained the chief justice's and the Court's apolitical role by declining to become involved publicly in partisan politics or to provide advice to policy makers. This overt political detachment was essential if the Court were to carry out its duty, as he perceived it, to find and interpret the law. Since Marshall, all chief justices to varying degrees have asserted the same prerogatives as leaders of the Court, even if they have been overshadowed temporarily by more commanding intellects or personalities among the associates.[3]

The Supreme Court and the federal judiciary could not perform the governmental function that Marshall thought the Constitution prescribed for them, however, unless their review power was secured and their jurisdiction was delineated, protected, and modified as needed—in short, unless their full authority was established and preserved. Marshall believed that the federal courts were the agencies best able to interpret the Constitution, and that the provisions of their authority to review acts of Congress and the state legislatures and their jurisdiction over legal controversies should be interpreted as broadly as the Constitution and congressional statutes permitted. He rejected the old Whiggish view of legislative supremacy that some Republicans were still espousing. Instead, drawing on his experience with the highly respected judges of the Virginia courts, and building on precedents from several states (including Virginia) in the 1790s, he affirmed the Supreme Court's judicial review power over congressional enactments in *Marbury v. Madison* (1803) and then extended it, much more frequently, to state laws beginning with *Fletcher v. Peck* (1810). Several milestone decisions by Marshall and his kindred spirit Joseph Story— including *United States v. Peters* (1809), *Martin v. Hunter's Lessee* (1816), *Cohens v. Virginia* (1821), and *Craig v. Missouri* (1830)—overcame challenges to the federal courts' authority under the Eleventh Amendment and attempts to question or obstruct the Supreme Court's power to hear appeals from the states' highest courts when federal questions were raised. "The judicial power," he wrote in *Cohens*, "must be capable of deciding every judicial question which grows out of the constitution and laws." "Just as the supremacy clause was essential to the operation of the federal Union," Herbert A. Johnson has written, "so *Cohens v. Virginia* was necessary to insure the authority of the Supreme Court to protect that Union." In *Osborn v. Bank of the United States* (1824), Marshall wrote that Congress may give federal courts original jurisdiction over anything the Constitution does not prohibit, not just over what it expressly allows. In the "steamboat case," *Gibbons v. Ogden* (1824), Marshall allowed that the states have police power in certain areas, but he explicitly reserved for the Supreme Court the authority to decide case by case whether the exercise of that power affected interstate commerce and thereby became a federal question. This simultaneous concession to the states and affirmation of national power, while seemingly balanced, in practice gave the Court greater influence than before. Marshall's sense of the proper scope of judicial authority remained constant even through changes in the national political climate. The rise of Jacksonian Democracy, with its suspicion of the federal courts, only made him more determined to assert their role. On separate occasions in 1831 he wrote that "we have never sought to enlarge the judicial power beyond its proper bounds nor feared to carry it to the fullest extent that duty required"; and "[a]s this Court has never grasped at ungranted jurisdiction, so will it never, we trust, shrink from the exercise of that which is conferred upon it."[4]

When the federal courts exercised their jurisdiction as Marshall, for the most part, broadly construed it, he adhered to a rule of constitutional and statutory construction that was consistent with his sense of law as a practical science. He succinctly expressed it in three decisions in 1804, 1820, and 1827, respectively: "[A] law is the best expositor of itself"; "The intention of the legislature is to be collected from the words they employ"; "[I]t is proper to take a view of the literal meaning of the words to be expounded, of their connexion with other words, and of the general objects to be accomplished by the prohibitory clause, or by the grant of power." The law was as the legislature stated it. Courts had no authority to go beyond the text of the law and delve into the lawmakers' "intent" because there were no hard and fast criteria for determining whose intent out of those variously expressed while the law was being drafted and debated should take precedence. Parsing speeches and other public statements, let alone figuring out what someone was thinking at the time, was a futile exercise and permissible only in rare circumstances. "The case must be a strong one indeed, which would justify a Court in departing from the plain meaning of words . . . in search of an intention which the words themselves did not suggest." Likewise, ethicality could not be determined with available legal standards and so was beyond the courts' purview. In *Fletcher v. Peck* (1810), despite the obvious corruption surrounding the sale of the Yazoo lands, Marshall would not inquire into the motives behind the deal. In this regard Marshall was an "originalist," but he also was an empiricist. The only sound "data" for a practitioner of legal science to use for interpreting what a law or the Constitution meant are what the legislators and the Framers *did*. The Constitution's meaning is ascertainable through reason, as it is a permanent collection of general principles to guide the government's actions. The literal meaning of the words of the law and the Constitution was the most reliable guide for respecting both their letter and spirit. The burden of proof was on those who argued for a more restricted or more expansive reading than the text would permit. When the words are ambiguous, the justices should then look at the consequences that would flow from various readings and choose the one most consistent with the government's purposes, and "where great inconvenience will result from a particular construction, that construction is to be avoided, unless the meaning of the legislature is plain." In addition, "in the exposition of statutes . . . every part is to be considered, and the intention of the legislature [is] to be extracted from the whole"; judges must not engage in prooftexting. Marshall's consistent application of these rules of construction to a large extent explains why he so rarely used arguments based on the extratextual concept of natural law, and why the opinion in which he did so most explicitly—his dissent in *Ogden v. Saunders* (1827)—stands out so starkly from his other major writings on the bench. Least of all should judges let their sentiments guide them, however tempting and "right" that may seem to be in the case at hand. "Nothing can be more irksome to a court than to perceive that principles, with an adherence to which it cannot permit itself to dispense, will produce great individual loss. But these feelings cannot controul the course of justice." Judges should seek justice, not perfection.[5]

Marshall's textual literalism did not mean that he was a "strict constructionist." He defined that attitude negatively as the placing of an unnecessarily constricted reading on general words and phrases. As he wrote in *Gibbons v. Ogden*: "What do gentlemen mean by strict construction? . . . If they contend for that narrow construction which . . . would cripple the government and render it unequal to the objects for which it is declared to be instituted, and to which the powers given, as fairly understood, render it competent; then we cannot perceive the propriety of this strict construction, nor adopt it as the rule by which the constitution is to be expounded." If "powerful and ingenious minds" employed this sort of "refined and metaphysical reasoning," he warned, they would "explain away the constitution . . . and leave it a magnificent structure . . . to look at, but totally unfit for use." Instead, he practiced what he called "fair construction"—"[a] medium between that restricted sense which confines the meaning of words to narrower limits than the common understanding of the world affixes to them, and that extended sense which would stretch them beyond their obvious import." Marshall's approach, in his words, "gives to language the sense in which it is used, and interprets an instrument according to its true intention." The Constitution is an enabling instrument, not a limiting one. Its principles are guidelines, not commands. It is not meant to codify the prejudices and interests of an historic elite but to be adapted to address novel contemporary problems. "[W]e must never forget, that it is *a constitution* we are expounding," he wrote in *McCulloch v. Maryland* (1819), "a constitution intended to endure for ages to come, and, consequently, to be adapted to the various *crises* of human affairs." But at the same time he did not regard the Constitution as "living," as an evolutionary document that each generation, wiser by experience than the one before, modifies in accordance with the needs of the time. Rather, he believed that the federal government's enumerated powers, though deliberately couched in general terms, must always be used in conformity with the purposes of the Constitution. "It was not Marshall's view that the Constitution must be kept in tune with the times," Walter Berns has written; "on the contrary, his view was the Framers' view that the times, to the extent possible, must be kept in tune with the Constitution. Why, otherwise, have a Constitution?"[6]

Marshall's expansive view of the Supreme Court's jurisdiction and his "broad" construction of the Constitution's grants of powers to the federal government may make him seem like an "activist" in the sense of being a jurist who went out of his way to find justifications for intruding into controversies and, in the next degree, taking those opportunities to read his own political preferences into the undefined interstices of the laws and the Constitution. Marshall's supposed "activism" has been a point of departure for numerous critics and defenders of his jurisprudence, but the stronger case seems to rest with analyses that question the validity of the label to begin with.[7] It is true that Marshall hardly ever looked for ways to keep the Court from deciding a case, but his willingness to rule derived more from his goal of strengthening the courts and asserting their coequality with the other branches in the federal governmental system than with a results-oriented purpose of pursuing a political program through constitutional interpretation. He used the power of judicial review sparingly and only when he deemed it essential to maintain the Constitution's vitality or to protect the federal judiciary from encroachments by the other branches or by the states. He was not an activist in diversity or admiralty cases, in extending the Bill of Rights to the states, or in creating a body of federal criminal common law. Several of his most important decisions illustrate the point. In *Cohens v. Virginia*, he affirmed the federal courts' authority to hear appeals when state courts ruled against claims of rights under the Constitution, adopting a literal application of the Judiciary Act of 1789 that was fully in keeping with the law's spirit. In Marshall's most famous discourse on "broad" construction, his ruling in *McCulloch v. Maryland*, he upheld the constitutionality of the economic policy of the Republican-controlled national government. As one scholar has incisively asked: "[H]ow can judges rationally be charged with activism when they defer to Congress, when they leave major policy issues to the processes of democracy?" The propriety of a national bank was a political question; no legal issue involving a universally supported individual right was at stake. He based his ruling in *Gibbons v. Ogden*, determining the scope of the federal government's power to regulate interstate commerce, by interpreting a mundane federal statute rather than embarking on a more adventurous analysis of the vaguer commerce clause of the Constitution. In *Barron v. Baltimore* (1835), he held to the clear language of the Bill of Rights in declining to apply it to state law. He concurred in Justice William Johnson's decision in *United States v. Hudson and Goodwin* (1812) abandoning the Federalist doctrine of a national criminal common law after quashing indictments based on it in an earlier circuit court ruling (*United States v. Hill* [1810]), and he later upheld Johnson in his own opinion in *United States v. Bevans* (1818). Only Congress through statute could designate behavior as criminal, the majority held. (Marshall later worked with Associate Justices Joseph Story and Bushrod Washington in drafting legislation to have that power conferred on the Court. They were not successful.) Lastly, in unclear instances Marshall was willing to defer to the state courts' interpretation of their own legislatures' enactments rather than have the Supreme Court trod a new path: "It is always with much reluctance that I break the way, in expounding the statute of a state; for the exposition of the acts of every legislature is, I think, the peculiar and appropriate duty of the tribunals, created by that legislature."[8]

Much of Marshall's success as a judicial statesman is attributable to his personal dominance over the Supreme Court for much of his tenure. Most contemporaries of the Marshall Court, and particularly its critics, perceived it as *Marshall's* Court. Thomas Jefferson captured the widespread sense of this purported control: "An opinion is huddled up in conclave, perhaps by a majority of one, delivered as if unanimous, and with the silent acquiescence of lazy or timid associates, by a crafty chief judge, who sophisticates the law to his

mind, by the turn of his own reasoning." The aggregate statistics of the
Marshall Court's decisions seem to support Jefferson's somewhat sinister
characterization. Of 1,111 opinions issued during 1805–33, only 74 (6.7
percent) were dissents, 35 (3.2 percent) were concurrences, and 25 (2.3 percent)
were seriatim. Marshall wrote 547 of the 1,121 opinions that the Court issued
during 1801–35—an average production of 16 per year that is noteworthy also
for its pace, as the Court met only three months a year until 1827 and never
more than five months after then through Marshall's tenure. He wrote well over
half of the constitutional decisions (36 of 62) that comprised the Court's most
substantively and politically significant work. Almost as important, Marshall
changed the way the Court issued its decisions. Drawing on the practice of the
Virginia Court of Appeals before which he argued many times as a lawyer in
Richmond, Marshall established the pattern of writing a single "opinion of the
Court" from his first case and adhered to it through the formative years of his
tenure. Of 26 decisions in Jefferson's first administration, he wrote the opinion
in all but the two on which he did not sit; through 1810, he wrote 124 of 141,
including all the important ones, and 209 of 378 through 1815; and the Court
issued its decision seriatim only seven times through the same period. This
departure from the prior desultory reading of seriatim opinions bolstered the
power and dignity of the Court, making it a distinct, collective entity in the mind
of the political public and a more formidable opponent to hostile Republicans.[9]

The notion, as Robert Wiebe has put it, that "[u]nique to its history, [Marshall]
transformed [the Supreme Court] into an agency for one man's vision" has been
revised significantly in recent years, however. Rather than being a monolith, the
Marshall Court went through several phases during which Marshall's
dominance fluctuated. The precise boundaries depend on the criteria of the
analyses, but the following periodization is as workable as any: 1801–12, when
Marshall substantially controlled the Court's decision-making process and its
output; 1813–18, when the justices divided over international law cases; 1819–
22, the apex of Marshall's influence during which the Court handed down most
of its landmark nationalist decisions; and 1823–35, when his power gradually
ebbed and his increasingly fractious colleagues forced the paring back of some
of the Court's most important constitutional rulings amid a resurgence of states'
rights theory. Despite the variations, Marshall's leadership was strongest when
from his vantage point it needed to be: at the start of his term, when he
established the patterns and practices that prevailed for much of the time that
followed, and during the years around 1820, when the country was under
unprecedented sectional stress and the Court heard several cases of potentially
monumental import.[10]

Marshall remained the ascendant figure on the Supreme Court for so long
mainly because of his personal attributes. He possessed nearly all the physical
and psychological characteristics that scholars have identified in the "great"
chief justices (the others being Charles Evans Hughes and Earl Warren): a
commanding appearance, vigorous health, natural dignity, self-discipline, the
ability to subordinate personal pettiness and partisanship to the public interest,

strong convictions combined with intellectual flexibility and humility, and professional dedication balanced with private ease. He and the other "greats" were "supremely fitted to the office," Robert Steamer has written, "not because they reflected the prevailing views of their time, but because they pursued their inner voices, their instincts, that aggregate of the innate and the attitudes acquired over the years from family, teachers, associates, and books." From the bench, Marshall impressed observers as strong but unintimidating, intellectually formidable but not overbearing. A contemporary wrote that he "presided in simple majesty, with perfect ease and naturalness of manner; without a trace of ostentation or self-consciousness of position. Amiability and firmness blended admirably in his expression, which alone seemed to guide and control, without need of utterance, the order and proceedings of the court." In 1808, Joseph Story, not yet on the Court and still a neutral observer, captured his first impressions of Marshall in words that describe a leader of unassuming authority:

Marshall is of a tall, slender figure, not graceful nor imposing, but erect and steady. His hair is black, his eyes small and twinkling, his forehead rather low, but his features are in general harmonious. His manners are plain, yet dignified; and an unaffected modesty diffuses itself through all his actions. His dress is very simple, yet neat; his language chaste, but hardly elegant; it does not flow rapidly, but it seldom wants precision. In conversation his is quite familiar but is occasionally embarrassed by a hesitancy and drawling. His thoughts are always clear and ingenious, sometimes striking, and not often inconclusive; he possesses great subtilty [sic] of mind, but it is only occasionally exhibited. I love his laugh,—it is too hearty for an intriguer,—and his good temper and unwearied patience are equally agreeable on the bench and in the study. His genius is, in my opinion, vigorous and powerful, less rapid than discriminating, and less vivid than uniform in its light. He examines the intricacies of a subject with calm and persevering circumspection, and unravels the mysteries with irresistible acuteness. He has not the majesty and compactness of thought of Dr. Johnson; but in subtle logic he is no unworthy disciple of David Hume.[11]

The Chief Justice's warmth, modesty, and political skill smoothed relations with the spectrum of characters he encountered among the fourteen associate justices he worked with during his 34-year tenure. They ranged from powerful and exuberant intellects like Joseph Story and contentious personalities like William Johnson, to ciphers like Thomas Todd and Gabriel Duvall; and included a boorish Federalist, Samuel Chase, and a decorous Jacksonian, John McLean. He was the fairest judge of his own intellectual limitations and had no conceit about his legal knowledge and abilities. He sought his brethren's advice, especially on circuit cases where he often sat alone and could not benefit from boardinghouse discussions and informal exchanges. By seeking their counsel and incorporating their differences into his opinions, he demonstrated his open-mindedness, made the associates feel that they actively contributed to decisions, and showed that he would not use his status to force decisions through. When other techniques of persuasion did not work, Marshall engaged in judicial bargaining to gain other justices' votes and achieve at least ostensible unanimity. The best example of this method was the state bankruptcy law case, *Sturgis v. Crowninshield* (1819), in which Marshall compromised on two important legal points with three associates to win full support for his opinion. When the Court heard appeals from the circuit courts on which the associates sat, Marshall assigned opinions in ways that avoided giving offense or exacerbating existing conflicts. In part because of his sensitivity to the justices' sensibilities, most circuit judgments were affirmed. The net effect of Marshall's methods for discouraging dissents and concurrences was at least the appearance, if not the reality, of consensus. The median rate of agreement between Marshall and the other justices in split decisions exceeded 80 percent, with only three associates—Johnson, Livingston, and the latecomer Baldwin—accounting for most of the dissents. Among those with whom Marshall served the longest, the agreement rates ranged from 88 percent with Duvall and 86 percent with Story, to 60 percent with Livingston and 52 percent with Johnson. Only one associate, Henry Baldwin, took a strong personal dislike to Marshall, and he was not appointed until 1830.[12]

Important commonalities among the associates made Marshall's leadership task easier. All fourteen were lawyers from solid middle- or upper-class backgrounds, had some legislative and judicial experience, and were professionally established and socially secure. They were imbued with a respect for American legal traditions and their importance in making the federal and state constitutions viable charters of government. They banded together to defend the federal judiciary from political pressures that included threats of impeachment and attempts to curtail its jurisdiction. Slow turnover in membership contributed to this unity. Between 1811 and 1823, for example, no new justices were appointed, and by the end of that period, the Court had 123 years of collective experience. The appointees to the Marshall Court also exhibited a tendency to think more independently than the Republican presidents who appointed them would have liked. Despite the influx of five Republican appointees during 1806–11, Jefferson complained that "the leaven of the old mass seems to assimilate to itself the new, and after twenty years . . . we find the Judiciary on every occasion still driving us into consolidation." As R. Kent Newmyer has observed, "Mutual respect, communal living, congenial principles, and personal friendship held dissent to an insignificant minimum, [and] bound the Court together as never before or since." Consequently, the "Revolution of 1800," the demise of Federalism, and the rise of Jacksonianism did not alter the Marshall Court radically. Ironically, the Supreme Court grew in independence as most of the Federalist holdovers from the Washington and Adams presidencies left the bench and were replaced by Republicans. Its resilience proved that the Framers were right in asserting that the Court would be able to resist the vagaries of factional and sectional politics. "It is hardly surprising," Robert McCloskey has concluded, "that the Supreme Court, an intrinsically national institution, should be drawn to the doctrine of nationalism."[13]

Marshall's mastery of small group dynamics was most evident in the special sociological setting in which the justices lived. Boardinghouses were the social and political centers of early Washington, ungenteel salons that brought a degree of camaraderie and professional cohesion to a group of transient, distracted inhabitants working in slovenly surroundings. Living together in a succession of them turned the working colleagues of the Supreme Court into a small fraternity. Almost all of the justices during Marshall's tenure lived at the same boardinghouse, sharing meals and private moments and discussing news of the day and the cases on the Court's docket. Marshall's amiable temperament and facile consensus-building skills were at their best in this informal setting that combined the ambience of home and office. As with his lawyer's dinners in Richmond, he made the justices' shared domicile into a sort of cozy men's club. Story thought working on cases in those intimate surroundings promoted a "most frank and unaffected intimacy" and "a pleasant and animated exchange of legal acumen." "[W]e are all united as one, with a mutual esteem which makes even the labors of jurisprudence light." "Our intercourse is perfectly familiar and unconstrained, and our social hours when undisturbed with the labors of law, are passed in gay and frank conversation, which at once enlivens and instructs." The casual conferences often led to quick decisions, largely on the Chief Justice's terms, because he stated the case and set the boundaries of discussion. Marshall believed that the boardinghouse lifestyle strengthened the Court. "If it be practicable to keep us together," he wrote Bushrod Washington, "you know how desirable this will be. If that be impracticable we must be as near each other as possible. Perhaps we may dine together should we even be compelled to lodge in different houses." He was distressed when the custom of sharing lodgings seemed to be going by the wayside late in his tenure. With his control already slipping since the early 1820s, he lamented to Story: "If the Judges scatter ad libitum, the docket I fear will remain quite compact, losing very few of its causes; and the few it may lose, will probably be carried off by seriatim opinion. Old men however are timid, and I hope my fears may be unfounded." They were not; the associates increasingly abandoned the group living arrangement, symbolizing the fracturing of consensus, or, according to Marshall, the rise of a "revolutionary spirit" within the Court that "will . . . work inconvenience and mischief in its progress."[14]

Marshall's overall philosophy of jurisprudence and his management of the Supreme Court's internal dynamics notwithstanding, it was the constitutional opinions he wrote that represented his greatest contribution to American history and the most compelling evidence of his judicial statesmanship. Their power lies in the august tone he adopted, the logical force of the arguments he employed, and his careful referral to the text of the Constitution as the basis for his decisions. Marshall's opinions had a timeless and capacious quality that magnified their authority and enabled them to withstand criticisms that they did not rely sufficiently on precedents or often spoke to extraneous matters or addressed political issues outside the judiciary's purview.

"The people made the constitution, and the people can unmake it"; "a constitution is framed for ages to come, and is designed to approach immortality as nearly as human institutions can approach it"; "the power to tax is the power to destroy"; "It is emphatically the province and duty of the judicial department to say what the law is"; "Commerce, undoubtedly, is traffic, but it is something more; it is intercourse": time and again, Marshall showed his ability to craft the felicitous phrase. Beyond his literary skill, however, they illustrate his use of tone as tactic. By taking the rhetorical "high ground" in his constitutional opinions, he avoided legalistic quibbles over interpretations of precedents that would call the decisions' legitimacy into question. He based his rulings on widely and long-held constitutional ideas, rather than constructing them one legal brick at a time. His "common law" approach was more evident in his nonconstitutional and circuit court decisions, where he demonstrated a great degree of acuity in handling precedents. "When private law was at issue," Herbert A. Johnson has observed, "Marshall was brilliant in the conventional sense." But in constitutional cases, he had a different mission, one for which a mere legal craftsman was less well suited. "If there was little precedent to guide him," writes Ben Palmer, "there was likewise little precedent to bind him." Instead of setting forth precise rules of constitutional law, Marshall intended to proclaim, often in seemingly incontrovertible language, the general outlines on which more explicit constitutional doctrines would be developed in the future.[15]

Although they were intended to be read, Marshall's constitutional decisions had an "oral/aural" quality that added to their power to persuade (or antagonize). This characteristic of his writing derived from his years of involvement in a setting that stressed verbal discourse, the courtroom. As a lawyer, Marshall knew how to appeal to a jury rhetorically—his main forensic shortcoming was his delivery, not his choice of words or structure of argument—and on the Supreme Court his linguistic abilities were supplemented by the performances of the many gifted attorneys who appeared before him, such as Daniel Webster, William Pinkney, William Wirt, and Luther Martin. During the extensive argument he allowed before the Court, Marshall not only listened to the contesting counsel to inform himself about the details of a case; he often captured their language in his opinions—their cadences, phrasing, and logic. Most of his best-known opinions sound more convincing (or alarming, by another view) when they are read aloud, as many were at a time when oratory was a major form of communication and printed materials often were disseminated by word of mouth in speeches and lectures and at taverns, shops, and clubs. The Chief Justice wanted his opinions to resonate far beyond the pages of the law reports, and the care he took with his literary craftsmanship showed how well he recognized that the reaction to a decision was often more consequential than the decision itself. Because he based his interpretations of the Constitution and the laws on their words, he made sure that his own words were as comprehensible and convincing as possible, in whatever form they were conveyed.

The grand-sounding phrases mentioned above often were the literary keystones of the argumentation that made Marshall's opinions seem so authoritative and so difficult to refute. In constitutional decisions he generally used the same argumentative technique that he had employed in the courtrooms of Virginia years before: the declaration of broad, often abstract, assumptions as self-evident truths; the investigation of the legal language at issue; the gradual accretion of intermediary implications through syllogisms; and the final pronouncement of an apparently inevitable decision, derived from those implications but incorporating the initial premise. Marshall's juristic "art," writes Robert Steamer, "consisted in laying his premises so remotely from the point directly at the base, or else in terms so general and spacious, that the hearer, seeing no consequences which could be drawn from them, was just as willing to admit them as not; but his premises once admitted, the demonstration, however distant, followed as certainly as cogently, as inevitably, as any demonstration in Euclid." "All wrong, all wrong," John Randolph reportedly said after reading one of Marshall's opinions, "but no man in the United States can tell why or wherein." Marshall's decisions were by no means unassailable on grounds of history, interpretation, or logic—two Virginia Jeffersonians, Spencer Roane and William Brockenbrough, subjected the *McCulloch* and *Cohens* opinions to withering criticism—but they withstood the attacks and retained their legitimacy as tools of judicial statecraft, in part because of the rhetorical devices Marshall employed so effectively.[16]

The Chief Justice believed that the Supreme Court's decisions would have greater effect in securing the national judiciary's influence as a unifying agency if they were publicized quickly and consistently, so he wanted the U.S. government to subsidize the reporting, printing, and distribution of the Court's opinions. The Supreme Court's reporters, the individuals responsible for recording arguments and oral decisions, at first did not have an official status or receive a salary. They were private citizens who collected the decisions, arranged for publication, and shared the returns with the publishers. This arrangement worked haphazardly in practice. It was not profitable for the reporters and did not guarantee that the rulings would be printed and distributed in a timely or accurate fashion. During its 1816–17, session Congress considering a bill to remunerate the reporter. Marshall—drawing on points already made by Justice Story and Attorney General Richard Rush—argued the case for a more professionalized system to the chairman of the Senate Judiciary Committee:

That the cases determined in the Supreme court should be reported with accuracy & promptness is essential to correctness & uniformity of decision in all the courts of the United States. It is also to be recollected that from the same tribunal the public receives that exposition of the constitution laws & treaties of the United States as applicable to the cases of individuals, which must ultimately prevail. It is obviously important that a knowledge of this exposition should be attainable by all. . . . It is certainly to be wished that independent tribunals having concurrent jurisdiction over the same subject, should concur in the principles on which they determine the causes coming before them. This concurrence can be obtained only by communicating to each the judgements of the other, & by that mutual respect which will probably be inspired by a knowledge of the grounds on which their judgements respectively stand. . . . From experience, the Judges think there is much reason to apprehend that the publication of the decisions of the Supreme Court will remain on a very precarious footing, if the Reporter is to depend solely on the sales of his work for a reimbursement of the expenses which must be incurred in preparing it, & for his own compensation. The patronage of the government is believed to be necessary to the secure & certain attainment of the object. . . . There is . . . much reason to believe that no Reporter will continue to employ his time & talents in preparing those decisions for the press, after he shall be assured that the government will not countenance his undertaking.

In March 1817, Congress passed the Reporter's Act that provided an annual compensation of $1,000 for the Reporter contingent on his arranging for publication of the decisions within six months of the close of each Court term, and his delivery of 80 copies of the reports to the secretary of state for distribution to federal officials. Together, this new legal status and the ambitions, personality, and social connections of the reporter when the act was passed, Henry Wheaton, transformed the office in the way Marshall had sought. G. Edward White has concluded that by the end of Marshall's tenure, the reporter's office had become "in some respects the nerve center of the Court's efforts to ensure that its decisions became authorities for as many Americans as possible."[17]

Marshall is not on record as trying to improve the Supreme Court's surroundings as a way to symbolize its rising prestige and authority. For Marshall's entire tenure, the Court had no separate facility in which to conduct its business. It met in a first-floor room in the Capitol until 1810, when it moved to the basement. After the British burned the Capitol in 1814, the Court had to meet in a private house on Pennsylvania Avenue for two years. They then returned to the basement room, refurbished but still unimpressive. A New York journalist wrote in 1824,

The apartment is not in a style which comports with the dignity of that body . . . it is like going down a cellar to reach it. The room is on the basement story in an obscure part of the north wing. . . . A stranger might traverse the dark avenues of the capitol for a week, without finding the remote corner in which Justice is administered to the American Republic . . . a room which is hardly capacious enough for a ward justice. The apartment is well finished; but . . . in size it is wholly insufficient for the accommodation of the Bar, and the spectators who wish to attend. . . . It is a triangular, semi-circular, odd-shaped apartment, with three windows, and a profusion of arches in the ceiling, diverging like the radii of a circle from a point over the bench to the circumference. . . .
    . . . Owing to the smallness of the room, the Judges are compelled to put on their robes in the presence of the spectators, which is an awkward ceremony, and destroys the effect intended to be produced by assuming the gown. The appurtenances of the Court are in no wise superior to the apartment itself. Two brown stone pitchers with a few glasses to furnish the speakers with water are the only moveables in the room; and the fixtures are not very remarkable for conveniences or elegance.

Marshall and his colleagues sat at chairs behind individual mahogany desks, slightly elevated and behind a rail from the chairs and tables for the lawyers. Other steps led up to another area, higher than where the justices sat, where spectators could observe the proceedings from chairs, sofas, and benches. The Washington community regarded arguments at the Court as social events, so if a renowned lawyer such as Webster, Pinkney, or Martin were scheduled to speak, the galleries would be packed. This overcrowding added to "the impression of justice being done in a corner," as one observer put it. Given the political difficulties the Court was having recurrently with the Republican administrations and Congress, Marshall and the associates may have thought it would be awkward to ask for money for their own building. Moreover, an unkempt dresser and lackluster decorator himself, Marshall may not have been that mindful of the aesthetics of power.[18]

Marshall also shaped the constitutional and legal contours of nineteenth-century America through his circuit court opinions. The circuit courts on which he and the associates spent much of their time were vital projectors of federal power and usually are overlooked as factors in the federal judiciary's success in defining its authority in the early republic. These courts involved Marshall and his colleagues in the daily legal life of the nation and often embroiled them in controversial and extremely politicized cases. Circuit riding had the important political effect of making the Supreme Court more "democratic" and accountable by keeping Marshall and his colleagues in touch with popular trends. In addition, much of the Court's docket of appellate work originated in the federal circuit courts. Marshall made his largest *legal* (as opposed to *constitutional*) contribution through his opinions in the important Fifth Circuit he handled, covering the districts of Virginia and North Carolina—one of the busiest in the federal system. His caseload emphasized economic matters, such as commercial law, business organization, contracts, and real estate, but he also wrote many opinions on cases dealing with admiralty and international law, criminal law, and civil procedure. His opinions contained 44 percent of the points of law raised in all federal circuit court opinions during 1801–35 (632 of 1,426). This disproportion is striking even when the length of his tenure is taken into account. Other long-serving associates addressed far smaller shares of the legal points through 1835. Story, appointed in 1811, considered the second most, 33 percent (303) in 24 years, followed by Johnson (118, or 8 percent, in 30 years) and Washington (86, or 6 percent, in 28 years). Moreover, Marshall's circuit opinions dealt with easily the largest share of the key legal categories: 48 percent of those cases raising points of constitutional law, 55 percent addressing courts and legal processes, 32 percent on admiralty or international law, 45 percent on domestic economic activity, and 32 percent on the status of persons. The weight of his individual contribution on this level of jurisprudence was a strong force in the transformation of the congeries of federal courts into a true national judiciary. The cases he and the associates heard on circuit also played a large part in making the Supreme Court a formative influence in law and economics. The preponderance of the cases the

Court heard came to it on appeal from the circuit courts—during 1801–15, over 95 percent.[19]

"That the United States form, for many, and for most important purposes, a single nation, has not yet been denied," Marshall wrote in *Cohens v. Virginia*.

In war, we are one people. In making peace, we are one people. In all commercial regulations, we are one and the same people. . . . In many other respects, the American people are one. . . . America has chosen to be, in many respects, and to many purposes, a nation. . . . [S]tates are constituent parts of the United States. They are members of one great empire.

This overriding sense of nationalism lay at the heart of Marshall's public life after he became chief justice. Directly attributable to his experiences in the Revolutionary War and the Confederation period, and intensifying as political and economic change accelerated during his tenure, Marshall's nationalism thoroughly infused not only his jurisprudence, but also his economic and social views and his political activities. It was not grandly philosophical, vaguely metaphysical, or romantically chauvinistic, and was not founded on intellectual constructs such as the social contract or common political ideals such as equality. Marshall's nationalism did, however, have several aspects. It applied beyond narrow legal and constitutional categories and included his conceptions of political economy and social development. It also formed the basis by which he tried to create an alternative source of order as the traditional political system in which he had grown up was gradually transformed by new popular political and commercial forces.[20]

The Republicans' "Revolution of 1800" ended the Federalists' "Augustan Age" and their dream of establishing a European-style state with a consolidated government, a powerful military-fiscal complex, a mercantilized economy, and a hierarchical patronage society. Instead, a liberal capitalist order began to emerge, formed from entrepreneurial energies, individual interests, egalitarian ideals, and localistic tendencies, and gradually to supersede the classical republican worldview that dominated the Revolutionary era—in large part because the Revolution itself unleashed powerful acquisitive and commercial tendencies. This decades-long transition created deep paradoxes within the culture. "Most Americans," writes Robert Shalhope, "clung to a harmonious, corporate view of themselves and their society even while behaving in a materialistic, utilitarian manner in their daily lives. Thus while rapidly transforming their society in an open, competitive, modern direction, Americans continued to idealize communal harmony and a virtuous social order." The conundrum that this inconsistency between ethos and action presented to Chief Justice Marshall can be expressed variously: how to defend the institutions and values of the Federalists' Old World paradigm of disinterested public leadership while simultaneously believing in the necessity and equity of a market economy; how to foster a sense of union and national purpose while controlling the democratizing power of what would come to be called the "market revolution"; how to insure that the pursuit of individual rights and private interests did not threaten the common good. He tried to resolve this tension between republican ideology and liberal behavior through constitutional nationalism. Insofar as the developing capitalist economy had inserted itself inside the traditional social order, changing the content but not the form of that order, Marshall sought to make the Constitution the bulwark of a new sense of nationhood, with the Supreme Court and the federal courts as the agents of unity. "On great commercial questions especially it is desirable that the judicial opinions of all parts of the Union should be the same," he wrote in 1817. America increasingly was becoming a middle-class business society that threatened to spin out of control in a commercial whirl at the same time that it was being beset by unprecedented sectional stresses. In such a potentially chaotic and contentious society, lawyers and judges would be the brokers of conflict. Faced with threats to domestic stability, Marshall used the rule of law as expressed through the opinions of the Supreme Court (which, by power of precedent, bound the lower courts) to tie dynamic economic interests to the federal government and create a national sense of enlightened self-interest ennobled by traditional conceptions of order, civic duty, and self-restraint. "Bench and bar," writes R. Kent Newmyer, would be "equal partners in unleashing the forces of commerce, which would in turn strengthen the bonds of Union and raise the tone of civilization." Hamilton had tried to realize a plan of unity in the 1790s with the funded national debt and the national bank, but his approach was too "European" and elitist to be popular and durable. Marshall's answer was more consistent with the Enlightenment principle of the rule of law and with rising liberal-capitalist expectations. In this sense, he linked the aristocracy of the eighteenth century and the capitalism of the nineteenth. Although the Progressive historians' portrayal of Marshall often was overdrawn, it correctly emphasized the nexus between his nationalism, constitutionalism, and views on political economy. Max Lerner, for example, perceptively noted that Marshall "had vision enough to see that political power had to be coterminous with the scale of economic activity," and that he "saw that the common man, who would not respond to Federal aristocratic theory, would respond to the same property interests when they were clothed in the rhetoric of the national interest." Marshall's opinions comprised this "rhetoric," and the "national interest" was embodied in the Constitution, as the Marshall Court interpreted it, which protected private gain as a public virtue. "Union was hypostatized into Nation," Newmyer concludes, "the government of limited authority . . . became a government of sufficient power. The constitution became the symbol of that Nation and the source of its vitality." Through constitutional nationalism, Marshall moved both to reclaim a world lost and control a world to come by forming a new union of interests.[21]

The constitutional nationalism that Marshall enunciated in his best-known opinions—probably most resoundingly in *McCulloch v. Maryland* and *Cohens v. Virginia*—was "negative" or "defensive" in the sense that it defended the federal government against encroachments by the states and protected the Union from their centrifugal and parochial interests. He asserted that the Constitution was the fundamental law of the sovereign people and not a compact among sovereign states; that the Supreme Court's interpretation of the Constitution should advance the purposes for which it was intended and not safeguard state prerogatives; and that the national government's powers, though limited, are supreme in their sphere and can be adapted to meet new circumstances. "Marshall was on guard against every tendency to continue treating the new Union as though it were the old Confederation," Justice Felix Frankfurter later wrote, and a sympathetic contemporary, John Quincy Adams, judged that he had succeeded: "Marshall has cemented the Union which the craft and quixotic democracy of Jefferson had a perpetual tendency to dissolve." Although the Chief Justice believed the federal government had plenary power to attain the ends for which it was created, he did not seek to enhance its power beyond what he believed the Constitution accorded it, nor did he proclaim his decisions as advancing a comprehensive program for developing a consolidated nation. For example, he did not regard the general welfare clause in Article I, Section 8 of the Constitution as a substantive grant of powers and wrote that it should not be interpreted as legitimizing an extensive program of internal improvements. To debate whether Marshall did or did not lay the constitutional groundwork for the "positive" state—the modern "liberal" government with vast powers to regulate the economy and promote social welfare—is to address a false and ahistorical issue. It is true that Marshall shared some of the "positive" nationalism of contemporary advocates of an interventionist federal government, such as Henry Clay, Daniel Webster, and John Quincy Adams; he was in some respects a "proto-Whig," a cautious modernizer seeking disciplined change. As a political or constitutional attitude, however, it is too remote conceptually to be evaluated in relation to its supposed twentieth-century descendant.[22]

The interplay between the "negative" and "positive" qualities of Marshall's nationalism during his chief justiceship can be discerned clearly in his perspective on territorial expansion and economic development.[23] He strongly supported westward expansion on political and economic grounds, and once the new territories matured into states, he wanted them kept free from provincial mercantilist restrictions so that entrepreneurial energy would be released, a national "common market" promoted, political unity encouraged, and independence from foreign economic pressure secured. Federal judicial power would combine with the rising market mentality, and vested interests would have a stake in supporting the national judiciary as a force against state impediments to commerce, contracts, and property rights. The goal was, as Daniel Webster put it, an economic "E Pluribus Unum." Marshall achieved much of it judicially through landmark economic decisions such as *Fletcher v. Peck* (1810), *Dartmouth College v. Woodward* (1819), *Sturgis v. Crowninshield* (1819), *Gibbons v. Ogden* (1824), *Brown v. Maryland,* (1827), and *Craig v. Missouri* (1830). His dissent in *Ogden v. Saunders* (1827), which placed the rights of acquiring and using property on the level of natural law, offers perhaps the purest distillation of his political economy because, voting in the minority, he did not have to temper his language to persuade other justices. These several judicial statements comprised another aspect of the same perspective that had characterized his approach toward western land speculation and internal improvements as a Virginia nationalist and southern Federalist before he joined the Supreme Court. Having lost faith in the utility of "republican remedies" to create social cohesion, he and other like-minded Federalists in the immediate postratification period sought practical, tangible mechanisms like a central bank, a national court system, and infrastructure building to bind the extended republic together. Marshall was among the most broadly economic minded of the Federalists, largely because the legal controversies he had experience with in his law practice and on the Court developed mainly from mercantile or property disputes, and because of his personal involvement with investments in internal improvements. This bias toward legal resolutions gave Marshall's political economy a more practical cast than Hamilton's often theoretical formulations, and consequently a more immediate impact on the society. As Marshall stated in 1829, "The Judicial Department comes home in its effects to every man's fireside: it passes on his property, his reputation, his life, his all." Moreover, his political economy was oriented toward internal commerce, not external trade as was Hamilton's. The "domestic intercourse" he championed would be facilitated over an expanding territory by transportation improvements, fluid investment practices, and legal predictability established by the federal courts through the contract and commerce clauses. Marshall did not have the political and constitutional reservations about acquiring the Louisiana Territory that Federalist critics of President Jefferson had at the time of the purchase, and he later ratified it juridicially. Federalist leaders did not want to strengthen the executive's hand right then, and those from the North feared that territorial expansion would strengthen the agrarian South at the expense of their commercial constituency. Southern Federalists such as Marshall did not worry that westward movement would dilute their power in the national government, as most of the new states would be tied economically and culturally to their region. In later years, Marshall endorsed most of the ideas of Daniel Raymond, a lawyer and author of *Thoughts on Political Economy* (1820), who rejected European laissez faire theories, regarded the nation as an aggregate economic unit, and, construing political economy as the science of public prosperity, concerned himself mainly with ways of increasing its productive power rather than protecting idle property and preserving a rentier lifestyle.

Marshall's opinion in *Gibbons v. Ogden* (1824), which struck down a state-granted monopoly on steamboat service, provides the clearest example of how he promoted national unity by encouraging economic enterprise. "In *McCulloch vs. Maryland* and *Cohens v. Virginia*," Albert Beveridge wrote, "he made the Government of the American people a living thing; but in *Gibbons v. Ogden* he welded that people into a unit by the force of their mutual interests." His decision in *Craig v. Missouri* (1830), denying a state authority to issue bills of credit, drew on his knowledge that such measures had been proven disruptive during the Confederation, and declared his belief that uniform currency regulations were needed to prevent the states from setting up barriers to economic growth and legal regularity. With *Dartmouth College v. Woodward* (1819) as the foundation, Marshall and the Court defined the legal status of the corporation—from his experience in Virginia, an ideal instrument for promoting private enterprise and economic development—and simultaneously regulate the interstate expansion of corporations while limiting the states' authority to control them inside state borders. Marshall was, in one scholar's apt phrase, "protransaction": willing, when other equities were not plainly unbalanced and when public interests were not clearly compelling, to protect from state action the contracts by which people conducted their personal affairs. In a society in which one's welfare depended increasingly on economic accomplishments, the stability of the network of voluntary, contractual relationships entered into was paramount. For the emerging middle class and the traditional elites trying to compete with it, a constitutional system that preserved what they already had while permitting ordered change and opportunity was especially desirable for maintaining social cohesion. Marshall's decisions dealing with political economy were crucial in melding the "private" realm of vested rights to the national interest.

In February 1812 the Old Dominion afforded the Chief Justice an ex officio opportunity to act on these beliefs. The General Assembly appointed him to head a commission to determine whether the headwaters of the James River could be linked with three tributaries of the Ohio River in present-day West Virginia—the Greenbrier, Kanawha, and New Rivers—across the Appalachians by a series of roads, canals, and riverbottom improvements. The legislature chose him to lend prestige and credibility to the survey and tried to build political support for its findings by selecting Federalists and commercially oriented moderate Republicans to serve on it. The 56-year-old Marshall's willingness to undertake an arduous trek into the Appalachian hinterlands demonstrated his long-standing strong commitment to the survey's larger economic and political purposes of drawing Ohio River commerce into Virginia's waterways and creating bonds of nationalism between East and West. With transmontane settlement burgeoning and Robert Fulton's steamboat proving that upstream navigation against strong currents was feasible, the time was right for Virginia to act on a vision that George Washington had set forth nearly three decades earlier, and which Marshall implicitly endorsed in his biography of the first president.[24]

Marshall and the other members of the 22-man party traveled 250 miles between Lynchburg and the Great Falls of the Kanawha from 1 September to 9 October—Marshall probably felt he was reliving some of his childhood days surveying with his father on the Fairfax domain—and submitted a report to Governor James Barbour, for transmittal to the assembly, on 26 December. Marshall was chiefly responsible for the report's preparation, and its style and themes, plus the fact that he was one of only two commissioners present on the entire trip, strongly suggest that he was its principal author. The *Report of the*

Commissioners Appointed to View Certain Rivers within the Commonwealth of Virginia set forth a cautiously optimistic, statesmanlike vision of the economic and political benefits that would result from linking Virginia's rivers to the Ohio River. Supportive but not "boosterish," the *Report* gave fair consideration to the geographic, technical, and economic obstacles that would impede the project but ultimately judged that its political and commercial benefits outweighed them. Agriculture and industry would be enhanced, and the population would grow. Perhaps more important for the long-term welfare of the nation,

That intimate connection which generally attends free commercial intercourse, the strong ties which are formed by mutual interest, and the interchange of good offices, bind together individuals of different counties, and are well calculated to cherish those friendly sentiments, those amicable dispositions which at present unite Virginia to a considerable portion of the Western people. At all times, the cultivation of these dispositions must be desirable; but, in the vicissitude of human affairs, in that mysterious future, which is in reserve, and is yet hidden from us, events may occur to render their preservation too valuable to be estimated in dollars and cents.[25]

The War of 1812 prevented the state government from acting on the commission's recommendations, but soon afterward it established a fund for public works that financed river improvements and road construction, and the commission's report helped bring about the James River and Kanawha Canal, the most important of Virginia's many transportation improvements during the pre–Civil War period. Marshall, already a stockholder in the James River Company that was responsible for navigation improvements along the waterway, actively supported the whole canals-and-highways enterprise in the Old Dominion for the rest of his life. He served as a delegate to a convention on internal improvements in Charlottesville in 1828. Chaired by James Madison and with James Monroe among the attendees, the convention recommended that the state government undertake more of the improvements to the James, Potomac, and Shenandoah Rivers suggested in the 1812 commission report and build turnpikes from Richmond to the southwest part of the state and the Ohio River. The convention, however, interpreted the term "internal" narrowly. When Marshall, Madison, and Monroe supported a motion that Virginia buy stock in the Chesapeake and Ohio Canal, they were voted down. Spending $500,000 in tax money in Maryland mainly to benefit Virginians living along the Potomac, the convention concluded, was too generous. A few years later, Marshall chaired a committee that sold stock in the James River and Kanawha Company after it was chartered in 1832. The campaign raised subscriptions for over 10,000 shares worth more than $1,000,000.[26]

Just before administering the oath of office to Jefferson on 4 March 1801, Marshall confided to his friend and fellow Federalist Charles Cotesworth Pinckney that he believed, "The Democrats are divided into speculative theorists & absolute terrorists: With the latter I am not disposd to class Mr. Jefferson."

After hearing the new president's inaugural address, Marshall remarked, "It is in the general well judgd & conciliatory. It is in direct terms giving the lie to the violent party declamation which has elected him; but it is strongly characteristic of the general cast of his political theory." The Chief Justice warned, however, that if Jefferson "arranges himself" with the "absolute terrorists" in his party, "it is not difficult to foresee that much calamity is in store for our country."[27] He did not have to wait long to see which side the president would choose.

"I shall . . . by the establishment of republican principles," Jefferson vowed in 1802, "sink federalism into an abyss from which there shall be no resurrection for it." Even before then, this spirit had determined the immediate target of the Republicans' revenge: the national judiciary, the last bulwark of Federalism in the government. The Federalists, Jefferson wrote, "have retired into the judiciary as a stronghold. There the remains of federalism are to be preserved and fed from the treasury, and from that battery all the works of republicanism are to be beaten down and erased." William Branch Giles, one of the more radical Jeffersonians in Congress who handled the attack on the national judiciary for the President, expressed the Republicans' intent: "[T]he revolution is incomplete so long as that strong fortress [the judicial branch] is in possession of the enemy," and "a pretty general purgation of office has been one of the benefits expected by the friends of the new order of things." The Republicans' complaints about the Federalist-controlled national judiciary were well founded, however, and Marshall and the Federalists could scarcely have been surprised that the new administration would try to undo what the extremists in their party had done to the courts while they were in power.[28]

When the federal judicial system was formed in 1789, it was something of an abstraction, with its nationalizing power limited by the historical influence of the state judiciaries. During the 1790s, however, the Federalists wielded the national courts as a blunt weapon of partisanship. Judges used charges to juries to deliver party polemics and berate opponents; they consistently supported Federalist political views in important cases, even against clear legal precedent; they harshly treated frontier dissidents and Republican journalists; and they openly campaigned for Federalist candidates. By the election of 1800, the political bias of the federal judiciary was pervasive and caused a popular backlash that contributed to the Republicans' victory. As a last measure to preserve its hold on "the least dangerous branch," the outgoing Federalist Congress passed, and the defeated John Adams signed, the Judiciary Act of 1801. The law enlarged the size and jurisdiction of the national courts, made it easier to remove litigation from state to federal courts, and, to deny Jefferson an opportunity to appoint a Supreme Court justice, reduced the number of justices from six to five starting with the next vacancy. As Gouverneur Morris explained, the Federalists "are about to experience a heavy gale of adverse wind; can they be blamed for casting many anchors to hold their ship through the storm?"[29]

The Republicans almost immediately set to work hauling in those anchors. Jefferson had indicated as much in his first annual message to Congress in

December 1801: "The judiciary system . . . and especially that portion of it recently erected will of course present itself to the contemplation of Congress." First, the Republicans repealed the Judiciary Act of 1801. Next, they passed another judiciary law in early 1802, the main effect of which was to put the Supreme Court out of business for a year by rescheduling its terms. In 1804, the Republicans removed a mentally unstable and bibulous Federalist judge, John Pickering, from office and tried to impeach an associate justice, the venomously partisan Samuel Chase. Some Federalists feared that had the Republicans succeeded in ousting Chase, William Paterson, a Hamiltonian, and Marshall were next. Meanwhile, Federalists were purged from positions in the national judicial bureaucracy. Of the 13 U.S. attorneys and 18 marshals replaced during Jefferson's first term, 11 and 13, respectively, were Federalists. Some of Marshall's relatives were caught up in the Republicans' machinations. Two of his brothers-in-law, George Keith Taylor and William McClung, were appointed circuit court judges under the Judiciary Act of 1801 but lost their positions when the law was repealed. Another brother-in-law, Joseph Hamilton Daveiss, was a U.S. attorney in Kentucky who first warned President Jefferson about Aaron Burr's conspiracy. Jefferson removed Daveiss in 1807 for failing to successfully prosecute Burr for treason. Daveiss retaliated by publishing a pamphlet that castigated Jefferson's handling of the Burr affair.[30]

Marshall "beleivd & feared that the tendency of the [Jefferson] administration will be to strengthen the state governments at the expence of that of the Union & to transfer as much as possible the powers remaining with the general government to the floor of the house of representatives." In response to what he regarded as a disquietingly particularist and populist agenda, Marshall affirmed "the importance of the judiciary at all times, but more especially the present," and pledged that "I shall endeavor in the new office to which I am calld [sic] not to disappoint my friends." Following this "strange revolution which has taken place in public opinion," Marshall determined to address probably the most formidable political problem of the time, rescuing Federalism from self-destruction, but the instrument he intended to use, the independent judiciary, itself soon fell under powerful attack. He did not respond immediately and vigorously, and in some ways his reaction had to be passive even though he was the most powerful Federalist in national office. His detachment was partly attitudinal, a holdover from his unpleasant experiences with factional strife when he served in state and national legislatures: "There is so much in the political world to wound honest men who have honorable feelings that I am disgusted with it & begin to see things & indeed human nature through a much more gloomy medium than I once thought possible." But his self-distancing posture was more a result of political and institutional imperatives. Jefferson and the Republicans had a great political advantage, having just swept into power over a discredited Adams and a gravely divided incumbent party. During the Republicans' first campaign against the federal courts, which not coincidentally coincided with Jefferson's first term, Marshall could hardly avoid being put on the defensive. The most he could do was to fight a holding action until Jefferson and the arch-Republicans spent themselves or more moderate elements in their party succeeded them.[31]

By deciding that he had to disengage from the Federalists' past politicization of the courts to restore their legitimacy, Marshall relinquished much of his ability to initiate action. He could not contest his opponents in public debate or otherwise promote Federalist policies because he feared that the judges, as he put it later, would be "condemned as a pack of consolidating aristocratics." To minimize the possibility that his grand jury charges would be misused or misinterpreted, he kept them bland and concise and would not allow them to be published. He had to wait for controversies to come to him in legal form. He then made the most of those limited opportunities to advance his political positions through artfully composed opinions that preserved the national judiciary's institutional authority and helped keep the Federalists alive as a political movement. Even then, however, he did not hand down decisions that directly challenged the Republicans' ideals or political dominance for the better part of a decade. He chose his battles carefully. Although he thought the repeal of the Judiciary Act of 1801 might be unconstitutional, he did not secure the backing of all his colleagues and submitted to this first blow from the Republicans ("policy dictates this decision to us all"). Later, in the relatively benign environment under Jefferson's successors, Marshall had more freedom to act, beginning with his first major defense of federal judicial authority against a recalcitrant state legislature (*United States v. Peters* [1809]), then with the first annulments of state laws under the contract clause (*Fletcher v. Peck* [1810]; *New Jersey v. Wilson* [1812]). For the most part, Marshall continued using the cautious, detached, statesmanlike approach that earlier, more hostile circumstances had dictated.[32]

"It is certainly devoutly to be wished that the politician may completely merge in the Judge," Marshall wrote privately in 1812, "for nothing is more to be deprecated than the transfer of party politics to the seat of Justice." If by this remark Marshall meant that as chief justice he would not participate in partisan politics or use the powers of the Court to undercut directly the domestic and foreign policy decisions of the Congress and the president, then he met the high standard implied. Notwithstanding his strong disagreements with the Republicans' policies, especially their diplomacy, and in spite of intense provocation from Jeffersonian critics in his home state, Marshall maintained a posture of partisan neutrality.[33]

The Republicans' policy toward the Napoleonic Wars provided the strongest test of Marshall's disengagement because he believed Jefferson's and Madison's strategy threatened American independence. Nonetheless, he held to the view he had expressed during the Jonathan Robbins affair in 1800 that the executive was supreme in foreign affairs, and so he did not hamper the Republicans' efforts to stay out of the Napoleonic Wars through nonimportation, embargo, and nonintercourse laws. Marshall believed that, as in the 1790s, the Republican party was dominated by Anglophobes whose ill-conceived policies aided France and would draw the United States into war with Great Britain, "the only power which protects any part of the civilized world from the despotism of that tyrant whom we shall then be arranged [Napoleon]." From the start of Jefferson's first term, he had thought that "there is a mass of violence & passion in the [Republican] party which seems to me disposd to press on to war," and by 1808 a crisis of national survival loomed, a rough replay of the Quasi-War with France during the Adams administration.

I have never known a time which I believed to be more perilous than the present. The internal changes which have been already made & those further changes which are contemplated by a party always hostile to our constitution & which has for some time ruled our country despotically, must give serious alarm to every attentive & intelligent observer; but these dangers lose their importance in the still greater perils which threaten us from without. Unless that system which has for some time guided our councils with respect to foreign powers can be changed[,] the independence of the United States will soon become an empty name & the name itself I fear will not long survive the substance.[34]

Even with these forebodings, Marshall did not inject himself into party politics. The Republican administrations relied on the federal courts to enforce their sanctions regime, and though Marshall's Federalist compatriots from New England argued that the embargo was unconstitutional, he did not question the legitimacy of it or the other trade restrictions when he addressed them in court. (Over a decade later, in *Gibbons v. Ogden* [1824], he mentioned that a government's power to impose embargoes was universally recognized.) In cases arising from seizures of British property and acts of piracy during the war, Marshall distinguished between questions of policy and law. With due regard for protecting individual rights against official abuse and for defending the rights of neutrals, he upheld the government's right to confiscate enemy property during wartime and to subordinate private rights to national security if Congress granted the executive branch that authority by passing a law or ratifying a treaty. Marshall believed that in cases with diplomatic import, the courts must consider the international implications of their decisions and accord the president and Congress greater deference than in domestic affairs. He also sought to balance the traditional neutral rights of the United States with its sovereign powers by giving maximum protection to American vessels without weakening the federal courts' power to deal with violations of American law. Moreover, by holding American merchantmen and privateers to a high legal standard, he avoided the political problem of seeming too pro-American, and thus pro-Republican, in his rulings.[35]

Marshall declined opportunities during these dire times to improve the Federalists' prospects by involving himself in either state or national politics. He knew that doing so would contradict his efforts to depoliticize the judiciary and might incite the Republicans to go after the courts again. Instead, by 1808, he "had absolutely withdrawn myself from the busy circles in which politics are discussed. I devoted to agricultural pursuits the time which could be drawn from professional duty & scarcely ever read a newspaper." He did not even vote in presidential elections. He claimed that his "attempts to produce in my own mind an indifference to what was passing around me" almost succeeded, but his correspondence betrays a continuing keen interest in party matters. He kept track of the Federalists in Virginia—"a small & oppressed minority"— noting the deleterious effect of a new election law that replaced the previous system of district balloting for presidential electors with a statewide ticket that clearly benefited the majority Republicans. He shared information about political developments with Federalist friends outside Virginia, especially Charles Cotesworth Pinckney of South Carolina, his fellow XYZ envoy. He endorsed Pinckney's nomination as the Federalist candidate for president in 1808, though he did nothing to assist him. It is not evident whether Marshall agreed with some Virginia Federalists' pragmatic decision to support the Republican James Monroe, a critic of the Madison administration, rather than the Federalist ticket, as the best way to take advantage of divisions in the Republican party and elect a more sympathetic president.[36]

The coming of war with Great Britain in 1812 may have tempted Marshall to oppose the Republicans more explicitly. "Although I have for several years forborne to intermingle with those questions which agitate & excite the feelings of party," he wrote to a disgruntled Republican, former Secretary of State Robert Smith, the declaration of war

has appeared to me, as it has to you, to be one of those portentous acts which ought to concentrate on itself the efforts of all those who can take an active part in rescuing their country from the ruin it threatens. All minor considerations should be waived; the lines of subdivision between parties, if not absolutely effaced, should at least be covered for a time; and the great division between the friends of peace & the advocates of war ought alone to remain. It is an object of such magnitude as to give to almost every other, comparative insignificance; and all who wish peace ought to unite in the means which may facilitate its attainment, whatever may have been their differences of opinion on other points.

Like nearly all Federalists, Marshall vehemently opposed the war for several reasons. He thought American prosperity required friendly relations with Britain; England and the Royal Navy were needed to check Napoleon's designs on North America; the country was woefully unprepared to fight a war and would suffer heavy losses; and if England won, the United States might lose its independence. Some Federalist leaders saw a chance to rally their party and win over disaffected Republicans by running a peace campaign in the 1812 election. Marshall, who agreed with the strategy, was mentioned as a possible presidential candidate—the thought was that no northern Federalist could do well in the South—but he spurned any efforts on his behalf. "It is not . . . for me to indulge these feelings" of "mortification" at the outbreak of hostilities by seeking political office. There was no precedent for a sitting justice to seek national elective office, and for Marshall to have done so then would have hopelessly politicized the Court. While Virginia Federalists were choosing presidential electors, he was miles away in the mountains heading the river survey commission. He could only enjoy vicariously the Federalists' significant gains in the congressional and state elections later in the year.[37]

Despite his political reservations about the war, Marshall subordinated them to the needs of national defense. When the war went badly for the United States in the Atlantic Seaboard theater and an invasion of Virginia seemed imminent in 1813, the city fathers of Richmond named Marshall as one of thirteen members of a "vigilance committee" charged with coordinating the capital's defensive preparations with the state government and the militia. Marshall headed a subcommittee on fortifications, whose work drew on his military knowledge from the Revolutionary War and his experience as a general in the city militia afterward. After surveying the topography around Richmond, the subcommittee concluded that it was not feasible to fortify the city. "It is to be saved by operations in the open field, by facing the enemy with a force which may deter him from any attempt to penetrate the interior of our country, and which may impress him with the danger of separating himself from his ships." The alternative was grim. "If this protection cannot be afforded, Richmond must share the fate of other places which are in similar circumstances. Throughout the world, open [undefended] towns belong to the army which is master of the Country." The capital was spared attack during the war, though there were other invasion scares. The vigilance committee met sporadically through mid-August 1814. Meanwhile, Marshall may have helped occasionally with drilling new recruits for the militia. Lastly, he made no recorded comments about the Hartford Convention of 1815, but he certainly would have disagreed with the secessionist ideas that emerged from it.[38]

As another aspect of his effort to save the judiciary from the twin corruptions of ideology and party, Marshall drew a paradigmatic distinction between law and politics in many of his decisions. He "set upon removing 'law' from the arena of politics, upon establishing a rule of law that did not bend to the vagaries of expediency and the uncertainties of legislative and executive action on sensitive political issues," George L. Haskins has written. If the federal courts continued to meddle in partisan politics as they had during the 1790s, they would lose their legitimacy, abdicate their authority, and sacrifice their independence. Accordingly, William E. Nelson concludes, "To conserve law's command over some spheres of social life, the judges had to concede law's irrelevance in others." Marshall was, in effect, carrying out the restrictive portrayal of the federal judiciary's power that Alexander Hamilton gave in *Federalist 78*: "The judiciary . . . has no influence over either the sword or the purse; no direction either of the strength or the wealth of the society, and can take no active resolution whatever. It may truly be said to have neither Force nor Will, but merely judgment." As Marshall put the idea in an 1814 decision, "Like all other questions of policy, it is proper for the consideration of a department which can modify it at will; not for the consideration of a department which can pursue only the law as it is written. It is proper for the consideration of the legislature, not of the executive or judiciary."[39]

In implementation, the law/politics distinction meant that though the Supreme Court handled legal controversies with political implications, it did not decide them on political grounds. Cases had to take the form of a legal dispute and follow accepted judicial procedures. The justices' decision was based on the relative merits of the litigants' arguments and evidence, not on concerns for the outcome's impact on policy or politics. The distinction was easiest to draw in civil and equity cases, where the political implications were small, and in international law, admiralty, and prize cases, where executive discretion was greatest. Of all the categories of law Marshall dealt with, his differentiation between law and politics is most pronounced in international cases—to some degree also because he regarded international law as one of humanity's great achievements toward creating civil society.[40] At least rhetorically, though, Marshall attempted to apply the distinction in constitutional disputes as well. Although it is true that the interpretations he placed on the Constitution fit the needs of the country as he perceived them, especially during the Court's "golden age" from 1819 to 1824, to him the fit was serendipitous (though salubrious). He believed the outcomes of that period's key cases—those concerning the national bank, state bankruptcy laws, corporate charters, the federal courts' appellate authority, and interstate commerce—was warranted by the principles inherent in them and not by the utilitarian needs of the time. Moreover, Marshall's distaste for legislative politics, based on his terms in the Virginia assembly and the House of Representatives, may have made him appreciate the value of the judge's detachment from politics all the more by demonstrating the discrepancy between the functions of the separate branches of government. Courts were to defer to the policy decisions of the legislature and the executive if it was determined that they had the authority to make them—even if the results of those policies achieved undesired results.

That an act ought so to be construed as to avoid gross injustice if such construction be compatible with the words of the law, will not be controverted; but this principle is never to be carried so far as to thwart that scheme of policy which the legislature has the power to adopt. To that department is confided without revision, the power of deciding on the justice as well as wisdom of measures relative to subjects on which they have the constitutional power to act. Wherever then their language admits of no doubt, their plain & obvious intent must prevail.[41]

The law/politics categorization loses its usefulness for analyzing Marshall, however, if it is cast too rigidly. The distinction between the two is sometimes artificial and retrospective, and it is hard to see the legal and constitutional issues at the time as so denatured of politics as the dichotomy requires. Law and politics were not seen then as separate in theory or distinct in reality—least of all by a man with Marshall's political acumen and experience. He accorded the legislative and executive branches wide latitude to perform their constitutional duties, but the process by which he demarcated their responsibilities from the judiciary's was at its heart political. Rather than confining the Supreme Court to deciding "legal" issues and avoiding "political" cases, Marshall assumed the essentially political role of defining those categories and deciding when and how he would invoke the Court's power. His opinion in *Marbury v. Madison* demonstrates this point perhaps better than any other. Although it was his most thoughtful exposition of the separation of powers, it was also probably his most "politicized" decision, as will be discussed below. In other major rulings, Marshall designated some concepts that were replete with "politics"—property rights, commercial regulation, and corporate privileges, for example—as "law," thereby taking them out of the direct processes of democratic politics and into the preserve of the courts. In practice the Marshall Court was not so much applying neutral, fixed principles of law as aligning itself with the Federalist side in the party conflict with the Republicans. In addition, Marshall tempered his nationalism and defense of property rights on numerous occasions for "political" reasons. He did not consistently take the most nationalist or procreditor views available to him in part because he calculated that overreaching would have diminished the political stature of the judiciary and encouraged unwanted public opposition. Important political issues had constitutional ramifications, and the converse certainly was true as well, to a great extent because the Marshall Court decided they did. Many legal and constitutional controversies were actually born of disputes over the allocation of power. The Supreme Court was in politics, and there was no way Marshall or anyone else could get it out.[42]

The Marshall Court's treatment of slavery was governed by three main considerations that show how it balanced legal and political concerns. First, it did not consider that many cases dealing with slavery because the law of "the peculiar institution" was essentially local and few federal questions were raised in litigation. Second, slavery was sanctioned in the Constitution and federal and state law, which substantially limited the Court's discretion in applying precepts of natural law and natural rights. The specific legal points at issue, rather than broad moral and philosophical appeals, set the parameters of its decisions. Finally, slavery quickly was becoming the most factious and pervasive issue of the day, and the Court had to take into account the repercussions its slavery decisions would have on the society and on itself at a time when it was vulnerable to critics who were trying to reduce its power.[43]

In trying to impose some order on this unstable mix of law, politics, and morality, Marshall's concerns for keeping the Court out of an insoluble issue, maintaining social peace, and preserving the Union overrode his moral reservations about slavery and his belief that it violated natural law. To him slavery always was a necessary evil, never a positive good, but the fulminations of slaveowners and abolitionists made him worry that even incremental advances toward to freedom through the courts would endanger their independence and further divide the nation. Even though he thought "every man has a natural right to the fruits of his own labour," on the Supreme Court he decided against the slaves in all suits for freedom and slave trade cases he heard. He followed his earlier pattern as a lawyer of giving precedence to legal over moral arguments, but in seeking what one scholar has called "judicial objectivity" as chief justice, he gave the Court's affirmation to proslavery statutes and the international slave trade. "Whatever might be the answer of a moralist to this question [the slave trade]," he wrote in his most important slavery opinion, *The Antelope* (1825), "a jurist must search for its legal solution in those principles of action which are sanctioned by the usages, the national acts, and the general assent of that portion of the world of which he considers himself a part." Even when the "criminal and inhuman traffic" in slaves was involved, "[the] Court must not yield to feelings which might seduce it from the path of duty, and must obey the mandate of the law." On other cases concerning disputed ownership of slaves, Marshall wrote brief decisions and stuck to the facts at hand or abided by traditional legal practices, such as the exclusion of hearsay evidence, that as implemented favored masters' property rights over slaves' claims to freedom. In the latter instance, he judged that greater harm to society would follow from modifying a libertarian principle without clear guidelines: "However the feelings of the individual may be interested on the part of a person claiming freedom, the Court cannot perceive any legal distinction between the assertion of this and of any other right, which will justify the application of a rule of evidence to cases of this description which would be inapplicable to general cases in which a right to property may be asserted." Occasionally, more sympathetic *obiter dicta* crept into his opinions, as when he observed that "a slave has volition, and has feelings which cannot be entirely disregarded." In private he could be more condemnatory of slaveholders. He wished that the antislavery views of economist Daniel Raymond, author of *The Missouri Question* (1819), circulated more widely in the South to "engage that share of our serious reflection to which they are entitled," and he criticized Southerners for refusing to entertain any limitations on slavery. The South, he wrote in 1826, "seemed to cherish the evil & to view with immovable prejudice & dislike every thing which may tend to diminish it. I do not wonder that they should resist any attempt . . . to interfere with the rights of property, but they have a feverish jealousy of measures which may do good without the hazard of harm that is, I think, very unwise."[44]

One of those "measures which may do good," Marshall thought, was colonization. Like many moderate opponents of slavery, Marshall doubted that whites and blacks could live peaceably in the same society. He was skeptical of compensated emancipation plans, believing that blacks would continue to be subjected to degrading treatment from causes that could not be altered. In keeping with a state legal requirement, he put a provision in his will emancipating his "faithful servant Robin" if the slave agreed to leave the state afterward, but Marshall did not think that practice provided any long-term solution to the underlying problem of race relations. He thought the best answer was for blacks to move to their ancestral homeland of Africa. He joined the American Colonization Society in 1819 and headed its Richmond chapter from 1823 to 1827, when he founded the independent Virginia Society for Colonization. He recommended Liberia as the best haven for freed blacks, with its good soil, hospitable climate, and friendly natives. Removal would apply to all blacks in America, "by no means confined to the slave states. . . . The whole union would be strengthened by it and relieved from a danger whose extent can scarcely be estimated." Marshall thought the proceeds from the sale of federal lands should be used to finance the export of blacks to Africa. Instead of the western lands "becoming an object for which the States are to scramble, and which threatens to sow the seeds of discord among us," they instead would become "a source of national wealth." Even with colonization's benefits, however, to Marshall it was only a palliative. Nat Turner's rebellion in Virginia in 1831 made him believe all the more urgently that the conflict over of slavery would only be resolved by a societal convulsion—a crisis that he certainly did not want the Court to help bring on.[45]

Marshall later claimed that he did not take the Republicans' antijudiciary offensive personally—"I have never allowed myself to be irritated by Mr. Jefferson's unprovoked and unjustifiable aspersions on my conduct and principles"—but their attacks on the national courts troubled him deeply. Their treatment of his relatives was unsettling, and he grew especially anxious when they began targeting federal judgments for impeachment, with him as the main quarry. These attempts, he wrote his brother James, "are sufficient to alarm the friends of a pure & of course an independent judiciary, if among those who rule our land there be any of that description." The attempt to oust Associate Justice Samuel Chase from the Supreme Court pulled Marshall in several directions. At a time when he was trying to depoliticize the courts, Marshall found it hard to defend a justice who had overstepped the bounds of judicial propriety by using a recent charge to a grand jury to revile the Jefferson administration. Marshall, besides disliking Chase, disapproved of his conduct, both on its merits and because it brought the judiciary into disrepute. His colleague deserved some rebuke, but Marshall naturally was loath to give any aid and comfort to the Republicans. The Chief Justice had to defend his fellow justice and the Supreme Court from what he regarded as a partisan vendetta without appearing partisan himself and imperiling his own tenure.[46]

Sorting out these sentiments was easy compared with the balancing act he had to execute when he appeared as a witness for the prosecution at the Senate trial. In that setting he had to testify truthfully without volunteering critical characterizations of Chase or, through clever questioning, being led to go on record as supporting Republican contentions. The whole situation posed such a quandary for Marshall that he even went so far as to entertain the idea of giving Congress a review power over decisions of federal courts in lieu of impeaching judges who misapplied the law—an idea that would have rendered the judiciary less independent than before. Under examination by the impeachment managers about Chase's behavior at the sedition trial of Republican journalist James Callendar in 1800, Marshall made a less than cooperative witness. He resisted being drawn into descriptions of Chase's actions and instead insisted on recounting the facts as he knew them. Other times his answers were unspecific and equivocal and tended to put Chase in a slightly bad light. Marshall's testimony was regarded by at least one prominent Federalist, Senator William Plumer of New Hampshire, as unhelpful to Chase. "The Chief Justice really discovered too much caution—too much fear—too much cunning—He ought to have been more bold—frank & explicit than he was. There was in his manner an evident disposition to accommodate the Managers. That dignified frankness which his high office required did not appear." Marshall's performance did not help Chase, but the Republicans' move against the justice failed. He was acquitted because they failed to prove their case on substance, mismanaged the proceedings, and lost support from some party members on some articles. The Republicans abandoned the impeachment tactic, but the fervid partisanship of which Chase had been guilty left the federal courts, rendering them, no doubt to Marshall's great relief, more independent and stable than before.[47]

A constant goad to Marshall throughout his chief justiceship was his intense— and, if anything, intensifying—dislike for Thomas Jefferson. Henry Adams overstated the case only slightly when he wrote in his history of the Jefferson and Madison administrations that Marshall "nourished one weakness."

Pure in life; broad in mind . . . almost idolized by those who stood nearest him, and loving warmly in return—this excellent and amiable man clung to one rooted prejudice: he detested Thomas Jefferson. He regarded with quiet, unspoken, but immovable antipathy the character and doings of the philosopher standing before him. . . . No argument or entreaty affected his conviction that Jefferson was not an honest man.

The Chief Justice's animus toward his cousin—dating back decades, originating in personal differences, and exacerbated by pronounced ideological differences and the Republicans' recurrent efforts to curb the federal courts—never diminished. With other Republicans it was different. He reconciled with his childhood friend James Monroe and could even get along with the cantankerous John Randolph, who had managed the attempt to impeach Chase and, if successful, would have gone after him. However, Marshall never tried to mend relations with the man he once snidely referred to as "the great Lama of the mountains." He thought Jefferson was a dangerous demagogue and held him responsible—not entirely fairly—for the antijudiciary campaign.

He is among the most ambitious, & I suspect among the most unforgiving of men. His great power is over the mass of the people & this power is chiefly acquired by professions of democracy. Every check on the wild impulse of the moment is a check on his own power, & he is unfriendly to the source from which it flows. He looks, of course, with ill will at an independent judiciary.

Late in life Marshall wrote, "I have never believed firmly in [Jefferson's] infallibility. I have never thought him a particularly wise, sound and practical statesman [and] I have not changed this mode of thinking." The Chief Justice's enmity toward Jefferson caused him to personalize the political battle with the Republicans and stiffened his resolve to resist their agenda. "The whole attack [on the federal courts], if not originating with Mr. Jefferson, is obviously approved & guided by him . . . it behooves the friends of the union to be more on the alert than they have been."[48]

Well aware that Marshall probably was his most troublesome adversary, Jefferson returned the Chief Justice's vitriol in full, accusing him of serious professional lapses and personal flaws. Marshall bore a "rancorous hatred . . . to the Government of his country" and committed "twistifications of the law" that "show how dexterously he can reconcile law to his personal biases." In his hands, law was "nothing more than an ambiguous text, to be explained by his sophistry into any meaning which may subserve his personal malice." He possessed a "gloomy malignity which will never let him forego the opportunity of satiating it on a victim." Jefferson was outraged at Marshall's critical depiction of the Republicans in the last volume of the *Life of Washington*, which appeared toward the end of his second term, and in retirement he set about correcting that "party diatribe." He charged that under Marshall's leadership the justices "sculk from responsibility . . . An opinion is huddled up in conclave, perhaps by a majority of one, delivered as if unanimous, and with silent acquiescence of lazy or timid associates, by a crafty chief judge, who sophisticates the law to his mind, by the turn of his own reasoning." He encouraged—though he did not, as Marshall claimed, instigate—the journalistic rejoinders by Virginia Republicans to the *McCulloch* and *Cohens* rulings (see below). The relatively small and closed political communities of Washington and Virginia did not keep personal secrets well, so Marshall and Jefferson certainly knew what one thought of the other.[49]

The two leaders of their respective branches of government confronted each other directly in three prominent public controversies during the first decade of Marshall's tenure. The first was the case of *Marbury v. Madison* (1803), which signaled that Marshall intended to resist the Republicans politically on constitutional grounds. His decision was, in Dumas Malone's words, "a Federalist counterattack, directed primarily at the executive." By declaring that the Court would order the president to grant a judicial commission if Congress had not exceeded its authority by giving the Court the power to do so, he made it clear that the judiciary was going to function as a coequal branch of government and scrutinize legislative *and* executive actions. In the context of his political and personal dispute with Jefferson, it should be noted that whereas Marshall spent half of his opinion in an *obiter dicta* inquiry into the nature of *executive* authority, in the rest he treated the issue of judicial review of *legislative* acts in an almost anodyne manner, as if it were a settled question— which, given the extensive body of precedent and practice in the state and national courts since the 1780s, it largely was. Marshall the historian even went so far as to take liberties with the historical record to craft a conclusion that achieved his political and constitutional objective of declaring the Court's power while minimizing the risk of a confrontation with Jefferson. Yet after all the assertions of authority, Marshall then denied that the Court had jurisdiction over the case—a result he could have reached without a full hearing, but only at the risk of appearing to surrender the field. Thus he carried out his counterattack as an adroit tactical retreat from the blatant partisanship of the national courts during the Adams administration. One legal scholar has rightly called Marshall's opinion "one of the great acts of political genius in American history: reaffirming the Court's power of judicial review in such a way that there was nothing the Jefferson administration could do about it." "Only a politician *would*—and only a *great* politician *could*—do what Marshall did in *Marbury*." As another possible example of Marshall's political acuity, a few days after *Marbury* the Court upheld the repeal of the Judiciary Act of 1801 in *Stuart v. Laird*. Perhaps Marshall had something to do with the timing of the two decisions. By deferring to the Republicans just after he admonished Jefferson, Marshall took some of the political heat off the Court. If it passed up a chance to annul a law that hurt it, could the Court really be such a threat to liberty? Jefferson, a strong believer in the "departmental theory" of constitutional interpretation, contended that the *Marbury* decision "would make the judiciary a despotic branch," and, an astute politician himself, he knew that his clever cousin had trumped him.[50]

The treason trial of Aaron Burr in 1807 arguably was the greatest political drama of the early national period and put Marshall and Jefferson on a public stage to act out their personal and official rivalries.[51] Burr's case—a result of his arrest for plotting to instigate a secessionist military movement in the West—fell under Marshall's federal circuit jurisdiction because one of the key sites in the conspiracy, an island in the Ohio River, lay within Virginia's boundaries. As presiding judge in the trial, his rulings on law and procedure would greatly influence the outcome. Moreover, anything he did during the trial would be interpreted by how it affected the conflict between the judicial and executive branches and the Federalist and Republican parties. Jefferson detested Burr for trying to take away his electoral victory in 1800 and for collaborating with some Federalists in an odd disunionist scheme called the Northern Confederacy in 1804, but he had dismissed earlier reports of Burr's filibustering as party intrigues, largely because they came from Joseph Daveiss, the district attorney for Kentucky, a Federalist, and a brother-in-law of Marshall's. When Jefferson later accepted that Burr was up to something, he believed the Federalists were suborning it—whatever "it" was—and pushed for Burr's apprehension and prosecution, publicly declaring that the renegade Republican was guilty. In these circumstances, compartmenting law and politics was impossible. In Marshall's words, "[Burr's] case presents many real intrinsic difficulties which are infinitely multiplied by extrinsic circumstances."[52]

The details of Burr's trial are available elsewhere, but a brief recapitulation is needed here to outline Marshall's involvement. Even before Burr entered a courtroom, Marshall had decided in a related case (*Ex parte Bollman and Ex parte Swartwout* [1807]) that under the Constitution, treason had a narrow and specific meaning, and that the standard of evidence needed to prosecute was quite high. "Conspiracy is not treason. To conspire to levy war, and actually to levy war, are distinct offenses. . . . There must be an actual assembling of men for the treasonable purpose, to constitute a levying of war." The proceedings against Burr comprised five different stages lasting from late March through late October 1807. In a preliminary hearing, Marshall—drawing on *Bollman*—determined that there was probable cause to order Burr's committal only for the misdemeanor of planning to launch a military expedition against a foreign power (Mexico) that was at peace with the United States, and not for treason, and released Burr after he made bail. That ruling angered Jefferson, and if he needed further convincing of Marshall's partisan intentions, the Chief Justice provided it with an inexplicable social blunder. While Burr was out of detention, one of his lawyers, John Wickham, hosted a dinner. Wickham was an old friend of Marshall's from the Virginia bar and the Quoits Club, so Marshall attended—but so did Burr. As one of Marshall's biographers has written, "In a case with so many political overtones, the spectacle of the judge and the accused dining together just before the trial seemed more than indiscretion."[53]

Next, Marshall empanelled a grand jury—comprising 14 Republicans and two Federalists—that indicted Burr for the misdemeanor and for treason. During that phase, Marshall, acting on Burr's request, issued a subpoena to the president requiring him to delivery evidence in his possession to the defense. The Chief Justice asserted that courts had the power to compel testimony from any citizen, including the president. Jefferson denied that he could be ordered to appear in court, but he did not claim executive privilege and provided the papers Burr wanted. The trial, held in the most torrid part of a Virginia summer in the crowded House of Delegates chamber, lasted four weeks and featured forensic combat among some of the Old Dominion's most illustrious legal talent. The prosecution, hampered by Marshall's *Bollman* ruling, could not place Burr at the scene of the crime and failed to argue successfully for his "constructive presence" there. Marshall issued a lengthy opinion on the law of treason that essentially forced the jury to acquit Burr. Speaking through its foreman Edward Carrington, another of Marshall's brothers-in-law, the jury announced with odd equivocation that "Burr is not proved to be guilty by any evidence submitted to us. We therefore find him not guilty." In the last two anticlimactic phases, Burr was acquitted on the misdemeanor charge—with Marshall again ruling that much of the prosecution's evidence was inadmissible—but was ordered to stand trial for it in Ohio. The government did not pursue Burr further, and he went free, though discredited as no American had been since Benedict Arnold.

Although it is true that "[s]cant foundation exists for the charge that Marshall used the Burr trial to carry out a political agenda or a vendetta against Jefferson," the political content of his activities should not be understated. No one misunderstood who he had in mind by his reference in his 1 April opinion to "the hand of malignity" that "may grasp any individual against whom its hate is directed, or whom it may capriciously seize, charge . . . with some secret crime, and put . . . on the proof of his innocence." He knew that historically treason had been loosely defined and invoked to suppress dissent, not just crimes against the state, and that Federalist prosecutors and judges had carried on that practice in the 1790s—especially during the Whiskey Rebellion and Fries's Rebellion. He also knew that the Republicans—in a turnabout for the rough treatment accorded some of them under the Sedition Act—might prosecute certain New England Federalists for treason if this loose definition held. The Framers, however, had defined treason strictly, consciously diverting from the broader usage under English common law. Marshall thus had both a political interest in, and a constitutional justification for, placing the Federalists on the "right" side of the issue. Moreover, he sided with the Jeffersonians in rejecting the Federalist concept of a criminal common law under which treason could be tried, thereby associating his party with a more moderate position. At the same time, Marshall could not be accused of trying to benefit personally or embarrass Jefferson by facilitating Burr's acquittal. Burr was very unpopular, and Marshall and the Federalists had nothing to gain by his exoneration. As Marshall put it after the trial, "I might perhaps have made it less serious to myself by obeying the public will instead of the public law & throwing a little more of the sombre upon others." Nor could Marshall be charged with aiding a friend or political ally; during the deadlock in the presidential election of 1800, he had decided that Burr was a greater evil than Jefferson and declined to support his bid for office.[54]

As in his major constitutional decisions, Marshall crafted his opinions in *U.S. v. Burr*—especially the most important one, on the law of treason, delivered on 31 August—with a sensitivity to their political impact. He solicited the advice of at least two associates, William Cushing and Bushrod Washington, citing his concern that the justices rule consistently on circuit, lest the variations "be disreputable to the Judges themselves as well as to our judicial system." He employed some of the techniques of literary craftsmanship that helped give his Supreme Court rulings such persuasive power. Mindful that he might be accused of usurping the role of the jury, he borrowed some pithy phrasing from *Marbury v. Madison* when he asserted that "[i]t is of necessity the peculiar province of the court to judge of the admissibility of testimony." Also, he framed the issue in general, overarching terms, in this case as a battle of judicial independence and the rule of law against the popular clamor and, inferentially, a zealous executive. In a notable departure from his other decisions, however, Marshall adopted a tone of careworn and dutiful independence in anticipation that he would be vilified—which begs the question whether such a preemptive political defense belongs in a judicial opinion. Jefferson's principal biographer is not too harsh in stating that here Marshall "assumed the mantle of self-righteousness" when he wrote:

That this Court dare not usurp power is most true.
That this court dares not shrink from its duty is not less true.
No man is desirous of placing himself in a disagreeable situation. No man is desirous of becoming the peculiar subject of calumny. No man, might he let the bitter cup pass from him without self-reproach, would drain it to the bottom. But if he has no choice in the case; if there is no alternative presented to him but a dereliction of duty or the

opprobrium of those who are denominated the world, he merits the contempt as well as the indignation of his country who can hesitate which to embrace.[55]

Marshall's only rhetorical lapse in the entire affair occurred when he was issuing his opinion on 13 June in favor of a defense motion to subpoena President Jefferson for evidence in his possession. When reading his decision, Marshall said the words, "Should it [the trial] terminate as is wished on the part of the United States." One of the government lawyers objected to Marshall's use of "wished," at which point the Chief Justice quickly recovered by offering assurances "that it was not his intention to insinuate, that the attorneys for the prosecution, or that the administration, had ever wished the conviction of [C]olonel Burr, whether he was guilty or innocent." He later apologized and changed the wording of his opinion to read "Should it terminate as is *expected*" (emphasis added). Although he was only declaring the obvious—that Jefferson wanted Burr convicted—his verbal blunder gave the Republicans an opening to attack him for political prejudice. Perhaps it was an honest slip by a weary presiding judge; or perhaps he could not resist giving Jefferson a jab. Either way, it was a gaffe, and all the worse when he was directing his chief political adversary to turn over material that might help the man Jefferson was trying to put in jail.[56]

Together, Marshall's two expositions of the law of treason, in *Bollman* and *U.S. v. Burr*, were not quite the sterling defenses of individual rights that most historians have portrayed them as being. A recent analysis argues convincingly that his opinion in the Burr case "fell somewhere in between the prosecution and defense, making him the first federal judge who did not swallow whole the government's argument in a treason case. . . . [He] was staking out ground in between the defense contention that some overt act of force . . . was a necessary component of levying war and the prosecution's argument that force was irrelevant where the intention to levy war was clear from spoken or written words or from deeds performed away from the purported scene of action." Marshall did not reject the English concept of constructive presence at an overt act of treason—Lord Coke's axiom that "in treason all be principals." He just did not think it applied to what Burr did. From the government's perspective, Marshall's holdings did not severely undercut its ability to prosecute for treason. The Chief Justice had tightened the definition of "overt act" and widened procedural protections for those accused of treason, but he had left the doctrine of constructive treason in place, and the meaning of "levying war" remained broad. His interpretations proved durable; none was reversed during the next 50 years.[57]

Marshall called the Burr episode "the most unpleasant case which has ever been brought before a Judge in this or perhaps in any other country which affected to be governed by laws." The Republican press took him to task briefly, and a Baltimore mob burned him (and Burr) in effigy, but the public outrage passed quickly. Jefferson blamed Marshall, not the faulty indictment or the weak case, for frustrating his retribution against Burr. Well before the trial was over, he already had accused the Chief Justice of ill motives: "The event has been what was evidently intended from the beginning . . . not only to clear Burr, but to prevent the evidence from ever going before the world." Afterward, believing that the verdict showed that "it now appears we have no law but the will of the judge," he decided to use Marshall's conduct as a justification for renewing the campaign against the courts. He sent the trial record to Congress and in his annual message pointedly stated that "[y]ou will be enabled to judge whether the defect was in the testimony, in the law, or in the administration of the law, and wherever it shall be found, the Legislature alone can apply or originate the remedy." Whether Jefferson was suggesting another impeachment, a constitutional amendment, or a statutory restriction is unclear, but he was ready for some action, as his appointments to the Supreme Court— William Johnson, Brockholst Livingston, and Thomas Todd—had not been the resolute Republicans he had wanted. The most widely discussed judicial "reform" was an amendment permitting the removal of federal judges on the vote of both the House and Senate. Congress, preoccupied with foreign affairs and the embargo, did not approve any antijudiciary measures. With the federal courts upholding the sanctions policy, and with James Madison—who did not share Jefferson's hostility toward the judiciary—serving as President, a truce settled in between the courts and the Republicans for several years.[58]

Marshall and Jefferson were not yet through with each other, however. The next direct clash between them was the "batture controversy," a politically charged legal dispute pitting Jefferson against Edward Livingston, a lawyer and former member of Congress, over title to land in Louisiana. Livingston had acquired an interest in potentially lucrative alluvial ground along the Mississippi River near New Orleans (the "batture"), but the U.S. government claimed the land as public property and evicted Livingston and his workers from it in 1808. Two years later, Livingston sued Jefferson, by then out of office, for trespass in the federal circuit court in Richmond. Jefferson apparently believed that Livingston chose that venue because he thought Marshall would favor him and, fearful of losing on the merits, framed his extensively researched defense on the issue of jurisdiction. Because the alleged trespasses happened in New Orleans, he contended, the federal court in Virginia should not hear the case. Marshall wanted to have the Supreme Court take up the matter, but the other circuit judge insisted that the case be decided at a lower level. Accusing the Chief Justice of "rancorous hatred . . . to the government of his country," the former president used the occasion to press for having reliable Republicans appointed to the federal bench. He called Justice Cushing's death "fortunate . . . and so timed as to be a Godsend to me." Though the court dismissed Livingston's suit, Jefferson must have read Marshall's opinion as an implied rebuke for pleading on jurisdiction in order to avoid a trial on substance. In the final paragraph, Marshall conveyed his frustration that the applicable law "produces the inconvenience of a clear right without a remedy." Neither Marshall nor Jefferson commented on the case at the time, but the Chief Justice later thought his decision exasperated Jefferson more than *Marbury*. In 1821, at the height of the debate over his opinion in *Cohens v. Virginia* (see below), he explained that Jefferson's "settled hostility" to the federal courts was attributable to the fact that "the Batture will never be forgotten." "The case of the mandamus [*Marbury*] may be the cloak, but the batture is recollected with still more resentment."[59]

Marshall enjoyed markedly improved relations with Jefferson's successors as president. James Madison and James Monroe supported Federalist policies such as a tariff, a national bank, and internal improvements and bore no malice toward the national judiciary. Their three appointments to the Supreme Court— Joseph Story, Gabriel Duval, and Smith Thompson—proved to be allies of the Chief Justice, especially Story. Madison, with whom Marshall had no personal differences, backed the Court in its test of wills with Pennsylvania that arose from its decision in *United States v. Peters* in 1809, and in 1812, he vetoed a bill that would have burdened the justices with more responsibilities on circuit. Marshall and Monroe had repaired their friendship and exchanged cordial letters of an official nature while Monroe was secretary of state and president. In 1822, Monroe apparently felt on good enough terms with the Court to ask it for an advisory opinion on the constitutionality of an internal improvements program. Marshall declined to express a view on the constitutional question, but he offered a bit of policy advice in suggesting that a measured approach "would be productive of no mischief, and of great good."[60]

In contrast to his amicable dealings with these Republican presidents, the Chief Justice soon found himself in a running battle with the ideological purists in Jefferson's party—the so-called "Old Republicans"—who took on the Supreme Court over the issue of national supremacy. After the War of 1812, Jeffersonian ideologues resisted the party's trend toward nationalist politics and demanded greater protection of states' rights. They also criticized the Court's use of section 25 of the Judiciary Act of 1789 to hear appeals of state court decisions in which constitutional issues were raised. Judge Spencer Roane of the Virginia Court of Appeals, a former legal associate of Marshall's in Richmond, was one of the most vociferous denouncers of the Marshall Court's constitutional nationalism and soon would become one of the Chief Justice's bitterest political enemies.[61]

Meanwhile, Roane and another judge on the Virginia court unsettled the Marshall family's possession of a portion of the land they had bought from Lord Fairfax's heir by upholding the state's prior grant of the land to a claimant. Believing that a legislative compromise reached in 1796 had resolved the dispute, Marshall decided to take the case to the Supreme Court on a writ of error under section 25 because a federal question was raised—whether a treaty took precedence over a state law—and personally took care of forwarding the case record to expedite a hearing. He had not contrived the appeal to get a definitive ruling on section 25 or to guarantee the profitability of his investment in the Fairfax manor lands; he only wanted to secure his brother's title to a valuable tract. Marshall's continuing personal involvement in the case was not regarded as improper at the time as long as he recused himself from any official role, so he refused to sit in any cases to which the Fairfax title might be connected. Unforeseen by him, the litigation produced a major conflict between federal and state authority and resulted in a landmark decision upholding national supremacy. First, the Supreme Court, in a ruling written by Justice Washington, upheld the validity of the title, but the Virginia Court of Appeals refused to execute the Court's order in a set of seriatim opinions highlighted by Roane's provocative exegesis on states' rights. Marshall drafted a second writ of error that resulted in Justice Story's ringing affirmation of judicial nationalism upholding the constitutionality of section 25. Story later wrote that the recused Marshall "concurred in every word" of his opinion. The Jeffersonians in Virginia reacted with excitement and indignation at what they regarded as a severe encroachment on state sovereignty, but for now they made no political moves against the Supreme Court.[62]

The next skirmish in Marshall's feud with the Jeffersonians resulted from his decision in the national bank case, *McCulloch v. Maryland* (1819).[63] His opinion linked several themes sure to arouse their ire: national supremacy, implied powers, broad construction, Federalist financial practices, restrictions on state prerogatives, and denial of the compact theory of the Union. Moreover, although few people outside Virginia had paid much attention to the protracted Hunter-Martin litigation over the Fairfax lands, changes in the economic and political situation assured that criticism of *McCulloch* would have more impact. The economy was suffering under the Panic of 1819, for which the Bank of the United States was partly blamed, and sectional tension over the expansion of slavery was building. In addition, in the same term the Court handed down decisions in *Dartmouth College v. Woodward* and *Sturgis v. Crowninshield*. Along with *McCulloch*, they marked a turning point in the constitutional relationship between the national government and the states. From then on, the Marshall Court's broad interpretation of national supremacy and implied powers would increasingly influence the public debate over the major domestic issues of the day—slavery, internal improvements, the tariff, and the bank. After the *Richmond Enquirer*, the journalistic organ of Virginia's Old Republicans, printed the *McCulloch* decision and editorialized that "[t]his opinion must be controverted and exposed," Marshall wrote to Story that the case "has aroused the sleeping spirit of Virginia, if indeed it ever sleeps."[64]

The Jeffersonians' rejoinder was fashioned as a series of essays written by Spencer Roane and another state judge, William Brockenbrough, and published in the *Enquirer* by its states' rights editor, Thomas Ritchie. Brockenbrough led off with two letters, under the pseudonym "Amphictyon," that argued for the compact theory of the Union and a narrow reading of the "necessary and proper" clause of the Constitution. Marshall was so irritated that Republicans in his own state would publicly attack what he regarded as a definitive exposition of constitutional nationalism, and was so concerned that a larger assault on the judiciary might be in the offing, that he intruded himself into public debate for the only time in his chief justiceship. He determined that the persistent parochialism of Virginia must be scotched for good. Under the pseudonym "A Friend to the Union," he wrote two essays rebutting "Amphictyon" that appeared in newspapers in Philadelphia in late April and in Alexandria in mid-May. Three weeks later, the *Enquirer* started running the four "Hampden" articles by Roane. More acerbic and inflammatory than the earlier pieces by Brockenbrough, Roane's essays were also more worrisome to Marshall. "The storm which has been for some time threatening the Judges has at length burst on their heads & a most serious hurricane it is," he informed Justice Washington. "I find myself more stimulated on this subject than on any other because I believe the design to be to injure the Judges & impair the constitution." The Jeffersonians' letters "were designed for the country & have had considerable influence there." Working feverishly over two weeks, Marshall wrote nine lengthy letters that were published in an Alexandria newspaper from late June to mid-July over the pseudonym "A Friend to the Constitution." Although not fully persuasive as learned propaganda, the essays should have dispelled any doubts about his intellectual attainments. As Gerald Gunther has noted, "Marshall took on Brockenbrough and Roane on the level of technical detail as well as of general philosophy. With great care, point by point—indeed, too tediously for polemic effectiveness—he replied to the state judges' invocations of common law and international law and engaged them toe to toe on the true meaning of the learned treatise writers, of Vattel and Grotius and Lord Coke." He arranged for sympathetic members of the General Assembly to receive copies in case some moves were made in the legislature to curtail the courts. Such an effort did occur in the December session, when the state's members of Congress were instructed to work for an amendment creating a separate tribunal to resolve conflicts between the federal government and the states. The House of Delegates adopted the resolution, but the Senate did not, and the attempt died.[65]

As Marshall remarked a bit earlier, though, "the opinion in the Bank case has brought into operation the whole antifederal spirit of Virginia. Some latent feelings which have been working ever since the decision of Martin & Hunter have found vent on this occasion, & are working most furiously."[66] Marshall's opinions in *Cohens v. Virginia* (1821) presented the Old Republicans with their next grievance. It involved another altercation over section 25 appeals of state court rulings to the federal judiciary and enabled both sides to revisit *Martin v. Hunter's Lessee*. "A case could not have been better designed to alarm the zealous guardians of states' rights," according to Charles Hobson. "That Virginia should be cited to appear at the bar of the Supreme Court to defend its right to enforce its own penal laws was regarded as a monstrous invasion of state sovereignty and independence." Marshall, closely following the text of the Constitution, the Judiciary Act of 1789, and the Eleventh Amendment, produced another carefully crafted ruling that decided narrowly for Virginia on the merits but delivered a comprehensive legal and political confutation of the states' rights doctrine. While trying to show that the Supreme Court was not driven to aggrandize its power and dissolve state sovereignty, he also responded to the

dangerous arguments about the limits of national authority that he had heard
Southerners voice in the Missouri Compromise debates the previous year.[67]

The Jeffersonians responded quickly and severely. *Enquirer* editor Thomas
Ritchie demanded that the Supreme Court be abolished. Spencer Roane,
encouraged by Madison and Jefferson, wrote another series of indignant letters,
this time signed "Algernon Sydney," that Marshall thought were unsurpassed
for "coarseness & malignity." Roane was "the champion of dismemberment"
whose "calumnies and misrepresentations" would go unanswered because
"[t]here is on this subject no such thing as a free press in Virginia." Unlike
when the torrent of protest fell after *McCulloch*, however, Marshall did not
march into the public arena this time. He may have thought Henry Wheaton's
"masterly" reply was sufficient; the Supreme Court reporter wrote seven essays
under the pen name "A Federalist of 1789," which appeared in the New York
American in July and August of 1821. He may also have decided not to risk
harming the Court's prestige by trading polemics again. If he were identified as
a participant in partisan exchanges, the Supreme Court would be more
susceptible to attempts to weaken it. Criticism of the *Cohens* decision spread
and intensified during the summer and fall of 1821, leading Marshall to
conclude that "the whole attack [on the Court], if not originating with Mr.
Jefferson, is obviously approved & guided by him." Marshall was
oversuspicious of his cousin, who nonetheless was more than an interested
bystander. Jefferson encouraged Ritchie to print Roane's essays in pamphlet
form so they could be sent to allies in other states "in the hope of exciting others
to attend to this cause"; he allowed publication of his letters praising John
Taylor's book *Construction Construed, and Constitutions Vindicated*, a treatise
on agrarian Republican provincialism; and he urged Justice William Johnson to
break the supposed Marshall Court monolith by resuming seriatim opinions and
letting differences in opinion be vented in public. "The practice [of one opinion
for the Court] is certainly convenient for the lazy, the modest & the
incompetent," whereas separate opinions "shews whether every judge has taken
the trouble of understanding the case . . . and of forming an opinion for himself,
instead of pinning it on another's sleeve." "The very idea of cooking up
opinions in conclave, begets suspicions that something passes which fears the
public ear." Misinformed, Marshall had felt "surprize & mortification" on
hearing that Madison shared the Old Republicans' hostility to the federal
judiciary. Actually Madison disagreed with the sweep of Marshall's rulings in
McCulloch and *Cohens*, but he never questioned that the national courts should
be the arbiters of disputes over federal and state authority.[68]

Marshall and Story have been accused of suppressing part of the Republicans'
response by successfully keeping Roane's "Sydney" essays out of a Philadelphia
law periodical. Given his complaints about the lack of a free press in
Republican-dominated Virginia, the Chief Justice's alleged actions seem highly
hypocritical, but the full story has a much duller edge. Marshall wanted to
counter an effort by Jefferson to have the editor of the *Journal of Jurisprudence*
print the Roane pieces along with the *Cohens* opinion. Jefferson thought the

journal was an appropriate forum for more widely disseminating the Republican response, but Marshall believed the set of essays was "in form & substance totally unfit to be placed there." He proposed instead that the periodical's publisher carry Wheaton's rebuttal along with the Court's decision and Roane's pieces. Marshall neither intervened with the editor nor encouraged Story to do so, writing to his colleague that "I do not suppose you would willingly interfere so as to prevent . . . the publication." Instead, the "proper reply" to Jefferson's proposal would be first to suggest to the publisher that "the coarseness of . . . language," "personal & official abuse," and "tedious prolixity" of the "Sydney" essays disqualified them from appearing in print, and if that argument did not persuade, then to urge that Wheaton's articles be run also. The *Journal of Jurisprudence* soon ceased publication, and Jefferson's idea ended with it. Marshall remained convinced that the former president was managing the opposition to the Court, but this brief contretemps does not demonstrate that when it came to civil liberties, he shared his cousin's "darker side."[69]

The debate that Marshall's *Cohens* ruling touched off continued with diminishing intensity for another year or so. Marshall perceived "a deep design to convert our government into a meer [*sic*] league of States" and claimed—in the manner of Federalists in the 1790s, who equated opposition to their party with disloyalty to the nation—that "the attack on the judiciary is in fact an attack upon the union." He exaggerated the extent of support for reining in the federal courts, as no curtailments were imposed on them by law or constitutional amendment, even though by 1826 the Supreme Court had annulled the laws of ten states. The Virginia legislature considered but declined to act on amendments submitted by Roane that would have sharply restricted the authority of the federal courts. Congress did not approve a proposed amendment giving the Senate appellate jurisdiction over cases arising between a state and the national government, and it rejected a move to repeal section 25. Another idea to expand the Supreme Court's membership to 10 while requiring concurrence of seven justices in a federal dispute met a similar fate. Meanwhile, Jefferson and Ritchie withdrew from the fight, Roane died in 1822, and the immediate threat from Virginia passed. Proposals to limit federal judicial power were introduced in Congress for the next several years, however, and during 1819–27, a total of 18 were considered. The breadth and virulence of the opposition to the Court, especially during 1819–22, seems to have chastened Marshall. Despite opportunities, he did not again propound such expansive views of national power, and he and his colleagues adopted a self-check to preempt resistance to some of the Court's decisions: If a case fell under section 25, it would rule only with the concurrence of at least four of the seven justices.[70]

Historical scholarship was one activity that Marshall could engage in to encourage his political purposes without seeming to violate the standard of judicial nonpartisanship he was trying to establish. His involvement took on a decidedly partisan cast, however, largely because of the subject he chose to write about and the timing of his enterprise. His authorship of *The Life of*

George Washington was one of the first developments of a cultural process of mythologizing Washington that began right after the first president's death. These "marmorealizing forces" of the early 1800s, as Daniel Boorstin has termed them, produced, among written products, Parson Weems's preachy apocrypha, several biographies of the Father of Our Country, and a collection of his writings; a campaign to build a sepulchre for his remains; an expanding catalog of paintings, sculptures, and other representations; and increasingly florid and bombastic observances of his birthday. The Federalists promoted the apotheosis of Washington as a political tactic of self-justification and self-preservation, to emphasize that the premier Founding Father and Republican also was the First Federalist whose followers merited a reserved place in American politics. Despite the partisan controversies surrounding him when he left office, Washington was elevated to secular sainthood remarkably soon after he died, becoming, in Marcus Cunliffe's apt phrase, both "man and monument," the embodiment of republican virtue and American values.[71]

Marshall's role in this emerging iconography began in early 1800 when he agreed to a request from Bushrod Washington to write a biography of his uncle, the late president.[72] The project would take far more time and effort and generate far more controversy than he had anticipated. It also was much less profitable than he had hoped, but he still accomplished an important financial objective and made a significant contribution to the historiography of the new nation. Washington bequeathed all his public and private papers to Bushrod, who began planning to write a biography two days after the former president died. Soon after, Bushrod decided not to go ahead with his original idea of collaborating with Washington's private secretary, Tobias Lear, and asked Marshall if he would be interested in helping to write the book. Marshall appears to have made at least a tentative commitment sometime between February and April, and had definitely consented by the fall. Patriotism, reverence for Washington, loyalty to Federalism, a desire to help establish the historical record, and financial pressures related to the Fairfax lands all influenced his decision to become a historian.[73]

In October, Marshall first corresponded with the book's prospective publisher, Caleb P. Wayne, the Federalist editor of the *Gazette of the United States*; in December, he received "a trunk containing sundry books and papers . . . relating to the late General Washington" from Lear; and in mid-1801, Bushrod sent him several more trunkloads. Marshall, Bushrod, and Wayne dickered over the publishing contract for two years, including Marshall's insistence on anonymity to minimize the political repercussions. Amazingly, Marshall expected to produce four or five volumes of 400 to 500 pages each in one year, or roughly 40 pages a week, not including time for research and editing. Besides the inherent difficulty of maintaining that frenzied pace, he had not studied much history, had not written any detailed or lengthy scholarly works, and had not examined any of Washington's papers or drafted an outline. In 1803, Marshall began writing the first of what would become by its completion in 1807 far more than a biography: a five-volume, 3,200-page history of the British colonies, the Revolutionary War, and the Federalist era that stressed Washington's indispensable role in the winning of independence and in America's successful experiment in republican government. More than 20 years before the work was complete, Marshall had hoped that Washington would "long enjoy those blessings he has secured to his country" and "ever experience from his Countrymen those attentions which such sentiments [of gratitude] of themselves produce." With the publication of the biography, Marshall had gone about as far as one man could toward realizing that hope. After some of the volumes had appeared, John Adams assured Marshall that his work would create "a more glorious and durable Memorial of your Hero, than a Mausoleum would have been, of dimensions Superiour to the proudest pyramid of Egypt."[74]

To Marshall's regret, however, *The Life of George Washington* provided apt evidence for the observation of his friend St. George Tucker that "American biography, at least since the conclusion of the peace of 1783, is a subject which promises as little entertainment as any other in the literary world. Our scene of action is so perfectly domestic as to afford neither novelty nor variety." Contemporary critics in the United States and England complained that Marshall's study of Washington had too much history and too little biography; even Federalists found the work disappointingly dull and tedious; and most Republicans excoriated it as partisan and libelous. The last volume on the 1790s, published in 1807, was the main target of detractors. Jefferson, who had thought that Marshall had conceived of the project to influence the 1804 presidential election, was so incensed by the final volume that he assembled the *Anas* partly as a rebuttal. Madison, who thought the rest of the work was "highly respectable," termed the last installment "quite inaccurate and ill-digested." Marshall anticipated the partisan condemnation. "I prepare myself for charges which are untrue & abuse which is unmerited," he wrote Oliver Wolcott, and to John Adams he stated that "I have reason to fear that the imprudent task I have just executed will draw upon me a degree of odium & calumny which I might perhaps otherwise have escaped." Twentieth-century commentators have reiterated most of the criticisms of the time, and some, using modern standards of scholarship, also have charged Marshall with plagiarism. Marshall was his own severest critic, often expressing "mortification on account of the careless manner in which the work has been executed" but nonetheless asking his publisher to convey to him "every condemnatory criticism which may reach you" so he could correct mistakes in subsequent editions.[75]

Even with its many flaws, the Washington biography provided a fitting literary capstone to Marshall's life before he became chief justice. It gave him an opportunity to reflect upon a period of time he had lived through, especially his public years; to recount many experiences that he had shared with his subject; and to set forth his views on the key political, military, and diplomatic events of America's founding decades. To a contemporary such as Marshall, Washington's life and times were inextricably intertwined; and to a Federalist, many of the events of that life seemed a fulfillment of long trends that had brought the proper sort of leaders to power—those "great men" embodying a classical code of republican virtue and selflessly committed to halting societal decay and democratic despotism. Historical writing of this period was intentionally didactic, not dispassionate, and borrowed freely from other works without attribution or far more expansively than modern "fair use" would allow. The *Life of Washington*, recently described as "a new kind of national history designed to promote national unity," set the pattern for interpretations of the first president for over a hundred years. The biography also proved valuable as a compendium of documentary sources, offering the first public access to Washington's papers and addresses. Marshall revised the book for many years—"a work which must be performed at liesure [sic]," he told Bushrod Washington—and by 1821 had abridged it to four volumes. He looked forward to publishing a corrected edition—"one of the most desirable objects I have in this life"—and decided to issue the first volume of colonial history at his own expense under a separate title in 1824. He chose to detach it from the main text because "it is considered rather as an incumbrance on the residue of the work" and "is so much improved that its publication may probably be useful to what is to follow. . . . my object being to do justice to my own reputation." The second edition of the main body of the *Life of Washington* was published in 1832, and the entire work was issued in a two-volume abridgement in 1838, making it available to a much broader public, including schoolchildren who could imbibe its lessons in civic virtue.[76]

Marshall had grossly overestimated his returns from the *Life of Washington*. Expecting to earn up to $75,000 from sales of at least 30,000 copies, he received less than $20,000 from sales of over 7,000. The high price per volume, the cumbersome use of postmasters as subscription handlers, and publication delays diminished interest in the project. Given the difficulty Marshall experienced writing in such detail under deadline—"I had to learn that under the pressure of constant application the spring of the mind loses its elasticity"—and all the fretting he did about corrections and revisions, the smaller return must have especially disappointed him. Despite the deflated hopes, the biography achieved commercial success domestically by the measures of the time. It also was published in London in 1807 and translated into French, German, and Dutch. Marshall's royalties enabled him at last to unburden himself of the vexing Fairfax lands debt and achieve and maintain a measure of prosperity he had sought for so long.[77]

By the end of the so-called "Era of Good Feelings" in the mid-1820s, Marshall to a large degree had achieved his political and constitutional goals for the national judiciary even though Republicans still controlled the Congress and the presidency and were the majority party on the state level. The Supreme Court itself enjoyed its highest stature ever. Under Marshall—with Story's important assistance—it had built a constituency of nationally minded politicians, economic interests, and lawyers who stood to benefit from a strong national government, a unified and stable legal system, and a common market that the Court's decisions did much to bring into being. Marshall's decision in *Gibbons v. Ogden* was widely hailed for breaking up a hated monopoly. The Court and Monroe's administration ended in 1825 on good terms. Marshall wrote to the departing president that "I feel sincere pleasure in the persuasion that your administration may be reviewed with real approbation by our wisest statesmen." The new president, John Quincy Adams, had been critical of the Court some years earlier but in his inaugural address praised it for having "expounded the Constitution and the laws, [and] settling in harmonious coincidences with the legislative will[,] numerous weighty questions of construction." Marshall was pleased with Adams's one successful appointment to the Court, Robert Trimble in 1826. Measures to restrict the federal courts' powers were still introduced in Congress and some state legislatures—as Marshall put it hyperbolically, "fuel is continually adding to the fire at which the *exaltées* are about to roast the judicial department"—but the most recent antijudiciary furor had passed.[78]

The Marshall Court benefited from the breakup of the first American party system and the brief period of uniparty government in the 1820s. For a while at least, he and the Court were freed from the stigma of partisanship by the demise of their principal defender, the Federalist party. Federalism never lost the image of disloyalty some extreme Northerners had placed on it with the Hartford Convention in 1815, and it soon disintegrated into factions, while the Republicans and then the National Republicans, having adopted much of the Federalist program, came to dominate an essentially single party system. The Federalists' candidate in the 1816 presidential election never had a chance, in the 1820 contest they did not run anyone, and in 1824 four "Republicans"— really representatives of sectional and economic factions—sought the presidency. As Henry Clay wrote in 1826, "[W]e really have in the Country no other than a Republican party. Names may be gotten up or kept up in particular states for local or personal purposes, but at this time there are but two parties in the Union, that of the Administration and the Opposition." In Marshall's home state, like in the South generally, Federalists did not adapt their organizing and electioneering techniques to a new era of nationwide "professional" politics as effectively as their counterparts in the North did. They instead remained localistic and deferential to a traditional leadership. Federalism lingered on in Virginia into the 1820s—it had pockets of support in the Blue Ridge and Shenandoah Valley regions and urban areas, Federalist candidates (including Marshall's son Thomas) ran for state and national legislative offices, and a party newspaper continued to be published in Richmond—but its strongholds in the 1790s lost population after 1800, and the party was unable to compete statewide. Except on the issue of internal improvements, Virginia Federalists opposed the nationalists' policies of territorial expansion, centralized banking, and protective tariffs, with which Marshall generally agreed. They were "antinationalist Federalists," an oxymoronic notion to him, and most eventually went over to the Democrats. The Chief Justice found more congenial the cosmopolitan, commercially minded components of the National Republican party, which in the South comprised the banking and entrepreneurial interests and outward-looking planters with whom Marshall had been connected for so long. Along with some regional variant groups, these elements of National Republicanism coalesced in the early 1830s to form the Whig party. Marshall and they shared a nationalist outlook and attitudes of social traditionalism, antipopulism, and antipathy toward Andrew Jackson, and his constitutional views promoted their economic policies. Although Marshall never was a partisan of what would become Whiggery as he had been of Federalism—there was no Whig party until after 1834—he was much in sympathy with its future leaders such as Henry Clay and Daniel Webster. Marshall, Clay, Webster, Nicholas Biddle (governor of the Bank of the United States), and other similarly minded men were "self-styled keepers of the union," in Robert Wiebe's apt phrase, sharing goals of "the strengthening of a national center, the formulation of nationwide policies, and the harnessing of a growing west to eastern authority."[79]

Marshall had a special affinity for Daniel Webster, the Massachusetts lawyer and Federalist-Whig politician whose views probably resembled his own more than any other prominent public figure. Webster was admitted to practice before the Supreme Court in 1814 and took an immediate liking to Marshall, and the admiration was mutual. Webster appeared in 127 cases that Marshall heard, including 10 of the 36 constitutional cases on which he wrote the Court's opinion. According to G. Edward White,

no advocate before the Court served simultaneously as a regular representative of clients litigating before the Court, as a celebrated publicist for the Court's doctrines, and as a close professional acquaintance and confidant of one of the Court's most influential justices [Story]. . . . Between 1819 and 1827, in the Marshall Court's most significant years, Webster was there, often on the winning side; he was there as promoter of the Court's version of history; he was there to support the Court's controversial sovereignty cases; and he was there to "overshadow all others in the importance of cases argued, and in the mastery of the great principles of constitutional law."

Marshall respected Webster's forensic skills and legal intellect, borrowed heavily from his briefs when writing the *McCulloch* and *Gibbons* opinions—though Webster certainly exaggerated when he stated about the latter that Marshall "did take it in, as a baby takes in its mother's milk"—and appreciated his efforts on behalf of their mutual political goals.[80]

Marshall also generally approved of the West's leader in the amalgamation known as National Republicanism, Henry Clay of Kentucky. Clay was the author of the "American System," a program of federally financed internal improvements and a protective tariff intended to spur territorial expansion and industrial and agricultural development. Marshall thought he was "an enlightened Statesman" with "enlarged and liberal views," believed he was "entitled to particular credit" for resolving the Missouri crisis, and encouraged him to oppose congressional attempts to restrict the Supreme Court's authority. Although he "abstain[ed] scrupulously from all intermedling in the election of President," Marshall indirectly endorsed Clay's candidacy in 1824 by circulating a letter written to him that raised doubts about one of the

Kentuckian's opponents. Clay was accused of making a "corrupt bargain" in the deadlocked 1824 presidential election by agreeing to end his candidacy and support John Quincy Adams in return for being appointed secretary of state. The charge has never been proven persuasively, and at the time Marshall, who hoped Clay would have won, defended him against it and warned him that Adams's opponents would use his besmirched reputation to attack the administration. Marshall and Clay also were fellow members of the American Colonization Society that encouraged the removal of blacks from America to Africa as a way to attenuate the problems of slavery and race relations.[81]

On 4 March 1829, as he had 28 years before, Chief Justice Marshall administered the oath of office to a president who would become a powerful adversary. The political phenomenon known as Jacksonian Democracy, and the austere and somewhat authoritarian personage of Andrew Jackson, deeply troubled Marshall. He had watched with mounting unease the growth of the bumptious egalitarian movement, with its manifestations of sectionalism and states' rights, and the assertive, much adored former general at its head. He did not harbor the same personal hostility toward Jackson as he did with Jefferson; his attitudes and motives were founded on major political differences. Jackson was an anomaly to Marshall—a democratic Unionist, a populist nationalist, hybrids unfamiliar to someone from the party of Washington, Hamilton, and Adams. Marshall had not voted in a presidential election since 1804, but in the spring of 1828, he indicated privately that he would support John Quincy Adams over Jackson. Late in the year he confided to Story that

I begin to doubt whether it will long be practicable peaceably to elect a chief magistrate possessing the powers which the Constitution confers on the President of the United States, or such powers as are necessary for the government of this great country with due regard for its essential interests. I begin to fear that our constitution is not to be so long lived as its real friends have hoped. . . . I shall not live to see and bewail the consequences of these furious passions which are breaking loose upon us.

The near riot that broke out at the inauguration just after Marshall administered the oath of office must have made him wonder whether mobocracy had taken over the republic.[82]

At first Marshall was willing to give the new president the benefit of the doubt. He was flattered that Jackson had invited him to dinner alone, and he thought that "a President . . . will always be more disposed to conciliate than exasperate; and must always feel some reluctance at inflicting injury." Two years into Jackson's term, however, Marshall's fear of the "furious passions" had returned in full. He suggested that "some less turbulent and less dangerous mode of choosing the Chief Magistrate" should be considered because "the passions of men are influenced to so fearful an extent, [and] large masses are so embittered against each other" under the current helter-skelter process. The bizarre idea he advanced—having the president selected by lot from among the members of the Senate—shows the depth of his disillusionment with the populist politics that had taken over the nation. In 1831, Marshall was considering retiring from the Court, but he decided to await the outcome of the 1832 election before deciding for sure. "You know," he wrote Story, "how much importance I attach to the character of the person who is to succeed me, and calculate the influence which probabilities on that subject [the presidential election] would have on my continuance in office." It was as if his apprehension from two decades before was coming true: "In popular governments it is I fear possible for a majority to exercise power tyrannically."[83]

Marshall thought that the tenets of Jacksonian constitutionalism endangered the national welfare, particularly its invigoration of the presidency, its bias toward decentralization and states' rights, and its populist attacks on supposedly illegitimate institutions such as the Bank of the United States (a "hydra-headed monster" that "impaired the morals of the people," "subverted the electoral process," and "threatened our liberty," contended President Jackson). He came to view Jackson as an autocratic demagogue, oblivious to established institutions and constitutional procedures as he pursued his policy objectives by appealing to the people. Marshall also disagreed with Jackson's claim of coequality in constitutional interpretation. In his message vetoing the national bank bill in 1832, Jackson asserted that "[t]he opinion of the judges has no more authority over Congress than the opinion of Congress has over the judges, and on that point the President is independent of both." In addition, Jacksonian Democracy shifted power from the federal government to the states in response to the growing localism in American politics and the need of an increasingly anxious slaveholding class to find a constitutional basis for protecting its interests. Strict construction had a resurgence as a way to check the exercise of national authority; Jackson's vetoes of the national bank recharter and an internal improvements bill rejected Marshall's reasoning in *McCulloch*; and local democracy and the state police power often seemed more relevant than judicial nationalism. The theory of dual federalism—the existence of separate and balanced spheres of state and federal power, neither superior to the other— facilitated the return of state mercantilism. Marshall thought the basic difference between the two parties was whether they believed the Constitution created "a league and not a government."[84]

Marshall came to grips with the Jacksonian phenomenon firsthand at the Virginia constitutional convention in 1829–30, to which he was summoned the same day he swore in the new Democratic president.[85] The convention was part of a trend underway for several years in other states to rewrite their constitutions to expand voting rights and equalize representation as population shifted westward. Residents of the Virginia frontier had agitated for years to have qualifications for voting reduced and legislative seats reapportioned based on universal white manhood suffrage. At the convention, however, delegates from the Tidewater and Piedmont joined forces to block meaningful changes, and Virginia's government remained one of the least "democratic" in the country. The two key issues were whether only freeholders should vote, and whether slaves should be counted in allocating seats in the legislature. The cleavage among the delegates was sectional: Westerners wanted no property qualifications and a "white basis" for representation; easterners wanted to retain the freehold requirement and inclusion of the slave population in calculations of apportionment.

Marshall initially declined the request of the citizens of Richmond to serve and feared the convention would do "much harm with some good"—such as liberalizing the franchise, "the contagion of universal example." He relented, however, and joined Virginia's two ex-presidents, Madison and Monroe, and 93 other delegates for a 14-week session in the chamber of the House of Delegates starting in October 1829. He attended every meeting and served on committees that dealt with the judiciary and the executive. He favored keeping the property qualification and voted against major reforms but did support Madison's compromise that extended the franchise to all householders and family heads who paid taxes. On representation, Marshall opposed using the "white basis" in the Assembly and the federal three-fifth's ratio in the Senate. As chairman of the judicial committee, he wrote the proposed article on the judiciary system and defended the justices of the peace as the "best men" and the "peacemakers" who guaranteed "complete internal quiet." He sensed that the new spirit of democracy might produce another attack on the judiciary, and, with uncharacteristic emotion, he implored the delegates to keep the courts free from political tampering. He argued for continuing the judges' lifetime tenure, intoning that "[t]he greatest scourge an angry Heaven ever inflicted upon an ungrateful and a sinning people, was an ignorant, a corrupt, or a dependent Judiciary. Will you draw down this curse upon Virginia?" The delegates accorded his remarks great weight and approved a new judiciary article to the constitution that was essentially unchanged from Marshall's draft except for a provision that judges could be removed by a two-thirds vote of the legislature; Marshall did not oppose that process. The final document, he wrote Story with evident relief, was "not precisely what any of us wished, but it is better than we feared."[86]

Marshall's experience at this last meeting of Virginia's Revolutionary generation underscored the conflict within him between his growing nostalgia for gentry politics and his approval of economic liberty. His father Thomas had embodied both phenomena, parlaying his material ambitions in the relative mobility of the Virginia frontier into a prominent place in the local governing class and material comfort for his family. Marshall, inheriting his father's enterprising spirit, did much the same in the Richmond political and legal elite. Although his father had made his mark in the Piedmont and Blue Ridge regions, and Marshall's homey manners seemed more suited to a rustic cottage than a city drawing room, professionally and sentimentally he was an easterner. His participation in the convention gave the clearest demonstration of his desire for what he called a "well-regulated democracy," for securing the political influence of the passing republican gentry generation over the pell-mell democratism of the Jacksonians. The description Marvin Meyers has offered of Federalists in

New York during that state's constitutional convention in 1821 fits Marshall at Virginia's in 1829 extremely well:

[They] found their ideal polity in an informally stratified republic, where a wholesome freeholder population chose leaders from among their well-born, well-trained, well-off neighbors—leaders who would maintain the rights and interests of the whole community, with a special regard for property rights. Their fear was for the imminent coming of anonymous democracy, detached from soil, neighborhood, custom, tradition—detached above all from the guiding influence of wise stewards. . . . Their remedies were designed to check not revolution but the coarsening and demeaning of public life, the erosion of minority rights and interests within the legal democratic framework, the careless dispossession of a natural republican elite.

By 1830, it was clear to Marshall that, in large part because of the intervention of judges and lawyers, the emergence of the liberal business society had also become a populist political movement. The threat of egalitarian democracy seemed too imminent for him to foresee that, just as property had been best protected by opening the traditional economy to middle-class entrepreneurship, the best guarantor of social stability was gradual political reform. He found himself in the classic dilemma of the conservative before and since—how much to change in order to preserve—and he, too, failed to find a lasting way out of it.[87]

The only time Marshall sided with the Jackson administration on a major issue was during the nullification crisis of 1828–33, when firebrands in South Carolina led by John C. Calhoun blamed the 1828 "tariff of abominations" for its economic woes, and, fearing that national power might be used against slavery, declared that a state could nullify a federal law.[88] Jackson supported states' rights, but he was too wedded to the exercise of executive authority to abandon the idea of federal sovereignty. He upheld national supremacy in his Nullification Proclamation of 1832 and asked Congress for authority to use troops to force South Carolina to comply with the tariff. Quelling this incipient secessionism was one of the few actions of the president's that Marshall commended, for, like Daniel Webster, he exalted both "Liberty *and* Union." Nullification—an idea so "extravagant . . . and so repugnant" that he could hardly "believe it was seriously entertained by any person"—went to the heart of the constitutional beliefs he had held for a half-century. The Constitution had been established to prevent the dissolution of the Confederation, but that would all be undone if the nullifiers had their way.

If the prospects of our country inspire you with gloom[,] how do you think a man must be affected who partakes of all your opinions and whose geographical position enables him to see a great deal that is concealed from you. I yield slowly and reluctantly to the conviction that our constitution cannot last. I had supposed that north of the Potowmack a firm and solid government competent to the security of rational liberty might be preserved. Even that now seems doubtful. The case of the south seems to me to be desperate. Our opinions are incompatible with a united government even among ourselves. The union has been prolonged thus far by miracles. I fear they cannot continue.[89]

As the darkening mood in South Carolina seemed to indicate that "the leaders are determined to risk all the consequences of dismemberment," he assigned blame to a familiar source: "We are now gathering the bitter fruits of the tree even before that time planted by Mr. Jefferson, and so industriously and perseveringly cultivated by Virginia." Presidential action was required to resolve the dispute; "[l]eaving [nullification] to the courts . . . will be leaving it to triumphant victory." Marshall was extremely pleased that Jackson took such a firm stand in upholding national authority over the nullifiers. "The Chief Justice and myself," Story wrote with some exaggeration, "have become [Jackson's] warmest supporters, and shall continue so just as long as he maintains the principles contained in them." Although he did not comment on Virginia's attitude on nullification, his state's strengthening embrace of states' rights certainly would have troubled him. The legislature had put down a marker already in 1829 when it denied that the federal courts could settle with finality conflicts between the national and state governments. By a two-to-one ratio, the legislators approved a resolution "that the Constitution of the United States, being a federative compact between sovereign States, in construing which no common arbiter is known, each state has the right to construe the compact for itself." Virginia politicians' muted support for South Carolina changed to vocal approbation after Jackson's proclamation. Marshall believed that states' rights ideologues and defenders of slavery—whom the Administration by and large supported—had become dangerously irrational, and perhaps irrevocably so. "In the South," he reported to Story after the crisis had passed, "we are so far gone in political metaphysics, that I fear no demonstration can restore us to common sense. The word 'State Rights' . . . has a charm against which all reasoning is in vain."[90]

For his part, Jackson did not leave any record of his feelings toward Marshall, though certainly after the Chief Justice ruled against the administration in the second Cherokee Indian case (*Worcester v. Georgia* [1832]; see below), he would not have agreed with the political architect of the Jacksonian movement, Martin Van Buren, that Marshall was "in all human probability the ablest Judge now sitting upon any Bench in the World." Jackson did not mount a campaign against the federal courts, as had Jefferson, but he did approve of an unsuccessful congressional effort to curtail their appellate authority. The most frequently noted example of Jackson's purported contempt for the Supreme Court probably is apocryphal. In all likelihood, after the *Worcester* ruling he did not say "John Marshall has made his decision; *now let him enforce it!*" Although the peremptory tone sounds like Jackson, he did not have to say anything like that because Marshall had not ordered him to do anything. The Court's ruling awaited Georgia's response, but the state ignored it. Marshall's decision could not be enforced, and Jackson knew that. If he said something in that vein, it was intended to support Georgia against the Court, not to defend the

presidency.   Either motive would have been followed from Jacksonian
constitutional doctrine, but the avowal of state sovereignty fit the case at hand.[91]

In addition to using the presidency to mobilize public opinion against the
constitutional nationalism that the Marshall Court espoused, Jackson sought to
affect its decision making by appointing Democratic justices. Anticipating this,
Marshall tried for the first time to influence a nomination to the Court. Working
through intermediaries to avoid being accused of impropriety, he asked Joseph
Story to recommend Senator John Crittenden to fill the seat vacated by Robert
Trimble, who had died in mid-1828, and he asked Henry Clay to make the
proposition directly to the lame-duck Adams. The president obliged, but the
Senate refused to go along and left the vacancy open so Jackson could fill it. As
it turned out, Marshall need not have been so worried that an influx of radical
Democrats would undo his work. During the remainder of Marshall's chief
justiceship, Jackson selected three associates: John McLean, Henry Baldwin,
and James Moore Wayne.   The newcomers wrote more dissents and
concurrences than their predecessors—the mentally unstable Baldwin was
especially querulous in conference—and broke up the boardinghouse lifestyle.
Marshall, moreover, having succeeded in removing the Court from overt
partisan activities, certainly would not have appreciated McLean's continuing
involvement in politics. Jackson's appointees, however, were not avatars of
anti-Federalist jurisprudence. McLean was something of an apostate, siding
with Marshall in cases dealing with state bills of credit and Indian treaty rights,
and Baldwin supported rechartering the national bank. It may have been a
measure of Jackson's lack of concern with the Court, or possibly his deference
to the Whig-controlled Senate, that he did not try to pack it with hardline
Democrats. For Marshall, the main problem with the Jacksonian cohort was that
they did not come from his political generation. They had not fought for
independence or served in government during the nation's formative years, and
so did not share his preoccupation with constitutional stability.[92]

Recognizing the disturbing realities the Jacksonian movement had thrust
before them, Marshall and his associates executed a strategic retreat from the
broad salient of nationalism they had established in 1819–24. The Court "saved
itself by accommodating history," according to R. Kent Newmyer—by refining
doctrine, especially on questions of state power and property rights. Ironically,
the accommodation may have began with *The Steamboat Thomas Jefferson*
(1825), wherein Story refused to extend the federal courts' admiralty
jurisdiction to inland waterways. Up to then he had interpreted the jurisdiction
broadly. Marshall joined in the decision but later disagreed with it. Over
Marshall's only dissent ever in a constitutional case, the Court in *Ogden v.
Saunders* (1827) stepped back from its holding in *Sturgis v. Crowninshield* and
showed a new willingness to allow states to regulate property by affirming a
state bankruptcy act that applied to contracts made after its passage. In two
other cases, Marshall modified some of his own important rulings. In *Willson v.
Blackbird Creek Marsh Co.* (1829), he ignored the same federal law he had
invoked in *Gibbons v. Ogden* to uphold a state's regulation of commerce as a

proper exercise of its reserved powers. Marshall amended the *Dartmouth College* decision in *Providence Bank v. Billings* (1830) by upholding a state tax on a bank in the absence of a specific provision in the bank's charter prohibiting such a levy.[93]

Marshall at first dodged a confrontation with the Jackson administration on the most politically charged constitutional question he faced during his last decade as Chief Justice: federal versus state authority over the Indians.[94] Jackson, consistent with his states' rights outlook and his enmity toward Indians, denied that they could be independent nations within sovereign states, and that the United States should not make treaties with tribes as if they were sovereign countries. He accordingly refused to act when Georgians violated Indians' rights supposedly secured by earlier treaties. In his history of colonial America, Marshall had written of Indians as savages; but by the late 1820s, he regarded them as "helpless people depending on our magnanimity and justice for the preservation of their existence," and he opposed the Administration's Indian removal policy. "I have followed the debate in both houses of Congress with profound attention and with deep interest, and have wished, most sincerely, that both the executive and legislative branches had thought differently on the subject. Humanity must bewail the course which is pursued." His humanitarian sentiments, political views, and concerns with judicial nonpartisanship were tested when Daniel Webster and other anti-Jacksonians seeking to discredit the president arranged to have a case about violations of Indian rights argued before the Supreme Court. In *Cherokee Nation v. Georgia* (1831), though he stated at the outset that "[i]f courts were permitted to indulge their sympathies, a case better calculated to excite them can scarcely be imagined," he dismissed the Cherokees' suit on the grounds that history, precedent, and international law prevented the Court from considering them as a foreign nation within the meaning of the Constitution.[95]

Marshall was so emboldened by this issue, however, that he tried what for him was an exceptional tactic: encouraging another suit in which the jurisdictional issue did not apply. He convinced two justices to read their dissents publicly, one of which, along with some *obiter dicta* in Marshall's own, suggested how another case might receive a sympathetic hearing by the Court. To sway public opinion, Marshall had the official reporter publish an account of the case that was weighted heavily in the Indians' favor. Aided by the Chief Justice's behind-the-scenes maneuvers, *Worcester v. Georgia* was heard in 1832. Marshall's opinion was his most resounding declaration of national supremacy since *Cohens v. Virginia* 11 years before. He ruled that the U.S. government had exclusive jurisdiction over Indian affairs and that all of Georgia's laws pertaining to Indians were unconstitutional. For Marshall, the decision was a victory on all counts. With the Jackson administration in the midst of the nullification controversy, the national bank up for recharter, and a presidential election approaching, it was an opportune time for him to reaffirm the authority of the federal government. Jackson could hardly dispute Marshall's assertion of national authority over Georgia while he was trying to exercise it over South

Carolina. On the general—and, in this instance, the more vital—issue of national supremacy, the two men were of one mind, and Marshall could also carry his points on judicial authority, Indian policy, and morality. "In this decision, perhaps more than in any other," Charles F. Hobson has rightly concluded, the jurist went beyond strict legal necessity to make a pronouncement that trenched upon the political sphere." Marshall also, as he had more than once with Jefferson, turned an adverse situation involving a hostile president to his advantage. In a final twist, the Force Bill—which Congress had passed at Jackson's request so he could use the military against the nullifiers in South Carolina—enabled the Court to enforce its decree in *Worcester* against Georgia. After South Carolina suspended its nullification ordinance, Georgia decided to comply with the decision.[96]

Worcester, however, stood out noticeably from the general trend of the Marshall Court's decisions during the Jacksonian period. By one accounting, Marshall wrote two thirds of his opinions supporting some sort of state right and denying protection to a vested property right (six of nine and two of three, respectively) during the 1826–35 period. The full Court followed the same pattern, handing down 17 of its 25 pro-states' rights decisions and 10 of its 11 denials of vested rights during those years. In sum, during its last years the Marshall Court showed flexibility in interpreting the Constitution in ways that upheld the basic nationalist principles it had set forth before, while preserving its independence by preempting attacks from a populist administration and Congress that bore a residual antijudiciary sentiment from earlier years.[97]

Besides the ill political winds, there were personal reasons for Marshall's apparent loss of leadership and his dispiritedness at "the gloom which lours over us." Even with his hardy personal constitution, age-related health problems forced him to curtail or absent himself from official duties. He was becoming, he told Story, "a mere inefficient pageant." A chronic bladder stone problem had become debilitating until he underwent harrowing, but successful, surgery in 1831—"My nerves, my digestion, and my head were seriously affected. I found myself unequal to the effective consideration of any subject"—and he was slow to mend from occasional injuries. Psychologically, Marshall was adjusting to his life's denouement. His later letters often refer to the passage of time, the effects of old age, and events of the past. Like many formerly healthy and active people, he had difficulty resigning himself to a less energetic lifestyle. "Could I find the mill which would grind old men, and restore youth, I might indulge the hope of recovering my former vigor and taste for the enjoyment of life. But as that is impossible, I must be content with patching myself up and dragging on as well as I can." His hold over the Court had weakened considerably, the Federalist party in which he had matured politically was dead, and a provincialism of outlook had set in. He wrote to Polly in 1826 that "I was in a very great crowd the other evening at Mrs. [John Quincy] Adams's drawing room, but I see very few persons there whom I know & fewer still in whom I take any interest. A person as old as I am feels that his home is his place of most comfort, and his old wife the companion in the world in whose society he is most happy." He partook little of the Washington social life and was more distressed than ever that he had to spend time away from Richmond. "Yesterday I dined with Mr. Van Buren, the Secretary of State. It was a grand dinner and the secretary was very polite, but I was rather dull through the evening. I make a poor return for these dinners. I go to them with reluctance and am bad company while there." Partisanship was dividing his family and making his role as patriarch—already filled with concerns about caring for his children and his nephews and nieces, superintending their education, and helping them find jobs and secure military appointments—more burdensome. "The Kentucky part . . . is I find a good deal divided in party politics and of course not very harmonious. I am sorry for it. Party success is but a poor compensation for family feuds."[98]

Then Marshall suffered the deepest loss of all. On Christmas Day 1831, his "dearest Polly" died after her shaky health failed earlier in the month. He grieved heavily in private and returned to court at the next term, but he never got over her death. Story once found him at the boardinghouse alone in tears, and he told his friend that he was that way most every night. "Never," he wrote one year later, "can I cease to feel the loss & to deplore it. . . . I have lost her! And with her I have lost the solace of my life!"[99]

Unlike Story, who had a plan of counterattack against egalitarian democracy that entailed mobilizing the "wise and good" of New England's former Federalist elite, Marshall pretty much gave up the struggle after 1832. Age and fatigue, depression after Polly's death, and the lack of a sectional or party base fed his despondency. He supported Story's idea—although he probably disliked the prominence it gave to the northeastern Federalists who had disparaged him so during the Adams administration—but he did nothing to advance it. In contrast to Story, who had made amends with Old Federalists like Harrison Gray Otis and Timothy Pickering, Marshall had no interest in sending out such feelers. The South's intransigence worried him more than ever. In that region, he wrote Story, "political prejudice is too strong to yield to any degree of merit; and the great body of the nation contains, at least appears to me to contain, too much of the same ingredient. To men who think as you and I do, the present is gloomy enough; and the future presents no cheering prospect." He regretted that—in a profound change from the time of Washington and the Federalists— "those who support the enormous pretentions of the Executive . . . do not support the government. They sustain the personal power of the President, but labor incessantly to impair the legitimate powers of the Government. Those who oppose the violent and rash measures of the Executive (many of them nullifiers, many of them seceders,) are generally the bitter enemies of a constitutional government." The new party system had produced no good choices. "As far as I can judge, the Government is weakened, whatever party may prevail."[100]

By this time, Marshall was, in his own words, "dragging on." As he prepared for retirement amid failing health, and as one associate died and another resigned, he no doubt began thinking about his successor, and the worrisome prospect that the choice would fall to Andrew Jackson. Some rumors circulated that Marshall would consider resigning if Webster replaced him. He could reasonably have assumed—incorrectly, it turned out—that Roger B. Taney, who was proposed and rejected for a vacancy on the Court in 1835, would not replace him. Marshall had approved of Taney's nomination. He had known Taney as attorney general and believed his legal abilities were respectable. However, the Whigs reviled Taney for his part as secretary of the treasury in closing the national bank, and, joined by John C. Calhoun's states' rights faction, succeeded in killing the appointment.[101]

In early June 1835, Marshall, described a month before as "very emaciated, feeble & dangerously low," collapsed while on one of his frequent walks to Polly's grave. He went to Philadelphia to consult the same doctor who had performed the lithotomy on him four years earlier. He was diagnosed as having grave liver disease. He remained in the former capital for four weeks and died on 6 July at age 80. His body was returned to Richmond and buried, with Masonic rites and artillery salutes, and amid a sudden heavy rain, next to Polly's in the family plot in Shockoe Cemetery. On hearing of his death, John Quincy Adams wrote a tribute that encapsulated the leadership qualities Marshall brought to the Supreme Court and the effect they had on its decisions and its influence on the U.S. political system: "[B]y the ascendancy of his genius, by the amenity of his deportment, and by the imperturbable command of his temper, [he] has given a permanent and systematic character to the decisions of the Court, and settled many great constitutional questions favorably to the continuance of the Union."[102]

Marshall wrote two epitaphs for himself, one intentional, one not. The former appears on his tombstone, and, like him, is notable for its humility. It offers no exhortations or laments, no bombast or didactic passages from the classics or literature, no litany of cherished accomplishments. It refers only to the people he truly cherished—his father, mother, and wife. The latter, constituting Marshall's judicial epitaph, came in his last reported pronouncement as chief justice. In just over a dozen words, he captured the essence both of his three-and-one-half decades as the country's foremost judicial statesman, and of his contribution to establishing the Supreme Court's place in American government. "The Court . . . must see with its own eyes, and exercise its own judgment, guided by its own reason."[103]

NOTES

1. On Marshall and Locke, see Robert K. Faulkner, *The Jurisprudence of John Marshall* (Princeton: Princeton University Press, 1968), which looks mainly at judicial opinions. On Marshall and republicanism, see Thomas C. Shevory, "John Marshall as a Republican: Order and Conflict in American Political History," and Richard A. Brisbin Jr., "John Marshall on History, Virtue, and Legality," in *John Marshall's Achievement: Law, Politics, and Constitutional Interpretation*, ed. Thomas C. Shevory (Westport,

Conn.: Greenwood Press, 1989), 75–93, 95–115; Thomas C. Shevory, *John Marshall's Law: Interpretation, Ideology, and Interest* (Westport, Conn.: Greenwood Press, 1994), 75–98; and Richard A. Brisbin Jr., "John Marshall and the Nature of Law in the Early Republic," *VMHB*, 98 (1990), 57–80, which rely heavily on the Washington biography. On the variations in the personal political philosophies of the leaders of the early republic, see Jennifer Nedelsky, *Private Property and the Limits of American Constitutionalism: The Madisonian Framework and its Legacy* (Chicago: University of Chicago Press, 1990), chaps. 1–4.

2. "Commission," *PJM*, 6:61–62; JM to Adams, 4 February 1801, *PJM*, 6:72; "The Supreme Court: Editorial Note," *PJM*, 6:69; Ben W. Palmer, *Marshall and Taney: Statesmen of the Law* ([Minneapolis]: University of Minnesota Press, 1939), 52; George L. Haskins and Herbert A. Johnson, *Foundations of Power: John Marshall, 1801–15*, Volume 2 of the Oliver Wendell Holmes Jr., Devise History of the United States Supreme Court (New York: Macmillan, 1981), 80–84; Jean Smith, *John Marshall: Definer of a Nation* (New York: Henry Holt, 1996), 285–86. Marshall's predecessors as chief justice were John Jay (1789–1795), John Rutledge (1795), and Oliver Ellsworth (1796–1800).

Marshall did not modify his standards of *personal* dress to make a political point, however, preferring the traditional knee breeches to the new-fashioned long trousers. In 1803, he recounted to Polly an amusing (at least afterward) incident that occurred while he was circuit riding in North Carolina and forced him temporarily to adopt the new style for a most unpolitical reason—necessity.

You will laugh at my vexation when you hear the various calamities that have befallen me. In the first place when I came to review my funds, I had the mortification to discover that I had lost 15 silver dollars out of my waist coat pocket. They had worn through the various mendings the pocket has sustaind & sought their liberty in the sands of Carolina. I determind not to vex myself with what coud not be remedied & ordered [his slave] Peter to take out my cloaths that I might dress for court when to my astonishment & grief after fumbling several minutes in the portmanteau, staring at vacancy, & sweating most profusely he turnd to me with the doleful tidings that I had no pair of breeches. You may be sure this piece of inteligence was not very graciously receivd; however, after a little scolding I determind to make the best of my situation & immediately set out to get a pair made. I thought I shoud be a sans culotte only one day & that for the residue of the term I might be well enough dressd for the appearance on the first day to be forgotten. But,"the greatest of evils, I found, was followd by still greater!" Not a taylor in town coud be prevaild on to work for me. They were all so busy that it was impossible to attend to my wants however pressing they might be & I have the extreme mortification to pass the whole term without that important article of dress I have mentiond.

JM to Polly, 2 January 1803, *PJM*, 6:145–46.

3. Robert J. Steamer, *Chief Justice: Leadership and the Supreme Court* (Columbia: University of South Carolina Press, 1986), 51–53.

4. JM to Story, 15 October 1830, *Massachusetts Historical Society Proceedings*, 2nd ser., 14 (1900), 342; Haskins and Johnson, *Foundations of Power*, 612–28; *Cohens v. Virginia*, 6 Wheaton 264 (1821), quote at 385; Charles F. Hobson, *The Great Chief Justice: John Marshall and the Rule of Law* (Lawrence: University Press of Kansas, 1996), 33–46; Herbert A. Johnson, "John Marshall," in *The Justices of the Supreme Court, 1789–1969: Their Lives and Opinions*, ed. Leon Friedman and Fred L. Israel, 4 vols. (New York: R. R. Bowker Co., 1969), 1:297; JM to William Rawle and others, [?] October 1831, quoted in John F. Dillon, comp. and ed., *John Marshall: Life, Character, and Judicial Services*, 3 vols. (Chicago: Callaghan and Co., 1903), 3:432; *Lessor of John Fisher v. William Cockerell*, 5 Peters 248, quote at 259 (1831). The Marshall Court overturned only one act of Congress, but did so to 18 state laws. David O'Brien, "The

Supreme Court: A Co-Equal Branch of Government," *Supreme Court Historical Society, Yearbook 1984*, 98.

5. *Pennington v. Coxe*, 2 Cranch 33, quote at 52 (1804); *United States v. Wiltberger*, 5 Wheaton 93 (1820), in *PJM*, 9:6; *Brown v. Maryland*, 12 Wheaton 437 (1827); Charles E. Umbanhower, "Marshall on Judging," *AJLH*, 7 (1963), 213–14, 220–23; Hobson, *Great Chief Justice*, 191–200; *Bond v. Ross* (U.S.C.C.Va., 1805), *PJM*, 6:419; *United States v. Fisher*, 2 Cranch 358 (1805), also in *PJM*, 6:360–69, quote at 361; JM to Richard Peters, 12 October 1815, *PJM*, 8:100; George L. Haskins, "Law versus Politics in the Early Years of the Marshall Court," *University of Pennsylvania Law Review*, 130 (1981), 20–21; Wallace Mendelson, "John Marshall's Short Way with Statutes," *Kentucky Law Journal*, 36 (1948), 284–89. See also *United States v. Burr* (1807), wherein Marshall applied the Constitution's definition of treason verbatim in deciding what evidence could be admitted at Burr's trial.

6. 9 Wheaton 188, quote at 222; *McCulloch v. Maryland*, in *PJM*, 8:263, 267; Hobson, *Great Chief Justice*, 192; Walter Berns, *Taking the Constitution Seriously* (New York: Simon and Schuster, 1987), 208.

7. Although "activism" is a modern term, the notion of the Supreme Court aggressively overreaching its authority to politicize jurisprudence was certainly around in Marshall's time under different rubrics.

8. Christopher Wolfe, *The Rise of Modern Judicial Review: From Constitutional Interpretation to Judge-Made Law* (New York: Basic Books, 1986), chaps. 2 and 3 passim; Wallace Mendelson, "Was Chief Justice Marshall an Activist?" in *Supreme Court Statecraft: The Rule of Law and Men* (Ames: Iowa State University Press, 1985), 85–92; Archibald Cox, *The Court and the Constitution*, (Boston: Houghton Mifflin, 1987), 82–83; Herbert A. Johnson, *The Chief Justiceship of John Marshall, 1801–1835* (Columbia: University of South Carolina Press, 1997), 198; G. Edward White, *The Marshall Court and Cultural Change, 1815–1835*, Volumes 3 and 4 of the Oliver Wendell Holmes Jr., Devise History of the Supreme Court (New York: Macmillan, 1988; abridged ed., New York: Oxford University Press, 1991) (references herein are to the more readily available abridgement), 455–60; *United States v. Hill* (U.S.C.C.Va., 1810), *PJM*, 7:249–52; Dwight W. Jessup, "Reaction and Accomodation: The United States Supreme Court and Political Conflict, 1809–1835" (Ph.D. diss., University of Minnesota, 1978), 38–39, 74; R. Kent Newmyer, *Supreme Court Justice Joseph Story: Statesman of the Old Republic* (Chapel Hill: University of North Carolina Press, 1985), 98–102; Charles Warren, *The Supreme Court in United States History*, 3 vols. (Boston: Little, Brown, 1922), 1:438–39, 441–42; Gary D. Rowe, "The Sound of Silence: *United States v. Hudson & Goodwin*, the Jeffersonian Ascendancy, and the Abolition of the Federal Common Law of Crimes," *Yale Law Journal*, 101 (1992), 919–48; Kathryn Preyer, "Jurisdiction to Punish: Federal Authority, Federalism, and the Common Law of Crimes in the Early Republic," *Law and History Review*, 4 (1986), 223–65; *Coate's Executrix v. Muse's Administrators* (1822), *PJM*, 9:212. Cf. Leonard Levy, *Original Intent and the Framers' Constitution* (New York: Macmillan, 1988), who hyperextends in his effort to rebut the "original intent" school—for example, by calling Marshall "[t]he most activist judge in our constitutional history" and discussing *Marbury v. Madison* in a chapter subtitled "Judicial Activism Run Amok" (54, 75–99). Rowe notes, in contrast, that in *U.S. v. Hudson and Goodwin* the Court disapproved at least eight circuit court cases that had affirmed the existence of a federal criminal common law; overrode the views of all the justices but one who had been on the court before 1804, when the concept of a federal criminal common law was most widely accepted; and arguably departed from the intent of the Framers and the drafters of the Judiciary Act of 1789.

Marshall joined in Johnson's opinion, having expressed similar views in two previous opinions. Rowe, "Sound of Silence," 920–21, 927.

9. Jefferson to Thomas Ritchie, 25 December 1829, *The Writings of Thomas Jefferson*, ed. Paul Leicester Ford, 12 vols. (New York: G. P. Putnam's Sons, 1904–5), 12:178; Donald Morgan, *Justice William Johnson: The First Dissenter* (Columbia: University of South Carolina Press, 1954) 45–46; White, *Marshall Court and Cultural Change*, 191; Warren, *Supreme Court in U.S. History*, 2:273 n. 1; Steamer, *Chief Justice*, 7; *Talbot v. Seeman*, 1 Cranch 1 (1801); Donald O. Dewey, *Marshall versus Jefferson: The Political Background of Marbury v. Madison* (New York: Alfred A. Knopf, 1970), 88–89; Johnson, *Chief Justiceship of Marshall*, 87 n. 6; Haskins and Johnson, *Foundations of Power*, 382, 652. Marshall's preeminence in the Court's decisions during 1801–15 is particularly notable when the rulings are broken down by the types of law involved. In cases dealing with conflicts of laws, he wrote 90 percent (9 of 10); on economic and commercial matters (the law merchant, bills and notes, business enterprise, real property, and public lands), 69 percent (103 of 149); nationality and the status of persons, 60 percent (12 of 25); international law (except prize), 58 percent (7 of 12); jurisdiction and procedure, 55 percent (70 of 127); admiralty and marine insurance, 54 percent (67 of 125); and constitutional (excluding seriatim and per curiam opinions), 48 percent (12 of 25); calculations derived from data in Haskins and Johnson, *Foundations of Power*, 654–64.

10. Robert H. Wiebe, *The Opening of American Society: From the Adoption of the Constitution to the Eve of Disunion* (New York: Alfred A. Knopf, 1984), 222; Robert G. Seddig, "John Marshall and the Origins of Supreme Court Leadership," *University of Pittsburgh Law Review*, 36 (1975), 785–833; Donald G. Morgan, "Marshall, the Marshall Court, and the Constitution," in *Chief Justice John Marshall: A Reappraisal*, ed. W. Melville Jones (Ithaca: Cornell University Press, 1956), 171–81; idem, "The Origin of Supreme Court Dissent," *WMQ*, 3rd ser., 10 (1953), 353–77; Newmyer, *Story*, 204–5; Albert Broderick, "From Constitutional Politics to Constitutional Law: The Supreme Court's First Fifty Years," *North Carolina Law Review*, 65 (1987), 947–48; Johnson, *Chief Justiceship of Marshall*, 86–96, 111; Gerald Garvey, "The Constitutional Revolution of 1837 and the Myth of Marshall's Monolith," *Western Political Quarterly*, 18 (1965), 27–34.

11. Steamer, *Chief Justice*, 37, 89; James A. Seddon quoted in Frances Norton Mason, *My Dearest Polly . . .* (Richmond: Garret and Massie, 1961), 318; Joseph Story to Samuel Fay, 25 February 1808, *The Life and Letters of Joseph Story*, ed. William Wetmore Story, 2 vols. (Boston: Little, Brown, 1851), 1:166–68.

12. Johnson, *Chief Justiceship of Marshall*, 135–37; Donald M. Roper, "Judicial Unanimity and the Marshall Court—A Road to Reappraisal," *AJLH*, 9 (1969), 125–32; Seddig, "Marshall and the Origins of Supreme Court Leadership," 793, 801; Johnson, *Chief Justiceship of Marshall*, 96–97, 122–23; White, *Marshall Court and Cultural Change*, 298, 372–73; John Stookey and George Watson, "John Marshall and His Court: Applied Behavioral Jurisprudence," in *John Marshall's Achievement*, 67.

13. Thomas Jefferson to Spencer Roane, 6 September 1819, *Writings of Jefferson*, ed. Ford, 10:140; Newmyer, *Story*, 80–81, 84; Johnson, *Chief Justiceship of Marshall*, 31–32, 51–52; Robert G. McCloskey, *The American Supreme Court* (Chicago: University of Chicago Press, 1960), 62.

14. James Sterling Young, *The Washington Community, 1800–1828* (New York: Columbia University Press, 1966), 98–109; Newmyer, *Story*, 78; Story to Fay, 24 February 1812, and to Sarah W. Story, 5 March 1812, *Life and Letters of Story*, 1:215–18; White, *Marshall Court and Cultural Change*, 160–61, 184–85, 190–91; Steamer,

Chief Justice, 52; JM to Bushrod Washington, 29 December 1814, *PJM*, 8:63; JM to Story, 3 May, 26 June, 12 October, and 10 November 1831, and 16 November 1833, in Charles Warren, "The Story-Marshall Correspondence (1819–1831)," *WMQ*, 2nd ser., 21 (1941), 22–25; Jessup, "Reaction and Accommodation," 435.

15. Quotes from *Cohens v. Virginia, McCulloch v. Maryland, Marbury v. Madison,* and *Gibbons v. Ogden*; Herbert A. Johnson, "John Marshall," in *The Justices of the Supreme Court, 1789–1969,* 1:290, 298; Palmer, *Marshall and Taney,* 66.

16. G. Edward White, *The American Judicial Tradition: Profiles of Leading American Judges* (New York: Oxford University Press, 1976), 25, 33; Steamer, *Chief Justice,* 68–69; Edward S. Corwin, *John Marshall and the Constitution* (New Haven: Yale University Press, 1919), 124. Thomas Jefferson found the Chief Justice's argumentation so maddening that, he reportedly told Joseph Story, "when conversing with Marshall, I never admit anything. So sure as you admit any position to be good, no matter how remote from the conclusion he seeks to establish, you are gone. So great is his sophistry you must never give him an affirmative answer or you will be forced to grant his conclusion. Why, if he were to ask me if it were daylight or not, I'd reply, 'Sir, I don't know, I can't tell.'" Charles R. Williams, *The Life of Rutherford Birchard Hayes,* 2 vols. (Columbus: Ohio State Archaeological and Historical Society, 1928), 1:33 (citing a diary entry by Hayes about a lecture he heard Story give at Harvard Law School).

17. White, *Marshall Court and Cultural Change,* chap. 6, esp. 385–89, 424–26; JM to Dudley Chase, 7 February 1817, *PJM*, 8:148–49. Story and Rush had lobbied for improving the reporting process since at least 1814.

18. Haskins and Johnson, *Foundations of Power,* 79–82; White, *Marshall Court and Cultural Change,* 158–59; *New York Statesman,* 7 and 24 February 1824, in *The Marshall Court, 1801–1835,* ed. Adrienne Siegel, Vol. 2 in the Supreme Court in American Life series (Millwood, N.Y.: Associated Faculty Press, 1987), 151; Warren, *Supreme Court in U.S. History,* 1:456–63.

19. On the circuit courts during Marshall's tenure, see Johnson, *Chief Justiceship of Marshall,* chap. 4; Shevory, *John Marshall's Law,* chap. 6; and Haskins and Johnson, *Foundations of Power,* 378. For the circuit courts of Virginia and North Carolina specifically, see the editorial notes in *PJM,* 6:126–28, 142–44. Sixty-four of Marshall's circuit opinions are extant, most of them dealing with suits in equity, and all from Virginia. In most cases he did not write an opinion.

20. *PJM*, 9:133. Cf. Faulkner, *Jurisprudence of Marshall,* 97–98.

21. JM to Dudley Chase, 7 February 1817, *PJM*, 8:148; George Dangerfield, *The Era of Good Feelings,* Harbinger ed. (New York: Harcourt, Brace and World, 1963), 162; Max Lerner, "John Marshall's Long Shadow," in *Ideas Are Weapons* (New York: Viking Press, 1943), 29, 34; R. Kent Newmyer, *The Supreme Court under Marshall and Taney* (New York: Thomas Y. Crowell Co., 1968), 55; Newmyer, *Story,* 154–56; Wiebe, *Opening of American Society,* 224–29. The variegated transformation of America referred to herein is thoroughly covered in Wiebe, *Opening of American Society*; Joseph Dorfman, *The Economic Mind in American Civilization, 1606–1865,* 2 vols. (New York: Viking Press, 1946), 1:241–499; Rowland Berthoff, "Independence and Attachment, Virtue and Interest: From Republican Citizen to Free Enterpriser, 1787–1837," in *Uprooted Americans: Essays to Honor Oscar Handlin,* ed. Richard L. Bushman et al. (Boston: Little, Brown, 1979), 99–124; Drew R. McCoy, *The Elusive Republic: Political Economy in Jeffersonian America* (Chapel Hill: University of North Carolina Press, 1980); Joyce Appleby, *Capitalism and a New Social Order: The Republican Vision of the 1790s* (New York: New York University Press, 1984); Cathy Matson and Peter S. Onuf, "Toward a Republican Empire: Interest and Ideology in Revolutionary

America," *American Quarterly*, 37 (1985), 496–531; James Oakes, "From Republicanism to Liberalism: Ideological Change and the Crisis of the Old South," *American Quarterly*, 37 (1985), 551–71; Steven Watts, *The Republic Reborn: War and the Making of Liberal America* (Baltimore: Johns Hopkins University Press, 1987); idem, "Ministers, Misanthropes, and Mandarins: The Federalists and the Culture of Capitalism, 1790–1820," in *Federalists Reconsidered*, ed. Doron Ben-Atar and Barbara B. Oberg (Charlottesville: University Press of Virginia, 1998), 157–75; Gordon S. Wood, "Interests and Disinterestedness in the Making of the Constitution," in *Beyond Confederation: Origins of the Constitution and American National Identity*, ed. Richard Beeman et al. (Chapel Hill: University of North Carolina Press, 1987), 69–109; James T. Kloppenberg, "The Virtues of Liberalism: Christianity, Republicanism, and Ethics in Early American Political Discourse," *JAH*, 74 (1987–88), 9–33; Charles Sellers, *The Market Revolution: Jacksonian America, 1815–1846* (New York: Oxford University Press, 1991); Robert E. Shalhope, "Republicanism, Liberalism, and Democracy: Political Culture in the Early Republic," and Peter S. Onuf and Cathy Matson, "Republicanism and Federalism in the Constitutional Decade," in *The Republican Synthesis Revisited: Essays in Honor of George Athan Billias*, ed. Milton M. Klein et al. (Worcester, Mass.: American Antiquarian Society, 1992), 37–90 (quote at 55), 119–41; and Gordon S. Wood, *The Radicalism of the American Revolution* (New York: Alfred A. Knopf, 1992).

22. Felix Frankfurter, "John Marshall and the Judicial Function," quoted in Mendelson, *Supreme Court Statecraft*, 230; *The Memoirs of John Quincy Adams*, ed. Charles Francis Adams, 12 vols. (Philadelphia: J. P. Lippincott, 1874–77), 9:243–44; JM to Timothy Pickering, 18 March 1828, quoted in Hobson, *Great Chief Justice*, 124; JM to James Monroe, 13 June 1822, *PJM*, 9:236–37.

23. Sources for this paragraph and the next are Joseph Dorfman, "John Marshall: Political Economist," in *Chief Justice Marshall: A Reappraisal*, 124–44; James W. Ely, Jr., *The Guardian of Every Other Right: A Constitutional History of Property Rights* (New York: Oxford University Press, 1992), chap. 4; James Willard Hurst, *Law and the Conditions of Freedom in the Nineteenth-Century United States* (Madison: University of Wisconsin Press, 1956), 44–45; Morton J. Horwitz, *The Transformation of American Law, 1780–1860* (Cambridge: Harvard University Press, 1977), 221–23; Sellers, *Market Revolution*, 57–59, 85–90, 145–48; C. Peter Magrath, *Yazoo: Law and Politics in the New Republic: The Case of Fletcher v. Peck* (Providence, R.I.: Brown University Press, 1966), chap. 7; Joseph M. Lynch, "*Fletcher v. Peck*: The Nature of the Contract Clause," *Seton Hall Law Review*, 13 (1982), 1–20; Francis N. Stites, *Private Interest and Public Gain: The Dartmouth College Case, 1819* (Amherst: University of Massachusetts Press, 1972); Bruce A. Campbell, "Social Federalism: The Constitutional Position of Nonprofit Corporations in Nineteenth-Century America," *Law and History Review*, 8 (1990–91), 149–88; Maurice G. Baxter, *The Steamboat Monopoly: Gibbons v. Ogden, 1824* (New York: Alfred A. Knopf, 1972); Gordon Wood, "Launching the 'Extended Republic': The Federalist Era," in *Launching the "Extended Republic,": The Federalist Era*, ed. Ronald Hoffman and Peter J. Albert (Charlottesville: University Press of Virginia, 1996), 1–24; Reginald Horsman, "The Dimensions of an 'Empire for Liberty': Expansion and Republicanism, 1775–1825," *JER*, 9 (1989), 7–9; Johnson, *Chief Justiceship of Marshall*, chaps. 6 and 7; Hobson, *Great Chief Justice*, chap. 4; John R. Nelson, "Alexander Hamilton and American Manufacturing: A Reexamination," *JAH*, 65 (1978–79), 971–95; John E. Crowley, *The Privileges of Independence: Neomercantilism and the American Revolution* (Baltimore: Johns Hopkins University Press, 1993), 146–54; W. Howard Mann, "The Marshall Court: Nationalization of

Private Rights and Personal Liberty from the Authority of the Commerce Clause,"
Indiana Law Journal, 38 (1962–63), 120–49, 173–238; Thomas McCraw, "The Strategic
Vision of Alexander Hamilton," *American Scholar*, 63 (1994), 31–57; JM's speech in the
Virginia constitutional convention, 11 December 1829, in *Proceedings and Debates of
the Virginia State Convention of 1829–30* (Richmond: Ritchie and Cook, 1830), 616;
Dumas Malone, *Jefferson the President: First Term, 1801–1805* (Boston: Little, Brown,
1970), chap. 17; *American Insurance Co. and Ocean Insurance Co. v. 356 Bales of
Cotton, David Canter, Claimant*, 1 Peters 511 (1828) ("The Constitution confers
absolutely on the government of the Union, the powers of making war, and of making
treaties; consequently, that government possesses the power of acquiring territory, either
by conquest or by treaty" [at 542]); JM to Daniel Raymond, 25 September 1821, *PJM*,
9:186; "Raymond, Daniel," *Dictionary of American Biography*, 8:406–7; Albert J.
Beveridge, *The Life of John Marshall*, 4 vols. (Boston: Houghton Mifflin, 1916–19),
4:429–30; Newmyer, *Supreme Court under Marshall and Taney*, 51–52, 150; *Craig v.
Missouri*, 4 Peters 410; Newmyer, *Story*, 73–76; Bruce A. Campbell, "John Marshall, the
Virginia Political Economy, and the *Dartmouth College* Decision," *AJLH*, 19 (1975),
40–65; Wallace Mendelson, "Chief Justice Marshall and the Mercantile Tradition,"
Southwestern Social Science Quarterly, 29 (1948–49), 27–37; idem, "Was Chief Justice
Marshall an Activist?," 97–98. Marshall initially agreed with Story's opinion in *The
Steamboat Thomas Jefferson*, 10 Wheaton 428 (1825), which followed English law in
holding that national commercial regulation ended on inland waters beyond the tidal
point. Later, however, he changed his mind, saying that American admiralty law must
cover the Mississippi River and its tributaries, and also perhaps the Great Lakes as inland
seas. This expansive interpretation of admiralty would effectively have given the
national government greater power over interstate commerce than *Gibbons v. Ogden*
allowed. White, *Marshall Court and Cultural Change*, 468–74.
   24. "River Commission Report: Editorial Note," "River Commission Report," and JM
to [Gov.] James Barbour, 26 December 1812, 8 January 1813, *PJM*, 7:355–79; John
Marshall, *The Life of George Washington*, 5 vols. (Philadelphia, C. P. Wayne, 1804–7;
rept., New York: Chelsea House, 1983), 4:77–79.
   25. "River Commission Report," *PJM*, 7:375.
   26. Wayland F. Dunaway, *History of the James River and Kanawha Company*
(Columbia University Studies in History, Economics, and Public Law, vol. 104 [1922];
rept., New York: AMS Press, 1969), 75, 100–104; Herbert C. Bradshaw, *History of
Prince Edward County, Virginia* . . . (Richmond: Dietz Press, 1955), 325–26; Leonard
Baker, *John Marshall: A Life in Law* (New York: Macmillan, 1974), 523; Irving Brant,
James Madison: Commander in Chief, 1812–1836 (Indianapolis: Bobbs-Merrill, 1961),
460.
   27. JM to Pinckney, 4 March 1801, *PJM*, 6:89.
   28. Jefferson to Levi Lincoln, 25 October 1802, *Writings of Jefferson*, ed. Ford., 8:175–
76; Jefferson to John Dickinson, 19 December 1801, *The Writings of Thomas Jefferson*,
ed. Andrew A. Lipscomb and Albert Ellery Bergh, 20 vols. (Washington, D.C.: The
Thomas Jefferson Memorial Association, 1905), 10:302; Giles to Jefferson, 1 June 1801,
quoted in Malone, *Jefferson the President: First Term*, 116; Giles to Jefferson, 16
March 1801, quoted in William S. Carpenter, "Repeal of the Judiciary Act of 1801,"
American Political Science Review, 9 (1915), 521.
   29. Charles Warren, "New Light on the History of the Judiciary Act of 1789," *Harvard
Law Review*, 37 (1923), 49–132; Julius Goebel Jr., *Antecedents and Beginnings to 1801*,
Volume 1 of the Oliver Wendell Holmes Jr., Devise History of the Supreme Court of the
United States (New York: Macmillan, 1971), 457–508; William R. Casto, *The Supreme*

Court in the Early Republic: The Chief Justiceships of John Jay and Oliver Ellsworth (Columbia: University of South Carolina Press, 1995); *Seriatim: The Supreme Court before John Marshall*, ed. Scott D. Gerber (New York: New York University Press, 1999); Carl E. Prince, *The Federalists and the Origins of the U.S. Civil Service* (New York: New York University Press, 1977), chap. 10; Charles G. Haines, *The Role of the Supreme Court in American Government and Politics, 1789–1835* (Berkeley: University of California Press, 1944), chaps. 4 and 5; Kathryn Turner, "Federalist Policy and the Judiciary Act of 1801," *WMQ*, 3rd ser., 22 (1965), 3–32; Erwin R. Surrency, "The Judiciary Act of 1801," *AJLH*, 2 (1958), 53–65; Gouverneur Morris to Robert R. Livingston, 20 February 1801, *The Life of Gouverneur Morris . . .*, ed. Jared Sparks, 2 vols. (Boston: Gray and Bowen, 1832), 153–54.

30. The Republicans' offensive against the federal courts is described in Richard E. Ellis, *The Jeffersonian Crisis: Courts and Politics in the Young Republic* (New York: W. W. Norton, 1974), chaps. 3–7; Haines, *Role of the Supreme Court*, chaps. 7–8; Haskins and Johnson, *Foundations of Power*, 136–81, 205–45; Robert M. Johnstone, Jr., *Jefferson and the Presidency: Leadership in the Young Republic* (Ithaca: Cornell University Press, 1978), chap. 6; Linda K. Kerber, *Federalists in Dissent: Imagery and Ideology in Jeffersonian America* (Ithaca: Cornell University Press, 1970), chap. 5; and Malone, *Jefferson the President: First Term*, chaps. 7 and 25. The Republicans' dismissal of Federalists from the civil service is discussed in Carl E. Prince, "The Passing of the Aristocracy: Jefferson's Removal of the Federalists, 1801–1805," *JAH*, 57 (1970–71), 563–75. On Marshall's relatives, see *PJM*, 6:77–78, 524; *Dictionary of American Biography*, 5:80, s.v. "Daveiss, Joseph"; Dumas Malone, *Jefferson the President: Second Term* (Boston: Little, Brown, 1974), 355; Milton Lomask, *Aaron Burr: The Conspiracy and Years of Exile, 1805–1836* (New York: Farrar, Straus, and Giroux, 1982), 126–27, 138–39, 142–48. Marshall's brother James was appointed as a circuit judge for the District of Columbia before the Judiciary Act of 1801 was passed. He and the other Federalist judge, William judge, William Cranch, ordered the district attorney to start a libel prosecution against the Republican editor of the *National Intelligencer* under the common law of sedition. The district attorney, a Republican, refused the order, and a grand jury would not indict the editor. Marshall did not comment on the incident but presumably would have disapproved of the prosecution. When he was in Congress, he had opposed a Federalist attempt to make the offenses enumerated in the Sedition Act punishable under the common law of seditious libel. Francis N. Stites, *John Marshall: Defender of the Constitution* (Boston: Little, Brown, 1981), 84. Cf. Randolph W. Church, "James Markham Marshall," *Virginia Cavalcade*, 13 (spring 1964), 28, which states incorrectly that James's judicial commission was never delivered and that he did not serve.

31. JM to Rufus King, 26 February 1801, to Pinckney, 4 March 1801, to Charles Cotesworth Pinckney, 21 November 1802, *PJM*, 6:82, 89, 125.

32. JM to Bushrod Washington, 27 March 1819, *PJM*, 8:281; Smith, *Marshall*, 313; JM to Oliver Wolcott, 5 April 1802, to William Paterson, 6 and 19 April and 3 May 1802, and to William Cushing, 19 April 1802, *PJM*, 6:104, 106, 108–9, 117; *Stuart v. Laird*, 1 Cranch 299 (1803); Ellis, *Jeffersonian Crisis*, 63–66.

33. JM to Timothy Pickering, 28 February 1811, *PJM*, 7:270.

34. JM to Rufus King, 26 February 1801, JM to Charles Cotesworth Pinckney, 21 September 1808, JM to Timothy Pickering, 19 December 1808, *PJM*, 6:83, 7:183, 188.

35. On Marshall and cases arising from the European conflict, see Haskins and Johnson, *Foundations of Power*, 292–311, 407–92, 526–58; Warren, *Supreme Court in U.S. History*, 1:342–52; Johnson, *Chief Justiceship of Marshall*, 66–68, 226–28, 236–42;

White, *Marshall Court and Cultural Change*, chap. 7 passim; Hobson, *Great Chief Justice*, 152–54. For examinations of Marshall's international jurisprudence, see Benjamin M. Ziegler, *The International Law of John Marshall: A Study of First Principles* (Chapel Hill: University of North Carolina Press, 1937); Edward Dumbauld, "John Marshall and the Law of Nations," *University of Pennsylvania Law Review*, 104 (1955), 38–56; and Frances H. Rudko, *John Marshall and International Law: Statesman and Chief Justice* (New York: Greenwood Press, 1991). Illustrative examples of Marshall's reasoning are his decisions in *U.S. v. Schooner Peggy*, 1 Cranch 103 (1801), also in *PJM*, 6:99–102; *United States v. Hill* (U.S.C.C.Va., 1810), also in *PJM*, 7:249–52; *Schooner Exchange v. McFadon and Greetham*, 7 Cranch 135 (1812), also in *PJM*, 7:307–15; *Brown v. United States*, 8 Cranch 121 (1814), also in *PJM*, 8:3–9; *The Venus*, 8 Cranch 288 (1814), also in *PJM*, 8:10–31; *The Nereide*, 9 Cranch 412 (1815), also in *PJM*, 8:67–80; *The Fortuna* (U.S.C.C.N.C., 1815), *PJM*, 8:91–98; *The Commercen*, 1 Wheaton 395 (1816), also in *PJM*, 8:128–34; *Schooner Thomas and Henry v. United States* (U.S.C.C.Va., 1818), *PJM*, 8:203–8. In a case arising from the Quasi-War with France, *Little v. Bareme* (2 Cranch 170 [1804]), Marshall wanted to uphold presidential authority to excuse the U.S. Navy for damages for stopping suspect neutral vessels. He believed it was inappropriate to punish good-faith obedience, and perhaps he did not want to overrule an order of the Adams administration. The other Justices convinced him to change his mind. *PJM*, 6:268 n. 7.

36. JM to Charles Cotesworth Pinckney, 19 October 1808, *PJM*, 7:184–85; James H. Broussard, *The Southern Federalists, 1800–1816* (Baton Rouge: Louisiana State University Press, 1978), 98–100, 202–3.

37. JM to Robert Smith, 27 July 1812, *PJM*, 7:337–39; Roger H. Brown, *The Republic in Peril: 1812* (New York: Columbia University Press, 1964), chap. 8; Broussard, *Southern Federalists*, chaps. 10 and 11; Beveridge, *Marshall*, 4:31–34, 47; Donald R. Hickey, *The War of 1812: A Forgotten Conflict* (Urbana: University of Illinois Press, 1989), 100ff. The Federalists' presidential candidate was DeWitt Clinton of New York, an antiwar Republican whom James Madison easily defeated.

38. "Report on Fortifications," [28 June 1813], *PJM*, 7:412–14; Mason, *My Dearest Polly*, 223–25; James M. Banner Jr., *To the Hartford Convention: The Federalists and the Origins of Party Politics in Massachusetts, 1789–1815* (New York: Alfred A. Knopf, 1970).

39. Haskins, "Law versus Politics in the Early Years of the Marshall Court," 5; William E. Nelson, "The Eighteenth-Century Background of John Marshall's Constitutional Jurisprudence," *Michigan Law Review*, 76 (1978), 954; *Brown v. United States*, 8 Cranch 121 (1814), also in *PJM*, 8:3, quote at 8. See also Hobson, *Great Chief Justice*, 150–68, and Haskins and Johnson, *Foundations of Power*, 395–406.

40. JM to Henry Wheaton, 24 March 1821, *PJM*, 9:147–48.

41. Charles E. Umbanhowar, "Marshall on Judging," *AJLH*, 7 (1963), 225; *Evans v. Jordan and Morehead* (U.S.C.C.Va., 1813), *PJM*, 7:406.

42. Jennifer Nedelsky, "Confining Democratic Politics: Anti-Federalists, Federalists, and the Constitution," *Harvard Law Review*, 96 (1982–83), 340–60; Mark A. Graber, "Federalists or Friends of Adams: The Marshall Court and Party Politics," *Studies in American Political Development*, 12 (1998), 229–66.

43. On slavery and the Marshall Court, and Marshall specifically, see Hobson, *Great Chief Justice*, 163–70; Stites, *Marshall*, 145–48; White, *Marshall Court and Cultural Change*, 681–703; Johnson, *Chief Justiceship of Marshall*, 242–48; Donald M. Roper, "In Quest of Judicial Unanimity: The Marshall Court and the Legitimation of Slavery," and Kent Newmyer, "On Assessing the Court in History: Some Comments on the Roper

and Burke Articles," *Stanford Law Review*, 21 (1969), 532–47. The legal and constitutional aspects of slavery in the early republic are covered comprehensively in the pertinent sections of William Wiecek, *The Sources of Antislavery Constitutionalism in America, 1760–1848* (Ithaca: Cornell University Press, 1977); Mark Tushnet, *The Law of Slavery in America* (Princeton: Princeton University Press, 1981); and Robert Cover, *Justice Accused: Antislavery and the Judicial Process*, rev. ed. (New Haven: Yale University Press, 1984). On the Federalists' antislavery inclinations, see Paul Finkelman, "The Problem of Slavery in the Age of Federalism," in *Federalists Reconsidered*, 135–56.

44. *The Antelope*, 10 Wheaton 66 (1825), quotes at 114, 120–21, 130; *Mima Queen and Child v. Hepburn*, 7 Cranch 290 (1813), quote at 294 (also in *PJM*, 7:382–85); *Boyce v. Anderson*, 2 Peters 150 (1829), quote at 154; Beveridge, *Marshall*, 4:473–76, 525 n. 1; Smith, *Marshall*, 489–90; JM to Bushrod Washington, 17 June 1819, *PJM*, 8:317; JM to Daniel Raymond, 25 September 1821, *PJM*, 9:186; JM to Timothy Pickering, 20 March 1826, *Massachusetts Historical Society Proceedings*, 2nd ser., 14 (1900), 321–22.

45. *Minutes of the Virginia Branch, American Colonization Society (1823–1859)*, and annual reports of the American Society for Colonization for 1823–35, summarized in Irwin S. Rhodes, *The Papers of John Marshall: A Descriptive Calendar*, 2 vols. (Norman: University of Oklahoma Press, 1956), 2:153–54, 169, 219, 248–49 (hereafter cited as Rhodes, *Calendar of Marshall Papers*); Marie T. McGraw, "The American Colonization Society in Virginia, 1816–1832: A Case Study in Southern Liberalism" (Ph.D. diss., George Washington University, 1980); JM to [?], 8 February 1835, in *American Depository and Colonial Journal*, 12 (May 1836), 165; JM's will and letters to R. R. Gurley, 14 December 1831, and Edward Carrington, 15 February 1832, in John E. Oster, *The Political and Economic Doctrines of John Marshall* (orig. publ. 1914; rept., New York: Burt Franklin, 1967), 45–47, 61, 201; Hobson, *Great Chief Justice*, 236 n. 44. The hardening of Virginia slaveholders' attitudes after the Turner rebellion is covered in Alison Goodyear Freehling, *Drift toward Dissolution: The Virginia Slavery Debate of 1831–1832* (Baton Rouge: Louisiana State University Press, 1982).

46. JM to Henry Lee, 20 January 1832, in Oster, *Political and Economic Doctrines of Marshall*, 48–49; JM to James Markham Marshall, 1 April 1804, *PJM*, 6:278. The Republicans' use of impeachment is discussed in Ellis, *Jeffersonian Crisis*, chaps. 5–7; Raoul Berger, *Impeachment: The Constitutional Problems* (Cambridge: Harvard University Press, 1973), chap. 8; Malone, *Jefferson the President: First Term*, chap. 25; Beveridge, *Marshall*, 3:157–222; Haskins and Johnson, *Foundations of Power*, 211–45; William H. Rehnquist, *Grand Inquests: The Historic Impeachments of Justice Samuel Chase and President Andrew Johnson* (New York: William Morrow, 1992), chaps. 1, 3–7; and Richard B. Lillich, "The Chase Impeachment," *AJLH*, 4 (1960), 49–72.

47. JM to Samuel Chase, 23 January 1804, and "Testimony in the Trial of Samuel Chase," 16 February 1805, *PJM*, 6:347 (Plumer quote at n. 12), 350–57.

48. Henry Adams, *History of the United States of America*, 9 vols. (New York: Charles Scribner's Sons, 1889–91), 1:194; JM to Story, 13 July and 18 September 1821, *PJM*, 9:179, 183–84; JM to Henry Lee, 25 October 1830, quoted in Smith, *Marshall*, 12.

49. Jefferson to Madison, 25 May 1810, to John Tyler, 26 May 1810, to Albert Gallatin, 27 September 1810, and to Thomas Ritchie, 25 December 1820, *Writings of Jefferson*, Ford ed., 9:275–76, 282, 10:171; Malone, *Jefferson the President: Second Term*, 356–59; idem, *The Sage of Monticello* (Boston: Little, Brown, 1981), 64–66, 351–54. Marshall's strained relations with Jefferson are recounted thoroughly in Donald O. Dewey, *Marshall versus Jefferson: The Political Background of Marbury v. Madison* (New York: Alfred A. Knopf, 1970).

50. Malone, *Jefferson the President: First Term*, 143; Jack M. Sosin, *The Aristocracy of the Long Robe: The Origins of Judicial Review in America* (Westport, Conn.: Greenwood Press, 1989), chaps. 13, 16; Maeva Marcus, "Judicial Review in the Early Republic," in *Launching the "Extended Republic*,*"* 25–53; Gordon S. Wood, "The Origins of Judicial Review," *Suffolk University Law Review*, 22 (1988), 1293–1307; idem, "Judicial Review in the Era of the Founding," in *Is the Supreme Court the Guardian of the Constitution?*, ed. Robert Licht (Washington, D.C.: American Enterprise Institute, 1993), 153–66; Susan Low Bloch and Maeva Marcus, "John Marshall's Selective Use of History in *Marbury v. Madison*," Supreme Court Historical Society, *Yearbook 1987*, 82–107; Scott D. Gerber, reviews of Smith, *Marshall*, and Paul W. Kahn, *The Reign of Law: Marbury v. Madison and the Construction of America*, in *JAH*, 84 (1997–98), 659, 1494; Malone, *Jefferson: First Term*, 151–56; Jefferson to Abigail Adams, 11 September 1804, *The Adams-Jefferson Letters . . .*, ed. Lester J. Cappon, 2 vols. (Chapel Hill: University of North Carolina Press, 1959), 1:279.

The literature on judicial review generally and *Marbury* specifically is massive but mostly falls into two groups that underscore the case's constitutional and political elements, respectively. Recent examples of the former are Robert L. Clinton, *Marbury v. Madison and Judicial Review* (Lawrence: University Press of Kansas, 1989), and Sylvia Snowiss, *Judicial Review and the Law of the Constitution* (New Haven: Yale University Press, 1990); and of the latter, James O'Fallon, "Marbury," *Stanford Law Review*, 44 (1992), 219–60, and Dean Alfange Jr., "Marbury v. Madison and the Original Understanding of Judicial Review: In Defense of Traditional Wisdom," *Supreme Court Review 1993*, 329–446. Useful attempts to synthesize the two views are Elizabeth McCaughey, "*Marbury v. Madison*: Have We Missed the Real Meaning?," *Presidential Studies Quarterly*, 19 (1989), 491–528; and Hobson, *Great Chief Justice*, chap. 3. Good synopses of the case are Ellis, *Jeffersonian Crisis*, 36–68; Haines, *Role of the Supreme Court*, 223–58; Haskins and Johnson, *Foundations of Power*, 182–204; the editorial note in *PJM*, 6:160–64; and Johnson, *Chief Justiceship of Marshall*, 57–62.

51. Sources used on the Burr conspiracy and trial are Marshall's opinions and the editorial notes on *Ex Parte Bollman and Ex Parte Swartwout* and *United States v. Burr, PJM*, 6:477–97, 7:3–31, 37–54, 56–59, 63–164; Malone, *Jefferson the President: Second Term*, 215–370; Lomask, *Burr: Conspiracy and Years of Exile*, chaps. 1–12; Haskins and Johnson, *Foundations of Power*, 246–91; Johnson, *Chief Justiceship of Marshall*, 124–31; Thomas P. Slaughter, "'The King of Crimes': Early American Treason Law, 1787–1860," in *Launching the "Extended Republic*,*"* 62–118; Smith, *Marshall*, 352–74; Beveridge, *Marshall*, 3:274–545; Corwin, *Marshall and the Constitution*, 86–113; Robert Faulkner, "John Marshall and the Burr Trial," *JAH*, 53 (1966–67), 247–58; Leonard W. Levy, *Jefferson and Civil Liberties: The Darker Side* (Cambridge: Harvard University Press, 1963), chap. 4; and Thomas P. Abernethy, *The Burr Conspiracy* (New York: Oxford University Press, 1954).

52. JM to William Cushing, 29 June 1807, *PJM*, 7:60.

53. *PJM*, 6:488; Stites, *Marshall*, 104.

54. "Editorial Note: *United States v. Burr*," *PJM*, 7:10; JM's 1 April opinion, *PJM*, 7:13; Slaughter, "'King of Crimes,'" 89–108; JM to Richard Peters, 23 November 1807, *PJM*, 7:165. Marshall clearly differentiated the applicability of English common law decisions made before and after the Revolution. "Those made since the revolution lose that title to authority which was conferred by the appellate character of the tribunals which made them, & can only be considered as the opinions of men distinguished for their talents & learning expounding a rule by which this country as well as theirs

professes to be governed." *Murdock & Company v. Hunter's Representatives* (U.S.C.C.Va., 1809), *PJM*, 7:209–10.

55. JM to William Cushing, 29 June 1807, *PJM*, 7:62; JM's 31 August opinion, *PJM*, 7:113, 115; Malone, *Jefferson the President: Second Term*, 341.

56. *PJM*, 7:48, 50 n. 15; Beveridge, *Marshall*, 3:447–49.

57. Slaughter, "'King of Crimes,'" 115–18.

58. JM to Richard Peters, 23 November 1807, *PJM*, 7:165; Jefferson to William Thomson, 26 September 1807, *Writings of Jefferson*, ed. Ford, 9:143–44; Malone, *Jefferson the President: Second Term*, 339–40, 351–54, 359–60, 367–69; Beveridge, *Marshall*, 3:530–44; Warren, *Supreme Court in U.S. History*, 1:313; Johnson, *Chief Justiceship of Marshall*, 31–37.

59. See generally Malone, *Sage of Monticello*, 55–73; George Dargo, *Jefferson's Louisiana: Politics and the Clash of Legal Traditions* (Cambridge: Harvard University Press, 1975), 74–101; William B. Hatcher, *Edward Livingston: Jeffersonian Republican and Jacksonian Democrat* (University: Louisiana State University Press, 1940), 180–89; and Ronan Degnan, "*Livingston v. Jefferson*—A Freestanding Footnote," *California Law Review*, 75 (1987), 115–28; JM's opinion in *PJM*, 7:278–88; JM to Story, 13 July and 18 September 1821, *PJM*, 9:179, 183.

60. Edward Dumbauld, "The Case of the Mutinous Mariner," Supreme Court Historical Society, *Yearbook 1977*, 52–58; Haskins and Johnson, *Foundations of Power*, 322–31; Warren, *Supreme Court in U.S. History*, 1:374–87; Jessup, "Reaction and Accomodation," 48–50; JM to Monroe, 8 November 1811, 25 June 1812, 13 June 1822, *PJM*, 7:272, 333, 9:236.

61. See generally Norman K. Risjord, *The Old Republicans: Southern Conservatism in the Age of Jefferson* (New York: Columbia University Press, 1964). On Roane's biography, beliefs, and judicial career, see Timothy S. Huebner, "The Consolidation of State Judicial Power: Spencer Roane, Virginia Legal Culture, and the Southern Judicial Tradition," *VMHB*, 102 (1994), 47–72; David Robarge, "Judge Spencer Roane and Jeffersonian Jurisprudence" (M.A. thesis, George Mason University, 1982); Margaret E. Horsnell, "Spencer Roane: Judicial Advocate of Jeffersonian Principles" (Ph.D. diss., University of Minnesota, 1967); and Rex Beach, "Judge Spencer Roane: A Champion of States Rights" (M.A. thesis, College of William and Mary, 1954). Whereas section 25 was a lightning rod for states' rights criticisms of the Marshall Court, in the 1790s cases that came to the Supreme Court under it caused little distress because the political context was very different and the Court had not emerged as a threat to state sovereignty. Marcus, "Judicial Review in the Early Republic," in *Launching the "Extended Republic,"* 28.

62. "Editorial Note: Marshall v. Hunter and Pendleton," and JM to James M. Marshall, 1 April 1804 and 13 February 1806, *PJM*, 6:94–96, 277–79, 426–27; "Editorial Note: Marshall and the Fairfax Litigation: From the Compromise of 1796 to *Martin v. Hunter's Lessee*," "Martin v. Hunter's Lessee: Petition for Writ of Error," c. 16 December 1815, and "Martin v. Hunter's Lessee: Fragment of Argument," c. December 1815–March 1816, *PJM*, 8:108–26; Charles F. Hobson, "John Marshall and the Fairfax Litigation: The Background of *Martin v. Hunter's Lessee*," *Journal of Supreme Court History*, 2 (1996), 36–50; Robarge, "Roane and Jeffersonian Jurisprudence," chap. 3; F. Thornton Miller, "John Marshall versus Spencer Roane: A Reevaluation of *Martin v. Hunter's Lessee*," *VMHB*, 96 (1988) 297–314; John A. Treon, "*Martin v. Hunter's Lessee*: A Case History" (Ph.D. diss., University of Virginia, 1970); White, *Marshall Court and Cultural Change*, 495–503; Haines, *Role of the Supreme Court*, 331–51; Beveridge, *Marshall*, 4:145–67; Charles Warren, "Legislative and Judicial Attacks on

the Supreme Court of the United States—A History of the Twenty-fifth Section of the Judiciary Act," *American Law Review*, 47 (1913), 6–17; *Fairfax's Devisee v. Hunter's Lessee*, 7 Cranch 603 (1813); *Hunter's Lessee v. Martin*, 4 Munford 1 (1815); *Martin v. Hunter's Lessee*, 1 Wheaton 304 (1816); Story to George Ticknor, 22 January 1831, *Life and Letters of Story*, 2:48–49. Marshall also thought he should not rule in any cases concerning the 1783 peace treaty's application to landholdings—in North Carolina, for example. See his remarks in *Granville's Devisee v. Allen* (U.S.C.C.N.C., 1805), *PJM*, 6:400.

63. Principle sources for this discussion of *McCulloch* are "Editorial Note: McCulloch v. Maryland," *PJM*, 8:254–59; Marshall's newspaper articles and related correspondence in *PJM*, 8:318–63; Hobson, *Great Chief Justice*, 116–26; White, *Marshall Court and Cultural Change*, 541–67; Haines, *Role of the Supreme Court*, 351–68; Harold J. Plous and Gordon E. Baker, "*McCulloch v. Maryland*: Right Principle, Wrong Case," *Stanford Law Review*, 9 (1957), 710–30; Gerald Gunther, ed., *John Marshall's Defense of McCulloch v. Maryland* (Stanford: Stanford University Press, 1969), 1–21; Robarge, "Roane and Jeffersonian Jurisprudence," 44–52; Eric Tscheschlock, "Mistaken Identity: Spencer Roane and the 'Amphictyon' Letters of 1819," *VMHB*, 106 (1998), 201–11.

64. JM to Story, 26 March 1819, *PJM*, 8:280. Unlike *McCulloch*, Marshall's *Dartmouth College* opinion attracted little public notice in Virginia—probably because it left intact the state's procedures for dealing with corporations and preserved civil liberties by protecting educational and religious institutions from legislative intrusions. Campbell, "Marshall, the Virginia Political Economy, and the *Dartmouth College* Decision," 64; idem, "*Dartmouth College* as a Civil Liberties Case: The Formation of Constitutional Policy," *Kentucky Law Journal*, 70 (1981–82), 643–706; Warren, *Supreme Court in U.S. History*, 1:487–90.

65. "Friend of the Union" and "Friend of the Constitution" letters, *PJM*, 8:287–308, 318–63; JM to Bushrod Washington, 6 May, 17 and 28 June, and 3 August 1819, *PJM*, 8:311, 316–17, 373; Gunther, ed., *Marshall's Defense of McCulloch v. Maryland*, 18; Haines, *Role of the Supreme Court*, 364–67.

66. JM to Story, 28 April 1819, *PJM*, 8:309–11. The purported Republican organization in Virginia called the "Richmond Junto" has been examined in Rex Beach, "Spencer Roane and the Richmond Junto," *WMQ*, 2nd ser. (1942), 1–17; Harry Ammon, "The Richmond Junto, 1800–1824," *VMHB*, 61 (1953), 395–418; Joseph H. J. Harrison, "Oligarchs and Democrats: The Richmond Junto," *VMHB*, 78 (1970), 184–98; Willard Ray Luce, "*Cohens v. Virginia* (1821): The Supreme Court and State Rights: A Reevaluation of Influences and Impacts" (Ph.D. diss., University of Virginia, 1978), 54–73; and Frederick T. Miller, "The Richmond Junto: The Secret All-Powerful Club—or Myth," ibid., 99 (1991), 63–80. Miller argues, with good corroboration, that the myth of the Junto grew out of a factional fight between two Richmond newspapers, and concludes that Roane could not have been the "boss" of the nonexistent organization. Marshall knew Roane, Brockenbrough, and Ritchie as neighbors, and his hurt pride and vexation at the Jeffersonians probably would have inclined him to see cabals if they existed, but in his private correspondence he never mentioned the Junto or any other Richmond-based Republican organization.

67. Sources for the *Cohens* case are Hobson, *Great Chief Justice*, 127–32; "Editorial Note: Cohens v. Virginia" and JM's opinions, *PJM*, 9:106–41, 143–47; Luce, "*Cohens v. Virginia*," passim; Johnson, *Chief Justiceship of Marshall*, 75–77, 152–54; White, *Marshall Court and Cultural Change*, 504–24; Haines, *Role of the Supreme Court*, chap. 12; Duncan Macleod, "The Triple Crisis," in *The Growth of Federal Power in the United*

States, ed. Rhodri Jeffreys-Jones and Bruce Collins (Edinburgh: Scottish Academic Press, 1983), pp. 13–24.

68. Charles H. Ambler, *Thomas Ritchie: A Study in Virginia Politics* (Richmond: Bell Book and Stationery, 1913), 81; JM to Story, 15 June, 13 July, and 18 September 1821, *PJM*, 9:167, 179, 184; Malone, *Sage of Monticello*, 355–60; Jefferson to William Johnson, 27 October 1822 and 4 March 1823, *Writings of Jefferson*, ed. Ford, 10:226, 248; Jefferson to Roane, 30 June 1821, "Roane Correspondence," in *The John P. Branch Historical Papers of Randolph-Macon College*, 2 (1905), 139; Hobson, *Great Chief Justice*, 208–12; Drew R. McCoy, *The Last of the Fathers: James Madison and the Republican Legacy* (New York: Cambridge University Press, 1989), 69–71, 99–103. Roane complained that "Jefferson and Madison hang back too much in this great crisis." Letter to Archibald Thweatt, 24 December 1821, *Branch Historical Papers*, 2:142.

69. White, *Marshall Court and Cultural Change*, 523; Johnson, *Chief Justiceship of Marshall*, 77; Malone, *Sage of Monticello*, 359; JM to Story, 18 September 1821, *PJM*, 9:183–84 and 185 n. 2.

70. JM to Story, 18 September 1821, *PJM*, 9:184; Warren, *Supreme Court in U.S. History*, 2:112–13; Luce, "*Cohens v. Virginia*," 174–79; Jessup, "Reaction and Accommodation," 425–28; Haines, *Role of the Supreme Court*, chaps. 13 and 14; Newmyer, *Story*, 222; Johnson, *Chief Justiceship of Marshall*, 105.

71. Daniel Boorstin, *The Americans: The National Experience*, Vintage ed. (New York: Random House, 1965), 337–56; Barry Schwartz, *George Washington: The Making of an American Symbol* (New York: Free Press, 1987), part two; Marcus Cunliffe, *George Washington: Man and Monument* (Boston: Little, Brown 1958), esp. chap. 1; Bernard Mayo, *Myths and Men* (New York: Harper and Row, 1963), 37–60; Garry Wills, *Cincinnatus: George Washington and the Enlightenment* (Garden City, N.Y.: Doubleday and Co., 1984), chaps. 3–5.

72. General sources for this section are the editorial notes in *PJM*, 6:219–30, 306–8, 430–32; Lawrence B. Custer, "Bushrod Washington and John Marshall: A Preliminary Inquiry," *AJLH*, 4 (1960), 34–48; Arthur H. Shaffer, *The Politics of History: Writing the History of the American Revolution, 1783–1815* (Chicago: Precedent Publishing, 1975), 139–40; Daniel R. Gilbert, "John Marshall and the Development of a National History," in *Early Nationalist Historians*, vol. 4 of *The Colonial Legacy*, ed. Lawrence H. Leder, 4 vols. (New York: Harper and Row, 1973), 197; Michael Kraus, *A History of American History* (New York: Farrar and Rinehart, 1937), 158; Marcus Cunliffe, "Introduction" to Chelsea House edition of *Life of Washington*, passim; Malone, *Jefferson the President: Second Term*, 356–59; Beveridge, *Marshall*, 3:223–73; Smith, *Marshall*, 328–34; Shevory, *John Marshall's Law*, 81–95.

73. Caleb P. Wayne to JM, 3 October 1800, Lear to JM, 12 December 1800, and JM, "Preface" to volume I of *Life of Washington*, December 1803, *PJM*, 4:314, 6:34–40, 230–36.

74. Lear to JM, 12 December 1800, JM to Charles Cotesworth Pinckney, 21 November 1802, JM to Wayne, 23 December 1803, *PJM*, 6:34, 124, 238; JM to James Monroe, 3 January 1784, *PJM*, 1:113; Adams to JM, 4 February 1806, *PJM*, 6:425. Adams would disparagingly invoke the same metaphor in an 1813 letter to Jefferson: "Marshall's [biography of Washington] is a Mausolaeum, 100 feet square at the base, and 200 feet high. It will be as durable as the monuments of the Washington benevolent Societies." 13 July 1813, quote in *PJM*, 6:425 n. 2.

75. Tucker to William Wirt, 4 April 1813, quoted in David D. Van Tassel, *Recording America's Past: An Interpretation of the Development of Historical Studies in America, 1607–1884* (Chicago: University of Chicago Press, 1960), 70; Dewey, *Marshall versus*

Jefferson, 101; Jefferson to Joel Barlow, 3 May 1802, in *The Writings of Thomas Jefferson*, ed. Paul Leicester Ford, 10 vols. (New York: G. P. Putnam's Sons, 1892–99), 8:151; JM to Wolcott, 28 June 1806, to Adams, 6 July 1806, and to Wayne, 20 July and 3 September 1804, *PJM*, 6:302, 328, 451. Bernard Mayo (*Myths and Men*, 43) describes the *Life of Washington* as "[m]ore history than biography, with the hero not born until volume two, with large parts lifted without credit from other writers, with volume five so partisan that Jefferson called it libelous, in it Washington always in military or court dress with godlike tread stalks stiffly through the many, many turgid pages."

The most critical look at Marshall's scholarship, but flawed by the misplaced application of modern standards of research, is William A. Foran, "John Marshall as a Historian," *AHR*, 43 (1937), 51–64. More useful for showing how the limitations of Marshall's research influenced his jurisprudence is Lindsay G. Robertson, "John Marshall as Colonial Historian: Reconsidering the Origins of the Discovery Doctrine," *Journal of Law and Politics*, 13 (1997), 759–77. According to Robertson—who calls the *History of the Colonies* "a cut-and-paste compilation of such secondary materials as he found it desirable to include"—Marshall misread the limited material available in the early 1800s on Britain's colonial policy and in 1823 erroneously decided a long-standing land title dispute between eastern speculators and Indian tribes in present-day Illinois and Indiana (*Johnson v. McIntosh*). With one exception, the sources Marshall used in the *History of the Colonies*—which he admitted at the time he wrote the decision were deficient—did not use British colonial records. Consequently, Robertson argues, it was not juristically sound for Marshall to draw on them through his own skewed history to substantiate the decision he reached in the case. Charles Hobson reaches a more favorable evaluation of Marshall's opinion in *PJM*, 9:281–83.

76. JM to Bushrod Washington, 3 April 1815 and 10 September 1816, *PJM*, 8:82–83, 140–41; same to same, 26 June 1820, 27 December 1821, 3 May, 12 July, 12 August, and 11 October 1823, *PJM*, 9:59, 195, 303, 333–34, 336, 340–41; JM to Caleb P. Wayne, 29 September 1823, *PJM*, 9:339; Smith, *Marshall*, 331, 629 n. 28; Beveridge, *Marshall*, 3:273 n. 1; Shevory, *John Marshall's Law*, chap. 3; idem, "John Marshall as a Republican," and Brisbin, "John Marshall on History, Virtue, and Legality," in *John Marshall's Achievement*, 75–93, 95–115. Marshall had to let the revised biography speak for him. When invited to give the principal oration at the centenary celebration of Washington's birth in 1832, he declined, citing the press of official duties and poor health: "My voice has become so weak as to be almost inaudible even in a room not unusually large." JM to Henry Clay, 10 February 1832, *The Papers of Henry Clay*, ed. James F. Hopkins et al., 10 vols. and supplement (Lexington: University Press of Kentucky, 1959–92), supplement, 235–56; Wesley Frank Craven, *The Legend of the Founding Fathers* (Ithaca: Cornell University Press, 1956), 106.

77. JM to Wayne, 5 July and 3 September 1804, *PJM*, 6:300–301, 328. The extensive correspondence between Marshall and Wayne in that volume of *PJM* well conveys their mutual frustrations with the project. A related undertaking that Marshall never finished was a compilation of the General's correspondence that he began with Bushrod Washington in 1815. They apparently intended to release the projected 10-to-12-volume collection at the same time as the revised biography. The work puttered on for over a decade until Marshall accepted an offer from Jared Sparks of Harvard to edit the papers. Marshall wrote the professor that he was "gratified at the expectation of seeing General Washington's works ushered to the world by a gentleman whose literary reputation ensures full justice to his memory"—and at the agreement that he and Bushrod Washington would share half the royalties from Sparks's work. JM to Bushrod Washington, 3 April 1815, 26 June 1820, 12 July, 11 October, and 6 December 1823,

PJM, 8:82–83, 9:59, 334, 340, 352–53; Smith, *Marshall*, 425, 482, 493; Herbert Baxter Adams, *The Life and Writings of Jared B. Sparks*, 2 vols. (Boston: Houghton Mifflin, 1893), 1:395–413.

78. Steamer, *Chief Justice*, 53; JM to Monroe, 10 March 1825, *The Writings of James Monroe*, ed. Stanislaus Murray Hamilton, 7 vols. (New York: G. P. Putnam's Sons, 1898–1903), 7:55–56; JM to Story, 26 September 1823, *PJM*, 9:338; Jessup, "Reaction and Accomodation," 50–51.

79. Clay to Daniel Webster, 10 November 1826, *Papers of Clay*, 5:889; Shaw Livermore Jr., *The Twilight of Federalism: The Disintegration of the Federalist Party, 1815–1830* (Princeton: Princeton University Press, 1962); Broussard, *Southern Federalists*, chaps. 13, 18–24; David Hackett Fischer, *The Revolution of American Conservatism: The Federalist Party in the Era of Jeffersonian Democracy* (New York: Harper and Row, 1965), 191, 216, 370–87; JM to Polly, 11 April 1823, *PJM*, 9:302–303; Wiebe, *Opening of American Society*, 209–33, quote at 216; Daniel Walker Howe, *The Political Culture of the American Whigs* (Chicago: University of Chicago Press, 1979); Glyndon G. Van Deusen, "Some Aspects of Whig Thought and Theory in the Jacksonian Period," *AHR*, 63 (1957–58), 305–22; Lynn L. Marshall, "The Strange Stillbirth of the Whig Party," *AHR*, 72 (1966–67), 445–68; Edward Pessen, *Jacksonian America: Society, Personality, and Politics* (Homewood, Ill: Dorsey Press, 1969), chaps. 9 and 10; Lawrence F. Kohl, *The Politics of Individualism: Parties and the American Character in the Jacksonian Era* (New York: Oxford University Press, 1989), chaps. 2–5. By the late 1830s, Virginia was split fairly evenly between Democrats and Whigs, and those state organizations looked and acted much like their counterparts elsewhere in the country. William G. Shade, *Democratizing the Old Dominion: Virginia and the Second Party System, 1824–1861* (Charlottesville: University Press of Virginia, 1996). See also the discussion of Virginia's Whigs in Michael F. Holt, *The Rise and Fall of the American Whig Party* (New York: Oxford University Press, 1999).

80. Russell Leon Caldwell, "The Influence of the Federal Bar upon the Interpretation of the Constitution by the Supreme Court under John Marshall" (Ph.D. diss., University of Southern California, 1948), 253–58; White, *Marshall Court and Cultural Change*, 288; Robert V. Remini, *Daniel Webster: The Man and His Times* (New York: W. W. Norton, 1997), 117–18, 208.

81. JM to Clay, 22 December 1823, JM to Charles Hammond, 28 December 1823, *PJM*, 9:365–67; JM to Clay, 4 April 1825, *Papers of Clay*, 4:211–12.

82. Beveridge, *Marshall*, 4:463–65; Smith, *Marshall*, 501; JM to Story, 1 May 1828, *Massachusetts Historical Society Proceedings*, 2nd ser., 14 (1900), 337; JM to Story, 30 December 1828, in *An Autobiographical Sketch by John Marshall*, ed. John Stokes Adams (Ann Arbor: University of Michigan Press, 1937); Robert V. Remini, *Andrew Jackson and the Course of American Freedom, 1822–1832* (New York: Harper and Row, 1981), 176. Marshall's preference in the 1828 election was leaked to a Democratic newspaper, causing a brief public row.

83. JM to Polly, 1 February 1829, quoted in Mason, *My Dearest Polly*, 304; JM to Joseph Hopkinson, 18 March 1829, quoted in Smith, *Marshall*, 503; JM to James Hillhouse, 26 May 1830, in Oster, *Political and Economic Doctrines of Marshall*, 188–90; JM to Story, 26 June 1831, in Warren, "Story-Marshall Correspondence," 23; JM to John Randolph, 18 June 1812, *PJM*, 7:332–33.

84. JM to Thomas Grimké, 6 October 1832, quoted in Baker, *Marshall*, 753; Alfred H. Kelly et al., *The American Constitution: Its Origins and Development*, 6th ed. (New York: W. W. Norton, 1983), 208–9; Major L. Wilson, "'Liberty and Union': An Analysis of Three Concepts Involved in the Nullification Controversy," *JSH*, 33 (1967),

331–55; idem, *Space, Time, and Freedom: The Quest for Nationality and the Irrepressible Conflict, 1815–1861* (Westport, Conn.: Greenwood Press, 1974), chaps. 3 and 4; Jackson's veto of the Bank bill, 10 July 1832, in *Documents in American History*, ed. Henry Steele Commager, 9th ed., 2 vols. (Englewood Cliffs, N.J.: Prentice-Hall, 1973), 1:272; Remini, *Jackson and the Course of American Freedom*, 366–69; Harold M. Hyman and William M. Wiecek, *Equal Justice under Law: Constitutional Development, 1835–1875* (New York: Harper and Row, 1982), chaps. 1 and 2.

85. The Virginia convention is treated comprehensively in Dickson D. Bruce, *The Rhetoric of Conservatism: The Virginia Convention of 1829–30 and the Conservative Tradition in the South* (San Marino, Ca.: Huntington Library, 1982). The debates are recounted in *Proceedings and Debates of the Virginia State Convention of 1829–30* (Richmond: Ritchie and Cook, 1830); Hugh Grigsby, *The Virginia Convention of 1829–1830* (orig. publ. 1854; rept., New York: Da Capo Press, 1969); and Robert P. Sutton, *Revolution to Secession: Constitution Making in the Old Dominion* (Charlottesville: University Press of Virginia, 1989), chap. 4. Marshall's role is detailed in Beveridge, *Marshall*, 4:467–508.

86. JM to Story, 11 June 1829 and 15 October 1830, *Massachusetts Historical Society Proceedings*, 2nd ser., 14 (1900), 127, 341–43; *Proceedings and Debates of the Convention*, 497–500, 615–19, 727–29.

87. Marvin Meyers, *The Jacksonian Persuasion: Politics and Belief*, Vintage ed. (New York: Alfred A. Knopf, 1960), 243–44.

88. On nullification generally, see William W. Freehling, *Prelude to Civil War: The Nullification Controversy in South Carolina, 1816–1836* (New York: Harper and Row, 1966); Richard E. Ellis, *The Union at Risk: Jacksonian Democracy, States' Rights, and the Nullification Crisis* (New York: Oxford University Press, 1987); James M. Banner, "The Problem of South Carolina," in *The Hofstadter Aegis: A Memorial*, ed. Stanley Elkins and Eric McKitrick (New York: Alfred A. Knopf, 1974), 60–93; Robert V. Remini, *Andrew Jackson and the Course of American Democracy, 1833–1845* (New York: Harper and Row, 1984), chaps. 2 and 3; and John Niven, *John C. Calhoun and the Price of Union* (Baton Rouge: Louisiana State University Press, 1988), chaps. 9 and 10.

89. JM to Edward Everett, 3 November 1830, quoted in Hobson, *Great Chief Justice*, 11; JM to Humphrey Marshall, 7 May 1833, quoted in *New York Tribune*, 7 February 1861; JM to Story, 22 September 1832, *Massachusetts Historical Society Proceedings*, 2nd ser., 14 (1900), 352.

90. JM to Story, 2 August and 25 December 1832, 3 June 1833, *Massachusetts Historical Society Proceedings*, 2nd ser., 14 (1900), 350, 354, 358; JM to Richard Peters, 3 December 1832, quoted in Beveridge, *Marshall*, 4:562; Story to Sarah W. Story, 27 January 1832, *Life and Letters of Story*, 2:119; Jessup, "Retreat and Accomodation," 340–41; Ellis, *Union at Risk*, chap. 6.

91. Smith, *Marshall*, 491; Remini, *Jackson and the Course of American Freedom*, 276–77.

92. JM to Clay, 28 November 1828, *The Life and Correspondence of Henry Clay*, ed. Calvin Colton, 5 vols. (New York: Barnes, 1855–57), 4:212; Johnson, *Chief Justiceship of Marshall*, 47–50; White, *Marshall Court and Cultural Change*, 294–302. In 1823, Marshall had felt "alarm" over what Story called "strange rumours" surrounding who would succeed the just-deceased associate, Brockholst Livingston. Nathaniel Macon, an Old Republican, was mentioned prominently. "Our Presidents I fear will never again seek to make our department respectable," Marshall wrote, but he did not intervene in the selection in any way. He "rejoiced" when Monroe picked Smith Thompson from the

New York Supreme Court. Story to JM, 22 June 1823, JM to Story, 2 July 1823, and JM to Bushrod Washington, 6 August 1823, *PJM*, 328, 331, 334.

93. Newmyer, *Story*, 87–88; idem, *Supreme Court under Marshall and Taney*, 81–88; Jessup, "Retreat and Accomodation," chap. 6; Haines, *Role of the Supreme Court*, chap. 16; Stanley I. Kutler, *Privilege and Creative Destruction: The Charles River Bridge Case* (Philadelphia: Lippincott, 1971), 61–73. *Barron v. Baltimore* (1833), in which Marshall declined to extend the Bill of Rights to the states, has been interpreted as a retreat from the exercise of national authority over state economic actions, but to Marshall it was a clear-cut case of merely applying the text of the Fifth Amendment as written. Hobson, *Great Chief Justice*, 108–10; Fred W. Friendly and Martha J. H. Elliott, *The Constitution: That Delicate Balance* (New York: Random House, 1984), chap. 1.

94. Sources used on the Cherokee cases are Joseph M. Burke, "The Cherokee Cases: A Study in Law, Politics, and Morality," *Stanford Law Review*, 21 (1969), 500–531; Hobson, *Great Chief Justice*, 170–80; Johnson, *Chief Justiceship of Marshall*, 81–84, 248–55, 257–60; White, *Marshall Court and Cultural Change*, 716–39; William F. Swindler, "Politics as Law: The Cherokee Cases," *American Indian Law Review*, 3 (1975), 7–20; Rennard J. Strickland and William J. Strickland, "The Court and the Trail of Tears," Supreme Court Historical Society, *Yearbook 1979*, 20–30; Jill Norgren, "The Cherokee Nation Cases of the 1830s," *Journal of Supreme Court History* (1994), 65–82; Beveridge, *Marshall*, 4:539–52; Warren, *Supreme Court in U.S. History*, 2:189 passim; Richard A. Monikowski, "The Actual State of Things: American Indians, Indian Law, and American Courts Between 1800 and 1835" (Ph.D. diss., University of New Mexico, 1997), part II.

95. JM to Story, 29 October 1828, *Massachusetts Historical Society Proceedings*, 2nd ser., 14 (1900), 337–38; JM to Dabney Carr, 26 June 1830, *Massachusetts Historical Society Proceedings*, 2nd ser., 60 (1927), 160; *Cherokee Nation v. Georgia*, 5 Peters 14 (1831).

96. *Worcester v. Georgia*, 6 Peters 515 (1832); Hobson, *Great Chief Justice*, 179.

97. Haines, *Role of the Supreme Court*, 610–11. Congress's last attempt during Marshall's tenure to repeal section 25 occurred in 1830–31. Despite Jackson's support, the measure lost by a wide margin in the House. The vote was overwhelmingly sectional; all but five votes for repeal came from Southern states. Warren, *Supreme Court in U.S. History*, 2:196ff.; Steamer, *Chief Justice*, 49.

98. JM to Story, 12 October 1831, *Massachusetts Historical Society Proceedings*, 2nd ser., 14 (1900), 346–48; JM to Richard Peters, 30 April 1835, quoted in Smith, *Marshall*, 211; JM to Polly, 12 March 1826 and 30 January 1831, "Letters from John Marshall to His Wife," *WMQ*, 2nd ser., 3 (1923), 86–88; JM to Polly, 7 March 1830, in Mason, *My Dearest Polly*, 321–22. Marshall's family difficulties are summarized in *PJM*, 8:xvii–xviii.

99. Story to Sarah W. Story, 4 March 1832, *Life and Letters of Story*, 2:86–87; Mason, *My Dearest Polly*, 343–44.

100. Newmyer, *Story*, 162–65, 170–71; JM to Story, 6 October 1834, *Life and Letters of Story*, 2:172.

101. Warren, *Supreme Court in U.S. History*, 2:238, 260 n. 1, 264; Remini, *Jackson and the Course of American Democracy*, 266.

102. Stites, *Marshall*, 167; Robert L. Scribner, "John Marshall, Deceased," *Virginia Cavalcade*, 5 (autumn 1955), 40–42; *The Memoirs of John Quincy Adams*, ed. Charles Francis Adams, 12 vols. (Philadelphia: J. P. Lippincott, 1874–77), 9:243. Associate Justice Henry Baldwin evidently reconciled with Marshall toward the end. "Judge

Baldwin . . . took an interest in the Chief Justice's dying hours," Story reported. "[T]here is no person on earth for whom he felt so much reverence and respect." Story to Richard Peters, 24 July 1835, *Life and Letters of Story*, 2:201. Baldwin accompanied Marshall's body back to Richmond.

103. *Mitchel et al. v. United States*, 9 Peters 711 (1835), quote at 725.

Bibliography

PUBLIC DOCUMENTS

[*Annals of the Congress of the United States.*] *Debates and Proceedings in the Congress of the United States, 1789–1824.* 42 volumes. Washington, D.C.: Gales and Seaton, 1834–56.

Bockstruck, Lloyd D. *Revolutionary War Bounty Land Grants Awarded by State Governments.* Baltimore: Genealogical Publishing Co., 1996.

Brumbaugh, Gaius M. *Revolutionary War Records. Volume I, Virginia. Virginia Army and Navy Forces with Bounty Land Warrants for Virginia Military District of Ohio, and Virginia Military Script; from Federal and State Archives.* Lancaster, Pa.: Lancaster Press, 1936.

Call, Daniel. *Reports of Cases Argued and Adjudged in the Court of Appeals of Virginia.* 6 volumes. 2nd edition. Richmond: Smith, 1833.

Cranch, William. *Reports of Cases Argued and Adjudged in the Supreme Court of the United States, 1801–1815.* 9 volumes. Philadelphia: Carey and Lea, 1830–54.

Hening, W. W., ed. *The Statues at Large: Being a Collection of All the Laws of Virginia, from the First Session of the Legislature, in the Year 1619.* 13 volumes. Richmond: Bartow, 1819–23.

Jillson, Willard R. *Old Kentucky Entries and Deeds.* Louisville: Standard Publishing Co., 1926.

John Marshall Bicentennial Celebration, 1955. Final Report of the United States Commission for the Celebration of the Two-Hundredth Anniversary of the Birth of John Marshall. Washington, D.C.: N.p., 1955.

Journals of the Council of State of Virginia. 5 volumes. Richmond: Division of Purchase and Printing, 1971–82.

Journals of the House of Delegates of the Commonwealth of Virginia. Richmond: Thomas W. White, 1828.

Palmer, W. P. et al., eds. *Calendar of Virginia State Papers and Other Manuscripts Preserved in the Capitol at Richmond.* 11 volumes. Richmond: N.p., 1875–93.

Peters, Richard Jr. *Reports of Cases Argued and Adjudged in the Supreme Court of the United States, from 1828 to 1843, Inclusive.* 17 volumes. Philadelphia: Nicklin, 1828–43.

Proceedings and Debates of the Virginia State Convention of 1829–30. Richmond: Ritchie and Cook, 1830.

Seymour, A. M. and W. T. Jewell, comps. *Fauquier County, Virginia, Court Records.* Unpublished typescript, Daughters of the American Revolution Library, Washington, D.C.

Swem, E. G. and John W. Williams, eds. *A Register of the General Assembly of Virginia: 1776–1918.* Richmond: Bottom, 1918.Thorpe, Francis Newton, ed. *The Federal and State Constitutions, Colonial Charters, and Other Organic Laws of the States, Territories, and Colonies Now or Heretofore Forming the United States of America.* 7 volumes. Washington, D.C.: Government Printing Office, 1909.

Washington, Bushrod. *Reports of Cases Argued and Determined in the Court of Appeals of Virginia.* 2nd edition. Philadelphia: Abraham Small, 1823.

Wheaton, Henry. *Reports of Cases Argued and Adjudged in the Supreme Court of the United States, 1816–27.* 12 volumes. Philadelphia: Carey and Lea, 1816–27.

Wythe, George. *Decisions of Cases in Virginia by the High Court of Chancery, with Remarks upon Decrees by the Court of Appeals Reversing Some of Those Decisions.* [Richmond: N.p.,] 1795.

CONTEMPORARY WRITINGS AND PUBLISHED COLLECTIONS

Adams, Charles Francis, ed. *The Memoirs of John Quincy Adams.* 12 volumes. Philadelphia: J. P. Lippincott, 1874–77.
———. *The Works of John Adams.* 10 volumes. Boston: Little, Brown, 1856.
Adams, Herbert Baxter. *The Life and Writings of Jared B. Sparks.* 2 volumes. Boston: Houghton Mifflin, 1893.
Adams, John Stokes, ed. *An Autobiographical Sketch by John Marshall.* Ann Arbor: University of Michigan Press, 1937.
Ames, Seth, ed. *Works of Fisher Ames, with a Selection from His Speeches and Correspondence.* 2 volumes. Boston: Little, Brown, 1854.
"Bank of the United States. Petitions of Virginia Cities and Towns for the Establishment of Branches, 1791," *Virginia Magazine of History and Biography*, 8 (1901), 287–95.
Boyd, Julian P. et al., eds. *The Papers of Thomas Jefferson.* 27 volumes to date. Princeton: Princeton University Press, 1950– .
Calumet, The, Volume T, November–December 1832.
Cappon, Lester J., ed. *The Adams-Jefferson Letters.* 2 volumes. Chapel Hill: University of North Carolina Press, 1959.
Colton, Calvin, ed. *The Life and Correspondence of Henry Clay.* 5 volumes. New York: Barnes, 1855–57.
Commager, Henry Steele, ed. *Documents in American History.* 9th edition. 2 volumes. Englewood Cliffs, N.J.: Prentice-Hall, 1973.
Cooke, Jacob E., ed. *The Federalist Papers.* Middletown, Conn.: Wesleyan University Press, 1961.
Duke, Maurice and Daniel P. Jordan, eds. *A Richmond Reader, 1773–1983.* Chapel Hill: University of North Carolina Press, 1983.

Fitzpatrick, John C., ed. *Diaries of George Washington, 1748–1799.* 4 volumes. Boston: Houghton Mifflin, 1925.

———. *The Writings of George Washington.* 39 volumes. Washington, D.C.: Government Printing Office, 1931–44.

Foner, Philip S., ed. *The Democratic-Republican Societies, 1790–1880: A Documentary Sourcebook of Constitutions, Declarations, Addresses, Resolutions, and Toasts.* Westport, Conn.: Greenwood Press, 1976.

Ford, Paul Leicester, ed. *The Writings of Thomas Jefferson.* 10 volumes. New York: G. P. Putnam's Sons, 1892–99.

———. *The Writings of Thomas Jefferson.* 12 volumes. New York: G. P. Putnam's Sons, 1904–5.

Garnett, James M. *Lectures on Female Education.* 4th edition. Richmond: Thomas W. White, 1825.

Gibbs, George. *Memoirs of the Administrations of George Washington and John Adams, from the Papers of Oliver Wolcott.* 2 volumes. New York: Van Norden Co., 1846.

Gilmer, Francis Walker. *Sketches, Essays, and Translations.* Baltimore: F. Lucas, 1818.

"Glimpses of Old College Life," *William and Mary Quarterly,* 1st series, 9 (1900), 18–23.

Grigsby, Hugh Blair. *The History of the Virginia Federal Convention of 1788, with Some Account of the Eminent Virginians of That Era Who Were Members of the Body.* 2 volumes. Richmond: Virginia Historical Society, 1890.

———. *The Virginia Convention of 1829–1830.* Originally published 1854. Reprint, New York: Da Capo Press, 1969.

Hamilton, Stanislaus Murray, ed. *The Writings of James Monroe.* 7 volumes. New York: G. P. Putnam's Sons, 1898–1903.

Henry, William Wirt. *Patrick Henry: Life, Correspondence, and Speeches.* 3 volumes. New York: Charles Scribner's Sons, 1891.

Hines, Christopher. *Early Recollections of Washington City.* Washington, D.C.: N.p., 1866.

"Historical and Genealogical Notes," *William and Mary Quarterly,* 1st series, 9 (1901), 141–44.

Hopkins, James F. et al., eds. *The Papers of Henry Clay.* 10 volumes and supplement. Lexington: University Press of Kentucky, 1959–92.

Hunt, Gaillard, ed. *The First Forty Years of Washington Society in the Family Letters of Margaret Bayard Smith.* New York: Frederick Ungar Publishing Co., 1965.

Hutchinson, William T. et al., eds. *The Papers of James Madison.* 17 volumes. Chicago: University of Chicago Press, 1962–91.

Jackson, Donald, ed. *Diaries of George Washington.* 6 volumes. Charlottesville: University Press of Virginia, 1976–79.

Jefferson, Thomas. *Notes on the State of Virginia.* Edited by William Peden. New York: W. W. Norton, 1982.

Jensen, Merrill et al., eds. *The Documentary History of the Ratification of the Constitution.* 10 volumes to date. Madison: State Historical Society of Wisconsin, 1976– .

Johnson, Herbert Alan et al., eds. *The Papers of John Marshall.* 9 volumes to date. Chapel Hill: University of North Carolina Press, 1974– .

King, Charles R. *The Life and Correspondence of Rufus King.* 6 volumes. New York: G. P. Putnam's Sons, 1894–1900.

"Letters from John Marshall to His Wife," *William and Mary Quarterly*, 2nd series, 3 (1923), 69–90.

Lipscomb, Andrew A. and Albert Ellery Bergh, eds. *The Writings of Thomas Jefferson.* 20 volumes. Washington, D.C.: The Thomas Jefferson Memorial Association, 1905.

Marcus, Maeva and James R. Perry, eds. *Documentary History of the Supreme Court of the United States, 1789–1800.* 4 volumes to date. New York: Columbia University Press, 1985– .

Marshall, Humphrey. *The History of Kentucky, Exhibiting an Account of the Modern Discovery; Settlement; Progressive Improvement; Civil and Military Transactions; and the Present State of the Country.* 2 volumes. Frankfort, Ky.: George S. Robinson, 1824.

Marshall, John. *A History of the Colonies Planted by the English on the Continent of North America, from Their Settlement to the Commencement of That War Which Terminated in Their Independence.* Philadelphia: Abraham Small, 1924.

———. *Life of George Washington.* 5 volumes. Philadelphia: C. P. Wayne, 1804–7; Reprint, New York: Chelsea House, 1983.

McRee, Griffith J., ed. *Life and Correspondence of James Iredell.* 2 volumes. New York: D. Appleton and Co., 1858.

"Minutes of the First Court." Annotated by H. C. Groom. *Bulletin of the Fauquier Historical Society*, number 4 (July 1924), 371–403.

Mordecai, Samuel. *Richmond in By-Gone Days, Being Reminiscences of an Old Citizen.* Richmond: West and Johnson, 1856.

Morris, Anne Cary, ed. *The Diary and Letters of Gouveneur Morris: Minister of the United States to France; Member of the Constitutional Convention; etc.* 2 volumes. New York: Charles Scribner's Sons, 1888.

Morris, Charles R., ed. *Burke's Speech on Conciliation with America.* New York: Harper and Brothers, 1954.

Munford, George Wythe. *The Two Parsons; Cupid's Sports; The Dream; and The Jewels of Virginia.* Richmond: J. D. K. Sleight, 1884.

Oster, John Edward. *The Political and Economic Doctrines of John Marshall.* Originally published 1914. Reprint, New York: Burt Franklin, 1967.

Paine, Thomas. *Common Sense.* Edited by Isaac Kramnick. New York: Penguin Books, 1982.

Rhodes, Irwin S. *The Papers of John Marshall: A Descriptive Calendar.* 2 volumes. Norman: University of Oklahoma Press, 1956.

"Roane Correspondence." In *The John P. Branch Historical Papers of Randolph-Macon College*, 2 (1905), 123–42.

Roche, John C., ed. *John Marshall: Major Opinions and Other Writings.* Indianapolis: Bobbs-Merrill, 1967.

Rutland, Robert A., ed. *The Papers of George Mason.* 3 volumes. Chapel Hill: University of North Carolina Press, 1970.

Schmidt, Gustavus. "Reminiscences of the Late Chief Justice Marshall," *Louisiana Law Journal*, 1 (1841), 81–83.

Siegel, Adrienne, ed. *The Marshall Court, 1801–1835.* Volume 2 in the Supreme Court in American Life series. Millwood, N.Y.: Associated Faculty Press, 1987.

Sparks, Jared, ed. *The Life of Gouverneur Morris.* 2 volumes. Boston: Gray and Bowen, 1832.

Story, William Wetmore, ed. *The Life and Letters of Joseph Story*. 2 volumes. Boston: Little, Brown, 1851.

Syrett, Harold et al., eds. *The Papers of Alexander Hamilton*. 27 volumes. New York: Columbia University Press, 1961–81.

Tarter, Brent, ed. "Orderly Book of the Second Virginia Regiment, September 27, 1775–April 15, 1775," *Virginia Magazine of History and Biography*, 85 (1977), 302–36.

Tyler, Lyon G. "Original Records of the Phi Beta Kappa Society," *William and Mary Quarterly*, 1st series, 4 (1896), 213–41.

Van Schreeven, William J., comp., and Robert L. Scribner, ed. *Revolutionary Virginia: The Road to Independence*. 7 volumes. Charlottesville: University Press of Virginia, 1973–83.

Warren, Charles. "The Story-Marshall Correspondence (1819–1831)," *William and Mary Quarterly*, 2nd series, 21 (1941), 1–26.

Weedon, George. *Valley Forge Orderly Book of General George Weedon of the Continental Army under the Command of Genl. George Washington, in the Campaign of 1777–78*. New York: Dodd, Mead, 1902. Reprint, New York: Arno Press, 1971.

Wirt, William. *Letters of the British Spy*. Originally published 1832. Reprint, Chapel Hill: University of North Carolina Press, 1970.

———. *Life of Patrick Henry*. Originally published 1836. Reprint, New York: Books for Libraries Press, 1970.

The Works of the Right Honorable Edmund Burke. 6th edition. 12 volumes. Boston: Little, Brown, 1880.

Wroth, L. Kilvin and Hiller B. Zobel, eds. *Legal Papers of John Adams*. 3 volumes. Cambridge: Harvard University Press, 1965.

BOOKS AND ARTICLES

Abernethy, Thomas P. *The Burr Conspiracy*. New York: Oxford University Press, 1954.

———. *Three Virginia Frontiers*. Baton Rouge: Louisiana State University Press, 1940.

———. *Western Lands and the American Revolution*. Charlottesville: University of Virginia Institute for Research in the Social Sciences, 1937. Reprint, New York: Russell and Russell, 1959.

Abraham, Henry J. *Justices and Presidents: A Political History of Appointments to the Supreme Court*. New York: Oxford University Press, 1974.

Adams, Henry. *History of the United States of America*. 9 volumes. New York: Charles Scribner's Sons, 1889–91.

Alden, John R. *The South in the Revolution, 1763–1789*. Baton Rouge: Louisiana State University Press, 1957.

Alexander, Jay. "Legal Careers in Eighteenth Century America," *Duquesne Law Review*, 24 (1984–85), 631–58.

Alfange, Dean Jr. "Marbury v. Madison and Original Understandings of Judicial Review: In Defense of Traditional Wisdom," *Supreme Court Review 1993*, 329–446.

Allison, Robert J. *The Crescent Obscured: The United States and the Muslim World, 1776–1815*. New York: Oxford University Press, 1995.

Ambler, Charles H. *Thomas Ritchie: A Study in Virginia Politics.* Richmond: Bell Book and Stationery Co., 1913.

Ammon, Harry. "Agricola Versus Aristides: James Monroe, John Marshall, and the Genet Affair in Virginia," *Virginia Magazine of History and Biography*, 74 (1966), 312–20.

———. *The Genet Mission.* New York: W. W. Norton, 1973.

———. "The Genet Mission and the Development of American Political Parties," *Journal of American History*, 52 (1965–66), 725–41.

———. *James Monroe: The Quest for National Identity.* New York: McGraw-Hill, 1971.

———. "The Richmond Junto, 1800–1824," *Virginia Magazine of History and Biography*, 61 (1953), 395–418.

"An Old Virginia Correspondence," *Atlantic Monthly*, 84 (1899), 535–49.

Appleby, Joyce. *Capitalism and a New Social Order: The Republican Vision of the 1790s.* New York: New York University Press, 1984.

Aptheker, Herbert. *American Negro Slave Revolts.* New York: Columbia University Press, 1943.

Arnebeck, Bob. *Through a Fiery Trial: Building Washington, 1790–1800.* Lanham, Md.: Madison Books, 1991.

Atkinson, Paul G. Jr. "The System of Military Discipline and Justice in the Continental Army: August 1777–June 1778," *Picket Post* (winter 1972–73), 12–23, 40–43.

Aumann, Francis R. *The Changing American Legal System: Some Selected Phases.* Columbus: Ohio State University Press, 1940. Reprint, New York: DaCapo Press, 1969.

Bailyn, Bernard. *The Ideological Origins of the American Revolution.* Cambridge: Harvard University Press, 1967.

Baker, Leonard. *John Marshall: A Life in Law.* New York: Macmillan, 1974.

———. "John Marshall's Federalist House," *Washington Post*, 28 March 1971, G1.

Baldwin, Leland D. *Whiskey Rebels: The Story of a Frontier Uprising.* Pittsburgh: University of Pittsburgh Press, 1939.

Bancroft, George. *The History of the United States of America.* 6 volumes. Boston: Little, Brown, 1885.

Banner, James M. Jr. "The Problem of South Carolina." In *The Hofstadter Aegis: A Memorial*, edited by Stanley Elkins and Eric McKitrick, 60–93. New York: Alfred A. Knopf, 1974.

———. *To the Hartford Convention: The Federalists and the Origins of Party Politics in Massachusetts, 1789–1815.* New York: Alfred A. Knopf, 1970.

Bartosic, Florian. "With John Marshall from William and Mary to Dartmouth College," *William and Mary Law Review*, 7 (1966), 259–66.

Bates, Whitney K. "Northern Speculators and Southern State Debts: 1790," *William and Mary Quarterly*, 3rd series, 19 (1962), 30–48.

Baxter, Maurice G. *The Steamboat Monopoly: Gibbons v. Ogden, 1824.* New York: Alfred A. Knopf, 1972.

Beach, Rex. "Spencer Roane and the Richmond Junto," *William and Mary Quarterly*, 2nd series, 22 (1942), 1–17.

Beard, Charles. *An Economic Interpretation of the Constitution of the United States.* New York: Macmillan, 1913.

Beeman, Richard R. *The Evolution of the Southern Backcountry: A Case Study of Lunenberg County, Virginia, 1746–1832*. Philadelphia: University of Pennsylvania Press, 1984.

———. *The Old Dominion and the New Nation, 1788–1801*. Lexington: University Press of Kentucky, 1972.

———. *Patrick Henry: A Biography*. New York: McGraw-Hill, 1974.

———. "The Political Response to Social Conflict in the Southern Backcountry: A Comparative View of Virginia and the Carolinas during the Revolution." In *An Uncivil War: The Southern Backcountry during the American Revolution*, edited by Ronald Hoffman et al., 213–39. Charlottesville: University Press of Virginia, 1985.

Bell, Rudolph M. *Party and Faction in American Politics: The House of Representatives, 1789–1801*. Westport, Conn.: Greenwood Press, 1973.

Bemis, Samuel Flagg. *Pinckney's Treaty: A Study of America's Advantage from Europe's Distress, 1783–1800*. Baltimore: Johns Hopkins University Press, 1926.

Bendini, Silvio A. "Marshall's Meridian Instrument," *Professional Surveyor*, 7 (July/August 1987), 26, (September/October 1987), 60.

Berg, Fred Anderson. *Encyclopedia of Continental Army Units: Battalions, Regiments, and Independent Corps*. Harrisburg, Pa.: Stackpole Books, 1972.

Berger, Raoul. *Impeachment: The Constitutional Problems*. Cambridge: Harvard University Press, 1973.

Berkeley, Edmund Jr. "Quoits, the Sport of Gentlemen," *Virginia Cavalcade*, 15 (summer 1965), 11–21.

Bernath, Stuart L. "George Washington and the Genesis of Military Discipline," *Mid-America*, 49 (1967), 83–100.

Bernhard, Winfred E. *Fisher Ames: Federalist and Statesman, 1758–1808*. Chapel Hill: University of North Carolina Press, 1965.

Berns, Walter. *Taking the Constitution Seriously*. New York: Simon and Schuster, 1987.

Berthoff, Rowland. "Independence and Attachment, Virtue and Interest: From Republican Citizen to Free Enterpriser, 1787–1837." In *Uprooted Americans: Essays to Honor Oscar Handlin*, edited by Richard L. Bushman et al., 99–124. Boston: Little, Brown, 1979.

Beveridge, Albert J. *The Life of John Marshall*. 4 volumes. Boston: Houghton Mifflin, 1916–19.

Biddle, Francis. "Scandal at Bizarre," *American Heritage*, 12 (August 1961), 10–13, 79–82.

Bill, Alfred Hoyt. *Valley Forge: The Making of an Army*. New York: Harper and Brothers, 1952.

Billias, George A. *Elbridge Gerry: Founding Father and Republican Statesman*. New York: McGraw-Hill, 1976.

Billings, Warren M. et al. *Colonial Virginia: A History*. White Plains, N.Y.: KTO Press, 1986.

Blackard, Raymond B. "Requirements for Admission to the Bar in Revolutionary America," *Tennessee Law Review*, 15 (1938), 116–27.

Blackburn, Joyce. *George Wythe of Williamsburg*. New York: Harper and Row, 1975.

Blaustein, Albert P. and Roy M. Mersky. *The First One Hundred Justices: Statistical Studies on the Supreme Court of the United States*. Hamden, Conn.: Archon Books, 1978.

————. "Rating Supreme Court Justices," *American Bar Association Journal*, 58 (1972), 1183–89.

Bloch, Susan Low and Maeva Marcus. "John Marshall's Selective Use of History in *Marbury v. Madison.*" In Supreme Court Historical Society, *Yearbook 1987*, 82–107.

Bloom, Robert S. *A Generation of Leaves*. New York: Ballantine Books, 1991.

Bloomfield, Maxwell. *American Lawyers in a Changing Society, 1776–1876*. Cambridge: Harvard University Press, 1976.

Boatner, Mark Mayo III. *The Encyclopedia of the American Revolution*. New York: David McKay Co., 1966.

Boorstin, Daniel. *The Americans: The Colonial Experience*. Vintage edition. New York: Random House, 1958.

————. *The Americans: The National Experience*. Vintage edition. New York: Random House, 1965.

————. *The Mysterious Science of the Law: An Essay on Blackstone's "Commentaries."* Boston: Beacon Press, 1958.

Borden, Morton. *The Federalism of James A. Bayard*. Columbia University Studies in the Social Sciences, 1955. Reprint, New York: AMS Press, 1968.

Bowers, Claude. *Beveridge and the Progressive Era*. New York: Literary Guild, 1932.

Bowling, Kenneth R. *The Creation of Washington, D.C.: The Idea and Location of the American Capital*. Fairfax, Va.: George Mason University Press, 1991.

Bowman, Albert H. *The Struggle for Neutrality: Franco-American Diplomacy during the Federalist Era*. Knoxville: University of Tennessee Press, 1974.

Boyd, Julian P. "The Chasm That Separated Thomas Jefferson and John Marshall." In *Essays on the American Constitution*. Edited by Gottfried Dietze. Englewood Cliffs, N.J.: Prentice-Hall, 1964.

Boyd, Steven R. *The Politics of Opposition: Antifederalists and the Acceptance of the Constitution*. Millwood, N.Y.: KTO Press, 1979.

Bradshaw, Herbert C. *History of Prince Edward County, Virginia, from Its Earliest Settlements through Its Establishment in 1754 to Its Bicentennial Year*. Richmond: The Dietz Press, 1955.

Braeman, John. *Albert J. Beveridge, American Nationalist*. Chicago: University of Chicago Press, 1971.

Brandow, James C. "John Marshall's Supreme Court Practice: A Letter Comes to Light," *Journal of Supreme Court History*, 1 (1995), 73–76.

Brant, Irving. *James Madison: Commander in Chief, 1812–1836*. Indianapolis: Bobbs-Merrill, 1961.

————. *James Madison: The Nationalist*. Indianapolis: Bobbs-Merrill, 1941.

Breen, T. H. *Tobacco Culture: The Mentality of the Great Tidewater Planters on the Eve of the Revolution*. Princeton: Princeton University Press, 1985.

Bridenbaugh, Carl. *Myths and Realities: Societies of the Colonial South*. New York: Atheneum, 1965.

Brisbin, Richard A. Jr. "John Marshall and the Nature of Law in the Early Republic," *Virginia Magazine of History and Biography*, 98 (1990), 57–80.

————. "John Marshall on History, Virtue, and Legality." In *John Marshall's Achievement: Law, Politics, and Constitutional Interpretation*, edited by Thomas C. Shevory, 95–115. Westport, Conn.: Greenwood Press, 1989.

Broderick, Albert. "From Constitutional Politics to Constitutional Law: The Supreme Court's First Fifty Years," *North Carolina Law Review*, 65 (1987), 945–56.

Broussard, James H. *The Southern Federalists, 1800–1816.* Baton Rouge: Louisiana State University Press, 1978.

Brown, Imogene E. *American Aristides: A Biography of George Wythe.* East Brunswick, N.J.: Associated University Presses, 1981.

Brown, Ralph Adams. *The Presidency of John Adams.* Lawrence: University Press of Kansas, 1975.

Brown, Richard D. "Shays's Rebellion and the Ratification of the Federal Constitution in Massachusetts." In *Beyond Confederation: Origins of the Constitution and American National Identity,* edited by Richard Beeman et al., 113–27. Chapel Hill: University of North Carolina Press, 1987.

Brown, Roger H. *The Republic in Peril: 1812.* New York: Columbia University Press, 1964.

Brown, Stuart E. Jr. *Virginia Baron: The Story of Thomas 6th Lord Fairfax.* Berryville, Va.: Chesapeake Book Co., 1965.

Bruce, Dickson D. *The Rhetoric of Conservatism: The Virginia Convention of 1829–30 and the Conservative Tradition in the South.* San Marino, Ca.: Huntington Library, 1982.

Bruce, Philip Alexander. *Institutional History of Virginia in the Seventeenth Century.* 2 volumes. New York: G. P. Putnam's Sons, 1910.

Bruce, William Cabell. *John Randolph of Roanoke, 1773–1833.* 2 volumes. New York: G. P. Putnam's Sons, 1922.

Bruchey, Stuart. "The Impact of Concern for the Security of Property Rights on the Legal System of the Early Republic," *Wisconsin Law Review* (1980), 1135–58.

Bryan, Wilhelmus B. *A History of the National Capital from Its Foundation through the Period of the Adoption of the Organic Act.* 2 volumes. New York: Macmillan, 1914.

Bryan, William A. *George Washington in American Literature, 1775–1865.* New York: Columbia University Press, 1952.

Brydon, George. *Virginia's Mother Church and the Political Conditions Under Which It Grew.* 2 volumes. Philadelphia: Church Historical Society, 1948–52.

Bryson, W. Hamilton. "The History of Legal Education in Virginia," *University of Richmond Law Review,* 14 (1979–80), 155–210.

Buckley, Thomas E. *Church and State in Revolutionary Virginia, 1776–1787.* Charlottesville: University Press of Virginia, 1977.

Buel, Richard Jr. *Securing the Revolution: Ideology in American Politics, 1789–1815.* Ithaca: Cornell University Press, 1972.

Burke, Joseph M. "The Cherokee Cases: A Study in Law, Politics, and Morality," *Stanford Law Review,* 21 (1969), 500–531.

Busch, Noel F. *Winter Quarters: George Washington and the Continental Army at Valley Forge.* New York: Liveright, 1974.

"Buyer Sought for John Marshall Estate," *Historic Preservation News,* October–November 1994, 20–21.

Callcott, George H. *History in the United States, 1800–1860: Its Practice and Purpose.* Baltimore: Johns Hopkins University Press, 1970.

Campbell, Bruce A. "*Dartmouth College* as a Civil Liberties Case: The Formation of Constitutional Policy," *Kentucky Law Journal,* 70 (1981–82), 643–706.

———. "John Marshall, the Virginia Political Economy, and the *Dartmouth College* Decision," *American Journal of Legal History,* 19 (1975), 40–65.

———. "Social Federalism: The Constitutional Position of Nonprofit Corporations in Nineteenth-Century America," *Law and History Review,* 8 (1990–91), 149–88.

Carp, E. Wayne. "Early American Military History: A Review of Recent Work," *Virginia Magazine of History and Biography*, 94 (1986), 259–84.

———. *To Starve the Army at Pleasure: Continental Army Administration and American Political Culture, 1775–1783.* Chapel Hill: University of North Carolina Press, 1984.

Carpenter, William S. "Repeal of the Judiciary Act of 1801," *American Political Science Review*, 9 (1915), 519–28.

Casto, William R. *The Supreme Court in the Early Republic: The Chief Justiceships of John Jay and Oliver Ellsworth.* Columbia: University of South Carolina Press, 1995.

Cayton, Andrew R. L. "Radicals in the 'Western World': The Federalist Conquest of Trans-Appalachian North America." In *Federalism Reconsidered*, edited by Doron Ben-Atar and Barbara B. Oberg, 77–96. Charlottesville: University Press of Virginia.

Chambers, William Nisbet. *Political Parties in a New Nation: The American Experience, 1776–1809.* New York: Oxford University Press, 1963.

"Chief Justice John Marshall: A Symposium," *University of Pennsylvania Law Review*, 104 (1955–56), 1–68.

Chitwood, Oliver P. *Richard Henry Lee: Statesman of the Revolution.* Morgantown: West Virginia University Libraries, 1967.

Christian, W. Asbury. *Richmond: Her Past and Present.* Richmond: L. H. Jenkins, 1912.

Chroust, Anton-Hermann. *The Rise of the Legal Profession in America.* 2 volumes. Norman: University of Oklahoma Press, 1965.

Church, Randolph W. "James Markham Marshall," *Virginia Cavalcade*, 13 (spring 1964), 22–29.

Clarfield, Gerard H. *Timothy Pickering and American Diplomacy, 1795–1800.* Columbia: University of Missouri Press, 1969.

Clarkin, William. *Serene Patriot: A Life of George Wythe.* Albany, N.Y.: Alan Publications, 1970.

Clinton, Robert L. *Marbury v. Madison and Judicial Review.* Lawrence: University Press of Kansas, 1989.

C. M. S. "The Home Life of Chief Justice Marshall," *William and Mary Quarterly*, 2nd series, 12 (1932), 67–69.

Coleman, Elizabeth Dabney. "Till Death Did Them Part," *Virginia Cavalcade*, 5 (autumn 1955), 14–19.

Coleman, Peter J. *Debtors and Creditors in America: Insolvency, Imprisonment for Debt, and Bankruptcy, 1607–1900.* Madison: State Historical Society of Wisconsin, 1974.

Combs, Jerald A. *The Jay Treaty: Political Battleground of the Founding Fathers.* Berkeley: University of California Press, 1970.

Cooke, Jacob E. *Alexander Hamilton.* New York: Charles Scribner's Sons, 1982.

"Cool Spring Church," *News and Notes of the Fauquier Historical Society*, 4 (fall 1982), 1–2.

Corwin, Edward S. "John Marshall." In *Dictionary of American Biography*, edited by Dumas Malone et al. 20 volumes and supplements, 12:315–25. New York: Charles Scribner's Sons, 1933– .

———. *John Marshall and the Constitution.* New Haven: Yale University Press, 1919.

Coulter, E. Merton. "Humphrey Marshall." In *Dictionary of American Biography*, edited by Dumas Malone et al. 20 volumes and supplements, 12:309–10. New York: Charles Scribner's Sons, 1933– .

————. "James Markham Marshall." In *Dictionary of American Biography*, edited by Dumas Malone et al. 20 volumes and supplements, 12:313–14. New York: Charles Scribner's Sons, 1933– .

Cover, Robert. *Justice Accused: Antislavery and the Judicial Process*. Revised edition. New Haven: Yale University Press, 1984.

Cox, Archibald. *The Court and the Constitution*. Boston: Houghton Mifflin, 1987.

Cox, Isaac J. "Joseph Hamilton Daveiss." In *Dictionary of American Biography*, edited by Dumas Malone et al. 20 volumes and supplements, 5:80. New York: Charles Scribner's Sons, 1933– .

Craigmyle, Thomas Shaw. *John Marshall in Diplomacy and Law*. New York: Charles Scribner's Sons, 1933.

Craven, Wesley Frank. *The Legend of the Founding Fathers*. Ithaca: Cornell University Press, 1956.

Cremin, Lawrence A. *American Education: The Colonial Experience, 1607–1783*. New York: Harper and Row, 1970.

Cress, Larry D. "The Jonathan Robbins Incident: Extradition and the Separation of Powers in the Adams Administration," *Essex Institute Historical Collections*, 111 (1975), 99–121.

Cress, Lawrence D. *Citizens in Arms: The Army and the Militia in American Society to the War of 1812*. Chapel Hill: University of North Carolina Press, 1982.

Cresson, W. P. *James Monroe*. Chapel Hill: University of North Carolina Press, 1946.

Crosskey, William Winslow. "Mr. Chief Justice Marshall." In *Mr. Justice*, edited by Allison Dunham and Philip B. Kurland. Chicago: University of Chicago Press, 1956.

————. *Politics and the Constitution in the History of the United States*. 2 volumes. Chicago: University of Chicago Press, 1953.

Crowley, John E. *The Privileges of Independence: Neomercantilism and the American Revolution*. Baltimore: Johns Hopkins University Press, 1993.

Cullen, Charles T. "Completing the Revisal of the Laws in Post-Revolutionary Virginia," *Virginia Magazine of History and Biography*, 82 (1974), 84–99.

————. "New Light on John Marshall's Legal Education and Admission to the Bar," *American Journal of Legal History*, 16 (1972), 345–51.

Cuneo, John R. *John Marshall: Judicial Statesman*. New York: McGraw-Hill, 1975.

Cunliffe, Marcus. *George Washington: Man and Monument*. Boston: Little, Brown, 1958.

————. "Introduction" to John Marshall, *The Life of George Washington*. 5 volumes. New York: Chelsea House, 1983.

————. *Soldiers and Civilians: The Martial Spirit in America, 1775–1865*. Boston: Little, Brown, 1968.

Cunningham, Noble. *The Jeffersonian Republicans: The Formation of Party Organization, 1789–1801*. Chapel Hill: University of North Carolina Press, 1957.

Custer, Lawrence B. "Bushrod Washington and John Marshall: A Preliminary Inquiry," *American Journal of Legal History*, 4 (1960), 34–48.

Dabney, Virginius. *Richmond: The Story of a City*. Garden City, N.Y.: Doubleday and Co., 1976.

Dangerfield, George. *The Era of Good Feelings*. Harbinger Books edition. New York: Harcourt, Brace and World, 1963.

Daniels, Jonathan. *The Randolphs of Virginia*. Garden City, N.Y.: Doubleday and Co., 1972.

Dargo, George. *Jefferson's Louisiana: Politics and the Clash of Legal Traditions*. Cambridge: Harvard University Press, 1975.

—————. *Roots of the Republic: A New Perspective on Early American Constitutionalism*. New York: Praeger, 1974.

Dauer, Manning J. *The Adams Federalists*. Baltimore: Johns Hopkins University Press, 1953.

Davis, Richard Beale. *Intellectual Life in Jefferson's Virginia, 1790–1830*. Chapel Hill: University of North Carolina Press, 1964.

—————. *Intellectual Life in the Colonial South, 1585–1763*. 3 volumes. Knoxville: University of Tennessee Press, 1978.

Davidson, Philip G. "Virginia and the Alien and Sedition Acts," *American Historical Review*, 36 (1931), 336–42.

Dawidoff, Robert. *The Education of John Randolph*. New York: W. W. Norton, 1979.

DeConde, Alexander. *Entangling Alliance: Politics and Diplomacy under George Washington*. Durham, N.C.: Duke University Press, 1958.

—————. *The Quasi-War: The Politics and Diplomacy of the Undeclared War with France, 1797–1801*. New York: Charles Scribner's Sons, 1966.

Degnan, Ronan. "*Livingston v. Jefferson*—A Freestanding Footnote," *California Law Review*, 75 (1987), 115–28.

Devitt, Fred B. Jr. "William and Mary: America's First Law School," *William and Mary Law Review*, 2 (1960), 424–36.

Dewey, Donald O. *Marshall versus Jefferson: The Political Background of Marbury v. Madison*. New York: Alfred A. Knopf, 1970.

Dickinson, Josiah L. *The Fairfax Proprietary*. Front Royal, Va.: Warren Press, 1959.

Dill, Alonzo Thomas. *George Wythe, Teacher of Liberty*. Williamsburg: Virginia Independence Bicentennial Commission, 1979.

Dillon, John F., comp. and ed. *John Marshall: Life, Character, and Judicial Services*. 3 volumes. Chicago: Callaghan and Co., 1903.

Dorfman, Joseph. *The Economic Mind in American Civilization, 1606–1865*. 2 volumes. New York: Viking Press, 1946.

Druyvesteyn, Kent. "With Great Vision: The James River and Kanawha Company," *Virginia Cavalcade*, 22 (winter 1972), 22–47.

Dumbauld, Edward. "The Case of the Mutinous Mariner," Supreme Court Historical Society, *Yearbook 1977*, 52–58.

—————. "John Marshall and the Law of Nations," *University of Pennsylvania Law Review*, 104 (1955), 38–56.

Dunaway, Wayland Fuller. *History of the James River and Kanawha Company*. Columbia University Studies in History, Economics, and Public Law, volume 104 (1922). Reprint, New York: AMS Press, 1969.

Eckenrode, Hamilton J. *The Randolphs: The Story of a Virginia Family*. Indianapolis: Bobbs-Merrill, 1946.

—————. *The Revolution in Virginia*. Boston: Houghton Mifflin, 1916.

—————, comp. *Virginia Soldiers of the American Revolution*. 2 volumes. Revised edition. Richmond: Virginia State Library and Archives, 1989.

Egerton, Douglas R. *Gabriel's Rebellion: The Virginia Slave Conspiracies of 1800 and 1802*. Chapel Hill: University of North Carolina Press, 1993.

Ekirch, Arthur A. *The Civilian and the Military: A History of the American Antimilitarist Tradition.* Colorado Springs: Ralph Myles, 1972.

Elkins, Stanley, and Eric McKitrick. *The Age of Federalism.* New York: Oxford University Press, 1993.

———. "The Founding Fathers: Young Men of the Revolution," *Political Science Quarterly,* 76 (1961), 181–216.

Ellis, Joseph J. "Maximum Justice," *New York Times Book Review,* 1 December 1996, 14.

Ellis, Richard E. *The Jeffersonian Crisis: Courts and Politics in the Young Republic.* New York: W. W. Norton, 1974.

———. *The Union at Risk: Jacksonian Democracy, States' Rights, and the Nullification Crisis.* New York: Oxford University Press, 1987.

Elting, John, ed. *Military Uniforms in America: The Era of the American Revolution, 1755–1795.* San Rafael, Calif.: Presidio Press, 1974.

Ely, James W. Jr. *The Guardian of Every Other Right: A Constitutional History of Property Rights.* New York: Oxford University Press, 1992.

Ernst, Robert. *Rufus King: American Federalist.* Chapel Hill: University of North Carolina Press, 1968.

Evans, Emory G. "Private Indebtedness and the Revolution in Virginia, 1776–1796," *William and Mary Quarterly,* 3rd series, 28 (1971), 349–74.

Farnham, Thomas J. "The Virginia Amendments of 1795: An Episode in the Opposition to Jay's Treaty," *Virginia Magazine of History and Biography,* 75 (1967), 75–88.

Faulkner, Robert K. "John Marshall and the Burr Trial," *Journal of American History,* 53 (1966–67), 247–58.

———. *The Jurisprudence of John Marshall.* Princeton: Princeton University Press, 1968.

———. "Marshall, John." In *Encyclopedia of the American Constitution,* edited by Leonard Levy et al. 4 volumes, 3:1205–8. New York: Macmillan, 1986.

Fauquier County Bicentennial Committee. *Fauquier County, Virginia, 1759–1959.* Warrenton, Va.: Virginia Publishing, 1959.

Fehrenbacher, Don E. *Prelude to Greatness: Lincoln in the 1850s.* Stanford, Ca.: Stanford University Press, 1962.

Ferguson, E. James. *The Power of the Purse: A History of American Public Finance, 1776–1790.* Chapel Hill: University of North Carolina Press, 1961.

Ferguson, Robert A. *Law and Letters in American Culture.* Cambridge: Harvard University Press, 1984.

Finkelman, Paul. "The Problem of Slavery in the Age of Federalism." In *Federalism Reconsidered,* edited by Doron Ben-Atar and Barbara B. Oberg, 135–56. Charlottesville: University Press of Virginia.

Fischer, David Hackett. *The Revolution of American Conservatism: The Federalist Party in the Era of Jeffersonian Democracy.* New York: Harper and Row, 1965.

Flanders, Henry. *The Lives and Times of the Chief Justices of the Supreme Court of the United States.* 2 volumes. Reprint, Philadelphia: T. and J. W. Johnson and Co., 1881.

Flexner, James Thomas. *George Washington in the American Revolution (1775–1783).* Boston: Little, Brown, 1967.

———. *George Washington in the New Nation (1783–1793).* Boston: Little, Brown, 1970.

————. *Steamboats Come True: American Inventors in Action.* Boston: Little, Brown, 1944.

Foner, Eric. *Tom Paine and Revolutionary America.* New York: Oxford University Press, 1976.

Foran, William A. "John Marshall as a Historian," *American Historical Review,* 43 (1937), 51–64.

Frankfurter, Felix . "John Marshall and the Judicial Function." In *Felix Frankfurter on the Supreme Court: Extrajudicial Essays on the Court and the Constitution,* edited by Philip Kurland. Cambridge: Harvard University Press, 1970.

Fratcher, William F. "History of the Judge Advocate General's Corps, United States Army," *Military Law Review,* 4 (1959), 89–92, 116–17.

Freehling, Alison Goodyear. *Drift Toward Dissolution: The Virginia Slavery Debate of 1831–1832.* Baton Rouge: Louisiana State University Press, 1982.

Freehling, William W. *Prelude to Civil War: The Nullification Controversy in South Carolina, 1816–1836.* New York: Harper and Row, 1966.

Freeman, Allen. "Buyer Sought for John Marshall Estate," *Historical Preservation News,* October–November 1994, 20–21.

Freeman, Douglas Southall. *George Washington.* 7 volumes. New York: Charles Scribner's Sons, 1949–54.

Friedman, Leon and Fred L. Israel, eds. *The Justices of the United States Supreme Court, 1789–1969: Their Lives and Major Opinions.* 4 volumes. New York: R. R. Bowker Co., 1969.

Friendly, Fred W. and Martha J. H. Elliott. *The Constitution: That Delicate Balance.* New York: Random House, 1984.

Frisch, Morton J. "John Marshall's Philosophy of Constitutional Republicanism," *Review of Politics,* 20 (1958), 34–45.

Furlong, Patrick J. "John Rutledge Jr. and the Election of a Speaker of the House in 1799," *William and Mary Quarterly,* 3rd series, 24 (1967), 432–36.

Furtwangler, Albert. *American Silhouettes: Rhetorical Identities of the Founders.* New Haven: Yale University Press, 1988.

Gaines, William H. Jr. "Bench, Bar, and Barbecue Club," *Virginia Cavalcade,* 5 (autumn 1955), 8–13.

Garraty, John A. "The Case of the Missing Commissions." In *Quarrels That Have Shaped The Constitution,* edited by John A. Garraty, 1–15. New York: Harper and Row, 1964.

Garvey, Gerald. "The Constitutional Revolution of 1837 and the Myth of Marshall's Monolith," *Western Political Quarterly,* 18 (1965), 27–34.

Gerber, Scott D. Reviews of Jean Smith, *John Marshall: Definer of a Nation,* and Paul W. Kahn, *The Reign of Law: Marbury v. Madison and the Construction of America,* in *Journal of American History,* 84 (1997–98), 658–59, 1494–95.

————, ed. *Seriatim: The Supreme Court before John Marshall.* New York: New York University Press, 1999.

Gilbert, Daniel R. "John Marshall and the Development of a National History." In *Early Nationalist Historians.* Volume 4 of *The Colonial Legacy,* edited by Lawrence H. Leder, 177–99. New York: Harper and Row, 1973.

Goebel, Julius Jr.. *Antecedents and Beginnings to 1801.* Volume 1 of the Oliver Wendell Holmes Jr., Devise History of the Supreme Court. New York: Macmillan, 1971.

Goldwin, Robert A. and William A. Schambra, eds. *How Capitalistic Is the Constitution?* Washington, D.C.: American Enterprise Institute, 1982.

Graber, Mark A. "Federalists or Friends of Adams: The Marshall Court and Party Politics," *Studies in American Political Development*, 12 (1998), 229–66.

Green, Constance McLaughlin. *Washington: Village and Capital, 1800–1878*. Princeton: Princeton University Press, 1962.

Greene, Francis Vinton. *General Greene*. Originally published 1893. Reprint, Port Washington, N.Y.: Kennikat Press, 1970.

Greene, Jack P. "From the Perspective of Law: Context and Legitimacy in the Origins of the American Revolution," *South Atlantic Quarterly*, 85 (1986), 56–77.

———. *The Quest for Power: The Lower Houses of Assembly in the Southern Royal Colonies, 1689–1776*. Chapel Hill: University of North Carolina Press, 1963.

———. "Society, Ideology, and Politics: An Analysis of the Political Culture of Mid-Eighteenth Century Virginia." In *Society, Freedom, Conscience: The American Revolution in Virginia, Massachusetts, and New York*, edited by Richard M. Jellison. New York: W. W. Norton, 1976.

Greenhouse, Linda. "Lives of the Judges," *New York Times Book Review*, 27 September 1998, 35.

Groome, H. C. *Fauquier during the Proprietorship: A Chronicle of the Colonization and Organization of a Northern Neck County*. Originally published 1927. Reprint, Baltimore: Regional Publishing Co., 1969.

Gummere, Richard M. *The American Colonial Mind and the Classical Tradition: Essays in Comparative Culture*. Cambridge: Harvard University Press, 1963.

Gunther, Gerald, ed. *John Marshall's Defense of McCulloch v. Maryland*. Stanford, Ca.: Stanford University Press, 1969.

Gwathmey, John H. *Historical Register of Virginians in the Revolution: Soldiers, Sailors, Marines, 1775–1783*. Richmond: Dietz Press, 1938.

Haines, Charles G. *The Role of the Supreme Court in American Government and Politics, 1789–1835*. Berkeley: University of California Press, 1944.

Hall, Kermit L. *The Magic Mirror: Law in American History*. New York: Oxford University Press, 1989.

Hammond, Bray. *Banks and Politics in America from the Revolution to the Civil War*. Princeton: Princeton University Press, 1957.

Hardy, Sallie E. Marshall. "John Marshall as Son, Brother, Husband and Friend," *Green Bag*, 8 (1896), 479–82.

Harrison, Fairfax. *Landmarks of Old Prince William: A Study of Origins in Northern Virginia*. 2 volumes. Originally published 1924. 2nd reprint, Baltimore: Gateway Press, 1987.

Harrison, Joseph H. J. "Oligarchs and Democrats: The Richmond Junto," *Virginia Magazine of History and Biography*, 78 (1970), 184–98.

Haskins, George L. "Law versus Politics in the Early Years of the Marshall Court," *University of Pennsylvania Law Review*, 130 (1981), 1–27.

Haskins, George L. and Herbert A. Johnson. *Foundations of Power: John Marshall, 1801–15*. Volume 2 of the Oliver Wendell Holmes Jr., Devise History of the Supreme Court. New York: Macmillan, 1981.

Hatcher, William B. *Edward Livingston: Jeffersonian Republican and Jacksonian Democrat*. University: Louisiana State University Press, 1940.

Hawke, David Freeman. *Paine*. New York: W. W. Norton, 1974.

Heitman, Francis B. *Historical Register of Officers of the Continental Army during the War of the Revolution, April 1775 to December 1783*. Revised edition. Washington, D.C.: Rare Book Shop Publishing Co., 1914.

Hibbard, Benjamin H. *A History of the Public Land Policies*. New York: Macmillan, 1924.

Hickey, Donald R. *The War of 1812: A Forgotten Conflict*. Urbana: University of Illinois Press, 1989.

Higginbotham, Don. "The American Militia: A Traditional Institution with Revolutionary Responsibilities." In *Reconsiderations on the Revolutionary War: Selected Essays*, edited by Don Higginbotham. Westport, Conn.: Greenwood Press, 1976.

———. *Daniel Morgan, Revolutionary Rifleman*. Chapel Hill: University of North Carolina Press, 1961.

———. *George Washington and the American Military Tradition*. Athens: University of Georgia Press, 1985.

———. "Military Leadership in the American Revolution." In *War and Society in Revolutionary America: The Wider Dimensions of Conflict*. Columbia: University of South Carolina Press, 1988.

———. *The War of American Independence: Military Attitudes, Policies, and Practices, 1763–1789*. Reprint, Boston: Northeastern University Press, 1983.

Hill, Peter P. *William Vans Murray, Federalist Diplomat*. Syracuse: Syracuse University Press, 1971.

Hobson, Charles F. *The Great Chief Justice: John Marshall and the Rule of Law*. Lawrence: University Press of Kansas, 1996.

———. "John Marshall and His Papers," *Journal of Supreme Court History*, 2 (1996), 30–35.

———. "John Marshall and the Fairfax Litigation: The Background of *Martin v. Hunter's Lessee*," *Journal of Supreme Court History*, 2 (1996), 36–50.

———. "The Recovery of British Debts in the Federal Circuit Court of Virginia, 1790 to 1797," *Virginia Magazine of History and Biography*, 92 (1984), 176–200.

Hofstadter, Richard. *The Idea of a Party System: The Rise of Legitimate Opposition in the United States, 1780–1840*. Berkeley: University of California Press, 1969.

"Hollow Needs Help, The," *News and Notes of the Fauquier Historical Society*, 6 (fall 1984), 3.

Holt, Michael F. *The Rise and Fall of the American Whig Party*. New York: Oxford University Press, 1999.

Horsman, Reginald. "The Dimensions of an 'Empire for Liberty': Expansion and Republicanism, 1775–1825," *Journal of the Early Republic*, 9 (1989), 1–20.

———. *The Diplomacy of the New Republic, 1776–1815*. Arlington Heights, Ill.: Harlan Davidson, 1985.

Horwitz, Morton J. *The Transformation of American Law, 1780–1860*. Cambridge: Harvard University Press, 1977.

Howe, Daniel Walker. *The Political Culture of the American Whigs*. Chicago: University of Chicago Press, 1979.

Howe, John R. "Republican Thought and the Political Violence of the 1790s," *American Quarterly*, 19 (1967), 147–65.

Huebner, Timothy S. "The Consolidation of State Judicial Power: Spencer Roane, Virginia Legal Culture, and the Southern Judicial Tradition," *Virginia Magazine of History and Biography*, 102 (1994), 47–72.

Hughes, Robert M. "William and Mary, the First American Law School," *William and Mary Quarterly*, 2nd series, 2 (1922), 40–48.

Hume, Ivor Noël. *1775: Another Part of the Field*. New York: Alfred A. Knopf, 1966.

Huntington, Samuel P. *The Soldier and the State: The Theory and Practice of Civil-Military Relations.* Vintage edition. New York: Alfred A. Knopf, 1957.

Hurst, James Willard. *Law and the Conditions of Freedom in the Nineteenth-Century United States.* Madison: University of Wisconsin Press, 1956.

Huston, James A. *Logistics of Liberty: American Services of Supply in the Revolutionary War and After.* Newark: University of Delaware Press, 1991.

Hutson, James H. "Court, Country, and the Constitution: Antifederalism and the Historian," *William and Mary Quarterly,* 3rd series, 38 (1981), 337–68.

———. "Riddles of the Federal Constitutional Convention," *William and Mary Quarterly,* 3rd series, 44 (1987), 411–23.

Hyman, Harold M. and William M. Wiecek. *Equal Justice Under Law: Constitutional Development, 1835–1875.* New York: Harper and Row, 1982.

Isaac, Rhys. "Evangelical Revolt: The Nature of the Baptists' Challenge to the Traditional Order in Virginia, 1765 to 1775," *William and Mary Quarterly,* 3rd series, 31 (1974), 345–68.

———. *The Transformation of Virginia, 1740–1790.* Chapel Hill: University of North Carolina Press, 1982.

Jensen, Merrill. *The New Nation: A History of the United States during the Confederation, 1781–1789.* Vintage edition. New York: Alfred A. Knopf, 1965.

John Marshall Foundation, The. Untitled guidebook for the John Marshall House. Richmond, Va.: N.p., n.d.

Johnson, Herbert A. "Albert J. Beveridge." In *Dictionary of Literary Biography.* Volume 17. *Twentieth-Century American Historians,* edited by Clyde N. Wilson, 70–74. Detroit: Gale Research Co., 1983.

———. *The Chief Justiceship of John Marshall, 1801–1835.* Columbia: University of South Carolina Press, 1997.

———. "John Marshall." In *The Supreme Court Justices: Illustrated Biographies, 1789–1993,* edited by Clare Cushman. 2 volumes, 1:61–65. Washington, D.C.: Congressional Quarterly, 1993.

Johnston, F. Claiborne, ed. "Federalist, Doubtful, and Antifederalist: A Note on the Virginia Convention of 1788," *Virginia Magazine of History and Biography,* 96 (1988), 333–44.

Johnstone, Robert M. Jr. *Jefferson and the Presidency: Leadership in the Young Republic.* Ithaca: Cornell University Press, 1978.

Jones, Howard Mumford. *O Strange New World: American Culture: The Formative Years.* New York: Viking Press, 1964.

Jones, W. Melville, ed. *Chief Justice John Marshall: A Reappraisal.* Ithaca: Cornell University Press, 1956.

Jordan, Winthrop D. *White over Black: American Attitudes toward the Negro, 1550–1812.* Penguin edition. Chapel Hill: University of North Carolina Press, 1968.

"Justice's Home Up for Auction," *Washington Times,* 11 October 1994, Nexis 94-00758889.

Kammen, Michael. *A Machine That Would Go of Itself: The Constitution in American Culture.* New York: Alfred E. Knopf, 1986.

Kaplan, Lawrence S. *Colonies into Nation: American Diplomacy, 1763–1801.* New York: Macmillan, 1972.

Kelly, Alfred H. et al. *The American Constitution: Its Origins and Development.* 6th edition. New York: W. W. Norton, 1983.

Kemper, Charles E. "The Early Westward Movement in Virginia," *Virginia Magazine of History and Biography*, 13 (1906), 362–70.

———. "Germantown, Fauquier's First Settlement," *News and Notes of the Fauquier Historical Society*, 3 (summer 1981), 1–2.

———. "The History of Germantown," *Bulletin of the Fauquier Historical Society*, 2 (July 1922), 125–33.

Kenyon, Cecilia. "Men of Little Faith: The Anti–Federalists on the Nature of Representative Government," *William and Mary Quarterly*, 3rd series, 12 (1955), 3–43.

Kerber, Linda K. *Federalists in Dissent: Imagery and Ideology in Jeffersonian America*. Ithaca: Cornell University Press, 1970.

Ketcham, Ralph. *James Madison: A Biography*. New York: Macmillan, 1971.

Kettner, James H. "Persons or Property? The Pleasants Slaves in the Virginia Courts, 1792–1799." In *Launching the "Extended Republic": The Federalist Era*, edited by Ronald Hoffman and Peter J. Albert, 136–55. Charlottesville: University Press of Virginia, 1996.

Kloppenberg, James T. "The Virtues of Liberalism: Christianity, Republicanism, and Ethics in Early American Political Discourse," *Journal of American History*, 74 (1987–88), 9–33.

Kohl, Lawrence F. *The Politics of Individualism: Parties and the American Character in the Jacksonian Era*. New York: Oxford University Press, 1989.

Kohn, Richard H. "American Generals of the Revolution: Subordination and Restraint." In *Reconsiderations of the Revolutionary War: Selected Essays*, edited by Don Higginbotham, 104–23. Westport, Conn.: Greenwood Press, 1978.

———. *Eagle and Sword: The Federalists and the Creation of the Military Establishment in America, 1783–1802*. New York: Free Press, 1975.

Kolp, John Gilman. *Gentlemen and Freeholders: Electoral Politics in Colonial Virginia*. Baltimore: Johns Hopkins University Press, 1998.

Kraus, Michael. *A History of American History*. New York: Farrar and Rinehart, 1937.

Kraus, Michael and Davis D. Joyce. *The Writing of American History*. Revised edition. Norman: University of Oklahoma Press, 1985.

Kuehl, John W. "Southern Reaction to the XYZ Affair: An Incident in the Emergence of American Nationalism," *Kentucky Historical Society Register*, 70 (1972), 21–49.

———. "The XYZ Affair and American Nationalism: Republican Victories in the Middle Atlantic States," *Maryland Historical Magazine*, 67 (1972), 1–20.

Kukla, Jon R. "A Spectrum of Sentiments: Virginia's Federalists, Antifederalists, and 'Federalists Who Are For Amendments,' 1787–1788," *Virginia Magazine of History and Biography*, 96 (1988), 277–96.

Kulikoff, Allan. *Tobacco and Slaves: The Development of Southern Cultures in the Chesapeake, 1680–1800*. Chapel Hill: University of North Carolina Press, 1986.

Kurtz, Stephen G. *The Presidency of John Adams: The Collapse of Federalism, 1795–1800*. Reprint, New York: A. S. Barnes, 1961.

Kutler, Stanley I. *Privilege and Creative Destruction: The Charles River Bridge Case*. Philadelphia: Lippincott, 1971.

Larson, John Lauritz. "'Bind the Republic Together': The National Union and the Struggle for a System of Internal Improvements," *Journal of American History*, 74 (1987–88), 363–87.

————. "'Wisdom Enough to Improve Them': Government, Liberty, and Inland Waterways in the Rising American Empire.'" In *Launching the "Extended Republic": The Federalist Era*, edited by Ronald Hoffman and Peter J. Albert, 223–48. Charlottesville: University Press of Virginia, 1996.

Lassiter, Francis Rives. "Arnold's Invasion of Virginia," *Sewanee Review*, 9 (1901), 78–93, 185–203.

Lerner, Max. "John Marshall and the Campaign of History," *Columbia Law Review*, 20 (1939), 396–431.

————. "John Marshall's Long Shadow." In *Ideas Are Weapons*. New York: Viking Press, 1943.

Levy, Leonard W. *Emergence of a Free Press*. New York: Oxford University Press, 1985.

————. *Jefferson and Civil Liberties: The Darker Side*. Cambridge: Harvard University Press, 1963.

————. *Original Intent and the Framers' Constitution*. New York: Macmillan, 1988.

Lewis, William Draper. *Great American Lawyers. The Lives and Influence of Judges and Lawyers Who Have Acquired Permanent National Reputation, and Have Developed the Jurisprudence of the United States. A History of the Legal Profession in America*. Philadelphia: John C. Winston Co., 1907. Reprint, South Hackensack, N.J.: Rothman Reprints, 1971.

Lillich, Richard B. "The Chase Impeachment," *American Journal of Legal History*, 4 (1960), 49–72.

Link, Eugene P. *Democratic-Republican Societies, 1790–1800*. New York: Columbia University Press, 1942.

Lipset, Seymour Martin. *The First New Nation: The United States in Historical and Comparative Perspective*. New York: W. W. Norton, 1979.

Little, Lewis P. *Imprisoned Preachers and Religious Liberty in Virginia. A Narrative Drawn Largely from the Official Records of Virginia Counties, Unpublished Manuscripts, Letters, and Other Original Sources*. Lynchburg, Va.: J. P. Bell Co., 1938.

Livermore, Shaw Jr. *The Twilight of Federalism: The Disintegration of the Federalist Party, 1815–1830*. Princeton: Princeton University Press, 1962.

Lockmiller, David A. *Sir William Blackstone*. Chapel Hill: University of North Carolina Press, 1938.

Loewenberg, Bert James. *American History in American Thought*. New York: Simon and Schuster, 1972.

Lomask, Milton. *Aaron Burr: The Conspiracy and Years of Exile, 1805–1836*. New York: Farrar, Straus, and Giroux, 1982.

————. *Aaron Burr: The Years from Princeton to Vice President, 1756–1805*. New York: Farrar, Straus, and Giroux, 1979.

Loth, David. *Chief Justice John Marshall and the Growth of the Republic*. New York: Greenwood Press, 1949.

Low, W. A. "Merchant and Planter Relations in Post–Revolutionary Virginia, 1783–1789," *Virginia Magazine of History and Biography*, 61 (1953), 308–18.

Lynch, Joseph M. "*Fletcher v. Peck*: The Nature of the Contract Clause," *Seton Hall Law Review*, 13 (1982), 1–20.

Mack, Maynard. *Alexander Pope: A Life*. New York: W. W. Norton, 1985.

Macleod, Duncan. "The Triple Crisis." In *The Growth of Federal Power in the United States*, edited by Rhodri Jeffreys-Jones and Bruce Collins, 13–24. Edinburgh: Scottish Academic Press, 1983.

Magrath, C. Peter. *Yazoo: Law and Politics in the New Republic: The Case of Fletcher v. Peck.* Providence, R.I.: Brown University Press, 1966.

Magruder, Allan B. *John Marshall.* Boston: Houghton Mifflin, 1885.

Mahon, John K. *History of the Militia and the National Guard.* New York: Macmillan, 1983.

Main, Jackson Turner. "The American Revolution and the Democratization of the Legislatures," *William and Mary Quarterly,* 3rd series, 22 (1966), 391–407.

———. *The Antifederalists: Critics of the Constitution, 1781–1788.* New York: W. W. Norton, 1974.

———. *Political Parties before the Constitution.* Chapel Hill: University of North Carolina Press, 1973.

———. *The Sovereign States, 1775–1783.* New York: Franklin Watts, 1973.

Malone, Dumas. *Jefferson and the Ordeal of Liberty.* Boston: Little, Brown, 1962.

———. *Jefferson the President: First Term, 1801–1805.* Boston: Little, Brown, 1970.

———. *Jefferson the President: Second Term, 1805–1809.* Boston: Little, Brown, 1974.

———. *Jefferson the Virginian.* Boston: Little, Brown, 1948.

———. *The Sage of Monticello.* Boston: Little, Brown, 1981.

Malone, Kathryn R. "The Fate of Revolutionary Republicanism in Early National Virginia," *Journal of the Early Republic,* 7 (1987), 27–51.

Mann, W. Howard. "The Marshall Court: Nationalization of Property Rights and Personal Liberty from the Authority of the Commerce Clause," *Indiana Law Journal,* 38 (1962–63), 117–238.

Marcus, Maeva. "Judicial Review in the Early Republic." In *Launching the "Extended Republic": The Federalist Era,* edited by Ronald Hoffman and Peter J. Albert, 25–53. Charlottesville: University Press of Virginia, 1996.

———. Review of Jean Smith, *John Marshall: Definer of a Nation,* in *American Historical Review,* 103 (1998), 584–85.

Marsh, Philip. "James Monroe as 'Agricola' in the Genet Controversy," *Virginia Magazine of History and Biography,* 62 (1954), 472–76.

Marshall, Lynn L. "The Strange Stillbirth of the Whig Party," *American Historical Review,* 72 (1966–67), 445–68.

Marshall, Maria Newton. "The Marshall Memorial Tablet," *Green Bag,* 14, August 1902, 372.

Martin, James Kirby and Mark Edward Lender. *A Respectable Army: The Military Origins of the Republic, 1763–1789.* Arlington Heights, Ill.: Harlan Davidson, 1982.

Mason, Frances Norton. *My Dearest Polly: Letters of Chief Justice John Marshall to His Wife, with Their Background, Political and Domestic, 1779–1831.* Richmond: Garrett and Massie, 1961.

Matson, Cathy and Peter S. Onuf. "Toward a Republican Empire: Interest and Ideology in Revolutionary America," *American Quarterly,* 37 (1985), 496–531.

Maurer, Maurer. "Military Justice under General Washington," *Military Affairs,* 28 (1964), 8–16.

Mayer, Henry. *A Son of Thunder: Patrick Henry and the American Republic.* New York: Franklin Watts, 1986.

Mayo, Bernard. *Myths and Men.* New York: Harper and Row, 1963.

Mays, David J. *Edmund Pendleton.* 2 volumes. Cambridge: Harvard University Press, 1952.

McCarty, Clara S., comp. and ed. *The Foothills of the Blue Ridge in Fauquier County, Virginia.* Warrenton, Va.: N.p., 1974.

McCaughey, Elizabeth, "*Marbury v. Madison*: Have We Missed the Real Meaning?," *Presidential Studies Quarterly,* 19 (1989), 491–528.

McCloskey, Robert G. *The American Supreme Court.* Chicago: University of Chicago Press, 1960.

McColley, Robert. *Slavery and Jeffersonian Virginia.* 2nd edition. Urbana: University of Illinois Press, 1973.

McConnell, Michael W. "Contract Rights and Property Rights: A Case Study in the Relationship between Individual Liberties and Constitutional Structure." In *Liberty, Property, and the Foundations of the American Constitution,* edited by Ellen Frankel Paul and Howard Dickman, 141–68. Albany: State University of New York Press, 1989.

McCoy, Drew R. *The Elusive Republic: Political Economy in Jeffersonian America.* Chapel Hill: University of North Carolina Press, 1980. Reprint, New York: W. W. Norton, 1982.

———. *The Last of the Fathers: James Madison and the Republican Legacy.* New York: Cambridge University Press, 1989.

———. "The Virginia Port Bill of 1784," *Virginia Magazine of History and Biography,* 83 (1975), 288–303.

McCraw, Thomas. "The Strategic Vision of Alexander Hamilton," *American Scholar,* 63 (1994), 31–57.

McCulloch, David. *Mornings on Horseback.* New York: Simon and Schuster, 1981.

McDonald, Forrest. *Alexander Hamilton: A Biography.* New York: W. W. Norton, 1982.

———. "Capitalism and the Constitution." In *How Capitalistic Is the Constitution?,* edited by Robert A. Goldwin and William A. Schambra. Washington, D.C.: American Enterprise Institute, 1982.

———. *E Pluribus Unum: The Formation of the American Republic.* Boston: Houghton Mifflin, 1965.

———. *Novus Ordo Seclorum: The Intellectual Origins of the Constitution.* Lawrence: University Press of Kansas, 1985.

———. *The Presidency of George Washington.* New York: W. W. Norton, 1975.

———. *We the People: The Economic Origins of the Constitution.* Chicago: University of Chicago Press, 1958.

McDonald, Forrest and Ellen S. McDonald. "On the Late Disturbances in Massachusetts." In *Requiem: Variations on Eighteenth-Century Themes.* Lawrence: University Press of Kansas, 1988.

McDonnell, Michael A. "Popular Mobilization and Political Culture in Revolutionary Virginia: The Failure of the Minutemen and the Revolution from Below," *Journal of American History,* 85 (1998–99), 946–81.

McMaster, John Bach. *A History of the People of the United States from the Revolution to the Civil War.* 8 volumes. New York: Appleton and Co., 1921.

Meade, Bishop [William]. *Old Churches, Ministers, and Families of Virginia.* 2 volumes. Philadelphia: J. P. Lippincott, 1910.

Meade, Robert D. *Patrick Henry, Practical Revolutionary.* Philadelphia: J. P. Lippincott, 1969.

Mendelson, Wallace. "Chief Justice Marshall and the Mercantile Tradition," *Southwestern Social Science Quarterly,* 29 (1948–49), 27–37.

———. "John Marshall's Short Way with Statutes," *Kentucky Law Journal*, 36 (1948), 284–89.

———. *Supreme Court Statecraft: The Rule of Law and Men*. Ames: Iowa State University Press, 1985.

Merk, Frederick. *History of the Westward Movement*. New York: Alfred A. Knopf, 1978.

Meyers, Marvin. *The Jacksonian Persuasion: Politics and Belief*. Vintage edition. New York: Alfred A. Knopf, 1960.

Miller, F. Thornton. "John Marshall versus Spencer Roane: A Reevaluation of *Martin v. Hunter's Lessee*," *Virginia Magazine of History and Biography*, 96 (1988) 297–314.

Miller, Frederick T. "The Richmond Junto: The Secret All-Powerful Club—or Myth," *Virginia Magazine of History and Biography*, 99 (1991), 63–80.

Miller, Helen Hill. *George Mason: Gentleman Revolutionary*. Chapel Hill: University of North Carolina Press, 1975.

Miller, John C. *Crisis in Freedom: The Alien and Sedition Acts*. Boston: Little, Brown, 1951.

———. *The Federalist Era, 1789–1801*. New York: Harper and Row, 1960.

Millett, Allan R., and Peter Maslowski. *For the Common Defense: A Military History of the United States of America*. New York: Free Press, 1984.

Millis, Walter. *Arms and Men: A Study in American Military History*. New York: Capricorn Books, 1956.

Mintz, Max M. *Gouverneur Morris and the American Revolution*. Norman: University of Oklahoma Press, 1970.

Monaghan, Jay. *John Jay: Defender of Liberty*. New York: Bobbs-Merrill, 1935.

Montague, Andrew J. "John Marshall." In *The American Secretaries of State and Their Diplomacy*, edited by Samuel Flagg Bemis. 18 volumes. New York: Cooper Square Publishers, 1963.

Morgan, Donald G. *Justice William Johnson, the First Dissenter: The Career and Constitutional Philosophy of a Jeffersonian Judge*. Columbia: University of South Carolina Press, 1954.

———. "The Origin of Supreme Court Dissent," *William and Mary Quarterly*, 3rd series, 10 (1953), 353–77.

Morgan, Edmund S. *Inventing the People: The Rise of Popular Sovereignty in England and America*. New York: W. W. Norton, 1988.

Morison, Samuel Eliot. *The Life and Letters of Harrison Gray Otis*. 2 volumes. Boston: Houghton Mifflin, 1913.

Morris, Richard B. *The Forging of the Union, 1781–1789*. New York: Harper and Row, 1987.

Morton, Richard L. *Colonial Virginia*. 2 volumes. Volume 2, *Westward Expansion and Prelude to Revolution, 1710–1763*. Chapel Hill: University of North Carolina Press, 1960.

Neagles, James C. *Summer Soldiers: A Survey and Index of Revolutionary War Courts-Martial*. Salt Lake City: Ancestry Inc., 1991.

Nedelsky, Jennifer. "Confining Democratic Politics: Anti-Federalists, Federalists, and the Constitution," *Harvard Law Review*, 96 (1982–83), 340–60.

———. *Private Property and the Limits of American Constitutionalism: The Madisonian Framework and Its Legacy*. Chicago: University of Chicago Press, 1990.

Neely, Sylvia. "Mason Locke Weems's *Life of George Washington* and the Myth of Braddock's Defeat," *Virginia Magazine of History and Biography*, 107 (1999), 45–72.

Neimeyer, Charles P. *America Goes to War: A Social History of the Continental Army.* New York: New York University Press, 1996.

Nelson, John R. Jr. "Alexander Hamilton and American Manufacturing: A Reexamination," *Journal of American History*, 65 (1978–79), 971–95.

———. *Liberty and Property: Political Economy and Policymaking in the New Nation, 1789–1812.* Baltimore: Johns Hopkins University Press, 1987.

Nelson, William E. "The Eighteenth-Century Background of John Marshall's Constitutional Jurisprudence," *Michigan Law Review*, 76 (1978), 893–960.

Nevins, Allan. *The American States during and after the Revolution, 1775–1789.* New York: Macmillan, 1924.

Newman, Simon P. *Parades and the Politics of the Street: Festive Culture in the Early American Republic.* Philadelphia: University of Pennsylvania Press, 1997.

———. "Principles of Men? George Washington and the Political Culture of National Leadership," *Journal of the Early Republic*, 12 (1992), 477–507.

Newmyer, R. Kent. "Marshall, John." In *The Oxford Companion to the Supreme Court of the United States*, edited by Kermit Hall et al., 523–26. New York: Oxford University Press, 1992.

———. "On Assessing the Court in History: Some Comments on the Roper and Burke Articles," *Stanford Law Review*, 21 (1969), 532–47.

———. *Supreme Court Justice Joseph Story: Statesman of the Old Republic.* Chapel Hill: University of North Carolina Press, 1985.

———. *The Supreme Court under Marshall and Taney.* New York: Thomas Y. Crowell Co., 1968.

Niven, John. *John C. Calhoun and the Price of Union.* Baton Rouge: Louisiana State University Press, 1988.

Nolan, Dennis R. "Sir William Blackstone and the New American Republic: A Study of Intellectual Impact," *New York University Law Review*, 51 (1976), 731–68.

Norgren, Jill. "The Cherokee Nation Cases of the 1830s," *Journal of Supreme Court History*, 1994, 65–82.

Oakes, James. "From Republicanism to Liberalism: Ideological Change and the Crisis of the Old South," *American Quarterly*, 37 (1985), 551–71.

Oberholtzer, Ellis Paxson. *Robert Morris, Patriot and Financier.* Reprint, New York: Burt Franklin, 1968.

O'Brien, David. "The Supreme Court: A Co–Equal Branch of Government," Supreme Court Historical Society, *Yearbook 1984*, 90–105.

O'Connor, John E. *William Paterson: Lawyer and Statesman, 1745–1806.* New Brunswick, N.J.: Rutgers University Press, 1979.

O'Fallon, James. "Marbury," *Stanford Law Review*, 44 (1992), 219–60.

Old Homes and Families of Fauquier County, Virginia. (The W.P.A. Records). Berryville, Va.: Virginia Book Co., 1978.

Oliver, Andrew. *The Portraits of John Marshall.* Charlottesville: University Press of Virginia, 1977.

Onuf, Peter S. *The Origins of the Federal Republic: Jurisdictional Controversies in the United States, 1775–1787.* Philadelphia: University of Pennsylvania Press, 1983.

Onuf, Peter S. and Cathy Matson. "Republicanism and Federalism in the Constitutional Decade." In *The Republican Synthesis: Essays in Honor of George Athan*

Billias, edited by Milton M. Klein et al., 119–41. Worcester, Mass.: American Antiquarian Society, 1992.

Ordonez, Jennifer. "A Supreme Effort At Preservation in Justice's Name; Marshall Admirer Takes a Last Stand," *Washington Post*, 26 July 1998, Loudoun County edition, V7.

Orieux, Jean. *Voltaire ou La Royauté de L'Esprit*. Paris: Flammarion, 1966.

Ott, Thomas O. *The Haitian Revolution, 1789–1804*. Knoxville: University of Tennessee Press, 1973.

Padover, Saul K. "The Political Ideas of John Marshall," *Social Research*, 26 (1959), 47–70.

Palmer, Ben W. *Marshall and Taney: Statesman of the Law*. [Minneapolis]: University of Minnesota Press, 1939.

Palmer, John McAuley. *General Von Steuben*. Originally published 1937. Reprint, Port Washington, N.Y.: Kennikat Press, 1966.

Parrington, Vernon Louis. "John Marshall: Last of the Virginia Federalists." In *Main Currents in American Thought*. 2 volumes. *Volume 2, The Romantic Revolution, 1800–1860*, 19–26. New York: Harcourt, Brace, 1927.

Paxton, William M. *The Marshall Family, or a Genealogical Chart of the Descendants of John Marshall and Elizabeth Markham*. Cincinnati: Robert Clarke and Co., 1885.

Peak, Mayme Ober. "Oak Hill: The Fauquier Home of Chief Justice Marshall," *House Beautiful*, 49 (April 1921), 288.

Pederson, William D. and Norman W. Provizer, eds. *Great Chief Justices of the U.S. Supreme Court: Ratings and Case Studies*. New York: Peter Lang, 1994.

Perkins, Bradford. *The First Rapprochement: England and the United States, 1795–1805*. Berkeley: University of California Press, 1967.

Perry, James R. "Supreme Court Appointments, 1789–1801: Criteria, Presidential Style, and the Press of Events," *Journal of the Early Republic*, 6 (1986), 371–410.

Pessen, Edward. *Jacksonian America: Society, Personality, and Politics*. Homewood, Ill: Dorsey Press, 1969.

Pfitzer, Gregory M. *Samuel Eliot Morison's Historical World: In Quest of a New Parkman*. Boston: Northeastern University Press, 1991.

Pincus, Walter. "Censure: A Debate with a Past," *Washington Post*, 19 November 1998, A27.

Plous, Harold J., and Gordon E. Baker, "*McCulloch v. Maryland*: Right Principle, Wrong Case," *Stanford Law Review*, 9 (1957), 710–30.

Powell, J. H. *Bring Out Your Dead: The Great Plague of Yellow Fever in Philadelphia in 1793*. Philadelphia: University of Pennsylvania Press, 1949.

Preyer, Kathryn. "Jurisdiction to Punish: Federal Authority, Federalism, and the Common Law of Crimes in the Early Republic," *Law and History Review*, 4 (1986), 223–65.

Prince, Carl E. *The Federalists and the Origins of the U.S. Civil Service*. New York: New York University Press, 1977.

———. "The Passing of the Aristocracy: Jefferson's Removal of the Federalists, 1801–1805," *Journal of American History*, 57 (1970–71), 563–75.

Proctor, John C., ed. *Washington, Past and Present*. 4 volumes. New York: Lewis Historical Publishing Co., 1930.

Ragsdale, Bruce A. *A Planters' Republic: The Search for Economic Independence in Revolutionary Virginia*. Madison, Wis.: Madison House, 1996.

Ray, Thomas M. "'Not One Cent for Tribute': The Public Addresses and American Popular Reaction to the XYZ Affair, 1798–1799," *Journal of the Early Republic*, 3 (1983), 389–412.

Reardon, John J. *Edmund Randolph: A Biography*. New York: Macmillan, 1974.

Reed, Alfred Z. *Training for the Public Profession of the Law: Historical Development and Principal Contemporary Problems of Legal Education in the United States with Some Account of Conditions in England and Canada*. New York: Carnegie Foundation for the Advancement of Teaching, 1921.

Rehnquist, William H. *Grand Inquests: The Historic Impeachments of Justice Samuel Chase and President Andrew Johnson*. New York: William Morrow, 1992.

Remini, Robert V. *Andrew Jackson and the Course of American Democracy, 1833–1845*. New York: Harper and Row, 1984.

———. *Andrew Jackson and the Course of American Freedom, 1822–1832*. New York: Harper and Row, 1981.

———. *Daniel Webster: The Man and His Times*. New York: W. W. Norton, 1997.

———. *Henry Clay: Statesman for the Union*. New York: W. W. Norton, 1991.

Reps, John W. *Washington On View: The Nation's Capital since 1790*. Chapel Hill: University of North Carolina Press, 1991.

Rhodes, Irwin S. "John Marshall and the Western Country: The Early Days," *Historical and Philosophical Society of Ohio Bulletin*, 18 (1960), 119–40.

Richardson, Edward W. *Standards and Colors of the American Revolution*. Philadelphia: University of Pennsylvania Press, 1982.

Riesman, Janet. "Money, Credit, and Federalist Political Economy." In *Beyond Confederation: Origins of the Constitution and American National Identity*, edited by Richard Beeman et al., 128–61 Chapel Hill: University of North Carolina Press, 1987.

Risjord, Norman K. *Chesapeake Politics, 1781–1800*. New York: Columbia University Press, 1978.

———. *The Old Republicans: Southern Conservatism in the Age of Jefferson*. New York: Columbia University Press, 1964.

———. "The Virginia Federalists," *Journal of Southern History*, 33 (1967), 486–510.

———. "Virginians and the Constitution: A Multivariant Analysis," *William and Mary Quarterly*, 3rd series, 31 (1974), 613–32.

Risjord, Norman K. and Gordon DenBoer. "The Evolution of Political Parties in Virginia, 1782–1800," *Journal of American History*, 60 (1973–74), 961–84.

Robertson, Lindsay G. "John Marshall as Colonial Historian: Reconsidering the Origins of the Discovery Doctrine," *Journal of Law and Politics*, 13 (1997), 759–77.

Rodell, Fred. "The Great Chief Justice," *American Heritage*, 7 (1955–56), 10–13, 106–11.

Roeber, A. G. *Faithful Magistrates and Republican Lawyers: Creators of Virginia Legal Culture, 1680–1810*. Chapel Hill: University of North Carolina Press, 1981.

Rohrs, Richard C. "The Federalist Party and the Convention of 1800," *Diplomatic History*, 12 (1988), 237–60.

Roper, Donald M. "In Quest of Judicial Unanimity: The Marshall Court and the Legitimation of Slavery," *Stanford Law Review*, 21 (1969), 532–39.

———. "Judicial Unanimity and the Marshall Court: A Road to Reappraisal," *American Journal of Legal History*, 9 (1965), 118–34.

Rose, Lisle A. *Prologue to Democracy: The Federalists in the South, 1789–1800*. Lexington: University of Kentucky Press, 1968.

Roth, David M. *Connecticut: A History*. New York: W. W. Norton, 1979.

Rowe, Gary D. "The Sound of Silence: *United States v. Hudson & Goodwin*, the Jeffersonian Ascendancy and the Abolition of the Federal Common Law of Crimes," *Yale Law Journal*, 101 (1992), 919–48.

Royster, Charles. *Light-Horse Harry Lee and the Legacy of the American Revolution*. New York: Alfred A. Knopf, 1981.

———. *A Revolutionary People at War: The Continental Army and American Character, 1775–1783*. New York: W. W. Norton, 1981.

Rudko, Frances H. *John Marshall and International Law: Statesman and Chief Justice*. New York: Greenwood Press, 1991.

Russell, T. Triplett and John K Gott. *Fauquier County in the Revolution*. Warrenton, Va.: Fauquier County American Bicentennial Commission, 1976.

Rutland, Robert A. *James Madison: The Founding Father*. New York: Macmillan, 1987.

———. *The Ordeal of the Constitution: The Antifederalists and the Ratification Struggle of 1787–1788*. Norman: University of Oklahoma Press, 1966.

Sanchez-Saavedra, E. M. "'All Fine Fellows and Well-Armed': The Culpeper Minute Battalion, 1775–1776," *Virginia Cavalcade*, 24 (summer 1974), 4–11.

———, comp. *A Guide to Virginia Military Organizations in the American Revolution, 1774 to 1787*. Richmond: Virginia State Library, 1978.

Schaffer, Alan. "Virginia's 'Critical Period.'" In *The Old Dominion: Essays for Thomas Perkins Abernethy*, edited by Darrett Rutman, 152–70. Charlottesville: University Press of Virginia, 1964.

Schoenbachler, Matthew. "Republicanism in the Age of Democratic Revolution: The Democratic-Republican Societies of the 1790s," *Journal of the Early Republic*, 18 (1998), 237–61.

Schultz, David. "Political Theory and Legal History: Conflicting Depictions of Property in the American Political Founding," *American Journal of Legal History*, 37 (1993), 464–95.

Schwartz, Barry. *George Washington: The Making of an American Symbol*. New York: Free Press, 1987.

Schwartz, Bernard. *A History of the Supreme Court*. New York: Oxford University Press, 1993.

Scott, Mary Wingfield. *Houses of Old Richmond*. New York: Bonanza Books, 1941.

Scribner, Robert L. "John Marshall, Deceased." *Virginia Cavalcade*, 5 (autumn 1955), 40–42.

Selby, John E. *Dunmore*. Williamsburg: Virginia Independence Bicentennial Commission, 1977.

———. *The Revolution in Virginia, 1775–1783*. Williamsburg: Colonial Williamsburg Foundation, 1988.

Sellers, Charles. *The Market Revolution: Jacksonian America, 1815–1846*. New York: Oxford University Press, 1991.

Shade, William G. *Democratizing the Old Dominion: Virginia and the Second Party System, 1824–1861*. Charlottesville: University Press of Virginia, 1996.

Shaffer, Arthur H. *The Politics of History: Writing the History of the American Revolution, 1783–1815*. Chicago: Precedent Publishing, 1975.

Shalhope, Robert E. "Republicanism, Liberalism, and Democracy: Political Culture in the Early Republic." In *The Republican Synthesis Revisited: Essays in Honor of George Athan Billias*, edited by Milton M. Klein et al., 37–90. Worcester, Mass.: American Antiquarian Society, 1992.

Sharp, James Rogers. *American Politics in the Early Republic: The New Nation in Crisis*. New Haven: Yale University Press, 1993.

Shaw, Peter. *The Character of John Adams*. New York: W. W. Norton, 1977.

Shepard, E. Lee. "Lawyers Look at Themselves: Professional Consciousness and the Virginia Bar, 1770–1850," *American Journal of Legal History*, 25 (1981), 1–23.

———. "'This Ancient and Honorable Class of Men': Practicing the Law in Old Virginia," *Virginia Cavalcade*, 36 (spring 1987), 148–57.

Shevory, Thomas C. "John Marshall as a Republican: Order and Conflict in American Political History." In *John Marshall's Achievement: Law, Politics, and Constitutional Interpretation*, edited by Thomas C. Shevory, 75–93. Westport, Conn.: Greenwood Press, 1989.

———. *John Marshall's Law: Interpretation, Ideology, and Interest*. Westport, Conn.: Greenwood Press, 1994.

Shockley, Martin S. "The Richmond Theatre, 1780–1790," *Virginia Magazine of History and Biography*, 60 (1952), 421–36.

Shuffelton, Frank. "Endangered History: Character and Narrative in Early American Historical Writing," *The Eighteenth Century*, 34 (1993), 221–42.

Shy, John. "American Society and Its War for Independence." In *Reconsiderations on the Revolutionary War: Selected Essays*, edited by Don Higginbotham, 72–82. Westport, Conn.: Greenwood Press, 1978.

———. "A New Look at the Colonial Militia." In *A People Numerous and Armed: Reflections on the Military Struggle for Independence*, 21–33. New York: Oxford University Press, 1976.

Sibley, Agnes Marie. *Alexander Pope's Prestige in America, 1725–1835*. New York: King's Crown Press, 1949.

Slaughter, Thomas P. "'The King of Crimes': Early American Treason Law, 1787–1860." In *Launching the "Extended Republic": The Federalist Era*, edited by Ronald Hoffman and Peter J. Albert, 54–135. Charlottesville: University Press of Virginia, 1996.

———. *The Whiskey Rebellion: Frontier Epilogue to the American Revolution*. New York: Oxford University Press, 1986.

Sloan, Herbert. Review of Jean Smith, *John Marshall: Definer of a Nation*, in *Political Science Quarterly*, 112 (1997), 526.

Sloan, Herbert and Peter S. Onuf. "Politics, Culture, and the Revolution in Virginia: A Review of Recent Work," *Virginia Magazine of History and Biography*, 91 (1983), 259–84.

Smelser, Marshall. "The Federalist Period as an Age of Passion," *American Quarterly*, 10 (1958), 391–419.

———. "The Jacobin Phrenzy: Federalism and the Menace of Liberty, Equality, and Fraternity," *Review of Politics*, 13 (1951), 457–82.

———. "The Jacobin Phrenzy: The Menace of Monarchy, Plutocracy, and Anglophilia," *Review of Politics*, 21 (1959), 239–58.

Smith, James Morton. *Freedom's Fetters: The Alien and Sedition Laws and American Civil Liberties*. Ithaca: Cornell University Press, 1956.

Smith, Jean. *John Marshall: Definer of a Nation*. New York: Henry Holt, 1996.

Smith, Page. *John Adams*. 2 volumes. Garden City, N.Y.: Doubleday and Co., 1962.

Smith, Stanley P. "The Northern Neck's Role in American Legal History," *Virginia Magazine of History and Biography*, 77 (1969), 277–90.

Smith, William Raymond. *History as Argument: Three Patriot Historians of the American Revolution.* The Hague: Mouton and Co., 1966.

Snowiss, Sylvia. *Judicial Review and the Law of the Constitution.* New Haven: Yale University Press, 1990.

Sosin, Jack M. *The Aristocracy of the Long Robe: The Origins of Judicial Review in America.* Westport, Conn.: Greenwood Press, 1989.

————. *The Revolutionary Frontier, 1763–1783.* New York: Holt, Rinehart, and Winston, 1967.

Spector, Robert M. "Judicial Biography and the U.S. Supreme Court: A Bibliographical Appraisal," *American Journal of Legal History*, 11 (1967), 1–24.

Starnes, George T. *Sixty Years of Branch Banking in Virginia.* New York: Macmillan, 1931.

Steamer, Robert J. *Chief Justice: Leadership and the Supreme Court.* Columbia: University of South Carolina Press, 1986.

Steinberg, Alfred. *John Marshall.* New York: G. P. Putnam's Sons, 1962.

Stinchcombe, William. *The XYZ Affair.* Westport, Conn.: Greenwood Press, 1980.

Stites, Francis N. *John Marshall: Defender of the Constitution.* Boston: Little, Brown, 1981.

————. *Private Interest and Public Gain: The Dartmouth College Case, 1819.* Amherst: University of Massachusetts Press, 1972.

Stookey, John and George Watson. "John Marshall and His Court: Applied Behavioral Jurisprudence." In *John Marshall's Achievement: Law, Politics, and Constitutional Interpretation,* edited by Thomas C. Shevory, 57–72. Westport, Conn.: Greenwood Press, 1989.

Strevey, Tracy E. "Albert J. Beveridge." In *The Marcus W. Jernegan Essays in American Historiography,* edited by William T. Hutchinson, 374–93. New York: Russell and Russell, 1937.

Strickland, Rennard J. and William J. Strickland. "The Court and the Trail of Tears," Supreme Court Historical Society, *Yearbook 1979,* 20–30.

"Subscribers in Virginia to Blackstone's *Commentaries,*" *William and Mary Quarterly,* 2nd series, 1 (1921), 183.

Surrency, Erwin R. "The Judiciary Act of 1801," *American Journal of Legal History,* 2 (1958), 53–65.

————. "The Lawyer and the American Revolution," *American Journal of Legal History,* 8 (1964), 125–35.

Sutton, Robert P. *Revolution to Secession: Constitution Making in the Old Dominion.* Charlottesville: University Press of Virginia, 1989.

Swem, E. G. "Some Notes on the Four Forms of the Oldest Building of William and Mary College," *William and Mary Quarterly,* 2nd series, 8 (1928), 217–307.

Swindler, William F. "John Marshall's Preparation for the Bar—Some Observations on His Law Notes," *American Journal of Legal History,* 11 (1967), 207–13.

————. "Politics as Law: The Cherokee Cases," *American Indian Law Review,* 3 (1975), 7–20.

Sydnor, Charles S. *American Revolutionaries in the Making: Political Practices in Washington's Virginia.* Reprint, New York: Free Press, 1965.

Szatmary, David P. *Shays's Rebellion: The Making of an Agrarian Insurrection.* Amherst: University of Massachusetts Press, 1980.

Tallentyre, S. G. *The Life of Voltaire.* 3rd edition. New York: G. P. Putnam's Sons, n.d.

Tate, Thad W. "The Coming of the Revolution in Virginia: Britain's Challenge to Virginia's Ruling Class, 1763–1776," *William and Mary Quarterly*, 3rd series, 19 (1962), 323–43.

———. "The Social Contract in America, 1774–1787: Revolutionary Theory as a Conservative Instrument," *William and Mary Quarterly*, 3rd series, 22 (1965), 375–91.

Taylor, Olive A. "Blacks and the Constitution: Chief Justice John Marshall," *Washington Post*, 4 July 1987, A19.

———. Interview with Bill Moyers on "In Search of the Constitution," Public Broadcasting System, 16 April 1987.

Thayer, James Bradley. *John Marshall*. Boston: Houghton Mifflin, 1901.

Thomas, Robert E. "The Virginia Convention of 1788: A Criticism of Beard's *An Economic Interpretation of the Constitution*," *Journal of Southern History*, 19 (1953), 63–72.

"Thomas Marshall," *Bulletin of the Fauquier Historical Society*, 1 (1922), 140–41.

Tillson, Albert H. Jr. *Gentry and Common Folk: Political Culture on a Virginia Frontier, 1740–1789*. Lexington: University Press of Kentucky, 1991.

———. "The Militia and Popular Political Culture in the Upper Valley of Virginia, 1740–1775," *Virginia Magazine of History and Biography*, 94 (1986), 286–306.

Titus, James. *The Old Dominion at War: Society, Politics, and Warfare in Late Colonial Virginia*. Columbia: University of South Carolina Press, 1991.

Tribe, Laurence H. *God Save This Honorable Court: How the Choice of Supreme Court Justices Shapes Our History*. New York: Random House, 1985.

Trussell, John B. B. Jr. *Birthplace of an Army: A Study of the Valley Forge Encampment*. Harrisburg: Pennsylvania Historical and Museum Commission, 1976.

Tscheschlock, Eric. "Mistaken Identity: Spencer Roane and the 'Amphictyon' Letters of 1819," *Virginia Magazine of History and Biography*, 106 (1998), 201–11.

Tucker, Glenn. *Dawn Like Thunder: The Barbary Wars and the Birth of the U.S. Navy*. Indianapolis: Bobbs-Merrill, 1963.

Turner, Kathryn. "The Appointment of Chief Justice Marshall," *William and Mary Quarterly*, 3rd series, 17 (1960), 143–63.

———. "Federalist Policy and the Judiciary Act of 1801," *William and Mary Quarterly*, 3rd series, 22 (1965), 3–32.

———. "The Midnight Judges," *University of Pennsylvania Law Review*, 109 (1961), 494–523.

Tushnet, Mark. *The Law of Slavery in America*. Princeton: Princeton University Press, 1981.

Tyler, Lyon G. *The College of William and Mary: Its Work, Discipline, and History, from Its Foundation to the Present Time*. [Williamsburg: College of William and Mary,] 1917.

———. "The Old Virginia Line in the Middle States during the American Revolution," *Tyler's Quarterly Historical and Genealogical Magazine*, 12 (1930–31), 1–42, 90–141, 198–203, 283–89.

Tyler, Lyon G., ed. *Encyclopedia of Virginia Biography*. New York: Lewis Historical Publishing Co., 1915.

Umbanhowar, Charles E. "Marshall on Judging," *American Journal of Legal History*, 7 (1963), 210–27.

[United States Army.] Judge Advocate General's Corps. *The Army Lawyer: A History of the Judge Advocate General's Corps, 1775–1975.* Washington, D.C.: Government Printing Office, [1975].

Upton, Anthony. "The Road to Power in Virginia in the Early Nineteenth Century," *Virginia Magazine of History and Biography,* 62 (1954), 259–80.

Van Deusen, Glyndon G. "Some Aspects of Whig Thought and Theory in the Jacksonian Period," *American Historical Review,* 63 (1957–58), 305–22.

Van Santvoord, George. *Sketches of the Lives, Times and Judicial Services of the Chief Justices of the Supreme Court of the United States.* New York: Scribner, 1854.

Van Tassel, David D. *Recording America's Past: An Interpretation of the Development of Historical Studies in America, 1607–1884.* Chicago: University of Chicago Press, 1960.

Varg, Paul A. *Foreign Policies of the Founding Fathers.* Pelican edition. Baltimore: Penguin Books, 1970.

Voorhees, Oscar M. *The History of Phi Beta Kappa.* New York: Crown Publishers, 1945.

Waldstreicher, David. *In the Midst of Perpetual Fetes: The Making of American Nationalism, 1776–1820.* Chapel Hill: University of North Carolina Press, 1997.

Wallace, Willard M. *Appeal to Arms: A Military History of the American Revolution.* Chicago: Quadrangle Books, 1951.

Walthall, David K. *History of Richmond Lodge, No. 10.* Richmond: Ware and Duke, 1909.

Ward, Christopher. *The War of the Revolution.* 2 volumes. New York: Macmillan, 1952.

Ward, Geoffrey. *Before the Trumpet: Young Franklin Roosevelt, 1882–1905.* New York: Harper and Row, 1985.

———. *A First Class Temperament: The Emergence of Franklin Roosevelt.* New York: Harper and Row, 1988.

Ward, Harry M. and Harold E. Greer Jr. *Richmond during the Revolution, 1775–83.* Charlottesville: University Press of Virginia, 1977.

Warren, Charles. *Bankruptcy in United States History.* Cambridge: Harvard University Press, 1935.

———. *A History of the American Bar.* Boston: Little, Brown, 1911.

———. "Legislative and Judicial Attacks on the Supreme Court of the United States—A History of the Twenty–fifth Section of the Judiciary Act," *American Law Review,* 47 (1913), 1–34, 161–89.

———. "New Light on the History of the Judiciary Act of 1789," *Harvard Law Review,* 37 (1923), 49–132.

———. *The Supreme Court in United States History.* 3 volumes. Boston: Little, Brown, 1922.

Watlington, Patricia. *The Partisan Spirit: Kentucky Politics, 1779–1792.* New York: Atheneum, 1972.

Watts, Stephen. "Ministers, Misanthropes, and Mandarins: The Federalists and the Culture of Capitalism, 1790–1820." In *Federalism Reconsidered,* edited by Doron Ben-Atar and Barbara B. Oberg, 157–75. Charlottesville: University Press of Virginia.

———. *The Republic Reborn: War and the Making of Liberal America.* Baltimore: Johns Hopkins University Press, 1987.

Wedgewood, Ruth. "The Revolutionary Martyrdom of Jonathan Robbins," *Yale Law Journal*, 100 (1990), 229–368.

Wehtje, Myron F. "The 1799 Congressional Elections in Virginia," *West Virginia History*, 29 (1968), 251–73.

Weigley, Russell F. *The American War of War: A History of United States Military Strategy and Policy*. Bloomington: University of Indiana Press, 1973.

———. *History of the United States Army*. New York: Macmillan, 1967.

Wernick, Robert. "Chief Justice Marshall Takes the Law in Hand," *Smithsonian*, 29 (November 1998), 156–73.

Wettereau, James O. "The Branches of the First Bank of the United States," *Journal of Economic History*, supplement to 2 (1942), 76–77.

White, G. Edward. *The American Judicial Tradition: Profiles of Leading American Judges*. New York: Oxford University Press, 1976.

———. "The Art of Revising History: Revisiting the Marshall Court," *Suffolk University Law Review*, 16 (1982), 659–85.

———. *The Marshall Court and Cultural Change, 1815–1835*. Volumes 3 and 4 of the Oliver Wendell Holmes Jr., Devise History of the Supreme Court. New York: Macmillan, 1988. Abridgement, New York: Oxford University Press, 1991.

White, Leonard D. *The Federalists: A Study in Administrative History, 1789–1801*. New York: Free Press, 1948.

White, William E. "The Independent Companies of Virginia, 1774–1775," *Virginia Magazine of History and Biography*, 86 (1978), 149–62.

Wiebe, Robert H. *The Opening of American Society: From the Adoption of the Constitution to the Eve of Disunion*. New York: Alfred A. Knopf, 1984.

Wiecek, William. *The Sources of Antislavery Constitutionalism in America, 1760–1848*. Ithaca: Cornell University Press, 1977.

Williams, Charles R. *The Life of Rutherford Birchard Hayes*. 2 volumes. Columbus: Ohio State Archaeological and Historical Society, 1928.

Wills, Garry. *Cincinnatus: George Washington and the Enlightenment*. Garden City, N.Y.: Doubleday and Co., 1984.

Wilson, Douglas L. *Honor's Voice: The Transformation of Abraham Lincoln*. New York: Alfred A. Knopf, 1998.

Wilson, Major L. "'Liberty and Union': An Analysis of Three Concepts Involved in the Nullification Controversy," *Journal of Southern History*, 33 (1967), 331–55.

———. *Space, Time, and Freedom: The Quest for Nationality and the Irrepressible Conflict, 1815–1861*. Westport, Conn.: Greenwood Press, 1974.

Wingo, Elizabeth B. *The Battle of Great Bridge*. Chesapeake, Va.: Norfolk County Historical Society, 1964.

Wish, Harvey. *The American Historian: A Social-Intellectual History of the Writing of the American Past*. New York: Oxford University Press, 1960.

Wolfe, Christopher. *The Rise of Modern Judicial Review: From Constitutional Interpretation to Judge-Made Law*. New York: Basic Books, 1986.

Wood, Gertrude. *William Paterson of New Jersey, 1745–1806*. Fair Lawn, N.J.: Fair Lawn Press, 1933.

Wood, Gordon S. *The Creation of the American Republic, 1776–1787*. Chapel Hill: University of North Carolina Press, 1969. Reprint, New York: W. W. Norton, 1972.

———. "The Father of the Court," *New Republic*, 17 February 1997, 39.

———. "Interests and Disinterestedness in the Making of the Constitution." In *Beyond Confederation: Origins of the Constitution and American National Identity*, edited by Richard Beeman et al., 69–109. Chapel Hill: University of North Carolina Press, 1987.

———. "Judicial Review in the Era of the Founding." In *Is the Supreme Court the Guardian of the Constitution?*, edited by Robert Licht, 153–66. Washington, D.C.: American Enterprise Institute, 1993.

———. "Launching the 'Extended Republic': The Federalist Era." In *Launching the "Extended Republic": The Federalist Era*, edited by Ronald Hoffman and Peter J. Albert, 1–24. Charlottesville: University Press of Virginia, 1996.

———. "The Origins of Judicial Review," *Suffolk University Law Review*, 22 (1988), 1293–1307.

———. *The Radicalism of the American Revolution*. New York: Alfred A. Knopf, 1992.

Wood, W. J. *Battles of the Revolutionary War, 1775–1781*. Chapel Hill, N.C.: Algonquin Books, 1990.

Woodfin, Maude H. "Thomas Marshall." In *Dictionary of American Biography*, edited by Dumas Malone et al. 20 volumes and supplements, 12:328–29. New York: Charles Scribner's Sons, 1932– .

Wren, J. Thomas. "The Ideology of Court and Country in the Virginia Ratifying Convention of 1788," *Virginia Magazine of History and Biography*, 93 (1985), 389–408.

Wright, John W. "The Rifle in the American Revolution," *American Historical Review*, 29 (1923–24), 293–99.

———. "Some Notes on the Continental Army," *William and Mary Quarterly*, 2nd series, 11 (1931), 81–105.

Wright, Louis B. *The Cultural Life of the American Colonies, 1607–1763*. New York: Harper and Row, 1957.

Wright, Robert K. *The Continental Army*. Washington, D.C.: U.S. Army Center for Military History, 1983.

Young, James Sterling. *The Washington Community, 1800–1828*. New York: Columbia University Press, 1966.

Zagarri, Rosemarie. "Festive Nationalism and Antiparty Partyism," *Reviews in American History*, 26 (1998), 504–9.

Zahniser, Marvin R. *Charles Cotesworth Pinckney, Founding Father*. Chapel Hill: University of North Carolina Press, 1967.

———. *Uncertain Friendship: American-French Diplomatic Relations Through the Cold War*. New York: John Wiley and Sons, 1975.

Ziegler, Benjamin M. *The International Law of John Marshall: A Study of First Principles*. Chapel Hill: University of North Carolina Press, 1939.

Zweiben, Beverly. *How Blackstone Lost the Colonies: English Law, Colonial Lawyers, and the American Revolution*. New York: Garland Publishers, 1990.

DISSERTATIONS AND THESES

Aldridge, Frederick S. "Organization and Administration of the Militia System of Colonial Virginia." Ph.D. dissertation, American University, 1964.

Beach, Rex. "Judge Spencer Roane: A Champion of States Rights." M.A. thesis, College of William and Mary, 1954.

Berlin, Robert H. "The Administration of Military Justice in the Continental Army during the American Revolution, 1775–1783." Ph.D. dissertation, University of California at Santa Barbara, 1976.

Caldwell, Russell Leon. "The Influence of the Federal Bar upon the Interpretation of the Constitution by the Supreme Court under John Marshall." Ph.D. dissertation, University of Southern California, 1948.

Campbell, Bruce A. "Law and Experience in the Early Republic: The Evolution of the Dartmouth College Doctrine, 1780–1819." Ph.D. dissertation, Michigan State University, 1973.

Chernow, Barbara Ann. "Robert Morris, Land Speculator, 1790–1801." Ph.D. dissertation, Columbia University, 1974.

Cox, Caroline H. "'A Proper Sense of Honor'": The Status of Soldiers and Officers of the Continental Army, 1775–1783." Ph.D. dissertation, University of California at Berkeley, 1997.

Cox, Harold E. "Federalism and Anti–Federalism in Virginia, 1787: A Study of Political and Economic Motivations." Ph.D. dissertation, University of Virginia, 1958.

Cullen, Charles T. "St. George Tucker and Law in Virginia." Ph.D. dissertation, University of Virginia, 1971.

Curtis, George M. "The Virginia Courts during the Revolution." Ph.D. dissertation, University of Wisconsin, 1970.

DenBoer, Gordon. "The House of Delegates and the Evolution of Political Parties in Virginia, 1782–1792." Ph.D. dissertation, University of Wisconsin, 1972.

Foard, Susan Lee. "Virginia Enters the Union: A Legislative Study of the Commonwealth, 1789–1792." M.A. thesis, College of William and Mary, 1966.

Holder, Jean S. "The John Adams Presidency: War Crisis Leadership in the Early Republic." Ph.D. dissertation, American University, 1983.

Horsnell, Margaret E. "Spencer Roane: Judicial Advocate of Jeffersonian Principles." Ph.D. dissertation, University of Minnesota, 1967.

Jessup, Dwight Wiley. "Reaction and Accomodation: The United States Supreme Court and Political Conflict, 1809–1835." Ph.D. dissertation, University of Minnesota, 1978.

Johnson, Robert. "Government Regulation of Business Enterprise in Virginia, 1750–1820." Ph.D. dissertation, University of Minnesota, 1958.

Kirtland, Robert B. "George Wythe: Lawyer, Revolutionary, Judge." Ph.D. dissertation, University of Michigan, 1986.

Kuehl, John W. "The Quest for Identity in an Age of Insecurity: The XYZ Affair and American Nationalism." Ph.D. dissertation, University of Wisconsin, 1968.

Kuroda, Tadahisa. "The County Court System of Virginia from the Revolution to the Civil War." Ph.D. dissertation, Columbia University, 1969.

Luce, Willard Ray. "*Cohens v. Virginia* (1821): The Supreme Court and State Rights: A Reevaluation of Influences and Impacts." Ph.D. dissertation, University of Virginia, 1978.

McGraw, Marie T. "The American Colonization Society in Virginia, 1816–1832: A Case Study in Southern Liberalism." Ph.D. dissertation, George Washington University, 1980.

Merz, Nancy M. "The XYZ Affair and the Congressional Election of 1799 in Richmond." M.A. thesis, College of William and Mary, 1973.

Miller, Frederick T. "Juries and Judges versus the Law: Virginia from the Revolution to the Confrontation between John Marshall and Spencer Roane." Ph.D. dissertation, University of Alabama, 1986.

Monikowski, Richard A. "The Actual State of Things: American Indians, Indian Law, and American Courts Between 1800 and 1835." Ph.D. dissertation, University of New Mexico, 1997.

Oliver, George B. "A Constitutional History of Virginia, 1776–1860." Ph.D. dissertation, Duke University, 1959.

Rice, Philip M. "Internal Improvements in Virginia, 1775–1860." Ph.D. dissertation, University of North Carolina, 1948.

Rich, Myra L. "The Experimental Years: Virginia, 1781–1789." Ph.D. dissertation, Yale University, 1966.

Richards, Gale Lee. "A Criticism of the Public Speaking of John Marshall Prior to 1801." Ph.D. dissertation University of Iowa, 1950.

Robarge, David. "Judge Spencer Roane and Jeffersonian Jurisprudence." M.A. thesis, George Mason University, 1982.

Sellers, John R. "The Virginia Continental Line, 1775–1780." Ph.D. dissertation, Tulane University, 1968.

Sheldon, Marianne P. B. "Richmond, Virginia: The Town and Henrico County to 1820." Ph.D. dissertation, University of Michigan, 1975.

Smith, Alan M. "Virginia Lawyers, 1680–1776: The Birth of an American Profession." Ph.D. dissertation, Johns Hopkins University, 1967.

Treon, John A. "*Martin v. Hunter's Lessee*: A Case History." Ph.D. dissertation, University of Virginia, 1970.

Index

About the Author

DAVID ROBARGE is a historian with the Central Intelligence Agency, where he has also worked as a political analyst. Prior to that he worked on the staff of David Rockefeller and at the Gannett Center for Media Studies at Columbia University. He has taught history at both Columbia and George Mason Universities.

Recent Titles in
Contributions in American History

ISBN 0-313-30858-6

HARDCOVER BAR CODE